NAPA & SONOMA

ELIZABETH LINHART VENEMAN

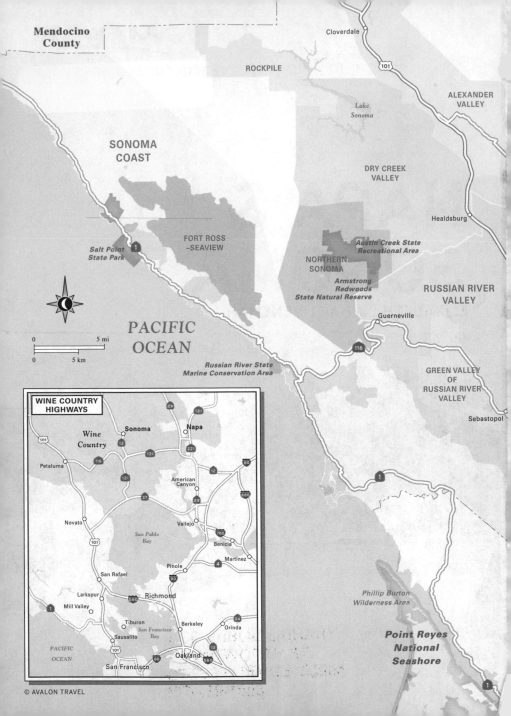

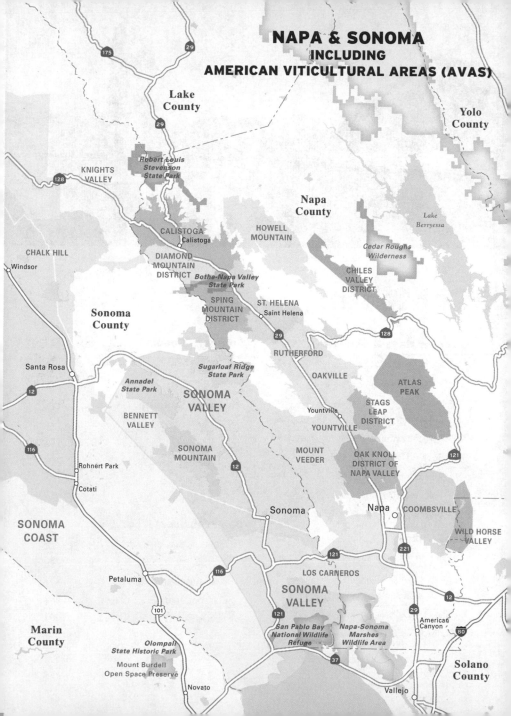

Contents

DISCOVER

Napa & Sonoma

Nowhere blesses the whims and tantalizes the senses quite like the valleys of Napa and Sonoma, California's garden of earthly delights. Soak in a soothing mud bath. Smell lavender wafting through the valley as you lounge poolside. Picnic on farmstead cheese and figs still warm from the sun. Dine on food prepared by some of the world's best chefs from ingredients cultivated only a few feet away.

And I haven't even started talking about the wine. Vines of chardonnay, cabernet, zinfandel, and sauvignon blanc grapes—just to name a few—cover the land in lush ribbed acres, while nearby tasting rooms of all sizes pour expertly crafted samples.

Wine has been integral to life here since the Spanish missionaries arrived and planted the first grapevines. It was later perfected by 19th-century European immigrants, who built the grand estates that today stand as monuments to their accomplishments.

Although it only produces 4 percent of the state's wine, Napa, with its world-class wineries, constellation of Michelin-starred restaurants, and luxurious spas, is the beating heart of Wine Country. Despite lacking the same name

---

Clockwise from top left: the Culinary Institute of America in St. Helena; vineyards in the fall; Safari West in Santa Rosa; the Napa River; Healdsburg Bar & Grill; Los Carneros.

recognition as its neighbor, Sonoma County often offers more diversity. It is home to sleepy villages, small farms, laid-back wineries, and the historic towns of Sonoma and Healdsburg. Eventually, the bucolic farmland yields to towering redwoods and the impressive and often unruly Russian River. Here, backpacks and canoes replace mud baths and massages, beer rivals wine for accolades and devotees, and celebrated farm-to-table restaurants rarely require a reservation.

It is hard to know whether the spirit of Bacchus came with the wine, or if it was already here. Either way, you will find it in Napa and Sonoma: along flat valley floors that invite bicycle tours through vineyards heavy with fruit, on top of rugged mountaintops and wild rivers, and in piping hot mineral pools, colorful country stores, and chic upscale boutiques. And through it all, there's enough farm-fresh food and award-winning wine to keep you fueled and inspired. There is no better place to savor the moment.

Clockwise from top left: Hale's Apple Farm along the Gravenstein Highway; chickens in the Russian River Valley; Dry Creek Valley; St. Francis Winery & Vineyards.

Planning Your Trip

Where to Go

Napa Valley

This *is* California Wine Country, as far as many people are concerned—arguably the most important winemaking region in the state with a name that is recognized around the world. The 30-mile-long Napa Valley is a valley of contrasts. Some **16 distinct appellations** are home to **hundreds of wineries,** ranging from the historic big names that make millions of cases of wine per year down to more modest wineries turning out some of California's best cabernet sauvignons. It can be expensive and crowded in Napa, yet it's not hard to find pockets of rural tranquility as you venture off the beaten path.

Southern Sonoma

Although it now lives in the cultural shadow of the Napa Valley, this is ground zero not only for California's modern wine industry but for California itself. The notable town of **Sonoma** is thoroughly at peace with itself, as though worn out from the tumultuous series of events more than 150 years ago that gave birth to the state. Life is more laid-back (and cheaper) here than in the larger, more famous neighboring valley, yet there are still plenty of cultural, culinary, and outdoor attractions alongside the first-class wineries, from the sleepy town of **Kenwood** to the cool flatlands of **Los Carneros.**

Northern Sonoma

If any region epitomizes the diversity of California's Wine Country, it is northern Sonoma, where scenery and wines from the multitude of hills and small valleys often have little in common other than their Sonoma County address. The cool, lush **Russian River Valley** has forests, rivers, small farms, and some of the best pinot noir and chardonnay in California. The warmer **Dry Creek Valley** and **Alexander Valley** are home to big red wines from small family-owned wineries. Bordering all three regions is the fascinating town of **Healdsburg,** itself a mix of the upscale and down-home.

San Francisco

If you're visiting Napa and Sonoma via San Francisco, spend a day or two in the city dining on **cutting-edge cuisine** at high-end restaurants and offbeat food trucks, touring classical and avant-garde **museums,** biking through **Golden Gate Park,** and strolling along **Fisherman's Wharf** before driving across the **Golden Gate Bridge** to Wine Country.

Clear Lake

Northern Sonoma

Napa Valley

Lake Berryessa

PACIFIC

Southern Sonoma

OCEAN

San Francisco

0   20 mi

0   20 km

© AVALON TRAVEL

Know Before You Go

When to Go

Summer and **fall** are when the weather is at its best and the wineries are at their most active, laying out lavish food and wine events, preparing for harvest, and releasing new vintages. The problem is that everyone seems to be here at this time of year. Hotel prices surge, traffic clogs the roads, and getting a restaurant reservation is like a game of roulette. Weekends can be particularly bad, as day-trippers from the Bay Area swell the already bulging tourist traffic.

Visiting **midweek** at this time of year can make a huge difference. St. Helena, Healdsburg, and Sonoma can feel deserted on an August or September weekday. After October, things quiet down a little bit, hotel rates drop, and the weather can still be fine as the vineyards turn glorious hues of red and gold.

Winter is the wettest but also the quietest period, when wineries can be blissfully devoid of visitors, enabling plenty of one-on-one time with tasting-room staff. In **spring** the weather warms up and the valley and mountains are a fresh, vivid green after the winter rains, making this one of the best times to visit the Wine Country ahead of the summer crowds.

Where to Stay

These towns stand out for their variety of accommodations and nearby wineries, eateries, and attractions.

- **Napa:** The biggest city in the Napa Valley, Napa is well on its way to having the most hotel rooms of any Wine Country town. Accommodations range from small and quiet bed-and-breakfasts to compounds devoted to high-end luxury to clean economy digs, all of which are close to downtown and its excellent and diverse dining scene.

- **Calistoga:** At the other end of the Napa Valley, Calistoga is filled with old-school resort

zinfandel grapes in the Russian River Valley

Ram's Gate in Carneros

accommodations that are affordable, filled with character, and have mineral pools and spa services. All are within easy walking distance from downtown.

- **Sonoma:** Historic, affordable, and family-friendly accommodations are scattered throughout the charming country town of Sonoma. With countless attractions within walking distance, Sonoma is easy on the traveler and the wallet.

- **Guerneville:** Nestled in the redwoods along the Russian River in northern Sonoma, Guerneville has recently been revitalized by the arrival of hip new hotels and restaurants. Prices haven't caught up, so this funky town remains an affordable place to stay.

Transportation

Most of Napa and Sonoma is rural and has little, if any, public transportation, making a **car** necessary.

You can park the car and explore some of the bigger towns like Napa and Healdsburg by foot, but you'll need wheels to fully appreciate Wine Country.

There's one obvious problem with this scenario—drinking and driving (or cycling) is not the best combination. If you're wine-tasting, planning a **designated driver** each day or for the duration of the trip is a good idea, or check out several companies that offer **daylong tours** either in a private vehicle with a driver or as part of a group in a small bus. If you must drive, having the discipline (and skill) to spit out wine in the tasting room is essential.

Be aware that **driving times** can be slower than you might expect. Average speeds can be very low on rural roads, especially in the mountains and in busy areas like Napa during rush hour. If you're cycling, keep in mind that distances between wineries and summer heat can be exhausting, so plan accordingly.

The Best of Napa & Sonoma

With so many wines to taste, restaurants to try, parks to visit, and spas to relax in, visiting Wine Country can be a dizzying proposition. To make the most of your time, pick a location and spend a day or two exploring it at your leisure.

If you plan on starting or ending your trip in **San Francisco,** see page 274 for a one-day itinerary.

Day 1: Carneros to Napa

Make your first drink in Wine Country a Bloody Mary at **Boon Fly Café** in Carneros. Pair it with a hearty breakfast, which will give you fuel for a tour through the 200 acres of modern art at the **di Rosa Preserve.** Toast the day with champagne across the street at **Domaine Carneros** before heading to Napa.

In Napa, head to the **Oxbow Public Market** for a casual lunch and a bit of souvenir-shopping. Afterwards, wander over to the eccentric **Mark Herold Wine** for some bold cabernets or drive into quiet Coombsville for an appointment with

chardonnay and pinot noir specialist **Ancien.** After other tasting rooms have closed, **1313 Main** pours great wine in a cool, lounge-like atmosphere. Slip out for dinner at the equally hip **Miminashi,** followed by some drinking and dancing at **Silo's** jazz and blues bar.

Day 2: Yountville to Calistoga

Head to Yountville first thing in the morning for a steaming espresso and buttery slice of coffee cake on the sun-dappled patio of **Bouchon Bakery.** Take a shopping detour at the historic **V Marketplace** before driving to the iconic **Robert Mondavi Winery** for a tour. Stop for a bite at Francis Ford Coppola's **Inglenook** or at **Cindy's Backstreet Kitchen** in St. Helena.

Farther up the valley, **Castello di Amorosa** impresses with its medieval largesse, and the historic **Chateau Montelena** pours such good chardonnays and Bordeaux blends that you'll see why the Paris judges swooned. Or, for a smaller, more intimate tasting experience,

Indian Springs Resort in Calistoga

the grave of Cyrus Alexander at Alexander Valley Vineyards

make an appointment at **Failla Wines** or take a drive up Spring Mountain for a tasting at **Pride Mountain Vineyards**. Afterwards, drive to Calistoga to take in the restorative waters at **Indian Springs Resort** or **Dr. Wilkinson's Hot Springs Resort** before indulging in a fun, low-key dinner at **Sam's Social Club**.

Day 3: Calistoga to Geyserville/Healdsburg

Fuel up on Brannan's Benedict at **Café Sarafornia**, then take the beautiful Highway 128 to the Alexander Valley. Make your first stop the friendly **Alexander Valley Vineyards**; enjoy the complimentary tasting and cave tour. Stop for a bite at the quirky **Jimtown Store** and a tasting at the lovely **Medlock Ames**. Either shoot west to Victorian Healdsburg or continue on to Geyserville.

If you head to Healdsburg, spend the rest of the day shopping for antiques and sipping on chardonnay at **Selby Winery** and **Banshee** or make the short drive to **Seghesio Family Vineyards** for a glass of sangiovese and a round of bocce ball. Enjoy Italian at **Scopa** and end

the day with a pint at **Bear Republic Brewing Company**.

If you head to Geyserville, try the boutique wine along the tiny but historic Main Street at **Meeker, Pech Merle**, and **Locals Tasting Room**. Dine on the delicious house-made charcuterie and thin-crust pizzas at **Diavola**.

Day 4: Dry Creek Valley to Guerneville

Have breakfast at **Geyserville Grille,** then cross U.S. 101 into the Dry Creek Valley and enjoy the sunshine and Rhône varietals at **Preston Farm & Winery**. Make a stop at the equally charming and rustic **Bella Vineyards** before heading south along the sleepy West Dry Creek Road. Lunch, as well as cute housewares and stiff drinks, can be found at the 1881 **Dry Creek General Store.** Nearby, try the famous zin at **Dry Creek Vineyard** or go higher to sample some famous cabernet at **Ridge Vineyards.**

Follow Westside Road down into the Russian River area and marvel at the original hop kilns at **Hop Kiln Winery** or its inky reds at the homespun **Porter Creek Winery.** Continue on for an

Hop Kiln Winery

outrageously original dinner at **Dick Blomster's Korean Diner** or make a reservation for the hip **boon eat + drink**. After dinner, trade wine for beer at the **Stumptown Brewery,** where pool and live music keep the fun going.

Day 5: Guerneville to Santa Rosa

Start your day with a big breakfast at **Big Bottom Market**. If the weather is nice, head to the **Russian River** to swim or kayak. If it's foggy, go for a hike at **Armstrong Redwoods State Natural Reserve**. Afterwards, get on the Gravenstein Highway to enjoy award-winning brut in the rustic surroundings at **Iron Horse Vineyards** or make an appointment for a food and wine pairing on the lovely patio at **Lynmar Estate**. Grab some fruit (Gravenstein apples if it's summer) to snack on at **Andy's Produce Market**.

Head to Sebastopol to browse the artsy shops at **The Barlow** before having a farm-to-table dinner at **zazu**. Shoot east to end your night in Santa Rosa with a pint (or two) of craft brew at **Russian River Brewing Company**.

Day 6: Santa Rosa to Sonoma

Fill up at **Omelette Express** before you head to Kenwood. Start at the manicured grounds of **Chateau St. Jean** for a tasting of its celebrated chardonnay. Next, pick up supplies at the **Glen Ellen Village Market,** then head on to **Imagery Estate Winery** or **Matanzas Creek Winery** to lay out your picnic blanket. Afterwards, try to squeeze in a stop at **Little Vineyards Family Winery** or **B. R. Cohn Winery** for a flight of reds before heading to the **Sonoma Plaza**. Jump from varietal to varietal at one of the many tasting rooms tucked through downtown or plant yourself on a couch at the lounge at **Pangloss Cellars** for a flight of Sonoma wines. Be careful not to fill up on delectable small bites before your reservation at **Oso** next door.

Day 7: Sonoma to SFO

Start your day with buttery biscuits at the **Fremont Diner** before making a final toast to Wine Country with some bubbly at **Gloria Ferrer**. Give yourself plenty of time to head back to San Francisco for your flight.

Varietals 101

California Wine Country is like no other in the world thanks to its unique geology and climate, which have created a patchwork of soil types with microclimates at varying elevations. Within Napa and Sonoma Counties' combined 2,320 square miles, there are 33 distinct AVAs, or American Viticultural Areas. These AVAs produce an astounding range of varietals, making it possible for you to start the day with a cool-weather sparkling wine and end it with a heat-loving cabernet.

Cabernet Sauvignon

Cabernet sauvignon, a grape from the Bordeaux region of France, creates a deep, dark, strong red wine. The grapes that get intense summer heat make the best wine, which makes the scorching Napa Valley a perfect fit for this varietal. A good dry cab might taste of leather, tobacco, and bing cherries. Cabs age well, often hitting their peak of flavor and smoothness more than a decade after bottling.

BEST PLACES TO SAMPLE:

• **Stag's Leap Wine Cellars** (page 64)

• **Silver Oak** (page 76)

• **Shafer Vineyards** (page 65)

Chardonnay

Most of the white wine made and sold in California is chardonnay. The grapes grow best in a slightly cooler climate, such as the vineyards closer to the coast. Most California chardonnays taste smooth and buttery and a bit like fruit, and they often take on the oak flavor of the barrels they sit in. Chardonnay doesn't keep (age), so most chards are sold the year after they're bottled and consumed within a few months of purchase.

BEST PLACES TO SAMPLE:

• **Grgich Hills Winery** (page 78)

• **Landmark Vineyards** (page 167)

• **Chateau St. Jean** (page 166)

chardonnay grapes

old vine zinfandel grapes in the Dry Creek Valley

One of the joys of wine tasting in Napa and Sonoma is the variety of winery tours available. Art, history, and education pair well with an earthy pinot noir or a crisp sauvignon blanc. Book a tour at one of the following wineries for an unforgettable afternoon.

HISTORY

- Established in 1876, **Beringer Vineyards** (page 88) is now on the National Register of Historic Places. Pay the extra expense for the reserve tasting, which takes place in the lavish and ornate Rhine House.

- Explore caves and check out the classic car collection at **Far Niente** (page 76), a winery from the 1880s.

- History was made at **Chateau Montelena** (page 110) in 1976 when the winery's chardonnay beat the French in the Judgment of Paris tasting. To learn more about all the château's history, book the 90-minute tour.

VINEYARD TOURS

- Book early if you want a spot on the popular tour at **Frog's Leap Winery** (page 80), which highlights the principles of organic farming and sustainability against a beautiful backdrop.

- **Long Meadow Ranch** (page 91) gives tours of its organic 650-acre Rutherford ranch and winery.

- **Benziger Family Winery** (page 159) shares the secrets of biodynamic farming on the 45-minute tractor drawn tours.

- The 380-acre organic Bell Weather Ranch at **Medlock Ames** (page 264) is home to an astonishing variety of varietals, as well as gardens, wildlife corridors, and a 100% solar -gravity flow winery.

CAVE TOURS

- **Gundlach Bundschu Winery** (page 138) has tours of the 430-foot-long hillside cave.

- With a 100,000-square-foot four-story cave system extending underground, **Palmaz Vineyards** (page 44) could be in a James Bond movie.

- **Schramsberg Vineyards** (page 113) has one of the best (and spookiest) tours in the valley, with bottle-lined caves that date back to the late 1800s.

WINE EDUCATION

- At **Ancien** (page 43), learn how climate, topography, and soil types combine to create great wine.

- **Robert Mondavi Winery** (page 75) offers tours geared toward the novice that illuminate the process of winemaking and tasting.

- Opt for the Palate Play experience at **Ram's Gate** (page 182), which includes an educational tour around the vineyards and winery.

EXPERIENCING THE CRUSH

- Lend a hand—err, foot—with the grape stomp held at **Grgich Hills Winery** (page 78) from mid-August to the end of October.

- High up Spring Mountain at **Schweiger Vineyards** (page 94), you can "help" the Schweigers prune, harvest, and crush the grapes (barefoot) on select weekends in September and October.

- Join the Battaglinis at their homey Russian River winery, **Battaglini Estate Winery** (page 213), for their fall stomp event.

ART AND ARCHITECTURE

- **The Hess Collection** (page 46) is home to a four-story gallery with contemporary art ranging from obscure to internationally famous artists.

- **HALL**'s (page 88) commitment to sustainable design is matched only by its cutting-edge aesthetics.

VIEWS

- Take in the views at the monastery-like **Sterling Vineyards** (page 110), perched above the valley floor and accessible only by gondola.

patio tasting at Domaine Chandon

Pinot Noir

Pinot noir grapes do best in a cool coastal climate with limited exposure to high heat. The Anderson Valley and the Monterey coastal growing regions tend to specialize in pinot noir, though many Napa and Sonoma wineries buy grapes from the coast to make their own versions. California vintners make up single-varietal pinot noir wines that taste of cherries, strawberries, and smoke.

BEST PLACES TO SAMPLE:

- **Robert Sinskey Vineyards** (page 65)
- **Ancien** (page 43)
- **Lynmar Estate** (page 213)

Zinfandel

These grapes grow best when tortured by their climate; a few grow near Napa, but most come from Dry Creek Valley. A true zinfandel is a hearty deep-red wine that boasts the flavors and smells of blackberry jam with the dusky hues of venous blood. Zinfandel often tastes wonderful on its own, but it's also good with beef, buffalo, and even venison.

BEST PLACES TO SAMPLE:

- **Ravenswood** (page 139)
- **Ridge Vineyards** (page 251)
- **Bella Vineyards** (page 255)

Sauvignon Blanc

When grown in cooler climates, sauvignon blanc grapes produce refreshingly crisp wine, and when grown in warmer climates, they produce a richer, more tropical wine, called fumé blanc. The California sauvignon blanc wine goes well with salads and fish, as well as vegetarian and spicy international dishes.

BEST PLACES TO SAMPLE:

- **Hanna Winery** (page 209)
- **Fritz Underground Winery** (page 254)
- **Medlock Ames** (page 264)

Merlot

Merlot is the second most widely planted red wine grape in California, though its popularity is now waning. In California it's often made into an easy-drinking wine that is less tannic and more plump than most cabernet sauvignons. Sometimes its subtler flavors can be lost, resulting in a bland wine, but a well-made merlot has just as much structure as other reds.

BEST PLACES TO SAMPLE:

• **Rutherford Hill Winery** (page 80)

• **Duckhorn Vineyards** (page 92)

• **Twomey Cellars** (page 109)

Syrah

Syrah is the rising star of California's red wines and the fifth most planted red grape in the state. Its traditional home is the Rhône region of France, and it is often made into Rhône-style wines in cooler parts of California, exhibiting telltale black pepper and chocolate flavors and an almost purple color. It makes a much denser, more powerful wine when grown in hotter climates.

BEST PLACES TO SAMPLE:

• **Loxton Cellars** (page 160)

Sparkling

Most California champagne-style wines are blends of both pinot noir and chardonnay, the grapes of which grow best in the cool climates of Carneros and the Russian River Valley. The key to making champagne is to bottle the wine while it is still fermenting so the yeast will generate both alcohol and carbon dioxide, the all-important gas that creates the fizz.

BEST PLACES TO SAMPLE:

• **Gloria Ferrer** (page 177)

• **Domaine Carneros** (page 182)

• **Domaine Chandon** (page 60)

A Romantic Weekend

Day 1

Start your day in **Sonoma Plaza.** Grab a cup of coffee, a pastry, and some picnic supplies at the **Basque Boulangerie Café,** then take a morning stroll through the **Sonoma Mission** and other historic sights of **Sonoma State Historic Park.** Venture over to **Gundlach Bundschu Winery,** where history is paired with Bordeaux- and Burgundy-style blends. Either plant yourself at one of the picnic tables on the estate's plentiful grounds or take your supplies up the **Sonoma Overlook Trail** and enjoy the view over lunch.

Next, venture up Highway 12 to **Glen Ellen.** Hop aboard the tram at the **Benziger Family Winery** for a tour of the beautiful biodynamic winery. Afterwards, wander over to the nearby **Jack London State Historic Park** for a stroll in the late afternoon. Enjoy a range of pinot noir at the cozy and relaxing tasting room at **Eric Ross Winery,** followed by a dinner at the **Glen Ellen Star.** Stay the night in Sonoma.

Day 2

Take the scenic Oakville Grade to Yountville and enjoy some pastries on the patio of **Bouchon Bakery,** then take a stroll through town. Afterwards, a glass of bubbly at **Domaine Chandon** is the perfect way to greet the day. Grab lunch at **Bistro Jeanty** before hitting the **Silverado Trail.** Stop in at the famous **Stag's Leap Wine Cellars** for some equally famous cabernet sauvignon or venture to organic champion **Robert Sinskey Vineyards.** Continue north to a seated tasting at **Mumm** or opt for an impressive cave tour at **Rutherford Hill Winery,** followed by a bottle of its fine merlot or sauvignon blanc on its expansive picnic grounds. Finish the day with a sunset dinner overlooking the valley at the **Auberge du Soleil** resort, high up in the hills. Stay in St. Helena.

Day 3

Coffee and pastries at the **Model Bakery** begins

Soaking in a hot spring or volcanic mud bath is the ideal way to pamper yourself after a tough day of wine tasting.

CALISTOGA (PAGE 116)

- Sitting on the site of Sam Brannan's original resort in Calistoga, **Indian Springs Resort** has an Olympic sized pool fed by hot springs, in addition to massages and body treatments such as the Chardonnay Scrub.

- **Dr. Wilkinson's Hot Springs Resort,** an old school establishment, is the gold standard for mud baths, with its proprietary blend of Calistoga mineral water and volcanic ash, Canadian peat, and lavender.

- **Lincoln Avenue Spa** offers a menu of refined pampering including massages, facials, mud treatments, and an Ayurvedic steam table in private rooms filled with candlelight.

- **Spa Solage** combines many of the highlights above in its serene compound devoted to health and beauty, where mineral pools, therapeutic massages, and aromatherapy unwind even the tightest muscle.

SONOMA (PAGE 147)

- At **Garden Spa,** treatments are inspired by the flowers, herbs, and fruit found in the garden that

a mineral pool at Spa Solage

surround this sanctuary at Sonoma's luxurious MacArthur Place.

- At the Fairmont Sonoma Mission Inn, **Willow Stream Spa** is the only spa in the Sonoma Valley with pools filled with hot mineral water from springs nearby.

the day in St. Helena. Spend the morning browsing the town's shops and galleries before heading to a tasting at **Velo Vino.** Pick up some picnic supplies at **Dean & Deluca** to enjoy at **Bothe-Napa Valley State Park,** where the redwoods beg for a hike. Alternatively, enjoy the quietude of the mountains by booking a tasting at **St. Clement Vineyards** for velvety cabernets or at **Schramsberg Vineyards** for a president-worthy blanc de blanc.

Next, it's time for some pampering,

Calistoga-style. Drive north for your appointment for a couple's restorative mud bath at the **Lincoln Avenue Spa.** Since it's a wine-themed weekend, choose the antioxidant-laden mud containing wine, grape seed oil, and green tea. Fully relaxed, stop in at **Up Valley Vintners** to sample wine from some of the northern valley's smaller wineries. Finally, end your weekend at the Michelin-starred **Solbar.** Try getting a table on the expansive patio alongside its floating fireplace.

Wine Country with Kids

Day 1

Start your tour of Wine Country with some inspiration from the Peanuts Gang at the **Charles M. Schulz Museum** in Santa Rosa. Ponder the Kite-eating Tree or wander the Snoopy Labyrinth before jumping in the car and heading to the redwoods of the Russian River. Stop by the back-to-the-land **Porter Bass** where kids are welcome to explore and visit with the resident chickens while you enjoy glasses of estate chardonnay and pinot noir. For lunch, grab picnic supplies at **Big Bottom Market**. If the fog has burned off, rent an umbrella and a couple of inner tubes at **Johnson's Beach** for an afternoon of picnicking and sandy fun. If not, take a nature hike in the fog-enshrouded giants of **Armstrong Redwoods State Natural Reserve**.

For an all-in-one stop, head north to the **Francis Ford Coppola Winery** in sleepy Geyserville. Kids will love the pool, the movie memorabilia, and the gelato; you will love relaxing poolside with a glass or two of Alexander Valley cabernet. For dinner, plan on pizzas at Guerneville's **Main Street Bistro**. Stay at one of Guerneville's rustic riverside resorts.

Day 2

Order a big breakfast at **Pat's Restaurant** before heading south on U.S. 101, then taking Highway 116 east to Carneros. Get out and stretch your legs at **Cornerstone Sonoma,** where you can taste small-lot chardonnay, pinot noir, and cabernet sauvignon, and the kids can explore the large and playful gardens filling the property. Not far away, down a long bumpy road, they'll love the farm animals at **Larson Family Winery** or simply beeline it to **TrainTown,** where carnival rides, a petting zoo, and a ride on a narrow gauge train will surely tire out any car-bound kid. For dinner, **Mary's Pizza Shack** is always a hit, but for something other than pie, **Murphy's Irish Pub** has a kids menu, plus plenty of brews for the grown-ups. Stay at **El Pueblo Inn** in Sonoma, which has a pool and is right across the street from TrainTown.

Sonoma City Hall at Sonoma Plaza

Epicurean Delights

RESTAURANTS

In Wine Country, options from diners to Michelin-starred restaurants tease the palate, inspire the novice, and make savoring the moment inescapable. Here is just a sampling of some of the best.

- Widely credited with putting Napa Valley on the culinary map, The French Laundry (page 69) continues to wow diners year after year.

- At The Restaurant at Meadowood (page 101), each dish is designed to inspire visceral experiences like the forest in spring or the sea after a storm.

- Adjacent to the historic Sonoma Plaza, the girl & the fig (page 148) serves French bistro fare utilizing Sonoma's agricultural bounty.

- In Guerneville, venture off the beaten Wine Country path at Dick Blomster's Korean Diner (page 227), where Korean street food meets American pop culture.

- Housemade charcuterie and woodfired pizzas draw many to Diavola (page 268) in tiny Geyserville.

PAIRINGS

Most restaurants in Wine Country tailor their cuisine to highlight local vintages. A chef's tasting menu paired with wine is an economical and adventurous option.

- In St. Helena, Press St. Helena (page 102) pairs its beef and veggie-heavy menu with the biggest Napa Valley wine list in the world.

- Bruschetteria Food Truck (page 103), parked out front of Velo Vino in St. Helena, serves up farm-to-fork Italian dishes that are perfectly savored with St. Helena cabernet.

- Scopa (page 244), an unpretentious favorite among Healdsburg locals, hosts a different winemaker every Wednesday.

PICNIC SUPPLIES

Great food emporiums, delis, shops, and markets hawk specialty cheese, bread, and charcuterie, plus produce, olive oil, and prepared food ready to take with you or eat at a table a few steps away.

- Oxbow Public Market (page 54), the king of food emporiums in Wine Country, has everything from cupcakes to kitchen supplies, with some of the biggest food names in the Napa Valley making an appearance.

- Oakville Grocery (page 83), the oldest grocery in the state, is known for stocking only the best food, wine, cheese, and other goodies.

- Healdsburg's one-stop shop for foodies, The Shed (page 244) has a sit-down restaurant, a fermentation bar, a coffee shop, and a casual deli counter.

- Jimtown Store (page 269) recalls country general stores with its mix of penny toys, kitchen gadgets, freshly baked pastries, and hearty lunch options—all with an epicurean sensibility.

- Nearly all Wine Country towns have their own farmers market (at least part of the year), and all are worth a stop. Two of the best are in Healdsburg (page 246) and Sonoma (page 152) during the summer and fall.

COOKING CLASSES

- With campuses in St. Helena and Napa, the Culinary Institute of America (page 96) has plenty of demos and hands-on cooking classes taught by some of tomorrow's best chefs.

- At Napa City College, the Napa Valley Cooking School (page 100) offers classes for the lay cook on everything from the concept of wine to the perfect steak at its St. Helena campus.

- Silverado Cooking School (page 51) is a small Napa cooking school that offers a range of classes, including cheese courses taught by local cheese expert Janet Fletcher.

- Relish Culinary Adventures (page 242) is a mom-and-pop operation that makes cooking fun, with classes geared toward making the most out of what's in season.

Cornerstone Sonoma

Day 3

For breakfast, take a table out on the patio at the **Sunflower Caffe.** Burn off any extra energy exploring the historic buildings at **Sonoma State Historic Park** before heading to Napa. Make a stop at **Starmont Winery and Vineyards,** which prides itself on its kid-friendly atmosphere almost as much as its estate pinot noir. You'll get a flight of five wines and they'll get their own menu of organic snacks, activity books, and a variety of lawn games. For lunch, the **Oxbow Public Market** can accommodate even the most fickle palate (with a noise level to match); however, you may get talked into a treat or two from **Kara's Cupcakes.**

Next, consider making a stop at **Robert** **Mondavi Winery, Beringer Vineyards,** or **Castello di Amorosa,** all of which have tours that accommodate and even entertain kids. Follow your tour up with a walk through **Bale Grist Mill.** The massive grinding stone turning wheat into flour never fails to impress. Or you may just want to plant yourself with a newly purchased bottle of rosé at the **Old Faithful Geyser,** while the kids wait for it to blow. Games, a petting zoo, and plenty of room to run around keep everyone happy while you relax in the sunshine. Stay at the surprisingly family-friendly **Dr. Wilkinson's Hot Springs Resort,** where kids will love the pool and you'll love the no-fuss atmosphere.

COOMBSVILLE

6 miles round-trip

Just east of downtown Napa, this sleepy AVA is filled with gently winding country roads and plenty of appoint-ment-only wineries pouring crafted cool-weather pinot noir and chardonnay.

Begin your ride in downtown Napa by taking 3rd Street across the Napa River to its junction with Coombsville Road. Just past the cemetery, make a stop at **Tulocay Winery** for barrel and stainless steel-fermented chardonnay beneath the resident oak tree. Then, go left on 3rd Avenue for a flight of chardonnay and pinot at **Ancien**. Continue on 3rd Avenue to reach **Farella Vineyard,** which offers varietals by a longtime Coombsville winemaker. From Farella, go back down 3rd Avenue, make a right on North Road, a left on 1st Avenue, and then another left to reach Coombsville Road back to Napa. Eat at **Taqueria Maria** in Napa for a filling post-ride meal.

SONOMA

10 miles round-trip

Downtown Sonoma is blessed with shaded country roads populated with historic wineries that sell picnic sup-plies and have fantastic picnic areas. Plan on eating lunch on the road.

Begin at the Sonoma Plaza and take Lovall Valley Road east to Gehricke Road, where **Ravenswood** il-luminates the wonders of zinfandel. Hop back on Lovall Valley Road to Castle Road and the history-laden **Bartholomew Park Winery.** It sits on the original estate of wine pioneer Agoston Haraszthy along with **Buena Vista Winery,** on the next road off Lovall Valley Road, aptly named Old Winery Road. Once back on Lovall Valley Road, take a right on Thornsberry Road until it winds its way to **Gundlach Bundschu Winery,** where you will be rewarded with wonderful views, beautiful wine, and even a cave tour. To get back to the plaza, take Bundschu Road to Denmark Street. Take a left. Take another right on 7th Avenue East, followed by a left on E. Macarthur Street, a right on 2nd Street East, then a left on East Napa Street.

CARNEROS

5 miles one-way

Just as flat as Sonoma, but a little cooler and with longer distances between wineries, Carneros offers a quiet ride through the vineyards. It's possible to tour the entire southeast section by bike, but it's a 20-mile round-trip.

Consider starting at **Etude Wines** close to Napa. Once you've had a flight of the estate wines, head south on Cuttings Wharf Road until it reaches Las Amigas Road, which will shortly veer left. Head straight until you reach Buchli Station Road, which will take you to the picturesque **Bouchaine Vineyards.** Flat and straight Las Amigas gives way to curvy and hilly Duhig Road when you turn right at the intersection. Ride the heart-pounding hill, then descend to reach chardonnay specialist **Cuvaison**'s modern tasting room. Finally, reward yourself with bubbly and small bites on the veranda at nearby **Domaine Carneros.**

DRY CREEK VALLEY

6 miles one-way

Northern Sonoma is packed with tiny country roads, but the best ride is up West Dry Creek Road, where the bumps and turns of this narrow country lane keep cars going slow. It gets hot in the summer.

Make your first stop the **Dry Creek General Store,** where you can stock up on plenty of water and picnic supplies or grab that last shot of espresso. Cross Dry Creek Road and ride a short way down Lambert Bridge Road to **Dry Creek Vineyard** to start your tour of heat-loving varietals. After your flight of old vine zinfandels, take Lambert Bridge Road to West Dry Creek Road and take a right. More zinfandel and flavorful sauvignon blanc can be found at **Quivira Vineyards.** Keep pedaling north until you reach **Göpfrich Estate Vineyard and Winery;** stop for some unusual late-harvest German white wines. At the top of West Dry Creek Road, **Bella Vineyards** makes good on its name, pouring beautiful zinfandel to match its beautiful farm-like setting. Backtrack slightly to **Preston Farm & Winery,** which is the ideal spot to conclude your ride with a flight of Rhône varietals, a loaf of hearty sourdough bread, and fresh fruit and aged cheese.

Napa Valley

Look for ★ to find recommended
sights, activities, dining, and lodging.

Highlights

★ **The Hess Collection:** Located in the mountains above Napa, this winery/gallery brings new meaning to the expression "the art of winemaking" (page 46).

★ **Domaine Chandon:** This Yountville winery offers one of the best tours in Napa as well as a gorgeous setting in which to sample its premier California champagne (page 60).

★ **Robert Mondavi Winery:** This pioneering winery is a great introduction to wine and the valley that grows it (page 75).

★ **Mumm:** This sophisticated yet easygoing winery excels in friendly service, sparkling wines, and generous pours (page 79).

★ **Frog's Leap Winery:** Revel in the laid-back vibe at this organic winery and garden. There's an excellent tour of the vineyards (page 80).

★ **Pride Mountain Vineyards:** Straddling the Napa and Sonoma border, this mountaintop winery has some of the best views in the valley and some of the best mountain wines (page 94).

★ **Bothe-Napa Valley State Park:** Stroll back in time through the redwoods and explore the **Bale Grist Mill** nearby (page 99).

★ **Schramsberg Vineyards:** If you plan to visit just one champagne cellar, why not make it the most historic one in the valley? Tour the spooky cellars once visited by Robert Louis Stevenson (page 113).

★ **Calistoga Spas:** Sink into a relaxing bath of Calistoga's famous mud at **Dr. Wilkinson's**

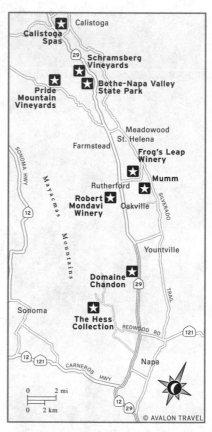

Hot Springs Resort, soak in California's largest mineral pool at **Indian Springs Resort,** or detox in the infrared sauna following your massage at **EuroSpa** (page 116).

T here's no escaping it—the Napa Valley is regarded as the center of everything wine in California, no matter how Sonoma, Santa Barbara, or Mendocino might jump up and down for attention.

The oft-mentioned Paris tasting of 1976, which pitted the valley's wines in a blind tasting against France's best, put the Napa Valley—and California—firmly on the international wine map: Napa Valley wines won both the red and white tasting, while other California wines placed in the top five.

The Napa Valley led the premium wine revolution in the 1980s and saw the building of some of California's most ostentatious wineries in the last two decades, including a grandiose castle near Calistoga. This little valley is now home to more than a quarter of all the wineries in California, despite the fact that it accounts for only about 4 percent of all the wine made in the state. The statistics speak for themselves—the Napa Valley turns out some of the best wine in California.

The valley is also a marketing manager's dream. Natural beauty, colorful history, some of the biggest names in the world of wine, and $100 bottles of cabernet all serve to draw hordes of visitors—almost five million a year at last count. They in turn are entertained by top chefs, luxury pampering, and lavish winery shows like no others in California, or probably anywhere else in the world.

It can all seem a bit like a giant wine theme park at times, especially when you are lining up at yet another ticket booth to empty your wallet for the privilege of being herded around another winery by guides who are probably as bored as they look.

While many visitors flock to the same big wineries, there are hundreds of others to choose from in the valley, big and small, glamorous and rustic. Such diversity is one of Napa Valley's big draws and the reason so many people keep coming back for more.

Art lovers could easily spend an entire vacation visiting the many wineries with art or sculpture displays, not to mention all the public art found in Yountville and the cutting-edge galleries of St. Helena. Photosensitive

Previous: Castello di Amorosa in Calistoga; old vine chardonnay in Coombsville. **Above:** vineyards on Spring Mountain.

Lower Napa Valley

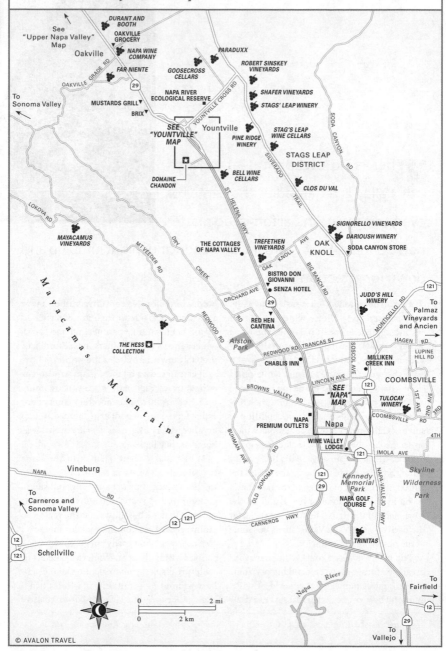

See
"Upper Napa Valley"
Map

Oakville

DURANT AND BOOTH

OAKVILLE GROCERY

NAPA WINE COMPANY

PARADUXX

ROBERT SINSKEY VINEYARDS

FAR NIENTE

GOOSECROSS CELLARS

OAKVILLE GRADE RD

29

NAPA RIVER ECOLOGICAL RESERVE

SHAFER VINEYARDS

STAGS' LEAP WINERY

To
Sonoma Valley

MUSTARDS GRILL

BRIX

YOUNTVILLE CROSS RD

SODA CANYON RD

SEE "YOUNTVILLE" MAP

Yountville

PINE RIDGE WINERY

STAG'S LEAP WINE CELLARS

STAGS LEAP DISTRICT

SILVERADO TRAIL

LOKOYA RD

DOMAINE CHANDON

BELL WINE CELLARS

CLOS DU VAL

ST. HELENA HWY

MAYACAMUS VINEYARDS

MT. VEEDER RD

THE COTTAGES OF NAPA VALLEY

TREFETHEN VINEYARDS

OAK KNOLL AVE

OAK KNOLL

SIGNORELLO VINEYARDS

DARIOUSH WINERY

SODA CANYON STORE

DRY CREEK

ORCHARD AVE

BISTRO DON GIOVANNI

SENZA HOTEL

BIG RANCH RD

121

M a y a c a m a s

29

JUDD'S HILL WINERY

To
Palmaz
Vineyards
and Ancien

MONTICELLO RD

REDWOOD RD

RED HEN CANTINA

HAGEN RD

THE HESS COLLECTION

Alston Park

REDWOOD RD

TRANCAS ST

CHABLIS INN

LINCOLN AVE

MILLIKEN CREEK INN

SOSCOL AVE

LUPINE HILL RD

COOMBSVILLE

M o u n t a i n s

BROWNS VALLEY RD

SEE "NAPA" MAP

121

TULOCAY WINERY

1ST AVE

2ND AVE

3RD

NAPA PREMIUM OUTLETS

Napa

COOMBSVILLE RD

BUHMAN AVE

WINE VALLEY LODGE

121

IMOLA AVE

4TH

Vineburg

NAPA

OLD SONOMA RD

121

Kennedy Memorial Park

NAPA VALLEJO HWY

Skyline Wilderness Park

To
Carneros and
Sonoma Valley

RD

29

NAPA GOLF COURSE

12

121

12

121

Schellville

CARNEROS HWY

TRINITAS

Napa River

To
Fairfield

12

© AVALON TRAVEL

0   2 mi

0   2 km

29

To
Vallejo

souls can hunt down all the wineries with cool, dark underground caves. Architecture buffs will have a field day at some of the more outlandish facilities, with design influences in the valley ranging from medieval to avant-garde.

And all of that happens before even considering wine itself. The valley is home to everything from boutique wineries making just a few hundred cases of wine a year to corporate behemoths turning out millions. The multitude of microclimates has given rise to a patchwork of 16 (and counting) distinct appellations, or AVAs, where just about every major type of grape can be grown. Although this is a red wine lover's paradise, there's a wine made here for almost every palate.

The valley's diversity extends well beyond wine: At one end are Napa's charming entertainment venues and museums, and at the other are the hot springs and spas of Calistoga. In between, nature offers plenty of diversions, and restaurants turn out delicacies that would put many in the world's finest dining capitals to shame.

The locals are remarkably sanguine about the endless stream of visitors clogging their valley. Clearly, they are wise enough not to discourage the hands that ultimately feed them. But they also get to experience the beauty and diversity of the valley, the quality of the food, and the strong sense of community when the rest of us have long since gone home.

And, of course, they get to toast their good fortune with some of the best wines in the world.

ORIENTATION

The Napa Valley, including Eastern Carneros, is roughly 35 miles long, with two main roads running up each side and about half a dozen roads traversing the 2-4 miles between them. As far as the world's major winemaking regions go, this is baby-sized, so don't be intimidated.

Just north of Carneros is the city of **Napa** itself, the biggest settlement in the valley,

home to many of the workers who keep the wine industry humming. The small city lacks the bucolic charm of the other towns up the valley and has traditionally been bypassed by tourists speeding to the big-name wineries and trendy destinations. However, over the years, Napa has transformed itself into a destination in its own right, thanks to a revamped riverfront and downtown commercial district, burgeoning dining scene, and its proximity to one of the valley's newest AVAs.

From Napa, the two main valley roads begin. The St. Helena Highway—more commonly known as **Highway 29**—is the well-beaten path up the valley. It passes the town of **Yountville,** dominated by increasingly upscale shops, restaurants, and hotels, then whistles past sleepy **Oakville** and **Rutherford** before hitting what has become almost the spiritual heart of the valley, **St. Helena.** Pretty, upscale, full of boutiques and restaurants, St. Helena still manages to be a fairly down-to-earth, functional place—except on those weekends when the world comes to visit and traffic slows to a crawl.

St. Helena and the surrounding big-name wineries are the main draw in this part of the valley, and rural tranquility quickly returns as Highway 29 continues north to the narrow top of the valley, where laid-back **Calistoga** has an almost frontier-town feel—seemingly torn between maintaining its slumber and being awakened by attracting more tourists to its up-and-coming wineries and famous volcanic hot springs.

Calistoga is also where the other main valley road, the **Silverado Trail,** ends. Named for a silver mine that it once served north of Calistoga, it runs from Napa along the foot of the eastern hills and is the shortcut used to get up and down the valley by locals in the summer when the other side is clogged. Anyone in a hurry to get to a spa appointment in Calistoga or a restaurant in Napa should consider cutting across the valley to the Silverado Trail if there is heavy traffic on Highway 29.

This undulating, winding two-lane road remains almost eerily quiet at times and feels

Upper Napa Valley

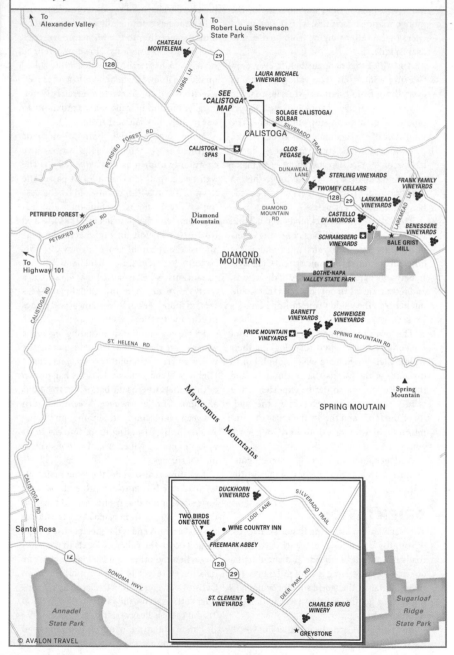

To Alexander Valley

To Robert Louis Stevenson State Park

CHATEAU MONTELENA

128

29

TUBBS LN

LAURA MICHAEL VINEYARDS

SEE "CALISTOGA" MAP

SOLAGE CALISTOGA/ SOLBAR

SILVERADO TRAIL

CALISTOGA

PETRIFIED FOREST RD

CALISTOGA SPAS

CLOS PEGASE

DUNAWEAL LANE

STERLING VINEYARDS

FRANK FAMILY VINEYARDS

TWOMEY CELLARS

128 29 LARKMEAD VINEYARDS

LARKMEAD LN

PETRIFIED FOREST ★

PETRIFIED FOREST RD

Diamond Mountain

DIAMOND MOUNTAIN RD

CASTELLO DI AMOROSA

BENESSERE VINEYARDS

SCHRAMSBERG VINEYARDS

BALE GRIST MILL

To Highway 101

CALISTOGA RD

DIAMOND MOUNTAIN

BOTHE-NAPA VALLEY STATE PARK

BARNETT VINEYARDS

SCHWEIGER VINEYARDS

PRIDE MOUNTAIN VINEYARDS

SPRING MOUNTAIN RD

ST. HELENA RD

Mayacamus Mountains

▲ Spring Mountain

SPRING MOUTAIN

CALISTOGA RD

Santa Rosa

DUCKHORN VINEYARDS

SILVERADO TRAIL

TWO BIRDS ONE STONE

LODI LANE

WINE COUNTRY INN

FREEMARK ABBEY

128 29

DEER PARK RD

12

SONOMA HWY

ST. CLEMENT VINEYARDS

CHARLES KRUG WINERY

Sugarloaf Ridge State Park

Annadel State Park

★ GREYSTONE

© AVALON TRAVEL

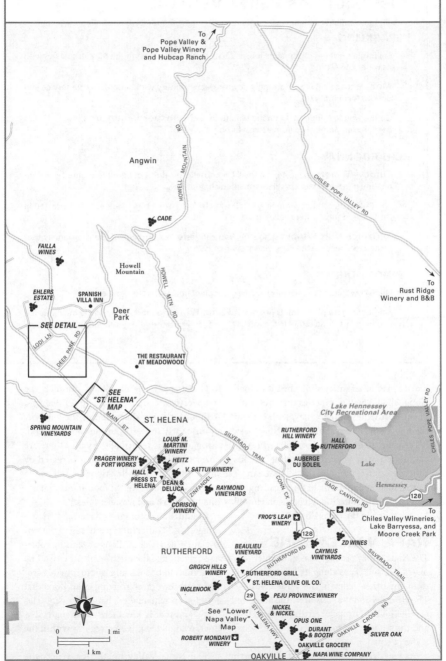

Best of Napa Valley Varietals

SPARKLING

- California's first big champagne house, **Domaine Chandon** (page 60) still sparkles with its wines and setting.

- **Mumm** (page 79) is a surprisingly down-to-earth winery with generous table service and options for nondrinkers.

- On the wooded slopes of Diamond Mountain, **Schramsberg Vineyards** (page 113) has been making some of California's best bubbly since 1862.

CHARDONNAY

- **Tulocay Winery** (page 44) is a small Coombsville producer of barrel-fermented chardonnay and unoaked, stainless steel-fermented chardonnay.

- The Oak Knoll estate chardonnays at **Trefethen Vineyards** (page 45) can be tasted in the historic Eshcol winery building.

- At **Grgich Hills Winery** (page 78), you can taste descendants of the chardonnay that bested the French in the Paris wine-tasting of 1976.

PINOT NOIR

- Learn how soil and climate mix to make great pinot noir at **Ancien** (page 43).

- Single-vineyard pinot noir is poured at **Failla Wines** (page 93), one of the most relaxed and friendly tasting rooms in the valley.

like it's in another valley altogether. It's a road along which smaller wineries turn out some of the best wines in the valley, with little of the hoopla of the big show-offs farther west. It's also a road down which serious wine lovers might prefer to travel, sampling famous cabernet sauvignons in the Stags Leap or Rutherford appellations before heading up into the hills to some hidden gems on Howell Mountain or in the rural Chiles Valley.

NAPA VALLEY WINES

The Napa Valley probably has more microclimates and soil types along its 35-mile length than any other valley in the Wine Country. The climates and the soils drew the attention of wine-loving European settlers in the 1800s, and the seeds of the modern-day wine industry were sown.

As you drive from the city of Napa north to Calistoga in the middle of summer, the temperature can rise by up to 20 degrees. Although the northern end of the valley is significantly hotter than the southern end, throughout the length of the valley there are dozens of unique microclimates created by small hills on the valley floor as well as the canyons and slopes of the mountains that define its eastern and western sides.

In addition, geologists have identified a staggering 33 different types of soil in the valley, laid down over millions of years by volcanoes, rivers, and the earth's shifting crust. The combination of soils and microclimates creates a patchwork of growing conditions that could keep winemakers happy for centuries more, and that is why there are so many distinct, recognized growing regions within the Napa Valley.

The Napa Valley north of Carneros is

CABERNET

- At **Shafer Vineyards** (page 65), you might be lucky enough to taste the Hillside Select cabernet.

- **Stag's Leap Wine Cellars** (page 64) is home to the vineyards that beat the best in the world in the famous Paris tasting of 1976.

- Splurge on the $125 clonal tasting at **Bell Wine Cellars** (page 63) and distinguish the characteristics from a distinct clone of cabernet.

- **Beaulieu Vineyard** (page 78) is a historic 1900 winery that makes bold cabernets laced with the distinct flavor of "Rutherford dust."

- Compare Napa and Alexander vintages at **Silver Oak** (page 76), a perennial favorite with cabernet enthusiasts.

- **St. Clement Vineyards** (page 90) pours cabernets from different appellations in the valley in one of the prettiest tasting rooms.

MERLOT

- High above Rutherford, **Rutherford Hill Winery** (page 80) specializes in well-structured merlot.

- **Duckhorn Vineyards** (page 92) is known for its outstanding merlot, personal service, and exclusive tasting lounge.

- **Twomey Cellars** (page 109) employs an ancient racking technique known as *soutirage traditionnel* in order to make rave-worthy merlot.

predominantly a red wine-growing region, thanks primarily to a warm climate that ensures the most popular red grape varietals can easily ripen and attain the sugar levels needed to make the big, powerful wines for which the valley is known. White grapes and some red varietals like pinot noir can get by in cooler climates because they generally reach their desired ripeness more easily while retaining the high acid levels desired by winemakers.

The one red grape for which Napa is most famous is cabernet sauvignon. There are roughly 45,000 acres of vineyards planted in Napa County, about three-quarters of which are planted with red grape varietals. Just over half of that red grape acreage is cabernet, which means that one varietal accounts for 40 percent of all the vineyards in Napa County (about 19,000 acres). The figure is probably closer to 50 percent of all the vineyards in the

Napa Valley north of Carneros, where pinot noir and chardonnay are the more dominant varietals.

That's not to say that other wines are not important here—far from it. The Napa Valley is where some of California's most distinctive chardonnay and sauvignon blanc are produced, together with increasing amounts of syrah, sangiovese, and many other minor varietals. But cabernet always has dominated the vineyards and probably always will, with chardonnay a distant second in terms of vineyard acreage, followed closely by merlot.

Most of the big Napa Valley wineries own vineyards all over the valley. They and smaller wineries also often buy fruit from other growers outside Napa Valley, so white-wine drinkers need not despair—there will usually be plenty of whites on offer, even at wineries in the big-cab appellations like Rutherford and Stags Leap. But ultimately this is a valley dominated by cabernet and chardonnay, and those looking for more unusual types of wine will want to choose the wineries they visit carefully.

TOURS

One way to visit wineries without having to worry about traffic, drinking, or cooking an expensive wine in a sunbaked car is to take a daylong organized wine tour. Someone else does the driving, you can drink until you can no longer stand, and any precious wine purchases will get transported back to your hotel probably in better shape than you.

Another advantage is that the local tour guides are knowledgeable about the valley, the wineries, and often about wines as well, making an organized tour an option worth considering if you have no idea where to start.

The **Napa Valley Wine Trolley** (877/946-3876 or 707/252-6100, www.napavalleywinetrolley.com, tours 6-6.5 hours, $99-129) departs every day from Napa and Yountville in a motorized cable car. Stops are made at four wineries, and a catered lunch from Oxbow Market is included. What is not included are the tasting fees, which can total $80-90 per trip, making it an expensive, albeit fun and relaxing, day out. Likewise, the **Napa Winery Shuttle** (707/257-1950, www.wineshuttle.com, $75) specializes in personal tours of the valley from Napa to Calistoga. The shuttle has a long list of local hotels it picks up from at about 10am (though they can often pick up at any hotel not on the list). It generally hits about five or six wineries with a stop for a gourmet lunch along the way. Unfortunately, the fee doesn't include tasting, but wineries will often throw in a deal or two for being with this long-standing Napa Valley business.

Beau Wine Tours (707/938-8001 or 800/387-2328, www.beauwinetours.com) is more of a custom touring company and often the owner of the limos seen parked at some of the bigger wineries. Rent a chauffeured car, SUV, limousine, or van for 3-13 people for

Napa Valley Wine Train

$65-90 per hour plus tax, tip, and (depending on gas prices) a fuel surcharge, and plan your own itinerary. Note that the size of the stretch limos and vans means they sometimes cannot visit smaller wineries at all, or only by prior arrangement. Beau Wine Tours has plenty of knowledge of the valley, however, and can offer lots of advice. It also offers private, preplanned, daylong tours (www.dynamicnapawinetours.com, from $125).

Napa Valley Wine Train

The **Napa Valley Wine Train** (1275 McKinstry St., Napa, 707/253-2111 or 800/427-4124, www.winetrain.com, $129-300) is surely the most glamorous touring option. You'll experience the valley aboard vintage train cars, while you can sit back and enjoy the food, wine, and views. The train runs from Napa to St. Helena and back, a 36-mile three-hour round-trip tour. Each package includes seating in a different historic railcar—you might lunch in the 1917 Pullman Car or take an evening tour of Grgich Hills aboard the

1952 Vista Dome Car. Visits to Grgich Hills, Raymond Vineyards, Castello di Amorosa, or Charles Krug can be tacked onto lunch, but to make this a true tour and tasting experience select the Quattro Vino tour, which stops at Robert Mondavi, Charles Krug, Merryvale, and V. Sattui. Advance reservations are strongly suggested.

PLANNING YOUR TIME

How can visitors make sense of all these wineries and avoid all the crowds? It's a $10,000 question with about 10,000 different answers. Many visitors seem to follow a similar pattern, never making it much farther north than St. Helena and sticking to the western side of the valley. If you can avoid that pattern, you're halfway to lowering your blood pressure.

The other key to enjoying the valley rather than being frustrated by it is plenty of planning. There's so much to do and so many wineries to visit that anyone simply turning up without a plan, however vague, will end up with a headache even before drinking too much wine in the sun. Visitors can get away with no preplanning in many other parts of Wine Country, but not in such a tourist mecca as the Napa Valley.

Research the type of wine that wineries specialize in before choosing which to visit, especially if you're not a big red-wine drinker. This is, after all, the land of endless cabernet sauvignon, but it is also a land where plenty of stunning white wines, including champagne, are made. And if you are a big cabernet drinker, this can be the place to learn much more about the king of wines—how and why a Spring Mountain cabernet is different from a Stags Leap cabernet, for example.

Alternatively, pick a theme not related to wine for a day of touring. Wineries in Napa have necessarily become adept at distinguishing themselves from their competitors to try to attract increasingly jaded visitors, a form of Wine Country evolution. Some rely on the reputation of their wines, others on **art, caves, car collections, architecture, gardens, tours, history**—the list is almost

endless and provides endless employment opportunities for marketing folks. Another option is to **abandon the car** altogether. From Napa to Calistoga, tasting rooms have opened along the valley's Main Streets, many of which are boutique wineries too small to have their own on-site tasting rooms. Fees are low, and the atmospheres are fun and relaxed. So pick what town most appeals to you, park the car, taste, shop, spa, and dine.

Or you can head for the hills, where healthy doses of nature help make the hidden wineries in the **Coombsville, Spring Mountain,** and **Chiles Valley** appellations that much more enjoyable. Unfortunately, most mountain wineries are appointment only and require some planning to visit.

If possible, avoid the peak season that runs roughly **July-October.** It brings peak crowds (particularly on weekends), peak hotel prices, and peak daytime temperatures. **April-June** is perhaps the best time to visit, when the wet winter season is finally drying out, the temperatures are mild, the creeks flowing, the hills green, and the vineyards full of vivid yellow wild mustard.

Most of all, the key to experiencing the best of the valley is to keep it simple and relaxed. Napa is about savoring the moment. Select three wineries at most to visit per day and consider carefully where you want to enjoy each meal (picnic or a fine dining restaurant?). If you are worried you won't see everything you want to, start planning your next trip!

GETTING THERE

There were far more ways to get to the Napa Valley a century ago, when trains and riverboats brought the visitors and goods that made the valley so successful. The car has long since become the main transportation mode, though the more adventurous can still get here on public transportation.

Car

The Napa Valley is almost the same driving distance from three major international airports—Oakland, San Francisco, and

A Case for Winter

Visiting the Napa Valley conjures dreams of long golden afternoons tasting cabernets, soaking in the sun at some the valley's most luxurious spas, and cycling along country lanes as the vineyards turn in the heat of an Indian summer. The unfortunate truth is that traveling during Napa's most spectacular seasons (summer and fall) can also mean horrendous traffic, crowded tasting rooms, and astronomical hotel prices. So, why not go in winter?

In fact, winter is the best-kept secret in Wine Country. Hotel prices drop by as much as 50 percent, and restaurants, eager to lure in diners, offer inexpensive prix fixe dinners and even coupons for 10 percent off or a free appetizer or dessert. In tasting rooms free of summer crowds, pourers have more time (and patience) to give you individual attention, even sharing with you some of their favorite vintages not on the tasting menu.

The beauty of traveling in the off-season is also the weather. Rarely does it dip below 55 degrees, and Napa is often blessed with crystal clear days. If it does rain, there are several wineries that are the perfect place to spend a drizzly day.

- **Beringer Vineyards, St. Helena:** Splurge on a reserve tasting and wait out the rain inside the ornate Rhine House, filled with carved wood and beautiful stained glass.

- **Prager Winery & Port Works, St. Helena:** Warm yourself with a tawny port.

- **Castello di Amorosa, Calistoga:** Listen to the rain hit Italian quarried stone as you sip wine or tour the vast armory and torture chamber.

- **Schramsberg Vineyards, Calistoga:** Wander through history-soaked caves and sample some of the finest sparkling wine in the country.

- **Vermeil Wines, Calistoga:** Cozy up with a glass of muscular cabernet in an overstuffed leather chair.

Sacramento. Driving from the airports to the city of Napa itself will take 1-2 hours, depending on traffic; from downtown San Francisco or Oakland, it's closer to an hour of driving time.

The most direct route from Oakland and Sacramento is on **I-80** (west from Sacramento, east from Oakland). Exit at Six Flags Discovery Kingdom (Highway 37), then take Highway 29 north into Napa and beyond. From Sacramento, a slightly more direct route is to exit at Jameson Canyon Road (U.S. 12), a little farther north of American Canyon. This also heads west and meets Highway 29 at the Napa airport.

From San Francisco (especially downtown), it takes about the same amount of time to drive across the Bay Bridge to I-80 and north to Napa as it does to go the prettier route through Marin. This route crosses the Golden Gate Bridge on **U.S. Highway** **101** to Marin County, then east on Highway 37 before Novato, which links with Highway 121 through Carneros, past the turnoff to the Sonoma Valley, and eventually to Highway 29 just south of Napa.

The Napa Valley is also easily accessible from other parts of the Wine Country, thanks to the numerous roads that cross the Mayacamas Mountains on the western side of the valley. From the Sonoma Valley, just north of Glen Ellen, **Trinity Road** winds its way east into the mountains, forking at **Dry Creek Road,** which heads south to Napa and the **Oakville Grade.** Farther north in the Sonoma Valley, just east of Santa Rosa, **Calistoga Road** heads to the hills and eventually to Calistoga, or you can turn off on St. Helena Road after about three miles to cross into the Napa Valley down through the Spring Mountain appellation and into St. Helena.

From the Russian River Valley, just north

of Santa Rosa, take **Mark West Springs Road** east, eventually turning onto Porter Creek Road, which leads down into Calistoga. And from the Alexander Valley, **Highway 128** runs south through Knights Valley to Calistoga.

Try not to be in a rush if you take these routes, because they are narrow, winding, and slow, but a lot of fun if time is not of the essence.

Boat and Bus

The most unusual way to get to the valley without driving, short of an epic bicycle ride, is on the **Baylink Ferry** (877/643-3779, www.baylinkferry.com) from San Francisco via Vallejo. The speedy catamarans leave San Francisco's Ferry Building about every 1-3 hours 6:30am-8pm daily for the hour-long crossing to Vallejo, which is about 12 miles south of Napa. The one-way fare is $13.40 for adults, $6.70 for children 5-18, and free for those 5 and under.

From the Vallejo Ferry Terminal, Route 11 of Napa Valley's **VINE** (707/251-6443 or 800/696-6443, www.ridethevine.com, $1.60-$5.50) bus service runs directly to downtown Napa about every hour until 7pm daily. The express Route 29 is faster, making only a handful of stops, including the El Cerrito BART station, thus linking Napa to the long arms of BART. The only drawback is that Route 29 only runs on weekdays. In the valley, Route 10 runs along Highway 29 from Napa to Calistoga every hour on the weekends and roughly every half hour on the weekdays. Check the schedule for details on this route.

Taking the ferry and bus to the valley and then renting a bike in downtown Napa, St. Helena, or Calistoga for a couple of days would certainly make for a memorable Wine Country experience, but it might not be for the impatient or those traveling on weekends.

GETTING AROUND
Car

Seemingly everyone drives to the Napa Valley, so you'd think everything would be geared up for the cars transporting those five million annual visitors to this part of the world. Wrong! This is essentially agricultural land that its custodians battle to protect, so the mighty vine and strict planning laws limit a lot of development—including, evidently, road widening.

The 28-mile drive from Napa to Calistoga up **Highway 29** can take less than 45 minutes in the middle of a winter day. Try that same drive on a summer weekend or a weekday during the evening rush hour and it might take close to double that time. The sheer volume of traffic is really what slows things down, especially with so much traffic coming and going from the multitude of wineries and the traffic bottleneck of St. Helena's Main Street.

Heading north on Highway 29, you can be lulled into a false sense of security as you zip toward St. Helena, only to hit a wall of traffic about a mile south of the town caused by traffic lights that seem to meter only a dozen cars at a time onto Main Street. Heading south from St. Helena from mid-afternoon until evening on many days, your average speed is likely to be less than 20 mph until well after Rutherford. The mid-valley traffic situation is not helped by the countless turnoffs for wineries from Rutherford to St. Helena that also slow traffic. Make your life easier and use the empty center lane of the road to turn left into wineries or when turning left out of wineries to merge into traffic. That's what it's there for.

The almost constant traffic jams on Highway 29 are also a reason to discover the **Silverado Trail,** running north-south on the other side of the valley. There might be the occasional slowdown caused by a valley visitor unfamiliar with its dips and bends or who is simply lost. Usually, however, this is the domain of merciless local speed demons zipping up and down the valley at 60 mph, a feat usually possible even when the road through St. Helena across the valley is at a standstill. Many locals will use the Silverado to bypass St. Helena altogether, cutting back to Highway 29 when necessary using one of the many small cross-valley roads.

Napa is the only city in the valley to have made an effort to ease traffic, with its brief stretch of smooth-flowing freeway and frustrating yet effective one-way system downtown. The irony, of course, is that so many valley visitors bypass the city for destinations up-valley, traffic is usually light anyway.

Bike

Picking the right route at the right time of the day and exploring a section of the valley by bike can be one of the most enjoyable ways to experience the Wine Country. Whether you plan a long bike ride up the Silverado Trail or a short hop around a few Rutherford-area wineries, there are a handful of established places to rent well-maintained bicycles in Yountville, St. Helena, Calistoga, and Napa. All know the area from a biker's perspective and so will have plenty of suggestions on routes—from easy rides of a few miles to epic loops through some of the best mountain appellations. Helmets, locks, bottle cages, and puncture repair kits are always included with rentals. It's also worth asking about free roadside assistance should you get a flat, or pickup service for any winery purchases.

Touring on a bike is easy in almost every part of the valley thanks to the flat landscape (on the valley floor, at least) and the proximity of all the wineries. The only place you might want to avoid is the stretch of Highway 29 between Oakville and St. Helena, which is the scene of regular car accidents—probably caused by inattentive, lost, or simply drunk visitors. It's also such a busy stretch of road that you might not want the hassle of car-dodging anyway. The **Napa Valley Vine Trail** makes navigating Highway 29 easier. Although still largely under construction, the 47-mile bike trail will connect Vallejo's Ferry Terminal with Calistoga largely paralleling the St. Helena Highway. As of this writing, many of the sections are complete, and it is now easy to pedal your way from Napa to Yountville and through many parts of Calistoga. For the most up-to-date information, visit the website www.vinetrail.org,

along the Silverado Trail

which has a map of the trail's progress. The best stretches of valley to explore on a bike include the **Silverado Trail** in the Stags Leap District, where big-name wineries like Clos Du Val, Pine Ridge, Shafer, Stag's Leap, and Robert Sinskey are all along a three-mile stretch of winding road. Just beware the speed demons on the trail. Other easy rides include many of the cross-valley roads, which sometimes have fewer wineries per mile but also have far less traffic. Biking the Rutherford Road from Highway 29 to the Silverado Trail, for example, takes in Beaulieu, Frog's Leap, and Caymus. Then a few hundred yards down the Silverado Trail are Mumm and ZD Wines.

The **Coombsville** area east of the city of Napa is also worth exploring on bike, not only because it has relatively quiet and flat roads but also because of its proximity to the hotels and amenities of the city. You could leave your hotel after breakfast, visit a couple of small wineries and have a relaxing picnic, then be back in Napa by mid-afternoon.

A couple of companies do all the work and

planning for your bike tour. All you need to do is show up and pedal. To explore the southern part of the valley by bike, stop by **Napa Valley Bike Tours** (6500 Washington St., Yountville, 707/944-2953, www.napavalley-biketours.com, daily 8:30am-5pm) in either Yountville or Napa. You'll have the option of joining half-day ($124) or full-day ($164) tours, or tack on a gourmet meal and spa treatment ($319) to your full day pedal. Expect to visit two to three wineries on each tour, and bear in mind that the fee does not include the tasting fees, but does include a catered gourmet picnic (all-day tour only). If you prefer to go your own way, the company also rents bikes for $45-75 per day and will bring the bikes to your hotel for $40-60. Up north, **Getaway Adventures** (2228 Northpoint Pkwy., Santa Rosa, 800/499-2453, www.getawayadventures.com) offers a five-hour tour ($149) of four wineries in the Calistoga area, and the price includes the bike, helmet, and lunch.

Napa and Vicinity

The blue-collar heart of the Napa Valley is the city of Napa, many of whose 80,000 residents work in banking, construction, the medical industry, and other businesses that serve the rest of the valley. Nathan Coombs laid out the city in grand style on a bend in the Napa River in 1848. The river was pivotal to the city's rapid growth (thanks to its connection to the San Pablo, and by extension San Francisco, Bay), but also to its setbacks. Massive floods, including those that wiped out downtown businesses in the 1980s, 1990s, and as late as 2005, kept the city economically vulnerable and a second-tier destination, despite its location and lovely Victorian past. The 2008 recession and the devastating 2014 earthquake didn't help. However, thanks to smart planning and a successful $300 million flood defense program, the city is on the rebound.

Now Napa has become a destination in its own right. Major luxury hotels have been moving into downtown Napa, including the Archer Hotel, which when completed will be the tallest building in Napa. At the feet of these great hotels, a new crop of restaurants has sprouted, plus many boutique winery tasting rooms. Big-city entertainment keeps Napa happening late into the night, and every year 100,000 people descend on the city for three days of food, wine, and music at the mega music festival BottleRock. The Oxbow Market, the valley's epicurean emporium, continues to shine, and the Culinary Institute of America has recently signed a deal to revamp the defunct Copia (the American Center for Wine, Food, and the Arts), promising to bring more vitality to this foodie district. Expect to find expanded cooking classes, a museum, restaurants, wine-tasting, food and wine demonstrations, and special events at the CIA at Copia beginning in 2017.

As for the river, it has regained its status as a boon to the city. A promenade along the water's edge provides scenic walks, and a new boat launch in the heart of downtown gives river access to kayaks, canoes, and stand-up paddleboards. A multiuse trail is in the works along the river through the city, as is native plant restoration. Beavers have already recolonized the city's stretch of river, and there is talk of a water taxi to the ferry terminal in Vallejo, creating a direct aquatic link to San Francisco. With plentiful accommodations and a vibrant dining scene, plus scores of attractions and recreation, visitors may find themselves tasting up-valley but returning to Napa for dinner and bed, or just sticking to Napa altogether.

The Wines

Napa is chock-full of tasting rooms, and the city is bordered by one of the best mountain appellations in the valley as well as two of the newest AVAs. All are home to historic and modern wineries, small and large.

Just east of the city of Napa is the newest of the Napa Valley's 16 appellations, **Coombsville.** Small in terms of vineyard acreage (under 1,000 acres) and the number of wineries, it has begun to nevertheless turn out some noteworthy wines as distinct as any in the valley thanks to a patchwork of different soils and microclimates, from sun-soaked hillsides to cool, breezy lowlands. It is an ideal place to grow both cabernet and Bordeaux varietals as well as cooler-climate varietals like pinot noir and chardonnay. Natural acidity and soft-focused tannins characterize the wines made here, so lovers of big, burly Napa Valley wines might be disappointed.

To the north, and stretching across the valley floor from the Silverado Trail to the St. Helena Highway and crossing the alluvial fan of the ancient Dry Creek is **Oak Knoll,** the other new addition to the Napa Valley's appellations. Here, the climate is a blend of the cooler weather in Carneros, south of Napa, and the hotter mid-valley temperatures. Just about every major grape varietal is grown here, though the appellation is probably best known for whites such as chardonnay and sauvignon blanc. It is also one of the few places in the valley where varietals such as pinot noir and riesling do well.

West of the Oak Knoll appellation is the **Mount Veeder** appellation, which extends from Napa up the middle of the valley on the slopes of the Mayacamas Mountains to the highest ridges and the Sonoma County line, and from Carneros to the Oakville Grade on the western side of the valley. Compared to the Spring Mountain and Diamond Mountain appellations farther north on the slopes of the same range, Mount Veeder wines have a leaner, more mineral edge to them, but with strong tannins. The thin volcanic soils provide little nourishment for the struggling vines, and the region is far enough south to feel the cooling effects of the bay. The conditions result in elegant, age-worthy cabernets with good acidity and an earthiness lacking from mountain appellations farther north. Likewise, Mount Veeder chardonnays are fresh and bright with an equally distinctive sense of place.

NAPA WINERIES

TRINITAS

Situated in a cool cave beneath a hilltop vineyard, the **Trinitas Tasting Room** (875 Bordeaux Way, 707/251-3012, www.trinitascellars.com, 11am-7pm daily, tasting $25) functions as the resort wine bar for the Meritage Inn. The bar is open to both hotel guests and passersby, offering tastings of Trinitas wines. Surprisingly balanced, these well-crafted wines are more than worth your time, even if (or especially if) you're serious about your vintages. Seats at the bar make it easy to get comfortable and stay awhile—which quickly becomes a possibility as soon as tasters get their nose inside a glass.

Downtown Tasting Rooms

You could spend a whole day, or even two, sampling wines from the dozen tasting rooms in the city of Napa itself—a process that's made a lot cheaper with the Taste Napa Downtown wine-tasting card, available at the **Napa Valley Welcome Center** (600 Main St., 707/251-5895 or 855/847-6265, www.visitnapavalley.com, 9am-5pm daily). The cards are also available online through the **Downtown Napa Association** (www.donapa.com), which produces the passes. However, you must allow enough lead time to make sure it reaches you by mail before you arrive in Napa. Costing $30, the card pays for tastings at eight downtown tasting rooms. Check online for participating wineries.

Without the card, tasting prices range from $5 up to $25 at the larger collectives. Many of Napa's tasting rooms are the only places to taste the wine from some of the valley's smallest wineries, and the winemakers themselves will sometimes be pouring the wines on weekends.

Napa

To Yountville

CALIFORNIA BLVD

LAUREL ST

OAK ST

3RD ST

2ND ST

1ST ST

300 yds
300 m

YORK ST

GEORGE ST

SPENCER ST

JEFFERSON ST

H ST

G ST

F ST

E ST

D ST

B ST

BEL ABRI INN

THE BEAZLEY HOUSE

WARREN ST

JEFFERSON ST

Fuller Park

BLACKBIRD INN

CLAY ST

CALISTOGA AVE

HAYES ST

BROWN ST

MAIN ST

SEMINARY ST

SEMINARY ST

J&M CELLARS

JOHN ANTHONY TASTING LOUNGE

LA BELLE EPOQUE

RANDOLPH ST

ARROYO DR

1313 MAIN

UVA TRATTORIA & BAR

NAPA ST

VALLEJO ST

YOUNT ST

VALLEJO ST

HENNESSEY HOUSE

ST CLAIR BROWN WINERY

VALLOME ST

ANDAZ NAPA

UPTOWN THEATRE

BETTY'S GIRL

2ND ST

1ST ST

ANTIQUES ON SECOND

PEARL ST

SHACKFORD'S KITCHEN STORE

AZZURRO PIZZERIA & ENOTECA

NAPA BOOKMINE

SOSCOL AVE

MCKINSTRY ST

IMPERIAL WAY

3RD ST

OAK ST

FRANKLIN ST

FIRST PRESBYTERIAN CHURCH

RANDOLPH ST

COOMBS ST

MIMINASHI

MAIN ST

4TH ST

NAPA VALLEY OPERA HOUSE

BOUNTY HUNTER WINE BAR & SMOKIN' BBQ

DOWNTOWN JOE'S AMERICAN GRILL AND BREWHOUSE

NAPA VALLEY WINE TRAIN STATION

LA TOQUE AND BANK CAFE & BAR

S COOMBS ST

CEDAR GABLES INN

5TH ST

NAPA RIVER INN

SILO'S

THE PEAR

MORIMOTO'S

NAPA VALLEY WELCOME CENTER

CELADON

THE PEAR

Veterans Memorial Park

SOSCOL AVE

MARK HEROLD WINE

OXBOW PUBLIC MARKET

CIA AT COPIA

BROWN ST

RIVERSIDE DR

NAPA MILL

ANGÈLE

NAPA GENERAL STORE

4TH ST

BURNELL ST

3RD ST

1ST ST

Napa River

TAQUERIA MARIA

SILVERADO COOKING SCHOOL

JUAREZ ST

SILVERADO TRAIL

To Coombsville Wineries

© AVALON TRAVEL

Downtown Napa Tasting Tour

Begin your day at the **Napa Valley Welcome Center** and pick up a wine-tasting card, a few free passes, and loads of helpful advice from the gracious staff. Take a stroll down Main Street and across the river to **Mark Herold,** where you'll start your day with some outrageous cabernets. For lunch, head across the street to **Oxbow Public Market.** Pick between burgers at **Gott's Roadside,** tacos at **C Casa,** or sushi at **Eiko's at Oxbow.** After lunch, browse for kitchen-related knickknacks at **Napastak** or hunt down rare spices at **Whole Spice Company.** Once fortified with food (and maybe a cupcake or two from **Kara's Cupcakes**), keep heading up Main Street to **Vintner's Collective,** Napa's biggest tasting room, and order a flight of six wines from the valley's premium boutique wineries. For one last tasting, walk across the street to **1313 Main,** a tasting room/restaurant/lounge that offers 13 whites and 13 reds and quickly becomes happy hour central in the early evenings. Alternatively, jump in the car and drive 10 minutes east into the quiet hills of Coombsville to taste delicate and aromatic chardonnay and pinot noir at **Ancien.** End your day in downtown Napa with *izakaya*-style small plates at **Miminashi,** a local hot spot. Plan a stay at the **Blackbird Inn,** which is conveniently located near downtown.

VINTNER'S COLLECTIVE

The biggest tasting room is the **Vintner's Collective** (1245 Main St. at Clinton St., 707/255-7150, www.vintnerscollective.com, 11am-7pm daily, tasting $10-25) in the historic stone Pfeiffer Building. A house of ill repute during its Victorian youth, it is now the public face of 31 different wineries and winemakers. The regular tasting includes a flight of three wines, while the more expensive tasting adds three more-expensive wines. Parking is free, although limited.

JOHN ANTHONY TASTING LOUNGE

As Napa continues to evolve and reach out to the younger set, its tasting rooms have taken on a city chic. **John Anthony Tasting Lounge** (1440 1st St., 707/265-7711, www.johnanthonyvineyards.com, 10am-10pm Sun.-Wed., 10am-midnight Thurs.-Sat., tasting $20-30), next to the new Andaz Napa, looks more like a classy café than your typical tasting room. The white and black color scheme is warmed up with dark wood that seems to glow, particularly in the after hours when John Anthony really comes alive. Whether you stop in during the day or swing by before or after dinner, you can opt for a flight of three wines ($20 or $30), a glass ($8-70—no kidding), or a bottle. For serious wine

lovers, a seated tasting is available during the day by appointment and includes a cheese pairing. The winery is principally known for its cabernet sauvignon, sauvignon blanc, and syrah.

JAM CELLARS

Also rocking the youth vibe is **JaM Cellars** (1460 1st St., 707/265-7577, www.jamcellars.com, 10am-10pm Sun.-Wed., 10am-midnight Thurs.-Sat., tasting $15-20), on the other side of the Andaz Napa. Pouring wine and spinning records late into the night, this hippie-chic tasting room/lounge/recording studio is the brainchild of the folks behind BottleRock, Napa's mega music festival. The wines are approachable and inexpensive (around $20), and can be enjoyed by the flight, glass, or bottle along with a menu of late-night comfort snacks. Every other Friday, an indie band takes the stage and, well, jams into the wee hours.

MARK HEROLD WINE

Across the river and next to the Oxbow Market, **Mark Herold Wine** (710 1st St., 707/256-3111, www.markheroldwines.com, noon-7pm daily, tasting $20-60) is a must-stop for both the casual drinker and the hardcore oenophile. Known up and down the valley for his cabernets, Herold's tasting room is filled with beakers, test tubes, and other science-oriented knickknacks. The result is a heady selection of not only great, but also approachable wines in a fun atmosphere. The tasting fee may seem steep, but the price gets you six tastes that include unusual Latin varietals such as grenache, tempranillo, and albariño that are made into the blends Flux and Acha. Cab lovers can indulge themselves with his hallmark wines in the pricier tasting. Either way, let your pourer know your preferences and they will be sure to accommodate you. Prices for bottles range $16-200.

ST. CLAIR BROWN

Follow the train tracks north and you'll run into **St. Clair Brown Winery** (816 Vallejo St., 707/255-5591, www.stclairbrownwinery.com, noon-8pm Mon.-Sat., noon-6pm Sun., tasting $20), an oasis of greenery. The small boutique winery produces fewer than 2,000 cases per year (everything from sauvignon blanc to cabernet) in the small downtown facility. You can taste many of these small lot wines at the charming Garden Eatery. Surrounded by a culinary garden, the Eatery serves small plates such as pork rillettes and farro salad ($9-18) to accompany its food-friendly wine. Order a

flight of four ($20), a glass ($6-20), or a bottle ($39-57), and enjoy an afternoon at this true labor of love.

COOMBSVILLE WINERIES

The rolling hills and country lanes to the east of the city of Napa are home to an increasing number of small wineries that coexist alongside horse farms, sheep pastures, and the giant Napa Valley Country Club. In a valley of big wineries and big traffic jams, exploring this area by car or on a bike is a welcome respite from the more hectic parts of the valley. In fact, Coombsville's only big traffic jam occurs when school lets out at 3 o'clock. Even the crush is low key. Due to local planning codes, all the wineries in this area require an appointment.

ANCIEN

At **Ancien** (4047 E. 3rd Ave., Napa, 707/255-3908, www.ancienwines.com, daily by appointment, tasting $35) you will learn what makes Coombsville wine special from the ground up. Standing in the 1885 Haynes vineyard, your tasting will start with a conversation about Coombsville's geology and volcanism, its unique wind patterns that

the cave at Ancien

create a myriad of microclimates, and the minutiae of grape farming from rootstock selection to owl boxes and deer fences. Not only will the beautiful historic vineyard help you to envision the ancient caldera upon which Coombsville sits, your guide will likely be owner and winemaker Ken Bernards, whose affability is equal to his infectious scientific curiosity and love of wine. Inside the cave, you'll see that this passion translates to restrained and elegant pinot noirs and chardonnays. Five wines are available to taste (three pinots and two chardonnays), all of which hail from different AVAs and are poured alongside soil samples of their home vineyards. With each sip and examination of the white volcanic ash of Coombsville or the red alluvial clay of Carneros, you'll have one of the best (and tastiest) lessons of *terroir*. Wines range between $30 and $60 per bottle.

FARELLA VINEYARD

Tom Farella has been a grape grower in this part of the Napa Valley for decades, so to say he knows Coombsville fruit well is perhaps an understatement. He still sells most of his estate fruit to other wineries, but he also makes about 1,200 cases of his own wines a year, which are known for their structure and balance. **Farella Vineyard** (2222 N. 3rd Ave., Napa, 707/254-9489, www.farella.com, by appointment daily, tasting $20) is nestled in the trees at the end of a long driveway cutting through the vineyards, and, depending on the time of year, Tom's personalized tour might involve a walk through the vineyards or a tasting of some barrel samples.

PALMAZ VINEYARDS

With a 100,000-square-foot four-story cave system extending underground complete with its own elevators and a computerized carousel of giant fermentation tanks, **Palmaz Vineyards** (4029 Hagen Rd., Napa, 707/226-5587, www.palmazvineyards.com, tours and tasting by appointment only, $80) was hailed as an architectural and engineering marvel when it was completed in 2009 after a reported eight years of construction costing $20 million. This is not just a wine aging cave like so many others in the Napa Valley; it's a huge gravity-flow winery facility built entirely underground with its own water treatment plant and the world's largest reinforced underground structure at its center. The wines are just as impressive as the structure, and most can be tasted as part of the pricey, appointment-only tour. Plan on spending two hours exploring the cave, learning about gravity-flow winemaking, and finally tasting five wines paired with small bites of gourmet food. Book well in advance because every tour is private, so only a handful of visitors can get their chance each week.

TULOCAY WINERY

On the other end of the spectrum, **Tulocay Winery** (1426 Coombsville Rd., Napa, 707/255-4064, www.tulocay.com, by appointment, tasting $20) could not be more down-to-earth. Since 1974, Tulocay has been making elegant, age-worthy pinot noir and traditional (for Napa, at least) barrel-fermented chardonnay and an unoaked, stainless steel-fermented version, and, of course, cabernet. Your host will likely be owner Bill Cadman, who has been making wines for over four decades. His winery is the oldest in Coombsville. While tasting beneath the oak trees (you are encouraged to bring a picnic lunch), you'll better understand what makes this part of the Napa Valley such a unique spot for growing cabernet and likely hear plenty of local history and gossip.

OAK KNOLL AREA WINERIES

Stretching across the base of the valley floor, Oak Knoll is blessed with light traffic, walk-in tasting rooms, and acres upon acres of vines. Several straight roads crisscross the AVA, making it easy to navigate and lending a distinctly low-key agricultural vibe.

TREFETHEN VINEYARDS

Both a driving force behind the decadelong quest to have Oak Knoll designated as an official AVA (successfully bestowed in 2004) and one of the oldest wineries in the Napa Valley, **Trefethen** (1160 Oak Knoll Ave., Napa, 866/895-7696, www.trefethen.com, check website for current schedule, tasting $25-35) offers both history and the diversity of this AVA. All the wines are estate, and you'll drive through some of Trefethen's 600 acres of vineyards on the long way to the original Eshcol winery building, built in 1886 and listed on the National Register of Historic Places. The building suffered major damage in the 2014 earthquake and was closed for restoration. As of this writing, work is scheduled to be finished in early 2017, complete with a new tasting room on the second floor of the historic building, overlooking the gardens, vineyards, and 100-year-old cork tree.

Trefethen is perhaps best known for its chardonnay, which grows well in the slightly cooler southern end of the valley, but you'll find plenty of reds on the tasting menu (you may select any four). Tours ($35) are available daily at 10:30am and include a tasting in the demonstration vineyard.

DARIOUSH

This Persian palace rising from the vineyard flatlands just north of Napa is one of the more unusual additions to the Napa Valley's ever-colorful architectural mash-up. The winery of Persian immigrants Darioush and Shahpar Khaledi, **Darioush** (4240 Silverado Trail, Napa, 707/257-2345, www.darioush. com, 10:30am-5pm daily, Sat.-Sun. by appointment only, tasting $40) is a hard-to-miss winery, thanks in part to the 16 giant sandstone pillars, each topped with a double-headed bull, that take the place of more traditional trees in front of the main entrance. The theme is continued in the luxurious interior, where carved sandstone looks like it's straight from the set of *Raiders of the Lost Ark*. The winery's lavish tasting options mirror its architecture. Options range in price from $40-300, with all but one offering caviar, boutique cheese, and small gourmet bites to accompany the winery's signature Bordeaux varietals. The cheapest option is a $40 flight of five wines either tableside or at the glass-topped tasting bar. For this walk-ins are welcome during the week, but on weekends it is appointment-only.

demonstration vineyards at Trefethen

Wineries by Appointment

JUDD'S HILL

This small winery at the southern end of the Silverado Trail is beginning to gain a big reputation. **Judd's Hill** (2332 Silverado Trail, Napa, 707/255-2332, www.juddshill.com, 10am-4pm daily by appointment, tasting $25-45) makes only 3,000 cases of wine here, but the complex cabernet sauvignon, with dusty tannins and a long finish, remains the mainstay and accounts for about half the production and many rave reviews. Another favorite is a proprietary red blend called Magic, so named because owner Judd Finkelstein not only works his magic on wines and the ukulele but also on audiences as an amateur magician. Tasting options include a current release and a reserve tasting. Both are flights of five wines and are $25 and $45, respectively. You can also opt for the 90-minute wine and food pairing seminar offered six days a week for $50.

SIGNORELLO VINEYARDS

Set back from the road on a hill with an idyllic view from its sunny poolside patio, **Signorello Vineyards** (4500 Silverado Trail, Napa, 707/255-5990, www.signorellovineyards. com, 10am-5pm Thurs.-Mon. by appointment, tour and tasting $65-175) is a gourmet stop on a daily tasting schedule. The winery is best known for its estate cabernet sauvignon and its limited-production estate chardonnay. These along with other varietals are paired with cheese and charcuterie or small bites for 90-minute to two-hour tastings, which also include a tour through the vineyard.

MOUNT VEEDER WINERIES

You'll find mostly grapes on Mount Veeder's terraced hillsides and few tasting rooms. Allow 15 minutes to get from downtown Napa to the heart of this appellation along the narrow country roads.

★ THE HESS COLLECTION

The art is probably going to be more memorable than the wines at the mountain estate of **The Hess Collection** (4411 Redwood Rd., Napa, 707/255-1144, www.hesscollection. com, 10am-5:30pm daily, tasting $25), but that's not to say the art of winemaking has not been perfected here. It certainly has, but the soaring four-story gallery linking the two historic stone winery buildings is the biggest draw. Most of the contemporary paintings and sculptures are by lesser-known European artists discovered by winery founder and Swiss entrepreneur Donald Hess, along with works by some big names like Francis Bacon, Frank Stella, and Andy Goldsworthy.

Visiting the museum is free, as is the audio tour, which you can download onto your phone. Docent-guided tours are available with advance reservations ($35) and conclude with a tasting of Hess's current release wines, including the Mount Veeder chardonnay and cabernet. For a more tailored experience select any one of the tour tasting combos ($35-85), but advance reservations are required.

SIGHTS

The city's **River Front District** and the historic commercial area along Main Street are bursting with new hotels, restaurants, shops, and tasting rooms, making the small city a wonderful place to spend the day. Stroll the wide **promenade** along the river that borders the **Riverfront Complex** and the charmingly revived **Napa Mill** (www.historicnapamill.com), which used to be where steamships docked before the automobile age. Both have been ushering in new upscale shops and noteworthy restaurants. The Riverbend Performance Plaza at the Napa Mill hosts free music and art shows on weekends.

Nearby, the cultural anchor of downtown is the recently restored **Napa Valley Opera House** (1030 Main St., 707/226-7372, http://nvoh.org). La Scala it isn't, but the 1880 Italianate building is a reminder of Napa's Victorian boom times. The opera house is one of a handful of pre-1890 buildings scattered around downtown. In fact, Napa has more buildings that survived the

the Uptown Theatre

There's usually something going on in the bars and restaurants along bustling Main Street in downtown Napa's River Front District, especially on Friday nights in the summer, when the **Downtown Napa Association** (www. donapa.com) organizes live music at the Veteran Memorial Park overlooking the river. The schedule changes frequently, so check their website for more information.

Napa might not be the center of the valley's wine scene, but it is the cultural center. The **Napa Valley Opera House** (1030 Main St., 707/226-7372, http://nvoh.org) is home to just about every performance art *except* opera. This 130-year-old Napa institution hosts comedians, musical acts, theater performances, and even old movie nights. In fact, you can count on something going on nearly every night of the week. Countless cultural icons from Jack London to Steve Martin have walked the stage over its long history. Jazz lovers will be thrilled to know that New York's famed **Blue Note** opened a jazz club in Opera House's lower theater in 2016.

At the Napa Mill complex, **Silo's** (530 Main St., 707/251-5833, www. napa.com, doors open at 6pm Mon.-Fri., and at 7pm Sat.-Sun.) is as popular for a predinner drink as it is for its entertainment. The eclectic mix includes everything from jazz to stand-up comedy to Johnny Cash tribute bands, and the cover charges (up to $25) vary just as much. There are plenty of Napa and Sonoma wines by the glass, and there is also a small food menu of appetizers, pizza, and desserts.

Bigger names appear at the recently renovated **Uptown Theatre** (1350 3rd St., 707/259-0123, www.uptowntheatrenapa.com). Originally opened in 1937, this art deco theater now hosts acts from Lindsey Buckingham to Steven Wright to Ani DiFranco. Shows generally start at 8pm.

Many restaurants also host live music. A popular casual jazz venue is **Uva Trattoria & Bar** (1040 Clinton St., 707/255-6646, www. uvatrattoria.com, until midnight Fri.-Sat.), where everything from funk to flamenco can

1906 earthquake than any other city or town in this part of the Wine Country. At one end of the spectrum is the fabulous Gothic Victorian **First Presbyterian Church** (1333 3rd St., 707/224-8693, www.fpcnapa.org) at 3rd and Randolph Streets, built in 1875, and at the other is the 1888 **Semorile Building** (975 1st St.), just around the corner from the opera house and now home to the **Bounty Hunter Wine Bar and Smokin' BBQ** (975 1st St., 707/226-3976, www.bountyhunterwinebar.com, 11am-10pm Sun.-Thurs., 11am-midnight Fri.-Sat., $14-35).

An easy-to-follow walking tour of Napa's historic buildings is available from the **Napa Valley Welcome Center** (600 Main St., 707/251-5895 or 855/847-6265, www.visitnapavalley.com, 9am-5pm daily). Also available are maps for the self-guided **Art Walk.** Over a dozen modern art installations can be found in the heart of downtown, mainly along 1st and Main Streets. Hunting for Napa's sculptures is another way to see the city.

be heard Friday and Saturday nights. You'll also find live music three nights a week at **Downtown Joe's** (902 Main St. at 2nd St., 707/258-2337, www.downtownjoes.com). Joe's stays open until 1:30am Friday-Sunday hosting music that ranges from rockabilly to Latin to jazz, with a live DJ spinning on Sunday nights. Wineries, or at least one, have gotten into the live music game. **JaM Cellars** (1460 1st St., 707/265-7577, www.jamcellars.com), owned by big sponsors of BottleRock, hosts indie rockers every other Friday night until midnight, while other nights, DJs spin tunes at this tasting room/lounge that also moonlights as a recording studio.

SHOPPING

Napa continues to be the place where locals up and down the valley come for their big-box needs. Many bargain hunters beeline it to the **Napa Premium Outlets** (629 Factory Stores Dr., right off Highway 29, 707/226-9876, www. premiumoutlets.com, all stores 10am-9pm Mon.-Sat., 10am-7pm Sun.), with its outposts of Michael Kors, J Crew, Tommy Hilfiger, and Calvin Klein.

The Oxbow and River Front districts are lovely places to pick up that special gift or while away an afternoon window-shopping. A great place to start is the **Historic Napa Mill** at the south end of Main Street. Formerly the Hatt Warehouse, the mill has since been converted into a shopping and dining center, decorated with rustic touches—weathered redwood, an abundance of trailing vines, and blooming planter boxes and hanging baskets.

From there, you'll find plenty of shops lining Main Street, with a string of antiques stores on 2nd Street. The aptly named **Antiques on Second** (1370 2nd St., 707/252-6353, 10am-5:30pm Mon.-Sat., 11am-5pm Sun.) has plenty of vintage cookware, clothing, and nostalgia-inducing knickknacks, as well as Napa prices.

For vintage clothes, check out **Betty's Girl** (1320 2nd St., 707/320-3739, 10am-5:30pm Mon. and Thurs.-Sat., 11am-5pm Sun.). A quirky and original clothing store (mainly for women), Betty's carries used clothes that are in great condition and somehow retain their hip edge.

Stocking everything from appliances to citrus zesters, **Shackford's Kitchen Store** (1350 Main St., 707/226-2132, 9:30am-5:30pm Mon.-Sat.) is where Napa home chefs shop for the tools of the trade. The shelves of this Napa institution are crammed to the gills with all sorts of gadgets and cookware, so give yourself enough time to take it all in.

Two blocks away, another local institution, **Napa Bookmine** (964 Pearl St., 707/733-3199, www.napabookmine.d7.indiebound. com, 10am-6pm Mon., 10am-8pm Tues.-Sat., and noon-5pm Sun.), has a huge collection of used and new books. Find plenty of literary fiction for your trip or swing by for one of its author events.

If you must find a gift to bring back home, the place to go is the **Napa General Store** (540 Main St., 707/259-0762, www.napageneralstore.com, 8am-6pm daily), which sells scores of wine-related knickknacks and local artwork, including leather crafts and fiber art, all of which have an arty ecological bent. The General Store also serves breakfast and lunch, plus wine-tasting to take the edge off.

Should the ideal Wine Country gift include something edible, head over to the **Oxbow Public Market** (610 and 644 1st St., 707/226-6529, www.oxbowpublicmarket. com, 9am-7pm daily) and pick through cooking- and kitchen-related knickknacks at the **Napastak;** get lost in the myriad spices and seasonings at the **Whole Spice Company;** sample and select your favorite olive oil at **The Olive Press;** or grab your favorite Napa vintage at the venerable **Wine Merchant.** No matter what, you won't leave empty-handed.

RECREATION
Skyline Wilderness Park

Most people don't associate Napa Valley with serious mountain biking, but just outside the city of Napa is **Skyline Wilderness Park** (2201 Imola Ave., 707/252-0481, www.sky-linepark.org, 8am-7pm daily), which hosted

Napa Valley Festivals and Events

JANUARY

Just as you have recovered from holiday excess, Napa Valley kicks off its year of festivals with the **Napa Valley Truffle Festival** (www.napatrufflefestival.com). Cooking demos, truffle hunting, and wine pairings fill four days mid-January. Tickets range $60-495 per event, but the Festival Marketplace at Oxbow has a bit of everything and is free.

MARCH

Flavor! Napa Valley (www.flavornapavalley.com), held the third week in March, has a higher purpose than simply indulgence—it raises money for scholarships to the Culinary Institute of America at Greystone. The festival lasts five days with events scattered up and down the valley that include wine-tasting, culinary demonstrations, and discussions with some of the area's biggest names, like Thomas Keller and Masaharu Morimoto.

MAY

Anyone thinking that Napa Valley food and wine don't mix with rock and roll could not be more wrong, at least during Memorial Day weekend. The three-day, three-stage music festival **BottleRock** (Napa Expo, 575 3rd St., Napa, www.bottlerocknapavalley.com) pairs 76 bands like The Shins, Flaming Lips, and Primus with 40 wineries and 28 Napa Valley eateries. Tickets are pricey: Expect to pay from $155 for a day pass to $275 for a three-day pass.

JULY-SEPTEMBER

The most all-American event of year is the **Napa County Fair and Fireworks** (www.napacountyfair.org). On the long Fourth of July weekend, Calistoga dons its best red, white, and blue (or "reds, whites, and blues") and puts on a summer festival that would make even Norman Rockwell nod in approval. There is a parade, fireworks, a Ferris wheel, bull riding, music, food, and, of course, plenty of wine to wash it all down.

The **Robert Mondavi Summer Music Festival** (888/769-5299, www.robertmondaviwinery.com) in July and August has become a summer institution in the Napa Valley and features big-name rock, jazz, blues, and Latin music artists (Blondie, Ziggy Marley, k.d. lang). The outdoor concerts are held Saturday evenings on the Robert Mondavi winery grounds, usually from the beginning of July through mid-August. Tickets cost $60-115.

The celebration of music continues with the month-long **Music in the Vineyards** (707/258-5559, www.napavalleymusic.com, $60) series of chamber music concerts. The festival kicks off in late July and features a concert every couple of days at wineries and other venues up and down the valley.

Downtown Napa is host to the **Napa Town & Country Fair** (www.napavalleyexpo.com, $13) in August at the Napa Valley Expo Fairgrounds, a kid-friendly arts, crafts, and culinary celebration.

NOVEMBER-DECEMBER

In November, the latest crop of independent films makes its way to big screen in Napa, Yountville, St. Helena, and Calistoga with the **Napa Valley Film Festival** (http://napavalleyfilmfest.org). Exclusive screenings, celebrity Q and A, and food and wine round out the event.

Grab a hot cocoa and join the locals for the **Calistoga Lighted Tractor Parade** (http://visitcalistoga.com), where all sorts of vintage tractors, modern construction equipment, and antique trucks are bedecked with lights for a truly agrarian Christmas celebration.

the U.S. round of the Mountain Bike World Cup three years in a row in the late 1990s. It's not the prettiest park in the valley—that distinction goes to Bothe-Napa Valley State Park near St. Helena—but it does offer 16 miles of trails for bikers, hikers, and horseback riders through its 850 acres of meadows and woodland. Spring is probably the best time to come, when the meadows are full of wildflowers doing their thing before the dry season turns the grassland to golden brown.

The park is reached from downtown Napa on Imola Avenue. The day-use fee is $5; be sure to pick up a map when you arrive because the trail system is more complex than most. Hikers should look out for bikers and horses— all users share all the trails.

Mountain bikers wanting to try their skills on the World Cup route should ride from near the park's entrance for about a mile up Lake Marie Road before turning right onto the murderous ascent of Passini Road and then descending on the rocky, sometimes steep single-track of the Bayleaf Trail. The next stage of the Cup was the Manzanita Trail, reached by climbing back up Lake Marie Road to the fig tree. The undulating two-mile trail was described as one of the best single-tracks on the Cup circuit.

Disc golf offers some less traditional exercise. You might know it as Frisbee golf, but the Professional Disc Golf Association would prefer you use the D word instead. It is played exactly as you might think, like golf but throwing a Frisbee instead of hitting a little white ball. There is an 18-hole course, and in case you don't always travel with one, Frisbees (sorry, discs) are available at the entrance kiosk, along with course maps. The dress rules are a little more relaxed than on most traditional golf courses—no collared shirts or fancy shoes are required. In fact, you don't even have to wear shirts or shoes.

Those who'd prefer to expend less energy can find **picnic areas** near the park entrance and about 2.5 miles up Lake Marie Road at the lake itself.

Kennedy Memorial Park

Napa's largest city park, **Kennedy Memorial Park** (2295 Streblow Dr., 707/257-9529, www.naparec.com, sunrise-sunset) sits along the southern bank of the Napa River. Within its 350 acres are the **Napa Valley Vine Trail**, the new **Napa Skatepark,** a boat launch, and plenty of picnic spots overlooking the recently restored wetlands. The park is also home to one of the few golf courses at this end of the valley open to the public. The 18-hole **Napa Golf Course** (707/255-4333, www.playnapa.com, $21-49) is a 6,500-yard, par-72 championship course. It has a driving range, practice putting greens, and a fully stocked golf shop.

The Napa River

With the success of the restoration of the Napa River, plus the revitalization of the River Front District (including the new boat launch), it is no surprise that the opportunity for river recreation is blossoming. To jump on a stand-up paddleboard, check out **Napa Valley Paddle** (100 Riverside Dr., 707/666-1628, http://napavalleypaddle.com). SUP and kayak rentals are available ($75/full day). You must make an appointment, as there are only two two-hour tours. The Oxbow Loop Tour ($89) takes guests from the Kennedy Park launch up through downtown, pointing out river and civic restoration along the way. The Living River Tour ($119) focuses mainly on the ecology of the river, beginning at the Napa Yacht Club, south of downtown, and traveling north to the Oakville district, where guests are then shuttled back.

To tour the river on a kayak, book a spot with **Kayak Napa Valley** (707/501-8585, www.kayaknv.com, $70). Tours last three hours and launch from the Napa Yacht Club, Kennedy Park, or Cuttings Wharf in Carneros around 9am. Another local outfit is **Enjoy Napa Valley** (707/227-7364, http://napariverhistorytour.com, $49-89), which offers the 1.5-hour Napa River History Tour. Launching near downtown, you'll explore the river's wetlands and no doubt see a river otter or beaver by the time you're through.

More Than Just Hot Air

Hot-air balloons have become so synonymous with the Napa Valley that locals don't even look up when balloons start floating around in the early morning.

Most companies are at the southern end of the valley, especially around Yountville, but a couple farther north can float the bleary-eyed over some of the volcanic scenery near Calistoga. Early morning winds tend to be southerly, so pick a company that launches north of any place you really want to see from the air. But bear in mind that balloons generally don't float far—often only a few miles over the course of a flight.

The drill is more or less the same for any ballooning adventure: get to a prearranged pickup point by 6am-7am (depending on the season), usually a hotel or restaurant near the launch site (some companies will also collect customers staying locally); drive to the launch site and watch or potentially help with the inflation of the balloon; and finally, take off with the roar of the burners for an hour-long, silent drift at elevations ranging from treetop to several thousand feet, depending on conditions. Brunch usually follows, either at a local restaurant or alfresco in a meadow. The whole experience usually lasts about four hours.

Some companies will do a "double hop," leaving those unfortunate enough to be assigned to the second hop, or flight, of the day following behind the balloons in a van to the landing spot before finally getting a flight. The drawback of the second flight (apart from the feeling of having woken up early for nothing) is that air currents can die down after the sun rises and the balloon might not float very far. Ask if a double hop is planned—they tend to be more common during the busy summer and fall seasons. If it is, insist on hopping on board with the first group.

Ask how big the basket is and how many groggy souls will be crammed in with you. Some companies limit riders to 8 or even 4 people; others take up to 16 per flight. For a large premium, most also offer the option of a private flight for two.

- Farthest north in the valley is **Calistoga Balloons** (707/942-5758, www.calistogaballoons. com, $239), which launches from the Calistoga area and offers a champagne breakfast at Solage afterward.

- With **Balloons Above the Valley** (707/253-2222 or 800/464-6824, www.balloonrides.com, $229), all tours begin and end at the Napa Valley Marriott. This company has been in the Napa Valley balloon business since the 1970s and frequently offers good online deals.

- Should it be foggy, **Napa Valley Aloft** (www.napavalleyaloft.com, $229) will launch in Pope Valley, or on the eastern edge of the Vaca Mountains, for a wholly unique experience. All tours meet at the Vintage 1870 Marketplace building in Yountville, and transportation to the launch site is available from Napa to St. Helena for an additional $20. The company offers a free shuttle from anywhere in the valley.

- Also launching near Yountville is **Napa Valley Balloons** (707/944-0228 or 800/253-2224, www.napavalleyballoons.com, $239), which includes a post-ballooning lunch at Domaine Chandon.

Cooking Schools

When Copia went bankrupt and closed its doors in 2008, it seemed to symbolize Napa's decline. For years, there was speculation about what would become of the 80,000-square-foot space sitting on 12 acres along the Napa River, but in 2015 the Culinary Institute of America at Greystone announced that it had acquired the property, to much adulation. As of this printing, classes are scheduled to begin in spring 2017 at the new **CIA at Copia** (500 1st St., 707/967-1010, https://enthusiasts.ciachef. edu/copia), including evening and weekend classes for lay cooks.

But Copia will not be the only game in town. Not far away on the Silverado Trail, the **Silverado Cooking School** (1552 Silverado Trail, 707/927-3591, http://

silveradocookingschool.com, $65-140) offers a multitude of classes for beginning and experienced cooks. Learn basic knife skills ($125), how to make a romantic dinner ($275 per couple), the secret to a great brunch ($140), or delve into the world of cheese ($65) with celebrated food writer Janet Fletcher. Classes last 2-4 hours, and many utilize (and even visit) produce from the school's two-acre farm.

FOOD

Over the last several years Napa's once empty storefronts have filled with an interesting mix of eateries from high-end notables to delicious old-school joints. Napa has yet to catch on as a dining destination, so enjoy to relatively uncrowded (at least compared the rest of the valley), eclectic foodie scene. Adding to cosmopolitan flair, many places serve food late into the night.

River Front District and Downtown

Anchoring one end of the Napa Mill Complex with views of the river is the pocket of Francophone charm **Angèle** (540 Main St., 707/252-8115, www.angelerestaurant.com, lunch 11:30am-2:30pm daily, dinner 5-9pm Sun.-Thurs., 5-10pm Fri.-Sat., $16-49). The interior and canopied riverside patio dressed in the colors of Provence are perfectly romantic settings for the classic French bistro food that has won plaudits from locals and critics. The restaurant has an outstanding Californian and French wine list that includes about a dozen wines available by the half bottle, as well as neatly crafted cocktails.

Nearby, **Celadon** (500 Main St., 707/254-9690, www.celadonnapa.com, lunch 11:30am-2:30pm Mon.-Fri., dinner 5pm-9pm daily, $22-46) goes international, dishing up "global comfort food." The shabby-chic exterior and huge sheltered patio give way to a pure bistro interior, the perfect match for the cross-cultural California menu. The wine list offers about the same balance of California and the rest of the world.

Sake in Wine Country? Not a bad idea, particularly if it's paired with dinner at **Morimoto** (610 Main St., 707/252-1600, www.morimotonapa.com, lunch 11:30am-2:30pm daily, dinner 5pm-10pm Sun.-Thurs. and 5pm-11pm Fri.-Sat., $25-40). This esoteric and sleek Japanese eatery is by none other than celebrity chef Masaharu Morimoto. The food includes traditional Japanese dishes, all with a unique and modern twist—*gyoza* with bacon foam and duck confit–fried rice are just some of the menu items. There are also a handful of non sequiturs like steak, lobster, and roasted fingerling potatoes. Should this sound like the ideal late-night snack, Morimoto keeps its lounge (5pm-midnight Sun.-Thurs., 5pm-1am Fri.-Sat) open into the witching hour.

Also in the riverfront complex is **The Pear** (720 Main St., 707/256-3900, 11:30am-9pm Mon.-Thurs., 11:30am-10pm Fri.-Sat., noon-9pm Sun., brunch 10am-noon Sun., $14-28), a 50-seat bistro specializing in farm-to-table fare from New Orleans and the Deep South. This is not the place for haute cuisine or exploring the *terroir* of an onion. Instead, you'll get big plates of fried chicken, bourbon barbecue ribs, and standout dishes like shrimp creole pasta. In fact, after some time in Wine Country, this large-plate Southern comfort food may be just what the doctor ordered. Still, the low lighting, open kitchen, and, of course, the wine list remind you that are in Napa, which is not a bad thing.

Trade in big plates for small plates and you get **ZuZu** (829 Main St., 707/224-8555, www.zuzunapa.com, lunch 11:30am-2:30pm Mon.-Fri., dinner 4:30pm-10pm Sun.-Thurs., 4:30pm-11pm Fri.-Sat., plates $8-13), a refreshingly down-to-earth tapas bar that's a great place to end a stressful day of touring without having to worry about reservations or the bill. The cozy interior with its exposed brick, beams, and tile is the perfect setting for the Spanish-inspired small plates, none of which (except the Moroccan glazed lamb chops) costs over $12.

Small plates *izakaya*-style are served at **Miminashi** (821 Coombs St., 707/254-9464, http://miminashi.com, lunch 11:30am-2:30pm

Mon.-Fri., dinner 5pm-11pm Mon.-Thurs., 5pm-midnight Fri.-Sat., 5pm-10pm Sun., $13-18), Napa's newest favorite eatery. Order the meat and vegetable skewers, or try the clam hot pot or the chicken tartare (yes, you read that right), and settle in with a sommelier paired sake in the smart and modern dining room. Be sure to leave room for dessert: house-made soft-serve ice cream complete with toppings, including rainbow sprinkles and miso caramel.

Downtown Joe's American Grill and Brewhouse (902 Main St., 707/258-2337, http://downtownjoes.com, 8:30am-10pm daily, dinner entrées $8-18) is a hopping alternative to the swanky restaurants and endless wine of the Napa Valley. Sure, it has a wine list (a short one), but most people come here for the more than half-dozen microbrews with the usual comical microbrew names, like Tantric India Pale Ale and Catherine the Great Imperial Stout. The menu is pretty standard if slightly pricey grill fare, but there is a decent kids menu. Live music entertains in the evening Thursday-Sunday with a late-night menu to go with it.

A completely original Napa joint is ★ **Bounty Hunter Wine Bar and Smokin' BBQ** (975 1st St., 707/226-3976,

www.bountyhunterwinebar.com, 11am-10pm Sun-Thurs., 11am-midnight Fri.-Sat., $14-35). This wineshop, tasting bar, and barbecue place, housed in a historic brick-walled Victorian building with wine barrels for table bases, is as relaxed as the comfort food served. The menu includes gumbo, a beer-can chicken (a Cajun-spiced chicken impaled on a Tecate beer can), chili, and big plates of barbecue pork, brisket, and ribs. Being Napa, 400 wines are sold here (40 by the glass) or served as part of a tasting flight. Since it's a wineshop too, you'll pay retail prices for bottles bought with a meal.

Also blurring the lines between tasting room and restaurant is the nightclub-esque **1313 Main** (1313 Main St., 707/258-1313, www.1313main.com, 5pm-10pm Wed.-Thurs., 5pm-11pm Fri.-Sat., 10am-1pm and 5pm-10pm Sun., $17-30), which serves upscale dishes with more than a little haute cuisine flare. Escargot, oxtail ravioli, and Australian lamb chop are just a few of the selections. The menu is slim, particularly compared with 1,300 different wines available, of which 13 reds, 13 whites, along with 13 kinds of beer, are poured nightly in two- or five-ounce tastes or sold by the glass. The atmosphere is more lounge like than high-end restaurant, catering

Bounty Hunter Wine Bar and Smokin' BBQ

to the young, hip set and serving small plates of cheese, charcuterie, and spreads late into the night.

The best pizza in town can be found nearby at **Azzurro Pizzeria & Enoteca** (1260 Main St., 707/255-5552, www.azzurropizzeria.com, 11:30am-9pm Sun.-Thurs, 11:30am-9:30pm Fri.-Sat., $14-19), from the veterans of the famous Pizzeria Tra Vigne in St. Helena. The menu includes classic Italian starters, salads, and a handful of pasta dishes alongside the dozen or so thin-crusted, wood-fired pizzas. The wine list is dominated by thoughtfully chosen Napa and Sonoma wines, yet another sign that this is a no-nonsense and hassle-free dining experience favored by locals.

Another Italian favorite is **Uva Trattoria** (1040 Clinton St. at Brown St., 707/255-6646, www.uvatrattoria.com, 11:30am-9pm Tues., 11:30am-9:30pm Wed.-Thurs., 11:30am-11:30pm Fri., 5pm-11:30pm Sat., 5pm-9pm Sun., $15-33), which has become a Napa institution for its rustic Italian food and lively bar, and as one of the few live music venues in the city.

A great place to grab a burrito after a day of tasting is **Taqueria Maria** (640 3rd St., 707/531-7741, 9am-9pm daily, $8-12). You'll see plenty of locals hunched over tacos con carne or big platters of enchiladas on the outdoor patio.

A little upriver, and certainly upscale, from the Oxbow Public Market is **La Toque** (1314 McKinstry St., Napa, 707/257-5157, www.latoque.com, 5:30pm-9:15pm daily, tasting menu $80-98). The Michelin-starred restaurant of the Westin Napa Verasa hotel gives Napa a touch of the Michelin magic felt farther north. Like you would expect, the food is French inspired, but generally less fussy and over the top than, say, at The French Laundry or Meadowood. But what really makes La Toque stand apart is the Truffle Menu of four savory courses, a cheese course, and dessert, all of which are centered around different truffles sourced from France and Italy. Such an experience will only set you back $200. If La Toque is slightly out of your range, try grabbing a table at the **Bank Café and Bar** (707/257-5151, http://bankcafenapa.com, 7am-11pm Sun.-Thurs., 7am-midnight Fri.-Sat., $16-36), La Toque's affordable sibling. This stylish alternative serves everything from breakfast to late-night bar snacks.

OXBOW PUBLIC MARKET

Want to try a bit of this and a bit of that? Venture across the river to the ★ **Oxbow**

Oxbow Public Market is the foodie epicenter of Napa.

Public Market (610 and 644 1st St., 707/226-6529, www.oxbowpublicmarket.com, see hours of individual venues), which showcases local artisanal food suppliers and restaurants. Oxbow is a one-stop shop for anyone looking for a quick fix of Napa Valley cuisine. The market is open daily and each business keeps its own hours, opening as early as 6:30am and closing as late as 10pm. Early birds will adore the **Model Bakery** (6:30am-6:30pm Mon.-Fri., 7am-7pm Sat., 7am-6:30pm Sun.) and the strong espresso at **Ritual Coffee** (7:30am-8pm daily). Hearty appetites will be satisfied at **Five Dot Ranch** (8am-8pm Sun.-Thurs., 8am-9pm Fri.-Sat.), while Latin lovers can savor egg, buffalo, spiced lamb, or citrus prawn tacos at **C Casa** (7:30am-9pm daily). Nearby, **Ca' Momi** (707/257-4992, 11am-9pm daily) slices wood-fired pizzas; **Hog Island Oyster Co.** (707/251-8113, 11:30am-8pm) shucks Tomales Bay Sweetwaters; and **Eiko's at Oxbow** (707/515-7026, 9am-9pm Mon.-Sat., 9am-8pm Sun.) plates sashimi and sushi rolls. Hamburgers are just out the side door at **Gott's Roadside** (10am-10pm daily summer, 10am-9pm daily winter), as are delectable take-out sandwiches made from some of the Valley's best charcuterie at the **Fatted Calf** (9am-7pm Mon.-Sat., 10am-6pm Sun.). Sweet tooth? Look no further. **Three Twins Ice Cream** (11:30am-8pm Mon.-Thurs., 11:30am-9pm Fri., 11am-9pm Sat., 11am-8pm Sun.) or **Kara's Cupcakes** (10am-9pm Mon.-Sat., 10am-8pm Sun.) will surely suffice.

To escape the loud congested interior, head to the market's **Kitchen Door** (707/226-6529, www.kitchendoornapa.com, 11:30am-8pm Mon., 11:30am-9pm Tues.-Fri., 10am-9pm Sat., 10am-8pm Sun.), and order a big plate of global gourmet comfort food. Most of what you'll get comes out of the white-tile wood oven, such as pizzas and roast chicken, but you'll also have your choice of noodle bowls, grilled fish, and ribs.

Vicinity of Napa

A few miles north of downtown Napa is the popular Italian restaurant **Bistro Don Giovanni** (4100 Howard Ln., Napa, 707/224-3300, http://bistrodongiovanni.com, 11:30am-10pm daily, dinner entrées $17-32). It's hard to miss on the east side of Highway 29 (though you might miss the turn for Howard Lane) and is a favorite of locals looking for casual Italian bistro food with a bit of California flair. On a warm summer night, ask for a table on the huge bustling outdoor patio. Anything from the wood-fired oven is worth trying here, especially the pizzas and oven-roasted fish. The wine list is dominated by Napa and Sonoma, but there's a good choice from the mother country too and an unusually wide selection by the half bottle.

If the relentless Wine Country-themed activities and food get to be a bit too much, you can escape it all at the **Red Hen Cantina** (4175 Solano Ave., Napa, 707/255-8125, 6am-9:30pm Sun.-Thurs., 7am-10:30pm Fri.-Sat., $10-23), a colorful and sometimes raucous Mexican bar and restaurant right off Highway 29. Just look for the giant red hen on the roof of the building.

Picnic Supplies

There is no better place to stock up on picnic items than at the **Oxbow Public Market** (610 and 644 1st St., 707/226-6529, www.oxbowpublicmarket.com). Grab cheese, charcuterie, bread, fruit, sandwiches, and sushi at this perfect one-stop shop.

Just south of the Darioush winery is the **Soda Canyon Store** (4006 Silverado Trail, at Soda Canyon Rd., 707/252-0285, www.sodacanyonstore.com, 6am-5:30pm Mon.-Fri., 7am-5:30pm Sat., 7:30am-5pm Sun.), just about the only decent place to buy box lunches, deli food, cheeses, and wine along the Silverado Trail.

Farmers Markets

Only the South Napa Century Center has enough space to hold 65 vendors that make up the **Napa Farmers Market** (195 Gasser Dr., 707/501-3087, https://napafarmersmarket.org, 8am-12:30pm Tues. and Sat. year-round). Spend the morning browsing the farm-fresh produce, along with local meat, cheese, bread, and crafts.

ACCOMMODATIONS

More than anywhere else in the valley, the city of Napa provides the widest choice of accommodation options. Many major chain hotels can be found here (including some recent upscale additions), as well as cheap independent motels, Victorian B&Bs, and a couple of modern boutique hotels. Best of all, rooms are generally cheaper than anywhere else in the valley, especially at the low end of the market.

Another advantage of staying in Napa, particularly if you're not a cabernet sauvignon fan, is its proximity to the Carneros region, the land of pinot noir and chardonnay. It's just a 15-minute drive south to many wineries in the eastern half of Los Carneros, or a 15-minute drive north to some of the Napa Valley's best cabernet producers. And for those traveling to or from Oakland or San Francisco, Napa has the shortest drive time of any of the valley's towns—a full 45 minutes closer to San Francisco than Calistoga, for example.

The city is also home to a good selection of restaurants, most within a short walk of downtown hotels and B&Bs. Indeed, if you don't want to drive to dinner but still want to choose from more than a handful of restaurants, then Napa is probably the best place to stay in the valley.

Under $150

There are more lodging options at the low end of the price spectrum in and around Napa than anywhere else in the valley. A little north of downtown Napa is the **Chablis Inn** (3360 Solano Ave., 707/257-1944 or 800/443-3490, www.chablisinn.com, $115-239). Some big-hotel touches (newspapers, HBO, CD players, coffeemakers and whirlpool tubs in the bathrooms) sweeten the appeal of the otherwise small and well-worn motel-style rooms. Its location right next to the St. Helena Highway (Highway 29) puts it in easy reach of wineries but also means there's some traffic noise to contend with, and you must drive to reach

local restaurants in Napa and Yountville. Dogs are welcome.

$150-250

For just a few dollars more a night than the nearby motels you could stay in, the more hotel-like **Napa Winery Inn** (1998 Trower Ave., 707/257-7220, www.napawineryinn. com, $190-265) is a sprawling building just off Highway 29 on the northern edge of Napa. The bland building is nothing much to look at, but it has nice gardens and plenty of clean and comfortable rooms that are a step up from most motel rooms. Standard amenities include flat-screen TV and in-room coffeemaker. Some have refrigerators and microwaves or full kitchenettes, and three of the deluxe king rooms have whirlpool tubs.

The **Wine Valley Lodge** (200 S. Coombs St., 707/224-7911 or 800/696-7911, www.winevalleylodge.com, $170) is a simple, clean, and bargain-priced independent motel about a mile south of downtown Napa, putting it just out of walking distance to most good restaurants and shops. It is just off Imola Avenue, however, which provides a quick connection to Highway 29. The guest rooms are simply but tastefully furnished, with microwaves and refrigerators, plus there is a complimentary breakfast. The Wine Valley Lodge boasts a significant past: In the late 1950s and early 1960s, several movies were filmed in Napa, and various A-list stars, including Rock Hudson, Jean Simmons, and even Elvis himself, stayed at the lodge during filming. If you're a movie buff, ask for the Elvis suite!

The choice of Victorian B&Bs in Napa can be a bit bewildering. One establishment that has some of the cheaper rates and plenty of room options is **Hennessey House** (1727 Main St., 707/226-3774, www.hennesseyhouse.com, $199-369), about six blocks north of downtown Napa. All rooms have private bathrooms, but those in the Carriage House have fireplaces, whirlpool tubs, and CD players. The full gourmet breakfast is enough to soak up plenty of wine during those morning wine-tastings, and the sauna is a place to relax tasting-weary feet at the end of a winter day. Allergy sufferers be warned: The resident cat has free rein in the common areas.

Anyone fed up with Victorian frills should check out the ★ **Blackbird Inn** (1755 1st St., 707/226-2450 or 888/567-9811, www.blackbirdinnnapa.com, $185-300), an Arts and Crafts-style shingled house dating from the 1920s with furnishings to match. It's just a few blocks from downtown Napa, directly opposite the West Coast home of *Wine Spectator* magazine, making it probably the most conveniently located B&B in Napa. The inn is owned by the Four Sisters group, which also owns a handful of other small Wine Country inns—although there's no corporate feel to the place. The only disadvantage is that there are no owners living there to take care of any late-night problems. But there are advantages, too: Unusual for a B&B, there are TVs with DVD players in every room (the walls supposedly have some decent soundproofing, unlike those at many B&Bs) and free wireless Internet access in addition to the more common fireplaces and whirlpool tubs in some rooms. You can opt to have your breakfast brought to your room ($10), and stop by the lobby for a predinner drink and hors d'oeuvres.

Just a couple of blocks from the Blackbird Inn and touted as Napa's first B&B when it opened in the 1980s, **The Beazley House** (1910 1st St., 707/257-1649, www.beazleyhouse.com, $205-390), with its own feline resident, is in another squat shingled mansion, this one dating from 1906 and adorned with blue-and-white canopies over the windows. Rooms contain the usual mix of what look like your great-grandmother's best furnishings. The five guest rooms in the main house have private bathrooms, though only one of the five has a claw-foot tub. The other five rooms are in the Carriage House and more luxurious, with whirlpool tubs, fireplaces, individual air-conditioning, and views of the lush garden.

Like a set for a real-life game of Clue, the sprawling mansion that is home to the **Cedar Gables Inn** (486 Coombs St., 707/224-7969, www.cedargablesinn.com, $219-349) might have you wondering if you'll bump into Colonel Mustard. Built in 1892 by a renowned English architect, the huge Tudor-style mansion was one of the grandest houses in Napa County in its heyday and the site of many lavish balls and gatherings. Today the labyrinth of stairways, passages, and secret doors is home to a lavish B&B with nine guest rooms, all exquisitely furnished with Victorian finery. All have private bathrooms, four have fireplaces, and five have whirlpool tubs. Other amenities include in-room massage service and a gourmet breakfast befitting the surroundings. The inn has an ideal location in a peaceful residential neighborhood about a 10-minute walk to downtown Napa.

La Belle Époque (1386 Calistoga Ave., 707/257-2161, www.labelleepoque.com, $209-529) is located in a glorious Queen Anne-style mansion built in 1893 with an antique-stuffed interior that looks like the movie set for an Agatha Christie mystery. The six guest rooms are all unique, most with stained-glass windows, some with canopy beds, and others with fireplaces or whirlpool tubs. For more room, consider booking one of the four suites in the adjacent Buckley House, where one of the perks is breakfast room service.

Despite being somewhat marooned right next to the freeway opposite the outlet stores, the **Bel Abri Inn** (837 California Blvd., 707/253-2100, www.belabri.net, $189-289) offers good value for the money and convenience, but is not the most stylish accommodation in the city. The clean, modern building is furnished in a playful modern style, including a few rooms with patios or fireplaces. In terms of amenities and services it lies somewhere between a motel and a hotel, but it does offer a few nice touches like complimentary breakfast and an evening wine and cheese tasting. Downtown Napa is a little too far to walk comfortably, but it is only a few minutes' drive.

Over $250

Napa's first and still most unique boutique

hotel, the **Napa River Inn** (500 Main St., 707/251-8500 or 877/251-8500, www.napariverinn.com, $250-509) has perhaps the best location in the city at the historic redbrick Napa Mill, a small riverside food and entertainment complex only a 10-minute walk to more shops and restaurants in downtown Napa. The 66 guest rooms are spread among three buildings—two are part of the historic mill itself and one (the Embarcadero building) was built in 1997. All rooms are furnished in an eclectic mix of contemporary and either Victorian or nautical styles, many with fireplaces, balconies, or views, though the views vary wildly from a parking lot to the river. Unlike at many hotels, even the boutique variety, there is a complimentary hot breakfast brought to your room. While pricey, the inn offers some great online deals.

Giving the Napa River Inn a run for its money is the 141-room **Andaz Napa** (1450 1st St., 707/687-1234, www.andaz.hyatt.com, $300-400), the chic hipster brand of Hyatt family. For many, the cool urbane style is a breath of fresh air in Wine Country. The standard room, known as the Andaz King, is roughly the same size as any other hotel room (but with far plusher amenities), while suites can get as large as over 900 square feet with deep bathtubs and dual-sided fireplaces. Downstairs, the Andaz **Farmers Table** restaurant serves relatively (at least for Napa) simple farm-to-table food that is tasty and filling.

Somewhere between a traditional B&B and a modern hotel like Andaz is **SENZA Hotel** (4066 Howard Ln., 707/253-0337, www.senzahotel.com, $300-450), on the northern edge of the city. It's actually more of a luxury country inn, with 41 guest rooms contained in five buildings set on two acres of wooded grounds with a hot tub, a small heated pool, and a spa. The smallest and cheapest rooms are in the main mansion house, dating from 1870; however, since this hotel is owned by Craig and Kathryn Hall of HALL Wines, don't expect any Victorian frills. Instead this updated hotel is dressed in modern design, with plenty of large art installations dotting the property. You'll also find an excellent complimentary breakfast and wine and cheese tasting, another HALL hallmark. Although the hotel is nowhere near downtown Napa, it does offer easy access to the rest of the valley and is virtually next door to the excellent **Bistro Don Giovanni** (4100 Howard Ln., 707/224-3300, http://bistrodongiovanni.com, 11:30am-10pm daily, $17-32).

There are luxurious resorts in the valley with views, others with wooded privacy, some with vineyards, but the **Milliken Creek Inn** (1815 Silverado Trail, 707/255-1197 or 888/622-5775, www.millikencreekinn.com, $450-650) has another twist—a riverside setting, an understated mix of Victorian and colonial Asian furnishings, and the sense of exclusivity that comes from having just 12 guest rooms to share the lush gardens and fountains. All rooms come with full entertainment systems, luxurious linens, and wireless Internet access. An exclusive spa sits riverside, and the staff is happy to deliver the hot complimentary breakfast to your room.

INFORMATION AND SERVICES

First stop for any visitors without a plan—whether staying in Napa, heading up to Calistoga—should be the **Napa Valley Welcome Center** (600 Main St., 707/251-5895 or 855/847-6265, www.visitnapavalley.com, 9am-5pm daily). The space is centered around a huge topographical map of the Napa Valley, educating visitors about the valley's AVAs, weather and geological influences, wineries and other points of interest. You'll also find, as well as plenty of wine and food-related knickknacks for sale, iPads loaded with information about the valley and a wall of pamphlets for local vendors, hotels, and tour guides. However, the best resource is the friendly and knowledgeable staff, who can provide tips and discounted wine-tasting coupons (don't be afraid to ask!) and even act as concierges.

For current events, *Wine Country This Week* (www.winecountrythisweek.com) has the best up-to-date information. It can be found at most tasting rooms throughout Wine Country, and as a casual read, it helps to get a feel for the valley. If it's local news you're seeking, you can find it in the daily *Napa Valley Register* (www.napanews.com).

For medical treatment (including alcohol poisoning), the **Queen of the Valley** (1000 Trancas St., 707/252-4411, www.thequeen.org) has both a 24-hour emergency room/trauma center and a walk-in urgent-care clinic (1621 W. Imola Ave., Napa, daily 10am-8pm). If the only thing hurting is an empty wallet, ATMs can be found at **Wells Fargo** (901 Main St.) and **Bank of America** (1700 1st St.).

GETTING THERE AND AROUND

Coming from the south, Napa is the first city on Highway 29, just past the Highway 121 intersection. Its size makes it hard to miss, but the numerous exits can be confusing. Just keep your eyes peeled for the 1st Street exit, which leads straight to downtown, Oxbow Public Market, the Silverado Trail, and Coombsville beyond. Unless you're a local,

you're not likely to need another exit. Once downtown, it is fairly easy to park either on the street or in relatively cheap public lots.

If you are considering going by bus, either to Napa or getting around once you're there, Napa Valley's **VINE** (707/251-6443 or 800/696-6443, www.ridethevine.com, $1.60-$5.50) bus service runs directly to downtown Napa from the El Cerrito BART station and the Vallejo Ferry Terminal. Check the schedule for details on this route. Once in town, there are a number of lines running through the city. Check the website for details.

If the bus doesn't get you where you need to be (or at least in a timely manner), exploring Napa by bike is also easy. **Napa River Velo** (680 Main St., 707/258-8729, www.naparivervelo.com, 10am-7pm Mon.-Fri., 9am-6pm Sat., 10am-5pm Sun.) is on the river side of the Riverside Plaza near the Napa Mill and rents bikes in the city of Napa for $40-90 per day, depending on whether you want a basic hybrid or a fancy road or mountain bike. If you are unsure of tackling hills, especially after an afternoon of wine-tasting, you can also opt for an electric bike ($55).

Yountville and Vicinity

Yountville was founded in 1867 by George C. Yount, who was the first to plant grapes in the Napa Valley on a Spanish land grant. Despite being the birthplace of Napa Valley wine, Yountville was considered to be on the wrong side of the tracks for years, known chiefly as the location of the Veterans Home of California (home to one-third of the small town's population) and a notorious dive bar. Little money flowed into the town until the 1990s, when a concerted effort to cash in on the valley's growing notoriety drew in big restaurant names, beginning with Thomas Keller. Today, Yountville is the tiny epicurean epicenter of the Napa Valley, known for its upscale shops, tasting rooms, spas, hotels, and of course its Michelin-starred dining. The

downside is that it attracts hordes of visitors during the day, destroying much of its rural charm and often making it feel more like a suburban mall than a historic town of 3,000 residents.

The Wines

While the **Yountville** name certainly goes far in the food world, you'll seldom see it mentioned on bottles, and the appellation certainly lacks the cachet of the hilly region to its east and the reputation for muscular cabs to the north. Still, Yountville can be relied on to produce tannic cabernets that age well in the bottle, as well as being cool enough for growing many other varietals, particularly chardonnay, sangiovese, zinfandel, sauvignon blanc, and even some pinot noir. Although wines from the Yountville AVA are certainly worthy of the Napa Valley pedigree, there is no one particular trait for which they are known.

The **Stags Leap District,** however, is different story. On the eastern side of the valley along the Silverado Trail, Stags Leap helped put California on the international wine map in the 1970s and is perhaps one of the most recognizable Napa AVAs to wine lovers. This fairly cool, hilly 1,300 acres of land rising up to the mountain crags (across which the legendary stag leapt to escape its hunters) is without doubt the land of cabernet sauvignon. The cabernets have been famously described by the founder of Stag's Leap Wine Cellars as "an iron fist in a velvet glove," and they certainly have a gentle elegance that belies their sometimes astonishing aging potential. The combination of volcanic soils and cool air channeled between the handful of knolls that make up the district are thought to play a role this being such a good place to create some of Napa Valley's best cabernets.

YOUNTVILLE WINERIES
★ DOMAINE CHANDON
Domaine Chandon (1 California Dr., 707/944-2280, www.domainechandon.com, 10am-5pm daily, tasting $20-25) is one of California's first big champagne houses. The buildings blend into the hillside beneath towering trees next to a giant pond and are almost invisible from the road. It's not the sort of modesty that one expects from such a big, glamorous operation producing several hundred thousand cases of sparkling and still wines each year; the surroundings are more earth mother than youthful bling.

Once across the bridge and into the cavernous reception, skip the PR presentations and head upstairs to the spacious tasting bar and salon, with its cozy club-like atmosphere and doors out onto a leafy terrace and lawn area. Four flights are available, including two that showcase Chandon's still wines. The terrace,

tasty appetizers, and sometimes energetic atmosphere are as much reasons to come here as the champagne. Another is the 1.5-hour tour ($40) offered daily at 10:30am and 3pm, which requires no reservations.

Downtown Tasting Rooms
While there are relatively few wineries to visit in Yountville, more and more are opening tasting rooms on Washington Street. All are in easy walking distance; even Domaine Chandon, a full-fledged winery and a must-see, is an easy stroll from the heart of town.

MA(I)SONRY
At the top of Washington Street is perhaps the most unusual tasting room in the valley, **Ma(i)sonry** (6711 Washington St., 707/944-0889, 10:30am-4:30pm Sun.-Thurs., 10:30am-5:30pm Fri.-Sat., tasting $35-55 for three wines). The space, located in a historic stone building, showcases high-dollar art and high-end furnishings and is home to a winery collective that pours flights from more than two dozen different small boutique wineries. With the exception of one Argentinean winery, all hail from California, if not Napa and Sonoma Counties. These are wines that you are unlikely to find anywhere else, as many of those featured only produce 300 cases or less. Tastings are seated with a "wine specialist," and appointments are necessary, particularly on weekends during the high season. Walk-ins are welcome, however, and the staff will try to accommodate you.

JESSUP CELLARS
It's hard to miss the large stucco and exposed-beam building that is home to **Jessup Cellars** (6740 Washington St., 707/944-8523, www.jessupcellars.com, 10am-6pm daily, tasting $10-20). Like Ma(i)sonry, Jessup offers tastes of incredible boutique red wines you'll have a hard time finding anyplace else, but instead of high art, you get a cute little bar, a few shelves with items for purchase, and staff that love their jobs. If you chat them up, you may find

Yountville to St. Helena Tasting Tour

If the line isn't too long, start your day with coffee and a croissant à la Thomas Keller at the **Bouchon Bakery,** then spend some time browsing the Napa lifestyle accessories found at the myriad of shops in the historic **V Marketplace.** Next, trade your latte for a glass of champagne at **Domaine Chandon,** Napa's premier champagne house, with landscaping that matches the caliber of its wines. Hit the road afterwards, stopping at **Oakville Grocery** for picnic provisions, and then at **Grgich Hills Winery** to taste the chardonnay (and pick up a bottle) made by the man who beat the French in the 1976 Judgment of Paris. Drive a bit farther to enjoy your goodies at **Bothe-Napa Valley State Park.** After packing up your basket, take a hike in the redwoods or explore the **Bale Grist Mill** nearby. Then, head over to **Failla Wines** to taste some cool-climate syrahs on the porch of a quiet farmhouse, or go back down to St. Helena for some bold and velvety cabernets at **Orin Swift.** Finish with a dinner at **Terra** in St. Helena to round out a star-studded day. To stay in town, splurge on a room at **Harvest Inn by Charlie Palmer.**

yourself tasting rare Jessup vintages that are not on the usual list.

HILL FAMILY ESTATE

Surfboards, baseball bats, a Fender electric guitar, and French antiques fill the tasting room of **Hill Family Estate** (6512 Washington St., 707/944-9580, www.hillfamilyestate.com, 10am-6pm daily, tasting $20). If you stand at the bar, you'll enjoy the company of the Hill family, who love to chat up customers tasting the small selection of light, balanced red and white wines. The cabernet sauvignons are not made in the typical heavy-handed Napa style, so even tasters with delicate palates will find them drinkable.

PRIEST RANCH WINES

The Tuscan-style building at the southern end of Washington Street is **Priest Ranch Wines** (6490 Washington St., 707/944-8200, www.priestranchwines.com, 11am-7pm daily, tasting $25-35). Sourced from the ranch vineyards, 2,800 feet above sea level deep in the Vaca Mountains, these estate wines score high with the critics. The tasting room, despite its exterior, draws in the beauty of the winery's remote location with oversize photos of sheep grazing on mountain slopes, tables made of reclaimed wood, and funky artistic flourishes. For a fuller tasting experience opt for the cheese and wine pairing ($45).

JCB TASTING SALON

If you were to make a collage of all the glossy ads in a luxury magazine, you might get something like **JCB Tasting Salon** (6505 Washington St., 707/934-8237, www.jcbcollection.com, 11am-7pm Sun.-Thurs., 11am-9pm Fri.-Sat., tasting $30-50). JCB stands for Jean-Charles Boisset, the Versace of the wine world, who has built an empire on his garish taste (some would say) and love of wine. JCB owns vineyards in Burgundy, several notable Napa and Sonoma wineries, and a tasting room like no other in Yountville. Think lots of mirrors, gold, leopard print, expensive stuff in glass cases, and dripping crystal chandeliers. As for wine, there are three tasting options, the cheapest being $30 for four pours of wine from Sonoma, Napa, and his home *terroir* in France. You can take your flute of pink bubbly to browse the collection of lifestyle tomes, perfume and jewelry, and Baccarat glassware (all for sale), or settle in for a guided tasting in the stunning Surrealist Room.

If your appetite is still intact, be sure to wander over to **Atelier by JCB** (11am-7pm daily), a gourmet food emporium that shares the same four walls as the JCB Tasting Salon. Despite the Sistine Chapel-esque ceiling, the aesthetic is considerably toned down, and browsing the goodies (local and European) is a delight. Cured meats, California caviar, truffles, foie gras, along with an immense cheese

Yountville

To
St. Helena
and Calistoga

To
Silverado Trail

LINCOLN AVE
MONROE ST
YOUNTVILLE CROSS RD
WASHINGTON ST
MADISON ST
REDD WOOD
JESSUP CELLARS
NORTH BLOCK INN & SPA
29
JEFFERSON ST
YOUNT ST
ST. HELENA HWY
MA(I)SONRY
THE FRENCH LAUNDRY
LAVENDER INN
FINNELL RD
WEBBER AVE
BOUCHON
WASHINGTON ST
MAISON FLEURIE
PETIT LOGIS
V MARKETPLACE/ BOTTEGA
BARDESSONO HOTEL
MULBERRY ST
HILL FAMILY ESTATES
NAPA VALLEY RAILWAY INN
OAK CIR
BISTRO JEANTY
CORNERSTONE CELLARS
JCB TASTING SALON & ANTELIER
YOUNTVILLE DELI
YOUNTVILLE WELCOME CENTER
MISSION
PRIEST RANCH
SAN CARLOS
VILLAGIO INN & SPA
REDD
AD HOC & ADDENDUM
SAN ANTONIO
HOTEL YOUNTVILLE
DOMAINE CHANDON
CHAMPAGNE DR
WASHINGTON ST

0   300 yds
0   300 m

CALIFORNIA DR
VINTNER'S GOLF CLUB

NAPA VALLEY MUSEUM

To
Napa
29

© AVALON TRAVEL

counter staffed by a true cheese monger, might make a picnic sound better than a long line at a celebrated restaurant.

CORNERSTONE CELLARS

Tucked behind the JCB Tasting Salon is the unassuming **Cornerstone Cellars** (6505 Washington St., 707/945-0388, www.cornerstonecellars.com, 11am-6pm daily, tasting $25-45). Pouring wine from the Napa and Willamette Valleys, the portfolio is diverse and showcases everything from bright Oregon chardonnay to a rich Howell Mountain cabernet. The cheapest tasting option is the white flight, but up it a few dollars to better enjoy the range of this winery. The Napa Valley syrah rosé is one of the specialties here, as are food pairings. For $45 (and with 48-hour advance reservations), enjoy small bites while learning the art of pairing wine in a tailored personal experience. Add another five and get a boxed lunch with a flight of three wines. The tasting room is a comfortable place to enjoy lunch with lovely wood tables, understated decor, and a friendly atmosphere.

Wineries by Appointment

BELL WINE CELLARS

Just a short jaunt out of town is the boutique **Bell Wine Cellars** (6200 Washington St., 707/944-1673, www.bellwine.com, 10am-4pm daily by appointment, tasting $20), surrounded by vineyards bordering the Napa River. Inside the stone winery you can taste whites and reds from Napa, as well as from Lake Country, the Sierra Foothills, and the Willamette Valley. However, Bell is best known for pioneering the single-vineyard, single-clone Napa Valley cabernet. True cabernet lovers might want to splurge on the $125 clonal tasting, which includes cheese and a chance to distinguish the characteristics of four wines, each made from a distinct clone of cabernet. Should you be a syrah fan, you may want to try the current release flight, which may include the Canterbury Vineyard Syrah, another Bell specialty. For $10 you can add a cheese plate to your tasting. Bell is also a great place to learn about the winemaking process. In the **Grape to Glass tour** (10:30am, 1pm, 3pm, daily by appointment, $50) you'll get out into the vineyards, a barrel tasting, and the five current release wines paired with cheese; in the **Sensory Tasting** (by appointment, $75) you'll learn to parse out different flavors and aromas through a series of blind tastings; and in the **Blending Seminar** (by appointment, $150) you'll learn to create your own blend guided by an expert.

GOOSECROSS CELLARS

One of the valley's smaller wineries open to the public, **Goosecross Cellars** (1119 State Ln., 707/944-1986, www.goosecross.com, 10am-4:30pm daily, tasting $15) has a refreshingly laid-back family vibe, especially considering its location. Opt for the lovely patio or the cozy tasting room, squeezed in next to the barrels, and select from any of the 10 wines that this family-owned winery makes, including the standout Howell Mountain cabernet sauvignon and the crisp but fruity Napa Valley chardonnay. Technically, Goosecross is appointment-only thanks to county regulations, but if as a small group you roll up unannounced, you won't be turned away.

PARADUXX

Another popular flight is offered by **Paraduxx** (7257 Silverado Trail, 866/367-9943, www.paraduxx.com, 10am-4pm daily, $35), which specializes in Napa Valley blends. Flights feature five pours that begin when you walk through the door of the modern farmhouse tasting room. From there it is table service of four reds either in the light and airy tasting room or out on the patio surrounded by vineyards. To make an affair of it, order the $25 cheese plate or try your own hand at blending at the **Blend Experience** (10:30am Thurs.-Fri. and Sun.-Mon., by appointment, $65).

STAGS LEAP WINERIES

Despite being a big name in Napa, Stags Leap is home to many low-key, if serious, wineries of history and pedigree. All are strung along the Silverado Trail, east of Yountville, and are a mix of walk-in and appointment-only. Still, expect to pay a premium to taste here.

CLOS DU VAL

Before the Judgment of Paris when Stag's Leap Wine Cellars bested the French, Frenchman Bernard Portet founded **Clos Du Val** (5330 Silverado Trail, Napa, 707/259-2200 or 707/261-5251, www.closduval.com, 10am-5pm daily, tasting $25), it is said, to make wines that rivaled Bordeaux. Established in 1972, Clos Du Val has succeeded. Cabernet sauvignon is the wine for which Clos Du Val is best known, especially the outstanding Stags Leap estate cabernet that comes from the vineyard right outside the winery door. White lovers will adore the estate white Bordeaux blend of semillon and sauvignon blanc called Ariadne. Tours of the ivy-clad winery and cellar are available daily at 10:30am by appointment and cost $35. Or you can bring a picnic to one of the many picnic tables overlooking the vineyards. On sunny Saturdays (which is often), the winery sets up a tasting bar out on the lawn, so you don't have to walk too far from your picnic spot or interrupt your game of *pétanque*, the French version of bocce, to try another wine.

STAG'S LEAP WINE CELLARS

Stag's Leap Wine Cellars (5766 Silverado Trail, Napa, 707/261-6410, www.cask23. com, 10am-4:30pm daily, tasting $40) is the winery that beat out the best of the French Bordeaux in the now-famous 1976 blind tasting in Paris and followed it up with another win in the anniversary tasting 30 years later in 2006. It still makes outstanding single-vineyard cabernet from that same SLV vineyard as well as the older Fay vineyard next to it. Such renowned wines command high prices, none more so than the Cask 23 cabernet, which retails at about $260. You can taste this, as well as other estate wines, for $40 in the new Fay Outlook and Visitor Center. Appointment-only tours ($60) take in the pristine-looking cave system and its fascinating Foucault pendulum (for measuring the earth's rotation), and conclude with the estate tasting. For years, the unassuming atmosphere belied the family-run winery's celebrity status, but the 2007 purchase by a major wine conglomerate has altered the

winery's personality, as evident by the replacement of the old intimate tasting room with a flashy visitors center and the upping of tasting prices from $15 to $40.

PINE RIDGE WINERY

Nestled in a small dell with its trademark ridge of pine trees above is another of the Stags Leap District's big cabernet houses, **Pine Ridge Winery** (5901 Silverado Trail, Napa, 800/575-9777, www.pineridgewinery. com, 10:30am-4:30pm daily, tasting $40), one of the few wineries to make highly rated wines from most of Napa's finest cabernet appellations—Stags Leap, Rutherford, Oakville, and Howell Mountain.

The charming tasting room is virtually devoid of merchandise, putting the wines firmly center stage as long as a tour bus has not just disgorged its passengers. The regular tasting includes wine from the various featured Napa Valley AVAs. Tours of the vineyard and aging caves, followed by a barrel tasting with cheese accompaniment, are offered three times a day by appointment (10am, noon, and 2pm, $50). You are also welcome to wander the Demonstration Vineyard of five Bordeaux varietals, at no additional cost, or reserve a picnic table in the Reserve Gardens.

The Stags Leap District is home to legendary cabernet.

Best Wineries for Lunch

There is no doubt that sipping and dining at the valley's very best can add up. To economize both time and money, consider making lunch a part of your tasting experience. Many wineries have excellent food programs that range from food pairings to café table service to pizzas served picnic-style. The price tag may seem outrageous, but in the end, it can be cheaper than tasting and then lunching elsewhere.

- **St. Clair Brown Winery, Napa:** The tasting room of this little winery is the charming Garden Eatery, where small plates of French-inspired food with ingredients plucked from the surrounding garden are served with flights, glasses, and bottles of wine.

- **Robert Sinskey Vineyards, Yountville:** There may be a wait, but walk-in tasting includes table service with each of the five pours paired with small bites prepared with ingredients from the vineyard's organic garden. The stone and weathered wood patio dripping with wisteria and lavender is an ideal spot to while away the afternoon.

- **Silver Oak, Oakville:** Splurge on the Food and Wine Pairing here and you'll find out how food-friendly their cabernets truly are. For $60, four wines are served alongside bites of ricotta agnolotti, lamb, morel mushrooms, and winery-cured speck.

- **Inglenook, Rutherford:** There is no tasting room at this famous estate, but you can savor Inglenook by grabbing a casual lunch at the Bistro. Executed with Hollywood precision, the Bistro has a charming Parisian vibe with seating inside and out on the leafy patio. Plenty of Inglenook wines are available by the glass.

- **Charles Krug Winery, St. Helena:** On weekends, the café in the new tasting room serves espresso, wine by the glass, cheese plates, and small wood-fired pizzas. There is plenty of seating in the stylish space, or better yet, you can take your food out to the lawn and eat surrounded by vineyards in the shadow of Krug's historic digs.

- **Velo Vino, St. Helena:** Parked out front, the winery's own Bruschetteria Food Truck plates excellent small bites to pair with the vino as well as bigger lunch platters that lure locals from as far away as Calistoga. The café-like tasting room and expansive back porch are perfect for lingering, and the staff couldn't be more welcoming.

ROBERT SINSKEY VINEYARDS

Robert Sinskey Vineyards (6320 Silverado Trail, 707/944-9090, www.robertsinskey.com, daily 10am-4:30pm, $40) is best known for its pinot noir, but the winery itself is a feast for the senses. Lavender and wisteria greet guests on their way to the stone and redwood cathedral-like tasting area. Here, a menu of small bites made with ingredients from the vineyard's organic garden is served alongside five pours off their list of current wines. While reservations are not required, there is a wait on busy days (they may even ask to make a reservation for you later in the day), so calling ahead is advised on peak weekends.

Robert Sinskey was one of the valley's earliest champions of organic farming. In 2007, the winery went a step further and was certified biodynamic, which explains all of the sheep photos around the winery. To boot, Rob Sinskey's wife, Maria, is a well-known chef and author of one of the better Napa Valley cookbooks, *The Vineyard Kitchen*. The **Full Circle Tour** ($95) aims to pull this all into focus. It includes a look in the cave and cellar, discussions about the art of winemaking, followed by small bites paired with Sinskey's current release wine.

Wineries by Appointment
SHAFER VINEYARDS

Tasting wine at **Shafer Vineyards** (6154 Silverado Trail, Napa, 707/944-2877, www.shafervineyards.com, tasting 10am and 2pm

Mon.-Fri. by appointment, $55) is about as close as many visitors might get to one of Napa's much-hyped cult wines without forking over hundreds of dollars. Shafer's limited-production Hillside Select cabernet sauvignon is regularly compared to the highly extracted wines from small producers like Screaming Eagle, Harlan Estate, and Bryant Family that are critically acclaimed and rare enough to command their cult status.

The secrets to success here are the rocky hillside vineyards behind the modest winery, which produce limited quantities of powerfully flavored grapes, and you can see this for yourself in the 90-minute, appointment-only tasting. The informative sit-down discussion and tasting on the patio overlooking the vineyards is limited to 10 people. Demand is high, so booking weeks in advance is sometimes necessary, as is a tolerance of the serious oenophiles who tend to flock here. There's no sign for the winery on Silverado Trail, so look for the cluster of property numbers at the end of the private road almost opposite the entrance to Silverado Vineyards.

STAGS' LEAP WINERY

North on the Silverado Trail, down a long driveway lined with ancient walnut trees, is the first winery to bear the area's name, **Stags' Leap Winery** (6150 Silverado Trail, 707/257-5790, www.stagsleap.com, tour and tasting by appointment 10am, 10:30am, 2pm, and 2:30pm daily, $65). Its wines might be less famous than those at Stag's Leap Wine Cellars, but its history and setting are far more impressive. The winery was founded in 1893, taking its name from the old Native American legend of a stag that evaded hunters by leaping across the craggy cliffs towering above the winery. The Victorian splendor remains fully intact today.

The tours take place in the Manor House, winemaking facilities, and wonderful gardens, which include an apothecary full of medicinal plants and a sensory garden devoted to flavorful and aromatic plants. Tasting is on the luxurious Manor House Porch and

includes the winery's current release of outstanding reds, such as the full-bodied petite sirah, a Rhône-style blend, an estate cabernet, and the estate merlot. Tie a visit here in with a tour of Shafer Vineyards, which shares the same driveway off the Silverado Trail, for the ultimate cabernet indulgence. Tours fill up fast, so book early.

SIGHTS

The history of Napa and the entire valley can be found at the **Napa Valley Museum** (55 Presidents Circle, 707/944-0500, www.napavalleymuseum.org, 11am-4pm Wed.-Sun., adults $7, seniors $3.50, children 17 and under $2.50). It has a fascinating mix of exhibits exploring the valley's natural and cultural heritage. You'll learn about the modern wine industry with an interactive high-tech exhibit on the science of winemaking. The upstairs gallery provides space for rotating exhibitions, and you're likely to find the work of local artists or art depicting food and wine.

To experience more than the culinary arts in Yountville, take the **Art Walk** (www.townofyountville.com) that stretches along Washington Street from California Street to Monroe Street, and hunt for the 40 pieces of installation art tucked around town. Look for the 200 stone mushrooms outside of the post office or the elegant *Great Blue Heron* hidden by the Vintage Inn. There are also plenty of rock and metal modern sculptures, like *Chaos Pamplona* by Jedd Novatt and *Belfry* by Napa's own Gordon Huether. The town's website has a printable map of the Art Walk, or you can pick one up at the **Yountville Welcome Center** (6484 Washington St., Ste. F, Yountville, 707/944-0904, www.yountville.com, 10am-5pm daily).

If you want to extend your walk, pick up a **Historical Walking Tour** map also at the visitors center. Along the two-mile loop you'll see parks, the local pioneer cemetery, original Victorian homes, century-old storefronts, wineries, and much more. If you do the full loop and stop to admire the various sights, this walk may take you as much as 2-3 hours.

ENTERTAINMENT

Nearly 60 years ago, the **Lincoln Theater** (100 California Dr., 707/944-9900, www.lincolntheater.com, $10-125) ran its first show at the Veterans Home in Yountville. Today, a packed year-round season brings top-end live entertainment of all kinds to quiet Yountville. You can see touring Broadway shows, locally produced plays, stand-up comedy, dance productions, music nights, and more. Although this large theater seats hundreds, purchase tickets in advance if you can—especially for one-night-only special performances or if you'll be in the area for only one weekend.

SHOPPING

The best shopping is found in and around the giant brick **V Marketplace** (6525 Washington St., 707/944-2451, 10am-5:30pm daily), which was once a winery and distillery. It was built in 1870 by German immigrant Gottlieb Groezinger, who made most of his fortune decades earlier in the California gold rush.

The building has been tastefully restored inside, with the exposed brick and giant wooden beams lending an air of sophistication to the little boutique shops selling everything from clothes and accessories to toys, art, and the usual Wine Country gifts. Groezinger might turn in his grave if he saw it today, but not every shopping center can boast of being on the National Register of Historic Places.

Most of the stores clearly thrive on tourist dollars, but it's still fun to get lost for half an hour exploring the nooks and crannies of the three floors. Some of the more memorable shops include **Domain Home & Garden** (707/945-0222, www.domainhomeandgarden.com), which sells fun items for the home and garden, while upstairs the specialty bath and body products found at **The Scents of Napa Valley** (707/947-7230) will allow you to take some Napa Valley pampering home with you. To pick up some wine, the **V Wine Cellar** (707/531-7053, www.vwinecellar.com) is a decent and fairly large wineshop that sells a lot of local and international wines and has occasional tastings. All stores in the building are open 10am-5:30pm daily.

If you're looking for an "art experience," head to the northern end of Washington Street, where art and design meet wine-tasting at one of the most unique shopping experiences in the valley, **Ma(i)sonry** (6711 Washington St., 707/944-0889, 10:30am-4:30pm Sun.-Thurs., 10:30am-5:30pm Fri.-Sat.). Inside a historic Victorian-era stone

the historic V Marketplace

house, the concept for Ma(i)sonry is to be a living gallery, where the work of both contemporary and classical artists and designers is part of the decor and also happens to be for sale. The reality is that it can be a little intimidating stepping into such a rarefied atmosphere with its immaculately dressed staff, but just pretend you have several thousand dollars to blow and you'll quickly feel relaxed poking around the imaginative and beautifully made home furnishings and design pieces. There are a few reasonably priced items that would make good souvenirs of the Napa Valley, from antique wine bottles to Native American arrows, and the beautifully designed garden is a relaxing refuge in which to taste the many wines on offer.

RECREATION
Napa River Ecological Reserve

A small patch of land next to the river in Yountville has been saved from the vineyards, and it's now a great place to see wildlife other than the flocks of tourists more commonly sighted in these parts. Almost 150 types of bird and 40 types of butterfly call this peaceful 73-acre patch of the valley home. The reserve has no specific hours but is probably best avoided during the rainy season (Dec.-Apr.) when it can be too wet to be accessible.

The small paved parking lot is on the north side of Yountville Cross Road, about halfway between Highway 29 and the Silverado Trail, just west of the small bridge over the river. There's just one trail, about a mile long, that dives into woodland, crosses the river (only possible during the dry summer and fall months), and eventually loops back on itself, but not before affording a unique view of the valley's native wildlife and plantlife.

The reserve is free, open 24 hours a day, and overseen by the California Department of Fish and Wildlife (707/944-5500, www.wildlife.ca.gov).

Golf

Just south of the Domaine Chandon winery

is the nine-hole, 2,800-yard **Vintner's Golf Club** (7901 Solano Ave., off California Dr., 707/944-1992, www.vintnersgolfclub.com, call for tee times). Fees for nonresidents range from $25 midweek to $30 weekends for nine holes, and up to $40 to play 18 holes.

Spas

An easy walk from anywhere in downtown Yountville, the **Spa Villagio** (6481 Washington St., 800/351-1133 or 707/948-5050, 7:30am-9pm daily, $85-280) has a beautiful space in which to pamper its patrons. You don't need to be a guest at the Villagio Inn to book a treatment at the spa, though you may wish for one of the five Spa Suites—private spaces where singles, couples, and friends can relax before, during, and after their treatments. Massages run $135-150 for 50 minutes and $250-280 for 100 minutes, and facials, manicures, and pedicures are also on the menu. But whatever your indulgence, be sure to show up an hour early—at the price you're paying for treatments here, you'll definitely want to take advantage of the saunas and hot tubs, relaxation rooms, and all the other chichi amenities. The spa recommends making reservations for your treatment at least three weeks in advance, especially during the summer and fall seasons.

Another purely Napa Valley option is the 50-minute "Uncorked" treatment at the **North Block Spa** (6757 Washington St., 707/944-8080, http://northblockhotel.com/spa, 8am-8pm daily), in which for 60 or 90 minutes you may have your feet rubbed with ground grape seeds and pressure points massaged with wine corks. It will cost you $145 or $215, respectively, or for about the same amount you can select one of the spa's other signature treatments, like the Stiletto Blues, which uses hot stone massage to heal well-heeled soles; a Hats Off scalp massage; and a massage designed just for moms. The spa also offers acupuncture, facials, and dry exfoliation treatments in its modern and minimalist setting.

FOOD

Anchored by The French Laundry, Yountville has become a restaurant mecca in the Napa Valley as the town continues to transform itself and move further upmarket.

Downtown Yountville

Good luck trying to get a reservation at ★ **The French Laundry** (6640 Washington St., 707/944-2380, www.frenchlaundry.com, dinner 5:30pm-9pm daily, lunch 11am-1pm Fri.-Sun., reservation only, $310). The famous restaurant is usually booked up two months in advance thanks to its world renown, limited seating, and strict reservations system. Reservations can only be made one month in advance, and such is the demand that all the slots for the two evening seatings two months hence are usually snapped up the first morning they are made available. This is the case for much of the year, particularly on weekend nights, so either be prepared to hit redial for the better part of a morning or persuade your hotel to make a reservation for you. If you are one of the lucky few to get in, you'll probably remember the seven- or nine-course prix fixe dinner as your best meal all year, but you'll want to forget the $310 price in a hurry. If you can't get a reservation, you can at least see some of the ingredients growing in the restaurant's own organic vegetable garden just across the street.

If you can't get into The French Laundry, try its little cousin down the road, **Bouchon** (6534 Washington St., 707/944-8037, www.bouchonbistro.com, 11am-midnight Mon.-Fri., 10am-midnight Sat.-Sun., $34). A French bistro that excels at *croque monsieurs* and *steak frites,* its brief menu evokes a relaxed Parisian hole, helped by a smattering of French wines on the otherwise Napa-dominated list. Reservations, while not necessary, are recommended. But, if you're just looking for a breakfast pastry or a sandwich, walk from Bouchon to the ★ **Bouchon Bakery** (6528 Washington St., 707/944-2253, www.bouchonbakery.com, 7am-7pm daily) next door. This ultra-high-end bakery supplies both Bouchon and The French Laundry with pastries and breads, as well as operating a retail storefront. Locals and visitors flock to the bakery at breakfast and lunchtime, so expect a line.

And then there is **Ad Hoc** (6476 Washington St., 707/944-2487, dinner 5pm-10pm Thurs.-Mon., brunch 9am-1:30pm Sun., prix fixe menu $52), Thomas Keller's most recent adventure in Yountville. Ad Hoc aims for (and hits with a perfect bull's-eye) a rustic American family style. The four-course menu changes nightly, and you'll get no choices, but considering the quality of the seasonal fare, that's not necessarily a bad thing. The only certainty is that there'll be either soup or salad followed by a meat or fish main course, a cheese course, and dessert. Usually, there are a couple of add-on options, if you can't get enough. While the food is decidedly American comfort food (think fried chicken, roasted corn, and peach cobbler), the wine list is a far cry from boxed-wine Americana. Expect a sommelier-crafted list, as well as an epicurean cocktail menu, with plenty of high-dollar French and local selections. Reservations are not quite as hard to get here as they are at The French Laundry, but don't expect to walk in and get a table most evenings either.

Next door to Ad Hoc is the sleek modern home of **Redd** (6480 Washington St., 707/944-2222, www.reddnapavalley.com, lunch 11:30am-2:30pm Fri.-Sun., dinner 5:30pm-9:30pm daily, brunch 11am-2:30pm Sun., $28-36), a critically acclaimed restaurant outside of the Keller constellation. The minimalist contemporary dining room reflects the modern American cooking, which has been compared favorably to the food at The French Laundry. If you're in the mood to splurge, the $85 five-course taster menu is well worth the price. On the other hand, a bacon-infused Bloody Mary ordered with the Hangtown Fry omelet and fried oysters is a perfect brunch after a late night of wining and dining.

If a visit to a Yountville restaurant is not complete without a celebrity chef sighting, make a reservation at **Bottega** (6525 Washington St. A9, 707/945-1050, www. botteganapavalley.com, lunch 11:30am-3pm Tues.-Sun., dinner 5pm-9:30pm daily, $15-36), where celebrity chef Michael Chiarello frequently strolls out into the dining room, wooing patrons. Aside from the finely executed Italian cuisine, the big draw here is the outside covered patio, where two large fireplaces, ringed by couches, invite you to sip a cocktail or glass of wine late into the evening or on a rainy afternoon.

But if celebrity sightings are not your thing and you're hungry for a local favorite, **Bistro Jeanty** (6510 Washington St., 707/944-0103, www.bistrojeanty.com, 11:30am-10:30pm daily, $21-41) just may be the place for you. The menu is a single page devoted to the classics of Parisian bistro cuisine. Tomato bisque served with a puff pastry shell, traditional salads, cassoulet, coq au vin, even a *croque monsieur* are all crafted with obvious joy. Every local Yountville resident will lovingly describe his or her own favorite dish. Service is friendly, and you'll see a few locals hanging at the bar, watching the TV tuned to a sports channel—something of a non sequitur here. Jeanty has two dining rooms, making walk-in dining easy on off-season weeknights, but definitely make a dinner reservation if you're in town on the weekend or in high season.

For a beer and pie, snag a table at **Redd Wood** (6755 Washington St., 707/299-5030, www.redd-wood.com, 11:30am-10pm Mon.-Thurs., 8am-10am and 11:30am-11pm Fri.-Sat., 8am-10am and 11:30am-10pm Sun., $15-35). This is Yountville's version of a pizzeria, meaning it is owned by an acclaimed chef (Richard Reddington of Redd); a farm-fresh egg can be added to your wood-fired pizza for an extra $3; and rustic Italian mains and house-made pasta are also available, as are craft cocktails.

Along St. Helena Highway (Highway 29)

One of the first big roadside restaurants north of Napa is **Brix** (7377 St. Helena Hwy.,

707/944-2749, www.brix.com, 11:30am-9pm Mon.-Sat., 10am-2pm and 4pm-9pm Sun., entrées $19-44), a cavernous place with a little bit of an expense-account atmosphere but that serves some nicely executed French-inspired cuisine. A standout feature of the restaurant is the big patio overlooking vineyards, which is perhaps best enjoyed on Sunday mornings when the kitchen serves a gourmet **brunch buffet** (adults $42.50, kids 7-12 $21, 6 and under free) complete with artisan cheeses, salads, eggs, pizzas, and a seafood bar. If the prices seem over the top, the restaurant serves a much more reasonable bar menu 4pm-7pm Monday-Saturday.

When locals want to get a steak, **Mustards Grill** (7399 St. Helena Hwy., 707/944-2424, 11:30am-9pm Mon.-Thurs., Fri 11:30am-10pm, 11am-10pm Sat., 11am-9pm Sun., $17-36) is where they go. Considered the king of the valley grills, it has been around for over 25 years, witnessing many more-fashionable restaurants in the valley come and go. Mustards is a thoroughly Napa Valley affair, run by Cindy Pawlcyn, who has also owned a couple of unique restaurants in St. Helena. It has spawned a cookbook and grows many of its own vegetables in its garden, as only a Napa restaurant could. The menu is filled with the sort of rich roasted and grilled meats that scream for a powerful Napa cabernet sauvignon, of which there are several dozen on the international wine list.

Picnic Supplies

Only in Yountville do picnic supplies have Michelin wattage. To take some Thomas Keller with you, **Bouchon Bakery** (6528 Washington St., 707/944-2253, www.bouchonbakery.com, 7am-7pm daily) has a limited selection of very good sandwiches for under $10, as well as fresh bread and some sweeter bakery delights (try the macarons).

For $16.50 you can have a picnic of pulled pork or fried chicken also à la Keller from **Addendum** (www.thomaskeller.com/addendum, 11am-2pm Thurs.-Sat.), the **to-go arm** of **Ad Hoc** (6476 Washington St.,

707/944-2487). If waiting to dig in is not an option, Addendum is blessed with plenty of picnic tables nestled in a garden surrounded by fruit trees.

Locals are usually to be found ordering lunch at the **Yountville Deli**, which is on the north side of the **Yountville Ranch Market** (6498 Washington St., 707/944-2002, 6am-10pm daily, deli 6am-3pm daily). A full range of sandwiches is available in the deli for $8-10, along with everything else you might need for a picnic, from bread and cheese to beverages, including plenty of half bottles of local wine.

ACCOMMODATIONS

The small town of Yountville has not only an impressive number of restaurants and shops but also a lot of hotel rooms for its size. Being right next to Highway 29 and a major cross-valley road, it is within easy reach of just about every valley winery but can suffer from almost constant traffic noise.

$150-200

In the heart of Yountville is the ★ **Maison Fleurie** (6529 Yount St., 800/788-0369, www.maisonfleurienapa.com, $170-395), which also does its best to be more French than Californian. The old ivy-covered stone-and-brick buildings around a pretty courtyard certainly evoke the French countryside, as do the vineyards almost across the street (if you ignore the contemporary Bardessono Hotel that sprouted up next to the vines). Inside the cozy lobby and the 13 guest rooms the French country theme continues. Cozy is also the word used by the hotel to describe its smallest and cheapest rooms—the Petite Full and the Petite Queen rooms are just 80 square feet. If you do get one, plan on spending time outside by the small pool to prevent claustrophobia. The biggest rooms are in the adjoining Carriage House and Bakery buildings and include fireplaces, views, and spa tubs in some.

Next to Bouchon Bakery, you can wake up to mouthwatering smells at the cozy five-room **Petit Logis Inn** (6527 Yount St., 707/944-2332, 877/944-2332, www.petitlogis.

com, $145-310). Each room has a fireplace, a jetted tub, and a fridge and is decorated in warm creamy colors with an occasional wall mural. Low-key and unpretentious, the inn is best described as "the place to come to pretend you live in Yountville." Unlike at many other inns, breakfast is not included but can be arranged at a nearby restaurant for an additional charge.

Over $200

The Yountville area has more than its fair share of upscale lodgings, many of which seem to be competing for conference and meeting business. That roughly translates to some slightly unjustified prices for the average visitor. The upshot is that the hotel concierges are actually able to get reservations at the best local restaurants when your own attempts might fail.

The Orient Express it is not, but this is the only place in the valley where you can sleep on a train. Sort of. The nine railcars and cabooses that constitute the **Napa Valley Railway Inn** (6523 Washington St., 707/944-2000, www.napavalleyrailwayinn.com, $225-260) took their last trip many decades ago and are now fitted out with king or queen beds, air-conditioning, skylights, flat-screen TVs, and private bathrooms, making surprisingly comfortable accommodations right in the middle of Yountville. For years, the Railway Inn was the economy option in town, but as Napa Valley rates skyrocketed, it jumped on board. Some of the perks include the in-house **Coffee Caboose,** where you can start your day with pastries and coffee; access to the nearby Yountville Fitness Center to burn off any unwanted calories; and a "Napa Valley Travel Packet" ($20), which includes tasting vouchers, maps, bottled water, and Advil.

If you're splurging on a no-expenses-spared trip to Napa Valley, enjoy the location and luxury of the **Vintage Inn** (6541 Washington St., 707/944-1112 or 800/351-1133, www.vintageinn.com, $330-675). Guest rooms in the elegant hexagonal buildings feature the softest sheets ever, L'Occitane toiletries in a big beautiful bath with plenty of storage for longer stays. The French country-meets-Wine Country decor extends to a private patio or deck overlooking the lush gardens. The dining room serves what might be the best complimentary hotel buffet breakfast in California. Because it's a sister property of the nearby Villagio, Vintage Inn guests get use of the Villagio's fitness center, tennis courts, and spa.

The **Villagio Inn & Spa** (6481 Washington St., 707/944-8877 or 800/351-1133, www.villagio.com, $340-675) has Tuscan-themed decor and similar amenities, but it is in a cluster of buildings that looks like an extension of the neighboring apartment complex despite the faux Roman gardens. All rooms have a private patio or balcony and may include a wood-burning fireplace. Like the Vintage Inn, the hotel serves an outstanding champagne breakfast every morning.

If you're looking for some contemporary luxury with plenty of green cred, the sprawling **Bardessono Hotel** (6526 Yount St., 707/204-6000, www.bardessono.com, $600-800) is the newest member of the Napa Valley's growing collection of super-resorts catering to those with money to burn for the ultimate in pampering. The 62-room hotel is one of only a few worldwide to be LEED-Platinum certified, thanks to a laundry list of nature-friendly design and operational features. Arranged around multiple courtyards with its own meandering streams, it resembles a contemporary luxury condo development more than a traditional hotel, but the amenities and services are what you'd expect when every room is a suite and costs upward of $600 per night—massive TVs, private patios, fireplaces, outdoor showers, giant Jacuzzi tubs, countless spa treatments, and the finest linens money can buy.

More intimate lodgings can be found at nine-room **Lavender Inn** (2020 Webber St., 707/944-1388 or 800/522-4140, www.lavendernapa.com, $275-495), a Provence-themed B&B. All rooms are spacious with fireplaces, and a few have private hot tubs and patios to take in the smell of the lavender gardens on warm summer nights. Guests are welcome to use the pool at Maison Fleurie down the road.

The **Hotel Yountville** (6462 Washington St., 707/867-7900 or 888/944-2885, www.hotelyountville.com, $475-600) is another with a distinctively French farmhouse appeal. The 80-room hotel has cobblestone exterior, exposed beams, and tons of natural light. The standard rooms, or "Deluxe Rooms," and the slightly bigger "Premium Rooms" have a vaulted ceiling, a four-poster bed, white Italian linens, a fireplace, a spa tub, and French doors opening onto a private patio. Suites are also available, with all the same amenities but with a lot more space. As you would expect, there is a full service spa, a pool, and complimentary wine-tasting.

Centered around a main courtyard, the **North Block Hotel** (6757 Washington St., 707/944-8080, http://northblockhotel.com, $300-650) resembles a Tuscan village with red-tiled roofs, earth-toned stucco, and stone archways. Should they want to, guests can look out onto the courtyard with its pool and communal fireplace from their own private balcony. Inside, the rooms start at 330 square feet and include an espresso machine, a soaking tub, and luxurious linens; some rooms have fireplaces. The hotel also includes the **North Block Spa** (http://northblockhotel.com/spa, 8am-8pm daily) and **Redd Wood** (6755 Washington St., 707/299-5030, www.redd-wood.com, 11:30am-10pm Mon.-Thurs., 8am-10am and 11:30am-11pm Fri.-Sat., 8am-10am and 11:30am-10pm Sun., $15-35), a pizzeria of sorts that, conveniently for guests, serves a limited breakfast menu Friday through Sunday. The hotel is located at the north end of town, making it a bit out of the fray, but it is still plagued by some traffic noise on Highway 29.

At **The Cottages of Napa Valley** (1012 Darms Ln., 2 miles south of Yountville, 707/252-7810, www.napacottages.com, $305-575), you'll pay to gain a home away from home in the heart of Wine Country. Each of the eight cottages has its own king bed, private garden, outdoor fireplace, and kitchenette. Every morning the quiet staff drops off a basket of fresh pastries from Bouchon Bakery and a pot of great coffee. A free shuttle will deliver you to your Yountville restaurant of choice for dinner that evening.

INFORMATION AND SERVICES

The tiny **Yountville Welcome Center** (6484 Washington St., Ste. F, 707/944-0904, www.yountville.com, 10am-5pm daily) is awash with guides, leaflets, magazines, and advice about the local area. The concierge desk at the **V Marketplace** (6525 Washington St., 707/944-2451, 10am-5:30pm daily) is also worth stopping at for some local tips and information.

GETTING THERE AND AROUND

Yountville sits snuggly on Highway 29, just nine miles north of Napa. Downtown is on the east side of the highway, and Washington Street is its main corridor. Easily enough, Washington Street connects with Highway 29 at the south and north end of town, but to get to the heart of Yountville, exit on California Drive in the south and Madison Street in the north. The Yountville Cross Road will take you from the north end of town to the Silverado Trail.

To get here via bus, jump aboard the **VINE** (707/251-6443 or 800/696-6443, www.ridethevine.com, $1.60-$5.50). Route 10 makes the daily trek from Napa to Calistoga, while Route 29, a commuter bus that runs from the El Cerrito BART station and the Vallejo Ferry Terminal up through Calistoga, runs on the weekdays only. Both make stops in Yountville.

Another option, particularly after an indulgent meal, is the **Yountville Trolley** (707/944-1234 or 707/312-1509 after 7pm, www.ridethevine.com/community-shuttles, 10am-11pm Mon.-Sat., 10am-7pm Sun, free). Running on a fixed track from Yountville Park, along Washington Street, to California Drive (conveniently near Domaine Chandon), the trolley is a cute historical ride through a cute historical town. It may also be a cheap and convenient way back to your hotel after imbibing a bit too much.

The Yountville area is great to explore by bike, particularly the Stags Leap District. The first section of the planned 47-mile **Napa Valley Vine Trail** was paved in Yountville and now gives cyclists a break from navigating cars at least for a little while. **Napa Valley Bike Tours** (6500 Washington St., 707/251-8687, www.napavalleybiketours.com, 8:30am-5pm daily) offers rentals by the day, as well as customized Self-Guided Bike Tours ($108) that include a picnic lunch, wine purchase pickup, and van support. On their own, bike rentals run $45 per day. Electric hybrids are also available ($75/day), as well as tandem bikes ($90). Loaner bikes at some of the posher hotels are increasingly coming into vogue, so be sure to ask about availability when making reservations or checking in.

Oakville and Rutherford

With populations of 71 and 164, Oakville and Rutherford are really agricultural districts that lack any real commercial or housing hub. Oakville began its life as a water stop for the railroad in the 1860s, and the last real vestige of the village that sprouted up around it is the now historic Oakville Grocery. Rutherford boasts 90 more people, some of whom work at the luxurious Auberge du Soleil on the eastern edge of the district. Grapes are the most famous (and numerous) residents of Oakville and Rutherford, which were both granted their AVA status in 1993.

The Wines

This is a part of the valley where the weather starts to get seriously warm in the summer, and the cabernets get seriously muscular. In fact, nearly 70 percent of the vineyards in this appellation are planted to cabernet sauvignon, and the area was home to some of the pioneering wineries in the Napa Valley.

Oakville begins just north of Yountville and stretches across the valley, earning its reputation from the sandy, well-drained soils. Here is where the land of big bold Napa cabernets begins in the valley, but the appellation also turns out some excellent sauvignon blanc and chardonnay. For this reason, it was also the home to some of the valley's famous wineries stretching back to the 1800s.

Like Oakville, **Rutherford** is a big appellation that spans the width of the valley. Some critics suggest there is not a great deal of difference between the two neighboring appellations—both have similar soils and weather, and both are capable of producing rich, muscular cabernets with exceptional balance. How Rutherford earned the bigger name over the years for cabernets might be partly due to the historic and influential wineries that made wine here, such as Inglenook and Beaulieu. Indeed, it was Beaulieu's famous winemaker, André Tchelistcheff, who made

the connection between the distinctive soils of the region and their influence on the characteristics of the equally distinctive wines. "It takes Rutherford dust to grow great cabernet," he famously said.

You might also often hear the term "Rutherford Bench," a section of the AVA down the western side of the valley that is not benchland in the traditional sense and was never granted its own appellation status. It has become an oft-used marketing term nonetheless, normally to suggest the best part of the Rutherford region.

East of Rutherford, hidden in the oak-studded peaks and valleys of the Vaca Mountains is the slender **Chiles Valley AVA.** Grapes have been grown here for more than 100 years, and the area was ripe for a new wave of viticultural development until the valley's biggest growers recently turned their attention farther north to Lake County, where land is cheaper and the promised investment return greater. Nevertheless, there are still some great wines made in these hills, most notably zinfandel and sauvignon blanc, which enjoy the warmer growing conditions.

OAKVILLE WINERIES

Oakville wineries are a mix of walk-in and appointment-only tasting rooms that hug Highway 29 and the Silverado Trail. In the thick of the valley's vineyards, you're not going to discover that small, unknown treasure. The ground here is pretty well trod, and any relatively quiet wineries owe their tranquility to high tasting prices and limited appointments.

DURANT & BOOTH

In the tiny commercial hub of Oakville, **Durant & Booth** (7856 St. Helena Hwy., 707/947-3180, 10:30am-4:30pm daily, tasting $35-55) occupies the historic home of the original owners of the Oakville Grocery.

While the elegant Victorian exterior remains untouched, the interior drips with decadent details such as crystal chandeliers and decidedly modern bric-a-brac, for a contemporary twist on the Victorian era. Tastings are seated (and pricey), and the wines are sophisticated and crafted with care, particularly the sauvignon blanc and the pinot noir. Bottles range $38-100. However, the proximity to the Oakville Grocery keeps things casual. Out back, the covered patio connects to Oakville Grocery's revamped picnic area and is perfect for lounging with a bottle or a glass ($13-19), plus some provisions from next door. A big-screen TV straddles the two spaces, playing Giants games and hosting the occasional movie night.

★ ROBERT MONDAVI WINERY

This sprawling mission-style complex with its distinctive giant archway and bell tower is considered by some to be the temple of modern Napa winemaking, with the late Robert Mondavi the high priest. Others are of the opinion that it's a classic example of the overcommercialization of the Napa wine industry—and judging by the crowds and limos that throng the winery, they have a point. The **Robert Mondavi Winery** (7801 Hwy.

29, 707/226-1395 or 888/766-6328, www.robertmondaviwinery.com, 10am-5pm daily) was once the crown jewel of the Mondavi Corporation, which started life in the 1960s, ushering in the valley's modern-day wine industry. While the wines are rather special, touring the impressive grounds and buildings while learning about their history and about winemaking is certainly the highlight of visiting the winery. Accordingly, there is a dizzying array of options at equally dizzying prices. Tour highlights include the 90-minute Signature Tour and Tasting ($35), with a 30-minute stroll through the vineyards and winery followed by a tasting of three wines; the Twilight Tour ($55), which is perfect for the end of a hot summer day; the Wine Basics tasting, which is a bargain at $20 for wine-tasting "beginners"; and the Discovery Tour, which is billed as good for parents with kids ($20), but only two wines are tasted. You can usually sign up for a same-day tour at the reception desk.

Without a tour the tasting options are limited to $5-30 per wine in the Vineyard Room. You may also retire to the To Kalon Room for a selection of reserve wines by the glass ($8-45) or opt for a flight of library wines ($55). Of course, if the modern-day Napa Valley

Robert Mondavi Winery

that Mondavi helped create has already bankrupted you, it's always free to wander around the courtyard to admire the architecture and views and imagine a time in the 1960s when this was virtually the only winery in the area.

SILVER OAK

"Life is a Cabernet" is the motto of **Silver Oak** (915 Oakville Cross Rd., 707/942-7022, www.silveroak.com, 9am-5pm Mon.-Sat., 11am-5pm Sun., tasting $25-60). Lovers of this winery's cabernet will undoubtedly recognize the old-fashioned water tower that graces Silver Oak's label. Inside the lovely timber-framed tasting room you'll get the opportunity to taste cabernets from both its Oakville and Alexander Valley wineries. The Silver Oak-Twomey Red tasting (appointment only, $40), throws Twomey's highly regarded merlot into the mix, making for a mouthful of reds. Silver Oak prides itself on the food-friendly nature of their very popular (and pricey) cabernets. Make the most of your tasting here and splurge on the Food and Wine Pairing (by appointment, $60). The menu includes Twomey's pinot noir and merlot, along with two Napa Valley Silver Oak cabernets, accompanying bites of ricotta agnolotti, lamb, morel mushrooms, and winery-cured speck. The price may seem steep, but it's a bargain when you consider how much it would cost to take a $100-plus bottle of Silver Oak to lunch.

Wineries by Appointment

Just across the road from the Oakville Grocery, **The Tasting Room at the Napa Wine Company** (7830 Hwy. 29, 800/848-9630, www.cultwinecentral.com, 10am-3:30pm daily by appointment, tasting $20) does not suggest that this is a huge winemaking and grape-growing operation. The tasting room is a cooperative of 25 small wineries and the Napa Wine Company itself, which manages to make its own wine as well, including a highly regarded cabernet sauvignon.

Some of the small wineries represented in the tasting room have links to major valley personalities, while others here are simply small or medium-size family affairs, making a stop here the best way to taste some outstanding Napa Valley wines made without the usual Napa Valley fanfare. Every week a different vintner is highlighted, and tastings involve five pours of their wines. While the tasting room is appointment-only, same-day appointments are never a problem.

OPUS ONE

Yup, that huge thing on the rise that looks like a missile silo really is a winery. **Opus One** (7900 Hwy. 29, 707/944-9442 or 800/292-6787, www.opusonewinery.com, 10am-4pm daily, reservations required) boasts a reputation as one of the most prestigious, and definitely one of the most expensive, vintners in Napa. The echoing halls inside the facility add to the grandeur of the place, as does the price of a tasting. You can shell out $45 for one four-ounce pour of the current release wine, or $65 will get you four ounces of a library wine. If curiosity gets the best of you, $20 will get you in the door with a glass of the winery's second label, Overture. If you don't mind the price tag or just can't get enough of the Opus One experience, tours ($75-125) of the estate are available daily and, like the tastings, are by appointment only.

FAR NIENTE

One of Napa's most well-respected wineries, **Far Niente**'s (1350 Acacia Dr., off the Oakville Grade, 707/944-2861, www.farniente.com, tours by appointment 11am-3pm daily, $65) appointment-only tour and tasting is among the best in the valley. The winery makes only two highly regarded (and expensive) wines—cabernet sauvignon and chardonnay—so the tasting of five wines will always include some older library vintages. Despite the $65 price tag, the tour is extremely popular, and booking in advance during the summer is essential.

Far Niente (Italian for "without a care") was established as a winery in the late 1800s by Gil Nickel, who also founded the nearby Nickel & Nickel winery. Among the highlights of the history-laden tour are a walk through the aging caves under the main house, which have been extended into a 40,000-square-foot labyrinth over the decades, and a chance to see Nickel's classic cars in the Carriage House.

NICKEL & NICKEL

Almost opposite the lavish Mondavi winery is the rather quaint Victorian farmstead of **Nickel & Nickel** (8164 Hwy. 29, 707/967-9600, www.nickelandnickel.com, tasting and tours by appointment 10am-3pm Mon.-Fri., 10am-2pm Sat.-Sun., $65), sister winery to Far Niente just down the road. Many of the buildings in the complex date from the late 1800s, but there is also a cunningly disguised state-of-the-art winery hidden in the huge barn built recently using Victorian building methods.

The collection of beautifully restored cottages and barns and the centerpiece 1884 Sullenger House can be seen on the appointment-only tour, a sedate and classy affair that culminates in the tasting of five of the single-vineyard wines paired with cheese. Although cabernet dominates the production, there are some outstanding chardonnays from Napa Valley and the Russian River Valley made in varying styles, as well as syrah, merlot, and zinfandel.

RUTHERFORD WINERIES

Highway 29 gets busier as it enters Rutherford, making ducking in and out of winery driveways difficult and nearly impossible if you are trying to cross the other lane of traffic. It is not a bad idea to strategize your tasting itinerary with the direction in which you are traveling.

PEJU PROVINCE WINERY

Peju (8466 Hwy. 29, 800/446-7358, www.peju.com, 10am-6pm daily, tasting $25-45, tour and barrel tasting $65), with its manicured gardens, koi pond, curiously shaped trees, and lofty tasting room in a tower replete with giant stained-glass window has the feel of a French country estate viewed through a hallucinogenic haze. This may reflect owner Anthony Peju's curious path to the Napa Valley from his homeland of Azerbaijan by way of France, England, and Los Angeles.

Apart from the curious trees, Peju is perhaps best known for its cabernet franc, but that's one wine that's usually not available for tasting due to its almost cultlike status. Instead, visitors can taste the equally outstanding estate cabernet sauvignon and the unusual Provence table wine, a dark rosé blend of almost all the other varietals Peju grows. Peju is open later than most in the area, but during particularly crowded times you might find getting into the tasting room involves a bit of a wait.

INGLENOOK

When a fabled Hollywood director buys one of the most storied of the historic Napa Valley wineries, it's somewhat inevitable that the result would be one of the most impressive winery shows in the valley. And so it is at **Inglenook** (1991 St. Helena Hwy., 707/968-1100, www.inglenook.com, 10am-5pm daily, tour and tasting $45-50), which was formerly Rubicon and formerly Niebaum-Coppola.

The Inglenook Estate was established in 1871 and bought by Francis Ford Coppola in 1975. The estate has been fully restored and now a great effort is underway to recreate the style of wines made in the winery's heyday. All this may sound like film (or wine) industry bluster, but the endeavor is taken very seriously. For example, there are no tasting rooms. To taste the wines, you must sign up (advance reservations are recommended) for a tour and tasting or a seated tasting paired with cheese or small bites. These generally last an hour and a half and occur daily. While the price is stiff (all around $50), the tours are fascinating, and the food pairings are significant enough to serve as lunch.

Another option is to simply stop by the **Bistro** (10am-5pm daily). Wines are available by the glass ($15-30) and the menu offers French-inspired food ($7-12) that is perfectly paired with the wine. If you want a casual tasting at Inglenook, buying a glass (or two) at the Bistro is your only option.

GRGICH HILLS WINERY

If you're looking for a showy Napa Valley experience, this might not be the best place for you. What you will find at **Grgich Hills Winery** (1829 St. Helena Hwy., 707/963-2784, www.grgich.com, 9:30am-4:30pm daily, $25-50) are some of the best wines in the valley, an entirely biodynamic winemaking operation, and the rich history of fine wine from California taking its rightful place alongside or even ahead of the great French vintages. When a winemaker at Calistoga's Chateau Montelena, Mike Grgich took his California chardonnay to the Paris Wine-tasting of 1976 and entered it in the white burgundy blind-tasting competition. It won, and French wine-makers were incensed; they demanded that the contest be held again, and Grgich's chardonnay won again.

Today, you'll learn about this history when visiting Grgich Hills. You'll also see plenty of information about biodynamic farming, a process that takes organic practices to the next level using all-natural processes and including phenomena such as the phases of the moon in the growing and harvesting cycles of the vineyards. The best wine might be the descendants of Mike's legendary chardonnay—arguably the best chardonnay made in Napa or anywhere else. But don't ignore the reds; Grgich offers some lovely zinfandels and cabernets.

BEAULIEU VINEYARD

A giant ivy-clad winery building that looks as dominant as any in the Napa Valley is a reminder of the huge role **Beaulieu Vineyard** (1960 St. Helena Hwy., 800/264-6918, www.bvwines.com, 10am-5pm daily, tasting $20-30) played in the modern California wine industry. Founded in 1900 by Frenchman Georges de Latour, BV is one of Napa's biggest wineries. It is best known for its powerful, dusty cabernet sauvignons, but BV also makes a full range of other red and white wines from its Napa Valley vineyards, four of which can be tasted in its beautifully constructed tasting room.

The impressive reserve tasting room, which has rich stonework, subdued lighting, and a marble-topped tasting bar, does a good job of conveying the appropriate degree of gravitas for wines that helped put California on the world wine map. Here you can opt for the Reserve Tasting ($40 by appointment) that

Inglenook combines history and Hollywood.

includes some of the winery's more exclusive cabernets or the Retrospective Reserve Tasting ($60 by appointment) in which you'll be treated to three library wines in addition to one current release. Tours are $35 by appointment and include an educational stroll through the winery, plus a barrel tasting followed by a flight of current release in the history-laden 1885 Heritage Room.

ZD WINES

While technically this winery is not appointment-only, it is still a good idea to call in advance if you are thinking about tasting at **ZD Wines** (8383 Silverado Trail, Napa, 800/487-7757, www.zdwines.com, 10am-4pm daily, tasting $40). For the extra effort (and dough) you'll be treated to a seated tasting where you'll be able to select four wines from an extensive list that includes outstanding chardonnay and pinot from its Carneros vineyards and Napa Valley cabernet sauvignon. You'll have to book a special tasting if you want a glass of ZD's most famous wine, Abacus, a cabernet made each year from a blend of all its previous vintages of reserve cabernet, starting from 1992. The idea is to combine the best aspects of aged wine with the fruit of more youthful wine. To know if it succeeds, you'll

have to pay $625 per bottle, or sign up with five other friends for a tasting ($900 for the entire group) that includes cheese, truffles, flights of some reserve wines, and a whole bottle of Abacus. To learn more about the grapes themselves and ZD's commitment to environmental stewardship, book a spot on the $85 tour, where you'll learn more about organic farming, the winery's efforts to promote biodiversity, and its use of renewable energy. The tour ends with a tasting paired with artisan cheese.

★ MUMM

Even for genuine wine aficionados, it's worth spending an hour or two at **Mumm** (8445 Silverado Trail, 707/967-7700, http://mummnapa.com, 10am-6pm daily, tasting $20-50), a friendly and surprisingly down-to-earth winery. Tastings happen at tables, with menus and service in restaurant fashion. The prices may look very Napa Valley, but you'll get more wine and service for your money at Mumm. Each pour is three ounces of wine—some of it high-end—and you get three pours per tasting. Good news for designated drivers: Nonalcoholic gourmet grape sodas or bottled water are complimentary as a thank-you for keeping the Silverado Trail safe. You can bring

Enjoy a tasting surrounded by vineyards at Mumm.

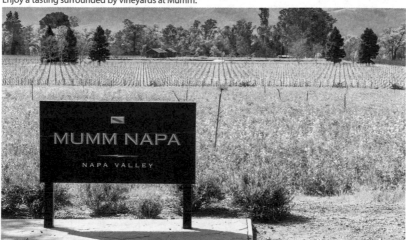

your dog into the tasting room too; dogs get water, gourmet doggie bones, and plenty of petting from the tasting-room staff.

For the best of the winery, join a tour (10am, 11am, 1pm, and 3pm daily, no reservation necessary, $40) of the sample vineyard and the working production facility, and learn from the knowledgeable and articulate tour guides who will describe the process of making sparkling wine in detailed comprehensible English. All tours wind up in a special treat of a place—the only gallery showing original Ansel Adams prints outside Yosemite Valley. Tasting is included in the price, as is your champagne flute.

RUTHERFORD HILL WINERY
One of the best merlots for the price and certainly the best winery picnic grounds in the valley can be found at **Rutherford Hill Winery** (200 Rutherford Hill Rd., 707/963-1871, www.rutherfordhill.com, 10am-5pm daily, tasting $25-40), housed in a giant barnlike redwood building just a mile up the hill from the Silverado Trail (and neighboring the Auberge du Soleil resort). Rutherford Hill also makes small quantities of a lot of other wines that never seem to garner quite the same praise as the merlot. They include cabernet sauvignon and a couple of chardonnays, syrah, cabernet franc, and sangiovese, all from Napa Valley vineyards.

But a chilled bottle of sauvignon blanc or rosé of merlot is perhaps the best wine to grab for a picnic in one of the two oak-shaded picnic grounds; both offer tantalizing glimpses through the trees of the valley far below. The picnic tables seat eight and are available with a $75 purchase of wine, equaling roughly two bottles. You may bring in your own food, however. While not required, reservations are recommended. To cool off, sign up for a tour ($40) of the winery, which includes its extensive cave system. Here, more than a mile of tunnels can store about 8,000 barrels of wine and impress even jaded wine lovers. Tours are offered three times a day at 11:30am, 1:30pm, and 3:30pm for $30 and include a tasting.

RAYMOND VINEYARDS
For nearly 50 years **Raymond Vineyards** (849 Zinfandel Ln., St. Helena, 707/963-3141, www.raymondvineyards.com, 10am-4pm daily, tasting $20-30) has earned accolades for elegant, complex, and well-balanced wines. But since charismatic wine icon Jean-Charles Boisset purchased the winery in 2009, the winery itself has garnered a number of awards for its signature style of luxury and touch of eccentricity. Boisset has created a fantasy palace for the senses—from the Crystal Cellar dripping with Baccarat chandeliers to the Corridor of Senses with its "Touch Station" to the educational outdoor Theater of Nature that describes the fundamentals of biodynamic farming. What eye-popping experience you have depends on how much you're willing to shell out: the Baccarat Crystal Cellar is reserved for the $30 tasting; the red velvet room is for the $85 private tasting; the electric blue Blending Room is for those willing to don a metallic coat for the $125 wine blending seminar; while the regular tasting room is a rather sedate affair for the lowest $20 tasting. The Boisset wine empire is vast, so expect to taste wine from Napa, Sonoma, the rest of Northern California, and France.

Wineries by Appointment
★ FROG'S LEAP WINERY
Mondavi and Grgich may have ushered in modern Napa Valley wine, but **Frog's Leap Winery** (8815 Conn Creek Rd., 707/963-4704, www.frogsleap.com, 10am-4pm daily, tour and tasting by appointment $20-25) was on the forefront of environmental stewardship and organic wine production. An understated breath of fresh air (the winery's motto is "Time's fun when you're having flies"), it is housed in a historic red barn and modest home, surrounded by vineyards and gardens. Recently, the winery became "appointment-only," but tasting here is still relaxing. The most casual (and cheapest) is the Garden/Cellar Tasting ($20), in which a flight of four current release wines is poured in either the

wine rush when they ripped up their prune orchards to plant vines in the early 1970s.

Since then, **Caymus Vineyards** (8700 Conn Creek Rd., 707/967-3010, www.caymus.com, 10am-4pm daily by appointment, tasting $50) gained a reputation for producing one of the best Napa cabernets, the Special Selection, made with the best grapes from the estate vineyard in Rutherford. It garners regular praise from all the major critics and is usually on the tasting flight of five at the sit-down, appointment-only tasting. The other well-known Caymus wine is a nonreserve cabernet that is equally impressive and half the price. A less well-known wine, but one to look out for nonetheless, is the outstanding zinfandel that is sold only at the winery.

HALL-RUTHERFORD

If you're looking for glitz and glamour, book a jaw-dropping tour at the exclusive **HALL-Rutherford** (56 Auberge Rd., 707/967-2626, www.hallwines.com, tours 11am and 2pm daily by appointment), located in the hills above Auberge du Soleil. It is owned by the modern art-loving Halls of HALL, presided over by Little Bunny Foo-Foo in St. Helena. HALL-Rutherford is where a high-end cabernet sauvignon is made from the Sacrashe estate vineyard. Tours are a pricey $125, but the centerpiece of the caves, a spectacular sculpture/chandelier of a grapevine root, might be, depending on your love of modern art, worth it. If not, the wine might be. It, along with HALL's more limited-release wines, is paired with small bites.

CHILES VALLEY WINERIES

The Chiles Valley is easy to reach. Take Highway 128 (Sage Canyon Road) up into the hills from the Silverado Trail at Rutherford, past Lake Hennessey, and go either left (Lower Chiles Pope Valley Road) or right (Capell Valley Road) at the junction. Both roads lead to the valley. Just be sure to leave plenty of time to drive there and back on the mountain

Frog's Leap Winery

garden or cellar depending on the weather. For $5 more you can have your own private tasting of these wines with a wine educator on the wraparound porch of the vineyard house, or go on the ever popular (book early!) tour and tasting (10:30am and 2:30pm Mon.-Fri.).

Whatever option you pick, expect to taste the excellent and well-priced sauvignon blanc. Frog's Leap is also known for its cabernet sauvignon, zinfandel, and the flagship Rutherford, a Bordeaux-style red blend that highlights the unique fruit-meets-earth characteristics of Rutherford appellation wines. You'll also find merlot, chardonnay, syrah, and a wine called (appropriately enough) Pink, which is another fun and cheap picnic wine.

CAYMUS VINEYARDS

This is a great example of how wineries on this side of the valley turn out some of the best wines with little fanfare. The Caymus family has been farming in the valley for more than 100 years but was ahead of the modern roads and to take lunch, because there's very little apart from farmland and vineyards up there. Be aware that all wineries here are appointment-only, but they can often accommodate same-day inquiries.

RUSTRIDGE RANCH & WINERY

In the heart of Chiles Valley, **RustRidge Ranch & Winery** (2910 Lower Chiles Valley Rd., St. Helena, 707/965-9353, www.rustridge. com, daily by appointment, tasting $20-75) is a very rustic part-winery, part-ranch, where thoroughbred horses are just as important as wine. Tastings at are held in an old cattle barn that now houses the winery workings, and a visit here is as much about smelling the horses as the wine. About 55 of the ranch's 440 acres are planted with grapes, and the winery makes zinfandel, both barrel- and tank-fermented chardonnay, cabernet sauvignon, and sauvignon blanc. Once seated, you'll taste five or six estate wines. There are also vertical cabernet ($75) and vertical zinfandel ($60) tastings available on weekdays. Afterward, guests are encouraged to picnic, visit the horses, and enjoy the scenery.

KULETO ESTATE

When one of the Bay Area's most successful restaurateurs turns his hand to winemaking, you can be sure the resulting winery is going to be quite a destination. The **Kuleto Estate** winery (2470 Sage Canyon Rd., St. Helena, 707/302-2209, www.kuletoestate.com, tasting and tours by appointment 10am-4pm daily, $45) does not disappoint. Pat Kuleto is the man behind such swank San Francisco restaurants as Boulevard and Farallon. On his expansive Napa estate, 800 acres of former grazing land, he has planted 90 acres of vineyards, predominantly cabernet sauvignon and sangiovese, with small blocks of zinfandel, syrah, pinot noir, and chardonnay. Such variety leads to a diverse portfolio of estate wines. Tours of the vineyards and modern winery, together with a comprehensive tasting of wines, are available four times a day by appointment.

RECREATION

Getting out of the thick of Wine Country is easy at **Moore Creek Park** (2607 Chiles Pope Valley Rd., 707/253-4417, http://napaoutdoors.org/parks/moore-creek-park, daily sunrise to sunset) on the north side of Lake Hennessey. The 1,600-acre park includes oak and fir woodlands, grassland, wetlands, and 15 miles of hiking trails. The **Bay Area Ridge Trail** cuts through the park and extends north on along Moore Creek. To get a bit of shore and ridgeline, connect the **Alta Hennessy, Shoreline,** and **Chiles Creek** trails for a 7-mile loop. This is a new park and fairly undeveloped (picnicking means spreading out a picnic blanket), but the trails are well marked, and signs at the gravel parking lots give some information about the park.

For anglers and kayakers, the emerald green water of **Lake Hennessey** may prove irresistible. If so, fishing ($1), kayaking, and small boats ($4) are permitted. The new boat launch is at 900 Sage Canyon Road, which also has a kiosk to drop fishing and boating fees. Be aware that Lake Hennessey is the municipal water supply for the city of Napa, so no swimming or paddleboarding is allowed.

For an even bigger lake adventure, continue on Highway 128 to **Lake Berryessa** (5520 Knoxville Rd., 707/966-2111, http://www.usbr.gov/mp/ccao/berryessa). On this large lake you can jump aboard powerboats, Jet Skis, kayaks, and canoes—or just sunbathe on the shore and splash about in the shallows with your family. If you've got your own boat, you can launch it at one of the marinas or the **Capell Cove Boat Ramp** (Berryessa Knoxville Rd.). Boat rentals are available at two of the lakeside resorts clustered around the southern tip of the lake: **Pleasure Cove Marina** (6100 Hwy. 128, Napa, 877/386-4383, www.goberryessa.com) is closest to Rutherford and rents all kinds of boats, including houseboats, while farther east, the larger **Markley Cove Resort** (7521 Hwy. 128, Napa, 707/966-2134, http://www.markleycoveresort.com) offers everything from patio cruisers to high-end ski-tow boats to personal watercraft to kayaks to water skis. You can also book a vacation rental here and pick up lunch or sunscreen at the fully stocked general store.

Campers can bed down at the **Steel Canyon Campground** (1605 Steele Canyon Rd., Napa, 877/386-4383, www.goberryessa. com) and **Spanish Flat Recreation Area** (4290 Knoxville Rd., Napa, 707/966-0200, www.spanishflatcamping.com), which also has a boat launch. The best picnic spots are at the **Olive Orchard** and **Smittle Creek Day** areas, which have tables, barbecues, restrooms, and access to both the lake and hiking trails. All areas are open to day-trippers.

Lake Berryessa also boasts some of the best fishing in California. You can fish for cold- and warm-water fish, including bass, rainbow trout, and kokanee salmon. Rent a boat from one of the resorts, launch your own, or enjoy some relaxed fishing from the shore. The resorts sell California fishing licenses and bait and will advise you about the season's hottest fishing holes. For additional information, stop by the **visitors center** (5520 Knoxville Rd., 707/966-2111, www.usbr.gov/mp/ccao/berryessa, noon-3pm Mon.-Tues. and Thurs.-Fri., 10am-5pm Sat.-Sun.).

FOOD

If a special occasion requires a special restaurant (and The French Laundry is not answering the phone), there's probably no better place in this part of the valley than ★ **Auberge du Soleil** (180 Rutherford Hill Rd., 707/967-3111 or 800/348-5406, reservations required, 7am-11am, 11:30am-2:15pm, and 5:30pm-9:30pm daily, brunch 11:30am-2:15pm Sat.-Sun., lunch entrées $20-36, dinner tasting menu $150). You don't need to be a guest to see why this resort restaurant has been wowing diners with its menu and stunning views of the valley since 1981. The wow factor is still as strong as ever and might make you want to stay at the resort on your next visit (after saving up, that is).

The exquisitely prepared French-Californian food is not as expensive as you'd think—the $150 set price buys you a four-course dinner with plenty of choices for every course (although that doesn't include wine, of course). Just make sure you choose a fine day, and try to get a table out on the terrace for the best views, especially at sunset. And casual as it might be, this is still a fancy restaurant, so don't turn up in baggy shorts and flip-flops.

If you're not ready to commit to such an indulgent affair, consider visiting the adjacent **Bistro & Bar** (11am-11pm daily, $17-31, walk-in only). You can choose from braised short ribs, a plate of charcuterie, or a light salad to accompany the rotating and wide selection of wines. You can still take in the luxurious atmosphere (wraparound deck, open fireplace) without quite the pinch to your belt or wallet.

For some more down-to-earth dining, often without the need for a reservation, the **Rutherford Grill** (1180 Rutherford Rd., Rutherford, 707/963-1792, www.hillstone. com, 11:30am-9:30pm Mon.-Thurs., 11:30am-10pm Fri., 11am-10pm Sat., 11am-9:30pm Sun., $20-44) offers traditional steak house fare in a slightly corporate setting that hints at the fact that it is owned by the Houston's restaurant chain. Nevertheless, it has become one of the most popular steak houses among Napa Valley residents and is a great place for a reliably cooked and aged steak to pair with a well-aged Rutherford cabernet. There's also a nice shady patio, although it's a little too close to the road to be classified as peaceful.

Picnic Supplies

Since 1881, the ★ **Oakville Grocery** (7856 St. Helena Hwy., Oakville, 707/944-8802, www.oakvillegrocery.com, 6:30am-5pm Sun.-Thurs., 6:30am-6pm Fri.-Sat., $10) has been providing the Napa Valley with its necessities. The oldest continually running grocery store in the state, Oakville Grocery is now known for stocking only the best food, wine, cheese, and other goodies. Browse the tightly packed shelves or order a hot lunch at the center counter, where you'll find everything from crab cakes to chimichangas to boxed lunches. The back picnic area has been recently revamped

Unpack Your Picnic Basket

Planting yourself for a picnic in Napa Valley is not as easy as you would expect. Thanks to certain zoning laws, most wineries are not able to accommodate outside food. A select few offer picnic tables (some require reservations, while all ask the purchase of a tasting or a bottle), and some public parks have shaded spots to unpack your picnic basket.

- **Clos Du Val, Yountville:** This Stags Leap winery has lovely picnic tables overlooking the vineyards, next to the *pétanque* courts (the French version of bocce courts). On the weekends the winery opens up a tasting bar out on the lawn.

- **Rutherford Hill Winery, Rutherford:** With a $75 purchase of wine, equaling roughly two bottles, you may claim a picnic table that seats eight overlooking the valley.

- **V. Sattui Winery, St. Helena:** The king of Napa Valley picnicking, this winery has two acres full of tables. Reservations are not required, but you can't bring in your own food—it must be purchased from V. Sattui's deli or ordered from the outside kitchen on sunny weekends.

- **Pride Mountain Vineyards, St. Helena:** Book a tasting, journey high up Spring Mountain, and unpack your lunch in front of a splendid view. While no reservations or bottle purchases are required, your gourmet provisions will taste better with Pride Mountain's aromatic cabernet franc or viognier.

- **Bothe-Napa Valley State Park, St. Helena:** Take a break from wineries at a shady picnic table at this beautiful state park. After lunch, explore the miles of hiking trails that begin close by.

- **Bale Grist Mill, St. Helena:** This historic park offers a scattering of picnic tables near the 1846 redwood mill. If you stop here during the weekend, take the tour—you might get to see the massive grinding stones in action.

- **Old Faithful Geyser, Calistoga:** This roadside attraction has been remade as a family-friendly picnic spot complete with an open prep area that offers utensils, wineglasses, and picnic blankets. Entertainment includes bocce ball, a petting zoo, and the famous geyser itself.

to include a take-out counter and plenty of canopied tables to enjoy a summer afternoon picnic. While the grocery is conveniently located in the heart of Oakville on Highway 29, keep a look out for the large *Coca-Cola* sign painted on the south side of the building if you are traveling north, at least, to not miss the quick turnout.

ACCOMMODATIONS

High up in the eastern hills of the valley, bathed in afternoon sun and buzzing with the sound of the golf carts used to ferry guests around, is **Auberge du Soleil** (180 Rutherford Hill Rd., Rutherford, 707/963-1211 or 800/348-5406, www.aubergedusoleil.com, $1,000), or the Inn of the Sun—one of the valley's most luxurious resorts, famous for

being the hangout of the rich, the famous, and lucky honeymooners. Even the most ardent oenophile will be hard-pressed to leave the lush sun-drenched grounds. And why would you leave? The compound features multiple dining options in addition to a pool, a fitness room, a store, and well-kept gardens accented by modern art. The guest rooms are appointed with Italian sheets, private patios, fireplaces, and TVs in both the living room and the bath. The smallest guest room is 500 square feet, suites can top 1,400 square feet, and the Private Mansion is 1,800 square feet. Auberge du Soleil is definitely the place to stay if you have the cash to focus on the inn's amenities and less interest in exploring the area.

If prices at Auberge du Soleil make you want to head for the hills, book a room at the

RustRidge Ranch B&B (2910 Lower Chiles Valley Rd., St. Helena, 707/965-9353, www. rustridge.com, $165-325). This very rustic winery/ranch not only breeds thoroughbred horses but also operates as a small B&B. Five rooms are available, each in a homey decor that makes you feel like you are staying at a relative's house. Each has its own bathroom, some have fireplaces, and all have views of the ranch's expansive landscape. For more privacy, you can opt for the detached cottage that has a sitting area plus a full kitchen. All guests enjoy a full country breakfast, hors d'oeuvres and wine-tasting in the afternoon, plus use of the tennis courts, sauna, and the ranch's 440 acres to explore.

INFORMATION AND SERVICES

Oakville and Rutherford are the only districts along Highway 29 without a visitors center or even a center of town. For more information on the area, go to the **visitors centers** in St. Helena (657 Main St., 707/963-4456, www. sthelena.com, 9am-5pm Mon.-Fri., 10am-4pm Sat., 11am-5pm Sun.) or Yountville (6484 Washington St., 707/944-0904, http://yountville.com, 10am-5pm daily). The people behind the desk will likely have the answers to your questions plus various coupons for tasting at Oakville and Rutherford wineries. Don't expect much in the way of free wireless Internet, but cell reception is generally reliable here. Any banking needs should be done in Napa or St. Helena.

GETTING THERE AND AROUND

A few miles north of Yountville, on Highway 29, you'll find Oakville and Rutherford, but their loose organization and rural character may cause you to miss them if you are not alert. You can reach the Silverado Trail on Oakville Road in Oakville and by Rutherford Road (also Highway 128) in Rutherford. The Oakville Grade is one of the few roads on Highway 29 that cross the Mayacamas Mountains into the neighboring Sonoma Valley, connecting with Highway 12 in Glen Ellen after 12 twisty miles.

The area is relatively easy to navigate, as there are few streets interrupting the acres of vineyards. However, street signs can be difficult to see, especially while watching out for tipsy drivers. Just in case you don't want to be one of those, Route 10 of the **Vine** (707/251-6443 or 800/696-6443, www.ridethevine.com, $1.60) makes regular stops here.

St. Helena and Vicinity

St. Helena has been the center of the valley's wine industry from the very beginning. George Crane first planted grapes in the area in 1861, followed by Charles Krug a few years later. With the new wine industry springing up all around, the town grew rapidly and was incorporated in 1876, only a few years after Napa and many years before Calistoga in 1885.

St. Helena's history has been inextricably linked to the valley's wine industry ever since. Calistoga to the north had its spas to draw visitors, and Napa to the south became a thriving commercial port city and gateway to the valley, but to a certain extent St. Helena has always been firmly planted in wine. Wealthy weekenders came here to wine and dine in the early 1900s, an influx of European immigrants created the thriving Italian and French heritage, and the town was the epicenter of the valley's bootlegging industry during Prohibition, making the St. Helena Highway (Highway 29, to locals) almost as busy in the 1930s as it is today.

Don't be fooled into thinking that St. Helena is resting on its Victorian charm. Behind the historic 19th-century storefront facades sits a sophisticated collection

St. Helena

To
Calistoga

29 128

BERINGER
VINEYARDS

MAIN ST

PRATT AVE

FULTON

LANE

ELMHURST AVE

OAK AVE

RAILROAD AVE

LIBRARY LANE

ROBERT LOUIS STEVENSON
SILVERADO MUSEUM/
NAPA VALLEY WINE LIBRARY

HUNT AVE

Lyman
Park

PINE ST

WOODHOUSE
CHOCOLATE

NAPA VALLEY
COFFEE ROASTING
COMPANY

TERRA
CAMINO
CINEMA

CINDY'S
BACKSTREET
KITCHEN
COOK TAVERN

ORIN
SWIFT

COOK ST.
HELENA

ANA'S
CANTINA

MARKET

GILLWOODS
CAFÉ

GIUGNI'S
GROCERY
& DELI

SUNSHINE
FOODS

MODEL
BAKERY

HOTEL
ST. HELENA

GOOSE &
GANDER

KEARNEY ST

MADRONA AVE

ADAMS ST

SPRING MOUNTAIN RD

STOCKTON ST

SPRING ST

To
PRIDE MOUNTAIN VINEYARDS,
Spring Mountain, and Santa Rosa

of modern art showcased in galleries, showrooms, and even tasting rooms.

The Wines

As the Napa Valley gets narrower farther north and the mountains ever more sheltering, the weather gets hotter. The **St. Helena** appellation includes the narrowest point of the valley and also some of the biggest and most historic winery names, like Beringer, Charles Krug, and Louis Martini. The heat and alluvial soils are responsible for wines that help give the Napa Valley its name for rich and highly extracted wines. You'll know a St. Helena cabernet when you taste one—big, bold, and powerful.

West of St. Helena, up the slopes of the Mayacamas Mountains, is the **Spring Mountain** appellation, an area with almost as much winemaking history as the valley floor below. The region gets its name from the many springs and creeks. The mountain wineries here make cabernet sauvignon and merlot with uncommon density and power. White wines are less common but include sauvignon blanc with a classic mountain minerality. As with many mountain-grown wines, however, the reds can be less approachable when young than those from the valley floor, but they tend to be more consistent year to year and usually only need a few years of aging to reach their full potential.

Looming above St. Helena to the east is the **Howell Mountain AVA.** Howell Mountain is known for its blackberry and tannic-rich cabernet sauvignon, merlot, and zinfandel, and for its chardonnay and viognier, which lean toward citrus instead of fruity. With an elevation of 1,400 to 2,600 feet above sea level, grapes see plenty of sun sitting above the fog line (there is no marine influence here) and high daytime temperatures that drop considerably at night. Infertile and well-drained volcanic ash and clay stress the vines enough to create wines that are well balanced between sugar and acidity, and with excellent aging potential.

Just beyond Howell Mountain is **Pope**

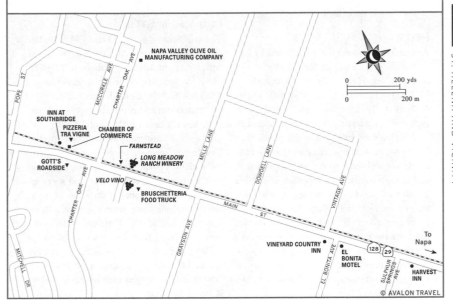

NAPA VALLEY OLIVE OIL MANUFACTURING COMPANY

INN AT SOUTHBRIDGE

PIZZERIA TRA VIGNE

CHAMBER OF COMMERCE

FARMSTEAD

GOTT'S ROADSIDE

LONG MEADOW RANCH WINERY

VELO VINO

BRUSCHETTERIA FOOD TRUCK

MAIN ST

VINEYARD COUNTRY INN

EL BONITA MOTEL

HARVEST INN

To Napa

© AVALON TRAVEL

Valley, a sliver of land between the folds of the Vaca Mountains. Advocates have been petitioning for the 14,000-acre growing area to be designated as its own AVA, pointing to the area's lighter cabernet and vibrantly flavorful sauvignon blanc. As of this writing, however, a decision has not been reached.

ST. HELENA WINERIES

St. Helena offers perhaps the widest range of wine-tasting experiences. Within its AVA borders are mega walk-in establishments, small appointment-only mom-and-pop operations, historic wineries, architectural marvels, and tasting prices that range from free to $50 just for the pleasure. Planning ahead is never a bad idea, especially as all kinds of wineries populate Highway 29 and the Silverado Trail, both south and north of town.

V. SATTUI WINERY

To say this place gets crowded in the summer is like saying the Napa Valley is an undiscovered wine region. The extensive deli and list

of well-priced wines has made the pretty **V. Sattui Winery** (1111 White Ln., 707/963-7774, www.vsattui.com, 9am-6pm daily, tasting $15) a victim of its own success. This is picnic central (and often party central) in this part of the valley.

The big tasting room boasts three spacious bar areas where you can taste (once a space opens up) six pours of vintage and estate wines from V. Sattui's vast portfolio. The dessert Madeira is particularly fine—if it's not on the tasting menu, ask your pourer at the bar if they've got a bottle open, and you might just get lucky. For a more intimate experience (and just a few more dollars), opt for the Tower Tasting Room, where you get a flight of six single-vineyard and limited release wines. Weekend tours are available (adult $30, children 6-20 $15) by appointment, but the big draw is the two-acre shaded picnic grounds. No reservations are required, just the purchase of a bottle of V. Sattui wine (many hover around the $20 mark) and deli provisions. On sunny weekends, the winery kicks it up a notch, offering hot wood-fired pizza, barbecue ribs, and tri-tip sandwiches from their outside kitchen.

HEITZ

A completely different experience can be had across the way at one of the oldest wineries in the valley, **Heitz** (436 St. Helena Hwy., 707/963-3542, www.heitzcellar.com, 11am-4:30pm daily, free tasting). The elegant, high-ceilinged tasting room is dominated by a stone fireplace with comfy chairs before it. To the happy surprise of many, Heitz's cabernets are well-balanced and easy to drink, and though costly, they approach affordable by Napa standards. Most of the grapes in these wines grow right in the Napa Valley. If you're lucky enough to visit Heitz in February, you can taste the current release of the Martha's Vineyard cabernet—a vintage grown in the first wine-designated vineyard (i.e., the first vineyard to grow grapes for wine rather than eating) in all of Napa.

HALL

When you visit **HALL** winery (401 St. Helena Hwy. S., 707/967-2626, www.hallwines.com, 10am-5:30pm daily, tasting $40), you will notice two things. One is that the Halls are big fans of modern art and design; the other is that their winery is the first LEED-Gold certified winery in California, a fact of which they are very proud. HALL's new "winery complex" with tasting room has an industrial chic different than the château aesthetic of the valley. Filled with art and surrounded by views of the mountains, you'll sip highly rated wines, but you are paying heavily for the privilege. Tastings are the same price as a tour, so to really make the most of the art, the wine, and the vision, book a spot on the **Hallmark Tour and Tasting** (daily $40) or **Wine and Art Exploration tour** (11am Sun., $40). Both walk the grounds, discuss art, design, and the Halls' environmental mission along with tasting several vintages. You'll also learn about the history of the winery's Napa Valley Cooperative Winery, a warehouse-like facility built around an old stone winery dating from 1885.

LOUIS M. MARTINI

The hulking winery of **Louis M. Martini** (254 St. Helena Hwy., 707/968-3362, www.louismartini.com, 10am-6pm daily, tasting $25-50) is the place to come for cabernet lovers. The bulk of the wine made here is dominated by various iterations of cabernet sauvignon, from appellation-specific bottlings to vineyard-specific and right down to lot-specific. The few other non-cabernet wines on the list include a petite sirah and meritage blend that is arguably a better value and more approachable than some of the cabs. Many of the best wines come from the Monte Rosso vineyard, including cabernets, a zinfandel, and a cabernet franc. A sheltered patio has tables and chairs for those who want to linger, and Martini is open at least half an hour later than most neighboring wineries, making it a good last stop.

BERINGER VINEYARDS

The oldest continuously operating winery in Napa Valley, **Beringer Vineyards** (2000 Main St., 707/302-7592, www.beringer.com, 10am-5:30pm daily, tasting $25-35) is now a huge tourist attraction that often contributes to St. Helena's summer traffic jams. It is still worth a visit (ideally midweek, when it's a bit quieter) for its significance in the valley's wine history and for some outstanding reserve wines.

Established in 1876, the entire winery and estate, including the lavish and ornate Rhine House built by German Frederick Beringer to remind him of home, was placed on the National Register of Historic Places in 2001. It is an impressive location to taste some of Beringer's reserve wines ($35-60); the regular tasting is in the old winery building up the hill and offers several themed flights of wine for less money and less atmosphere. Outdoors, you can stroll in the beautiful estate gardens that stretch for acres on prime land next to Highway 29. The **Taste of Beringer Tour**

(10:30am, 1pm, and 3:30pm daily, $50, 21 and over, reservation only) takes guests throughout the property and finishes at the Rhine House kitchen for small bites paired with reserved wines. If you have children in tow, you may want to opt for the 30-minute **Legacy Cave Tour** (11:30am, 12:30pm, 2pm, 3pm, and 4pm daily, $30 by appointment), free for those under 21.

CHARLES KRUG WINERY

It's probably fitting that the winery founded by the grandfather of the Napa Valley wine industry, Charles Krug, was also the winery that helped start the modern-day wine dynasty of the Mondavis. Krug arrived in California in the heady days after the gold rush and fell in with the likes of Agoston Haraszthy, credited with being the first serious winemaker in the state; George Yount, father of Yountville; and Edward Bale, who built the nearby Bale Grist Mill. Krug opened his winery in 1861 and even had the first tasting room in the valley. In 1943 the Krug winery was purchased by Cesare Mondavi, who built a new family wine business around it, creating one of the leading wineries in the valley. After Cesare's death in 1959, however, there was a bitter feud between his two sons,

Robert and Peter, which resulted in Robert establishing his own separate winery (which has since become an empire), while Peter's side of the family held on to and still controls the Charles Krug business. Peter passed away in 2016.

With a history like that, it's hardly surprising that parts of the **Charles Krug Winery** (2800 Main St., 707/967-2229, www.charleskrug.com, 10:30am-5pm daily, tasting $15-60) are historic landmarks, including the stately old Carriage House and giant redwood cellar building. The interior of the Redwood Cellar has been stylishly redesigned with reclaimed wood from the winery's original redwood tanks and features an intimate tasting bar and lounge with table service. Charles Krug produces a wide variety of wine, appealing to many palates. The Classic Tasting is five wines for $20. Hardcore cabernet lovers should focus on the reserve tasting (five for $40), which includes some of the vineyard-specific, some small-lot wines, and the flagship Vintage Selection cabernet. If you are on a budget, you can opt for the barrel tasting (two wines for $15). On weekends, the small **café counter** (11am-4pm Sat.-Sun., $19-25) opposite the tasting bar, serves espresso, wine by the glass ($9-13), cheese plates, and small,

the Rhine House at Beringer Vineyards

wood-fired pizzas. Eat at the long communal table or take your pizza and glass (or bottle!) of wine out to the lawn to round out the experience.

ST. CLEMENT VINEYARDS

After passing the big boys of Napa wine like V. Sattui, Beringer, and Krug, it's hard not to miss the quaint Victorian house perched on the side of the hill west of the main road. That is **St. Clement Vineyards** (2867 St. Helena Hwy. N., 707/257-5783, www.stclement.com, 10am-5pm Thurs.-Mon., tasting $35), a small winery that is perhaps the prettiest in this part of the valley.

St. Clement specializes in cabernets from different appellations in the valley, many of which can be tasted seated on the front porch of the 1878 Victorian house, surrounded by sloping vineyards, lush English gardens, and heavy-limbed oaks. The views alone will make you want to linger. While walk-ins are welcome, tasting is a pricey, intimate affair. If you are a cabernet lover, you will definitely want to make a reservation for the **Armstrong Ranch Vertical Tasting** (11am Fri.-Sun., $55), in which you'll get four pours of limited-production cabernet from the Diamond Mountain appellation.

FREEMARK ABBEY

Despite the name, there is no religious connection with the weathered stone **Freemark Abbey** (3022 St. Helena Hwy. N., 800/963-9698, www.freemarkabbey.com, 10am-5pm daily, tasting $20-30). Instead, it got its current identity in the 1940s from the nickname of Albert "Abbey" Ahern and the names of partners Charles Freeman ("Free") and Markquand Foster ("Mark"), who bought the former Lombarda Winery and its stone building, which date from 1899.

Today, Freemark Abbey is probably best known for its cabernet sauvignon, from the generic Napa Valley version to a couple of vineyard-designates. Plenty of other wines (merlot, petite sirah, chardonnay, sauvignon blanc, and viognier) are available to try in one of the more relaxing and spacious tasting rooms in the valley. The winery recently got a face-lift to better show off its historical digs, while adding the highly regarded **Two Birds One Stone** restaurant (3020 St. Helena Hwy. N., 707/302-3777, www.twobirdsonestone-napa.com, lunch noon-5pm Fri.-Sun., dinner 5pm-9pm Thurs.-Mon., $16-30). To take best advantage spend an extra $10 and enjoy a select tasting seated on the patio. Light snacks are available from the small market café.

Charles Krug Winery

Downtown Tasting Rooms

St. Helena has a few downtown tasting rooms, making it easy to spend a day here shopping, sipping, and dining. **Orin Swift** (1325 Main St., 707/967-9179, www.orinswift.com, 11am-5pm Sun.-Thurs., 11am-6pm Fri., 10am-6pm Sat., tasting $10-20) created great buzz when the cult winery announced it would open a tasting room on Main Street. Dave Phinney, the wunderkind winemaker, cut his teeth at Robert Mondavi, Whitehouse Lane, and Bennett Lane before venturing out on his own to make velvety and aromatic cabernets and rich Bordeaux blends, which gained instant notoriety. Many are available to taste (including a sauvignon blanc and chardonnay); simply step into the black Victorian storefront tasting room and select from three tasting menus, each offering four pours including a dessert wine made with cabernet sauvignon. In 2016 Orin Swift was bought by the mega E&J Gallo. The word is still out on how this will affect this once edgy boutique winery.

Farther south on Main Street where the walking is less scenic, **Long Meadow Ranch** (738 Main St., 707/963-4555, www.longmeadowranch.com, 11am-6pm daily, tasting $25-40) pours flights of highly regarded food-friendly wine with grapes sourced from estate vineyards in Rutherford, the Mayacamas Mountains, and the Anderson Valley. The tasting room is located in Long Meadow Ranch's General Store, where you can also browse shelves of jams, vinegar, honey, sauces, and other food products, as well as taste olive oil and whiskey. The bounty here is the happy result of Long Meadow Ranch's commitment to organic and integrated farming, which produces not only great vineyards, but also extensive organic gardens, olive orchards, beehives, farm-fresh eggs, and grass-fed beef.

Across the street, perhaps the best downtown tasting experience can be found at **Velo Vino** (709 Main St., 707/968-0625, www.cliffamily.com, 10am-6pm daily, tasting $20-40), the tasting room for Clif Family Winery. If the name rings a bell, you'll understand why when you enter the tasting room and see energy bars lining the walls and a chunk of space devoted to cycling. Yes, this is the enological endeavor of the man behind Clif Bar. Gary Erikson and his wife Kit moved to the Napa Valley in 1999 and have given valley living the sort of gusto you would expect from a physical fitness enthusiast. In that short time, they started an organic farm; began bottling their own olive oil; developed a Wine Country snack food line that includes fruit preserves, spice blends, nut mixes, and mustards; and, of course, began making a variety of wines from gewürztraminer to cabernet.

Not only are the wines good, but the tasting is fun. Arranged like a café, the tasting room has tables for privacy and an outdoor patio. At the bar, you are likely to see locals come in for a glass of wine ($8-15) and horse around with the staff. The tastings tend to focus on cabs and zins, but you can also customize your flight by ordering two-ounce pours ($4-7). Cheese, small bites, food pairing, and a delicious lunch are available from Velo Vino's **Bruschetteria Food Truck** (11:30am-4pm Tues.-Sun., $5-12). With pours so generous, food so good, and the atmosphere so friendly, you may not want to leave. But if you must, there is an espresso machine behind the counter to get you going. And, oh yeah, you can rent bikes here, too.

Wineries by Appointment

CORISON

A rarity in the ritzy Napa Valley, **Corison** (987 St. Helena Hwy., 707/963-0826, www.corison.com, 10am-5pm daily, tour and tasting $55) is the genuine article—a tiny single-proprietor winery producing great wines in small quantities. Tours and tastings begin through the huge white door that leads to the tasting/barrel/stockroom. A tiny bar sits right next to the entrance, offering tastings from the 3,000 cases the winery produces each year. You'll also learn about the winemaking process as well as observe it in action. Expect the attentive staff to talk in loving and knowledgeable terms about the delicious wines they're pouring. Corison's flagship cabernet sauvignon tastes of luscious fruit and perfect balance.

PRAGER WINERY & PORT WORKS

Right opposite the entrance to the Louis M. Martini Winery is the little wooden sign and driveway leading to **Prager Winery & Port Works** (1281 Lewelling Ln., 707/963-7678 or 800/969-7678, www.pragerport. com, 10:30am-4:30pm daily, tasting $20), a funky, family-owned port producer that is a refreshing change from the commercial atmosphere of most wineries in the area. The closest you'll find to a winery museum here is the Web Window, a masterpiece of spiderweb engineering that's supposedly been untouched since 1979.

The Prager family makes a few regular wines here (a couple are usually included in the tasting), but the emphasis is on an unusual selection of ports and late-harvest dessert wines, including a fruity white port made from chardonnay and the more usual vintage and tawny ports made predominantly with cabernet sauvignon and petite sirah grapes. Bring a cigar to enjoy with port out in the garden.

DUCKHORN VINEYARDS

The impressive farmhouse-style home of **Duckhorn Vineyards** (1000 Lodi Ln. at Silverado Trail, 707/963-7108 or 888/354-8885, www.duckhorn.com, 10am-4pm daily, tasting $35) is known for some outstanding merlot and cabernet sauvignon. The stylish lounge and the big circular tasting bar beyond, surrounded by neatly arranged tables and chairs, resemble an upscale club or restaurant, so it's no surprise that trying the wines can be pricey. But the personal service, quality wines, and peaceful veranda overlooking the vineyards make the tasting experience far more relaxing and fulfilling than at some other wineries. While appointment-only, during the week it's usually possible to get on the list right away.

EHLERS ESTATE

If wine consumption is good for the heart, then consumption of Ehlers Estate wines is most certainly good for hearts in general. Established in 1886, the historic stone **Ehlers Estate** winery (3222 Ehlers Ln., 707/963-5972, www.ehlersestate.com, 9am-3:30pm daily, tasting $35), just north of St. Helena, is owned by the Leducq Foundation, a French charity that funds cardiovascular research at high-profile medical schools around the world including Harvard, Columbia, and the University of California at San Diego. Visiting such a nonprofit enterprise is a refreshing idea in a valley known more for unashamed hedonism.

Unlike many valley wineries, Ehlers Estate makes only estate wines from the surrounding organic vineyards. For the price of the tasting, you'll get a flight from the relatively diverse portfolio that includes sauvignon blanc, a cabernet franc rosé, and cabernet sauvignon. Perhaps owing to good heart health, Ehlers opens earlier than other Napa Valley wineries and even offers an early bird experience. The Start Your Day tour and tasting begins with a tour of the winery (including a barrel tasting) followed by a flight accompanied by fresh croissants from Bouchon Bakery.

BENESSERE VINEYARDS

The family that established **Benessere Vineyards** (1010 Big Tree Rd., 707/963-5853, www.benesserevineyards.com, 10am-5pm daily, tasting $20-40) in 1994 does not publicize the fact that the winery used to be owned by Charles Shaw, a name that will forever be associated with the Two-Buck Chuck phenomenon of cheap and cheerful wines. Shaw owned the winery from the early 1970s but eventually sold it to the Central Valley Bronco Wine Company, which now churns out those cheap wines. The winery property itself and 42 acres of neglected vineyards were eventually bought by John and Ellen Benish in the early 1990s.

They have since transformed it into a producer of increasingly well-regarded Italian varietal wines, with the help of some expert Italian winemaking consultants. The lively and light Italian wines here are a nice diversion from the more intense cabernet and chardonnay that dominate the scene in this part of the Napa Valley, and the winery itself is at the end of a small road far off the beaten path of the St. Helena Highway (Hwy. 29), surrounded by aromatic gardens. An appointment for tasting is technically necessary, but calling ahead by even an hour is usually fine during the week.

FAILLA WINES

Before the Silverado Trail enters Calistoga, the road seems to narrow as it passes through thickets of pine and oak. Up one of these hillside drives you'll find **Failla Wines** (3530 Silverado Trail N., 707/963-0530, www.faillawines.com, 10am-4pm daily, tasting $20) in a modest yellow farmhouse that acts as the tasting room, office, and general ground zero. The location makes Failla feel removed from the fray of the famous valley, as does the relaxed and friendly staff, but the wines remind you of where you are.

Failla is primarily known for its elegant single-vineyard pinot noir. Food-friendly, these wines are bigger and more complex than other more aromatic pinots. Likewise, the chardonnays (Failla's other specialty) are also single vineyard and versatile and subtle. Tastings (a flight of four) take place either on the front porch or inside the cozy living room in plush chairs in front of a great stone fireplace. The tours ($30-50) are another great way to experience this very personable winery. You'll taste five or six wines, explore the cave behind the winery, and learn about winemaking in the concrete egg, the latest trend.

SPRING MOUNTAIN WINERIES

Escape the bustle of St. Helena by turning off Highway 29 and onto Spring Mountain Road (via Madrona Road in town and Elmhurst Road, south of Beringer Vineyards). Within moments your blood pressure and your jaw will drop as the road winds steeply through redwoods and oak trees, past many small wineries with terraced mountain vineyards and stunning views of the valley.

If you're on a schedule, be sure to leave plenty of time to visit these Spring Mountain wineries; the drive is slow and quickly becomes frustrating (and potentially dangerous) if you're in a hurry. Allow at least 30 minutes to drive one-way from St. Helena to Pride Mountain Vineyards, for example. All the wineries on Spring Mountain are appointment-only (thanks to a county ordinance that aims to prevent the small road from becoming too busy), but with the exception of Pride Mountain you can usually secure an appointment a day or two ahead.

SPRING MOUNTAIN VINEYARDS

Not far out of St. Helena is one of the oldest Spring Mountain wineries, almost as famous for being the set of the 1980s television soap opera *Falcon Crest* as for its history and wines. Established in the 1880s as the Miravalle estate, **Spring Mountain Vineyards** (2805 Spring Mountain Rd., St. Helena, 707/967-4188 or 877/769-4637, www.springmtn.com, 10am-4pm daily by appointment, tasting $40) is perhaps best known for its sauvignon blanc and cabernet sauvignon, in particular the meritage blend called Elivette. A critically praised syrah is also made here, as well as some pinot noir (thanks to a cool spot in the mountain vineyards), a wine not normally made this far north in the valley. Spring Mountain's vineyards stretch from the valley floor almost to the top of Spring Mountain, giving the winery a huge variety of soils and microclimates to work with.

Tours ($75) of the beautiful grounds and some of the historic buildings, including its famous mansion and caves, are offered three times a day at 11am, 1pm, and 3pm by appointment. The short tours are followed by a seated tasting of four or five reserve wines for a total experience of close to two hours.

SCHWEIGER VINEYARDS

Schweiger Vineyards (4015 Spring Mountain Rd., St. Helena, 707/963-4882, www.schweigervineyards.com, tasting 10am-4pm daily, tasting $50) is another of Spring Mountain's small makers of highly regarded cabernet sauvignon, also with spectacular views from its vineyards. The vast majority of the wine is cabernet, but Schweiger also makes small amounts of merlot and chardonnay, all from the estate vineyards at about 2,000 feet in elevation, and a nice sauvignon blanc from a vineyard over the hill in the Sonoma Valley. The flagship wine is the reserve cabernet, called Dedication, which competes with the best from Spring Mountain. Another perennial favorite is the cabernet port, which is made in true nonvintage style by blending wines dating back more than a decade.

BARNETT VINEYARDS

A more formal experience can be found nearby down the long and winding driveway of **Barnett Vineyards** (4070 Spring Mountain Rd., St. Helena, 707/963-7075, www.barnettvineyards.com, 10am-4pm daily, tasting $50). This boutique winery takes care to keep guests to a minimum to ensure the wines and the tranquility of the panoramic Napa Valley view can be enjoyed in all their glory. It's one of the best views from a vineyard you'll find in this part of the world.

A visit to the winery starts at the tasting bar, tucked away in a corner of the cool dark barrel room, where most of the half-dozen wines are usually available to taste. Spring Mountain vineyards are the source of Barnett's cabernet and merlot, both of which exhibit the classic concentration and robust tannins of Spring Mountain fruit. Also on the menu may be a tangy Sonoma chardonnay and a Russian River Valley pinot noir, and if you're lucky the flagship Rattlesnake Hill cabernet, sourced from vines on a small knoll above the winery at 2,400-foot elevation. If the weather is cooperating, guests can often continue tasting the wines and learn more about the winery and its vineyards on one of two small decks perched at the end of rocky paths among the terraced vineyards. You feel a little like a mountain goat traversing the terraces, and heels are not recommended.

★ PRIDE MOUNTAIN VINEYARDS

When you reach the line on the road that marks the border of Napa and Sonoma Counties, you're as far up Spring Mountain as you can go and just outside the estate of

Pride Mountain Vineyards

Pride Mountain Vineyards (4026 Spring Mountain Rd., St. Helena, 707/963-4949, www.pridewines.com, 10am-3:30pm Mon. and Wed.-Sat. by appointment, tasting $20), a winery that has been receiving wine reviews almost as lofty as its location 2,000 feet up in the Mayacamas Mountains. It is known for its powerful and intense cabernet sauvignon and merlot. Other wines that regularly score over 90 points with the critics include an aromatic cabernet franc, chardonnay, and viognier. Many of these can be tasted for $20, a relative bargain considering the quality of the wines and the attentive, often entertaining service.

Grapes have been grown here since 1870 by some accounts, and the size of the burned-out shell of the old Summit winery building, constructed in 1890, suggests that a fair amount of wine was produced until Prohibition ended the party. The elevated **Summit Experience** (10:45am and 2pm Mon., and Wed.-Fri., $75) showcases Pride's views and history on the private tour and tasting in the formal tasting salon in the cave. If you packed a picnic for your long trip up Spring Mountain, Pride has several picnic tables available to enjoy your bag lunch before or after your tasting.

HOWELL MOUNTAIN WINERIES

The appointment-only wineries of Howell Mountain are nestled in the wooded slopes surrounding the small town of Angwin, only eight miles away from St. Helena, up Deer Park Road from the Silverado Trail. With a population of just over 3,000, Angwin is home to the valley's only four-year college, the small liberal arts Pacific Union College. The school is affiliated with the Adventist Church, which has a tradition of refraining from caffeine and alcohol—somewhat ironic as vineyards keep getting planted around this town.

CADE

Make the trip up Howell Mountain to visit Napa's the first LEED-Gold certified winery, **Cade** (360 Howell Mountain Rd. S., Angwin, 707/965-2746, www.cadewinery.

com, 10am-4pm daily, $40-80). This impressive structure is made from recycled steel and concrete, insulated by old blue jeans, and uses renewable cork flooring. Naturally, it is topped with solar panels and has outlets to plug in your electric car. Stylish and modern with a signature green chic, Cade is a part of the Plumpjack group, Gavin Newsom's wine and hospitality venture. The one-hour current release tasting includes four wines, including Howell Mountain sauvignon blanc and cabernet. Bump it up to $80 and you can get a tour of the winery while sipping its current releases and nibbling on small bites. Winning the most raves, however, is the unparalleled view of the Napa Valley, which for many makes the climb up to Cade worth it.

POPE VALLEY WINERIES

While winemakers may be fighting to make Pope Valley an AVA, the small appellation has only one tasting room. Still, Pope Valley is a quirky yin to the valley's stylized yang, making this scenic and funky detour worthwhile. The drive from St. Helena takes less than half an hour, up Howell Mountain road, through Angwin, and down through the forest. Downtown Pope Valley, which constitutes an auto-repair shop, a junkyard, and a general store, sits at the intersection of Pope Valley Road.

To taste wine, turn left here. This is also the way to California Historic Landmark No. 939, also known as **Hubcap Ranch** (6654 Pope Valley Rd., two miles past the Pope Valley Winery). Yes, the state of California designated this collection of thousands of hubcaps strung from posts, fences, and trees as a historic landmark. It was created by Emanuel "Litto" Damonte in the 1950s when he began hanging lost hubcaps found near his ranch in case their hapless owners wanted them back. The growing collection proved to be a magnet, and soon neighbors and anonymous visitors were leaving hubcaps rather than taking them. Now, half a century later, there are, it is said, about 5,000 of the things glinting in the sun, from lavish chrome 1960s trim to the present-day plastic wannabes. It is still a private ranch, so don't expect any Wine Country-style tours, though you're welcome to leave a hubcap from the rental car or your own to ensure the collection keeps growing. The ranch's dogs seem to love trying to scare visitors, so don't be surprised when they hurl their snarling bodies at the fence behind the landmark plaque.

POPE VALLEY WINERY

Pope Valley's sole tasting room is the aptly named **Pope Valley Winery** (6613 Pope Valley Rd., 707/965-1246, www.popevalley-winery.com, 10am-5pm daily, tasting $10). While the AVA status has yet to be confirmed, Pope Valley Winery was founded in 1897 and now produces 5,000 cases of, among others, zinfandel, cabernet sauvignon, sangiovese, and chenin blanc from its 80 acres of vineyards. Part of the fun of tasting here is the relaxed atmosphere and rural character. Taste, picnic, play bocce ball, and explore the original homestead, 100-year-old farm equipment, and the old blacksmith shop. You'll likely encounter a member of the Eakle family, who now own the historic winery and are applying their youthful energy to expand its potential. Complimentary tours of the winery and caves are available daily, as are introductions to the winery pets, Gus, Kitten, and Boo Boo.

SIGHTS

Much of St. Helena's Victorian heyday is on display on Main Street (mainly between Hunt and Adams Streets)—even the unusual street lamps on Main Street date from 1915.

At **1302 Main Street** (at Hunt Street), a brass inlay in the sidewalk is the only sign that the wonderfully named Wonderful Drug Store had its home for half a century in this building constructed in 1891 by local businessman Daniel Hunt (as a sign of the times, the building is now home to a clothing store).

In the middle of the block is the former **Odd Fellows Hall** (1350 Main St.), built in 1885 as Lodge 167 of the Independent Order of Odd Fellows, the social fraternity established

in 1810 in England. The building is said to have a sealed granite memorial stone containing a time capsule of articles from the era. Today, you will find the eclectic **Martin Showroom** (1350 Main St., 707/967-8787, www.martinshowroom.com, 10am-6pm Tues.-Sat.) filling the hall.

Almost opposite at 1351 Main Street is what used to be the **Bank of St. Helena,** established and built in the 1880s by a group of local winemakers, including Charles Krug. A lot of the original interior features and stone walls are still evident, and add atmosphere to the olive oil tasting here. Farther south (1305-1309 Main St.) is the incomparable 1881 Italianate structure that is now home to **Hotel St. Helena** (1309 Main St., 707/963-4388, www.hotelsthelena.net, $195-300) and several gift stores.

Culinary Institute of America

The Napa Valley takes food very seriously, so it's fitting that the West Coast outpost of the **Culinary Institute of America** (2555 Main St., 707/967-1100, www.ciachef.edu, 10:30am-6pm daily) is housed in one of the grandest old winery buildings in California, the fortress-like former Greystone Winery just north of downtown St. Helena. Built in 1890, the building later found fame as the Christian Brothers winery, but today, chefs and sommeliers are busy being trained behind the imposing stone walls.

Thankfully, you don't need the dedication they have to learn a secret or two from the Napa Valley's top chefs. Hour-long **cooking demonstrations** (reservations 707/967-2320, www.enthusiats.ciachef.edu, 1:30pm weekends, $25) are open to the public and include a tasting of the finished dish paired with a glass of wine, so the fee is worthwhile, especially at lunchtime. Don't expect to go more than once over a single weekend, though, because the same demonstration is given on both days. If you have more time (and money), you can delve deeper into the art of food and wine at one of the many classes open to the public. Options range from the Wine 101 classes (2.5

Wine Spectator Restaurant

thebakerycafeatgreystone.com, 10:30am-5pm daily, $8-13), where you can grab an espresso and a light lunch, and the **Café Bar,** a cozy nook surrounded by books and overlooking the **Ghirardelli Chocolate Discovery Center,** if a glass of wine seems more in order. If you're ready for a meal, book a table at the highly celebrated **Wine Spectator Restaurant** (707/967-1010, www.ciarestaurantgroup.com, lunch 11:30am-2pm, dinner 5:30pm-8:30pm Tues.-Sat., $19-34), which serves California cuisine at fairly reasonable prices in a beautiful setting.

Robert Louis Stevenson Silverado Museum

One of the valley's most famous literary visitors, the Scottish writer Robert Louis Stevenson, spent his honeymoon in the valley just as St. Helena's Victorian building boom was getting under way in 1880. His life and visit are celebrated in the compact **Silverado Museum** (1490 Library Ln., 707/963-3757, www.silveradomuseum.org, noon-4pm Tues.-Sat., free), right next to the small library a few blocks from Main Street.

There are more than 9,000 of Stevenson's personal artifacts on display, including original manuscripts of some of his many books. The most famous in these parts is *The Silverado Squatters,* published in 1883, which chronicles his Napa Valley travels and meetings with early wine industry pioneers. Stevenson is probably best known elsewhere in the world for some of his other books, including *Treasure Island* and *The Strange Case of Dr. Jekyll and Mr. Hyde.*

Also housed in the library building is the **Napa Valley Wine Library** (St. Helena Public Library, 1492 Library Ln., 707/963-5244, www.shpl.org, 10am-6pm Mon., 10am-7pm Tues.-Wed., 10am-9pm Thurs., 2pm-6pm Fri.-Sat.). There you will find 3,500 titles and 6,000 items all related to wine in the valley and in general. It is a wonderful place to brush up on your knowledge while taking a break from tasting.

hours, $95) to the longer Saturday Kitchen cooking and baking classes (9:30am-2:30pm, $250) to the Boot Camps that can last 2-5 days ($895-2,195) and cover everything from cheese making to Mediterranean cuisine.

If you're not looking for such a commitment, just explore the historic building on your own. The first two floors are open to the public. Downstairs you'll find a small exhibit that illustrates the history of the Greystone Winery with some of the original Christian Brothers barrels, casks, and brandy-making stills, and a display of more than a thousand corkscrews, some of them hundreds of years old. Opposite is the **Spice Islands Marketplace** (707/967-2309, www.ciastore.com, 10:30am-6pm daily), considered one of the best kitchen stores in the valley, supplying all those trainee chefs and sommeliers (and you) with the best culinary equipment, spices, cookbooks, and other essentials from around the world. You'll also find the **Bakery Café by Illy** (707/967-2320, www.

Bale Grist Mill

About three miles north of St. Helena is one of the more unusual sights in a valley dominated by the wine industry, the **Bale Grist Mill** (3369 N St. on Hwy. 29, 3 miles north of St. Helena, 707/942-4575 or 707/963-2236, www.parks.ca.gov, grounds open daily, buildings 10am-5pm Sat.-Sun., $5). The small, redwood mill building with its oversize, 36-foot-high waterwheel was built in 1846 by Edward Bale and is now part of a small State Historic Park.

It originally had a 20-foot waterwheel, but a later owner made a few power upgrades, adding the bigger wheel and iron cogs in the 1850s, a few years after Bale died. In an age of supermarkets it can be difficult to see the relevance of this relic of 19th-century farming, but the mill was a major part of valley life. People came from far and wide to grind their grain, making it a major social hub.

The weekend-only tours (10am and 4pm) shed more light on both the man and the milling, and when the mill is operating, it is truly a sight to behold. For a small donation you can buy a bag of cornmeal, polenta, whole wheat, or other whole grain flour that has been ground on this historic mill, just as it would have been 150 years ago. The mill itself and a handful of picnic tables are reached from the parking lot along a quarter-mile trail that ends up looping back to the main road.

You can also turn left before reaching the mill to take the pretty mile-long hike through the madrone woods, past the remains of the valley's first church and into neighboring **Bothe-Napa Valley State Park** (3801 St. Helena Hwy. N., 707/942-4575, www.parks.ca.gov, sunrise-sunset daily, $8 day-use fee).

ENTERTAINMENT

It might seem like this part of the valley goes to sleep after the restaurants have closed down for the evening, and sadly that's more or less true. Things can get hopping in the summer when **Long Meadow Ranch** (738 Main St., St. Helena, 707/963-4555, www.longmeadow-ranch.com) hosts its **Bluegrass Fed Concert** series. The outdoor concerts are held, for the most part, once a week on Saturday or Sunday night, costing $45-75.

But if you're looking for a little late-night fun, join the locals at the casual hangout **Ana's Cantina** (1205 Main St., 707/963-4921, 10am-2am daily). It's a Mexican restaurant by day and a bar by night, when beer and margaritas are the drinks of choice, and pool, karaoke, and live weekend music provide the entertainment, usually until 1am. Although the bartenders know how to mix some good cocktails, this falls just shy of being a dive bar, so don't expect to see much, if any, of the usual "Wine Country" ambience. Local favorite Cook St. Helena also got into the late-night scene when it opened **Cook Tavern** (1304 Main St., 707/963-8082, http://cooksthelena.com/cooktavern, 11:30am-10pm Mon.-Thurs., 11:30am-midnight Fri., 10am-midnight Sat., 10am-10pm Sun.), a sports bar, St. Helena style. In the stylish interior bedecked with flat-screen TVs, a delicious comfort food menu is served into the wee hours with plenty of top-notch libations to wash it down.

If catching a flick sounds like the perfect evening out, the historic **Cameo Cinema** (1340 Main St., 707/963-9779, www.cameo-cinema.com, $6-8) sits in the heart of Main Street and offers an old-school movie experience. Expect to see a wide range of films on the schedule, everything from the last blockbuster to indie and international films.

SHOPPING

It's hardly surprising in a valley that was built on the guilty pleasures of consumption that shopping is a close third to eating and drinking for many visitors. The short stretch of Main Street in downtown St. Helena is quick and easy to explore, with an eclectic mix of shops that draw crowds and help create some horrendous traffic jams as visitors look for parking.

Whether you have a green thumb or not, swing by **Acres Home and Garden** (1219 Main St., 707/967-1142, http://acreshome-andgarden.com, 10am-5:30pm Mon.-Sat., 11am-5:30pm Sun.). Not only will you find the most beautiful trowel and gardening gloves you've ever seen, but this slender shop also has a beautiful selection of delicate silver and gold jewelry, sumptuous soaps and candles, the quirkiest handcrafted gifts, and the most perfect array of cut flowers filling the back of the store.

While St. Helena is dominated by small boutiques that tend to cater to tourists, high-end contemporary art and design are gradually supplanting the more traditional Wine Country paraphernalia. Two of the best examples sit side by side in the historic Independent Order of Odd Fellows building on Main Street. The **Martin Showroom** (1350 Main St., 707/967-8787, www.martinshowroom. com, 10am-6pm Tues.-Sat.) is a showcase for designer Erin Martin, who fashions contemporary pieces with a rustic or industrial chic from natural and reclaimed materials. While you may not take home a $15,000 table or bronze statue as a souvenir of the Wine Country, there is nonetheless plenty of inspiration on offer from the works of Erin and a handful of other artists and designers represented here, along with plenty of more-affordable, whimsical items for sale, from jewelry to housewares.

Right next door is the St. Helena outpost of the **Aerena Gallery** (1354 Main St., 707/603-8787, www.aerenagalleries.com, 10am-5:30pm daily), which is represented at four locations in the Napa Valley, including Ma(i)sonry in Yountville. Unlike the Martin Showroom, this is a more traditional gallery with rotating exhibitions of contemporary works from Bay Area artists and sculptors.

Foodies might drool on entering the only West Coast outpost of New York's super-deli **Dean & Deluca** (607 St. Helena Hwy. S., 707/967-9980, www.deandeluca.com, 7am-7pm Sun.-Thurs., 7am-8pm Fri.-Sat.), just south of downtown St. Helena. This being the Wine Country, of course, it stocks some 1,400 wines plus countless local cheeses, meats, and produce, all alongside the already unmatched selection of gourmet foods from around the world.

Venture off Main Street to find a taste of old-school Napa Valley (and some of its best olive oil) at the **Napa Valley Olive Oil Manufacturing Company** (835 Charter Oak Ave., 707/963-4173, 9am-5:30pm daily). While it no longer presses its oils in its great barnlike retail space, this family operation has been here since 1931. You'll be able to taste their organic olive oil in addition to shopping for thoroughly Italian deli items out of a small, colorful, and chaotic store.

Chocoholics might get a sugar rush just by looking at the neat rows of dozens of handmade bonbons at **Woodhouse Chocolate** (1367 Main St., 800/966-3468, www.woodhousechocolate.com, 11am-6pm daily). It's a good old-fashioned chocolatier with interior decorations as sumptuous as the confectioneries. Indulging is not as expensive as you'd think, particularly in this valley of pricey wine-tasting. For less than a flight of wines at a local winery, you can walk out of here with a small box of chocolate bliss.

RECREATION
★ Bothe-Napa Valley State Park

Just a few miles north of St. Helena and right off the main highway, **Bothe-Napa Valley State Park** (3801 St. Helena Hwy. N., 707/942-4575, www.parks.ca.gov, sunrise-sunset daily, $8 day-use fee) is the most accessible place up-valley to escape anything wine related and also the inside of the car. Proximity to the wineries and shops of St. Helena makes the park a popular picnic spot, but most people packing a lunch don't venture far beyond the shady picnic area just beyond the parking lot near the Pioneer Cemetery (and the road). They miss the best reason to come here, which is to experience the relative wilderness that's so close to the beaten path and home to some of the most easterly stands of coastal redwood trees.

Most of the best hiking trails start from the **Redwood Trail,** which runs from the main parking lot through the cool redwood forest along Ritchey Creek for just over a mile

Hiking in Wine Country

- **Bothe-Napa Valley State Park, St. Helena:** A favorite park in Wine Country, Bothe has scores of trails through redwoods that ascend to dry oak shaded peaks. At the top of the Coyote Peak Trail, you'll enjoy commanding views of the valley.

- **Robert Louis Stevenson State Park, Calistoga:** While home to the cabin site where Robert Louis Stevenson spent his honeymoon, the big draw to this park is the five-mile hike to the top of Mount St. Helena, from which you can San Francisco's skyline and Mount Shasta on clear day.

- **Jack London State Historic Park, Glen Ellen:** Miles of hiking trails surround the former residence of Jack London at this 800-acre park. To access the miles of hiking trails, take the Lake Trail uphill past the vineyards and through the redwoods for about half a mile to the forest-fringed lake created by London.

- **Sugarloaf Ridge State Park and neighboring Mount Hood Regional Park, Kenwood:** These two parks have the largest network of trails in Wine Country, and include such sights as a 25-foot waterfall, a pygmy forest, and the 2,729-foot Bald Mountain.

- **Armstrong Redwoods State Natural Reserve, Guerneville:** This 800-acre forested reserve offers some of the most diverse hiking in the area. Take a stroll through the cool, damp redwoods on the Pioneer Trail, or continue on to the 5,700-acre wilderness of Austin Creek State Recreation Area.

before meeting the **Ritchey Canyon Trail.** That trail more or less follows the creek for about another mile to the site of an old homestead, an ideal destination for adventurous picnickers.

More strenuous hikes start from the Redwood Trail and climb steeply into the heat to some rewarding lookout points. The closest is Coyote Peak, accessed via the **Coyote Peak Trail** and just under a mile from the creek. From the lookout spur, the trail continues to the **South Fork Trail.** Turn right here to head back down to the creek for a loop of about four miles, or go left to climb again to another lookout. These trails are not for the fainthearted, especially in the summer when it can get very hot, so don't underestimate the dehydrating power of too many glasses of wine.

Mountain bikers (or anyone on a Wine Country bike tour tired of dodging weaving rental cars) also have a few miles of trails to explore here, but these mainly stick to the creek near the campground. If you need to cool off, Bothe-Napa has a pool open on summer weekends noon-6pm for an additional $5 per swimmer.

Cooking Classes

Napa City College has an excellent Culinary Arts program, the **Napa Valley Cooking School** (1088 College Ave., 707/967-2900, http://napavalleycookingschool.org). Classes for lay cooks include The Concept of Wine, Demystified Emulsions, and The Perfect Steak and are offered weekday evenings 6pm-9pm, and on a Saturday or Sunday 11am-2pm. Each class costs about $85. With a diverse schedule and offerings at least twice a week, the Napa Valley Cooking School has more options than the slightly more famous cooking school up the road.

FOOD

There's an ongoing tug-of-war between up-valley and down-valley restaurants for the limited tourist food dollars. St. Helena's ever-changing restaurant scene with its big-name chefs continues to compete with Yountville for the title of Napa Valley's culinary epicenter.

California Cuisine

Typically, one of the first things that happens when you sit down at a restaurant is a server hands you a menu; at ★ **The Restaurant at Meadowood** (900 Meadowood Ln., 707/967-1205, www.therestaurantatmeadowood.com, 5:30pm-9:30pm Tues.-Sat., $300) it comes at the end of the meal, with your name on it. Garnering three Michelin stars (the only other in Napa is The French Laundry), Meadowood has been the talk of the St. Helena dining scene. For $330 (wine pairing is extra), diners are treated to a nine-course tasting menu carefully crafted with farm-to-table ethos executed with French precision. Diners will be surprised by sumptuous bites of duck with persimmon and maple, fermented pear puree and seared sturgeon, Asian pear soda served with warm frankincense sabayon, and the list goes on and on. Despite the haute cuisine, the restaurant works hard to maintain a reasonably relaxed atmosphere (clean dark denim pants are okay!). What you may not be as comfortable about is how far in advance you need to make a reservation (three months) or the many questions you're asked once you do (your name, the names of all your guests, and any dietary restrictions or preferences). The cancellation policy may make you downright queasy: 48 hours' notice or your credit card will be charged $330 per person. If it's all too much to stomach, Meadowood has some "affordable" options: **The Restaurant Bar** (5pm-midnight Tues.-Sat.) offers a snack menu ($40 pp) or a full three-course prix fixe ($90).

Another Michelin-starred favorite is **Terra** (1345 Railroad Ave., 707/963-8931, http://terrarestaurant.com, 6pm-9:30pm Thurs.-Mon., entrées $20-36) in the historic stone Hatchery Building. A romantic restaurant, it competes with the best restaurants in the valley (with its food and spin-off cookbook) thanks to chef Hiro Sone, who won the prestigious James Beard Foundation award for Best Chef in California in 2003. The menu is French and Californian with Asian flourishes and might include such eclectic creations as sake-marinated Alaskan black cod with shrimp dumplings. Diners create their own prix fixe menu by selecting four ($85), five ($104), or six ($121) courses from the 17 savory dishes on the menu. For something more casual but with the same fusion flare, step to the right at the entrance and dine at **Bar Terra**. With a full liquor license and an à la carte menu ($13-22), you can nibble on any one of Terra's signature dishes for considerably less.

Next door on Railroad Avenue is **Cindy's Backstreet Kitchen** (1327 Railroad Ave., 707/963-1200, www.cindysbackstreetkitchen.com, 11:30am-9pm daily, $17-27). The Cindy is Cindy Pawlcyn, who is largely credited with bringing casual yet sophisticated dining to the Napa Valley when she opened Yountville's Mustards Grill in 1983. Done with her usual panache, her "backstreet" kitchen feels just as it is: a charming local favorite. The menu goes for the same homey charm, with large plates including meat loaf, wood-oven duck, and *steak frites*. The small plates and sandwiches for lunch can be ordered to go. Be aware, however, that the quiet patio is a hive of activity at lunchtime and can require a wait.

★ **Farmstead** (738 Main St., www.longmeadowranch.com, 707/963-4555, 11:30am-9:30pm Mon.-Thurs., 11:30am-10pm Fri.-Sat., 11am-9:30pm Sun., $18-34) may not have a Michelin star or a famous chef at the helm, but it does take the idea of farm-fresh to a new level. It is run by the Long Meadow Ranch, a winery and farm based in Rutherford and the Mayacamas Mountains that supplies many of the ingredients, including vegetables, herbs, olive oil, eggs, and grass-fed beef (a specialty). The rustic restaurant is housed in the barn of the former Whiting Nursery, where salvaged farm equipment and even old tree stumps have found new life as fixtures, fittings, and furnishings. Even the booths are covered in leather sourced from the ranch's cattle. Complementing the atmosphere, the food hits just the right balance of sophistication and familiarity. If none of the well-priced wines in the varied California-heavy wine list appeals, the restaurant imposes only a $5 charitable donation to open a bottle of your own. To escape the echo chamber noise in the barn, ask for one of the coveted tables on the outdoor patio surrounded by fruit trees. Early risers will especially appreciate the outdoor café, which opens at 7am and serves Stumptown coffee and fresh pastries.

Another solid choice, and one where you might be able to bypass the reservation line, is **Market** (1347 Main St., 707/963-3799, www.marketsthelena.com, 11:30am-9pm Mon.-Thurs., 11:30am-10pm Fri.-Sat., 10am-9pm Sun., $14-35). The American bistro-style food is sophisticated yet familiar, with dishes like pan-roasted crispy chicken sharing the menu with mac and cheese made, of course, with the best artisanal cheeses. The stone walls, Victorian bar, and elegant tables might suggest an astronomical bill at the end of your meal, but instead the prices and atmosphere are very down-to-earth, and jaded locals have grown to love the place.

Goose and Gander (1245 Spring St., 707/967-8779, www.goosegander.com, 11:30am-11pm Mon.-Thurs., 11:30am-midnight Fri.-Sun., $19-42) channels the cocktail-driven, meaty farm-fresh cuisine, faux turn-of-the-20th-century aesthetic that has colored the San Francisco dining scene over the last couple of years. Here, the low-lit interior is warmed with dark wood, back-tufted leather booths, and a deep bar that showcases a stable of high-caliber, hard-to-find spirits that are made into "retro-fresh" cocktails. If you're detouring from wine, this is the place to order a Manhattan. Thankfully, the menu is tailored around a highball. Plates of cheese, charcuterie, or dishes of steak tartare, pork loin, and octopus stew keep tipsy stomachs full.

California farm-to-fork fowl gets some *izakaya* treatment at **Two Birds One Stone** (3020 St. Helena Hwy. N., 707/302-3777, www.twobirdsonestonenapa.com, lunch noon-5pm Fri.-Sun., dinner 5pm-9pm Thurs.-Mon., $16-30) next to Freemark Abbey north of town. Small plates and "poultry forward," the food is dressed in Asian flavors such as tamarind,

wasabi, and miso, while showcasing local produce. If you ever crave to just dine on plate after plate of carefully crafted appetizers, this is your place (don't pass up the Japanese pancake). The atmosphere is equally refined, housed in a historic weathered stone building. Beverages run from cocktails, to whiskey, to sake, to beer and, of course, wine. A sommelier is on hand to help you select the ideal choice to wash down dinner.

When you ask the locals where they go for dinner, they will invariably say **Cook St. Helena** (1310 Main St., 707/963-7088, www.cooksthelena.com, 11:30am-10pm Mon.-Sat., 4pm-10pm Sun., $19-24). This slender restaurant, painted in steel blue and accented with dark wood and white linen, serves classic rustic Italian-style food. You'll find linguine with clams, pappardelle with pork, braised lamb, and seared flat iron steak; a healthy Napa-centric wine list; and a full bar with fresh and inventive cocktails. While this is not one of the big Napa Valley tourist draws, reservations are recommended.

Next door, **Cook Tavern** (1304 Main St., 707/963-8082, http://cooksthelena.com/cooktavern, 11:30am-10pm Mon.-Thurs., 11:30am-midnight Fri., 10am-midnight Sat., 10am-10pm Sun., $16-19) gives locals that sports bar that all towns need. Being St. Helena, however, expect microbrews, an excellent wine list, craft cocktails, and great pub food to match. Brunch is served Saturday and Sunday 10am-2pm.

Steak Houses

You won't find the traditional steak house atmosphere of dim lighting, bold cabs, and big slabs of beef alongside boiled potatoes and blanched vegetables at ★ **Press St. Helena** (587 St. Helena Hwy., 707/967-0550, www.pressnapavalley.com, 5pm-10pm Wed.-Mon., $40). After all, this is a steak house Napa Valley-style: The interior is light-filled and modern, the wine list's breadth is breathtaking, and produce shares the spotlight with the meat. Everything is separately priced (including steak sauce), which can add up quickly.

The best bet is to go with the filling Tasting Menu ($125). While you may not get that huge hunk of mouthwatering steak, you'll taste the unusual swordfish with peaches and purslane salad and the amazing beef tartare with lightly fried oyster.

Pairing wine is a big part of the fun at Press, which has the largest Napa Valley wine list in the world. In fact, sommelier Kelly White wrote the book about Napa wine, literally. The list is delivered to your table on a svelte iPad, and can be arranged by price, varietal, or alphabetically. Should it still be too overwhelming, the friendly and knowledgeable staff can help you pair your wine, and even split glasses to offer you the most variety.

A light bar menu is also available and includes Wagyu corn dogs, a bacon flight, and a burger and *steak frites*. Beer, scotch, and cocktails are also available.

Cafés and Bakeries

Fortunately for St. Helenians, the quick stop for a morning cup of joe also happens to be one of the most celebrated bakeries in the valley. Known chiefly for its bread, the **Model Bakery** (1357 Main St., 707/963-8192, www.themodelbakery.com, 6:30am-5:30pm Mon.-Fri., 7am-5:30pm Sat., 7am-5pm Sun., $5-15) has been around, in one form or another, since 1920. Not overly fussy, there are shelves of flour-dusted bread, display cases full of pastries, and an array of scones, muffins, and croissants. Everything is here to please the most fickle sweet tooth, especially the divine Espresso Bundt cake, which goes perfectly with the café's Blue Bottle Coffee. You can also opt for the "healthy" option of the exceedingly moist whole wheat muffin made with brown sugar and dried fruit. Sandwiches, wood-fired pizzas, and salads also make this an easy stop for lunch or provisions for a picnic.

If quick refreshment is all you need to keep going, the **Napa Valley Coffee Roasting Company** (1400 Oak Ave., 707/963-4491, www.napavalleycoffee.com, 7am-7pm daily) offers some peace and quiet on its patio a block from Main Street.

Casual Dining

For the best breakfasts and no-nonsense lunches in St. Helena, head to **Gillwoods Café** (1313 Main St., 707/963-1788, 7am-3pm daily, $9-15). It's a friendly, no-frills diner popular with locals and perfect for some good old-fashioned hearty food to prepare you for a day of exploring or to help you recover from yesterday's overconsumption of wine.

Although St. Helena's food scene is constantly changing, there is one place that the term "institution" could apply to, and that's the half-century-old **Gott's Roadside** (933 Main St., 707/963-3486, www.gottsroadside.com, 10am-9pm daily in winter, 10am-10pm daily in summer, $10-13), formerly Taylor's Automatic Refresher. This unmistakable old diner just south of downtown is home of the ahi burger and other diner delights, many given a Wine Country gourmet twist but also with prices that have been given a Wine Country lift. A big grassy picnic area with plenty of tables gives a little respite from the traffic, or perch on a stool at the counter. It's a unique experience, but after dropping $30 or more for lunch for two people in the summer, and waiting in a long line for the restrooms, you might wish you'd gone to a more traditional restaurant with more traditional air-conditioning and facilities. More civilized outposts of Gott's have opened in Napa and San Francisco, but this is the original and still the best if you want some old-school kid-friendly outdoor fun.

If you're tired of waiting in line at Gotts, drive up the road to the ★ **Bruschetteria Food Truck** (709 Main St., 707/968-0625, www.cliffamily.com, 11:30am-4pm Tues.-Sun., $5-12) at Velo Vino. The small menu is farm-to-fork Italian with such seasonal offerings as peach and burrata cheese salad and spiced lamb meatballs. Take your goodies to the back patio at the very friendly Velo Vino to pair it with a glass of wine for an excellent lunch.

For a slice, head over to **Pizzeria Tra Vigne** (1016 Main St., 707/967-9999, http://pizzeriatravigne.com, 11:30am-9pm

Sun.-Thurs., 11:30am-9:30pm Fri.-Sat., $13-21), where locals come for the famous thin-crust Italian pizzas. Hearty plates of pasta or heavy Italian salads are also available, and servers are happy to deliver pitchers of any number of beers they have on tap. If you're traveling with kids, Pizzeria Tra Vigne is a great place to stop and relax over a meal. They even have a pool table. You can also get your selection to go.

Picnic Supplies

You'll find plenty to pack in the picnic basket all over St. Helena. Many restaurants offer almost all their lunch menu items to go, including **Cindy's Backstreet Kitchen, Market, Farmstead**, the **Bruschetteria Food Truck**, and the **Model Bakery.** But even they cannot compete with the gourmet paradise of **Dean & Deluca** (607 St. Helena Hwy. S., 707/967-9980, www.deandeluca.com, 7am-7pm Sun.-Thurs., 7am-8pm Fri.-Sat.). Just don't lose track of time while browsing the food you never knew existed. A cheaper and altogether quirkier place to buy sandwiches is the old-fashioned deli counter at **Giugni's Grocery & Deli** (1227 Main St., 707/963-3421, 9am-4:30pm daily), an old St. Helena institution that's chock-full of fascinating family memorabilia. Be sure to ask for some Giugni juice, a trademark marinade that's delicious. Those planning to build their own sandwich can also battle through the crowds to the well-stocked deli at the **V. Sattui Winery** (1111 White Ln., 707/963-7774, www.vsattui.com, 9am-6pm daily).

And don't shun the local grocery store, **Sunshine Foods** (1115 Main St., 707/963-7070, www.sunshinefoodsmarket.com, 7:30am-8:30pm daily), next to the Wells Fargo bank at the southern end of the downtown zone. It's a quality grocery store with a remarkably broad range of deli sandwiches and salads, wines, and even freshly made sushi.

Farmers Markets

The place to buy local produce direct from the farmers is the **St. Helena Farmers Market** (8am-1pm Fri. May-Oct.), held at Crane Park west of Main Street; access is via Sulphur Springs Road or Mills Lane. Plenty of local crafts also fill the booths, as do ready-to-eat goodies like crepes, local cheese, and samosas with dips.

ACCOMMODATIONS

St. Helena has a wide range of accommodations, but at far higher prices than the equally diverse Napa and Calistoga, justified perhaps by the convenient location in the middle of the valley, the pretty Main Street, the thriving restaurant scene, or maybe simply because, in world-famous St. Helena, they can get away with it.

Under $150

With its retro neon sign, the 1940s-era **El Bonita Motel** (195 Main St., 707/963-3216 or 800/541-3284, www.elbonita.com, $120-279) is not the most glamorous place to stay in St. Helena, but it's still pretty fancy for a motel. The Poolside rooms, laid out around a small pool and hot tub, are the cheapest and suffer from less privacy and more road noise than the Homestead and Garden rooms, which are set farther back on the property and quieter but less of a bargain, though many have kitchenettes to make up for it. All contain modern furnishings and include air-conditioning, refrigerators, coffeemakers, and microwave ovens.

$150-250

The **Hotel St. Helena** (1309 Main St., 707/963-4388, www.hotelsthelena.net, $195-300) is about as central as can be, down a little alley through the impressive 1881 Italianate building on Main Street. The old Victorian building is full of original features, as are the 18 guest rooms with brass beds, a smattering of antiques, and plush carpeting and fabrics. You might also have to tolerate some less charming Victorian traits such as temperamental plumbing and poor sound insulation. The four smallest and cheapest rooms share a bathroom. The best deals are the North Wing rooms, which are still on the small side but have private bathrooms, or you can go big with the queen suite that has a claw-foot bathtub and a sitting area.

Right next to El Bonita Motel is the **Vineyard Country Inn** (201 Main St., 707/963-1000, www.vineyardcountryinn. com, $185-325), a combination of hotel and B&B with 21 spacious suites, each with fireplaces, refrigerators, and comfortable but unexceptional country-style furniture. All suites are in a main two-story building or several cottages around the pool and pleasant brick patios—just be sure to ask for a room away from the main road, which is noisy enough to render the balconies of some suites next to useless. A complimentary breakfast is served each morning.

For some true peace and quiet, skip the valley floor and head for the hills. Northeast of St. Helena near the small community of Deer Park is secluded **Spanish Villa Inn** (474 Glass Mountain Rd., 707/963-7483, www.napavalleyspanishvilla.com, $207-275), a small Mediterranean-style B&B set in several acres of beautifully tended grounds with bocce and croquet courts as well as roses galore. There are six rooms and two suites. All have private bathrooms and unusual touches like hand-painted sinks, plantation-style shutters, and carved headboards but, alas, an overabundance of floral prints. Downstairs rooms open onto a patio overlooking the garden, while one of the upstairs suites has its own balcony. None accommodate pets or children.

Over $250

On the southern edge of St. Helena, hidden from the road behind a thicket of trees, is the mock-Tudor mansion of the ★ **Harvest Inn by Charlie Palmer** (1 Main St., 707/963-9463 or 800/950-8466, www.harvestinn.com, $218-408), set in eight acres of lush gardens shaded by mature trees. The place is crammed with stylish antiques, fancy brickwork, and other often-surreal English country features. There's nothing surreal about the luxury of the 78 rooms and suites, however: All have

flat-screen TVs, fireplaces, featherbeds, and minibars; some have their own private terrace or views of neighboring vineyards. If that isn't enough, the grounds include two outside heated swimming pools, a wine bar, spa, fitness center, and **Harvest Table** (lunch 11:30am-2:30pm Wed.-Fri., dinner 5:30pm-9:30pm Tues.-Thurs., 5:30pm-10pm Fri.-Sat., brunch 11:30am-2:30pm Sat.-Sun., $18-50), Palmer's 110-seat, indoor-outdoor restaurant, which serves a complimentary breakfast to all inn guests (7am-10am daily).

Its location surrounded by vineyards a few miles north of St. Helena makes the **Wine Country Inn** (1152 Lodi Ln., 707/963-7077 or 888/465-4608, www.winecountryinn. com, $365-650) a slightly cheaper alternative to some of the other luxury resorts out in the wilds. This family-run establishment offers an unusual down-home atmosphere, good amenities, and a decent breakfast. Rooms are decorated with a mix of modern and rustic, which you'll either love or regret paying so much for. If you splurge on a room with a view, there'll be no questioning it. There are a variety of rooms (and prices) to choose from, with fireplaces and private porches and patios on the high end, and five luxury cottages each with 800 square feet of lounging space.

In the thick of downtown St. Helena, the **Wydown Hotel** (1424 Main St., 707/963-5100, www.wydownhotel.com, $290-370) offers a break from Victorian excess and the landed gentry aesthetic. The 12 rooms are all smartly decorated, while the lobby downstairs outdoes itself in urban chic. If you want to saturate yourself in St. Helena's modern art scene, this is the place to stay. The boutique hotel has little in the way of luxury amenities, but the Wydown offers a convenient location and historic digs that are modern and stylish.

The luxurious **Meadowood Napa Valley** (900 Meadowood Ln., off Silverado Trail, 707/531-4788 or 877/963-3646, www.meadowood.com, $500-1,400) resort is facing increasing competition in this astronomical price bracket, but it's still worth considering if you're planning to splurge, not least because of its spectacular setting on 250 lush acres in the hills above the Silverado Trail. The rooms are in 20 country-style lodges spread around the grounds and range from simple two-room studios up to spacious suites. All have fireplaces, beamed ceilings, private decks or terraces, and every conceivable luxury trapping. For those who actually venture out of the rooms, there are plenty of distractions, including miles of hiking trails, two swimming pools surrounded by vast expanses of lawn, tennis courts, a nine-hole golf course, and croquet. And to make sure visitors never have to venture down into the valley, there's a small spa, wine-tasting events, and two highly regarded restaurants on-site.

Camping

The Napa Valley might be touted by every marketing brochure as a bank-breaking hedonistic playground, but it actually has a remarkably good campground where two people can stay for less than it would cost them to taste wine at most of the nearby wineries. So forget about matching a Napa cabernet with an entrée at the latest Michelin-starred restaurant—instead see how it goes with s'mores around a campfire under a warm summer night sky.

You can light your fire and unpack the marshmallows just a few miles north of St. Helena in the leafy **Bothe-Napa Valley State Park** (3801 St. Helena Hwy. N., 707/942-4575, www.parks.ca.gov, reservations www.reserveamerica.com or 800/444-7275). There are 39 sites, 30 of which can accommodate RVs up to 31 feet long (though there are no hookups). The other nine sites are walk-in tent-only, and all cost $35 per night. Most sites offer some shade beneath oak and madrone trees, and there's a swimming pool as well as flush toilets, hot showers, and that all-important fire ring at every site.

If camping isn't quite your style, consider glamping in one of the park's 10 yurts or stay in its recently refurbished historic cabins. Three of the yurts sleep six ($60-75), while seven sleep four ($55-70). Each comes with

cots and beds, but you need to bring your bedding as well as your other camping gear. Each yurt site comes with picnic table, fire pit, and storage locker. You won't need any of these if you opt to stay in a six-person cabin ($225-250), as all are fully furnished, including a complete kitchen stocked with pots, pans, dishes, and silverware. The cabins are also heated and have showers and a private deck; however, they don't include Wi-Fi, TV, linens, or towels.

INFORMATION AND SERVICES

The **St. Helena Welcome Center** (657 Main St., 707/963-4456, www.sthelena.com, 9am-5pm Mon.-Fri., 10am-4pm Sat., 11am-5pm Sun.) has maps, information, and discounted wine-tasting vouchers. Thankfully, there is parking in the back; turn on Vidovich Lane just north of the visitors center.

If you're in town for a few days, the local **St. Helena Star** (http://napavalleyregister.com/star) is worth picking up at any local café, as much for the latest Wine Country gossip as for information about local events and some entertaining wine-related columns.

For any health concerns, the **St. Helena Hospital** (10 Woodland Rd., 707/963-6425, http://sthelenanowaiter.org) has a 24-hour emergency room that provides quick and reliable service. Urgent care can be found also at **Ole Health** (1222 Pine St., Ste. A, 707/963-0931, www.olehealth.org, 8:30am-5:30pm Mon., 8:30am-5:30pm Tues.-Wed., 10am-7pm Thurs., 8:30am-5:30pm Fri.).

If you need to withdraw some cash, try **Wells Fargo** (1107 Main St.) or **Bank of America** (1001 Adams St.).

GETTING THERE AND AROUND

The next town north on Highway 29 after Rutherford, St. Helena is in the center of the valley and only eight miles south of Calistoga. To jump over to the Silverado Trail, take Zinfandel Lane or Pope Street east.

If you want to avoid the constant headache

of parking and driving in traffic around town, consider hopping aboard Route 10 of Napa Valley's **VINE** (707/251-6443 or 800/696-6443, www.ridethevine.com, $1.60-$5.50) that travels between Napa and St. Helena multiple times a day. The express 29 Route runs from the El Cerrito BART station, but it only runs on weekdays. In town, the VINE's **St. Helena Shuttle**, which also runs on a fixed track, offers on-demand service (707/963-3007). After calling, expect a wait time of 15-30 minutes.

Like elsewhere in the valley, the St. Helena area is great to explore by bike. Right downtown is the **St. Helena Cyclery** (1156 Main St., 707/963-7736, www.sthelenacyclery.com,

9:30am-5:30pm Tues.-Sat., 10am-5pm Sun.), which rents basic hybrid bikes for $15 per hour or $45 per day and more advanced road bikes $85-125 per day. Delivery is available to your hotel for an additional cost ($40-85). You can also rent bikes at **Velo Vino** (709 Main St., 707/968-0625, www.cliffamilywinery.com, 10am-6pm daily), which has a partnership with Calistoga Bike Shop. Road bikes are available for $60 per day, while hybrids can be rented for $39 per day. While you are arranging your tour, the folks at the tasting counter will help you plan your route, pour you an espresso, and sell you any Clif family snacks for the road.

Calistoga

No other town in the Napa Valley retains a sense of its pioneer Victorian roots more than Calistoga, with the remaining stretch of its old boardwalk and Victorian storefronts framed by views in all directions of mountains and forests. Replace the cars and paving with horses and mud, and things would probably look much like they did a hundred years ago when the spa town was at its peak, drawing visitors from far and wide to its natural hot springs and mud baths.

The town was built on mud, literally and figuratively. San Francisco businessman Sam Brannan bought up thousands of acres of land in the 1850s, drawn by the development potential of the hot springs. He opened a very profitable general store in the late 1850s (now a historic landmark at 203 Wappo Ave.), followed by his lavish Hot Springs Resort in 1868. He was also instrumental in bringing the railroad this far up the valley to transport visitors to his new resort, making the town a destination for the masses and a gateway to Sonoma and Lake Counties to the north.

What Brannan is perhaps best known for, however, is an alcohol-induced slip of the tongue. Legend has it that in a speech promoting his resort he planned to say that

it would become known as the "Saratoga of California," referring to the famous New York spa town, but his words instead came out as the "Calistoga of Sarafornia."

Perhaps more than in any other valley town, all this history does not seem that far away, but Calistoga is not preserved in amber. The funky town is the most affordable place to live in the valley, and its population reflects that. While wine is certainly the main economic engine, Calistogans are not easily wooed by the promise of big resorts such as farther down-valley. Most agree that the Solage resort has been a boon, but with two more on the way (one on Diamond Mountain and a Four Seasons on the Silverado Trail), many are concerned that Calistoga's earthy vibe may turn upscale.

The Wines

As the valley narrows into a box canyon, the **Calistoga AVA** stretches seven square miles along the valley and creeps up the slopes of the Vaca and Mayacamas Mountains. Not only is Calistoga the hottest part of the valley, reaching 100°F in the summer, it also has the greatest diurnal variation, dropping as much as 50 degrees at night thanks to the influence

Calistoga

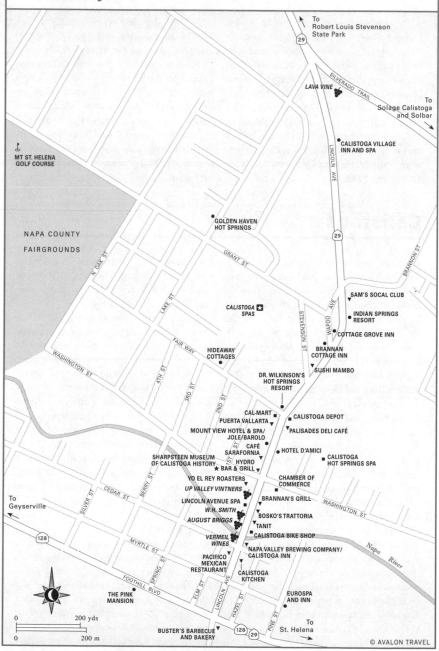

To
Robert Louis Stevenson
State Park
29

SILVERADO TRAIL

LAVA VINE

To
Solage Calistoga
and Solbar

CALISTOGA VILLAGE
INN AND SPA

LINCOLN AVE

MT ST. HELENA
GOLF COURSE

GOLDEN HAVEN
HOT SPRINGS

NAPA COUNTY
FAIRGROUNDS

GRANT ST

29

N OAK ST

SAM'S SOCAL CLUB

CALISTOGA
SPAS

LAKE ST

STEVENSON ST

WAPOO AVE

INDIAN SPRINGS
RESORT

COTTAGE GROVE INN

FAIR WAY

HIDEAWAY
COTTAGES

WASHINGTON ST

4TH ST

3RD ST

BRANNAN ST

BRANNAN
COTTAGE INN

SUSHI MAMBO

DR. WILKINSON'S
HOT SPRINGS
RESORT

2ND ST

CAL-MART
PUERTA VALLARTA

CALISTOGA DEPOT

MOUNT VIEW HOTEL & SPA/
JOLE/BAROLO

PALISADES DELI CAFÉ

CAFÉ
SARAFORNIA

1ST ST

HOTEL D'AMICI

CALISTOGA
HOT SPRINGS SPA

SHARPSTEEN MUSEUM
OF CALISTOGA HISTORY

HYDRO
BAR & GRILL

YO EL REY ROASTERS

UP VALLEY VINTNERS

BERRY ST

CHAMBER OF
COMMERCE

CEDAR ST

LINCOLN AVENUE SPA

W.H. SMITH

BRANNAN'S GRILL

WASHINGTON ST

SILVER ST

AUGUST BRIGGS

BOSKO'S TRATTORIA

TANIT

To
Geyserville

128

MYRTLE ST

SPRING ST

VERMEIL
WINES

CALISTOGA BIKE SHOP

NAPA VALLEY BREWING COMPANY/
CALISTOGA INN

Napa River

FOOTHILL BLVD

PACIFICO
MEXICAN
RESTAURANT

CALISTOGA
KITCHEN

ELM ST

LINCOLN AVE

HAZEL ST

THE PINK
MANSION

EUROSPA
AND INN

0   200 yds

0   200 m

BUSTER'S BARBECUE
AND BAKERY

128
29

PINE ST

To
St. Helena

© AVALON TRAVEL

Calistoga Tasting Tour

After a hearty breakfast at **Café Sarafornia,** begin your day with a gondola ride up to **Sterling Vineyards,** where sunshine and chardonnay share equal brightness over commanding views of the valley. After a long, relaxing visit, jump over to the Silverado Trail and have lunch at **Solbar,** the Michelin-starred restaurant at **Solage Calistoga.** Finish with a dip in **Spa Solage**'s mineral pool or go old school with a mud bath and massage at the famous **Dr. Wilkinson's Hot Springs Resort.** Go for wine-tastings along **Lincoln Avenue** or take a tour at **Chateau Montelena,** a historic 1882 winery with ornamental Chinese gardens and home of the chardonnay that won first place in the Judgment of Paris. For dinner, make it social at **Sam's Social Club,** where the farm-to-table food, outdoor fireside seating, and cool ambience are a winning combination. Stay the night at the charming, affordable, and centrally located **Calistoga Inn,** or if you can't resist one last soak before lights out, take the plunge at **Indian Springs Resort.**

of the Russian River basin just over the hill. Calistoga is also the highest part of the valley (300 feet above sea level) and founded entirely on well-drained volcanic bedrock. These unique factors, among others, produce mainly cabernet, zinfandel, syrah, and petite sirah, which become wines with ripe fruit, minerals, well-balanced acidity, and good structure.

On Calistoga's western slopes is the Diamond Mountain AVA. Temperatures are cooler with less daily variation, while sharing the same volcanic soil with Calistoga. Cabernet and cabernet franc occupy most of the vineyards and produce wines of mineral and black currant notes given structure by strong tannins that soften and age well.

CALISTOGA WINERIES

Many visitors never really explore the wineries this far north in the valley, and they are missing out. Wineries pepper Calistoga, but tasting here is surprisingly casual and relaxing compared to the often congested St. Helena just a few miles away. There's plenty of diversity with seemingly an equal number of downtown tasting rooms, small boutiques and appointment-only wineries, and grand architectural palaces. The area's latest claim to fame is the impressive Tuscan castle built by valley son Dario Sattui just south of Calistoga.

FRANK FAMILY VINEYARDS

In the heart of the Larkmead area (so christened by Lillie Hitchcock Coit of San Francisco Coit Tower fame for the area's preponderance of larks) is **Frank Family Vineyards** (1091 Larkmead Ln., 707/942-0859 or 800/574-9463, www.frankfamilyvineyards.com, 10am-5pm daily, tasting $30). The winery is home to the imposing sandstone building of the historic Larkmead Winery established in 1884 and now on the National Register of Historic Places. Yet the winery is perhaps as well known for an unpretentious and slightly quirky tasting experience as for its wines. Producing about 15,000 cases of still and sparkling wines a year, the increasing emphasis is on still wines, particularly cabernet sauvignon from Rutherford-area vineyards and pinot noir from Carneros. Sparkling wine remains an important part of the portfolio, however, and a dry blanc de blancs is offered as the first part of the tasting in the tasting room in the original Craftsman bungalow on the property.

TWOMEY CELLARS

In the heart of cabernet country, you'll find **Twomey Cellars** (1183 Dunaweal Ln., 707/942-2489, www.twomey.com, 10am-5pm Mon.-Sat., 11am-5pm Sun., tasting $15-20). This charming winery is owned by the same family behind Silver Oak, who in Oakville and

Geyserville have perfected cabernet sauvignon to an art form. At Twomey Cellars, however, they turn the gaze (and palate) to merlot. It is crafted through an ancient racking technique known as *soutirage traditionnel*, a slow method of decanting wine that was developed over centuries in Bordeaux. Sauvignon blanc and pinot noir are also on the tasting menu at the elegant curved bar that opens onto a sunny courtyard with views of the lush, rolling vineyards.

STERLING VINEYARDS

When it opened in 1973, this contemporary, monastery-like winery, perched high on a wooded knoll rising straight from the valley floor just south of Calistoga, was hailed as one of the most spectacular wineries in the valley. Now **Sterling Vineyards** (1111 Dunaweal Ln., 800/726-6136, www.sterlingvineyards. com, 10:30am-5pm Mon.-Fri., 10am-5pm Sat.-Sun., visitor fee $29, under 21 $15, children 3 and under free), famously accessible only via aerial gondola, remains one of the most striking and has become a serious tourist attraction.

At first glance the gondola, ticket booths, and giant parking lot make it feel more like an out-of-season ski resort than a winery, but once at the top of the hill it's all about wine and views. Once visitors have paid the $29 to get up the hill, everything is pretty much free, including a fun self-guided tour of the winery on elevated walkways, the views, a sit-down tasting of five wines either inside or out on the patio (weather permitting), and the souvenir wineglass. At any time you can take a seat and order a cheese and charcuterie plate. A large winery, Sterling has more than 1,200 acres of vineyards in just about every Napa appellation, from Los Carneros, from which come some highly rated pinot noir and chardonnay, to high up on Diamond Mountain, the source of some powerhouse cabernet sauvignon. Those more interested in the wines than the views should opt for one of the pricier tasting options that include the limited-release and single-vineyard wines for which

Sterling is better known ($39). The only thing sometimes missing is the sort of personal service found at smaller wineries, so you might have to persevere to get any detailed information from the staff about what you're drinking.

CLOS PEGASE

Sterling might be easy to spot perched atop its nearby hill, but just down the road, **Clos Pegase** (1060 Dunaweal Ln., 707/942-4981, www.clospegase.com, 10:30am-5pm daily, tasting $20-30) is truly hard to miss. Designed as a "temple to wine and art" in 1987, it could be mistaken for the Napa outpost of a modern art museum, as postmodern design touches grace almost every part of the giant boxy building.

You'll learn about the estate on the **Connoisseur Cave Tour and Tasting** ($60 by appointment), which ends with a seated tasting in the dramatic Cave Theater. Otherwise, you can explore the grounds on your own and step into the tasting room for a flight of approachable pinot noir, merlot, and chardonnay from Carneros behind the counter, as well as a local cabernet sauvignon.

CHATEAU MONTELENA

The beautiful French- and Chinese-inspired **Chateau Montelena** (1429 Tubbs Ln., 707/942-5105, www.montelena.com, 9:30am-4pm daily, tasting $25) wine estate will forever be remembered for putting Napa Valley on the map when its 1973-vintage chardonnay trounced the best French white burgundies at the famous 1976 Paris tasting. Today, the soft, plush cabernet sauvignon is now just as acclaimed as the rich chardonnay at Montelena, and the winery makes an excellent estate zinfandel. These are all available at the walk-in tasting located in the top floor of the château.

But if the wines aren't enough, the grounds are also worth a visit. The stone château was built in 1882 by Alfred Tubbs (after whom Tubbs Lane is named), and the ornamental Chinese garden was added in 1965. It is centered around the lush five-acre Jade Lake, crisscrossed with lacquered bridges. For $40 you can take the vineyard tour on Monday and Wednesday at 10am, for which reservations are not required, but reservations are required to tour the entire estate with the 90-minute tour on Tuesday and Thursday at 10am.

LAVA VINE

At **Lava Vine** (965 Silverado Trail, 707/942-9500, www.lavavine.com, 10am-5pm daily, tasting $10) you'll find no tour buses or big architectural spectacle, only chickens, rustic farm equipment, funky art, and good wine. The tasting room is tiny, with a friendly atmosphere that eschews the enological navel-gazing (i.e., pretention) that you can find at other wineries in the valley. Instead, this is the place to enjoy some of the best the valley has to offer, including sunshine and live music, which frequently happens spontaneously Sunday afternoons as many pourers are also musicians. For $10 you get five generous pours of whatever they happen to have on hand, but expect to find chenin blanc, chardonnay, cabernet, and syrah.

Downtown Tasting Rooms

Like elsewhere in the valley, more small wineries and vintners are getting into the tasting room game. Nearly all are located on Lincoln Avenue in the heart of downtown Calistoga.

VERMEIL WINES

For anyone itching to watch the Niners games while sipping a cabernet, **Vermeil Wines** (1255 Lincoln Ave., 707/341-3054, www.vermeilwines.com, 10am-5:30pm Sun.-Thurs., 10am-8pm Fri.-Sat., tasting $20-40) is the place to go. With a large flat-screen TV, several deep armchairs, and a wall of football memorabilia, this tasting room may resemble a man-cave more than a Napa Valley tasting room. In fact, it is home to hometown boy Dick Vermeil's latest venture. If you can't quite place the name, Vermeil was the NFL coach who took the St. Louis Rams to win the Super Bowl in 2000 and was a popular commentator on CBS and ABC Sports. While you might be tempted to think the appropriate beverage here is beer, think again. Vermeil turns out some great wines. The sauvignon blanc is delightful, while the cabernet sauvignon and zinfandel have scored above 90 points from *Wine Enthusiast*. The tasting room has two bars, and if you're lucky, one of the winery partners will be on hand to do the pouring.

AUGUST BRIGGS

The crowded tasting room of **August Briggs** (1307 Lincoln Ave., 707/942-4912, www.augustbriggswinery.com, 11am-5pm Wed.-Mon., Tues. by appointment only, tasting $10) is a local favorite, perhaps because this small winery produces 16 different wines using seven varietals locally grown in the Napa and Sonoma Valleys—meaning there is something for everyone. For the price of a tasting, you'll get five healthy pours. Out of the long menu, be sure to ask for the old vine zinfandel ($35), which is wonderfully full but not too peppery. The Napa Valley "Dijon Clones" pinot noir is another standout, as it is big and bold, especially for the usually shy grape.

W.H.SMITH

W.H.Smith (1367 Lincoln Ave., 707/942-1194, www.whsmithwines.com, 11am-5pm daily, tasting $10) is known for cabernets and particularly pinot noirs, many of which are made from grapes grown on the Sonoma Coast. The tasting room also hosts the Wine Sensory Experience, a two-hour class held every day at 10am. For $65, students learn how to identify different aromas and flavors in wine, as well as how each is cultivated by the winemaker in the first place. It is the only class of its kind in this part of the valley, and the winery keeps it small and intimate with a maximum of only eight students at a time.

UP VALLEY VINTNERS

Up Valley Vintners (1371 Lincoln Ave., 707/942-1004, www.upvalleyvintners.com, noon-6pm Sun.-Thurs., noon-8pm Fri.-Sat., tasting $15) is the shared tasting room of two highly regarded boutique wineries. Located east of Calistoga at the foot of the Palisades Mountains, the 125-acre **Kenefick Ranch** has been a pioneer in the resurgence of bottling cabernet franc as a stand-alone varietal. Its Bordeaux-style blends are equally celebrated: The flagship Picket Road Red and the winery's other single varietals have frequently earned over 90 points from *Wine Advocate* and *Wine Spectator*. From **Tofanelli Wines,** a historic winery started in 1929, you'll find sophisticated zinfandels, charbono, and petite sirah designed for the dinner table. The Rosé di Carignane is particularly good (especially with a meal) and a great deal at $25. Flights of four wines are offered in a relatively spare tasting room free of the typical tchotchkes. You can also retire with a glass (or two) to the secluded back patio, where umbrella-topped tables, brick walls, and climbing vines invite you to stay awhile ($12-15).

Wineries by Appointment

LARKMEAD VINEYARDS

Driving up to the farmhouse tasting room of **Larkmead Vineyards** (1100 Larkmead Ln., 707/942-0167, www.larkmead.com, 10am-3:30pm daily, tour and tasting $75) gives you a sense of what the Napa Valley was like when it was simply farmland that happened to grow grapes. It is modest by Napa Valley standards, a sign that it is more serious about wines than tourists. And this certainly shows in the wines it pours. Over the years, Larkmead has come to produce very sophisticated wines and won particular praise for its opulent and elegant cabernets made in a classic European style. Those interested in tasting here must book a 90-minute tour and tasting in which you stroll through the vineyards, learn about the winemaking process here, and sample four wines on the terrace surrounded by the winery's aromatic native plants. If this sounds like an ideal way to spend a summer afternoon, be sure to book several weeks in advance as you are not alone.

LAURA MICHAEL WINES

On Highway 29, just as the highway heads over the mountains toward Clear Lake, is a little cluster of modest buildings belonging to this family-owned boutique winery. **Laura Michael Wines** (2250 Lake County Hwy., 707/942-9251, www.zahtilavineyards.com, 10am-4:30pm daily, tasting $10-20) makes some fine cabernet sauvignon and zinfandel. Its relaxed atmosphere and smooth-drinking wines offer a nice change of pace (and price) from the Napa Valley crush. The specialty here is zinfandel, which is grown in the small Oat Hill Vineyard next to the winery and sourced from the Russian River Valley. Napa Valley chardonnay and cabernet sauvignon are also on the menu. The staff in the cozy tasting room is a mine of information about other small local wineries.

DIAMOND MOUNTAIN WINERIES

Known to produce big reds with powerful tannins and strong black currant and mineral characteristics, the few wineries of Diamond Mountain are worth a visit.

CASTELLO DI AMOROSA

Driving up to **Castello di Amorosa** (4045 N. St. Helena Hwy., Calistoga, 707/967-6272, www.castellodiamorosa.com, 9:30am-5pm daily Nov.-Feb., 9:30am-6pm daily Mar.-Oct., general admission ages 21 and over $25-35, children 5-20 $15), it is difficult to remember that it is a winery. Everything from the parking attendant who directs you through the large and crowded parking lot to the "general admission" prices (includes a tasting of five wines and juice for the kids) screams "Disneyland." And then there is the castle itself: complete with 107 rooms, eight floors, and made from 8,000 tons of stone and 850,000 European bricks. Everything from the hand-forged nails to the antique tiles and Italian quarried stone has been painstakingly recreated by an army of artisans. Taking it all in will make anyone want a drink.

Thankfully, the wines are good. Expect

big Diamond Mountain powerhouse reds, plus plenty of whites, including a late harvest semillon. General admission gets you five tastes, plus you can amble around the castle's first two floors at your leisure. To make the most of your time here, tack on an extra $15 for the guided tour. On it, you'll marvel at a two-story marvel of frescoes, coffered ceilings, and the towers, which offer strategic views over the valley and chutes to pour hot oil on the advancing hordes below; you'll descend to catacombs and vaulted cellars, including the breathtaking, 130-foot-long barrel room with its vast cross-vaulted ceiling; and imagine some gruesome things in the dungeon stocked with some particularly heinous torture instruments—including an original iron maiden and a door leading to the aptly named "pit of despair," into which victims were thrown to starve to death. Then comes the barrel and reserve tasting! Not surprisingly, this is a big destination, particularly for parents eager to make their Wine Country visit palatable to their young children. It is wise to make a reservation on busy weekends.

Wineries by Appointment
★ SCHRAMSBERG VINEYARDS

If you plan to visit just one of the valley's big champagne makers, you should consider the historic **Schramsberg Vineyards** (1400 Schramsberg Rd., via Peterson Dr. off Hwy. 29, Calistoga, 707/942-4558 or 800/877-3623, www.schramsberg.com, 10am-4pm daily, tour and tasting $65). The winery was established high on the wooded slopes of Diamond Mountain in 1862 by German immigrant Jacob Schram, who had soon made such a name for himself that he was memorialized in Robert Louis Stevenson's book *Silverado Squatters.*

The winery was immortalized again in 1972 when its 1969 blanc de blancs was served to President Richard Nixon and China's Premier Zhou Enlai in Beijing for a toast to the normalization of diplomatic relations. In fact, the sales room is full of photos and menus from various White House events at which Schramsberg wines have been served.

Today Schramsberg still makes that historic blanc de blancs, along with a rich, creamy blanc de noirs and its flagship J. Schram wine, regarded as one of the best California champagnes. The wines are all very complex, thanks to the 67 different vineyards in four California counties from which Schramsberg sources its grapes. To taste them, however, you must sign up for one of the 1.25-hour appointment-only tours of the winery, which include a visit to the Victorian mansion, a trip into the spooky bottle-lined caves that date from the late 1800s, and a lesson on the art of champagne making, all culminating in a sit-down tasting. The price is on the high side, but the setting, the history, and the quality of the wines you taste make it worthwhile.

Even if you cannot book yourself on a tour, it's worth a quick detour from Highway 29 up the perilously narrow wooded road (with almost invisible speed bumps) just to see the mansion and ornate gardens. You can also buy any of the wines and look at the old photos in the sales room, which is open all day.

SIGHTS
Sharpsteen Museum

The quirky little **Sharpsteen Museum** (1311 Washington St., 707/942-5911, www.sharpsteenmuseum.org, 11am-4pm daily, $3 donation requested) was donated to Calistoga in the 1970s by its creators, Ben and Bernice Sharpsteen, and depicts up-valley life from the days of the Wappo people to the early 1900s. Its main claim to fame is a beautifully painted diorama depicting Calistoga in its hot springs heyday, but it also has some more traditional exhibits, many no doubt enhanced by the skills of Ben Sharpsteen, who was an Academy Award-winning animator.

Next door is one of the frilly little cottages built by Sam Brannan in the 1860s for his groundbreaking Hot Springs Resort in Calistoga. It was moved here in the 1970s, leaving only one of Brannan's cottages where it was built—at the Brannan Cottage Inn on Wappo Avenue.

Old Faithful Geyser

Anyone familiar with Calistoga's **Old Faithful Geyser** (1299 Tubbs Ln., 707/942-6463, www.oldfaithfulgeyser.com, 8:30am-7pm daily, adults $15, seniors $13, children 4-12 $9, under 4 free) may be pleased to hear that the popular 1960s era roadside attraction has had a makeover. Although it's a bit of a shame that the retro sign is gone, it is now a family-friendly destination with picnic tables, bocce ball, and an open prep area that offers utensils, wineglasses, and picnic blankets. For road-weary travelers with kids in tow, this may be the place to stop. Kids can play games, scamper around the gardens, feed the animals in the small petting zoo (even try their hand at making fainting goats faint), and be thrilled when the geyser suddenly erupts, shooting water 60 feet into the air. Meanwhile, their grown-ups get to enjoy their wine country goodies in peace. Be aware the geyser erupts usually every 30-40 minutes for 2-6 minutes depending on the season (the highest and longest eruptions occur June-July, as if to coincide with tourist season), so if you are anxious to see Old Faithful blow, check the website for the latest updates.

Old Faithful Geyser

Petrified Forest

A natural attraction that illustrates the area's volcanic past but with far more scenic value than Old Faithful (though no goats) is the **Petrified Forest** (4100 Petrified Forest Rd., 707/942-6667, www.petrifiedforest.org, 10am-7pm daily summer, 10am-5pm daily winter, spring and fall 10am-6pm, adults $12, seniors $11, juniors $8, children 6-11 $6, under 6 free), a couple of miles west of Calistoga on the road to Santa Rosa. Like Old Faithful Geyser down the hill, the experience feels very homespun with little in the way of glossy corporate tourist facilities. You also might start wondering what you paid for, because the short trails meander through what seem like recently fallen redwood trees. In fact, they were long ago turned to stone at such a microscopic level that they still look almost like real wood rather than the fossils they are. In the distance looms Mount St. Helena, believed to have been the source of the volcanic eruption that buried the trees millions of years ago and started the long petrification process. To learn more about it, join one of the 1.5-hour docent-led tours (11am, 1pm, and 3pm daily). Maps are also available for self-guided tours. You can also learn more about the forest by browsing the lovely little visitors center and gift shop. There are lots of rocks and minerals, earthy handcrafted gifts, books on geology, and a few rare shards of the petrified trees from this very forest.

Pioneer Cemetery

You'll find the graves of many of Napa's earliest nonnative settlers and some of the more prominent early pioneer families at the **Pioneer Cemetery** (Bothe-Napa Valley State Park, 3801 St. Helena Hwy. N., www.parks.

ca.gov, $8). The paths are kept clear and walkable, but many of the graves are overgrown with vines—some even have full-size oak trees growing through them—while others are old wooden planks, their lettering worn away. The whole area is covered by a dense canopy of forest foliage, making it a pleasantly cool place to visit on hot summer days. If you're interested in genealogy, start at the front entrance of the cemetery, where a map and an alphabetical survey of the cemetery are posted. One warning about visiting this cemetery: no, not ghosts, but a lack of parking. There's enough room at the front gate for one small car; otherwise, you have to park elsewhere and walk carefully along and across Highway 29 to the gate.

ENTERTAINMENT

For the sleepiest and most mellow town in the Napa Valley, Calistoga has some of the best nightlife. This is still Wine Country, however, so don't expect too much beyond live local bands and the ability to buy a beer after 11pm. The **Hydro Bar & Grill** (1403 Lincoln Ave., 707/942-9777, bar open until 11pm daily) hosts local live music on weekend nights, and the **Calistoga Inn Restaurant and Brewery** (1250 Lincoln Ave., 707/942-4101, www.calistogainn.com, 11am-9pm daily) offers live jazz or blues Friday through Sunday on the creek-side patio during the summer. **Lava Vine** (965 Silverado Trail, 707/942-9500, www.lavavine.com, 10am-5pm daily) is in the process of building its lounge to host local bands late into the evening. Should you want a true dive bar experience, **Susie's Bar** (1365 Lincoln Ave., 707/942-6710, http://susiescalistoga.com, noon-2am Mon.-Fri., 10am-2am Sat.-Sun.), with its cheap well drinks and domestic beer, will surely fit the bill.

SHOPPING

Like many things in Calistoga, shopping is a little more down-to-earth than elsewhere in the valley. Sure, there are plenty of gift shops, but there's a decidedly artisanal feel to most of them. **Calistoga Pottery** (1001 Foothill Blvd., 707/942-0216, http://calistogapottery. com, 9am-5pm Mon.-Sat., 11am-5pm Sun.) is one example in the sunny yellow cottage on Highway 29, just south of Lincoln Avenue. You'll find something original from local artists who have supplied some of the valley's biggest wineries and restaurants with their stoneware. Calistoga also has a string of secondhand and consignment stores, the quality of which is exceptional. For example, don't be surprised if you see a mink stole outside **Sugar Daddy's** (1333 Lincoln Ave., 707/942-1600, 10am-5pm Mon.-Fri., 10am-4pm Sun.). Inside there is everything from a $10 trash can to a $250 set of silver. You can also find fondue pots, bamboo cutting boards, used DVDs, a ton of hats, and great deals on women's clothing.

Not to be left out, **A Man's Supply** (1343 Lincoln Ave., 707/942-2280, www.amanssupply.com, 10am-6pm daily) satisfies the needs of the Y chromosome with plenty of work clothes, outdoor gear, watches, pocketknives, and boots. And everyone will find something to pique their interest at **Copperfields Books** (1330 Lincoln Ave., 707/942-1616, http://copperfieldsbooks.com, 10am-8pm daily) or pique their taste buds at **Calistoga Olive Oil Company** (1441 Lincoln Ave., 707/942-1329, http://calistogaoliveoilcompany.com, 9am-7pm daily), which not only produces its own label of local olive oil, but has a dizzying array of infused salts.

At the eastern end of Lincoln Avenue, poke around the historic **Calistoga Depot** (1458 Lincoln Ave.), the second-oldest remaining railroad depot in the country, built by Sam Brannan in 1868. It is now home to a handful of funky little stores, some of them in six old railroad cars parked on the tracks that lead to nowhere. **Calistoga Wine Stop** (707/942-5556, http://calistogawinestop.net, 10am-6pm daily) is in the main depot building and has a great selection of wines from both Napa and Sonoma. Most are from smaller producers (usually 3,000 cases or less) that are hard to find elsewhere. Each day a red and a white are available for tasting. Wine aficionados will also probably enjoy sniffing around the small **Enoteca Wine Shop** (1348 Lincoln Ave., 707/942-1117, http://enotecawineshop.com, 11:30am-5:30pm daily), which specializes in smaller (sometimes cult) producers of wines from California and beyond.

RECREATION
★ Calistoga Spas

During his stay in 1880, Robert Louis Stevenson observed that Calistoga "seems to repose on a mere film above a boiling, subterranean lake." That mineral-laden boiling water fueled the growth of one of the biggest spa destinations in California, thanks to Sam Brannan, who first recognized that there was gold to be made in Calistoga's mud (he also alerted the world to gold in the Sierra foothills in 1848), opening the first Hot Springs Resort in 1862. Since then, mud and mineral devotees continue to make their pilgrimages to Calistoga to indulge in its restorative and curative powers. Unlike the over-the-top luxury found at spas in other areas of Wine Country, Calistoga's soaking culture is, as it were, down-to-earth. You'll find no-nonsense spa treatments with minimal fuss.

The region's Wappo people were the first to discover the unlikely pleasure of soaking in the local mud (one wonders who first had the idea and why). These days the mud is usually a mixture of dark volcanic ash, peat (for buoyancy), and hot mineral water that suspends your body, relaxes muscles, and draws out impurities in the skin, all accompanied by a rather off-putting sulfurous smell. A 10- to 15-minute soak is usually followed by a rinse in crystal clear mineral water and a steam wrap with or without piped music. Aromatherapies, massages, and other hedonistic treatments can be added afterward but will quickly run up the price. Those worried about lying in someone else's impurities can take comfort from the claims that the mud is regularly flushed with fresh springwater. There is evidently such a thing as "clean" mud.

Wherever and whatever the treatment, remember that the heat can rapidly dehydrate your body, so lay off the wine beforehand and don't plan to hike to the top of Mount St. Helena afterward. Reservations are usually needed, but you might luck out just by walking in, especially midweek. Most spas are also open late, making them an ideal way to wrap up a long day of touring (pun intended).

On the site of Brannan's original resort is the **Indian Springs Resort** (1712 Lincoln Ave., 707/942-4913, www.indianspringscalistoga.com, 9am-9pm daily), which specializes in 100 percent volcanic mud bath treatments ($95), using the volcanic ash from its 16 acres of land, and mineral baths ($80). A slew of massages are also available, as are facials and body treatments such as the Chardonnay Scrub. Indian Springs has what is said to be California's oldest and largest continuously operating swimming pool, an Olympic-size version built in 1913 and fed by warm springwater. In fact, you can usually see the puffs of steam from the natural hot springs on-site. Spa customers can lounge by the pool as long as they want, but if it is too crowded, sneak away to the meditative Buddha Pond.

For an old-school Calistoga spa experience, head over to **Dr. Wilkinson's Hot Springs Resort** (1507 Lincoln Ave., 707/942-4102, www.drwilkinson.com, 8:30am-3:45pm daily, $89-184). The spa is part of the perfectly preserved mid-century compound rigorously dedicated to health and relaxation opened by "Doc" Wilkinson in 1952. Doc's proprietary blend of Calistoga mineral water and volcanic ash, Canadian peat, and lavender is still the gold standard for the Calistoga mud bath today. "The Works" includes the mud bath (complete with a soothing mud masque for your face), mineral bath, sauna, a blanket wrap, and a massage. Facials are also available. The men's and women's spa areas are separated, and the whole experience is refreshingly free of pretention. If you're a guest of the hotel, be sure to take a swim or a soak in one of the three mineral-water pools (there are two outdoor pools and one warm pool inside).

Another old-school option (though this time think 1980s teal and mauve Formica)

Dr. Wilkinson's Hot Springs Resort

antioxidant-laden wine mud containing wine, grape seed oil, and green tea. It also offers salt scrubs, with or without accompanying mud, and a full range of massages and facials. Rooms are private with a whirlpool tub and candlelight. For those wanting pool time, an appointment at Lincoln Avenue Spa comes with a day long pass at **Golden Haven** (1713 Lake St., 707/942-8000, www.goldenhaven. com). No jokes about spa treatments breaking the bank here—this spa is in an impregnable-looking stone building that was a Victorian-era bank.

EuroSpa (1202 Pine St., 707/942-4056, www.eurospa.com, 9am-6pm Mon.-Sat., 10am-5pm Sun., $95-220) may have a smaller pool area, but the charm and massages more than make up for it. Pick from one of the many massages (Thai Swedish or the signature Euro Stone Soother), or maybe a Chakra Reading and Balancing is in order. But whatever you decide, be sure to book some time in the Infrared Sauna ($15-60), where dry radiant heat draws out toxins and relaxes deep muscle tissues.

Treatments take on an urban chic at **Mount View Spa** (1457 Lincoln Ave., 707/942-1500, www.mountviewhotel.com, 8am-8pm daily) in the namesake hotel. Massages ($125-215), facials ($13-200), and mud baths ($70-90) are on the menu. You'll also find high-tech approaches to beauty like the oxygen bath and Coolsculpting, a noninvasive method of reducing body fat. Pile on a variety of different treatments with one of the spas packages, which culminate with a three-hour $400 extravaganza called the Mount View Deluxe package. The hotel's pool can also be used by spa customers.

For that glossy magazine spread spa experience, book a treatment at **Spa Solage** (755 Silverado Trail, 855/790-6023, www.solagecalistoga.com, 8am-8pm daily, $110-400). Inside the exclusive compound serenely dressed in white, a full menu of massage, facials, and scrubs aims to rejuvenate and beautify through a thoroughly personal experience. Aromatherapy, meditation, and lymphatic

is the **Calistoga Hot Springs Spa** (1006 Washington St., 707/942-6269, www.calistogaspa.com, 8:30am-4:30pm Tues.-Thurs., 8:30am-9pm Fri.-Mon., $57-165), where you can step into a mud bath ($65) or stay still for a deep tissue massage ($57-165). What sets Calistoga Hot Springs apart are its prices and four outdoor mineral pools. The lap pool is the coolest at 80°F and set up for serious swimmers. The 90°F wading pool with fountains offers fun health benefits for the whole family. Another large soaking pool is set to 100°F and meant primarily for adults. Finally, the enormous 104°F octagonal jetted spa sits under a gazebo—the perfect location to relax and enjoy the serenity of spa country.

The **Lincoln Avenue Spa** (1339 Lincoln Ave., 707/942-2950, www.lincolnavenuespa. com, 10am-6pm daily, $85-410) saves you from total immersion, instead applying the mud as you would a facial mask followed by a relaxing rest in a covered Ayurvedic steam table. There is a choice of six types of mud, including an Ayurvedic herbal mud and an drainage are also on the menu, as are private fitness sessions, men's only and couple's treatments, and complete body renewal packages. Guests have access to the mineral pools before and after treatment, or can top off their massage with a power nap in the spa's sound chair. It is not surprising with its range of options that combine both scientific and New Age approaches to beauty and health, plus its immaculate indoor/outdoor space, that Spa Solage has been named one of the world's best spas by *Condé Nast Traveler.*

Robert Louis Stevenson State Park

By far the best views in the valley, and perhaps the entire Wine Country, are from the top of Napa's highest peak, Mount St. Helena, which is near Calistoga in **Robert Louis Stevenson State Park** (Hwy. 29, 707/942-4575, www.parks.ca.gov, open sunrise-sunset daily, free) named for the mountain's most famous Victorian visitor.

Stevenson honeymooned in a cabin here after traveling from his native Scotland to marry Fanny Osbourne, the woman he met at an artists' retreat. The area had just been abandoned by silver miners following the rapid rise and fall of the **Silverado mine** in the 1870s, after which the Silverado Trail and Stevenson's account of his brief stay in the valley, *Silverado Squatters,* are named.

The happy couple's cabin is long gone, marked only by a small monument partway up the five-mile trail to the summit. Look out for two big dirt parking lots on either side of the road about eight miles north of Calistoga on Highway 29. The **Mount St. Helena Trail** starts from the western lot and has virtually no shade, together with some particularly steep sections—it climbs about 2,000 feet in five miles to the 4,339-foot summit of the mountain—so hiking it in the middle of a hot summer day is not recommended. On the clearest days, usually in spring, the 360-degree views stretch for nearly 200 miles, and sometimes you can even see San Francisco's skyline or Mount Shasta far to the north. In winter there is often a dusting of snow near the peak. Those not so determined to get to the summit can take a spur off the main trail at about the 3.5-mile point to the 4,000-foot South Peak, which has impressive views of the valley.

East from the parking lot is the start of the **Table Rock Trail,** a shorter and less strenuous 2.2-mile trail that climbs out of the woodland and past volcanic rock outcroppings to a ridge overlooking the flat moonscape known as Table Rock and the entire valley to the south. The more adventurous can connect to the **Palisades Trail,** which crosses Table Rock and eventually meets the historic Oat Hill Mine Road leading down into the valley, though that turns the hike into a daylong expedition and ends miles from the parking lot.

Hiking

If you want to stretch your legs, the 8.25-mile **Oat Hill Mine Trail** departs from a trailhead (street parking only) at the intersection of Highway 29 and the Silverado Trail. It winds up 2,000 feet above the valley through volcanic formations, groves of Douglas fir, gray pine, and cypress as well as chaparral and grassland, which is known to yield an exceptional bounty of wildflowers. The trail was constructed in 1893 for access to nearby quicksilver mines. You can still see the ruts carved by heavy wagons in the soft volcanic rock. Midway, there are ruins of the Holmes homestead settled in 1893. You'll see many locals on the trail, and it crosses parkland as well as private property. Unfortunately, there is no loop, but the views and backcountry setting are worth the up and back trek. The trail is open to hikers, mountain bikers, horseback riders, and unleashed (but still within voice command) dogs. For information about trail conditions check www.napaoutdoors.org.

Golf

Like elsewhere in the valley, there is plenty to lure visitors out of the tasting room. The Napa County Fairgrounds in the heart of Calistoga has its own nine-hole golf course. The **Mt.**

St. Helena Golf Course (2025 Grant St., 707/942-9966, www.mtsthelenagolfcourse. org, 7am-dusk daily; $12-20 Mon.-Fri., $14-26 Sat.-Sun.) is charming and inexpensive—perfect for any player. For those younger or less experienced, it is flat and straight, with easier lines than some other courses, while intermediate-level players will appreciate the challenge of the trees along the fairways.

FOOD

Calistoga is often overlooked in the valley's food scene, eclipsed by the culinary destinations of Yountville and St. Helena. High-end restaurants have struggled to survive here, as illustrated by the seemingly endless stream of restaurants that have tried, and failed, to make money in the town's fancy Mount View Hotel. Still, Calistoga continues to have great food at good prices, perhaps just a little more casual than its Napa Valley neighbors.

California Cuisine

In Calistoga, even Michelin-starred dining is casual and relaxed. **Solbar** (755 Silverado Trail, 707/226-0850, breakfast 7am-11:30am and lunch 11:45am-2:30pm daily, dinner 5:30pm-9pm Sun.-Thurs., 5:30pm-9:30pm Fri.-Sat., $26-38), part of the Solage Calistoga resort, has garnered the coveted star every year since 2009 for its sleek indoor/outdoor dining room, friendly yet impeccable service, and, of course, for its inventive and classic farm-to-table fare. You'll find veal sweetbreads, foie gras, crab, and an amazing peach salad. If the business casual vibe is not casual enough, you can order off the lounge menu with its oysters, hand-tossed pizzas, and legendary fish tacos ($14-21), and even kids are honored with their own fairly large menu ($6-13). The wine list is comprehensive with abundant selections from local vintners. Some wines are on tap and offered by the glass ($10-13) or carafe ($40-45). Flights of three wines are also available, as are retro-fresh cocktails, beer, and hard cider.

Walking past the ★ **Calistoga Inn Restaurant and Brewery** (1250 Lincoln Ave., 707/942-4101, www.calistogainn.com, 11am-9pm daily, $15-38) on a cool dark winter evening, it's tempting to go into the restaurant just for the cozy rustic atmosphere exuding through its Victorian windows. During the warmer months the draw is the creek-side patio, but nonetheless, all year the food is equally good international bistro-style fare. The menu is a perfect fit for pints of **Napa Valley Brewing Company** beer, made in the old water tower in the back of the property. Founded in 1989, it is said to be the first brewery established in the valley since Prohibition. The inn also usually has some sort of evening entertainment, from open-mike nights to jazz.

A block down is **Brannan's Grill** (1374 Lincoln Ave., 707/942-2233, lunch 11:30am-4pm daily, dinner 5pm-9pm Mon.-Thurs., 5pm-9:30pm Fri.-Sun., happy hour 3pm-6pm, $27-35). White tablecloths, dark wood bar, and the giant murals of the valley's past lend an air of elegance to accompany the pricey all-American menu, which usually includes two or three steaks. The wine list offers a smattering of choices from Oregon, Europe, and Australia alongside Napa and Sonoma regulars. The emphasis is on the high-end, but offset by the $15 burger and side of mac and cheese. Desserts are particularly good, especially the crème brûlée, if it happens to be on the menu that night.

Locals love the leafy patio and classic California cuisine of **Calistoga Kitchen** (1107 Cedar St., 707/942-6500, www.calistogakitchen.com, lunch 11:30am-3pm Fri.-Sat, dinner 5:30pm-9pm Thurs.-Sat., brunch 9:30am-3pm Sun., $20-30). The ingredients-driven menu, while slight, succeeds because everything on it is executed perfectly; you may never taste a more tender steak or a more delicate (and generously portioned) ahi. Even the salads, with toppings of duck and Cornish game hen, can stand alone as entrées. The wine selection is relatively short but carefully selected, with glasses available for under $8. Lunch and brunch are a great bargain, and all (dogs, kids, and philistines) are welcome, an attitude not always found in the valley.

Calistoga's newest hot spot is ★ **Sam's Social Club** (1712 Lincoln Ave., 707/942-4913, http://samssocialclub.com, breakfast 8am-10:30am Mon.-Fri., lunch 11:30am-2:30pm Mon.-Fri., dinner 5:30pm-9pm Mon.-Wed., 5:30pm-9:30pm Thurs.-Sun., snacks 2:30pm-5:30pm daily, brunch 8am-2:30pm Sat.-Sun., $17-38), adjacent to Indian Springs Resort. There is good reason for this—Sam's is the whole package: great outside seating with covered tables and open fire pits beneath an oak canopy; interior done up in a stylized remembrance of 1970s diners; and fresh, flavorful food that crosses over from comfort to farm-to-fork California cuisine. Should you arrive between lunch and dinner, Sam's offers a light snack menu that includes deviled eggs, bacon-wrapped dates, and ricotta crostini. The wine list is an excellent cross section of Napa and Sonoma wines, and their cocktail menu stands out even in this era of high-caliber mixology. The beer menu is smaller, though carefully crafted, and includes three or four house-made seasonal brews.

American

You can't miss the boxy brick **Hydro Bar & Grill** (1403 Lincoln Ave., 707/942-9777, 8:30am-10pm Mon.-Wed., noon-11pm Thurs., 8:30am-11pm Fri.-Sat., $10-18), with its neon lights, central location, and booming music. This is the place to get your standard American favorites, a live music fix, or to be in a restaurant that's louder than your kids. Burgers, mac and cheese, salads, pork loin, and *steak frites* are on the menu, but the bar is the draw. In addition to countless cocktail concoctions, there are plenty of microbrews, plus a full page (in small type) of wines, nearly all from the Napa Valley. It stays open well after most other restaurants have closed, which is good because the service can often be unbearably slow.

Asian

Sometimes nothing goes better with cucumber spa water and detoxing volcanic mud than Asian food. Locals line up for their take-out orders at the pan-Asian **Tanit** (1350 Lincoln Ave., www.tanitpanasian.com, 11:30am-3pm and 5pm-9pm Wed.-Mon., $15). You'll find spring rolls, coconut soups, curries, kimchi fried rice, and noodle bowls at this minimal-frills eatery.

For lunch try **Sushi Mambo** (1631 Lincoln Ave., 707/942-4622, 11:30am-9pm Mon.-Thurs., 11:30am-9:30pm Fri., noon-9:30pm Sat., noon-9pm Sun., $15). Unlike at Tanit,

dining alfresco at Sam's Social Club

the menu here is expansive with tiny type, which amounts to a variety of small sushi bites. There are teriyaki, katsu, and tempura mains, and the rolls (scores of them) are fresh and inventive. Real crab California rolls are available, but you have to ask for them.

Barbecue

You'll know you've left behind the fussiness of St. Helena when you reach Calistoga's first intersection at Lincoln Avenue and see the Harleys lined up outside of **Buster's Barbecue and Bakery** (1207 Foothill Blvd., 707/942-5605, 707/942-5606, www.busters-southernbbq.com, 10am-8pm Mon.-Sat., 10am-7pm Sun., $12). Opened in 1961, this walk-up eatery serves mostly locals looking for a quick bite to bring home. While the portions aren't huge, and prices are a bit high compared to other barbecue joints, the tri-tip sandwiches and barbecued chicken, pork, and ribs are often worth the trip and outshine the sides. The sweet-potato pie is a reputed local favorite, and for those eager to sit down with the food and a pile of napkins, there is a low-key dining area.

Italian

Bosko's Trattoria (1364 Lincoln Ave., 707/942-9088, www.boskos.com, 11:30am-9:30pm Sun.-Thurs., 11:30am-10pm Fri.-Sat., $17-20) is a Calistoga institution with a reputation for its Italian comfort food as solid as the stone building it calls home. The simple salads, handmade pastas, and wood-fired pizzas are served in the homey surroundings, as well as a good selection of delicious, well-stuffed panini sandwiches and kid-friendly options.

Mexican

Wondering where Calistogans stop to snag dinner after softball practice? **Puerto Vallarta** (1473 Lincoln Ave., 707/942-6563, 10:30am-8pm daily, $8-12), down a skinny alley next to the Cal Mart. Standing in line, you'll see on-duty police officers, moms with kids in tow, and workers just coming off long days in the vineyards here to pick up fat burritos, steaming plates of fajitas, or one of its traditional seafood dishes. And this is not just because it is affordable and convenient; it is very good. The one drawback is the lack of ambience, but if you dine in, opt for the outdoor seating beneath the leafy grape arbor and chase down your hearty Mexican dinner with a beer or two.

To replace that beer with a margarita, **Pacifico Mexican Restaurant** (1237 Lincoln Ave., 707/942-4400, 11am-9:30pm Mon.-Thurs., 11am-10pm Fri., 10am-10pm Sat., 10am-9:30pm Sun., $10-20) on the corner of Lincoln and Cedar Street is just the place. The food may not have that hole-in-the-wall authenticity to it, but it makes up for it in atmosphere, particularly outside at the sidewalk tables lining Cedar.

Breakfast and Brunch

The beauty of Calistoga is how well the locals rub shoulders with the tourists. Just take a booth at the ★ **Café Sarafornia** (1413 Lincoln Ave., 707/942-0555, http://cafesarafornia.com, 7am-2:30pm daily, $9-18) and see. Farmers and tradespeople of all sorts sidle up next to out-of-towners for a down-home breakfast and bottomless cups of coffee. The huevos rancheros stand up to their claim of being "the best," and the Brannon Benedict is a one-of-a-kind take on a brunch staple. It is quite possible that breakfast here may be your most expensive meal of the day in the otherwise quite affordable Calistoga. Still, it is worth it: Café Sarafornia has been a Calistoga institution for over 120 years, and the hearty breakfast will stick to your ribs all day.

If you're just looking for a quick cup of coffee and a pastry, head around the corner to **Yo El Rey Roasting** (1217 Washington St., 707/321-7901, www.yoelreyroasting.com, 6:30am-5pm daily). Here coffee is taken as seriously as wine. Roasted in small batches, the coffee, whether you order an espresso or just stick to drip, is velvety and rich while the service is warm and friendly. For a cool afternoon pick-me-up after several stops along the wine trail, pick up a bottle of 16-hour cold-brewed coffee. Rotating art shows and the random open-mike night add to collegiate vibe.

Delis

The ultracasual **Palisades Deli Café** (1458 Lincoln Ave., 707/942-0145, https://palisadesdelicafe.com, 7am-6pm daily, $8-12) occupies the bottom floor of the Calistoga Depot's yellow station house. This counter-service deli has a huge selection of hot and cold sandwiches, burritos, tacos, salads, and wraps; all are flavorful, good size, and tasty without feeling like a calorie bomb. The Reuben sandwich (known here as the Geyser) may rival any other made in the valley. Espresso drinks are also available, as is a small but nice outside patio.

Picnic Supplies

A great stop is the **Palisades Deli Café** (1458 Lincoln Ave., 707/942-0145, https://palisadesdelicafe.com, 707/942-0145, 7am-6pm daily). In addition to coffee and other café staples, it sells a range of deli meats and cheeses, chips, and cold drinks. You can also get any one of their freshly made sandwiches or wraps to go. If the line is too long, walk across the street to the **Cal Mart** supermarket (1491 Lincoln Ave., 707/942-6271, 7am-9pm daily), which sells even cheaper deli sandwiches (although not as good), a wide selection of cheese, and local wine.

Farmers Markets

The **Calistoga Farmers Market** (http://calistogafarmersmarket.org) is held 8:30am-noon on Saturday year-round at the Sharpsteen Museum Plaza at 1311 Washington Street. It sells crafts, cut flowers, oils and vinegars, crepes, to-go lunches, and fresh seafood as well as produce. A kids craft table makes this a great stop for families.

ACCOMMODATIONS

Calistoga is one of the cheapest places in the valley for most purchases, from food and gas

to a place to stay. This is still Wine Country, however, so "cheap" is a relative term, and prices have risen faster than the valley average in the past few years. Calistoga might finally be cashing in on its charms.

Some of the Victorian B&Bs strung along Highway 29 and Foothill Boulevard seem downright reasonable during the week, but rates can almost double on summer weekends (and let's not forget those two- or three-night minimums!), much like everywhere else in the valley. The best bargains are probably the numerous spa resorts, which offer slightly less elegant motel-style rooms for slightly more reasonable prices. As always, book plenty of time in advance July-October.

Under $150

The ★ **Calistoga Inn** (1250 Lincoln Ave., 707/942-4101, www.calistogainn.com, $129-169) has been in continuous operation for over 100 years, and offers an old-school hotel experience, complete with small charming rooms and shared bathrooms, all perched above a pub that serves lunch and dinner. Be sure to make reservations in advance—at these prices, rooms go quickly, especially in summer and fall! And be aware that the pub downstairs has live music acts four nights a week, so the party can get loud (and fun!) on weekends.

$150-250

Like most of the accommodations in Calistoga, **Golden Haven Hot Springs** (1713 Lake St., 707/942-8000, www.goldenhaven.com, $150-275) began its life as a 1950s motel. Most of the accommodations line the main drive, each with parking right outside the door. Inside, the rooms are clean and quite spacious with lofted ceilings, king beds, widescreen TVs, and roomy bathrooms. Each has a smaller second bedroom with queen bed (the low-slung ceiling hints to its life as a carport during the motel's Eisenhower era). There are three pools (one hot, one warm, and one large cold), a lovely picnic area with bocce ball courts, and an old farm building with

Napa Valley Hotel Bargains

Napa Valley can be a very expensive place to stay, particularly July-October. Still, a few old-school valley hotels remain low on cost and high on charm. Calistoga has the greatest concentration of these, but there are a couple of hidden gems in Yountville and St. Helena as well.

- **Petit Logis Inn, Yountville:** This charming five-room inn may not serve breakfast, but its prices are low enough to ensure that you can afford a great meal or two in the Michelin-studded town.

- **El Bonita Motel, St. Helena:** Each of the rooms in this 1940s-era motel has a refrigerator, coffeemaker, and microwave oven, as well as access to the small pool and hot tub. Spend a little more to get a room with a kitchenette and save on eating out.

- **Bothe-Napa Valley State Park, St. Helena:** A tent is by far the cheapest accommodation in Napa, and thankfully this state park is a beautiful place to pitch one. You can also opt for a yurt or a six-person cabin. Either way, you'll get to enjoy the complimentary pool and hiking trails.

- **Calistoga Inn, Calistoga:** Despite upgrades and new furnishings, little has changed over the 100 years that this Calistoga institution has been in operation. Bathrooms are still down the hall, there is a pub downstairs, and rates are unbelievably low.

- **Golden Haven Hot Springs, Calistoga:** This former motor lodge has spacious rooms, a funky pool area, a back lawn, and bikes for guests' use. In addition to the already low rates, keep an eye out for their online deals.

- **Hideaway Cottages, Calistoga:** At first glance, these 1940s-era bungalows might not seem to be the cheapest rates in Calistoga, but each sleeps four comfortably, has a full kitchen, and comes with a gourmet breakfast basket every morning. The privacy and the pools add to the value.

a small rec room and complimentary coffee and packaged pastries and granola bars in the morning. Golden Haven also runs a small **spa** ($75-265). Mud and a variety of massage and one-hour-long facials are available.

The Sunburst Calistoga (1880 Lincoln Ave., 707/942-0991, www.thesunburstcalistoga.com, $160-270) adds some splashy colors to its motel kitsch. Stylish bursts of orange, black, and lime green accent the white walls and furnishings in each of the 50 cozy rooms. All are pet-friendly with mini-fridges, tiled showers, flat-screen TVs, coffeemakers, and free wireless Internet. You'll find three mineral pools and one large hot tub. The vibe at The Sunburst is low-key economy style as only Calistoga can do.

For mid-century charm par excellence stay at ★ **Dr. Wilkinson's Hot Springs Resort** (1507 Lincoln Ave., 707/942-4102, www.

drwilkinson.com, $180-285). Everything in the 1950s resort has been meticulously maintained and feels as though it is still in the time of Sputnik. There are multiple accommodations available, from the motel's main rooms to bungalows with kitchens to rooms in the adjacent restored Victorian. All guests are welcome to use the pools and patio area, including the indoor hot mineral pool with its Eichler-esque touches. In addition to the complimentary bathrobes, all rooms have coffeemakers, cable TV, refrigerators, and hypoallergenic bedding. Dr. Wilkinson's even has bathing suits on loan if you forget yours.

Equally old-school (and also owned by Dr. Wilkinson's), **Hideaway Cottages** (1412 Fair Way, 707/942-4108, www.hideawaycottages.com, $180-350) is made up of 1940s-era bungalows that retain their original details. Most have sitting rooms, full kitchens, and outside sitting areas. All face the communal leafy grounds, where lawns offer plenty of spots to lounge around the outdoor mineral pool and hot tub. In the interest of quiet, no pets or children under 18 are allowed. The property has been added onto over the years and also includes the main house built in 1877, where guests pick up their complimentary "tote" breakfast, filled with fruit and pastries.

Another inexpensive option is the **EuroSpa and Inn** (1202 Pine St., 707/942-6829, www. eurospa.com, $180-225), a motel-style establishment on a peaceful residential street just a block from Lincoln Avenue. Rooms are arranged around a central parking lot and are tastefully furnished with a long list of standard features including whirlpool tubs, air-conditioning, gas fireplaces, Internet access, and refrigerators. Because it's on the edge of town, the inn's pool looks onto vineyards and is where the continental breakfast is usually served in summer.

If you're able to get a reservation for one of the four rooms at the **Hotel d'Amici** (1436 Lincoln Ave., 707/942-1007, www.hoteldamici. com, $215-305), consider yourself lucky. The charming hotel in the center of downtown offers spacious and comfortable junior suites in the heart of Calistoga for very reasonable rates, which makes it very popular. The two smaller suites at the back of the hotel are the cheapest, while the larger suites at the front of the building have fireplaces and share a balcony looking over Lincoln Avenue. All the rooms are decorated in a simple, clean style and offer private bathrooms with soaking tubs, down comforters, cable television, and a bottle of Rutherford Grove wine (the Pestoni family owns both the winery and the hotel). A continental breakfast appears as if by magic outside the door every morning, but the lack of on-site staff can make late-night arrivals challenging. Be sure to keep the confirmation letter for the code to get into the hotel.

Hats off to the owners of **The Pink Mansion** (1415 Foothill Blvd., 707/942-0558 or 800/238-7465, www.pinkmansion.com,

$195-395) for not even attempting to come up with a clever name for their bright pink Victorian, which dates from 1875. The honest name is matched by some unique features— like the small heated pool in what looks like a Victorian parlor. The woodsy surroundings, quaint but not overly frilly furnishings, and features like claw-foot tubs and air-conditioning make this one of the pricier establishments along this stretch of road, however. The smallest rooms have no shortage of charm, but the gargantuan and luxurious Master Suite, dripping with period features and exotic woods, includes a wood-burning fireplace, marble bath for two, and a separate sitting room and deck.

Over $250

You could say that it all began at **Indian Springs Resort** (1712 Lincoln Ave., 707/942-4913, www.indianspringscalistoga.com, $250-500), where Sam Brannan first set up his Victorian-era mineral spring resort. Today, it is pricey to stay at the birthplace of Calistoga's soaking culture, but for many the pools and style make it worth it. The compound has a variety of accommodations. You can pick from rooms in the main lodge or those in smaller micro lodges scattered around the property. For a bit more you can stay in the 1940s-era cottages, for which the resort is best known. Surrounding the palm-lined driveway, these cozy one- and two-bedroom duplexes are probably the best bargains with their separate sitting area with a sofa bed. Ask for number 16 or 17—they back onto open fields for some extra isolation.

You can stay at one of Brannan's original cottages at the **Brannan Cottage Inn** (109 Wappo Ave., 707/942-4200, www.brannancottageinn.com, $300-350). The Victorian cottage with its white picket fence is the only cottage from Sam Brannan's original Calistoga resort that still stands where it was built, on a quiet street just off Calistoga's main drag. It is now on the National Register of Historic Places and has been recently revamped to retain its original Victorian charm but with a modern sensibility. The six cozy rooms are appointed with espresso makers, mini-fridges, plush bathrobes, views of the pretty gardens, and private entrances from the wraparound porch.

As its name suggests, the **Cottage Grove Inn** (1711 Lincoln Ave., 707/942-8400 or 800/799-2284, www.cottagegrove.com, $300-425) is actually 16 private cottages strung along a small road under a pretty grove of old elm trees on the edge of Calistoga. The cottages were built in 1996 and offer some modernity along a strip dominated by older motels. Despite their individual names, all 16 are furnished in a similar Mediterranean style with vaulted ceilings, beautiful antique wood floors, and a long list of luxury features, including double Jacuzzi tubs, CD and DVD players, and front porches on which to sit, sip, and watch the world go by.

One of the biggest old buildings in downtown Calistoga (though that's not saying much) is home to the **Mount View Hotel** (1457 Lincoln Ave., 707/942-6877, www.mountviewhotel.com, $249-450), which brings a bit of urban style within walking distance of almost everything Calistoga has to offer. The cheapest queen and king rooms can be a bit on the small side, but all 29 rooms and suites have a slightly eclectic mix of modern furnishings with Victorian antique and art deco touches that harken back to the hotel's 1920s and 1930s heyday. The list of standard features includes the in-room espresso machine, and all have access to the hotel's mineral pool and hot tub. Best of all are the three separate cottages, each with its own small outdoor redwood deck and hot tub.

Nothing caps a day of wine-tasting in the hot Napa Valley better than a soothing dip in the mineral pool at **Solage Calistoga** (755 Silverado Trail, 707/266-7531 or 866/942-7442, www.solagecalistoga.com, $500). This compound of cottages and duplexes offers several places to soak and swim, plus a high-end spa and Michelin-starred dining. Winding paths and prim gardens give the resort a quiet and private atmosphere, despite its 83 rooms, and the sleek style and abundant technology in each room appeal to the young, urban, and moneyed set. In true Calistoga form, there is an ode to health with a full schedule of complimentary fitness, yoga, and meditation classes; a scrumptious room service menu complete with antioxidant breakfast smoothies (but watch out for the $9 lattes!); and a slew of beautifying, rejuvenating, and indulgent spa treatments. Cruiser bikes parked outside each room shorten the trek to Pilates and the pool, and though they're not touring quality, they'll certainly get you into downtown Calistoga, a half mile away, and maybe to a few nearby wineries.

INFORMATION AND SERVICES

The spacious **Calistoga Visitors Center** (1133 Washington St., 707/942-6333, http://visitcalistoga.com, 9am-5pm daily) in the heart of downtown has two walls where local wineries, restaurants, hotels, and spas leave brochures and discount passes for wineries, spa treatments, and restaurant meals. You'll even be able to grab the *Weekly Calistogan* for a dose of local news and up-and-coming events.

Bank of the West has a branch at 1317 Lincoln Avenue, and you can find a **Bank of America** ATM at 1429 Lincoln Avenue. A block away, **Ole Health** (911 Washington St., 707/709-2308, www.olehealth.org, 8:30am-5:30pm Mon.-Tues. and Thurs., 3pm-7pm Wed., 8:30am-12:30pm Fri.) treats nonemergency health concerns. For something more serious, the **St. Helena Hospital** (10 Woodland Rd., 707/963-6425, http://sthelenanowaiter.org) has a 24-hour emergency room.

GETTING THERE AND AROUND

Calistoga is eight miles north of St. Helena on Highway 29. Highway 128 also runs through Calistoga, connecting it to U.S. 101 north near Geyserville. From Santa Rosa, take exit 494 off U.S. 101, labeled "River Rd/Guerneville." Turn onto Mark West Springs Road and continue up the mountain. The road will miraculously change its name to Porter Creek Road in the process. Eventually, you'll come to a T intersection with Petrified Forest Road. Turn left and travel a few miles until you reach Highway 128. You can also connect to Porter Creek Road from the Highway 12 east exit off U.S. 101. A left on Farmers Lane, then a right on Sonoma Highway will take you to Calistoga Road, onto which you turn left. After 7.1 miles, Calistoga Road intersects with Porter Creek Road.

You can reach Calistoga by bus on the VINE (www.ridethevine.com, $1.60) on Route 10, which makes daily runs up the valley from Napa. On the weekdays, you can jump onboard the Route 29 Express from the El Cerrito BART and the Vallejo Ferry Terminal; the trip takes a little over two hours.

In Calistoga, catch the **Calistoga Shuttle** (707/963-4229), the VINE's on-demand shuttle service. All you have to do is call. Service extends from Dunweal Lane in the south to Tubbs Lane in the north and the St. Helena Highway and Silverado Trail to the west and east. Wait time is roughly 15-20 minutes.

As elsewhere in the valley, biking in Calistoga is a fun and scenic alternative to sitting in congested traffic. **Calistoga Bike Shop** (1318 Lincoln Ave., 707/942-9687, http://calistogabikeshop.com, 10am-6pm daily, $28 for two hours or $42-90 per day) offers guided tours, self-guided tours, and bike rentals. Hybrids run $39 per day; road bikes, $60 per day; and mountain bikes, $120 per day. For $110 you can opt for their self-guided "Calistoga Cool Wine Tour," with which the bike shop will book your tastings, pay the fees, pick up any wine you buy, and provide any roadside assistance you may need. Many hotels in the area also offer loaner bikes that are decent enough on which to navigate through town and visit some nearby wineries.

Southern Sonoma

Look for ★ to find recommended
sights, activities, dining, and lodging.

Highlights

★ **Gundlach Bundschu Winery:** Witness Shakespeare or Mozart performed on a summer day at this historic winery's outdoor amphitheater (page 138).

★ **Sonoma Plaza:** Spend an afternoon exploring the eclectic shops, tasting local boutique wine, and touring the historic sites (page 141).

★ **Mission San Francisco Solano:** The last established California mission has been immaculately restored. Its museum sheds light on the important role it played in the region's history (page 142).

★ **Benziger Family Winery:** See Benziger's biodynamic vineyards from a tractor-drawn tram, the most entertaining tour in the valley (page 159).

★ **Jack London State Historic Park:** Scenic hiking trails surround the former residence of the valley's prolific author and adventurer (page 161).

★ **Chateau St. Jean:** Enjoy the reserve tasting while relaxing on the patio overlooking the valley (page 166).

★ **Sugarloaf Ridge State Park:** Meander down the short nature trail or hike to the top of Bald Mountain for the best valley views (page 170).

★ **Cline Cellars:** Enter an oasis of green at this historic winery next to a natural spring. You can also explore all of California's missions in miniature (page 176).

★ **Domaine Carneros:** Take a private tour and learn how champagne is made, all with a glass of bubbly in hand (page 182).

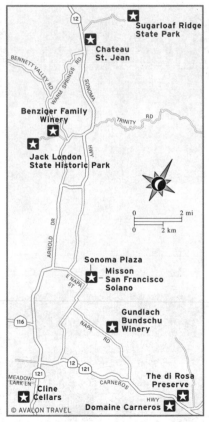

★ **The di Rosa Preserve:** Enter a wonderland of art and leave the Wine Country behind (page 184).

Southern Sonoma, made up of the Sonoma Valley and neighboring Carneros, is just so laid-back and slow-going that even finding parking is unnervingly easy.

Apparently it has always been a pretty good, stress-free life in these parts. Mother Nature might mix things up a bit with the occasional fire or earthquake, but she also provides hot springs, redwood forests, burbling streams, fertile soils, and a friendly climate. In terms of climate, scenery, and growing conditions, the Sonoma Valley is a mini Napa Valley, but it has been spared the same level of development by some favorable rolls of the historical dice.

In a sense, southern Sonoma is fairly close to paradise: a place where wine, history, scenery, and some of the best California produce combine in an area small enough to tour in a day or two. A visitor can spend the morning sipping splendid wine and be strolling through historic Victorian splendor by the afternoon, or might traverse a muddy mountain one hour and spend the next relaxing in a spa covered in therapeutic mud. There are few other parts of the Wine County as compact yet packed with opportunity.

Hundreds of years ago, these same natural attributes attracted numerous Native American tribes, who lived peacefully side by side without the turf battles common elsewhere. Even author Jack London sensed something intoxicating in the air. He relocated from Oakland to put down deep roots in the Sonoma Valley, transforming himself from working-class hero to gentleman farmer and landowner. The main characters in his 1913 novel *Valley of the Moon* spend months wandering up and down California in search of their nirvana, the Sonoma Valley.

The lucky locals have worked hard against the odds to keep their valley and flatlands so inviting. In the 1960s, they fought off a plan developed by car-crazed California to run a freeway down the middle of Sonoma Valley. Instead it was built through the middle of Santa Rosa to the west. While fame and freeways brought the heaving masses to Napa and northern Sonoma, the valley became the land that development forgot.

By 1980 there was a grand total of two sets

Previous: vineyards in Carneros; Gundlach Bundschu Winery. **Above:** a bike trail in southern Sonoma.

of traffic lights—and there aren't many more now. One of the busiest intersections in the valley, on the south side of Sonoma Plaza, is still very politely controlled by four simple stop signs. The valley's modern custodians are still a potent force, as is the passion here to keep the "slow" in this place the locals call Slownoma.

Can the valley keep its identity amid modern population and development pressures? It's trying hard, but it's hard to swim against the tide of tourism. Wineries and hotels are being mopped up by bigger and bigger conglomerates. The local food is transforming into ever more expensive "cuisine." An average family home in the valley now costs more than $1.5 million. Visit quickly before Napa hops over the mountains, pushes up the prices, and ends the mellow fun.

In the long term, there's more hope for Carneros, simply because there is no "there" there. The vineyards that are slowly covering any remaining pastureland (that is, the land that's not already underwater) are effectively spiking future development. Chances are that nothing much will change here anytime soon—except perhaps that rush-hour traffic on the two-lane roads may worsen as more people visit or move to the Napa and Sonoma Valleys.

TOURS

To take a tour powered by something besides your own two feet, jump aboard the **Sonoma Valley Wine Trolley** (707/938-2600, www.sonomavalleywinetrolley.com, 10:30am-4:30pm, $99). Departing from the Sonoma Plaza daily at 10:30am, the trolley (actually a four-wheeled replica of a San Francisco cable car) visits four wineries (tasting fees not included), where guests enjoy private tastings and the occasional tour. Along the way the driver points out sites of historical interest and, around noon, lays out a gourmet picnic lunch supplied by **the girl & the fig** (110 W. Spain St., Sonoma, 707/938-3000, www.thegirland-thefig.com, 11:30am-10pm Mon.-Thurs.,

11am-11pm Fri.-Sat., 10am-10pm Sun., $19-28).

You can also tour the wineries via Segway, albeit a little less leisurely and gracefully. **Sonoma Segway** (707/938-2080, www.sonomasegway.com, $129/tour, $40/hour rental), an offshoot of the Goodtime Touring Company, offers a 4.5-hour tour that includes a visit to a couple local wineries, a stop at a local food-based business, and a full-fledged visit to historic Sonoma.

PLANNING YOUR TIME

The Sonoma Valley and Carneros are two of the easiest parts of Wine Country to visit, each having just one main road running its entire length. A visit to Carneros can be slightly harder to plan due to the lack of major towns, but it's easy enough to stop there for a few hours on the way to or from Sonoma and Napa.

Within the 17-mile-long Sonoma Valley, the wineries, shops, and hotels are generally centered around the towns of **Glen Ellen** and neighboring **Kenwood,** and Sonoma itself. Without a well-planned strategy, it can be time-consuming to try to visit wineries at both the northern and southern ends of the valley, especially when the Sonoma Highway (Hwy. 12) slows down with northbound rush-hour traffic in the afternoon.

If you do find yourself traveling slower than you like on Highway 12, it's worth heading a few miles west at Glen Ellen or Boyes Hot Springs to pick up Arnold Drive, an alternative north-south route in the valley. It runs mainly through residential areas, but sticking to the 30 mph speed limit on this quiet road might be more relaxing than being tailgated on Highway 12. It runs right down to the junction with Highway 121 in **Carneros.**

It can easily take a full day to visit three wineries around Sonoma and Kenwood, or in Carneros, and still have enough time for lunch without getting indigestion. This means it's a good idea to carefully pick the wineries you want to visit based on the wine in which they specialize, any historical significance, or for beautiful grounds and gardens. An alternative strategy is to spend a full day exploring the shops and historic sights of Sonoma while tasting wine at several dedicated tasting rooms on the Sonoma Plaza. With over 20 tasting rooms surrounding the square, you'll have plenty to pick from. If you do plan to visit wineries throughout the valley, get an early start. Their busiest times are mid-late afternoon, especially for the wineries around Kenwood, which most visitors only get to toward the end of the day. Most wineries open at 10am (a few at 11am) and close between 4:30pm and 6pm, depending on the season. Wineries along the Carneros Highway (Hwy. 121) are generally clustered at the eastern and western ends of Carneros, with fairly great distances in between. To hunt for those far off the highway, it is helpful to have a map close at hand.

Both Carneros and the Sonoma Valley have a dearth of any sizable trees, particularly in winery parking lots. Consequently there's usually no shade, and for the nine months of the year that the sun shines, parked cars quickly heat up to the temperature of an oven. Take a cooler if you plan a picnic or want to prevent that $100 bottle of wine from trying to become vinegar.

Compared to the Napa Valley, wine-tasting in the Sonoma Valley is less expensive, but this is changing. For years, you could expect free or a modest tasting fee of $5. The average price for a flight is creeping up toward $20, just as Napa's is nearing $30. As in many other parts of the Wine Country, the tasting fee can sometimes be recouped when you buy one or more bottles of wine. Another way to curb expenses is to stop in at the **Sonoma Valley Visitors Bureau** (453 1st St. E., Sonoma, 707/996-1090 or 866/996-1090, www.sonomavalley.com, 9am-5pm Mon.-Sat., 10am-5pm Sun.) and pick up free passes or "2 for 1" tasting specials dropped off by many nearby wineries.

GETTING THERE

A century ago there were more ways to get to Sonoma than there are today—by ferry, train, stagecoach, automobile, or plane. The train is long gone, ferries come nowhere near, the tiny local airports have no scheduled services, and there is no direct bus service to Sonoma, just some local connections to Santa Rosa and Petaluma—all of which leaves the car with a monopoly.

Getting there by car, however, is straightforward. From San Francisco the most traveled route is via **U.S. 101, Highway 37,** and **Highway 121,** which leads to the heart of Carneros and to the junction of **Highway 12** to Sonoma and the Sonoma Valley. The drive from the Golden Gate Bridge to Sonoma takes just under an hour, longer if you hit afternoon rush-hour traffic.

To avoid Sonoma and go straight to Glen Ellen, go straight on **Arnold Drive** at the junction and gas station about five miles after joining Highway 121. It is a slower road but avoids heavy traffic and leads to the heart of Glen Ellen.

Other routes to the area from the north and east include Highway 12 east into the valley from U.S. 101 at Santa Rosa, or Highway 37 west from I-80 at Vallejo to the junction of Highway 121. Be warned that Highways 37 and 121 through Carneros are infamous for nasty accidents due to the unexpected bends and dips, dawdling tourists, and high volume of commuter (in other words, speeding) traffic. One accident seemingly far away can clog all surrounding roads and highways for hours.

GETTING AROUND
Car

Most people get around Carneros and the Sonoma Valley by car. While navigating the area is fairly straightforward, keep in mind that the many local highways double as roads with their own names. This can be confusing, particularly when you stumble upon addresses written two different ways. While making your way around southern Sonoma, keep in mind that Highway 12 is also the Sonoma Highway from Santa Rosa to Sonoma, Broadway in the town of Sonoma, and the Carneros Highway when it joins Highway 121

Best of Southern Sonoma Varietals

Thanks to its cool climate, chardonnay and pinot noir often dominate the portfolio of southern Sonoma wineries, particularly in Carneros. As the valley shoots north, the temperatures rise and the diversity broadens. Syrah, cabernet, merlot, and even zinfandel begin popping up on tasting room menus, but even these reflect the restraint of more temperate temperatures.

SPARKLING

- **Gloria Ferrer** (page 177) boasts the largest selection of sparkling wines in Carneros. They're poured in the Italian farmhouse tasting room, which overlooks the vineyards and wetlands beyond.

- **Domaine Carneros** (page 182) is a grand French château that pours flights of bubbly, including the Le Rêve blanc de blancs, made from 100 percent chardonnay and considered one of California's top champagnes.

CHARDONNAY

- One of the few grand wineries in the Sonoma Valley, **Chateau St. Jean** (page 166) is primarily known for its variety of excellent chardonnays.

- Another large Sonoma winery, **Landmark Vineyards** (page 167) also focuses nearly exclusively on chardonnay sourced from its estate vineyards, as well as other regions in California.

- At **Nicholson Ranch** (page 179), a small winery in the hills of Carneros, you'll find chardonnay options like the flagship Cuvée Natalie, which not only gets good reviews from critics but is also quite affordable.

- The modern indoor/outdoor tasting room at **Cuvaison** (page 183) matches the clean and bright elegance of its Carneros chardonnay.

PINOT NOIR

- **Walt Wines** (page 140) pours flights of pinot noir from grapes sourced from the Sonoma Coast, Anderson Valley, the Santa Rita Hills near Santa Barbara, and Oregon's Willamette Valley at a tasting room just off the Sonoma Plaza.

and bends east toward Vallejo. Highway 121 runs the length of Carneros from Napa until it T's with Arnold Drive, joining it south toward U.S. 101. Along this stretch it is known both as Highway 121 and Arnold Drive. North of the T, Arnold Drive is also Highway 116, until the highway shoots off to the west toward Petaluma.

Bus

If driving sounds too confusing, you can opt for public transit. **Sonoma County Transit** (707/576-7433 or 800/345-7433, www.sctransit.com, $1.50-4.80) has several routes through the Sonoma Valley and to Santa Rosa, Guerneville, and other spots in the Russian River Valley as well.

Bicycle

Biking is a great way to see the valley and avoid the car-to-winery-to-car relay. To keep it fun instead of tiring, stick to the wineries around Sonoma and Glen Ellen and avoid long distances, summer heat, and tipsy drivers on major thoroughfares. Cruising around the empty flatlands of eastern Carneros on two wheels is a rewarding way to get off the beaten track and visit less-crowded wineries.

- At **Eric Ross Winery** (page 159), a cozy tasting room in Glen Ellen, Russian River pinot noir takes center stage among a portfolio of excellent wines.

- **Hanzell Vineyards** (page 141) is a Moon Mountain winery that makes award-winning and limited-production wines from the oldest pinot noir vineyard in California.

- At **Bouchaine Vineyards** (page 180), a winery bordering the Carneros wetlands, the tasting menu is dominated by award-wining pinot noir sourced from estate vineyards and elsewhere in Carneros.

- The stylish **Etude Wines** (page 180) is best known for its refined but pricey Carneros pinot noir. Try the Study of Pinot Noir tasting, which includes six vintages, each from a major pinot-growing region.

SYRAH

- The only Sonoma winery focusing on syrah, **Loxton Cellars** (page 160) is a one-man Aussie operation. Grapes are sourced from the five-acre estate vineyard to produce an earthy syrah, robust syrah port, and an unusual cabernet-shiraz blend.

ZINFANDEL

- **Ravenswood** (page 139) is a fun-loving Sonoma winery that produces a dizzying amount of vineyard-designate zinfandels from Dry Creek Valley, Amador County, Mendocino, and the Russian River Valley.

- **Homewood Winery** (page 179) is a small production winery that produces small batches of red wine, including several zinfandels, which can be enjoyed in a vertical tasting. Try the affordable Flying Whizzbangers, a zinfandel-dominated red blend.

CABERNET

- **B. R. Cohn Winery** (page 158) produces highly regarded cabernet from its Olive Hill vineyard, which has its own microclimate thanks to an underground geothermal aquifer.

- A small but elegant winery, **Arrowood Vineyards & Winery** (page 158) produces celebrated cabernets from Sonoma County's diverse microclimates and offers cabernet-only flights.

Unfortunately, the western region is dominated by the busy (and narrow) thoroughfares, making for a white-knuckled cycling experience rather than a relaxing afternoon ride. The area around downtown Sonoma, however, is perfect for exploring by bike. The visitors bureau has a helpful map that gives the best bike routes, including one that hits all the historic downtown sites as well as the Ravenswood, Buena Vista, and Gundlach Bundschu wineries, which are within a mile or two of the plaza.

Some hotels and B&Bs have their own bicycles to rent or borrow. Otherwise, several shops rent bikes and supply tour maps near the Sonoma Plaza. **Sonoma Valley Cyclery** (20091 Broadway, Sonoma, 707/935-3377, www.sonomacyclery.com, 10am-6pm Mon.-Sat., 10am-4pm Sun., $7-15/hour, $30-75/day) and **Wine Country Cyclery** (262 W. Napa St., Sonoma, 707/996-6800, www.winecountrycyclery.com, 10am-6pm daily, $10-20/hour, $30-75/day) rent bikes, including mountain, road, and tandem bikes, as well as bike trailers for kids. You can also find rentals and organized tours at **Sonoma Valley Bike Tours** (1254 Broadway, Sonoma, 707/996-2453, http://sonomavalleybiketours.

com, 8:30am-5pm daily, $10-20/hour, $30-75/day). The company offers plenty of resources (boxed lunches, wine pickup, roadside assistance) to go with its easy-to-follow self-guided tours. To join something more organized, select one of its three touring options: the half-day tour ($108), which includes stops at two wineries; the full-day Sonoma Valley tour ($144) that visits three wineries and includes lunch; and the Cycling in the Vineyards Tour ($124), a half-day excursion through the back roads of Carneros. Note that tasting room fees are not included and may run $20-25 per winery.

If you want something delivered to your hotel, **Goodtime Touring Company** (707/938-0453 or 888/525-0453, www.goodtimetouring.com, $30-65/day) rents bikes for adults and kids, bike trailers, and tandems. The company also offers organized tours ($124, 10am-3:30pm) of Carneros, Glen Ellen, and Kenwood that include lunch and a visit to two to three wineries. Tasting fees are not included.

Sonoma Valley

The picturesque Sonoma Valley is a fitting end point for the bells of the original El Camino Real, which march up the middle of California and mark the route of the Franciscan friars and their string of missions. The Mission San Francisco Solano de Sonoma, or simply Sonoma Mission, is the northernmost mission and the last, established in 1823. It and the neighboring plaza anchor the historic town of **Sonoma.** Despite its heavy dose of history, which includes some of California's first wineries and the sprawling historic park that weaves through its downtown, Sonoma manages to retain its small-town atmosphere without selling its soul to the tourist trade.

The road north out of town passes fast-food outlets and a strip mall, about as close to urban sprawl as there is. In keeping with the valley's laid-back nature, it's a spaced-out, relaxed sort of sprawl linking Sonoma and three spring towns: Boyes Hot Springs, Fetters Hot Springs, and Agua Caliente, all of which look like they could do with a rejuvenating spa treatment themselves.

The towns end abruptly, and the serene valley lies ahead. Plum, walnut, and peach orchards once shared the valley with cows that must have thought they'd died and gone to heaven to be grazing here. Now the mighty vine has taken over the valley floor. Along

the way, there is the tiny town of **Glen Ellen,** just slightly off the main highway. It is a sleepy town, but a couple epicurean eateries and delightful inns hidden in the surrounding woods let you know you're in Wine Country, Sonoma-style. One of the biggest buildings is an auto shop, a sign that real life still takes place in this part of the valley.

Farther north, the valley spreads out around the loose-knit community of **Kenwood.** Here the wineries get grander and the parks wilder, but the lodging and dining options get slimmer. Still, a hike or an estate winery tour is not a bad way to end the day before Highway 12 takes you north into Santa Rosa.

The Wines

The volcanic soils of the hot mountainsides and the rich alluvial plains of the valley floor make Sonoma an ideal place to grow a plethora of grape varietals, a fact the missionaries and immigrants of the 1800s quickly discovered. The valley doesn't have quite the number of different growing conditions and soils of the larger Napa Valley, but winemakers maintain that its wines can be just as good.

In many ways the Sonoma Valley and Napa Valley are more alike than different. Both have productive mountain growing regions, both are proportionally similar, face the same

Sonoma Valley

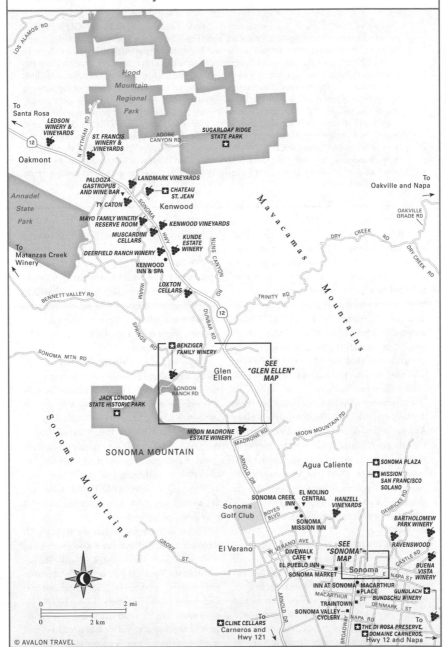

To Santa Rosa

Hood Mountain Regional Park

LOS ALAMOS RD

LEDSON WINERY & VINEYARDS

N PYTHIAN RD

ST. FRANCIS WINERY & VINEYARDS

ADOBE CANYON RD

SUGARLOAF RIDGE STATE PARK

12

Oakmont

Annadel State Park

PALOOZA GASTROPUB AND WINE BAR

LANDMARK VINEYARDS

CHATEAU ST. JEAN

TY CATON

Kenwood

MAYO FAMILY WINERY RESERVE ROOM

KENWOOD VINEYARDS

MUSCARDINI CELLARS

KUNDE ESTATE WINERY

To Matanzas Creek Winery

DEERFIELD RANCH WINERY

KENWOOD INN & SPA

SONOMA HWY

LOXTON CELLARS

BENNETT VALLEY RD

WARM SPRINGS RD

DUNBAR RD

12

TRINITY RD

NUNS CANYON RD

Mayacamas Mountains

To Oakville and Napa

OAKVILLE GRADE RD

DRY CREEK RD

SONOMA MTN RD

BENZIGER FAMILY WINERY

Glen Ellen

SEE "GLEN ELLEN" MAP

LONDON RANCH RD

JACK LONDON STATE HISTORIC PARK

Sonoma Mountains

MOON MADRONE ESTATE WINERY

MADRONE RD

MOON MOUNTAIN RD

SONOMA MOUNTAIN

ARNOLD DR

Agua Caliente

SONOMA PLAZA

MISSION SAN FRANCISCO SOLANO

SONOMA CREEK INN

EL MOLINO CENTRAL

HANZELL VINEYARDS

Sonoma Golf Club

BOYES BLVD

SONOMA MISSION INN

GEHRICKE RD

BARTHOLOMEW PARK WINERY

GROVE ST

W VERANO AVE

El Verano

DIVEWALK CAFE

EL PUEBLO INN

SONOMA MARKET

SEE "SONOMA" MAP

Sonoma

RAVENSWOOD

CASTLE RD

BUENA VISTA WINERY

E NAPA ST

INN AT SONOMA

MACARTHUR PLACE

MACARTHUR ST

GUNDLACH BUNDSCHU WINERY

TRAINTOWN

SONOMA VALLEY CYCLERY

DENMARK ST

NAPA RD

ARNOLD DR

BROADWAY

To Carneros and Hwy 121

CLINE CELLARS

THE DI ROSA PRESERVE, DOMAINE CARNEROS, Hwy 12 and Napa

To

0   2 mi

0   2 km

© AVALON TRAVEL

Sonoma Valley Tasting Tour

Start with a plate of brioche french toast on the Sonoma square at **El Dorado Kitchen,** then spend some time wandering **Sonoma Plaza** and checking out the **Sonoma Mission.** Spend the rest of the morning on the historic grounds of **Bartholomew Park Winery** and **Buena Vista Winery** and grab some picnic supplies to go while you're there. For one last flight before leaving Sonoma, make a stop at **Ravenswood** and explore the world of zinfandel, which is larger than you might expect. Then hit the road and enjoy the rolling scenery of the Sonoma Valley. Unpack that picnic at **Kunde Estate Winery,** where you'll find picnic spots next to the lake, as well as a flight of estate wines, which you can enjoy in the tasting room or out on the patio. Work off lunch with a stroll to the 25-foot waterfall at **Sugarloaf Ridge State Park.** If you're spending the night in Santa Rosa, head to **St. Francis Winery** for more outstanding views and some serious merlot, and finish the day with dinner at hip **The Bird and the Bottle.** If you're spending the night in Sonoma, backtrack to Glen Ellen for one last tasting at the valley's only biodynamic winery, **Benziger Family Winery,** and plan for an amazing dinner at the **Glen Ellen Star.**

direction, and are affected by the same wind and rain patterns. The fact that Sonoma's early head start in winemaking in the mid-1800s petered out by the early 1900s seems to have had more to do with chance and bad business decisions by the early pioneers like Agoston Haraszthy. The larger Napa Valley wineries established in the late 1800s gained more commercial traction, perhaps due to the greater availability of land. Once a critical mass of winemaking had been reached, there was no turning back.

Climate-wise, the Sonoma Valley has three distinct appellations. The **Sonoma Valley** AVA is the largest and includes some or all of the other two. It stretches from the top of the valley near Santa Rosa all the way down to the bay, bordered by 3,000-foot-high mountains on each side and encompassing 116,000 acres of land and about 65,000 acres of vineyards (this number includes those in Carneros to the south).

The valley acts like a giant funnel, channeling cooler air (and sometimes fog) up from the bay, leaving the mountainsides to bask in warm sunshine. Zinfandel loves the higher, hotter elevations, while cabernet and merlot ripen well on hillsides and the warmer north end of the valley. Pinot noir, chardonnay, and other white varietals prefer the slightly cooler

valley floor, especially farther south toward Carneros.

The 800 acres of vineyards in the cooler and rockier **Sonoma Mountain** appellation just up the hill from Glen Ellen vary widely depending on their exposure, but the region is known mostly for its cabernet, although chardonnay, pinot noir, and other white varietals are also grown here.

Opposite Sonoma Mountain on the eastern side of the valley sits Sonoma's newest appellation, **Moon Mountain** AVA. While the AVA was established in 2013, the rocky volcanic mountainsides have been planted with grapes since the 1800s. The well-drained red volcanic and ash soils, aided by hotter elevations, produce cabernet, zinfandel, and merlot, full of dark fruit and notes of cocoa. Today, only 1,500 acres out of the AVA's total 17,000 acreage are covered in vines, and the few wineries here are appointment-only.

To the northwest, and just overlapping with Sonoma Valley, **Bennett Valley** stretches northwest from the Sonoma Mountains toward Santa Rosa. Its 650 acres of vineyards are primarily planted with cabernet, merlot, and chardonnay and generally have rocky, volcanic-based soils. A gap in the low mountains west of the Bennett Valley lets ocean air and fog through and keeps growing conditions cool compared to the Sonoma Valley and the mountains.

SONOMA

As if by accident, Sonoma is perhaps the most idyllic town in Wine Country. It is often credited as being the birthplace of modern California, thanks to the relatively ragtag Bear Flag Revolt, but this notoriety, including being the home of the last of California's missions, comes with little fanfare. Instead, history weaves itself through the town (literally), as the middle-class population of 10,000 continues to raise families, farm fields, and yes, make wine. The historic plaza that draws tourists to its shaded picnic tables is still the center of Sonoma life, and is even home to City Hall. Within blocks from the plaza residential neighborhoods yield to pasture without notice, making a stroll through town especially quaint and relaxing. Sonoma is one of those places where you may find yourself browsing the real estate listings toward the end of your stay.

Wineries

The town Sonoma is blessed with a mix of downtown tasting rooms, historic wineries tucked in its back roads, and hip new appointment-only wineries, all within minutes of each other. The town's age and rural character make a map helpful navigating the small town, which is in turns residential and rural, often block by block.

BARTHOLOMEW PARK WINERY

History is the big draw of **Bartholomew Park Winery** (1000 Vineyard Ln., 707/939-3026, www.bartpark.com, 11am-4:30pm daily, tasting $10-20), or **Bart Park** as it's known locally. Not only was it part of Sonoma wine pioneer Agoston Haraszthy's original estate, but the winery was also once home to a widow and her 200 Angora cats, the site of a hospital, and an institution for "delinquent women." When the Bartholomew family bought the property in the 1940s, they returned it to its original purpose. For decades it was a family-owned

winery until it was bought by the nearby Gundlach Bundschu Winery in 1994, and they still operate it today as a sister winery.

Bart Park's colorful history is detailed in a small but packed museum housed in the old hospital building, along with the small tasting room where you can sample the estate chardonnay, cabernet sauvignon, and merlot, as well as several wines from other vineyards around Sonoma. The real charm of Bart Park, however, has nothing to do with history or wine. The winery sits in some glorious open space, including what remains of the formal gardens of an old mansion that was burned down (reportedly by the delinquent women) and the small garden of the reproduction Haraszthy home. You can wander freely throughout as if it's your own private garden and find great shaded picnic spots with sweeping views of the valley. Miles of hiking trails start from the winery and wind up the nearby hillsides. Where they start is not obvious, however, so ask someone in the winery for directions. Palladian Villa, a replica of Haraszthy's home, is open to the public free of charge noon-3pm Saturday and Sunday.

BUENA VISTA WINERY

Buena Vista Winery (18000 Old Winery Rd., 800/325-2764, www.buenavistawinery.com, 10am-5pm daily, tasting $20) sits on some of the land used by the original Buena Vista Winery, established by Agoston Haraszthy in 1858. Among the old winery structures that remain are the original hand-dug caves, the original champagne cellar, and the old stone press house, which is today the visitors center and helps the site qualify as a California Historic Landmark.

Such status does not preclude Buena Vista from being a thoroughly commercial operation. Owned by the multinational conglomerate Ascentia Wine Estates, it attracts an estimated 120,000 visitors a year, and there is no doubt that the winery plays into its status as a tourist destination. As such, there are various touring options in addition to flights of mid-priced estate wines, from chardonnay

Sonoma

To Sonoma Overlook Trail

Sonoma State Historic Park

★ DEPOT MUSEUM

VELLA CHEESE COMPANY

HAWKES WINERY

BUNGALOWS 313

COTTAGE INN & SPA/ MISSION B&B

SONOMA HOTEL/ THE GIRL & THE FIG

WALT WINES

MISSION TER

W SPAIN ST

ROCHE WINERY & VINEYARDS

SWISS HOTEL

LA CASA GRANDE

★ SONOMA BARRACKS

To Ramekins and Lachryma Montis

EL DORADO HOTEL

MARY'S PIZZA SHACK

▼ SONOMA CHEESE FACTORY

★ ▤ MISSION SAN FRANCISCO SOLANO

BLUE WING INN

E SPAIN ST

SUNFLOWER CAFFE

SONOMA WINE SHOP

SIGN OF THE BEAR KITCHENWARE

BEAR FLAG MONUMENT

▼ LA BODEGA CHEESE SHOP

▼ LA SALETTE

To Sebastiani Vineyards & Wineries

W NAPA ST

12

★ SONOMA PLAZA

CITY HALL

★ VISITORS BUREAU

▼ MURPHY'S IRISH PUB

▼ BASQUE BOULANGERIE CAFÉ

■ SEBASTIANI THEATRE

● LEDSON HOTEL

▼ HIGHWAY 12 VINEYARDS WINERY

0   200 yds

0   200 m

THE RED GRAPE

▼ OSO

▼ MAYA

▼ CAFÉ LA HAYE

E NAPA ST

To Inn at Sonoma, MacArthur Place, Train Town, and Sonoma Valley Cyclery

12

PANGLOSS CELLARS

▼ SIGH

ENKIDU

▼ ENOTECA DELLA SANTINA

▼ DELLA SANTINA'S

© AVALON TRAVEL

to cabernet. The most original experience is the 20-minute play about the founding of the winery, followed by a tasting of current release wines (11am, 1pm, and 3pm daily, $25, children free). Access to the winery's caves comes with the **Barrel Tour** (11am and 2pm daily, $40, by appointment), which includes a flight of reserve wines as well as barrel tastings. Private reserve tastings are available ($35-50), as is a seminar on the art of blending (10:30am and 1:30pm daily, by appointment, $100). You can also explore the winery on your own. Like most other large wineries, the tasting room has an array of picnic food to be taken out to one of the plentiful hillside picnic tables. While well-shaded, none of them offer much privacy on summer weekends when the winery tends to be swamped by busloads of visitors.

★ **GUNDLACH BUNDSCHU WINERY**
Not many wineries in California can boast that they won awards for their wines almost 100 years ago, but **Gundlach Bundschu** (2000 Denmark St., 707/938-5277, www.gunbun.com, 11am-4:30pm daily Nov.-May,

11am-5:30pm daily June-Oct., tasting $20-30), or **GunBun** as it's known, is one of them. The 19 Gundlach Bundschu wines entered into the 1915 Panama-Pacific International Exhibition in San Francisco all won medals. Today the winery focuses on squeezing the highest-quality wines possible out of its estate vineyards, including pinot noir, chardonnay, and gewürztraminer, in addition to cabernets and merlots that tend to have plenty of tannic backbone.

The tasting room is housed in one of the original stone winery buildings, which can feel cramped when full of visitors—but the fun atmosphere makes it more bearable. Browse the historical memorabilia, including old wine posters from the 1800s. If small spaces aren't for you, consider calling ahead and booking a seated tasting on the courtyard (11am-4pm Fri.-Mon., $30). Otherwise, the **Winemaking Tour and Cave Tasting** (2:30pm Thurs.-Mon., reservations required $40) explores the 430-foot-long hillside cave, just a short walk away. During the summer months, GunBun also offers a tour of the estate vineyards in a quirky former Swiss military vehicle called a

Pinzgauer, followed by a tasting of some of the best estate wines (11:15am Thurs.-Mon., reservation required, $60).

GunBun also provides a picnicking area at the top of Towles' Hill overlooking the valley, and even a grassy amphitheater where you can hear performances of Mozart during the summer. Overall it has one of the nicest outdoor spaces of any winery in the valley. Check the website for event schedules, or just pack a picnic before visiting.

SEBASTIANI VINEYARDS & WINERY

Within walking distance from the square, the **Sebastiani Vineyards & Winery** (389 4th St. E., 707/933-3230, ext. 3230, www.sebastiani.com, 10am-5pm daily, tasting $10-15) was founded by one of the city's most important benefactors and philanthropists, Samuele Sebastiani. Today, the winery offers visitors a fair dose of history and a vast portfolio of Sonoma wines to taste, including the flagship Cherryblock cabernet sauvignon that routinely scores above 90 points with the critics and is sourced from an old vineyard near the winery.

The cool, vaulted visitors center is chock-full of Italian-themed gifts, but is on a scale that can feel slightly impersonal, with more of a corporate than a family atmosphere. For the $20 tasting fee, visitors can taste seven wines and order wine by the glass ($7-10). But really, it's worth taking one of the three daily historical tours of the cellars and old stone buildings to see some of the original winemaking equipment from the early 1900s and learn more about the history of the winery and its family. Tours are given at 11am daily and cost $5. Other tours, seminars, and food pairings are available by appointment. These generally cost $35-65, and reservations should be made a week or so in advance.

RAVENSWOOD

"To err is human but to zin is divine" is just one of the many droll mottoes you'll find at the tasting room of this fun and friendly zinfandel specialist a few blocks north of downtown Sonoma. The vineyard-designate zins at **Ravenswood** (18701 Gehricke Rd., www.ravenswoodwinery.com, 10am-4:30pm daily, tasting $18) exhibit the full range of flavors and styles that the humble zinfandel is capable of producing, from the full-throttle fruitiness of Dry Creek Valley and Amador County zins to the subtler spiciness of cooler-climate versions from Mendocino and the Russian

Gundlach Bundschu Winery

River Valley. Ravenswood also offers a tasting flight of its remarkably good small lot cabernet blends. If you're up early enough, the daily tour at 10:30am ($25) is an entertaining start to the day and usually includes tasting of barrel samples.

PLAZA TASTING ROOMS

Tucked in the small alleyways and pedestrian paths that snake through Sonoma's downtown are scores of tasting rooms. Most are small family enterprises (5,000 cases or fewer) specializing in one or two varietals. This proximity makes for a fun tasting experience in which you can create your own flight from bubbles to cabernet.

If starting with sparkling, head over to **Sigh** (29 E. Napa St., Ste. C, 707/996-2444, www.sighsonoma.com, noon-6pm Sun.-Thurs., noon-9pm Fri.-Sat., tasting $14-55) in the retail courtyard of Sonoma Court Shops and order a flight ($14-55) or a glass ($8-18) of bubbles. It is not affiliated with any winery and carries an assortment of bubbles, from cava to locally made sparkling wine to true champagnes from France. You won't find any Veuve Cliquot here, but instead only wine that has been hand selected by the proprietor, Jayme Powers.

On the same block you'll find **Enkidu** (520 Broadway, 707/833-6100, www.enkiduwines.com, noon-6pm daily, tasting $15-25), where a slightly acidic chardonnay is offset with notes of pear and brown sugar, and the excellent and creamy syrah rosé is also worth a taste. Made by Sonoma native son Phillip Staehle, Enkidu wines are offbeat and challenge the senses. Round out your tasting with the bold Bedrock zinfandel and the popular and age-worthy Rhône blend.

If you're in the mood for pinot, cross the plaza to **Walt Wines** (380 1st St. W., 707/933-4440, www.waltwines.com, 11am-6pm daily, tasting $30), which produces pinot noir from grapes sourced from the Sonoma Coast, Anderson Valley, the Santa Rita Hills near Santa Barbara, and Oregon's Willamette Valley. By buying fruit from such a large

swath, winemaker Steve Leveque, formerly of Robert Mondavi Winery, is able to draw out the grape's delicate characteristics, each uniquely amplified in different appellations. For those in your party still content with whites, Walt offers one Sonoma Coast chardonnay with its pricey current release tasting. True pinophiles may want to go double or nothing with the Root 101 tasting (11am and 2pm daily, reservation required, $60) of single-vineyard pinot noir paired with small bites from **the girl & the fig** (110 W. Spain St., 707/938-3000, www.thegirlandthefig.com, 11:30am-10pm Mon.-Thurs., 11am-11pm Fri.-Sat., 10am-10pm Sun., $19-28).

Cabernet rules across the street at **Hawkes Winery** (383 1st St. W., 707/938-7620, www.hawkeswine.com, 11am-6pm daily, tasting $15), but you're not going to find your typical bold Napa varietal here. Instead, Hawkes gets its fruit from the hotter Alexander Valley. The result is handcrafted cabernets that are balanced, lower in alcohol, and exceptionally food-friendly. The winery also offers a chardonnay and a merlot, just to shake things up. The chardonnay is particularly striking among California whites for lacking the oak-inducing malolactic fermentation, leaving a crisp, citrusy wine. It is also the best value at $26, while the rest hover around the $50 mark.

For an all-in-one stop, the homey 1940s Craftsman-style cottage just around the corner houses the Carneros-based **Roche Winery & Vineyards** (122 W. Spain St., 707/935-7115, www.rochewinery.com, 11am-7pm Mon.-Sat., 11am-6:30pm Sun., tasting $15-20), where you can taste chardonnays to pinots to merlots to a variety of dessert wines. All are sourced from the estate vineyards and cost no more than $40, quite a deal for tasting rooms in the area. Taste them indoors, or buy a glass ($10-25) to accompany snacks from the deli case. If you have packed your own picnic, you are invited to unpack it with any glass or tasting on the laid-back patio, where families and dogs are also welcome.

A bit of the Sonoma winemaking establishment can be found at the southeast corner of

the Bear Flag Monument on Sonoma Plaza

largely Sonoma wines, including a sauvignon blanc, chardonnay, pinot noir, and a cabernet from the new Moon Mountain AVA. Take a seat at the tasting bar or at one of the couches scattered around the large space for a flight of five wines, wine by the glass, or a flight paired with farm-to-fork bites ($35-50).

Wineries by Appointment
HANZELL VINEYARDS
Siting on the slopes of the Moon Mountain AVA, **Hanzell Vineyards** (18596 Lomita Ave., 707/996-3860, www.hanzell.com, 10am-3:30pm daily, tour and tasting $45) was established in 1948 by industrialist James D. Zellerbach and is today renowned for its luxury-priced but limited-production chardonnays and pinot noirs that regularly score over 90 points in reviews. The secret to its success is its very own Hanzell clones of both pinot and chardonnay. In fact, the pinot noir vineyard overlooking the Sonoma Valley is said to be the oldest in California. The tour and tasting fee is pricey for Sonoma but buys a very personalized experience, including a jaunt into the vineyards, a tour of the winery and caves, and a sit-down tasting.

Sights
Sonoma is not the only Wine Country town with a rich history stretching back hundreds of years, but it holds the distinction of being ground zero both for the turbulent events that led to the creation of the state of California in the 1840s and for the beginnings of California's booming wine industry. Many of the most important buildings from that active period in the mid-1800s are still standing, making Sonoma the most historically alive Wine Country town in Northern California.

★ SONOMA PLAZA
Created in 1835 by General Vallejo for troop maneuvers, **Sonoma Plaza** (Broadway or Hwy. 12 and Napa St.) has seen religious uprisings, revolution, and fires in its history. Today it is both California's largest town square and the hub of civic life in Sonoma.

the plaza next to the Ledson Hotel. As the name implies, **Highway 12 Vineyards & Winery** (498 1st St. E., 707/938-8091, www.highway12winery.com, 10:30am-5:30pm daily, free tasting) makes wines from vineyards along the highway that runs through the Sonoma Valley and Carneros. Highlights include the chardonnays, which are made in a plush, full-bodied style. Among the reds, the most interesting wines are the blends, particularly the Sonoma red blend of sangiovese, primitivo, and zinfandel. This should come as no surprise, as one of Highway 12 Winery's principal partners is Michael Sebastiani, member of Sonoma's famed Sebastiani winemaking clan and former winemaker at Viansa.

The place to finish a day of wine-tasting is at the hot new **Pangloss Cellars** (35 E. Napa St., 707/933-8565, 11am-6pm Sun.-Thurs., 11am-7pm Fri.-Sat., tasting $25). Inside, the high ceilings, stone walls, and lounge atmosphere belie the cozy laid-back charm of other Sonoma tasting rooms. On hand to taste is Pangloss's relatively modest portfolio of

At the northeast corner is the **Bear Flag Monument,** a bronze statue that stands roughly where the flag was raised by settlers in 1846, heralding the eventual creation of the state of California and the demise of Mexican rule. Smack in the middle of the plaza is **Sonoma City Hall,** built from locally quarried stone and completed in 1909, while on the eastern side is the **Sonoma Valley Visitors Bureau** (453 1st St. E., 707/996-1090 or 866/996-1090, www.sonomavalley.com, 9am-5pm Mon.-Sat., 10am-5pm Sun.). In addition to loads of helpful information, the visitors center also has the free *Sonoma Valley Guide,* which has an excellent self-guided walking tour of the plaza and the many historic buildings surrounding it.

★ MISSION SAN FRANCISCO SOLANO

At the corner of the historic plaza, the **Mission San Francisco Solano** (114 E. Spain St., 707/938-9560, www.parks.ca.gov, 10am-5pm daily), also known as the **Sonoma Mission,** is the northernmost of the chain of Spanish missions in California. The last mission established (1823) and one of the first restored as a historic landmark, the Sonoma Mission isn't the prettiest or most elaborate of the 21 missions, but its beautiful interior and historic value make it worth a stop.

The mission is part of **Sonoma State Historic Park.** The park's $3 entrance fee includes a docent-led tour of the mission, which starts every hour 11am-3pm Friday-Sunday. You can also explore the mission on your own, checking out the tiny museum where displays and large watercolors depict life in the missions, or observe a moment of silence at the Native American mortuary monument situated in the dusty courtyard full of giant prickly pear cactuses (said to be as old as the mission itself).

SONOMA STATE HISTORIC PARK

While the Sonoma Mission is a central part of the rambling **Sonoma State Historic Park** (363 3rd St. W., 707/938-9560, www.parks.ca.gov, 10am-5pm daily, adults $3, children 6-17 $2, under 6 free), the majority of the sites in the rest of the park were built by or in the heyday of General Mariano Vallejo, the Mexican army commander who became a key figure in California's transition from a Mexican province to one of the 50 American states. A stroll through this well-maintained park is a window into California during that time. These include the two-story adobe

Mission San Francisco Solano

Sonoma Barracks, the old **Toscano Hotel,** and Vallejo's opulent home, **Lachryma Montis.** Tours for both Lachryma Montis and the Toscano Hotel are included in the park's $3 entrance fee and are available Saturday and Sunday. Next to the Lachryma Montis is the wood-framed **Swiss Chalet** originally used to store the estate's fruit and now home to the park's visitors center and museum (10am-5pm daily).

The one building not currently open to the public is the wobbly-looking adobe building with a long second-floor veranda, the **Blue Wing Inn.** Across the street from the mission entrance on Spain Street, it was a gold rush-era saloon and stagecoach stop that is thought to be one of the oldest unaltered buildings in the city and the oldest hotel north of San Francisco. The park hopes to open the building once the required earthquake retrofitting has been completed; however, with the state park's budget as tight as it is, these plans are set in the very distant future.

DEPOT PARK MUSEUM

If you haven't had enough of history in Sonoma, stop by the **Depot Park Museum** (270 1st St. W., 707/938-1762, http://depotparkmuseum.org, 1pm-4pm Fri.-Sun., free) right down the street from the plaza and around the corner from the mission. The museum hosts a small set of exhibits inside a reproduction of the historic Northwestern Pacific Railroad depot, hence the name. Inside are reconstructions of the depot, along with exhibits about the Bear Flag Revolt, the indigenous Miwok people, and memorabilia from Sonoma life 1850-1900.

TRAINTOWN

Riding the only trains left in town requires a visit to the brightly painted station of **TrainTown** (20264 Broadway, 707/938-3912, www.traintown.com, 10am-5pm daily June-Aug., 10am-5pm Fri.-Sun. Sept.-May, $2.75-6.75/ride). The often crowded combination of amusement park, model railway, and petting zoo is a great treat for little ones who couldn't care less about history or wine. Ride the 15-inch scale railroad that winds through the park's 10 cool forested acres, take a spin on the roller coasters and rides, or ride the vintage carousel and Ferris wheel. Be aware, however, that rides are paid for with coupons, which quickly add up, so buy a Family Pack (six for $14.75); it will be worth it.

TrainTown

Southern Sonoma Festivals and Events

Throughout the year, residents of Sonoma celebrate everything from the smell of lavender to the full glass in their hand. Thankfully, these celebrations are plentiful and eagerly include residents and visitors.

JANUARY

The Sonoma Valley is as much about olives as wine during the winter when the annual **Sonoma Valley Olive Festival** (www.olivefestival.com) is in full swing. The festival kicks off with the Blessing of the Olives at Sonoma's mission the beginning of December, then runs through February. Check the website for a full list of the 30 or more events, including plenty of tastings and fun cooking demonstrations organized at wineries, restaurants, and outdoors. There is even a departure from the wine world with Martini Madness, in which bartenders from all over the valley are challenged to stir (or shake) the best new martini. Many of the events are free, but the biggest usually require tickets, which are available through the event link on the festival's website.

FEBRUARY

Among the big wine events in the valley during the year is the **Vinolivo,** usually held on the last weekend in February. Organized by the **Sonoma Valley Vintners & Growers Alliance** (707/935-0803, www.sonomavalleywine.com), the event is a two-day affair in which 40 wineries up and down the valley throw themed parties with free food, wine, and entertainment for those lucky enough to have a festival passport. One- or three-day tickets are available ($25 and $50, respectively), but dinners and bigger events must be reserved separately and cost $125-150.

APRIL

Both big and small wineries open their doors during the **April in Carneros** event, usually held on the third weekend in April. Just visit one of the participating wineries for a ticket ($45), which gets you a glass and access to special tastings and events at all the other wineries.

JUNE

June is **Lavender Month** in the Sonoma Valley, when many farmers and makers of aromatic soaps, oils, and other delights open their doors and fields to the public. One of these is the **Sonoma Lavender Barn** (8537 Hwy. 12, Sonoma, 707/523-4411, www.sonomalavender. com/festival.html) next to the Chateau St. Jean winery in Kenwood. There you can learn about growing countless varieties of lavender, how to use the oil, and even how to cook with the tiny purple flowers. There's also a lavender festival held in early June at the **Matanzas Creek Winery** (6097 Bennett Valley Rd., Santa Rosa, 707/528-6464, www.matanzascreek.com), near Glen Ellen, where festivities include bocce ball, live music, fantastic food, and the first pourings of their sauvignon blanc.

AUGUST

Shakespeare in Sonoma celebrates the town's theatrical heritage and its great summer weather with weekend performances of Shakespeare's plays in the outdoor amphitheater at the **Buena Vista Winery** (18000 Old Winery Rd., Sonoma, 800/926-1266, www.buenavistawinery. com). Put on by the local Avalon Players group, tickets cost $35. For more information, contact the **Avalon Players** (707/996-3264, www.sonomashakespeare.com).

NOVEMBER

Holiday in Carneros is usually held on the weekend before Thanksgiving. For a list of wineries and more information about the events, visit www.carneroswineries.org, where you can also buy tickets in advance.

Entertainment

NIGHTLIFE

In quiet Sonoma, you won't find any late-night partying—the town goes dark around 10pm. What nightlife Sonoma does have centers around its nascent beer scene. For a fun evening of drinking and live entertainment, head to **Murphy's Irish Pub** (464 1st St. E., 707/935-0660, www.sonomapub.com, 11am-11pm Sun.-Thurs, 11am-midnight Fri.-Sat.) on the Sonoma Plaza. Grab an imported Irish pint or a glass of local wine, some barbecued oysters or downhome pub fare, and enjoy an evening of live music, literary entertainment, or perhaps a lively trivia game. Unlike many pubs and wine bars in Wine Country, Murphy's welcomes kids in its dining room, so feel free to bring the whole family for a meal and a good time.

Another option is the local outpost of the **Hopmonk Tavern** (691 Broadway, 707/935-9100, www.hopmonk.com, 11:30am-11pm Sun.-Wed., 11:30am-midnight Thurs.-Sat.), a Sonoma county chain of three brewpubs. You'll find tasty pub food (including a kids menu), live music either inside on weekend nights or in the beer garden on Saturday and Sunday afternoons, and Hopmonk's four craft beers, plus scores of other microbrews, international beer, wines, and cocktails.

Purists may just want to head over **Sonoma Springs Brewing Company** (19449 Riverside Dr., 707/938-7422, www.sonomaspringsbrewing.com, 4pm-9pm Mon.-Tues., 1pm-9pm Wed.-Sun.), which doesn't offer any food or entertainment, just award-winning craft beer. The modest taproom on Highway 12 offers flights and pints of California-style ales, German beer, and barrel-aged brews. The brewery is best known for its light and dry Sonoma Springs Kolsch, the caramel and citrus Lil Chief Strong Pale Ale, and the Roggenbier, a Bavarian-style rye with lingering notes of clove. The brewery has a dozen beers on tap at a time, so keep a lookout for its seasonal brews and special barrel-aged beers.

THE SEBASTIANI THEATRE

Not only was California born in Sonoma, but so was California theater. What was believed to be California's first theatrical presentation, Benjamin Webster's *The Golden Farmer,* was put on by American soldiers in an old adobe storehouse converted to a theater in 1849.

Today, a theater of the silver screen era is one of the most prominent buildings on the plaza. **The Sebastiani Theatre** (476 1st St. E., 707/996-2020, www.sebastianitheatre.com, $9), built to replace the burned-down Don Theatre, was funded by Samuele Sebastiani, city benefactor and founder of the eponymous winery. It opened its doors in April 1934 with the film *Fugitive Lovers,* starring Robert Montgomery. Today the theater still shows mainly art house movies with the occasional classic thrown in as part of its Vintage Film Series.

RAMEKINS SONOMA VALLEY CULINARY SCHOOL

The Napa Valley has the famous Culinary Institute of America, but the Sonoma Valley, not to be outdone, has its own renowned culinary school in **Ramekins** (450 W. Spain St., 707/933-0450, www.ramekins.com, $95-115), just four blocks from the plaza. Since it was established in 1998, such culinary luminaries as Jacques Pepin, Thomas Keller, and Joyce Goldstein have taught at the school, which has far more in the way of a hands-on cooking experience for casual visitors than the CIA over in St. Helena. You'll find cooking classes on how to make fresh cheese, the perfect pizza, grilled meat, and what to do with the profusion of great produce in summertime Sonoma. Classes don't cost too much more than a fancy meal out, but reservations are a necessity and can be made on the school's website, where you can also find an updated schedule.

Shopping

Shopping is another major draw to this historic small town. Packed around the leafy plaza are countless shops. Many sit on the four main streets bordering the square, but most you have to hunt for in the nooks and crannies in remodeled historic buildings and tiny retail alleyways that penetrate each block. Some are throwbacks to the town's working-class and farming past, and others are upscale boutiques banking on Sonoma's future as a Napaesque Wine Country destination. Simply put, there is something for everyone.

Coming into town on Broadway you'll pass **Fat Pilgrim** (20820 Broadway, 707/721-1287, www.fatpilgrim.com, 10am-5pm Mon.-Sat., 11am-5pm Sun.). Billing itself as a "contemporary general store," this little roadside shop stocks eclectic and earthy housewares, jewelry, and garden supplies. You'll find quirky napkin rings, dime-store toys, and old-fashioned candies and preserves under the Fat Pilgrim label.

At the plaza, a good first stop for food lovers is **Sign of the Bear Kitchenware** (435 1st St. W., 707/996-3722, 10am-6pm daily). It is chock-full of kitchen gadgets, gleaming countertop appliances, Dansk and Le Creuset crockery, and everything you would need to set a gorgeous table. While the store carries big-name labels, look for the "Sonoma Grown" stickers that highlight local products.

Where Sign of the Bear is general, **Bram** (493 1st St. W., 707/935-3717, www.bramcookware.com, 11am-6pm Thurs.-Mon., 11am-5pm Tues.) is specific. Devoted entirely to clay pot cooking, the dark shelves are stocked with a beautiful selection of deep skillets, stew pots, rondeaux, open casseroles, tagines, rectangular bakers, brams, and roasters. In fact, most shoppers will be astounded by the range and diversity of clay pots available. If you're not sure how to use one of these beautiful pots, stacks of cooking books fill the other side of the shop. Furthermore, the staff is extremely knowledgeable and eager to share their own experiences and prejudices.

Despite its name, **Large Leather** (481 1st St. W., 707/938-1042, www.large-leather.com, 10am-6pm daily) is a pint-size store filled to the brim with purses, backpacks, belts, wallets, and bracelets. In fact, anything you can think of that is or can be made out of leather,

you can find here. All their items are handcrafted and designed by the two owners, Paul Terwilliger and Jessica Zoutendijk.

For more handcrafted artistry, but with a bit more polish, stroll just a few doors down to **Sonoma Silver Company** (491 1st St. W., 707/933-0999, www.sonomasilver.com, 11am-6pm daily), where the slender shop is awash in silver rings, pendants, bracelets, and earrings. Multiple local jewelers sell and showcase their work here, but many of the shiny trinkets are made in-house by the company's resident jeweler of 20 years.

Bibliophiles can get their fix at **Readers' Books** (130 E. Napa St., 707/939-1779, www.readersbooks.com, 10am-7pm Mon.-Sat., 10am-6pm Sun.), a well-stocked general-interest bookstore specializing in contemporary fiction. The bookstore hosts literary events in the evenings including local poets, Bay Area travel writers, and book clubs.

Not far away, the **Figone Olive Oil Company** (483 1st W. 707/282-9092, www.figoneoliveoil.com, 10am-6pm Sun.-Thurs., 10am-7pm Fri.-Sat.) sells oils from olive groves in the Central Valley and Sonoma Valley. There are usually several oils and vinegars to taste (for free), and the variety can be dizzying to both the imagination and the taste buds. Taking home selections like Persian Lime and Blood Orange olive oils and the 20-year-old aged balsamic vinegar will breathe new life to any old homemade salad.

Recreation

SONOMA OVERLOOK TRAIL

Nowhere is the spirit of Slownoma better represented than in this three-mile trail just north of Sonoma Plaza that winds through woods and meadows to the top of Schocken Hill, with fine views over the town below. Grab picnic supplies and head for the trailhead near the entrance to the Mountain Cemetery on West 1st Street about a half mile north of the plaza beyond Depot Park. Within an hour you'll feel like you're in the middle of nowhere. Hikers eager to extend their trek can jump on the newly constructed connector trail that links the Overlook Trail with those in the neighboring Montini Preserve, including treks along the ridgeline to lookouts at Coyote View and Two Goat View. Dogs, bikes, and smoking are not allowed on any of the trails.

The **Sonoma Ecology Center** (707/996-0712, www.sonomaecologycenter.org) offers free docent-led weekend hikes along the Overlook Trail, during which guests learn more about the local ecosystem and the area's natural highlights. Springtime is a big draw as the knowledgeable guides identify the abundant spring wildflowers and birds nesting in the area. Contact the center for more information.

GOLF

The grande dame of the valley golf scene is the **Fairmont Sonoma Mission Inn Golf Club** (17700 Arnold Dr., 707/996-0300, $175-225), opened in 1928 with hopes to rival the famous Del Monte course in Monterey. The 18-hole, par-72 course is on 177 acres bordered by the Sonoma Mountains and vineyards. Only club members and guests at the neighboring **Fairmont Sonoma Mission Inn** (100 Boyes Blvd., 707/938-9000 or 866/540-4499, www.fairmont.com/sonoma, $300-500) can play here, however.

On the other hand, the public **Los Arroyos Golf Club** (5000 Stage Gulch Rd., 707/938-8835) is open to all comers. Great for newer players, Los Arroyos offers nine holes, par 29, and good fun for everyone.

SPAS

Aware that local Native American tribes had long talked about the healing properties of Sonoma Valley's numerous hot springs, Captain Henry Boyes spent two years drilling all over his property at the southern end of the valley in search of them. In 1895 he hit what would turn out to be liquid gold—a 112°F gusher that ushered in decades of prosperity for the valley's hotel owners. Within a few years, more springs were tapped, resorts established, and the towns of Boyes Hot Springs and Agua Caliente were born.

Today, the **Willow Stream Spa** at the **Fairmont Sonoma Mission Inn & Spa** (100 Boyes Blvd., 707/938-9000 or 866/540-4499, www.fairmont.com/sonoma, 7:30am-8pm daily), opened in 1927, is the only spa in the valley with its own natural source of hot mineral water. Even if you're not a guest at the Fairmont-owned hotel, basic spa packages are available for $89-239, depending on how many extra salon pamperings are added on. The basic spa includes an exfoliating shower, warm and hot mineral baths, and herbal steam room and sauna, interspersed with various cold showers and baths (which include indoor and outdoor pools). There are yoga classes, stone treatments, and mud baths to purify and relax you (until you see the bill).

Just south of the Sonoma Plaza, the **Garden Spa** (29 E. MacArthur St., 707/933-3193, www.macarthurplace.com/spa.php, 9am-8pm daily, $125-250) at the luxurious MacArthur Place inn is good for some luxury pampering, with a list of spa treatments that could cause you to tense up with indecision. All their signature treatments are made from or inspired by the flowers, herbs, and fruit found in the garden. These are distilled into such luscious effusions as the pomegranate body polish, golden passionflower body wrap, peppermint foot soak, and the red wine grapeseed bath. The spa also offers mud bath soaks, massages, and facial and waxing treatments. Couples can get their treatments together, and all spa guests also have full use of the inn's tranquil outdoor pool and fitness center. It is encouraged to book whatever you choose to do here at least two weeks in advance, as space in this fragrant spa fills up.

Food

Sonoma's food scene has gradually been transformed over the years from rustic to more stylish, but the change has not been nearly so dramatic and universal as in some other Wine Country towns. There's a strong European theme to food in the valley, but ingredients will likely be fresh and local, representing the giant produce basket that is Sonoma County.

SOUTHERN SONOMA VALLEY

Expect to see menus change throughout the year as vegetables, fish, and meats come in and out of season.

CALIFORNIA CUISINE

★ **the girl & the fig** (110 W. Spain St., 707/938-3000, www.thegirlandthefig.com, 11:30am-10pm Mon.-Thurs., 11am-11pm Fri.-Sat., 10am-10pm Sun., $19-28) is somewhat of a valley institution. The French country menu includes main courses like free-range chicken and duck confit, Sonoma rabbit and *steak frites*, an excellent cheese menu, and delicious salads, including the signature arugula, goat cheese, pancetta, and grilled fig salad. The Thursday evening Plat du Jour menu is a bargain at $38 for three courses. To match the Provençal cuisine, the wine list focuses on Rhône varietals, with many from local Sonoma producers. There's not a cabernet to be seen. But thirsty patrons can also opt for a shot of Pernod or an aperitif of absinthe. The restaurant usually closes at 10pm, but a smaller brasserie menu is offered until 11pm on Friday and Saturday.

Inside the El Dorado Hotel is the equally stylish farm-to-fork **El Dorado Kitchen** (405 1st St. W., 707/996-3030, breakfast 8am-11am Mon.-Sat., lunch 11:30am-2:30pm Mon.-Sat., dinner 5:30pm-9pm Sun.-Thurs., 5:30pm-10pm Fri.-Sat., brunch 9:30am-2:30pm Sun., $20-30). Several Thomas Keller alums have been at the helm, giving the restaurant the notoriety it deserves. Under the tutelage of the current chef, Armando Navarro, the menu has a regional comfort-food bent with entrées of roasted pork shoulder, corn ravioli, and steamed clams with chickpeas and chorizo. The inside of the restaurant is all cool dark wood and slate minimalism, while outside by the pool is more Miami than Sonoma. There is a pared-down bar menu (2:30pm-5:30pm daily) for those in just for a nibble or a chance to taste one of their original cocktail creations.

The bustle of the open kitchen speaks to the success and creativity of the small plate Sonoma newcomer, **Oso** (9 E. Napa St., 707/931-6926, http://ososonoma.com, 5pm-10pm Mon.-Wed., 11:30am-10pm Thurs. and Sun., 11:30am-11pm Fri.-Sat., $17-40). Opened in 2014, it has received praise from Bay Area critics and a nod in the Michelin Guide. The menu is exclusively small plate, but portions are large and the fare is California comfort food infused with international flavors. The restaurant is known for its crab and yellow curry deviled eggs, but don't pass up the mole-braised pork shoulder tacos. Oso has a good local wine list, but the food and the atmosphere in this small, dimly lit modern space are perhaps best paired with one of its original cocktails. On a weekend night, its popularity makes getting a table tricky without calling ahead, but the bar is reserved for walk-ins only and will put you in the center of the action.

A little off the square, **Café La Haye** (140 E. Napa St., 707/935-5994, 5:30pm-9pm Tues.-Sat., $18-32) is a trusted and well-loved restaurant. Local ingredients are the backbone of simple yet polished dishes like beef carpaccio, pan-seared steelhead trout, and a daily risotto, while the wine list is dominated by smaller wineries from all over Sonoma and farther afield. The uncluttered, split-level dining room is small, so either book well in advance or be prepared to sit at the bar in front of the tiny kitchen. The café is part of La Haye Art Center, which contains studios and the work of several local artists.

If dining in Wine Country isn't complete without a Michelin star, Sonoma has its very own celestial eatery, **Santé** (100 Boyes Blvd., 707/939-2415, breakfast 7am-11am and dinner 6pm-9pm daily, $25-40) in the exclusive Fairmont Sonoma Mission Inn. With white tablecloths, walls painted slate, and plush chairs the color of cabernet, Santé stands out in Sonoma's laid-back, albeit excellent, dining scene. The menu drips with decadence, from the foie gras appetizer to the 20-ounce wagyu beef steak entrée. Expect a level of excellence in execution as well as sophistication in the service and style. To keep dinner from surpassing the entire budget of your trip, opt for the generous four-course tasting menu, which is a relative steal at $149 (wine pairing $89).

ITALIAN

Ask any of the valley's winemakers where they like to eat and the list will likely include the family-owned Italian trattoria **Della Santina's** (133 E. Napa St., 707/935-0576, www.dellasantinas.com, lunch 11:30am-3pm and dinner 5pm-9:30pm daily, $18-28). The big outdoor patio and the simple Italian country food garner consistently good reviews, so reservations are usually essential despite the casual atmosphere. As you would expect, the restaurant excels at pastas, fish, and spit-roasted meats. Budget-conscious travelers may want to opt for the prix fixe that includes three large courses plus dessert for only $45.

Right next door to the restaurant is the wine bar and wine shop **Enoteca Della Santina** (127 E. Napa St., 707/938-4200, www.enotecanextdoor.com, 4pm-10pm Mon.-Thurs., 4pm-11pm Fri., 2pm-11pm Sat., 2pm-10pm Sun., $8-22), which serves 30 California and international wines by the glass ($8-16), accompanied by appetizers at its copper-topped bar. It's a great place for a predinner drink while you wait for your table at a nearby restaurant, or for a late glass of port to end your day.

Sonoma's Italian heritage is not only represented by fancy trattorias. **Mary's Pizza Shack** (8 W. Spain St., 707/938-8300, www.maryspizzashack.com, 11am-10pm Sun.-Thurs., 11am-11pm Fri.-Sat.), founded by Italian New Yorker Mary Fazio in 1959, has been around longer than many other Sonoma restaurants and now has 19 branches throughout the North Bay. It might now be a chain, but you will at least be eating in the town where it all started. The traditional or build-your-own pizzas (starting at $17 for a medium) are consistently good, and there's a big selection of traditional pasta dishes ($11-18), including spaghetti with baseball-size meatballs. This is a great place to eat with kids on the plaza. Mary's has another location in **Boyes Hot Springs** (18636 Sonoma Hwy., Sonoma,

707/938-3600, 11am-10pm Sun.-Thurs., 11am-11pm Fri.-Sat.).

Slightly more inventive pizzas are made across the plaza at **The Red Grape** (529 1st St. W., 707/996-4103, http://theredgrape.com, 11:30am-9pm daily, $14-20). Some of the selections of thin-crust pizza include a bacon, caramelized onion, and crème fraîche pizza, and another with marinated flank steak and cheddar cheese. There are plenty of less-inspired but cheap pizza, pasta, and panini options. The restaurant is named after a type of particularly sweet tomato and is surely a nod to its home in Wine Country. And befitting any Wine Country eatery, the Red Grape has an impressive wine menu with over 30 mostly local wines, which you can order by the glass or by the bottle. Both are a bit pricey for a casual pizza joint, but if you score a table out on the patio, you may not mind.

MEXICAN

Looking for something with a little more bite? Pull up a bar stool at **Maya** (101 Napa St. E., 707/935-3500, www.mayarestaurant.com, 11:30am-close daily, $10-21), at the corner of 1st and Napa Streets, and pick from one of the 60-plus tequilas on the menu. You can opt for a cool margarita on the rocks or take it straight with lime and salt. Either way, the food, especially the addictive spicy roasted pumpkin seeds or the "Really Good Nachos," will help wash it down. Influenced by the cuisine of the Yucatán Peninsula, the menu relies heavily on fresh fish and locally grown fruits and vegetables. Ceviche, fish tacos, and *carnitas* slow-roasted in banana leaves sit alongside taquitos, nachos, and enchiladas. Like the food and the tequila, the atmosphere is both casual and sophisticated with a decor of worn wood, exposed brick walls, and colorful peasant paintings à la Diego Rivera.

If Mexican comfort food is what you crave, particularly to soak up excess wine or to refuel after a long bike ride, try **El Molino Central** (11 Central Ave., 707/939-1010, www.el-molinocentral.com, 9am-9pm daily, $10), a foodie-inflected taco stand in Boyes Hot

Springs. The stars of the menu are Sonoma Valley produce and the freshly ground corn made into tortillas and masa for its tamales. Swiss chard, heirloom tomatoes, and pickled cabbage fill the menu of enchiladas, tamales, and fish tacos. Lest you think dining here is a light affair, the portions are huge and filling, just as you'd expect in a proper taqueria. Should you need to, however, you can perk yourself back up with a cup of Blue Bottle coffee.

PORTUGUESE

It's rare when locals and travelers agree on the best restaurant in any given town. The fact that it's a traditional Portuguese eatery in a sea of California cuisine makes it all the more special. ★ **LaSalette** (452 1st St. E., 707/938-1927, www.lasalette-restaurant.com, 5pm-9pm Tues.-Sat., $22-30) has a simple charming atmosphere with a wood-fired oven facing a bar and a large outdoor patio that is popular with dinners in the summer. The unswervingly Portuguese menu features fresh fish and hearty meat dishes plus some good meatless options.

CAFÉS

If you just want a cup of coffee or a quick pastry, swing by the **Basque Boulangerie Café** (460 1st St. E., 707/935-7687, http://basqueboulangerie.com, 6am-6pm daily, $6-12); pay attention after ordering as customer names are only called once when food is ready. The line to order often snakes out the door on weekend mornings and at lunchtime throughout the week, but it usually moves fast. The wide selection of soups, salads, and sandwiches can also be bought to go, which is handy because table space inside and out is usually scarce.

There are more seating options at the colorful **Sunflower Caffe** (421 1st St. W., 707/996-6645, www.sonomasunflower.com, 7am-4pm daily, $5-15) across the plaza, but the line, and the wait, can be just as long. It sells fairly basic breakfast selections and upscale salads and sandwiches, but the real gem is a big patio hidden down the side passageway of the El Dorado Hotel. It is an oasis of greenery with plenty of tables. Later in the day, you can swap your espresso for a beer, a glass of wine, or a champagne cocktail.

Take a walk to the **Divewalk Café** (19449 Riverside Dr., 707/334-3175, www.divewalkcafe.com, 11am-4pm Thurs.-Fri., 9am-3pm Sat.-Sun., $10), whose tent on the sidewalk lends authenticity to the French and Vietnamese street food it serves. Sweet and savory crepes, pho, and banh mi sandwiches are on the menu and served on mismatched plates and colorful tablecloths at this indoor/outdoor space. This homespun labor of love was opened in 2015 and has been steadily drawing local foodies (especially foodies with families) since. Its location in front of the Sonoma Springs Brewing Company is delightfully convenient should you need something to soak up those craft brews.

PUBS

The best place to enjoy a pint with dinner is at **Murphy's Irish Pub** (464 1st St., 707/935-0660, www.sonomapub.com, 11am-10pm Sun.-Thurs., 11am-11pm Fri.-Sat., $11-15), just off the plaza behind the Basque Boulangerie. It's one of the few places in the valley where beer trumps wine and live music, usually of the Irish variety, gets people dancing four nights a week. The food includes pub standards like fish-and-chips, shepherd's pie, and Irish stew, as well as sandwiches and a kids menu. Unfortunately, the pub also stays true to its Irish roots with its beer selection, which includes international favorites but little in the way of Northern California brews. But the upshot is that there is a healthy selection of whiskeys: Irish and Scotch, single malt, blended, and bourbons. There is even a Welsh whiskey. And this being Wine Country, you can taste a flight for $23 or $44.

PICNIC SUPPLIES

The Sonoma Valley is like one giant picnic ground. Many of the wineries have large open spaces or picnic tables, and the more

Unpack Your Picnic Basket

In a valley where nearly every winery has at least one picnic table, it may be more useful to list those places at which you *can't* picnic. To help you decide, here are the best spots to open your basket.

- **Bartholomew Park Winery, Sonoma:** Not far from downtown Sonoma, this winery boasts expansive grounds, including plenty of shaded picnic spots with sweeping views. After lunch, consider taking a small hike on one of the many trails that depart from here and wind up the nearby hillsides.

- **Buena Vista Winery, Sonoma:** Commercial, picturesque, and loaded with history, Buena Vista has beautiful grounds, a well-stocked deli, and plentiful shaded hillside picnic tables.

- **Gundlach Bundschu Wine, Sonoma:** The last of the big historic Sonoma wineries, this 100-year-old venue has perhaps the best picnicking in Sonoma, with shaded picnic tables perched at the top of Towles' Hill overlooking the valley.

- **Benziger Family Winery, Glen Ellen:** High up on Sonoma Mountain, this biodynamic winery has a variety of picnic spots, including some blanketed in wireless access.

- **Imagery Estate Winer, Glen Ellen:** Reserve a two-hour picnic spot for $50 at one of the tables at this art-infused winery. Included in the fee is access to bocce ball, Jenga, and horseshoes, plus a bottle of one of Imagery's select white wines.

- **Matanzas Creek Winery, Glen Ellen:** At this Bennett Valley winery, picnickers are welcome to unpack their baskets and enjoy the surrounding fragrant, buzzing fields and a round or two of bocce ball.

- **Sonoma Valley Regional Park, Glen Ellen:** This 202-acre park, located in the heart of the Sonoma Valley, has picnic tables with barbecues along the paved and unpaved trails that wind through open oak woodland.

- **Kunde Estate Winery, Kenwood:** There are plenty of good picnic spots in the shady lakeside picnic area at the largest winery in the west.

- **Sugarloaf Ridge State Park, Kenwood:** Spread a blanket out beneath redwoods and oak trees at the most beautiful park in the valley. In spring, take the 0.75-mile trail from the picnic area out to see the 25-foot waterfall.

- **Viansa Winery, Carneros:** Get a view of the neighboring 90-acre wetlands with the bay in the distance at one of the numerous picnic tables on this winery's long terrace. If you forgot supplies, there is plenty of deli-style food available inside.

- **Gloria Ferrer, Carneros:** The bubbly at this hillside winery pairs perfectly with a picnic on the terrace tables. Outside food is welcome, or you can pick up supplies at the winery's gift store.

- **Larson Family Winery, Carneros:** Out near the wetlands in Carneros, you'll find a regulation-size bocce ball court and a grassy picnic and play area behind this winery's tasting room. For $15 you can reserve a picnic table that will include a flight of wines to go with your own picnic lunch.

adventurous can drive or hike into one of the many parks in the valley, such as the Overlook Trail above Sonoma, Jack London State Park, or up into the western hills in Sugarloaf State Park.

Many wineries now offer a limited selection of deli-style food in their visitors centers or gift stores, but some offer more than most, including **Bartholomew Park Winery** (1000 Vineyard Ln., 707/939-3026, www.bartpark.

com, 11am-4:30pm daily), with its selection of Sonoma Valley cheeses, and **Buena Vista Winery** (18000 Old Winery Rd., 800/325-2764, www.buenavistawinery.com, 10am-5pm daily). Still, you may want to take advantage of the excellent (and cheaper) offerings in town.

Good bread can usually be found at most delis, though many places run out by lunchtime. Centrally located and supplying most of the valley's bread is the **Basque Boulangerie Café** (460 1st St. E., 707/935-7687, http://basqueboulangerie.com, 6am-6pm daily). Inside the bustling bakery, you'll find not only sandwiches and salads to go but also freshly baked breads and pastries.

Three good cheese shops are around the plaza. On the north side is the **Sonoma Cheese Factory** (2 Spain St., 707/996-1931 or 800/535-2855, www.sonomacheesefactory.com, 9am-6pm Mon.-Thurs., 9am-7pm Fri.-Sat.), home of Sonoma Jack cheese and also other strangely flavored cheeses (which, thankfully, you can usually taste first), as well as a limited selection of salads and fancy sandwiches. A less crowded place to buy cheese is the historic **Vella Cheese Company** (315 2nd St. E., 707/938-3232 or 800/848-0505, www.vellacheese.com, 9:30am-6pm Mon.-Fri., 9:30am-5pm Sat.), a block north of the plaza and the latest incarnation of the cheese store opened in the 1930s by Thomas Vella. Some of the best cheese in Northern California can be found directly on the plaza at the **Sonoma Wine Shop** (412 1st St. E., 707/996-1230, http://sonomawineshop.com, 11am-6pm Thurs.-Mon.), which has a small but very select assortment of cheeses plus excellent wine. Perhaps the easiest option for getting everything in one place is to visit one of the valley's excellent general grocery stores.

The **Sonoma Market** (500 W. Napa St., 707/996-3411, https://sonomamarket.net, 5am-9:30pm daily) is not far from the plaza. Here you can find a surprisingly great selection of lunch options, some hot, some gourmet, as well as local wine and good cheese. Another option is the **Vineburg Deli &**

Grocery (997 Napa Rd., 707/938-3306, 6am-6pm daily), just south of Sonoma not far from the Gundlach Bundschu Winery. Perhaps not as upscale as the Sonoma Market, this smaller deli sells hearty lunches and barbecue that lean more toward the picnics of your childhood.

FARMERS MARKETS

One way to soak up the atmosphere while picking up supplies is to visit one of Sonoma's **farmers markets.** The valley's prolific farmers congregate in Depot Park, a block north of the plaza on 1st Street West, 9am-12:30pm every Friday year-round, and in front of City Hall 5:30pm-dusk on Tuesday May-October. At either event you can browse local produce as well as cheese, meat, and bread in addition to the odd art or craft.

Accommodations

Apart from a few big resort or chain hotels, the accommodations in the Sonoma Valley are small, usually independent or historic establishments with a handful of rooms. The smaller the hotel or inn, the more likely there is to be a two-night minimum over weekends, especially during the busiest summer and early fall months. Cancellation policies might also be less than flexible. The peak hotel season is generally from the end of May through October, roughly corresponding to the best weather in the region. For years, Sonoma was a cheaper alternative in Wine Country, but that no longer holds true. Over the last couple years, prices have shot up, making finding a room for under $150 nearly impossible.

$150-250

This price point is blessed with a great diversity of charming inns and lodges, many historic, and several on the square. The ★ **Sonoma Hotel** (110 W. Spain St., 707/996-2996, www.sonomahotel.com, $150-288) is one of these. You'll find affordable rooms, a superb location in a historic building right on Sonoma Plaza, and a highly rated restaurant, **the girl & the fig** (110 W. Spain enjoy a meal at the restaurant or have a drink at the historic bar and take in the history.

Kitty-corner from the Swiss Hotel is another historic inn dating from 1843. It is now home to the **El Dorado Hotel** (405 1st St. W., 707/996-3030, www.eldoradosonoma.com, $165-295), which offers stylish 21st-century accommodations for not much more money than a pricey Wine Country motel. The lobby looks the part of a classy boutique hotel, but the size of the 27 guest rooms reminds you this is a budget boutique in historic digs. A decent list of amenities includes CD players, flat-screen TVs, and wireless Internet access but doesn't stretch to bathtubs—only showers—or room service. The courtyard swimming pool is inviting, but you'll be swimming and sunbathing just yards away from diners spilling onto the patio from the hotel's bar and restaurant. Still, for the price and a location right on the plaza, it's hard to complain. All rooms have a view of some sort from their small balconies—the best overlook the plaza, although they suffer from some associated street noise.

The **Sonoma Chalet** (18935 5th St. W., 707/938-3129 or 800/938-3129, www.sonomachalet.com, rooms $150-190, cottages $210-235) takes its history to a fabulously over-the-top Swiss Family Robinson-meets-Wild West theme with its alpine murals, dark wood, antiques, and colorful fabrics. There are four individually decorated rooms in the main Swiss-style farmhouse: The two cheapest share a bathroom, while the larger of the other two has a fireplace and balcony. Several small cottages on the three acres of wooded grounds have claw-foot tubs and wood-burning stoves. These are also the only accommodations that accept small children. The leafy location on the edge of Sonoma is peaceful but a fairly long walk to most of Sonoma's shops and restaurants.

The adobe may not be authentic, but all guest rooms at **El Pueblo Inn** (896 W. Napa St., 707/996-3651, www.elpuebloinn.com, $189-249) face a lush central courtyard with a pool and a hot tub in true Spanish style. Some of the guest rooms boast walls of adobe bricks

the Swiss Hotel

St., 707/938-3000, www.thegirlandthefig.com, 11:30am-10pm Mon.-Thurs., 11am-11pm Fri.-Sat., 10am-10pm Sun., $19-28), occupying the ground floor. Even the four cheapest rooms have views of something worthwhile, but don't expect luxury in the bright and cozy rooms. In keeping with the price and the hotel's heritage (the building dates from 1880), there are few amenities, and you're likely to hear your neighbor's nighttime antics. Also be warned that the bathroom for one of the cheapest rooms (room 34), although private, is out in the hallway past the friendly ghost.

Since the late 1800s, the **Swiss Hotel** (18 W. Spain St., 707/938-2884, www.swisshotelsonoma.com, $150-280), also on the square, has offered a bed and a meal to travelers from near and far. With a renovation in the 1990s, the five guest rooms have plenty of modern amenities (plus private bathrooms), while the outside of the building and the public spaces retain the historic feel of the original adobe. You'll find your room bright with fresh paint and pretty floral comforters. Downstairs, or lounge areas with fireplaces, but many are standard hotel accommodations—clean and modestly decorated. For the price and location, not to mention views of the garden, it's a good deal. The inn also offers a fitness room, complimentary breakfast, and an in-room safe. Near TrainTown, it is a great option for families.

Only a few blocks from the plaza, the equally contemporary **Inn at Sonoma** (630 Broadway, 888/568-9818 or 707/939-1340, www.innatsonoma.com, $220-395) is a Four Sisters Hotel, which are known for quality at reasonable prices. The 19 guest rooms are furnished in modern Wine Country style and have a full range of modern amenities, including fireplaces, DVD players, and luxury bathrooms. Some of the larger rooms have patios. The price, although not cheap, does include a hot breakfast, which for $10 more can be brought to your room, and an afternoon cocktail hour that includes a glass of wine, a selection of cheese, and house-made hors d'oeuvres.

Although located in the relative no-man's-land of Boyes Hot Springs just north of Sonoma, the **Sonoma Creek Inn** (239 Boyes Blvd., 707/939-9463 or 888/712-1289, www.sonomacreekinn.com, $155-195) is one of the cheapest non-chain hotels in the valley. At this price point it's more common to see IKEA furniture, but the furnishings here are delightfully quirky, and some look like spoils from local antiques stores. The 15 rooms are small and laid out in motel style; all are clean and have air-conditioning and refrigerators, and some have tiny private patios.

OVER $250

History anchors the modern **MacArthur Place** (29 E. MacArthur St., 707/938-2929 or 800/722-1866, www.macarthurplace.com, $450). The original structure was built in 1850, but it has since been remade into a 21st-century, seven-acre exclusive spa resort. Nevertheless, the cookie-cutter faux-Victorian cottages and landscaped gardens that now fan out from the original Manor

House provide 64 luxurious and spacious guest rooms, making it one of the larger hotels in Sonoma. All rooms are sumptuously furnished in a cottage style that makes it seem more like a luxurious B&B. Other amenities include an outdoor pool, free DVD library, evening cheese and wine, and the on-site steak house and martini bar, **Saddles** (breakfast 7am-10pm daily, lunch 11:30am-2pm daily, dinner 5:30pm-8:30pm Sun.-Thurs., 5:30pm-9pm Fri.-Sat., $20-32), which also serves the hotel's complimentary breakfast buffet. Suites and cottages also come with a fireplace and decadent hydrotherapy tub. Try to avoid the rooms on the south side of the complex that overlook the neighboring high school or those bordering the street to the west.

The Chapel Suite with its vaulted ceilings and skylight above the bed is one of the more unusual rooms at the **Cottage Inn & Spa** (310 1st St. E., 707/996-0719, www.cottageinnandspa.com, $140-445), just a block north of Sonoma Plaza. This self-styled "micro resort" with its mission-style architectural flourishes is an oasis of calm and style. Accommodations are billed as suites, even those with only one room, but all are luxurious and full of character with thick white walls, tile floors, and deep tubs ringed in cerulean blue tile; some include private patios, fireplaces, and a full kitchen.

Just a bit farther up the street is the small **Bungalows 313** (313 1st St. E., 707/996-8091, www.bungalows313.com, $179-479). As the name implies, this is a cozy collection of six bungalows around a peaceful courtyard fountain. Each suite is decorated in Italian country style with modern luxuries like sumptuous linens, an LCD television, and a DVD player. All are spacious, with seating areas, a kitchen or kitchenette, and private patio, yet all are unique in some way. One has a fireplace, another a jetted tub, and the largest is 1,200 square feet. Like everywhere in Wine Country, prices vary due to time of year, but keep a lookout for specials on the website. Planning ahead will benefit you, but beware of the 14-day cancellation policy.

With all of its spot-on Victorian flare, it's

hard to believe that the **Ledson Hotel** (480 1st St. E., 707/996-9779, www.ledsonhotel.com, $250-395), a sibling to the **Ledson Winery** up the valley, was honored by *Condé Nast Traveler* magazine in 2004 for best *new* hotel. The Victorian-style brick building looks as old as the plaza itself. Three of the six rooms have balconies looking onto the plaza, and all include state-of-the-art entertainment systems, fireplaces, and marble bathrooms with whirlpool tubs. Downstairs, the **Zina Hyde Winery** (707/895-9462, www.zinawinery.com, 10:30am-7pm daily, tasting $15), founded in 1865, pours flights and glasses ($5-30) of its Sonoma and Mendocino wine.

At the other end of the scale from the intimate Ledson Hotel is the 228-room **Fairmont Sonoma Mission Inn & Spa** (100 Boyes Blvd., 707/938-9000 or 866/540-4499, www.fairmont.com/sonoma, $300-500), which dates from 1927 and is now owned by Fairmont Hotels. It is luxurious, even by Fairmont standards. The well-heeled are drawn to the 40,000-square-foot full-service spa, use of the exclusive **Sonoma Golf Club** (17700 Arnold Dr., 707/996-0300) next door, and one of the best (and most expensive) restaurants in the valley, the Michelin-starred **Santé** (707/939-2415, breakfast 7am-11am and dinner 6pm-9pm daily, $25-40). Many of the rooms have tiled floors and plantation-style wooden shutters to complement their colonial-style furnishings, and some have fireplaces. Despite the exclusivity, the in-room amenities are typical of a chain hotel, albeit a high-end one.

Information and Services

First stop for visitors to the Sonoma Valley should be the **Sonoma Valley Visitors Bureau** (453 1st St. E., 707/996-1090 or 866/996-1090, www.sonomavalley.com, 9am-5pm Mon.-Sat., 10am-5pm Sun.) in the Carnegie Library building in the middle of the plaza right next to City Hall and across from the Sebastiani Theatre. It publishes a free valley guide, and its staff is happy to dispense all sorts of local information, answer any questions, and offer advice for nothing more than an entry in the visitors book. Furthermore, don't be shy to ask for any complimentary tasting passes often dropped off here by neighboring wineries, or for an "I Heart Sonoma" sticker, which when worn will frequently get you discounts and other perks at certain tasting rooms. There's a branch of the visitors bureau at the **Cornerstone Sonoma** (23570 Arnold Dr., 707/933-3010, www.cornerstonegardens.com, 10am-4pm daily) in Carneros.

If you're staying in the valley, be sure to pick up a copy of the *Sonoma Index-Tribune* (www.sonomanews.com), which has been published for more than 100 years and now comes out twice a week. It is full of local news, gossip, event information, and reviews. For wine-related information, including events at individual wineries, check the website of the **Sonoma County Wineries Association** (www.sonomawine.com), which represents all of Sonoma's wineries. You can get cash on the plaza at the **Bank of America** at 35 West Napa Street and **Wells Fargo** just down the street at 480 West Napa Street. If you are faced with a medical emergency, head for the **Sonoma Valley Hospital** (347 Andrieux St., 707/935-5000, www.svh.com), which has a full-service emergency room.

Getting There and Around

The town of Sonoma lies over the mountains west of the Napa Valley. The main route through the valley is Highway 12, also called the Sonoma Highway. From Napa, drive south on Highway 29, turning west onto Highway 12/121. Turn north on Highway 12 to reach downtown Sonoma.

If driving from San Francisco, take U.S. 101 north to Highway 37. Turn north onto Highway 121 and follow it as it bends east and intersects with Highway 12. If you're driving south on U.S. 101, you can turn off onto Highway 12 South in Santa Rosa and take a scenic journey down into the Sonoma-Carneros wine region.

Once downtown, parking is easy in the

Glen Ellen

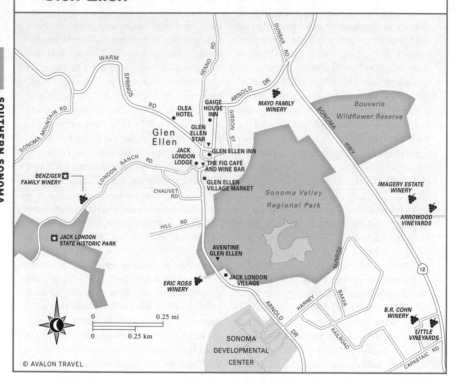

© AVALON TRAVEL

off-season and tougher in the high season (summer and fall). Expect to hunt hard for a spot during any local events, and prepare to walk several blocks. For your public transit needs, use the buses run by **Sonoma County Transit** (707/576-7433 or 800/345-7433, www.sctransit.com, $1.50-4.80). Several routes service the Sonoma Valley on both weekdays and weekends. You can use SCT to get from the Sonoma Valley to Santa Rosa, Guerneville, and other spots in the Russian River Valley as well.

GLEN ELLEN

Only six miles up Highway 12 from Sonoma, but tucked away in the leafy glen of Sonoma Creek, Glen Ellen gives very little sign of being a part of "Wine Country." The sleepy town hugs Arnold Drive, which parallels Highway 12. Its population is just 784, and on the main drag through town there are only two grocery stores, a handful of good but casual restaurants, a hardware store, and a couple of tasting rooms. Even in the height of summer, this town, cool under its shady oak canopy, can feel deserted.

But Glen Ellen has always been a popular draw, particularly with the literary set. M.F.K Fisher spent her final years here, and Hunter S. Thompson lived in Glen Ellen in the mid-1960s. But its most famous writer in residence was Jack London, whose presence can be felt throughout the area, from his haunt up on Sonoma Mountain, now Jack London State Park, to the redbrick Jack London Saloon, which first opened its doors in 1905.

Wineries

Glen Ellen is home to the Sonoma Mountain AVA, which produces unique cabernets from its rocky soils and cooler temperatures. Within the diverse microclimates also can be found chardonnay, pinot noir, sauvignon blanc, semillon, and zinfandel. Tasting here is a low key affair. You won't find any big historic wineries but plenty of laid-back tasting rooms with relatively modest tasting fees that make the most of their rustic locations.

MADRONE ESTATE WINERY

A little bit of history can be found at the **Madrone Estate Winery** (777 Madrone Rd., 707/939-4500, www.madroneestatewinery.com, 10am-5pm daily, tasting $15). Since the Civil War era, this Sonoma institution has passed through many hands (including George Hearst's, father of William Randolph) and produced hundreds of wines. In 2012, the winery was changed once again from the well-known Valley of the Moon winery to the Madrone Estate Winery. Renovated and rebranded, the winery continues to produce Valley of the Moon's vast and diverse portfolio, but in the 1880s stone tasting room, you'll taste wine from the 60 acres of estate vineyards, including sauvignon blanc, barbera,

sangiovese, an award-winning cabernet, and zinfandel made from the area's oldest zinfandel clones. To explore the workings of the winery and the historic barrel cellar, consider taking a tour (10:30am and 1pm Mon.-Thurs., 10:30am Sat.-Sun., $25). Reservations are recommended, but walk-ins are welcome. The winery also offers seating on the stone patio and a bocce ball court.

LITTLE VINEYARDS FAMILY WINERY

Step back in time to Sonoma in the 1980s at **Little Vineyards Family Winery** (15188 Sonoma Hwy, 707/996-2750, www.littlevineyards.com, 11am-4:30pm Thurs.-Mon., tasting $15-25), an unpretentious must for aficionados of big reds and seekers of the laid-back, bohemian attitude for which Sonoma is known. The century-old farmhouse vineyard, planted with 17 acres of grapes, is the dream creation of Joan and Rich Little for the production of premium reds. Zinfandel, syrah, and cabernet sauvignon are the primary varietals, as well as a small block of cabernet franc, malbec, petite sirah, and merlot. The tasting room walls, lined with guitars, reflect another of Rich Little's passions—music. Taste a fusion of both in the acclaimed Band Blend. A true

Glen Ellen

boutique winery, Little produces only 2,200 cases a year. Tours of the vineyards and winery are available by appointment Saturday-Monday at 11am ($40).

B. R. COHN WINERY

More red can be found at the nearby **B. R. Cohn Winery** (15000 Sonoma Hwy., 800/330-4064, www.brcohn.com, 10am-5pm daily, tours by appointment, tasting $20), which produces highly regarded cabernet from its Olive Hill vineyard, which has its own microclimate warmed by an underground geothermal aquifer and shielded from cool air by Sonoma Mountain. Also available to taste are Russian River pinot gris, Carneros chardonnay, and Sonoma malbec, zinfandel, and merlot.

The olive trees surrounding the buildings and lining the driveway give the vineyard not only its name but also some award-winning olive oil available in the tasting room. The estate oil as well as various blended oils and unusual vinegars, such as raspberry champagne vinegar and cabernet vinegar, are sold in the tasting room, and many can be sampled.

You might also hear Doobie Brothers songs wafting over the patio, giving away Bruce Cohn's other profession as the manager of the Doobies since the early 1970s and some other bands in the 1980s, including Bruce Hornsby and Night Ranger. The music connection continues to this day—the winery hosts musicians on Sunday afternoons in the summer.

ARROWOOD VINEYARDS & WINERY

The professional vibe at picturesque **Arrowood Vineyards & Winery** (14347 Sonoma Hwy., 707/935-2600 or 800/938-5170, www.arrowoodvineyards.com, 10am-4:30pm daily, tasting $15-25) may seem more in line with Napa's Silverado Trail than Sonoma's Valley of the Moon, but the wines are exceptional. You'll find wines from grapes grown exclusively in Sonoma County's diverse microclimates, including a variety of cabernet for which the winery

is best known, as well as a Russian River rosé, an Alexander Valley sauvignon blanc, a Carneros chardonnay, and a late harvest vineyard-specific riesling from the Russian River Valley. Many of these can be tasted in the Signature flight ($15), or for $25 you can just stick to Arrowood's cabernets with a flight of four, or opt for the wine and cheese pairing (reservations required). Located in a New England-style farmhouse with a wraparound veranda, the airy tasting room overlooks well-manicured vineyards and commands lovely views of the Sonoma Valley from its place on the eastern hillside.

IMAGERY ESTATE WINERY

The world's largest collection of wine-label art by some well-known contemporary artists (including Sol LeWitt and Terry Winters) is one reason to visit **Imagery Estate Winery** (14335 Sonoma Hwy., 707/935-3020 or 877/550-4278, www.imagerywinery.com, 10am-4:30pm Mon.-Fri., 10am-5:30pm Sat.-Sun., tasting $15). Another is the wide variety of small-lot wines that are available only at the winery itself. Imagery was established as a boutique offshoot of the **Benziger Family Winery** in the 1980s when art labels were catching on. Thirty years later, visitors can view much of the artwork in Imagery's gallery/tasting room.

The wines poured in the modern light-filled tasting room are sourced from estate vineyards near the valley floor and up in the higher elevations of Sonoma Mountain and Pine Mountain-Cloverdale Peak, an AVA since 2011, located at the northernmost point of the Mayacamas Mountains. From these come several blends and stand-alone varietals of malbec, petite sirah, and riesling, along with some unusual Italian and Spanish varietals. You can pick five to taste for $15. To make an afternoon of it, you can reserve one of Imagery's picnic tables for two hours. Included in the $50 fee is bocce ball, Jenga, and horseshoes, plus a bottle of one of Imagery's select white wines.

ERIC ROSS WINERY

You can almost imagine author Jack London himself relaxing with a book in the cozy tasting room of the **Eric Ross Winery** (14300 Arnold Dr., 707/939-8525, www.ericross. com, 11am-5pm daily, tasting $15), across the street from the Jack London Village complex. The bright red rustic building throngs with visitors on summer weekends, but during the week you'll likely have the comfy leather sofa inside to yourself. On winter days the fireplace makes it all the homier. The metal-topped corner tasting bar almost seems like an afterthought, but it's where all the action is to be found. The pinots in particular are worth trying, and there are usually two or three available to taste, each with a distinct character featuring classic Russian River complexity and smoothness. You'll also find a Sonoma Valley cabernet plus an old vine zinfandel from the Dry Creek Valley. More unusual is the Struttin Red blend of Portuguese varietals, co-fermented to create a wine with good acidity and structure, full of fruit and spice.

★ BENZIGER FAMILY WINERY

With vines poking out from the hillside grass, free-range cockerels crowing, and its collection of rustic wooden buildings hidden among the trees, the mountainside **Benziger Family Winery** (1883 London Ranch Rd., 707/935-3000 or 888/490-2739, www.benziger.com, 10am-5pm daily, tasting $20-30) seems like an old family farm rather than a commercial wine business. Started in the 1980s, Benziger is a family-run operation (some 30 Benziger folk call this land home) and the valley's only biodynamic winery.

To get a better understanding of this complex style of land stewardship, hop aboard one of their 45-minute tractor-drawn tours ($25, under 21 $10). You'll wind through the gorgeous and slightly wild-looking estate, while learning about biodynamic principles, the natural environment, and of course, the vines, the vintages, and winemaking in general. The tour concludes with stops at the winemaking facility and hillside storage cave and a special tasting of biodynamic wines. It's the best tour in the valley for the money and culminates with a basic tasting back at the large commercial tasting room. Tours are offered every half hour 11am-3:30pm, but the tram isn't big, so in the summer you should buy a ticket as far in advance as possible. If you miss the tour, check out the Biodynamic Discovery Trail just off the parking lot. The short walking tour guides you through the basics of biodynamics, while also providing a lovely place to sit in the shade and take in the scenery.

Once you're in the tasting room, you'll be reminded that this is a large-scale operation. The long bar pours a mix of organic and biodynamic Bordeaux blends, cabernet, zinfandel, and sauvignon blanc, many of which are estate grown. Prices are reasonable, starting at $25 and hovering around $45 per bottle. The tasting room is also filled with wine-related gifts and the standard cheese and salami fare, made more exciting with beautiful, handcrafted pickled veggies. Once you have selected your wine and snacks, head out to one of the many picnic options. Nibbling on food purchased elsewhere is also fine, and some of the shady spots even have wireless Internet.

MATANZAS CREEK WINERY

It's worth the 10-minute drive up scenic Bennett Valley Road (off Warm Springs Rd.) from Glen Ellen to visit **Matanzas Creek Winery** (6097 Bennett Valley Rd., Santa Rosa, 707/528-6464, www.matanzascreek. com, 10am-4:30pm daily, tasting $15-25), especially in May and June when the lavender is in full bloom and quite a sight (and smell) to behold. The winery is in the Bennett Valley AVA, nestled at the foot of the hills and surrounded by woods, flower-filled gardens, and the largest planting of lavender in California. Like the fields outside, the tasting room is filled with the scent of lavender in the form of soaps, oils, cut stems, and all sorts of other aromatic products for pampering and cooking. You'll also find wine, of course, including syrah and sauvignon blanc. But the winery is particularly well known for its chardonnays and limited-production merlots. Walk-in tastings run $15-25, while cheese paired with a current release flight costs $25. Private tours and tastings are available ($20-40 by appointment only), as is a round or two of bocce ball and picnicking surrounded by the fragrant, buzzing fields.

MAYO FAMILY WINERY

Founded in 1993, the **Mayo Family Winery** (13101 Arnold Dr. at Hwy. 12, 707/938-9401, www.mayofamilywinery.com, 10:30am-6:30pm daily, $10-15) boasts a big presence in the Sonoma Valley, with two winemaking facilities and a few tasting rooms. The winery is known for some of its unusual varietals, such as its smoky rich carignane and its fruity white viognier. Grapes are sourced largely from Sonoma vineyards, including two estate vineyards, one just south of Healdsburg in the Russian River AVA and the other at the foot of Sonoma Mountain. Outside the stone and wood tasting room are several oak shaded picnic tables where guests are invited to bring their lunch (and their pooch). Should you want your Mayo wine indoors, book a seated tasting at the winery's prized **Mayo Family Reserve Room** (9200 Sonoma Hwy., 707/833-5504, 10:30am-6:30pm daily,

reservations recommended, $40) up north in Kenwood. At the reserve tasting room, your experience includes seven tasting pours of Mayo's very best wines, each paired with a small bite of gourmet California cuisine created by on-site chefs. Bon appétit!

LOXTON CELLARS

Visiting **Loxton Cellars** (11466 Dunbar Rd., 707/935-7221, www.loxtoncellars.com, 11am-5pm daily, free tasting) is as unpretentious an experience as you can have in a valley that is already pretty laid-back. Owner and winemaker Chris Loxton hails from four generations of grape growers in his native Australia and has been making wines in the Sonoma Valley for over 20 years. He focuses mainly on syrah, which is sourced both from the five-acre estate vineyard surrounding the winery and from other growers in Sonoma County. In the makeshift tasting bar set up in the corner of the spotless, warehouse-style barrel room, you'll taste an earthy syrah from hillside fruit, a robust syrah port, a shiraz from Australian vine clones, and a cabernet-shiraz blend—a sure sign that there's an Aussie at work. The sole white is a delicate and bright chardonnay from the Russian River Valley. On Saturdays and Sundays at 10:30am, Loxton will take

Benziger Family Winery

guests on "walkabout" tours (by advance reservation, $25) of the vineyard and winery, followed by a sit-down tasting.

Recreation

Nothing screams picnic quite like Glen Ellen's shaded glens, oak-studded grasslands, and gently rolling hills. Thankfully this little hamlet has plenty of open space to spread a picnic blanket or stretch your legs after an afternoon of touring. Wedged between Highway 12 and Arnold Drive is the **Sonoma Valley Regional Park** (13630 Sonoma Hwy., 707/539-8092, www.sonoma-county.org/parks, sunrise-sunset daily, parking $7). A favorite with locals, the 202-acre park has paved and unpaved trails that wind through open oak woodland on the valley floor. Horseback riders, mountain bikers, and hikers are all welcome here, as are dogs, especially at the park's one-acre, fenced-in dog park. Picnic tables with barbecues can be found along the paved multiuse trail that bisects the park.

If you want to take full advantage of the beauty of the valley, it is worth it to plan ahead and book a guided tour at the nearby **Bouverie Preserve** (13935 Hwy. 12, 707/868-9244, www.egret.org/visit_bouverie). Home to 130 species of birds, 350 species of flowering plants, and diverse ecosystems that range from chaparral to mixed evergreen forest, the 535-acre preserve is accessible only on docent-led tours. Despite the lost spontaneity, a guided tour through this beautiful spot gives visitors a window into the natural world that gives the valley such beauty and produces such great wine. Tours take place 9:30am-1:30pm on select Saturdays in the spring and fall. A donation of $15 is suggested.

★ JACK LONDON STATE HISTORIC PARK

Literary travelers come to Sonoma not just for the fine food and abundant wine but for the chance to visit **Jack London State Historic Park** (2400 London Ranch Rd., 707/938-5216, www.parks.ca.gov or http://jacklondonpark.com, 9:30am-5pm daily, $10), the site of the 130-acre Beauty Ranch, where the famed author wrote and spent the last five years of his life. Inside the **House of Happy Walls** (10am-5pm daily) is the former residence of Jack London's widow, Charmian, who built it following London's death in 1916. It is now a museum dedicated to the author's life and adventures. From there it's only a half-mile walk on a paved trail to London's grave and the ruins of the spectacular **Wolf House,** his 17,000-square-foot dream home that burned down accidentally just before it was completed in 1913. Today, only the monumentally thick stone walls remain in the dappled shade of the surrounding redwoods.

Near the upper parking lot, you can also poke your head into the **London Cottage** (noon-4pm daily, adults $4, seniors $2, children 12 and under free), where he wrote many of his later books and died at a youthful 40 years old. Also available to explore is the piggery known as the Pig Palace and built by London himself, as well as many of the other buildings, which once belonged to the 19th-century Kohler and Frohling winery, including a barn, an old distillery building, and the ruins of the winery itself. Docents offer tours of the park, which include talks on London's life and history. Tours of Jack London's gravesite and the nearby Wolf House leave the Happy Walls museum at 11am and 1pm Saturday and Sunday, while tours of Beauty Ranch depart at 1:30pm on weekends. Both tours are free and last 1-1.5 hours.

To access the miles of **hiking** trails in the 800-acre park, take the **Lake Trail** uphill past the vineyards and through the redwoods for about half a mile to the forest-fringed lake created by London. There, you'll find **picnic spots,** restrooms, and trails that loop through oak woodland and meadows. To get your heart pumping, jump on the long **Mountain Trail** to the park summit next to Sonoma Mountain. That hike is about seven miles round-trip but can be lengthened by taking loops off the main trail. Another long hike is the **Sonoma Ridge Trail** (7-8 miles, moderate to strenuous), which leaves the

Mountain Trail and twists through forests and clearings with sweeping views before reaching the **Vineyard, Orchard, and Coon Trap Trails,** which together lead back to the lake.

Mountain biking is allowed on all the trails in the park except the Cowan Meadow, Fallen Bridge, and Lake Trails, plus the Mountain Spur Trail leading up to the park summit (2,370 feet). You might see a member of the Benziger family from the winery down the road hurtling by, but be aware that all trails are shared with hikers and some with horses. The Sonoma Ridge Trail loop is recommended over the Mountain Trail to the summit, which is a steep uphill and perilously rocky downhill.

To explore the park on **horseback,** book a trail ride with **Triple Creek Horse Outfit** (707/887-8700, www.triplecreekhorseoutfit. com). Public tours last 1 and 1.5 hours and cost $75 and $95, respectively. Riders meet just off the upper parking lot, and groups don't usually exceed six riders. Private 2-hour tours ($220) are also available, as are those that include a picnic lunch beneath the redwood trees (2.5 hours, $275). All rides are limited to those over eight years old and weighing less than 220 pounds. Wear long pants and appropriate footwear, and make reservations in advance (however, sometimes same-day calls get lucky). At the conclusion of your ride, you'll get a free pass to London's cottage and complimentary tasting passes to Benziger Family Winery.

Food

A big reason to stay in Glen Ellen is to take advantage of its excellent eateries. The number and diversity is disproportionate to the town's tiny population, which helps in getting a table. Calling ahead on busy weekends is never a bad idea, however.

CALIFORNIA CUISINE

Some of the most reasonably priced food in the valley, together with free corkage all the time, can be found in the heart of Glen Ellen at ★ **The Fig Café** (13690 Arnold Dr., 707/938-2130, 5pm-close Mon.-Sat., 11am-close Sun., $12-25). It is the North Valley offshoot of the popular **the girl & the fig** restaurant in Sonoma. The café serves up some of the same French bistro fare, although slightly scaled down. The menu leans more toward comfort food with grilled sandwiches, thin-crust pizzas, and main courses like braised pot roast. The bright, art-infused interior and Sunday brunch make it a sure bet. The

the House of Happy Walls at Jack London State Historic Park

Sonoma-dominated wine list is also more compact, but markups are modest enough that you might not even decide to take advantage of the free corkage.

Down the road is the yellow-ochre **Glen Ellen Inn** (13670 Arnold Dr., 707/996-6409, www.glenelleninn.com, 11:30am-8:30pm Thurs.-Tues., $16-28). With low ceilings, warm lighting, and lush earth tones, the restaurant of the Glen Ellen Inn can feel like either a cool retreat from a hot valley afternoon or a cozy hideaway on a cold wintry night. The restaurant seats 80, but thanks to patio seating, tables on both a covered and an open-air deck, and more tucked throughout the old building, it feels like a much smaller operation. A well-stocked bar sits just off the main entrance, encouraging a quiet cocktail in a romantic atmosphere, while you pore over the California-style menu. Changing with the seasons, the menu is unpretentious and offers items like the Kobe burger, a range of oysters, and a Wine Country cioppino. Desserts are something to behold though bordering on a little too fussy.

Since it opened in 2012, the ★ **Glen Ellen Star** (13648 Arnold Dr., 707/343-1384, www. glenellenstar.com, 5:30pm-9pm Sun.-Thurs., 5:30pm-9:30pm Fri.-Sat., $18) has been a favorite, representing the newest wave of California and also Wine Country cuisine. It serves locally sourced, wood oven-fired fare (i.e., pizzas, roasted meats, vegetables, and iron skillet quickbreads) that leans heavily toward comfort food with a slightly urban sensibility. The wood and brushed metal interior is spare, with a gleaming, stainless steel open kitchen. Reservations are encouraged, but the patio and bar seating remain open to walk-ins. On Wednesdays the restaurant offers a special Neighborhood Night menu of two courses and free corkage for $30.

Aventine Glen Ellen (14301 Arnold Dr., 707/934-8911, http://glenellen.aventinehospitality.com, 4:30pm-9pm Wed.-Thurs. and Sun., 4:30pm-10pm Fri.-Sat., $14-32), housed in an old gristmill, offers classic Italian dishes revamped with an epicurean delight, plus a wide selection of beer, wine, and craft cocktails. With the 40-foot waterwheel outside, the restaurant has an earthy, historic feel, and the patio is surrounded by a thick forest of evergreens.

PICNIC SUPPLIES

Glen Ellen not only has top-notch places to picnic, but also a great local grocery to pick up supplies, the **Glen Ellen Village Market** (13751 Arnold Dr., 707/996-6728, https://sonomamarket.net, 5am-9pm daily). Owned by the same partners as the Sonoma Market, this full-service grocery is stocked with all the essentials in addition to an outstanding deli that serves upscale treats like asparagus wrapped in prosciutto and golden beet and goat cheese salads, along with down-home favorites like fried chicken. There is a whole deli case devoted to specialty cheeses and one of the best and most diverse olive bars around. If you're looking for a bottle to take on your picnic, there is a whole aisle of just local vintages (many of which cannot be found at most grocery stores) at exceptionally good prices.

While only open seasonally May-December and one day a week, the **Red Barn Store** (15101 Sonoma Hwy., 707/996-6643, 9am-3pm Sat.) sells produce from the organic Oak Hill Farm and some fabulous freshly cut flowers, as well as handmade wreaths, making it worth a stop. You can find this little gem of a store off Highway 12 just north of Madrone Road near Glen Ellen.

Accommodations
UNDER $150

Attached to the redbrick Jack London Saloon and Wolf House Restaurant, the **Jack London Lodge** (13740 Arnold Dr., 707/938-8510, www.jacklondonlodge.com, $95-185) anchors central Glen Ellen. The 22-room lodge is modern, with a broad patio, a kidney-shaped pool, and groomed lawns. The inn's interior offers a more Victorian feel with dark wood furniture, rich linens, and low lighting, but the relative newness of the building shines through. Vines draping the balcony are a nice touch, as is the hot tub and the creek running through the back of the property.

$150-250

To stay in authentic historic lodgings, book a room, suite, or cottage at the ★ **Olea Hotel** (5131 Warm Springs Rd., 707/996-5131, www.oleahotel.com, $215-475), a B&B tucked away behind Glen Ellen. Built at the turn of the 20th century to accommodate railroad travelers, it has been receiving guests for over a hundred years. Today, spare and modern furnishings grace the rooms, which are all equipped with flat-screen TVs and Internet access. Some rooms come with a stone fireplace, while others boast an expansive porch overlooking the charming and well-maintained grounds. For more privacy, 300-square-foot cottages dot the property. All guests receive a hot two-course breakfast and are encouraged to end their day with a soak in the outdoor communal hot tub and the complimentary wine-tasting in the lobby. The revamped hotel also offers massage services ($110-160) and accommodations for your pooch (an extra $25) that include a welcome basket full of treats, doggie bags, bowls, and towels.

A little less polished but loaded with charm is the **Glen Ellen Inn** (13670 Arnold Dr., 707/996-1174, www.glenelleninn.com, $149-275), right in the center of town. Billed as cottages, the seven rooms are more like 1940s-style bungalows that each open out to a shared overgrown courtyard with a hot tub overlooking the creek. Like the restaurant only feet away in a separate building, the rooms are decorated in bold earth tones with overstuffed beds and chairs. The interiors feel a little dated, but they are still exceptionally cozy, surrounded by the lush greenery of the glen with the creek bubbling outside. Each room is outfitted with a deep whirlpool tub and a gas fireplace. Many have mini-fridges.

Just outside of Glen Ellen, the **Beltane Ranch B&B** (11775 Sonoma Hwy., 707/996-6501, www.beltaneranch.com, $185-295) looks like a little piece of the Deep South landed in the vineyards. The Victorian-era house with its New Orleans-style wraparound veranda and lush gardens sits in the middle of the valley at the end of a long driveway, far from the madding crowds of Highway 12. The five tastefully furnished, white-paneled rooms evoke a bygone era without going over the top, and all except the one downstairs room open onto the veranda. Additional privacy can be found in the two-room cottage for not too much more per night. The ranch is actually 105 acres of vineyards, pasture, and woods at the foot of the Mayacamas Mountains, with miles of hiking trails and a tennis court for guests.

OVER $250

An alternative to the big-name luxury resorts in the valley is the lavishly appointed and fantastically Zen **Gaige House Inn** (13540 Arnold Dr., 800/935-0237, www.gaige.com, $275-595), where the serene setting is complemented by contemporary Asian-inspired furnishings, gourmet breakfasts, a big outdoor pool, and indulgent spa treatments to help soften the financial blow. The cheapest of the 23 rooms are in the main Victorian house, and as the price increases the features include fireplaces and small private Japanese Zen gardens. The more expensive suites include truly indulgent bathrooms, while the Creekside rooms add a private patio overlooking Calabazas Creek to the package. Vaulting into the next price category are stunning, Asian-minimalist spa suites, each with its own freestanding granite soaking tub, sliding glass walls, and contemporary furnishings.

Information and Services

The small town of Glen Ellen does not have a visitors center, so stock up on your maps and tips before you leave Sonoma. The **Sonoma Valley Visitors Bureau** (453 1st St. E., Sonoma, 707/996-1090 or 866/996-1090, www.sonomavalley.com, 9am-5pm Mon.-Sat., 10am-5pm Sun.) will have information for Glen Ellen. Online you can check out the website of the **Sonoma County Wineries Association** (www.sonomawine.com) and the **Heart of Sonoma Valley Association** (www.heartofthevalley.com), which represents only those wineries around Glen Ellen and Kenwood.

Likewise, don't expect to find much in the way of banks, gas stations, wireless Internet access or reliable cell phone reception, so be sure to take care of any of these needs before leaving Sonoma.

Getting There and Around

The heart of Glen Ellen is just off Highway 12 over seven miles north of Sonoma. Arnold Drive is the main street through town and runs all the way to Sonoma. To get there from Santa Rosa, take Highway 12 east, through Kenwood, for 15.7 miles.

KENWOOD

Kenwood is the last town in the Sonoma Valley before you hit Santa Rosa to the north. Here the valley fans out and the Mayacamas Mountains to the east grow wilder and more rugged. Thankfully, this translates to three large state and regional parks for picnicking, hiking, mountain biking, horseback riding, and even stargazing. Unlike the towns of Sonoma and Glen Ellen, Kenwood is loosely arranged on Highway 12 and lacks a traditional main street. Instead, the center of town sits in the Kenwood Village Plaza, with its post office, a couple tasting rooms, and a popular restaurant. You will also find the most renowned and luxurious spa in the valley, but that does not mean that the funky town has been minted in Napa's upscale image.

Wineries

Firmly planted in the Sonoma Valley AVA, Kenwood is home to a couple of large wineries with big architectural ambition, in addition to smaller, mostly independent operations.

DEERFIELD RANCH WINERY

At **Deerfield Ranch Winery** (10200 Sonoma Hwy., 707/833-5215, http://deerfieldranch.com, 10:30am-4:30pm daily, tasting $15-20), all tastings, despite the beauty of the ranch,

take place inside the cave. It's pretty cool, and not in that musty cold cave kind of way. The winery is set off from the highway, deep in the Sonoma countryside, with two life-size rusted metal giraffes standing sentinel by the lake. The winery itself looks both quaint and industrial. This feeling follows as you pass the crush pad, the fermenting tanks, and barrels of wine on the way to the cave. Once there, you'll be amazed at the warmth and coziness of the wineglass-shaped cave. Filled with plush couches and overstuffed chairs instead of the standard tasting bar, the room makes you feel like you have paid a premium for a VIP or reserve tasting, but the price is only $15. To add to the bargain, you are likely to get a seasoned employee or partner who knows their wine. Deerfield makes an impressive range of wines, from sparkling to cabernet, from Sonoma grapes, each of which is carefully crafted to minimize the "red wine headache" that the winemaker believes is an allergic reaction to various components of wine. Careful sorting of grapes, a rigorous commitment to cleanliness, and the limited use of sulfites are all employed as means to this end.

KUNDE ESTATE WINERY

Unlike the small Deerfield Ranch Winery, the **Kunde Estate Winery** (9825 Sonoma Hwy., 707/833-5501, www.kunde.com, 10:30am-5pm daily, tasting $15-30) sprawls across 2,000 acres of valley land, making it the largest family-owned winery in the West. A whopping 800 acres of estate vineyards grow 20 varietals of grapes from the valley floor up to elevations of 1,000 feet on the terraced hillsides. In fact, the winery has enough vineyards, and varied enough growing conditions, to make only estate wines and still have enough fruit left to sell to neighboring wineries.

Grapes have been grown here by the Kunde family since 1904, and today it is best known for its zinfandel, cabernet sauvignon, and vineyard-designate chardonnays. There are also plenty of good picnic wines to complement an alfresco lunch in the shady lakeside picnic area.

The spacious tasting room rarely seems crowded, but if you want to escape it, you can take your flight to the outside 202 Lounge open April-October. Otherwise the price goes up to $30 with the private reserve tasting paired with cheese in the Kinneybrook Room. Free tours of the aging caves stretching half a mile under the hillside behind the winery occur daily 11am-3pm on the hour. All you have to do is ask. Other tours (also read hikes) are led around the vast estate on various Sundays starting at 9am and lasting four hours. These cost $30, require a reservation, and conclude with a flight of current release wines in the tasting room. To skip the perspiration, pay another $50 and jump aboard one of the winery's passenger vans to the mountaintop tasting room (10:30am, noon, 1:30pm, 3pm daily, 21 and over only). Along the way, you will explore the caves and vineyards and learn about the winery's sustainable practices. The tour ends with a tasting 1,400 feet above the valley floor. Reservations are recommended, but walk-ins can be accommodated.

SUNCE

If you are driven to try a variety of varietals, make a stop at **Sunce** (9580 Sonoma Hwy., Kenwood, 707/282-9387, www.suncewinery. com, 10:30am-5:30pm daily, tasting complimentary), the redwood-sided tasting room in the heart of Kenwood. The Russian River winery grows an astonishing number of varietals (41 as of the winery's 24th harvest), including regional standards such as chardonnay and pinot noir and also lesser known varietals like Alicante bouschet and negroamaro. All are produced in small quantities, under 16 barrels each, and many win awards. There will often be as many as 20 wines on the tasting menu; you can pick any five for a complimentary tasting.

MUSCARDINI CELLARS

Occupying Kenwood's historic 1860 Red Schoolhouse is **Muscardini Cellars** (9380 Sonoma Hwy., 707/933-9305, www. muscardinicellars.com, tasting $15-25,

11am-6pm Wed.-Mon., Tues. by appointment). Channeling his grandfather Emilio, who made table wine for the family, Michael Muscardini planted his first grapes in 2000 and soon thereafter began making award-winning wine, most notably his organic sangiovese. He continues to focus on Italian varietals, growing many of his own grapes while sourcing the rest from growers inside the Sonoma Valley. As such, the tasting room is chock-full of barbera, tesoro, syrah, and, of course, sangiovese. A real treat is the dry and crisp Rosato di Sangiovese, a rosé given 91 points by *Wine Enthusiast*. Flights of five ($15-25) are available in the relaxed tasting room, or you can take your wine out on the patio or shaded picnic tables beyond.

TY CATON

Ty Caton (8910 Hwy. 12, 707/938-3224, www. tycaton.com, 11am-6pm daily, tasting $15-25), located in the Kenwood Village Plaza, has become a favorite in the valley, known for producing excellent wine at extremely affordable prices. In the tasting room, which also sells mustards, vinegars, and olive oil, you'll find bold cabernets, big syrahs, and zesty zinfandels sourced from grapes grown in its Moon Mountain vineyards. The award-winning Tytanium is a blend of five varietals that includes cabernet sauvignon, syrah, petite sirah, merlot, and malbec, but its price point is $80, putting it out of range of many wine enthusiasts. Instead, for a terrific value, look for Ty's Red, another blend that, while not taking home the gold, is, for $34, a great value. If you're visiting on an off-season weekday, you may find yourself alone in the shop, discussing the wine regions of California and various varietals for more than an hour. Even in-season, this small tasting room preserves the kind of wine-tasting experience that wine lovers have been coming to Sonoma for decades to enjoy.

★ CHATEAU ST. JEAN

If you were to build your own personal château in the Sonoma Valley, you couldn't pick a much better location than this. A long driveway through the vineyards leads up to **Chateau St. Jean** (8555 Sonoma Hwy., 707/833-5284, www.chateaustjean.com, 10am-5pm daily, tasting $15-25), a white turreted mansion at the foot of the mountains. The walk from the parking lot to the tasting rooms leads through a manicured formal garden, and on the other side of the reserve tasting room is a patio and expanse of lawn overlooking the valley and its vineyards.

Although St. Jean is best known for its white wines (which include multiple chardonnays, pinot blanc, riesling, and fumé blanc), it also has its share of big reds, including Cinq Cepages, a Bordeaux-style red blend of five varietals—some grown in a tiny vineyard perched on a steep slope above the winery— that is always rated highly by critics. Flights of five are available in the spacious main tasting room, which has a small deli and countless Wine Country gifts, but it's worth spending a little extra to taste wines in the more comfortable and intimate reserve tasting room. Chateau St. Jean also offers a pairing of cheese and charcuterie out on the patio (reservation required, $45), or you can grab your own picnic supplies (plus a bottle or glass of wine) and find a seat at one of the estate's many outdoor picnic tables.

LANDMARK VINEYARDS

Landmark Vineyards (101 Adobe Canyon Rd., 707/833-0053, www.landmarkwine.com, 10am-5pm daily, tasting $10-20) was one of the first California wineries to make only chardonnay, though it has since expanded to include pinot noir, and the rare syrah, grenache, and pinot gris, all made using grapes from the 11 acres of estate vineyards and others sourced from all over California.

Chardonnay still accounts for the majority of the production, with pinot noir a close second. Prices for both range $25-60. Flights of five are available in the main tasting room, or you can ascend to the Tower Tasting for a private flight of single-vineyard chardonnay and/or pinot noir (by reservation, $40). Outside, the large shady Spanish-style courtyard leads to a fountain and gardens with a view straight over the vineyards to Sugarloaf Mountain in the distance. On Saturday afternoons (noon-3pm, May-Oct.) you may hop aboard the horse-drawn carriage for a tour of the vineyards for no additional charge (or reservation). You may also just take advantage of the few picnic tables where you can enjoy a flight of current release wines with a premade box lunch ($35 with at least 24-hour notice) or snack on the selection of cheese and charcuterie offered inside. There is also a free bocce ball court to test how straight you can throw after a few glasses of wine.

ST. FRANCIS WINERY & VINEYARDS

Named to honor the Franciscan monks who are widely credited with planting California's first wine grapes, **St. Francis Winery & Vineyards** (100 Pythian Rd., 707/538-9463 or 888/675-9463, www.stfranciswine.com, 10am-5pm daily, tasting $15) is a place for red-wine lovers, and particularly merlot fans and fans of Spanish architecture. The spacious tasting room is one of the best designed in the valley. Windows running the length of the room look out onto the vineyards and mountains, and you can easily escape into the garden if it gets too crowded.

Picnickers are welcome on the sun-drenched patio across the lawn from the tasting room, while the tables just outside the large picture windows are reserved for those indulging in the charcuterie and wine pairing (11am-4pm daily, no reservation required). The $35 fee includes a selection of local cheese, charcuterie, and house-made rillettes, and either a flight of reserve wines or a full glass of your selection. Want to make it into a lunch? For $68 (11am, 1pm, and 3pm Thurs.-Mon.), you can get five courses that highlight the diversity of the wine selection. Call or check the website for the current menu and to make a reservation; walk-ins can also often be accommodated.

LEDSON WINERY & VINEYARDS

At the top of the valley, the "Castle," as it's known to locals—a description that at first was meant more in a derogatory sense but has now been embraced by the **Ledson Winery & Vineyards** (7335 Sonoma Hwy., 707/537-3810, www.ledsonwinery.com, 10am-5pm daily, tasting $15-20)—is about as ostentatious as Sonoma gets, and it's still a far cry from the palaces (and actual castles) in the Napa Valley.

Enter through the grand front door, pass the sweeping staircase, polished oak accents, and marble fireplaces, and you almost feel like you're walking onto the set of some Wine Country soap opera. There are no fewer than six tasting bars in various rooms, together with a small marketplace stocked with wines, mustards, vinegars, a selection of cheeses, sandwiches, and other not-too-exciting picnic supplies including macaroni and potato salad. You can picnic on the grounds in the shade of a giant oak tree, although there's limited space and you can only eat food bought at the winery itself. Almost every grape varietal is represented in the portfolio, from pinot grigio to the estate merlot, so there's bound to be a wine to please everyone in the flights of five ($15) or seven ($20) wines.

Shopping

There is not much in the way of shopping in Kenwood, but a few shops stand out and deserve a stop. The wacky **Swede's Feeds Pet Garden Gifts** (9140 Sonoma Hwy., 707/833-5050, www.swedesfeeds.com, 10am-6pm Mon. and Wed.-Fri., 10am-5pm Sat., 11am-4pm Sun.) is technically a country feed store, but it carries everything from chicken feed to decorative pots to unusual succulents, outside fireplaces, garden sculptures, and bright pinwheels. Even if you don't have a garden, this is a great place to stop and spend some time browsing. Quality gifts can also be found across the highway at the **Kenwood Farmhouse** (9255 Sonoma Hwy., 707/833-1212, 11am-5:30pm Wed.-Fri., 11am-5pm Sat.-Sun.). A cute little red farmhouse, it showcases local artisans and has a selection of fair-trade clothing and various household, garden, and kitchen wares.

Recreation

ANNADEL STATE PARK

Redwoods, oaks, meadows, and a large well-stocked lake make **Annadel State Park** (6201 Channel Dr., Santa Rosa, 707/539-3911, www.parks.ca.gov, 8am-sunset daily, $6/car) one of the most diverse of Sonoma Valley's

A tasting at St. Francis Winery & Vineyards comes with beautiful views.

Ledson Winery & Vineyards

Trail loop; and the rockier Orchard and Cobblestone Trails (including the Orchard Loop). Lake Ilsanjo is pretty much the center of the park and a good start and end point for many biking loops, although it can be relatively crowded on summer weekends. The best way to reach it from the main parking lot is to ride up the Warren Richardson fire road, saving the single-track for going downhill.

An alternative entrance that avoids the entrance fee and is popular with mountain bikers is on Lawndale Road. From Highway 12, take a left just north of the Landmark Vineyards; the unmarked dirt parking lot is on the right about a mile down the road. Farther up Lawndale Road, forking off to the right, is Schultz Road, leading to the Schultz Trailhead. It's better to bike up the Schultz Trail and come down Lawndale, but you will have to bike up to the Shultz Trailhead as there is no parking there.

The best time to go **hiking** in Annadel is spring or early summer when the wildflowers are in full bloom in the meadows around Lake Ilsanjo. The two-mile trek from the parking lot up the Warren Richardson Trail to the lake gives a good cross section of the park's flora, starting in a forest of redwoods and Douglas fir and climbing up through oaks to the relatively flat area around the lake where miles of other trails converge.

Steve's "S" Trail, which branches off and then rejoins the Richardson Trail, is one of the few trails off-limits to bikes and therefore worth taking if you'd prefer to avoid speeding bikers. Allow about four hours to make the round-trip and explore the lake area. At the lake are picnic areas and restrooms, plus access to the rest of the trail network.

Fishing at the lake is also popular, with largemouth bass and bluegill the most common catch. The Park Service suggests the purple plastic worm as the best bait for bass, and garden worms or grubs are favored by bluegills. Anyone over age 16 must have a California fishing license.

parks. The rocky trails throughout this 5,500-acre park that make Annadel a bone-jarring ride for mountain bikers today also give away its previous life as an important source of obsidian for Native American tools and cobblestones for cities up and down the West Coast in the early 1900s. There's still some evidence of quarrying on many of the trails, including the aptly named Cobblestone Trail, which used to be the route of a tramway carrying rock down the hill to the railroad.

Mountain bikers love the fact that most of the trails are either single-track or double-track and strewn with rocks for a bit of added fear. This is probably not the best place for novice bikers to find their wheels, but it offers some of the best midlevel mountain biking in the Bay Area, with plenty of technical trails and an elevation gain and drop of about 1,000 feet for most loops.

Popular downhills include the Lawndale Trail from Ledson Marsh, a smooth, fast single-track through the forest; the Marsh

★ SUGARLOAF RIDGE STATE PARK

Sugarloaf Ridge State Park (2605 Adobe Canyon Rd., 707/833-5712, www.parks. ca.gov, sunrise-sunset, $8) is perfect for either a quick fix of shady redwood forests or for hikes to some of the best views, both terrestrial and extraterrestrial, in the valley. It's about a 10-minute drive up Adobe Canyon Road from the Landmark Winery and has the only campground in the valley. Winter to early summer, the park draws visitors to admire the 25-foot waterfall that tumbles just a few hundred yards from the parking lot. Take the Canyon Trail or the 0.75-mile-long shady Creekside Nature Trail that runs from the picnic area.

The big **hiking** draw is the seven-mile round-trip slog up to the summit of 2,729-foot Bald Mountain, rewarded by spectacular 360-degree views of the North Bay. It starts off on paved fire roads, but the paving soon ends as the trail climbs 1,500 feet in about three miles with no shade at all, so take a hat and plenty of water in the summer. From the summit, the Grey Pine Trail offers an alternative route downhill, and on the way up there's a short detour to the peak of neighboring Red Mountain, which sits, technically, on private property.

To get 12 inches closer to the sun, there's an equally long and hot hike from the parking lot to the 2,730-foot summit of Hood Mountain, which lies in neighboring Hood Mountain Regional Park. The dirt parking lot for the Goodspeed Trailhead is on the left of Adobe Canyon Road next to a stand of redwood trees just before the road starts climbing steeply.

From the lot, the **Nattkemper-Goodspeed Trail** crosses Bear Creek through the forest, eventually steepening for the next three miles into exposed grass and scrubland. At the ridge you can bear left for the sweeping views west from the Gunsight Rock Overlook, or turn right and trek the remaining half mile up to the Hood Mountain summit. Allow at least five hours round-trip. During fire season (June-Oct.) the trail is occasionally closed about halfway up but is still a good place to go for a picnic.

For a walk around the sun, park at the main lot ($8 parking fee) and follow the interpretive path through the solar system. Beginning at the sun, each planet is proportionally correct in size and distance from the sun and the other planets, demonstrating the size and scope of our solar system. The walk takes over an hour and you'll enjoy lovely views along the way. Nearby, the **Robert Ferguson Observatory** (707/833-6979, www.rfo.org, $3 for night viewing, under age 18 free, daytime solar viewing free), the largest observatory open to the general public on the West Coast, offers daytime solar viewing and regular stargazing through 8-, 14-, and 40-inch telescopes. There are usually one or two public day- and night-viewing sessions per month, plus regular astronomy classes throughout the year ($23 for one class, $75 for a series of six). Check the website or call for the current schedule.

MOUNT HOOD REGIONAL PARK

Just to the north of Sugarloaf Ridge State Park is **Mount Hood Regional Park** (1450 Pythian Rd., Santa Rosa, 707/539-8092, http://parks.sonomacounty.ca.gov, 7am-sunset daily, $7/car). It also sits not too far up the road from the valley's tasting rooms (the closest being St. Francis Winery), but with less of a big-name reputation the picnic tables, situated beneath bay laurels, oaks, and redwoods just off the trailhead parking lot, are more likely to be empty.

With no campgrounds or special facilities like an observatory, **hiking** the park's 19 miles of trails is the big draw here. From the Pythian picnic area, the Lower Johnson Ridge Trail hugs Hood Creek, switchbacking two miles up 2,000 feet through riparian woodland to the exposed higher elevations of the park. The Pond and the Valley Loop Trails veer off the main trail to the right and, true to their names, offer excellent valley vistas and picnic sites around Merganser and Blue Heron Ponds. This area is also abundant in natural springs. If you are eager to summit the valley's highest peak, Hood Mountain (2,730 feet), Lower Johnson Ridge Trail turns into Panorama Ranch Trail, which connects to Hood Mountain Trail for a moderate to strenuous eight-mile hike. To make it all strenuous, veer off the Panorama Ranch Trail at the Orchard Meadow Trail, which becomes Upper Johnson Ridge Trail, leading to the summit. Hood Mountain is less than a mile from where Upper Johnson Ridge Trail departs from Orchard Meadow, but it is a steep, dusty climb. Gunsight Rock Overlook is less than half a mile away and showcases the occasional glimpse of the Golden Gate Bridge in addition to its peregrine falcon resident in the spring and summer.

Sharp changes in elevation and rocky, challenging trails are considered by some to be the ideal conditions for adrenaline-filled **mountain biking.** The mixed-use Hood Mountain funnels mountain bikers from the 3000 Los Alamos Road trailhead in Santa Rosa to the large network of multiuse trails both in Mount Hood Regional Park and in the neighboring Sugarloaf Ridge State Park. Nearly all the trails are open to bikers, but if you are looking for a quiet backcountry experience, take the hiking-only Summit Trail as an alternative to Hood Mountain. An added benefit is that the trail slices through the pygmy forest that sits in the saddle of Hood Mountain's northeastern slope. Mostly made up of Sargent cypress, the forest is roughly 10-15 feet high and extends for nearly a quarter mile. Despite the riparian and forested reprieves, the majority of the park is exposed chaparral and home to wonderful rock outcroppings, poison oak, and, in the summer, rattlesnakes and blistering temperatures. Bring plenty of water and sunscreen.

THE KENWOOD SPA

If you are looking for some famous Wine Country pampering after all that wine-tasting and dusty exploring of the area's regional parks, make an appointment at **The Kenwood Spa** (10400 Sonoma Hwy.,

800/353-6966, www.kenwoodinn.com/spa. php, 9am-9pm daily). It might not have its own source of mineral water like its cousin down in Sonoma, but the spa makes full use of the surrounding vineyards and has been declared one of the top resort spas in the United States by *Condé Nast Traveler* every year 2007-2015. The wraps, baths, and other treatments use vine and grape-seed extracts to purify body and mind. Choose between the Pinot Noir, Chardonnay, and Sparkling baths to fully immerse yourself in Wine Country ($69). If you are looking to purify your body *of* wine, you can choose from other edible treatments like Hot Chocolate Body Wrap or the Spicy Mud Slimming Wrap, both $199. For treatments that don't sound like you're ordering something at a restaurant, the spa also has an array of clinical facials, Hollywood-esque oxygen treatments ($159-299), and plain old massages ($149-279). Reservations are a must.

Food

If you're hungry in Kenwood the only option is **Palooza Gastropub and Wine Bar** (8910 Sonoma Hwy., 707/833-4000, www.paloozafresh.com, 11:30am-9pm Sun.-Thurs., 11:30am-10pm Fri.-Sat., $9-18). While it may not be the height of Wine Country cuisine, it is a fun, affordable option for everyone from families to travelers with a foodie bent. The menu is pure pub food with hot dogs, burgers, fish-and-chips, and barbecued ribs, served with house-made pickles, potato chips, and original sauces. For $16 you can opt for the cheese board with a glass of Sonoma wine ($7-11). Plenty of beer is also available and $1 cheaper at the Monday-Friday happy hour 4pm-6pm. Table tennis, pool, a giant Jenga, and a patio also make this a relaxed and fun option.

PICNIC SUPPLIES

Despite Kenwood's dearth of dining options, you will find plenty in the way of picnic supplies at **Ledson Winery** (7335 Sonoma Hwy., 707/537-3810, www.ledsonwinery.com, 10am-5pm daily, tasting $15-20). The gift shop doubles as a deli, serving premade salads, to-order sandwiches, and cheese and charcuterie. While it may not be the most gourmet option in the valley, it is certainly convenient to the excellent picnic spots in the nearby parks.

FARMERS MARKETS

To stock up on picnic supplies on your way down the valley, stop by the **Kenwood Community Farmers Market** (9000 Sonoma Hwy., 415/999-5635, 11am-3pm Sun., June 15-Sept. 18) in front of St. Patrick's Church near the Kunde Estate Winery. In addition to valley's freshest fruits and vegetables, you can also find eggs, cheese, sweet treats, locally crafted oils and vinegars, art, and even music.

Accommodations

In Kenwood, lodging options are limited to the extremes. You can either sleep under the stars or just pay astronomical prices for a room at Wine Country's most exclusive spas. Nonetheless, whatever your pocketbook or temperament can afford, both options are heavenly.

To make your stay in Kenwood a fabulous wine-and-spa getaway, stay at the **Kenwood Inn & Spa** (10400 Sonoma Hwy., 707/833-1293 or 800/353-6966, www.kenwoodinn.com, $425-475, no children under 18, no pets). The Tuscan-style villa has 27 posh guest rooms attached to its world-renowned spa. The on-site restaurant serves a complimentary breakfast (7:30am-10am daily); dinner (6pm-9pm Tues.-Sat., $28-48) of elegant Italian dishes such as pancetta-rolled pork tenderloin and Sonoma-raised lamb, paired with the carefully selected wine menu; a wine bar menu (4pm-10pm daily) that pours from the Kenwood Inn's award-winning cellar; and an Intermezzo Menu (all day, $9-19) of snacks for those peckish moments in between. Every room has a private patio, fireplace, and luxurious bathroom, which for an extra $65 you can outfit as your own private spa with the hotel's Bath Butler Service. Proper spa treatments only climb in price from there. You will be relaxed and beautiful, even if you never manage to leave the hotel.

With cheap rooms at a premium in the valley and not a drop of rain falling for about five months of the year, camping starts to look attractive, especially when the campground also happens to be just 10 minutes from many wineries and a stone's throw from some of the best hiking trails in the area.

The year-round campground at **Sugarloaf Ridge State Park** (2605 Adobe Canyon Rd., 707/833-5712, www.parks.ca.gov, reservations 800/444-7275 or www.reserveamerica.com, $35) is the only one in the valley and has a lot going for it if you can stand the summer heat (it does get cooler at night). It's a somewhat typical state park campground, with a small ring road serving the 49 mostly shady sites for tents and small RVs (up to 27 feet), with drinking water, restrooms, fire pits, and picnic tables. Be sure to bring quarters for the showers. Sites 1-11 and 26-28 back onto a small creek, across which is the start of a popular hiking trail. Most of the rest of the sites are at the foot of a hill and get the most shade, although none can be described as truly secluded. Reservations are a must on weekends April-October.

Information and Services

Like Glen Ellen, Kenwood is shy of visitor services, but many of the hotels and wineries are accustomed to directing visitors to the best places to see. The *Kenwood Press* is the local rag and is published twice a month. Either in their print or online edition (www.kenwoodpress.com), you can find out about local events and get a flavor for the town. Cell phone reception is better here than in Glen Ellen, due to its proximity to Santa Rosa.

Getting There and Around

Kenwood is on Highway 12, 11 miles east of downtown Santa Rosa and 4 miles north of Glen Ellen.

Los Carneros

Replace the vineyards with grass, throw in a few more cows, and the Carneros area would probably look a lot like it did 100 years ago. *Carneros* is Spanish for sheep or ram, and grazing was the mainstay of the region for hundreds of years. In fact, it has more of a Wild West feel to it than most of the Wine Country and was home to the annual Sonoma Rodeo until 1950. These days it's car and bike racing at the Sonoma Raceway that draws adrenaline addicts, but even here the area's bovine history is celebrated by the supercharged cow that sits atop the giant raceway billboard.

In addition to the grazing land that used to dominate the Carneros area, there were also fruit orchards growing every type of soft fruit. The first vineyards were thought to have been planted in the 1830s, and by the end of the 1800s the advent of the ferries and railroad had made Carneros a veritable fruit and wine basket.

Phylloxera and Prohibition wiped out the small wine industry in Carneros in the early 1900s, and it didn't get back on its feet again until the 1960s. By then the fruit growers had moved elsewhere, and the march of the vineyards across the pastureland began.

Today, the western part of Carneros primarily resembles grazing land, and huge marshes still merge at the edge of the bay with the low-lying flatlands. Drive east and the low-rolling hills are now covered with vineyards as far as the eye can see, a sign that cows will probably not return anytime soon.

The Wines

Established in 1983, the **Los Carneros** AVA encompasses 8,000 acres planted in grapes. It borders San Pablo Bay and straddles the county line dividing Napa and Sonoma Counties, though the majority of its vineyards are actually on the Sonoma side. Hence it's included in this chapter and not in the Napa

Valley chapter, although both regions claim it as their own. The cool winds that blow off the bay and through the Petaluma Gap from the west, plus the murky cloud cover that often takes half the morning to burn off in the summer, help make this one of the coolest appellations in California, ideal for growing pinot noir, chardonnay, and other grapes with a flavor profile that makes crisp, aromatic, and well-balanced wines.

Not surprisingly, those two varietals fill 85 percent of the vineyards, but more winemakers are now discovering that very distinctive wines can be made from syrah and merlot grapes grown here. Carneros is about as cool as it can be for merlot to ripen completely, and the resulting wines have a greater structure and subtlety than their hot-climate cousins.

Despite its cool, damp appearance, Carneros gets less annual rainfall than any other part of Napa or Sonoma County. In addition, the fertile-looking topsoil is usually only a few feet deep and sits on top of a layer of dense cold clay that is unforgiving to vines and forces them to put more energy into producing fruit than leaves.

WINERIES

There are far fewer wineries in the Carneros region than its size might suggest. Its prized cool growing conditions mean that most of the vineyards seen from the road are either owned by, or sell their grapes to, wineries based outside the area. Those that are open range from international champagne houses to tiny family-owned businesses where you're more likely to experience informative (and occasionally free) tasting sessions that used to be the norm in Napa and Sonoma but are, alas, no more.

Finding some of the wineries can be a test, best taken when sober. Plenty of big white signs mark the vineyard owners, but they're of absolutely no help in actually finding a

Los Carneros

To Glen Ellen

To Sonoma

To Sonoma Raceway and Hwy 37

ROBLEDO FAMILY WINERY

SCHUG CARNEROS ESTATE

GLORIA FERRER

CLINE CELLARS

ANABA

FRUIT BASKET

VINEYARD INN

ANGELO'S WINE COUNTRY DELI

CORNERSTONE SONOMA

VINTAGE AIRCRAFT COMPANY

JACUZZI FAMILY VINEYARDS

VIANSA WINERY

LOS ARROYOS GOLF CLUB

Schellville

SCHELLVILLE GRILL

LARSON FAMILY WINERY

CEJA VINEYARDS

TIN BARN VINEYARDS

CARNEROS BREWING COMPANY

HOMEWOOD WINERY

W. WATMAUGH RD.

STAGE GULCH RD

BONNESS RD

MEADOWLARK LN

ARNOLD DR

MILLERICK RD

BURNDALE RD

RAMAL RD

5TH ST E

8TH ST E

BROADWAY

NAPA RD

DENMARK ST

VINEBURG DELI & GROCERY

PATZ & HALL

Vineburg

GUNDLACH BUNDSCHU WINERY

FREMONT DR

RAMAL RD

NICHOLSON RANCH

ARTESA VINEYARDS & WINERY

DOMAINE CARNEROS

THE DI ROSA PRESERVE

CUVAISON ESTATE

DUHIG RD

LAS AMIGAS RD

BOUCHAINE VINEYARDS

MCKENZIE-MUELLER

BUCHLI STATION RD

ETUDE WINERY

CUTTINGS WHARF RD

SOUTH AVE

HENRY RD

DELAY LN

OLD SONOMA RD

CARNEROS RESORT AND SPA/ BOON FLY CAFÉ/ THE FARM

STARMONT WINERY & VINEYARDS

Sonoma Creek

Napa River

To Truchard Vineyards and Napa

To Napa

0
0

1 km

1 mi

N

Champagne Central

The French fiercely guard the word *champagne,* and over the last few decades they have forced much of the rest of the world to accept that a sparkling wine can only be called champagne if it comes from the Champagne region of France, just east of Paris. Their hardest-won battle was with the United States, and it wasn't until 2006 that the U.S. government agreed to prevent American wineries from using traditional French regional names like Burgundy and Champagne on their labels.

The agreement was part of broader trade talks, but there was a small catch for the French: American wineries already using the term *champagne* on their labels could continue to do so. Most California wineries, however, have long stuck to the term *sparkling wine* to describe their bubbly and *méthode champenoise* to describe how it's made.

Champagne-style wines have popped up all over the world over the centuries, from the sophisticated cava wines of Spain that have been made for hundreds of years to the more recent rise of sparkling wines in California, where Carneros is the center of it all.

In the 1980s and 1990s, the world's top producers of cava and champagne saw the potential of Carneros to produce world-class sparkling wines, and many set up shop in the area. The two biggest cava makers in Spain, Freixenet and Codorníu, are represented by the Carneros wineries **Gloria Ferrer** and **Artesa,** while **Domaine Carneros** is the American outpost of champagne house Taittinger.

The local wineries of many other big French champagne houses, including Mumm and Moët & Chandon, might be located in the nearby Napa Valley, but all grow a large proportion of their champagne grapes in Carneros.

The cool climate of Carneros is ideally suited for growing the two most important champagne grape varietals, chardonnay and pinot noir. Brisk winds and overcast summer mornings might not be the best conditions for touring with the top down, but a taste of some crisp local champagne more than makes up for the morning chill.

SOUTHERN SONOMA
LOS CARNEROS

winery, so a sharp eye is needed to spot the tiny signs tied to trees and posts. Most of the bigger wineries are fairly obvious from the main road, however, and there are only a few back roads on which to get lost.

Western Carneros

The gateway to Sonoma and Napa, western Carneros is largely flat with wineries, large and small, strung along the Highway 121.

VIANSA WINERY & ITALIAN MARKETPLACE

Traveling from San Francisco, the **Viansa Winery & Italian Marketplace** (25200 Arnold Dr., Sonoma, 800/995-4740, www.viansa.com, 10am-5pm daily, tasting $15-20) is the first you'll come across. The Italian heritage of its founders, Sam and Vicki Sebastiani of the famed Sonoma family, is obvious from the Tuscan-style architecture of the

terra-cotta-roofed villa, but the real smoking gun is the Italian varietals filling the tasting menu. Of course there are the usual Carneros characters like cabernet sauvignon, merlot, pinot noir, and chardonnay, but you'll largely find red Italian varietals like sangiovese, barbera, primitivo, and freisa, and whites including pinot grigio and arneis. If you've never heard of most of those grapes, the $15 tasting of four wines will be a good introduction. For $5 more, you can opt for the premier tasting of the winery's reserve wines.

Either way, the crisp, food-friendly reds and whites will get your mouth watering for some antipasti. Luckily, Viansa is geared heavily toward food, which it sees as a natural pairing to its wines. In the ample tasting room, there is plenty of deli-style food available, and even wood-fired pizzas in the summer. Many of the wines are also a perfect accompaniment (and price) for a picnic, and you can buy most by the glass from the tasting bar. In the summer months, you might end up feeling more like a Mediterranean sardine yourself, as it is such a popular destination for busloads of visitors.

The neighboring 90-acre wetlands restored by Viansa with the bay in the distance make a fine view from the numerous picnic tables on the long terrace, marred only by the constant drone of traffic and the sometimes brisk winds. To tour the estate, book the 45-minute **Viansa Summit Tour and Tasting** (by appointment, $25).

★ CLINE CELLARS

Taste Rhône varietals next to one of the bells marking the original El Camino Real at the beautiful and historic **Cline Cellars** (24737 Arnold Dr., Sonoma, 707/940-4044, www.clinecellars.com, 10am-6pm daily, free tasting). Tasting Cline's large portfolio is free and takes place in a modest farmhouse with wraparound porch that dates from 1850. Natural springs feed the three ponds and help sustain the giant willow trees, magnolias, and colorful flower beds surrounding small patches of lawn that are ideal for picnics. The tasting room contains a small deli, and the wines include several picnic-friendly options,

including the Nancy Cuvee sparkling wine and a dry mourvèdre rosé.

The area was also the site of a Miwok Indian village and later used by Father Altimira as a forward camp while investigating a site for what would become the Sonoma Mission. The winery's colorful history comes alive in the three tours offered daily at 11am, 1pm, and 3pm, and in its **California Missions Museum** (10am-4pm daily) located in a barn right behind the tasting room. The small museum displays intricately detailed scale models of every single Californian mission, from the first in San Diego to the last just north of here in Sonoma.

JACUZZI FAMILY VINEYARDS

Located across the road from Cline Cellars is another Cline family venture in the form of a giant Tuscan farmhouse, paying homage to the family's Italian heritage. **Jacuzzi Family Vineyards** (24724 Arnold Dr., Sonoma, 707/931-7575, www.jacuzziwines.com, 10am-5:30pm daily, free tasting) is modeled after the Jacuzzi family home in Italy—the same Jacuzzi family that invented the eponymous bubbling bathtubs. In that sense it could be considered as another Carneros producer of bubbly.

Cline Cellars

Unlike Cline, Jacuzzi focuses on classic Italian varietals such as montepulciano, sangiovese, primitivo, and pinot grigio as well as the more common varietals in this part of the world like chardonnay, pinot noir, cabernet sauvignon, and merlot. As at Cline, tasting is free, but you can choose to spend a little and book an advance reservation to have a private tasting and a tour ($20), or pair your tour and tasting with an assortment of cheese ($35).

Jacuzzi is also the new home of Sonoma olive oil producer **The Olive Press** (www.theolivepress.com), which used to be based in Kenwood. Its small tasting room is on the right as you enter the winery (for wine, turn left) and is the place to discover that olive oils can be as diverse in taste as wines. A small tasting bar usually features oils ranging from a light and grassy taste up to a rich, mellow one, with flavors generally determined by the olives used and where they're grown (sound similar to wine-grape lore?). The Olive Press is also a functioning production center, processing olives from growers across Northern California, and it sells a full range of oil-related gifts, from cookbooks and oil containers to soaps.

GLORIA FERRER

Jump back across the road to taste some upscale Carneros sparkling wines at the Spanish farmhouse of **Gloria Ferrer** (23555 Arnold Dr., Sonoma, 707/933-1917, www.gloriaferrer.com, 10am-5pm daily, tasting $25-33). The champagnerie now has the largest selection of sparkling wine in Carneros, priced from a modest $22 for the classic Brut to the $80 flagship Carneros Cuvee in a distinctly curvaceous bottle that matches its smooth elegance. In addition to the champagnes, Gloria Ferrer also makes an increasing quantity of still wines. Both still and sparkling regularly score above 90 with *Wine Enthusiast* and/or *Wine Spectator*, and you can taste either by flight or by glass ($7-20).

Every day at 11am, 1pm, and 3pm, tours explore the long, cool cellars in the hillside behind the winery and are as good a lesson in how to make champagne as you'll find at any other sparkling wine producer. The cost is $25 and comes with two sparkling wine tastes and a still. Elevated dining experiences are available that pair flights with small bites (10am, noon, 2pm daily, $50-60 by appointment), as is a Glassware Exploration where you can learn how the shape of a glass enhances the flavor profile of your wine (10am, noon, 2pm daily, by appointment, $45).

The more affordable sipping and tasting option is at the visitors center shop, where you can buy a bottle plus pick up all sorts of edibles, from picnic supplies and Spanish cooking ingredients to cookbooks and striking, pop art-inspired posters for some of the wines. You can also bring your own food and snag a terrace table. If it's not too foggy, there are few better places in Carneros to enjoy a picnic or an early evening aperitif.

ANABA

In a quaint, modest 100-year-old farmhouse near the intersection of Highways 121 and 116, **Anaba** (60 Bonneau Rd., Sonoma, 707/996-4188, www.anabawines.com, 10:30am-5:30pm daily, tasting $15) pours elegant wines that are handcrafted from premium Rhône and Burgundian grape varietals grown on the Carneros Estate vineyard and on select vineyards throughout Sonoma County. Anaba's wines are artistic blends, inspired by the rugged earthiness of France's Rhône Valley and replicated in the rocky soils found in Sonoma. And as you might expect, the chardonnays and pinot noirs reflect the flavors and aromas that the gently sloping vineyards of the Burgundy, Sonoma Coast, and Carneros appellations are renowned for. If you are looking for an intimate, unpretentious boutique winery, Anaba is a great place to kick back on the patio overlooking the vineyards and enjoy expertly crafted wine. The engaging and knowledgeable staff is an added bonus.

SCHUG CARNEROS ESTATE

You might recognize the labels at the **Schug Carneros Estate** (602 Bonneau Rd., Sonoma,

707/939-9363 or 800/966-9365, www.schug-winery.com, 10am-5pm daily, tasting $10). One of the Carneros region's elder statesmen, Walter Schug has made wine that's set the tone for California vintages for many years. The estate itself is worth a visit; the Tudor-esque tasting room sits in the middle of barns and fields of mustard (the brilliant yellow flowering plants) on the valley floor, with views of the surrounding mountains all around. Schug's hallmarks are chardonnays and pinot noirs, grapes that grow well in this cooler region, so be sure to try the latest releases of both.

ROBLEDO FAMILY WINERY

If you ever wondered about the fate of the laborers who hand-pick the grapes throughout the Wine Country, a visit to this winery will provide one answer. In the 1970s, Mexican immigrant Reynaldo Robledo was one of those laborers working in local vineyards, a job that was the beginning of his path to realizing the American Dream. He eventually formed a successful vineyard management company and finally created his dream winery, making his first commercial vintage in 1998.

The **Robledo Family Winery** (21901 Bonness Rd., Sonoma, 707/939-6903, www.robledofamilywinery.com, 10am-5pm Mon.-Sat., 11am-4pm Sun., tasting $10-15) is a low-key affair down a sleepy, semirural residential street off Highway 116 (Arnold Dr.) just north of the busy junction with Highway 121. Despite the lack of architectural flourishes of the big wineries nearby, the small tasting area with a giant oak communal table at its center is located in the barrel room, providing a wonderfully cool and intimate atmosphere in which to sample the wines. You're also likely to be served by one of the Robledo family, so be sure to ask about the story of Reynaldo. The winery also boasts a large covered patio with long communal tables, perfect for picnicking and festive occasions. Thankfully, the tasting room stocks plenty of cheese and salami from the local Sonoma Vella Cheese Company.

LARSON FAMILY WINERY

To get to this historic patch of land, you must turn off Highway 121 and head toward the wetlands, down a small country road almost as far as dry land will take you. Only the whimsical, hand-painted signs along the way suggest there's civilization at the end of the road. The **Larson Family Winery** (23355 Millerick Rd., Sonoma, 707/938-3031, www.larsonfamilywinery.com, 10am-5pm daily, tasting $10-20) is situated next to Sonoma Creek at the edge of the San Pablo Bay. It's pretty, but being surrounded by wetlands has its disadvantages. The area is prone to flooding during winter rains, and summer days can be a bit chilly this close to the water.

Despite its relatively small size, Larson's portfolio is large and dominated by cool-climate Carneros wines, including pinot noir, barrel-aged chardonnay, and a gewürztraminer. Standouts include a pinot noir rosé that got a nod at the state fair. You won't find Larson wines on many reviewers' lists, but part of the fun of visiting here is the unique location and the down-home family-farm atmosphere. The winery tasting room is in an old redwood barn with a small enclosure of goats and sheep and usually a couple of the winery dogs lounging nearby. You might also be lucky enough to see the pet llama.

There's a regulation-size bocce ball court and a grassy picnic and play area behind the tasting room to enjoy a bite to eat with a bottle of Larson's rosé or gewürztraminer. For $15 you can reserve a picnic table that will include a flight of wines to go with your own picnic lunch. This is highly recommended on busy weekends. Jeep tours of the surrounding vineyards and wetlands are sometimes available through an unaffiliated company—just look for the bright green Jeep in the parking lot.

TIN BARN VINEYARDS

It might look like you're driving into a storage locker complex, but don't be fooled by the industrial park setting. The tasting room at **Tin Barn Vineyards** (21692 8th St. E., #340, Sonoma, 707/938-5430, www.

tinbarnvineyards.com, noon-5pm Fri.-Mon., tasting $15) is located in a spare, industrial building near the Sonoma airport. There are no cutesy aprons or corkscrews with clichéd Wine Country sayings here. Instead, visitors see a modern tasting room with clean lines, corrugated ceilings, and large windows that overlook the adjacent wine production cellar. The staff is gregarious and knowledgeable. The name was derived from Tin Barn Road, a rocky appellation high atop the ridges of the Sonoma Coast, where the five friends and collaborators of the vineyard sourced their first grapes. The Tin Barn portfolio of wines includes a Russian River zinfandel, a Napa Valley merlot, and a Sonoma Valley zinfandel, as well as a syrah and sauvignon blanc.

CEJA VINEYARDS

Amelia and Pedro Ceja met picking grapes behind Robert Mondavi's house in 1967. Thirteen years later they bought their first vineyard in Carneros, and shortly thereafter **Ceja Vineyards** (22989 Burndale Rd., Sonoma, 707/255-3954, www.cejavineyards. com, 11am-5pm Fri.-Sun., tasting $10-15), the first Mexican American winery, was born. The story is an inspiring demonstration of the American Dream. Amelia Ceja has even become a celebrated chef, been named Woman of the Year by the California State Legislature, and has visited the White House and cooked for the Smithsonian. Thankfully, at least one member of the extended Ceja family is likely to be behind the bar at the modest tasting room to tell the colorful story.

Today Ceja makes only 5,000 cases of wine a year, 10 different varietals, sourced only from estate vineyards in Stags Leap, Carneros, and the Sonoma Coast. Taste five off the list, and you'll likely get one extra, usually the sweet late harvest chardonnay Dulce Beso (sweet kiss). Bottles range $25-65 in price and can be enjoyed on the small patio outside the tasting room. You can also take your bottle to the larger picnic area outside the **Carneros Brewing Company** (22985 Burndale Rd., Sonoma, 707/938-1880, www.

carnerosbrewing.com, noon-5:30pm Mon.-Fri., 10am-5:30pm Sat.-Sun.), also a Ceja operation, which makes handcrafted beer. On the weekend, the older generation of Cejas sell superb tacos and quesadillas with handmade tortillas and flavorful salsas.

HOMEWOOD WINERY

Across from the Ceja compound on Burndale Road, is the down-home atmosphere of **Homewood Winery** (23120 Burndale Rd., Sonoma, 707/996-6353, www.homewoodwinery.com, 10am-4pm daily, tasting $10), which produces small batches of mainly red wines like zinfandel, merlot, syrah, pinot noir, and a late-harvest cabernet sauvignon and merlot. Most wines are very reasonably priced, with the best bang for the buck being the Flying Whizzbangers, a zinfandel-dominated red blend.

The staff will happily spend an hour or more with visitors in the tiny tasting room explaining the wines, conducting some vertical tastings, and teaching some tasting tricks, like how to identify the oak used in the barrels. That is, if no big groups arrive; otherwise the small indoor tasting area can quickly get claustrophobic, and it's best to spill out onto the back porch "lounge" if it's open. Be sure to check out the olive oils also sold at the winery.

NICHOLSON RANCH

Though just outside the Los Carneros appellation boundary by literally a few yards (it's technically in the Sonoma Valley appellation), the mission-style **Nicholson Ranch** winery (4200 Napa Rd., Sonoma, 707/938-8822, www.nicholsonranch.com, 10am-6pm daily, tasting $15-25) is perched on a small hill above the intersection of the Carneros Highway and Napa Road.

Nicholson Ranch is predominantly a pinot and chardonnay producer, in addition to small quantities of syrah and merlot from local vineyards, both of which exhibit the classic aromas and restraint of cool-climate wines. The chardonnays, and in particular the flagship Cuvée Natalie, garner some good reviews from critics, and bottle prices are generally reasonable. For $15 you can taste four wines and for $26 you can bump it up to six. For just $5 more, you can take an appointment-only tour of the winery caves and winemaking facilities with a couple of extra tastes thrown in along the way.

Inside the bright and spacious tasting room with limestone floors and a cherrywood central tasting bar topped with granite, you'll find a modest selection of picnic supplies. Tables on the veranda overlook the surrounding hills, while those on a grassy area next to the pond are perfect for those days when the weather's cooperating. When it's not, take time to peruse the Overlook Gallery, appropriately overlooking the tasting room, which showcases local artists, sculptors, and photographers. The selection is well chosen and urbane, eschewing the typical wineglass still life. The tasting room is open later than most in the area, even in winter, so those on a hectic schedule should make this their last winery of the day.

Eastern Carneros

As soon as the land begins to swell in rolling hills, you'll know you have entered eastern Carneros, or the Napa side, as locals call it. The same mix of big and boutique wineries apply, but instead of strung along the central highways, you'll find them tucked on bumpy back roads and hidden throughout rolling vineyards. The land is especially suited to pinot noir made into wine here or sold up to other wineries in other areas of Wine Country.

ARTESA VINEYARDS & WINERY

Near Napa, the vast infinity pools surrounding **Artesa Vineyards & Winery** (1345 Henry Rd., Napa, 707/254-2139, www.artesawinery.com, 10am-5pm daily, tasting $15-35) draw Carneros's wetlands high into its rolling hills. The outpost of the historic Spanish sparkling wine producer Codorníu, this grass-covered winery was designed by Barcelona architect Domingo Triay to blend in with the surrounding land. Yes, it blends in, but it also astounds with its sublime marriage of wine, art, and design.

The sleek tasting room with its adjoining patio overlooking the vineyards offers several tasting options. On weekdays these range from a single glass of sparkling ($15) to a flight of reserve wines for $25. On weekends, the salon and patio are opened for seated tastings ($45) as well as a variety of food and wine pairings, which include tapas, cheese platters, and chocolate ($45-60). While the prices may seem steep, these don't cost much more than a fancy lunch out, especially considering the food, wine, and location. To truly experience the architectural and artistic scope of the winery, take a tour offered at 11am and 2pm daily ($40), which includes a flight of five wines. However, perusing the art and the small museum of the history of champagne making and the Codorníu family is free.

BOUCHAINE VINEYARDS

On the other side of the highway (and on the opposite side of the spectrum) the charming **Bouchaine Vineyards** winery (1075 Buchli Station Rd., Napa, 707/252-9065 or 800/654-9493, www.bouchaine.com, 10:30am-4:30pm daily Nov.-Apr., 10:30am-5:30pm daily May-Oct., tasting $25) is tucked away on the edge of eastern Carneros's wetlands.. Grapes have been growing on the property since 1899, and today Bouchaine produces mainly Carneros chardonnay and pinot noir, which both regularly win gold medals at various competitions and score above 90 points with the critics. The cozy tasting room offers flights of five wines or pours wine by the glass, which you may take out to the garden or to the porch overlooking the vineyards with San Pablo Bay in the distance. Bouchaine is a popular stop for bikers who relish the quiet, straight, and flat roads of the area.

ETUDE WINES

Closer to Highway 121 and the city of Napa is **Etude Wines** (1250 Cuttings Wharf Rd.,

Best Wineries for Lunch

More and more wineries in southern Sonoma are adding food to their wine-tasting experiences. Consider splurging on a food and wine pairing to maximize your time and budget in Wine Country.

- **Pangloss Cellars, Sonoma:** Sitting on the Sonoma Plaza, this lounge-like tasting room pairs flights of its Sonoma wine with farm-to-fork bites that include rabbit terrine, duck liver mousse, artisanal cheese, and charcuterie.

- **Mayo Family Reserve Room, Glen Ellen:** One of the earliest wineries to adopt a food program, the Mayo Family Winery pairs seven reserve wines with a seasonal menu that goes way beyond the standard cheese and charcuterie plates. Expect small plates of gnocchi, savory tarts, a meaty main, and a sweet cake. You'll need to make reservations in advance.

- **St. Francis Winery & Vineyards, Kenwood:** Out on the terrace with the vineyards nearly tableside, indulge in a casual flight of wine plus a cheese and charcuterie plate, or book a $68 five-course food and wine pairing ahead of time. The St. Francis Winery has rightfully earned the reputation as the best food program in the valley.

- **Ram's Gate, Carneros:** At this stylish Carneros winery, the Palate Play experience for $90 is a pricy but filling option. Four healthy pours are paired with small tasty bites that may include shrimp wontons, pork belly, and lamb tenderloin sliders. An added bonus is the lovely pinot blanc that you'll get to enjoy with the in-depth tour of the vineyards and winery before sitting down.

- **Domaine Carneros, Carneros:** As soon as you sit down inside the stylish salon or out on the terrace overlooking the vineyards, you'll get a menu with flights of sparkling wine and plates of cheese, charcuterie, and smoked salmon, as well as a selection of caviar.

Napa, 707/257-5782, www.etudewines.com, 10am-4:30pm daily, $20-35). The understated stone château-like winery is surrounded by trim grounds and lush vineyards, and the tasting room has a Euro-chic air. High ceilings, blond wood, and modernist chandeliers complement the vertical (and artful) array of wines on display behind the bar. Style aside, the winery is known for its refined but pricey Carneros pinot noir, but also produces chardonnay, pinot blanc, and pinot gris from local Carneros vineyards together with some Napa Valley cabernet. Tastings include five wines ($20) or five reserve wines ($30) and a seated tasting of reserve wines ($35) out on the lovely stone patio. To take advantage of Etude's portfolio of pinot noir, book the Study of Pinot Noir (10am, 1pm, 3pm daily, $50 by appointment), in which you'll taste six vintages each from a major pinot-growing region: Carneros, the Sonoma Coast, the Willamette Valley, and Santa Barbara County.

STARMONT WINERY AND VINEYARDS

At the very eastern edge of Carneros is **Starmont Winery and Vineyards** (1451 Stanly Ln., Napa, 707/252-8001, www.starmontwinery.com, 10:30am-5:30pm daily, tasting $25-40). The winery sits on some of the 1860 Stanly Ranch, where some of Carneros's first grapes were planted at the end of the 19th century. Today, Starmont grows chardonnay and pinot noir, along with small amounts of syrah and viognier on these historic vineyards, while employing a number of sustainable practices to keep its impact on the land light. You can hear about these endeavors, from solar panels to cover crops and bird boxes, while tasting the wine in the modern indoor/outdoor tasting room.

For $25, you'll get a flight of five wines and maybe a splash of something else that the pourer is particularly excited about that day. The staff is friendly and likely to hand your dog a milk bone or your kid a special tasting menu that includes juice, milk, organic snacks, and activities, should either be in tow. According to Starmont, parents like to go wine-tasting too, and it wants to be the place to accommodate them. Grown-up snacks are available in the tasting room, as are wines by the glass ($9-15), both of which can be taken outside to the comfy couches or out on the lawn where corn hole, jump rope, games, and coloring books create a delightful afternoon for all. To get out and stretch your legs book a two-hour tour ($65) of Stanly Ranch that includes barrel and seated tastings.

Wineries by Appointment

In Carneros, wineries by appointment vary hugely from big wineries trying to control their numbers to tiny ones who simply can't staff a full-time tasting room. However, most, particularly the biggies, can accommodate walk-ins on slow days and even same-day appointments on busy ones.

PATZ & HALL

The new home of **Patz & Hall** (21200 8th St. E., Sonoma, 707/265-7700, www.patzhall. com, 10am-4pm Thurs.-Mon., tasting $30-60, by appointment) lends a bit of Napa glamour to the industrial 8th Street winery scene in Carneros. The entrance is through a gate and down a long drive to the Sonoma House, a grand compound that includes a tasting salon with a fireplace, views of the Mayacamas Mountains, and single-vineyard pinot noirs and chardonnays. Three tasting options are available: the Tasting Bar ($30), with a flight of four wines; the Appellation Series ($45), with a flight of four wines plus a cheese plate on the terrace; and the Salon Experience ($60), with a flight of six wines paired with small bites.

RAM'S GATE

Aptly named, **Ram's Gate** (28700 Arnold Dr., Sonoma, 707/721-8700, http://ramsgatewinery.com, 10am-6pm Thurs.-Mon., tasting $40) stands sentinel at the entrance to Carneros

from San Francisco and points south and west. High up on a hill, it overlooks its estate vineyards planted mainly in chardonnay and pinot noir, with views of the San Pablo Bay beyond. The winery is smartly designed, influenced by the old barns dotting Carneros and utilizing ponderosa pine reclaimed from Wyoming snow fences, to create an indoor/outdoor space that is contemporary yet rustic in feel. For $40 you can sit at the elegant tasting bar and sample a flight of four wines (two chardonnay, two pinot noir). The wines are good, but the steep price and marginal pours don't quite add up. However, if you'll willing to fork out $90, the Palate Play experience is exceptional. You'll start with a glass of the lovely pinot blanc and get an in-depth tour of the vineyards and winery, a true education about the process behind making great wine. This is followed by a seated tasting of four healthy pours, including the Vent de Colline, a blend of syrah and pinot noir, paired with small bites that may include shrimp wontons, pork belly, and a lamb tenderloin slider. The menu changes with the season and is hearty enough to count as a light lunch. This experience lasts 90-120 minutes and is available at 10:30am, 1pm, and 3:30pm Thursday-Monday.

★ DOMAINE CARNEROS

The first winery you'll see as you roll into eastern Carneros is the stately **Domaine Carneros** (1240 Duhig Rd., Napa, 800/716-2788, www.domainecarneros.com, 10am-5:45pm daily, tasting $30-40), built in the style of the 18th-century Chateau de la Marquetterie, home of one of the winery's principal founders, Champagne Taittinger. The sweeping staircase leading from the parking lot and the palatial interior leave no doubt about the winery's fancy French pedigree. It all feels a little over-the-top, particularly when contrasted with the rustic, windswept Carneros landscape on a foggy day. With some sun on a less crowded day, however, it can feel magical.

The refinement follows you in as you take

a table either in the salon or out on the terrace overlooking the vineyards. You'll have your pick of four flights of four wines that include sparkling or pinot noir only or a mix of both for $30-40; wines by the glass ($10-30); and cheese, charcuterie, and smoked salmon plates, as well as a selection of caviar. To taste the cream of the crop, splurge on the Grande Tasting Flight ($40), which includes the flagship Le Rêve blanc de blancs made from 100 percent chardonnay and considered one of California's top champagnes. However, all the wines here are meant to be savored with food and atmosphere, at which this establishment excels.

To learn about how bubbly is made, take the Art of Sparkling Wine tour (11am, 1pm, and 3pm daily), which lets visitors peer into the squeaky-clean, modern production and bottling areas. At $50 per person, the tour includes a tasting of four wines along the way, and you get to keep the tasting glass. The winery is by appointment only; however, same-day reservations are frequently, and gladly, accepted.

CUVAISON

Opposite to Domaine Carneros and its fancy French architectural excesses is the modern and minimalist home of **Cuvaison** (1221 Duhig Rd., Napa, 707/942-2455, www.cuvaison.com, 10am-5pm daily, tasting $25), a winery that takes its name from an old French term describing the part of the winemaking process that gives red wine its color. Also unlike its neighbor, Cuvaison is a bubble-free zone. Instead, you'll find Carneros-grown highly rated pinot noir and chardonnay poured in the indoor/outdoor tasting lounge. The minimal fuss, in addition to the airy tasting room built from concrete, wood, and glass, lets the wine, and nature, do the talking. From the patio, you can practically reach out and touch the vines. Although Cuvaison advertises this tasting room as appointment-only, there's usually no problem rolling up unannounced. It's worth calling ahead if you can, however, because it can get crowded at certain times of the day.

MCKENZIE-MUELLER

If you're looking for a small family-run winery out in the wilds of Carneros, the **McKenzie-Mueller** winery (2530 Las Amigas Rd., Napa, 707/252-0186, www.mckenziemueller.com, 10am-4:30pm by appointment, tasting $10) is your place. Owned and operated by Napa Valley wine veterans Bob

Domaine Carneros is styled after an 18th-century château.

and Karen Mueller, McKenzie-Mueller produces only 2,500 cases of wine, sourced from their 50 acres of estate vineyards in Carneros and in the Oak Knoll district in the Napa Valley. In the homespun tasting room that opens out onto the vineyards, you can taste the estate merlot, pinot noir, malbec, cabernet sauvignon, and the standout, an aromatic cabernet franc. On quiet days you'll likely be the only person there and may even be treated to a peek in the cellar and an impromptu barrel tasting.

TRUCHARD VINEYARDS

Another beloved boutique winery is **Truchard Vineyards** (3234 Old Sonoma Rd., Napa, 707/253-7153, www.truchardvineyards. com, Mon.-Sat. by appointment, tour and tasting $30), located across Highway 121 high up Old Sonoma Road. The highly acclaimed wines made here come from the huge 270-acre Carneros vineyard, where 10 varietals are grown, including cabernet, tempranillo, and zinfandel grapes that reflect the vineyard's site near the border with the warmer Napa Valley. However, the best of these premium limited-release wines, the elegant syrah and pinot noir, can be tasted as part of the tour and tasting, which includes a vineyard walk and a look at the winery's 100-year-old barn.

SIGHTS
★ The di Rosa Preserve

In 1960, writer Rene di Rosa bought some old grazing land in Carneros. In 1997, the largest collection of Northern California contemporary art opened at **The di Rosa Preserve** (5200 Carneros Hwy./Hwy. 121, Napa, 707/226-5991, www.dirosaart.org, 10am-4pm Wed.-Sun., $5). Today the preserve has more than 2,000 works on display throughout its 217 acres, including a colorful cow that has floated on the 35-acre lake since 1989, although it occasionally tips over. While Rene di Rosa passed away in 2010, the foundation continues his work collecting and displaying art from Northern California artists.

Visiting the preserve is to enter an eclectic,

artistic wonderland, where giant sculptures march up into the hills, a car hangs from a tree, and every indoor space is crammed with photographs, paintings, and video installations of sometimes mind-bending strangeness. Even nature seems to do its part to maintain the sense of whimsy, as the preserve's 85 peacocks (including two albinos) strut, screech, and occasionally crash-land around the galleries.

The preserve is on the north side of the Carneros Highway (Hwy. 121), almost opposite the Domaine Carneros winery. Look for the two-dimensional sheep on the hillside. The $5 fee will get you into the Gatehouse Gallery, which displays rotating exhibits along with some pieces from the permanent collection, but to wander around the property or explore other indoor gallery space, including the 125-year-old winery, you have to join a tour. Luckily, they are in abundance. Three to four are scheduled daily, depending on the time of year, and all last 1.5 or 2 hours and cost $12-20. During the dry summer months, the Nature Hike (10am-noon, Sat. May-Oct., $20) takes visitors up Milliken Peak, a 2.5-mile round-trip to the highest peak in Carneros. You might be able to sign up for one of the tours on the day, but chances are you'll need a reservation (call 707/226-5991 or visit www. dirosaart.org), especially on weekends.

Cornerstone Sonoma

It's hard to classify this sprawling collection of shops, studios, cafés, tasting rooms, and gardens, but **Cornerstone Sonoma** (23570 Arnold Dr., Sonoma, 707/933-3010, www. cornerstonegardens.com, 10am-5pm daily, gardens 1pm-4pm daily) should certainly be on the list of any architecture or gardening enthusiast. The centerpiece of Cornerstone is a nine-acre plot of land that's a showcase for several dozen well-known landscape architects, each of whom designed and planted separate plots. The result is a fascinating blend of traditional and contemporary gardens that make art and sculpture out of plants. To learn more, book an hour-long tour ($10) by contacting Ruth Roberson (ruth@cornerstone.com) at least 48 hours in advance.

Over the years, restaurant and retail space has grown up around the gardens, making it a great stop for folks needing to get out of the car. Kids particularly love the garden exclusively made of pinwheels and the oversized Adirondack chairs, while their parents will love the opportunity to shop, taste wine, and select from low-stress eating options. *Sunset*, the West's lifestyle magazine since 1898, now has its test kitchen and demonstration gardens here, giving Cornerstone a more foodie vibe.

The **Sonoma Valley Visitors Bureau** (23570 Arnold Dr., Sonoma, 707/996-1090 or 866/966-1090, www.sonomacounty.com, 10am-4pm daily) has a useful outpost here and is a first stop for many visitors to the region. Be sure to stop in and inquire about any discounted or free tasting passes to nearby wineries. The shops (10am-5pm daily) at Cornerstone have been carefully curated to focus primarily on home, garden, and lifestyle, so that any inspiration you may have gotten from the beautiful gardens can be translated into a myriad of purchases. Some of the most fascinating shops and studios include **Artefact Design & Salvage** (707/933-0660, www.artefactdesignsalvage.com), which sells antiques and whimsical home and garden accessories made from salvaged materials (bar stools with giant railroad springs in place of legs, for example); **Eurasian Interiors** (707/933-8006, http://eurasianinteriors.com), with its mix of Chinese and French antiques, incense, and handcrafted trinkets; and **Nomad Chic** (415/381-9087, http://nomadchic.mx), which sells clothes, jewelry, and knickknacks to fit the modern jet-set lifestyle.

No Wine Country stop is complete without a couple of tasting rooms. **Keating Wines** (707/939-6510, http://keatingwines.com, tasting $10) pours flights of zinfandel and Bordeaux varietals that frequently score above 90 points with critics; **Poseidon Vineyards & Obsidian Ridge** (707/255-4929, www.tricyclewine.com, tasting $15) sources its grapes from two vineyards (one at sea level, the other

high in the Mayacamas Mountains) to make small lot chardonnay, pinot noir, and cabernet sauvignon; and **Meadowcroft** (707/934-4090, http://meadowcroftwines.com, tasting $15-20) makes a relatively diverse portfolio that includes chardonnay, pinot noir, zinfandel, and cabernet sauvignon sourced from all over Napa and Sonoma and offers a variety of tasting options, including a wine and food pairing ($25-40). Should the shopping and tasting get you hungry, **Park 121 Café and Grill** (707/938-8579, www.park121.com) is the perfect blend of casual and quality, tying the whole Cornerstone Sonoma experience together.

RECREATION
Sonoma Raceway

Not every inch of ground in Sonoma County grows grapes or houses inns and restaurants. One huge plot of invaluable dirt has long been given over to the **Sonoma Raceway** (29355 Arnold Dr., Sonoma, 800/870-7223, www.infineonraceway.com), known locally as Sears Point. This massive motor-sports complex hosts almost every sort of vehicular race possible, with several NASCAR events each year, various American Motorcyclist Association motorcycle races, an Indy car race, and, of course, a National Hot Rod Association drag race. The raceway sees more action than many of the country's most popular racetracks, with events scheduled 340 days per year, although many of these are local track days and small-time club races. Ticket prices vary widely, so check the website for the cost of events.

The turnoff to the Sonoma Raceway is near the intersection of Highways 37 and 121, and wretched traffic jams, truly more stop than go, can last for hours as people exit the racetrack into the unsignaled intersection. Check the race schedule online to avoid this area for at least four hours after the scheduled or estimated end of a big race.

Water Tours

Water and bird lovers may find it difficult not to explore the wetlands bordering Carneros. If so, **Napa Valley Paddle** (100 Riverside Dr., Napa, 707/666-1628, http://napavalleypaddle.com, tours Sat. and Sun., and by appointment, $99) takes enthusiasts out to the snaking waterways of the Carneros Wildlife Refuge and Hudeman Slough, where one can stand-up paddleboard alongside osprey, egrets, and blue herons. The tours last two hours, travel four to six miles, and depart from Cuttings Wharf Boat Ramp in Eastern Carneros morning and evening for maximum wildlife viewing.

Flying

Balloons might be the traditional way to see Wine Country from above, but Carneros prefers a more adventurous way to take to the air. The **Vintage Aircraft Company** (23982 Arnold Dr., Sonoma, 707/938-2444, www.vintageaircraft.com, walk-in 10:30am-4pm Sat.-Sun., by appointment only Mon. and Thurs.-Fri.) offers rides in its fascinating collection of old planes, which include biplanes and a World War II-era training aircraft.

Simply pick your adrenaline level for the biplane flights, and the FAA-certified pilots can oblige. For a modest rush, pick the 20-minute Scenic ride over the vineyards and mountains of the Sonoma Valley ($175, $270 for two people) or double the flying time (and price) for a trip out to the ocean, down to San Francisco, or over the Napa Valley. To really get the adrenaline pumping, try the Aerobatic ride with a few loops and rolls thrown in for fun for an additional $50. Acrobatics are free in the World War II SNJ-4 "Texan" plane, but flights in the navy fighter start at $399 for 20 minutes.

The Vintage Aircraft Company's home is the Sonoma County airport, a thriving base for vintage aircraft restoration and flights. You'll probably see an old plane or two parked close to the Carneros Highway as you drive by.

ENTERTAINMENT
Carneros Brewing Company

The **Carneros Brewing Company** (22985 Burndale Rd., Sonoma, 707/938-1880, www.carnerosbrewing.com, noon-5:30pm

Mon.-Fri., 10am-5:30pm Sat.-Sun.) is a venture of the Ceja family, owners of **Ceja Vineyards,** the first Mexican American winery, which is located just feet away from the brewery's warehouse-like tasting room. The brewery makes, stores, and pours flights of its craft brews, from the light Cerveza Pilsner to the dark Negra IPA. Pick five from the 12 beers on tap (including house and seasonal brews) for a generous $16 flight of 5-ounce pours, or grab a pint and see beer being made right next to your table. TVs and a pool table are also inside the tasting room. On the weekends, the taps out in the oasis-like beer garden start to flow (during the week, you can just carry your pint from the tasting room) and the elder Cejas set up a stand selling homemade tacos and quesadillas.

FOOD
California Cuisine

If you can't resist the luxury of the **Carneros Resort and Spa,** book a table at **The FARM** (4048 Sonoma Hwy., Napa, 707/299-4880, www.carnerosresort.com, dinner 4pm-10pm daily, brunch 10am-2pm Sun., $20-49), which serves up the expected upscale California cuisine, complete with a chef's tasting menu and big white service plates topped with tiny artistic piles of food (five courses $115, wine pairing $85). The dining room feels more comfortable than many of its ilk, with cushy banquettes and padded chairs that spill out to the patio, perfect for enjoying a warm Carneros night. But that's dinner. If you want to soak in the atmosphere but have a more casual experience, ask about the bar menu. You'll find a burger, flatbread, even grilled ham and cheese for considerably less ($16-32).

The truly casual option at Carneros Resort and Spa is the ★ **Boon Fly Café** (4048 Sonoma Hwy., Napa, 707/299-4870, www.boonflycafe.com, 7am-9pm daily, entrées $14-28); its bright red exterior brightens up the gray prison-like walls of the upscale inn on the Sonoma-Napa Highway. The food is rustic and full of fresh ingredients—the kind of food that would be eaten by a local known as Boon Fly who used to farm the surrounding land. Breakfast and brunch are the fortes here, priced low enough to make you want to fill up for the day, but the simple yet elegant main courses and the fresh flatbread pizzas are also worth a stop in the evening. There is a healthy beer, wine, and cocktail menu, but the bar gives a careful nod to the rare nondrinker, with its "zero proof" beverages, such as the delicious pomegranate spritzer.

Casual Dining

The **Schellville Grill** (22900 Broadway, Sonoma, 707/996-5151, www.schellvillegrill. com, 9am-3pm Mon. and Thurs., 8am-3pm and 5pm-8:30pm Fri., 8am-4pm and 5pm-8:30pm Sat., 8am-4pm Sun., $11-32) at the intersection of Highways 12 and 121 represents the old-school, blue-collar side of Carneros. You'll find hearty plates of comfort food delivered by a crew of relaxed locals who seem unimpressed by all the Wine Country fuss. There is plenty of seating in the checkered tablecloth dining room, but if the weather is nice, take a table on the covered back patio. This is primarily a sandwich joint with plenty of burgers, pulled pork, and fish sandwiches. The real standout is the Hot Matty's Smoked Tri-Tip Sandy, which bursts with strips of tender, flavorful meat.

For those looking for a casual bite on the way into Wine Country, **Park 121 Café and Grill** (23570 Arnold Dr., Sonoma, 707/938-8579, www.park121.com, 10am-5pm daily, $8-15) is a versatile and casual spot in Cornerstone Sonoma. Pastries and a cup of Verve coffee provide fuel for a day of wine-tasting, while the flavorful and locally sourced menu of salads and sandwiches, plus hot dishes such as herb marinated skirt steak and the house-made empanadas, make for a casual lunch in the bustling café. You may decide to linger over a cheese and salami plate plus a glass or two of local wine on the patio shaded by olive trees, or take it all to go, finding a sunny picnic spot on the back lawn as the kids run around the pinwheel flower bed. At Park 121, the choice is yours.

Further towards Napa, the **Fremont Diner** (2698 Fremont Dr., Hwys. 12 and 121, www.thefremontdiner.com, Mon.-Wed. 8am-3pm, Thurs.-Sun. 8am-9pm, $13-16) has reinvented the country café with a hip farm-to-fork ethos. You'll find hush puppies, fried chicken and waffles, fried egg sandwiches, and grits. Any rough lines here look deliberate (i.e., country shabby chic), but all the ingredients are responsibly sourced from local farmers and ranchers. The food is excellent and the Mississippi mud pie is to die for.

Picnic Supplies

Carneros is often chilly and windy compared to the Napa and Sonoma Valleys just to the north and so might not be the most inviting part of Wine Country for a picnic, but there are plenty of places to stop for supplies if the weather's nice or you're en route to warmer climes.

Angelo's Wine Country Deli (23400 Arnold Dr., Sonoma, 707/938-3688, http://angelossmokehouse.com, 9am-5pm daily) is renowned for its smoked meats and jerkies but also sells a wide range of other deli food and has become a bit of a Carneros institution. Sandwiches ($8-10) and prepared salads are available, plus imported Italian meats. Despite being small, the store is hard to miss—there's a large model of a cow on its roof.

Just up the road is the **Fruit Basket** (24101 Arnold Dr., Sonoma, 707/938-4332, 7am-7pm daily), which looks a little like a shack in the middle of its dusty parking lot but is actually a comprehensive open-air market and one of the best places to buy local in-season fruit and vegetables along with almost every other grocery staple, including bread, cheese, and a good selection of wine by the half bottle. There's a second shop in **Boyes Hot Springs** (18474 Sonoma Hwy., Sonoma, 707/996-7433, 7am-8pm daily).

And then, of course, there are the wineries. Most of the large wineries have a selection of deli meats, local cheeses, crackers, and even some prepared food. Both **Gloria Ferrer** (23555 Arnold Dr., Sonoma, 707/933-1917, www.gloriaferrer.com, 10am-5pm daily) and **Robledo Family Winery** (21901 Bonness Rd., Sonoma, 707/939-6903, www.robledofamilywinery.com, 10am-5pm Mon.-Sat., 11am-4pm Sun.) have good selections, but perhaps the best is found at **Viansa Winery** (25200 Arnold Dr., Sonoma, 800/995-4740, www.viansa.com, 10am-5pm daily), which sells a broad range of Italian-themed deli foods, soups, sandwiches, and even pizzas in its tasting room. There are some nice spots nearby to eat, but when the winery gets crowded in the summer months, you'd do better to flee to somewhere more peaceful.

ACCOMMODATIONS

There's not much in the way of lodging in this part of Wine Country. Carneros thinks of Sonoma as its main town, and that's where most of the "local" hotels can be found. There are, however, a couple of options for those looking for either an out-of-the-way bargain or some out-of-this-world luxury.

$100-200

The Spanish-style **Vineyard Inn** (23000 Arnold Dr., Sonoma, 707/938-2350 or 800/359-4667, www.vineyardinnsonoma. com, $179-315) offers 22 modern and comfortable rooms just minutes from some of the biggest wineries in Carneros. The standard queen rooms are the cheapest and include the usual motel amenities, including a continental breakfast and use of the very small outdoor pool. One drawback is the inn's location at one of the busiest intersections in Carneros, which makes some of the cheaper rooms at the front of the building a bit noisy. Other than the constant traffic and a gas station opposite, there's not much else around, so you'll have to drive to dinner; Sonoma Plaza is only about 10 minutes away.

Over $200

Carneros Resort and Spa (4048 Sonoma Hwy., Napa, 707/299-4900, www.carnerosresort.com, $365-1,600) is an expansive and expensive cottage resort. The immense property, which backs onto real countryside, was once a trailer park and is now home to three restaurants, a spa, two pools, a fitness center, and even a small market. The unprepossessing (from the outside) cottages are spread out in small clusters for acres, each group surrounding its own garden paths and water features. Inside, the cozy (yes, that does mean "smallish") cottages sparkle with white linens, alfresco showers, tile floors, and windows overlooking sizable private backyards with decks and comfy chaises. Not surprisingly, there's a hefty price to pay in the Wine Country for a personal cottage that's bigger than some apartments. The cheapest places start at $365 per night. The price rockets past $600 for a vineyard view and up to four figures for the 10 walled compounds they call suites. The popularity of the place also means that rates change very little with the seasons, although you might find some special deals in winter.

INFORMATION AND SERVICES

Although you won't find much in the way of services here, you will find the **Sonoma Valley Visitors Center** (23570 Arnold Dr., Sonoma, 707/996-1090 or 866/996-1090, www.sonomacounty.com, 10am-4pm daily) at Cornerstone Gardens. The visitors center is well stocked with maps, discounts on tastings, and general advice for where to go and what to do in the area.

GETTING THERE AND AROUND

Carneros sits at the tip of the San Pablo Bay and is the crossroads for many highways heading north-south and east-west. The region is also the gateway to the Napa and Sonoma Valleys from San Francisco along Highway 121 and from Vallejo and the East Bay on Highway 12. Those two highways are the major roads through Carneros. While in the west, wineries hug Highway 121, in the east, many can be found off the main road (Hwy. 12) to the north or south.

Expect to stay behind the wheel in western

Carneros, where traffic along the main highways would make for a white-knuckled bike ride even without a flight or two of wine. The quiet back roads of eastern Carneros, however, practically scream for the bike. Pack a picnic and cycle through the vineyards either along the relative flatlands bordering the bay or through the heart-pumping hills on the north side of the highway. To cycle in the vineyards, take a tour (9am-1:30pm Mon., Wed., Fri., Apr.-Oct., $124) with **Sonoma** **Valley Bike Tours** (1254 Broadway, Sonoma, 707/996-2453, http://sonomavalleybiketours. com, 8:30am-5pm daily). You'll stop at two wineries (tasting fees not included) along the way, pedaling through rows of pinot noir and chardonnay, bordering wetlands and a wildlife preserve filled with herons, egrets, and other shorebirds. The company also rents bikes ($10-20/hour, $30-75/day) that you can pick up from their downtown Sonoma location, an easy ride from Carneros.

Northern Sonoma

There's probably no other wine-producing region in California that has as much to offer visitors as northern Sonoma. Famed Victorian horticulturist Luther Burbank called it the "chosen spot of all this earth as far as Nature is concerned," and he was pretty well traveled.

This is also a place where living off the land has always been, and still is, a way of life. That land provides some of California's best wine and food and countless recreational possibilities. You can mix wine with almost anything outdoors here: kayaking, mountain hikes, apple picking, camping, fishing, lounging on a sandy beach, flying, or even a safari.

While "Hop Country" and "Prune Country" don't have quite the same ring as "Wine Country," those crops and others once dominated the land but have long since vanished (at one point in the last century, a silkworm farm was planned, and a frog farm briefly found fame with its edible amphibians). There's even a major road named after the slowly disappearing Gravenstein apple. It would be easier to name crops that had *not* at some point been grown on these hills and valleys, helped along by the vast number of microclimates. There are probably more here than in any other part of the Wine Country—which is saying something in this climate-blessed part of the world. One day vines too might disappear, only to be replaced by the next big agricultural cash generator.

That's not to say that all is peace and rural tranquility—far from it. The freeway that was carved through the region in the 1960s brought with it suburban sprawl and rush-hour traffic that sucked the soul out of the largest city, Santa Rosa. But while Santa Rosa continues to bulge outward, it doesn't take much to get back to the land and step back in time. Less than a half hour away, deep in the woods, are towns like Guerneville and Occidental that still retain some feeling of the frontier towns they once were, even as they become overrun in the summer by an unlikely mix of urbanites, hippies, and

Previous: Lynmar Estate; tasting at Porter Bass. **Above:** Dry Creek zinfandel grapes.

Look for ★ to find recommended
sights, activities, dining, and lodging.

Highlights

★ **Luther Burbank Home & Gardens:**
Learn about the Victorian horticulturist who created hundreds of new plants in his greenhouses and see many of those plants in the historic gardens (page 201).

★ **Iron Horse Vineyards:** An unassuming barn off the beaten track is home to some of the Russian River Valley's best sparkling wines and a view to die for (page 211).

★ **Kendall-Jackson Wine Estate and Gardens:** Enjoy excellent small bites paired with a daily selection of wines, served in an elegant tasting room (page 219).

★ **Korbel Champagne Cellars:** In a forest clearing in Victorian times, two Czech brothers started making wine. Their historic stone winery still makes sparkling wine fit for presidents and plebeians alike (page 220).

★ **Hop Kiln Winery:** The towering hop kilns are so well preserved that this small winery could almost produce beer in addition to its unusual range of well-priced wines (page 221).

★ **The Russian River:** Rent a canoe for a day and drift along the river, stopping at the many secluded beaches (page 224).

★ **Armstrong Redwoods State Natural Reserve:** Take a break from the car and the heat on a short hike through the cool, damp redwood forest (page 226).

★ **Ridge Vineyards:** This winery, built with rice-straw bales, takes the principle of organic wines to a whole new level (page 251).

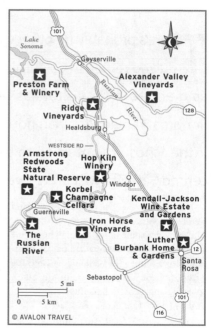

★ **Preston Farm & Winery:** Grab a loaf of bread, some fresh produce, and a bottle of your favorite Rhône varietal at this back-to-the-land fantasy come to life (page 255).

★ **Alexander Valley Vineyards:**
Incorporating part of the homestead of the valley's first settler, Cyrus Alexander, the grounds of this winery are peppered with historic buildings (page 263).

bikers, who all seem to coexist happily for a few months.

Even the Victorian town of Healdsburg has managed to keep in touch with its historic past, despite trying ever so hard to sell its soul to those marketing an imaginary Wine Country lifestyle.

The whole area is slowly being dragged up-market, however, as the burgeoning Bay Area population seeks out bigger backyards. At the southernmost edge of this part of the Wine Country, Sebastopol is starting to resemble a hip San Francisco neighborhood. Property prices everywhere are soaring, contributing to the mechanisms of change that have continually transformed the land since European immigrants first arrived here in the 1800s and carved out a life for themselves in the soil and forests.

Winemakers still produce wines to rival the best in the world, but as the cost of doing so rises, the conglomerates are beginning to take over, much as they've already done in the Napa and Sonoma Valleys. You increasingly have to be big to survive in the wine world here, and many new winemakers are looking farther north in Mendocino and Lake Counties for a chance to get in on the action.

Nevertheless, there's still plenty of life left in the northern Sonoma scene, with an amazing diversity of wine, scenery, and activities. There might be challenges in paradise, but it's still paradise.

PLANNING YOUR TIME

Parts of northern Sonoma are easy to get around; others are not. The **Russian River Valley** is definitely in the "not" category. This sprawling appellation encompasses forests and mountains, hills and dales, and has the navigational inconvenience of a large river cutting almost straight through the middle of it. A map is essential, as is a bit of planning to ensure you spend more time in wineries than backtracking on the roads. The **Russian River Wine Road** (707/433-4335 or 800/723-6336, www.wineroad.com) publishes

one of the best maps, which is downloadable from the website.

The **Dry Creek Valley** and **Alexander Valley** are relatively straightforward to navigate by comparison, with most of the wineries strung along a few long, relatively straight roads. These valleys are almost like miniature Sonoma or Napa Valleys as far as climate, shape, and scenery, and it's easy to get a good feel for the area in a day or even a half day.

The three main appellations are like night and day when it comes to wine, which makes planning a wine route either exciting or daunting. Sample some velvety Alexander Valley cabernets, for example, before crossing into the Dry Creek Valley to try to find your favorite Dry Creek zinfandel. Then, head down Westside Road to explore some leaner, cool-climate chardonnay or hunt out the next big pinot noir in the Russian River Valley.

If all the possibilities just seem too overwhelming, there's always the option of staying in **Healdsburg,** which has enough tasting rooms to satisfy the fussiest wine drinker, as well as plenty of shops and restaurants to occupy those less curious about the region's wines. Healdsburg is the most central town in the region, and its hotels and restaurants make it an almost essential staging post for any trip to this part of the world.

As in other parts of the Wine Country, wineries generally open late and close early, so don't expect to get started until late morning, and plan to be finished touring by about 5pm, closer to 4pm during the winter. Unlike in the rest of Sonoma and Napa, free tasting is still fairly commonplace here, but is increasingly less so. But even when there is a fee for tasting regular or reserve wines, it will be far more palatable than in some other parts of Wine Country.

And of course, non-wine-related activities also abound. Check out the burgeoning Santa Rosa Arts District, the multitude of hiking options in wilderness areas such as Armstrong Redwoods State Natural Reserve, and of course the endless water fun on the Russian River. As for food, the scene in the

Best of Northern Sonoma Varietals

Northern Sonoma has the widest variety of growing conditions in Wine Country, from the cool and damp Green Valley AVA on the western edge of the Russian River to the hot and dry Rockpile AVA at the top of Dry Creek. With such a diversity of soil, climate, and elevation comes a breadth of varietals, including rare Rhône and Italian varietals. Chardonnay and pinot noir thrive in the cooler Russian River Valley, while jammy zinfandels and plush cabernets dominate the drier and hotter Dry Creek and Alexander Valleys.

SPARKLING

- **Iron Horse Vineyards** (page 211) makes award-winning sparkling wine from grapes grown in the cool Green Valley AVA.

- **J Vineyards & Winery** (page 221) pours flights of Russian River sparkling wine in a setting that is almost as effervescent as its wine.

CHARDONNAY

- Boutique winery **Banshee** (page 236) specializes in distinctive chardonnays from the Sonoma Coast, including its incomparable Heintz vineyard chardonnay.

- The reserve chardonnay at **Selby Winery** (page 236) has been served at the White House. Try it for yourself in the relaxed Healdsburg tasting room.

- In operation since 1881, **Simi Winery** (page 261) is now best known for its Russian River chardonnay.

- Chardonnay dominates at **Robert Young Estate Winery** (page 265), a sixth-generation run winery. They make a particularly rich, full-bodied version of the versatile varietal.

PINOT NOIR

- **Merry Edwards Winery** (page 209) is an unpretentious (and free) winery that serves a celebrated pinot noir made by a legend in the field.

- Surrounded by lush gardens at **Lynmar Estate** (page 213), guests can try the winery's 15 pinot noirs, some of which are vineyard select from the surrounding Quail Hill estate vineyards.

Russian River Valley is one of the most varied in Wine Country. It certainly has its share of pricey, stylish establishments, particularly at the many inns hidden away in the woods. But since it's a down-to-earth, outdoorsy sort of place, there are also plenty of cheap and homey establishments where the lack of an uptight reservation system can make the experience instantly relaxing.

GETTING THERE
Car
Convenient, but ugly, **U.S. 101** runs up the center of this region, leaving strip malls in its wake. Still, the drive time from San Francisco up the freeway to almost every major Russian River Valley town is usually not much more than an hour, to Healdsburg and beyond about an hour and a half. Be aware that traffic on 101 can get sticky, particularly during the morning commute and 3pm-7pm. It is also slow on sunny summer afternoons when all the folks return to their Bay Area homes after cooling themselves along the Russian River.

From the freeway, **Highway 116** West runs up through Sebastopol to Guerneville. In the Santa Rosa area, River Road runs west to Forestville and Guerneville. The Healdsburg

- One of the pioneers of pinot in the Russian River Valley, **Joseph Swan Vineyards** (page 218) now pours flights in its off-the-beaten-path rustic tasting room.

- Serious cork dorks recommend the tiny tasting room at **Porter Creek Winery** (page 220) for its carefully crafted pinot noirs, sourced from the organic vineyards just outside the tasting room door.

ZINFANDEL

- A fixture in the valley since the 1900s, **Martinelli Winery** (page 218) makes one of the most noteworthy zinfandels in the Russian River Valley from the Jackass Vineyard, planted in the 1800s.

- **Ridge Vineyards** (page 251) makes over a dozen different zins, sourced from vineyards as far south as Paso Robles to north of Geyserville. The winery is striking for its mid-century style and environmental credentials.

- **A. Rafanelli Winery** (page 256) is a fourth-generation run Dry Creek winery whose zinfandels have achieved an almost cultlike status.

- One of the prettiest wineries in Dry Creek, **Bella Vineyards** (page 255) produces outstanding single-vineyard zinfandels.

CABERNET

- The Monte Bello cabernet at **Ridge Vineyards** (page 251) placed fifth out of 10 in the notorious Judgment of Paris. It can now be tasted with the estate flight or vertical Monte Bello vintage tasting.

- **Hawkes** (page 264) is a family-run winery that specializes in estate cabernet sourced from its vineyards in Alexander Valley. It offers a cabernet-only tasting.

- At **Silver Oak Cellars** (page 266), red-wine lovers can compare the leggy Napa Valley cabernet with the plush and aromatic Alexander Valley version in a cabernet-only tasting.

Avenue exit leads straight into downtown Healdsburg, and the Westside Road exit is the entry to the Dry Creek Valley and Russian River regions. The next four exits serve Dry Creek and Alexander Valleys before the freeway reaches Geyserville and then heads into the hills toward Hopland and Mendocino.

Bus

Although most people come to this part of the Wine Country by car, there are other transport options. Santa Rosa is served by **Golden Gate Transit** (415/455-2000, www.goldengatetransit.org, $13), which runs scheduled bus service to and from San Francisco hourly for much of the day. Routes 72 and 74 are the most expeditious, but these are commuter buses that only travel south in the morning and north in the afternoon Monday-Friday. Route 101 makes trips up and down U.S. 101 seven days a week, but it is a slower two-hour trek. From Santa Rosa, **Sonoma County Transit** (707/576-7433 or 800/345-7433, www.sctransit.com, $2-3) runs regular services to Healdsburg and Guerneville. From Sebastopol there's service to Guerneville through Graton and Forestville. Things are so spread out in the Russian River Valley, however, that once you arrive there by bus you'll still need some mode of transport to see anything.

GETTING AROUND

Car

The Russian River Valley is roughly square in shape, with an arm stretching from its northeastern corner up to Healdsburg. The major towns are Guerneville in the northwest corner of the square, Sebastopol on the southern edge, Occidental on the western edge, and Santa Rosa on the eastern side. In the middle is a patchwork of farmland and vineyards, together with the hamlets of Graton and Forestville. Highway 116, also called the **Gravenstein Highway,** is the main road running north-south through them.

Wineries cluster along Eastside and Westside Roads, which both run on either side of the river from Healdsburg to east of Guerneville, and throughout the patchwork in the middle of the area. Many of the region's food and lodging options lie in Healdsburg and in tiny Guerneville. Unlike in the Dry Creek and Alexander Valleys farther north, roads here tend to meander as they follow the river and hills, often making driving times longer than anticipated.

By comparison, the Dry Creek Valley could be navigated with your eyes shut. Just two roads run the length of the valley, and the wineries are roughly spread out along them, making it the easiest part of northern Sonoma to visit in a day, even without a map. Along the other side of the freeway is the longer and wider Alexander Valley. Even here, the wineries are concentrated along Highway 128, which runs from Calistoga to Geyserville. Worth noting is that there are virtually no gas stations in Dry Creek, Alexander Valley, and west of Sebastopol and Guerneville.

Bike

Of course, driving is not the only way to get around. Wine Country would not be complete without cycling. The compact, flat **Dry Creek Valley** and relatively flat **Westside Road** from Healdsburg down into the Russian River Valley are two of the most bikeable routes. The Alexander Valley is also relatively flat, but distances between wineries are greater. In all areas, temperatures get high in the summer, so plenty of water is essential.

The best place to rent bikes is in Healdsburg, where there are several options. The friendly folks at **Spoke Folk Cyclery** (201 Center St., Healdsburg, 707/433-7171,

bikes for rent in Healdsburg

www.spokefolk.com, 10am-6pm Mon.-Fri., 10am-5pm Sat.-Sun.) will rent you a bike ($60/day) and send you on your way with maps for biking routes that range from leisurely 12-mile loops in Dry Creek Valley to 40-mile adventures down to Guerneville. At the other end of town next to the Old Roma Station winery complex, **Wine Country Bikes** (61 Front St., Healdsburg, 707/473-0610, www.winecountrybikes.com, 9am-5pm daily) rents bikes ($39-85/day) and offers a casual six-hour tour ($139) of Dry Creek that includes stops at a couple wineries and a gourmet picnic catered by the Oakville Grocery.

Russian River Valley

The Russian River Valley is one of Sonoma's largest and most diverse geographic regions. It covers about 150 square miles of forest, orchards, vineyards, and pastureland from trendy Sebastopol in the south to chic Healdsburg in the north, and from the suburban freeway sprawl in the east to rural Occidental in the west. Running right through it is the mighty Russian River, shaping the climate, scenery, and recreational opportunities in the region.

The Russian River Valley attracted immigrants in the late 1800s to exploit its vast forests, and many of the towns that exist today were established as logging or railroad outposts. Once the redwood forests had been largely cleared, sheep ranches, cattle pasture, orchards, and even hops farms took over the land. The Gravenstein apple, now an endangered piece of local agricultural history, was embraced as the region's very own, though its roots remain somewhat ambiguous.

It wasn't until the 1980s, when the cool growing climate was recognized as ideal for the increasingly fashionable pinot noir and chardonnay grapes, that the area's wine industry took off, and the Russian River Valley has long since been recognized as one of the best cool grape-growing regions in California.

This is not an easy part of Wine Country to explore compared to the relatively self-contained valleys elsewhere in Sonoma, however. Roads wind through forests, over hills, and along the snaking river, making wineries sometimes hard to find. Large parts of the region are rural, dotted with small communities like **Forestville** and **Graton,** which hide their already small populations very well in the surrounding hills and woods.

The center of the action is **Guerneville** and neighboring **Monte Rio,** both slightly faded Victorian resort towns that are transformed each summer into a surreal scene of leather-clad bikers and plaid-clad outdoors enthusiasts, hipsters, and hippies. Guerneville is something of a gay mecca and party town, and the rustic resorts and bars often pulsate with the beat of dance music and drunken hordes on summer evenings.

The eastern and western edges of the appellation could not be more of a contrast. The suburban sprawl of **Santa Rosa** is just outside the eastern boundary of the appellation and almost a poster child for how not to grow a city. It is by far the biggest city in the region—a place where culture meets characterless malls—but a far cry from the peaceful and remote Bohemian Highway running along the appellation's western edge, where the picture-postcard town of **Occidental** exists in the midst of dense forests. In between sits **Sebastopol,** which has long drawn aging hippies and young families in search of nature, an agrarian vibe, and an artistic community all served with a gourmet cup of artisan coffee.

The Wines

Almost a third of all the grapes grown in Sonoma County come from the Russian River Valley, but there's the potential for it to be a far higher proportion. Only 15,000 acres, or

Russian River Valley

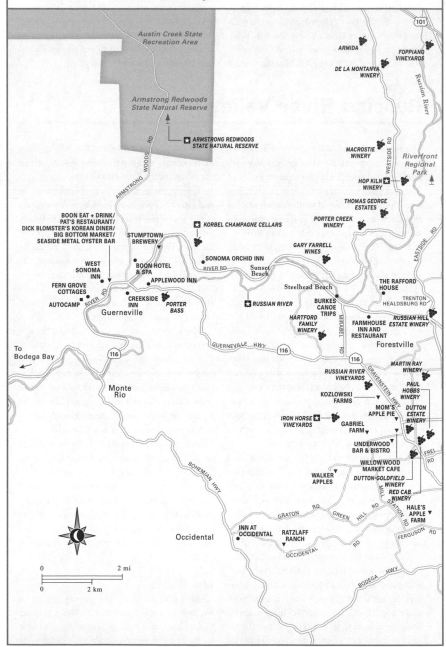

Austin Creek State
Recreation Area

ARMIDA

FOPPIANO
VINEYARDS

DE LA MONTANYA
WINERY

Armstrong Redwoods
State Natural Reserve

⭐ ARMSTRONG REDWOODS
STATE NATURAL RESERVE

MACROSTIE
WINERY

Riverfront
Regional
Park

HOP KILN ⭐
WINERY

THOMAS GEORGE
ESTATES

PORTER CREEK
WINERY

⭐ KORBEL CHAMPAGNE CELLARS

GARY FARRELL
WINES

BOON EAT + DRINK/
PAT'S RESTAURANT/
DICK BLOMSTER'S KOREAN DINER/
BIG BOTTOM MARKET/
SEASIDE METAL OYSTER BAR

STUMPTOWN
BREWERY

WEST
SONOMA
INN

BOON HOTEL
& SPA

SONOMA ORCHID INN

RIVER RD   Sunset
            Beach

Steelhead Beach

THE RAFFORD
HOUSE

TRENTON
HEALDSBURG RD

FERN GROVE
COTTAGES

APPLEWOOD INN

AUTOCAMP

CREEKSIDE
INN

PORTER
BASS

⭐ RUSSIAN RIVER

BURKES
CANOE
TRIPS

RUSSIAN HILL
ESTATE WINERY

Guerneville

HARTFORD
FAMILY
WINERY

FARMHOUSE
INN AND
RESTAURANT

Forestville

To
Bodega Bay

116

GUERNEVILLE   HWY   116

116

MARTIN RAY
WINERY

Monte
Rio

RUSSIAN RIVER
VINEYARDS

PAUL
HOBBS
WINERY

KOZLOWSKI
FARMS

MOM'S
APPLE PIE

DUTTON
ESTATE
WINERY

IRON HORSE ⭐
VINEYARDS

GABRIEL
FARM

UNDERWOOD
BAR & BISTRO

WILLOW WOOD
MARKET CAFE

FREI
RD

WALKER
APPLES

DUTTON-GOLDFIELD
WINERY

RED CAB
WINERY

BOHEMIAN   HWY

GRATON   RD   GREEN   HILL   RD

HALE'S
APPLE
FARM

INN AT
OCCIDENTAL

RATZLAFF
RANCH

FERGUSON   RD

Occidental

OCCIDENTAL

BODEGA   HWY

0   2 mi

0   2 km

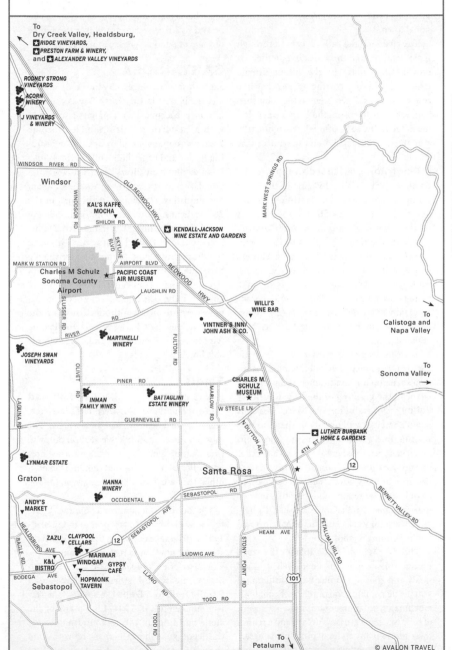

To
Dry Creek Valley, Healdsburg,
★ RIDGE VINEYARDS,
★ PRESTON FARM & WINERY,
and ★ ALEXANDER VALLEY VINEYARDS

RODNEY STRONG
VINEYARDS

ACORN
WINERY

J VINEYARDS
& WINERY

WINDSOR RIVER RD

OLD REDWOOD HWY

Windsor

WINDSOR RD

KAL'S KAFFE
MOCHA

SHILOH RD

SKYLINE BLVD

★ KENDALL-JACKSON
WINE ESTATE AND GARDENS

MARK W STATION RD

AIRPORT BLVD

REDWOOD HWY

Charles M Schulz
Sonoma County
Airport

★ PACIFIC COAST
AIR MUSEUM

LAUGHLIN RD

MARK WEST SPRINGS RD

WILLI'S
WINE BAR

To
Calistoga and
Napa Valley

SLUSSER RD

RIVER RD

MARTINELLI
WINERY

FULTON RD

VINTNER'S INN/
JOHN ASH & CO.

JOSEPH SWAN
VINEYARDS

OLIVET RD

PINER RD

CHARLES M.
SCHULZ
MUSEUM
★

To
Sonoma Valley

INMAN
FAMILY WINES

BATTAGLINI
ESTATE WINERY

MARLOW RD

W STEELE LN

GUERNEVILLE RD

N DUTTON AVE

★ LUTHER BURBANK
HOME & GARDENS

LAGUNA RD

LYNMAR ESTATE

4TH ST

12

Graton

HANNA
WINERY

Santa Rosa

★

ANDY'S
MARKET

OCCIDENTAL RD

SEBASTOPOL RD

BENNETT VALLEY RD

HEALDSBURG AVE

RAGLE RD

ZAZU

CLAYPOOL
CELLARS

12

SEBASTOPOL AVE

HEAM AVE

PETALUMA HILL RD

K&L
BISTRO

MARIMAR
WINDGAP

GYPSY
CAFÉ

LUDWIG AVE

STONY POINT RD

BODEGA AVE

HOPMONK
TAVERN

LLANO RD

101

Sebastopol

TODD RD

TODD RD

To
Petaluma

© AVALON TRAVEL

just over 10 percent, of the 126,000 acres in the valley are actually planted with vineyards. The rest is still pasture, forest, and the occasional town.

The river and the valley it carved through the coastal mountain ranges over millennia provide the region with the unique climate that is perfect for growing grapes that like cool conditions. There's enough strong sunlight each day to ensure the grapes ripen, but the air remains cool, often downright chilly at night, and keeps a lid on the fruit's sugar levels.

Pinot noir and **chardonnay** are the dominant varietals in this part of the Wine Country, but **zinfandel** is almost as important, and the resulting wines have a subtlety that is often lacking in the brawny zins from the warmer valleys to the north. Growers are also having increasing success with **syrah** and some other Rhône varietals, while **gewürztraminer** is starting to make more of an appearance. The ubiquitous cabernet sauvignon and merlot are largely absent, however, except on the warmest eastern hills of the region.

The cool layer of damp marine air from the Pacific Ocean just a few miles west is the region's natural air-conditioner and was a big factor in the granting of the **Russian River Valley**'s AVA status in 1983. Marine fog rolls down the river valley during the summer, snaking into gullies and canyons and keeping the temperature here lower than any other inland portion of Sonoma County. As the ripening process slows, the fruit can gain in complexity and retain enough acidity to keep the wines interesting. Grapes are usually harvested several weeks later here than in some hotter Sonoma regions.

The river is also responsible for the area's unique soils, depositing deep, well-drained sandy and gravelly sediments over millions of years. The combination of relatively cool microclimates, no summer rain, and a patchwork of soils is a grape grower's dream and a reason there are so many styles of pinot made here.

Within the southwest corner of the Russian River appellation is the even cooler **Green Valley** AVA, thanks to a persistent layer of fog. This is just about as cool as a climate can be and still ripen grapes, and it is the source of some of Sonoma's best pinot noir.

SANTA ROSA

Santa Rosa is the biggest city in Wine Country and the largest in the North Bay. As such, it is more preoccupied with big-city issues than with wine-tasting. This is a mixed-income area where many people work in the building trades and other blue-collar professions. It is also ethnically diverse, with a large Latino population as well as strong Southeast Asian communities. Developed at the turn of the 20th century, the older neighborhoods are filled with charming Craftsman-style bungalows. Downtown boasts some historic buildings, but many did not survive the big earthquakes of 1906 and 1969. Santa Rosa's size and proximity to Wine Country make it a good jumping-off point for a day of exploring, plus there are plenty of things to do with the kids, such as the Charles Schulz and Pacific Air Museums, Safari West, and lots of affordable hotels with pools.

Sights

In the heart of the sprawl sit **Railroad Square** and the **Downtown Arts District,** Santa Rosa's downtown and tourist areas. The most compact and walkable section of town, these feature a number of restaurants, shops, and galleries. While located right next to each other, they are divided by the ugly, eight-lane U.S. 101.

On the west side, Railroad Square is home to some of Santa Rosa's precious few pre-1906-earthquake buildings that have been restored and now house restaurants and shops. The district encompasses 3rd, 4th, and 5th Streets, near the historic **Northwestern Pacific Railroad Depot,** a small stone station house built in 1904. Like many of the stone buildings in the surrounding blocks, the depot is as solid as it looks and withstood the 1906 earthquake that leveled much of

Santa Rosa

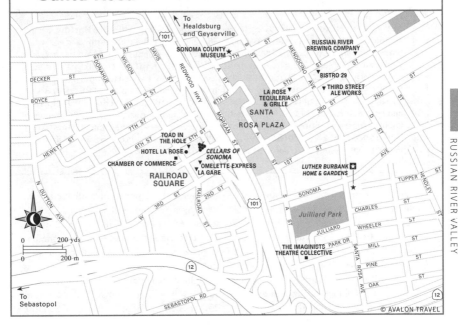

downtown Santa Rosa. Its claim to fame was acting as a backdrop in the Alfred Hitchcock film *Shadow of a Doubt,* and it is now home to a California Welcome Center that includes the **Santa Rosa Convention & Visitors Bureau** (9 4th St., 707/577-8674 or 800/404-7673, 9am-5pm Mon.-Sat., 10am-5pm Sun.). Pick up a walking map from the visitors bureau to see some of the other historic buildings made from the locally quarried basalt stone.

Maps are also available online for the Arts District, east of U.S. 101, by the **South of A Street Art District Association** (http://sofasantarosa.com). Framed by Sonoma, Mendocino/Santa Rosa, Sebastopol Avenues, and South A Street, this area is home to over 30 art studios, galleries, cafés, and countless pieces of installation art amid Santa Rosa's working downtown. The district may lack the historical charm of Railroad Avenue, but the comparatively modern and gritty area adds a bit of urban chic to its artistic endeavors. Thankfully, these endeavors can be seen at open studio weekends spread throughout the year.

★ LUTHER BURBANK HOME & GARDENS

At the southeast corner of the Arts District sits the **Luther Burbank Home & Gardens** (204 Santa Rosa Ave., 707/524-5445, www.lutherburbank.org, 8am-dusk daily, free). Burbank was a pioneering horticulturist best known for his cross-breeding experiments and is credited with creating more than 800 new strains of flowers, fruits, trees, and other plants over his 50-year science career. He was well connected in the scientific circles of the time, counting Thomas Edison and Henry Ford, among others, as friends.

Burbank's home, where he lived until 1906, is preserved along with a small greenhouse and the gardens as part of the 1.6-acre National and State Historic Landmark. The gardens contain many of Burbank's horticultural creations and are open 8am-sunset

Russian River Valley Tasting Tour

Nothing starts off a day of wine-tasting better than a stop at Sebastopol's **The Barlow,** a large compound of shops, restaurants, and vendors reflecting Sebastopol's arty, earthy, and epicurean tendencies. Sample a crepe at **Ultra Crepes** and get a cup of joe at **Tailor Maid Farms,** and you'll be ready for some wine. Stroll over to the hip **Wind Gap** for a flight of cool climate varietals or a pint of hard cider. Continue up the Gravenstein Highway for a seated tasting at pinot specialist **Merry Edwards Winery,** followed by lunch and a flight on the porch of **Russian River Vineyards.** Or, if the beauty of the day calls for a picnic, grab supplies at **Kozlowski Farms** and head over to **Korbel** for a flight of bubbly and a picnic beneath the redwoods. Spend the last bit of sunshine at **Sunset Beach** on the Russian River or beneath the giants at **Armstrong Redwoods State Natural Reserve.** Finally, head into downtown Guerneville and finish the day with some oysters and crudo at **Seaside Metal Oyster Bar.**

every day. The **museum** and **greenhouse** (10am-4pm Tues.-Sun. Apr.-Oct.) include some of his tools and explain the significance of his work. **Guided tours** (adults $10, students and seniors $8.50, children under 12 free) are available 10am-3:30pm Tuesday-Sunday April-October. Check the website for a list of what's in bloom during your visit, as something will be showing off its finest flowers every month of the year.

MUSEUMS

History and modern art come together at the **Sonoma County Museum** (425 7th St., 707/579-1500, www.sonomacountymuseum. org, 11am-5pm Tues.-Sun., adults $7, children under 12 free). Located in the city's historic former main post office building, the museum includes permanent exhibits of historic artifacts and photos that help tell the story of the county. Rotating modern art shows and the permanent collection of contemporary art tell about the Sonoma of today. Thrown into the mix are works by world-famous artists Christo and Jeanne-Claude, generously donated by a Sonoma resident. Be sure to step out to the sculpture garden, where a combination of art, landscape design, and Sonoma sunshine provides a lovely reprieve.

North of downtown, the slightly offbeat **Charles M. Schulz Museum** (2301 Hardies Ln., 707/579-4452, www.schulzmuseum.org, 11am-5pm Mon.-Fri., 10am-5pm Sat.-Sun.

summer, 11am-5pm Mon. and Wed.-Fri., 10am-5pm Sat.-Sun. fall-spring, adults $12, seniors $8, children 4-18 $5, 3 and under free) celebrates the man who drew the beloved *Peanuts* comic strip for almost 50 years and called Sonoma home from 1958 until his death in 2000. Inside the 27,000-square-foot building, you'll find most of the original *Peanuts* strips, a large collection of Schulz's personal possessions, and an astonishing array of tribute artwork from other comic-strip artists and urban installation designers the world over. Outside the building, the grounds include attractive gardens, the Snoopy Labyrinth, and even the infamous Kite-eating Tree.

Nearby, the **Pacific Coast Air Museum** (1 Air Museum Way, 707/575-7900, www. pacificcoastairmuseum.org, 10am-4pm Wed.-Sun., adults $10, seniors $7, children 6-17 $5, under age 6 free) is worth a stop even if you're not an aviation buff. Learn about the history of flying in the United States through interpretive and photographic exhibits. Many of the planes here are examples of modern war machines—such as those you'd see on the deck of an aircraft carrier. Or if you prefer to see civilian craft, check out the funky little Pitts aerobatic plane, the sort of thing you'll see doing impossible-looking tricks during the museum's annual **Wings over Wine Country** air show, held each September.

larger animal enclosures and learn why the rhino is endangered, the zebra has strips, and what makes the Cape buffalo one of the most dangerous animals in Africa. You may get eye to eye with a curious giraffe. The on-site café offers an excellent lunch and dinner (adults $15-29, children 4-17 $12-17) plus beer and wine. The more adventurous might consider sleeping overnight in one of the luxurious tent cabins ($285-400).

Entertainment and Events

Santa Rosa's entertainment scene is somewhat dispersed, but the city does have a well-established local theater group. **The Imaginists Theatre Collective** (461 Sebastopol Ave., 707/528-7554, www.theimaginists.org, $15-25) puts on an eclectic series of original and imaginative plays year-round at a small theater that was once home to an auto-repair shop. The evening performances are usually concentrated in a two-week stretch each month. Check the website for a performance schedule.

Beer, and specifically craft beer, is really the bread and butter of Santa Rosa nightlife. **Third Street Ale Works** (610 3rd St., 707/523-3060, www.thirdstreetaleworks.com, 11:30am-midnight Sun.-Thurs., 11:30am-1am Sat.-Sun.) challenges drinkers to take the plunge with Brass Parachute Barleywine and Puddle Jumper Pale Ale, or a flight of everything on the menu for only $13. High-caliber pub food is also available, served either in the bustling but charming bar or outside on the sidewalk patio.

A few blocks away is the **Russian River Brewing Company** (725 4th St., 707/545-2337, www.russianriverbrewing.com, 11am-midnight daily), which brews dozens of ales and lagers with names that probably sound funnier when drunk, like Hop 2 It, Pliny the Elder, and Blind Pig IPA. Pizza, sandwiches, munchies, and even a kids menu are available to order alongside your $5 pint. The Brewing Company is a popular local hangout, so expect a wait on weekends.

In Railroad Square, **Toad in the Hole** (116 5th St., 707/544-8623, www.thetoadpub.

Safari West

SAFARI WEST

Wine Country might not exactly bring to mind the savannas of Africa, unless you happen upon **Safari West** (3115 Porter Creek Rd., 707/579-2551 or 800/616-2695, www.safariwest.com, adults $83-115, seniors $80-100, children 4-12 $45-50), a 400-acre wildlife preserve dedicated to saving endangered species (mostly African) through education and propagation. Over 900 animals and around 90 different species happily call the reserve home, and the public is invited to see them by joining one of the many three-hour tours given daily. You'll walk through the newly constructed aviary and peer into the enclosures of hyenas, lemurs, monkeys, and blue duikers, a tiny species of antelope. The fun and informative guides make this much more than your standard zoo experience with interesting facts and a clear affection for the animals here. Part two of the tour begins by boarding a jeep, customized with three wide bench seats in the back and one on top for maximum viewing and thrill. You'll drive through the

Beer Before Wine

It's hard to imagine a time before vineyards in Wine Country, but another type of vine was once the mainstay of the agricultural economy in Sonoma County. From Sebastopol to Healdsburg and up into Mendocino, hop vines rather than grapevines once lined the roads and covered the hillsides. The tall hop kilns that rear up over the landscape from Guerneville to Hopland, some now converted into wineries, are reminders of the time before wine.

These days, however, craft beer is going strong in Wine Country. In every town in Northern Sonoma, you are likely to find at least one microbrewery.

- **Russian River Brewing Company, Santa Rosa:** Local beer lovers are drawn with growlers in hand to the dozens of ales and lagers brewed at Russian River. It's also a popular place to eat, so expect a wait on weekends.

- **Third Street Ale Works, Santa Rosa:** Third Street Ale Works leans heavily on English-style beer but also experiments with lagers, stouts, porters, and IPAs in an ever-changing menu.

- **Hopmonk Tavern, Sebastopol:** Hopmonk Tavern has a modest portfolio of four brews and pours a hearty selection of other West Coast microbrews. There are a couple of locations around the North Bay in addition to its Sebastopol location.

- **Woodfour Brewing Company, Sebastopol:** Woodfour brews an astonishing array of complex German, French, Belgium, and American beer, including a sour wheat ale and a black lager fortified with Taylor Maid cold brew coffee.

- **Stumptown Brewery, Guerneville:** Try one of the potent-sounding microbrews like Red Rocket or Death and Taxes.

- **Bear Republic Brewing Company, Healdsburg:** The quiet, sunny outdoor patio is the perfect place to tap into Bear Republic's Racer 5 IPA.

com, noon-midnight Sun.-Thurs., noon-2am Fri.-Sat.) pours pints, serves plates of greasy fish-and-chips, and keeps the telly turned to rugby, soccer, and football; in other words, it is a proper English pub. You'll also find darts, live music, and an annual Monty Python festival that spills out onto the street with plenty of silly walks.

Craft beer comes with wine at the boutique wine collective, **Cellars of Sonoma** (133 4th St., 707/284-3487, www.cellarsofsonoma. com, 3pm-8:30pm Sun.-Wed., 11am-10:30pm Thurs.-Sat.). Order a glass of pinot noir or perhaps a coastal chardonnay and enjoy small bites and live music Thursday through Saturday when the tasting room transforms into a relaxed lounge.

Big-time live-music venues are few and far between in the Russian River region, but the **Luther Burbank Center for the Arts** (50 Mark West Springs Rd., 707/546-3600, http://

lutherburbankcenter.org, ticket prices vary) is a full-size theater that hosts any number of national acts on tour each year, plus the occasional play or headlining comic. Recent acts have included Emmy Lou Harris and Tracy Morgan.

One of the biggest annual events in this agricultural region is the **Sonoma County Fair** (Sonoma County Fairgrounds, 1350 Bennett Valley Rd., 707/545-4200, www.sonomacountyfair.com, 13 and up $12, children 7-12 $6, children 6 and younger free), held during two weeks at the end of July through the beginning of August. Even the biggest Sonoma wineries prize the awards they win at their local county fair, and you'll see fair ribbons displayed proudly in many Russian River tasting rooms. If you're lucky enough to be able to attend, you'll find far more than just wine—live entertainment, family shows, amusement rides for the kids, and an amazing array of contests and exhibitions featuring the work of folks from all over the Sonoma region.

Shopping

The best shopping in Santa Rosa is found at Railroad Square, where many pre-1906 buildings are now antiques stores, jewelry stores, and other boutiques. Glamorous vintage jewelry and watches, from Victorian to mid-century and 21st-century periods, can be found at **Olde Towne Jewelers** (125 4th St., 707/577-8813, www.oldetownejewelers. com, 10am-5:30pm Mon.-Sat.), while across the street, **Whistlestop Antiques** (130 4th St., 707/542-9474, http://whistlestop-antiques.com, 10am-5:30pm Mon.-Sat., 11am-5pm Sun.) is a collective of dozens of antiques dealers.

For timeless pieces that you can wear, stroll over to **Hot Couture Vintage Fashion** (101 3rd St., 707/528-7247, www.hotcouturevintage.com, 10am-6pm Mon.-Sat., 11am-5pm Sun.), where clothes mostly from the 1940s to the 1970s fill the racks, and hats for both men and women line the shelves along the walls. This store takes great pride in selling fashionable vintage clothing in great condition, so as not to be confused with just any old used clothing store. Complement your vintage wardrobe with the modern bric-a-brac at **Rococo Mercato** (127 4th St., 707/526-7500, www.rococomercato.com, 11am-5:30 daily). Fancy soaps, handbags, scarves, and cool knickknacks fill the store and provide ample opportunity for that needed gift and maybe not so needed treat.

Check out Santa Rosa's art scene at **Chroma Gallery** (312 South A St., 707/293-6051, http://chromagallery.net, 11am-4pm Thurs.-Sat., 11am-2pm Sun.), across U.S. 101 in the Arts District. You'll find rotating shows of fine art, as well as jewelry and ceramics for sale. Conveniently located in the same building, **Christie Marks Fine Art** (312 South A St. Ste. 7, 707/695-1011, http://christiemarksfineart.com, noon-5pm Thurs.-Sat.) showcases Marks's own work as well as other Bay Area artists. Expect to see vibrant and

contemporary oil and mixed media painting, as well as photography and sculptures.

Recreation

Just as in Napa, one of the popular ways to get a great view of the Russian River Valley is from the basket of a hot-air balloon. **Wine Country Balloons** (707/538-7359 or 800/759-5638, www.balloontours.com, adults $225, children $195) meets at **Kal's Kaffe Mocha** (397 Aviation Blvd., 707/566-8100, 7am-9pm Mon.-Fri., 8am-9pm Sat.-Sun.) and gets you up in the air to start the day high above Wine Country. This big company maintains a whole fleet of balloons that can carry 2-16 passengers. Expect the total time to be 3-4 hours, with 1-1.5 hours in the air, and reservations should be made a month in advance in the summer. You'll end your flight with a brunch at Kal's and a handful of wine-tasting coupons.

For a bit of open space during your visit, **Spring Lake** (393 Violetti Dr., 707/539-8092, www.sonoma-county.org, parking $7) has a little something for everyone. Picnic tables and hiking and paved cycling trails skirt this 72-acre lake. Anglers out to stalk the wily largemouth bass can launch electric-motor boats (but not gas-powered boats) into the water, while lifeguards watch over a cordoned swimming lagoon that's perfect for kids. A nearby concession stand rents paddleboats and canoe-like craft during summer and sells beer, burgers, and $1 oysters at happy hour. The Environmental Discovery Center has interactive displays eager to teach kids and adults alike about the lake's ecosystem and environmental stewardship in general.

Golfers can take a swing at the **Bennett Valley Golf Course** (3330 Yulupa Ave., 707/528-3673, www.srcity.org/golf, $26-45). A par-72 medium-length 18-hole course, it provides challenging play for beginners, intermediates, and advanced golfers. Practically next door are two 18-hole courses at the **Oakmont Golf Club** (7025 Oakmont Dr., 707/539-0415, www.oakmontgc.com, $20-70). The Oakmont

East course offers executive-length par-63 play—perfect for a shorter or slightly easier game, while Oakmont West is a little bigger and more challenging, at regulation length and par 72.

Food

Santa Rosa has an eclectic dining scene that better reflects its size, diversity, and largely working-class population instead of its location in the heart of Sonoma Wine Country. Still there are several standouts, including a couple of excellent French bistros in the downtown area.

CALIFORNIA CUISINE

Surrounded by vineyards north of Santa Rosa, **John Ash & Co.** (4350 Barnes Rd., 707/527-7687, www.vintnersinn.com, 5pm-9pm daily, $26-44) stands out as one of the best high-end California cuisine restaurants in the Russian River region. A part of the Vintners Inn, the elegant dining room is done up in Mediterranean style, and the food runs to pure California cuisine, with lots of local and sustainable produce prepared to show off its natural flavors. Select appetizers and mains off the fairly short menu or pick the four-course tasting menu ($68), which is a very affordable way to taste the best John Ash has to offer. The wine list is also something special, with some amazing local vintages that are tough to find anywhere outside of the Russian River Valley.

Locals love **Willi's Wine Bar** (4404 Old Redwood Hwy., 707/526-3096, www.starkres-taurants.com/willis_winebar, 11:30am-9:30pm Tues.-Thurs., 11:30am-10pm Fri.-Sat., 5pm-9:30pm Sun.-Mon., $9-15), also just north of Santa Rosa. Here, sipping wine or cocktails is as much a part of the fun as nibbling on one of the many small plates on the globally inspired menu. Pick from oysters Rockefeller, curried crab tacos, or pork belly pot stickers. The sophisticated wine list belies the casual vibe and makes for a delightful night out.

The same team behind Willi's Wine Bar is also behind Santa Rosa's hippest new restaurant, **Bird and the Bottle** (1055 4th St., Santa Rosa, 707/568-4000, http://birdandthe-bottle.com, 11:30am-9:30pm Sun.-Thurs., 11:30am-10pm Fri.-Sat., $12-28). Located in a converted Craftsman style home (complete with a lovely outdoor patio) in an unassuming part of town, Bird and the Bottle calls itself a modern tavern. The menu is broken into seafood, poultry, pork, beef, and "food without a face" (vegetarian) sections, and each dish blends comfort food with bright, international flavors. Like any good tavern, the restaurant has a healthy drink list with plenty of beer, local and international wine, and original cocktails.

FRENCH

There is no doubt about it, downtown and the historic Railroad Square are the best dining districts in the sprawling and somewhat suburban Santa Rosa. Railroad Square was obviously an inspiration when naming **La Gare** (208 Wilson St., 707/528-4355, www.lagarerestaurant.com, 5pm-9pm daily, $18-36), which serves simple but sophisticated French-Swiss food, including some lavish steaks, in an old-school setting of starched white tablecloths (the French influence) and mountain ambience (the Swiss). It was established in 1979, and such longevity is rare for a Sonoma restaurant, which means it must be doing something right.

Across U.S. 101 in the Arts District, **Bistro 29** (620 5th St., 707/546-2929, www.bistro29.com, 5pm-9pm Tues.-Thurs., 5pm-9:30pm Fri.-Sat., $21-28) serves food inspired by Breton regional cuisine from northwestern France (29 is the number of the district in Brittany). An assortment of savory buckwheat crepes and old French standbys like cassoulet and *steak frites* grace the menu. The modern decor hints at French country style, and the wine list also gives a nod to French regional wines, with choices from Bandol, the Rhône, the Loire, and Languedoc complementing the extensive Northern California options. Happy hour offers $5 wine paired with $5 crepes, and the three-course prix fixe dinner menu served weekdays is a steal at $34 (wine pairing $11).

MEXICAN

Also downtown, the cavernous ★ **La Rosa Tequileria & Grille** (500 4th St., 707/523-3663, http://larosasantarosa.com, 11am-9pm Sun.-Thurs., 11am-1:30am Fri.-Sat., $11-20) is the place to go for a casual lunch or a late night out with friends. The large restaurant has multiple dining rooms and a large back patio, each styled with deep booths, luscious murals of roses, and collections of crucifixes. Served is classic south-of-the-border cuisine that is excellent and delivered with artistic panache. La Rosa also specializes in tequila, so steel yourself for a flight or several rounds of margaritas.

BREAKFAST

Get in line for breakfast, brunch, or lunch at the ★ **Omelette Express** (112 4th St., 707/525-1690, http://omeletteexpress.com, 6:30am-3pm daily, $11-13). Owned by local character Don Taylor, who might even be acting as host at the front door on the weekend, this spot is definitely favored by locals. Don calls many of his customers by their first names, but he also welcomes newcomers with enthusiasm. The very casual dining rooms are decorated with the front ends of classic cars, and the menu—no surprise—involves lots of omelets. Portions are huge and come with a side of toast made with homemade bread, so consider splitting one with a friend.

For just coffee, stop by **Atlas Coffee** (300 South A St., 707/978-3199, 7:30am-5pm Mon.-Fri., 8am-5pm Sat.-Sun., $5) and soak in some hip downtown culture. Espresso, bagels, outside seating, and a record player spinning tunes makes this a hangout for those with an arty bent.

FARMERS MARKETS

Santa Rosa has two farmers markets worth checking out. The **Santa Rosa Downtown Market** (www.wednesdaynightmarket.org) includes a beer garden, chef demonstrations, and other entertainment alongside farm stands. It is held on 4th Street from Mendocino Avenue to E Street on Wednesday evenings (5pm-8:30pm May-Aug.). The more traditional **West End Farmers Market** (9 4th St., http://wefm.co) is held every Sunday 9:30am-2pm April-November next to Depot Park in Railroad Square. The biggest market is **Santa Rosa's Original Certified Farmers Market** (50 Mark West Springs Rd., http://thesantarosafarmersmarket.com, 8:30am-1pm Wed. and Sat. year-round) in the parking lot of the Luther Burbank Center for the Arts. You'll find everything from fresh fruit and veggies to honey, seafood, pastries, and pottery. The farmers market is a great place to pick up picnic provisions or shop for that unique Wine Country gift.

Accommodations

In the city of Santa Rosa, you'll find all the familiar chain motels along with a couple that channel that motel-era kitsch. You'll also see a few upper-tier hotels that show off the unique aspects of the region.

UNDER $150

The **Sandman Motel** (3421 Cleveland Ave., 707/293-2100, www.sandmansantarosa.com, $100-161) offers clean, comfortable motel rooms for reasonable prices. Amenities include a big heated swimming pool, an outdoor whirlpool tub that is heated year-round, coffee and continental breakfast in the lobby each morning, and in-room fridges and satellite TV. The Sandman is a great place to bring the family.

$150-250

The neon pink retro kitsch at the **Flamingo Resort and Spa** (2777 4th St., 707/545-8530 or 800/848-8300, www.flamingoresort.com, $125-260) is such that the hotel was declared a Historic Landmark in 1996. Since then the mid-century design has only gotten cooler thanks to numerous upgrades. Upon arriving, and even from a distance, you won't miss the 1950s styling of the giant rotating neon sign with the flamingo perched on top. Guest rooms surround a central garden and immense swimming pool. Each sizable room has comfortable beds, a clean bath, minifridge and coffeemaker, and nearby parking. The Flamingo is a great place to bring the kids during the hot Sonoma summer—they'll love the pool, while grown-ups will love the easy access to the Russian River wine roads, the in-house spa, and the late-night lounge.

In the historic Railroad Square, **Hotel la Rose** (308 Wilson St., 707/579-3200, www.hotellarose.com, $109-205) offers historic and modern accommodations for very reasonable prices. In the stone-clad main building, guests enjoy what the hotel might have been like when it opened back in 1907, with antique furniture and floral wallpaper, while across the street the carriage house offers modern decor and amenities. Because Hotel la Rose has only 47 guest rooms, you'll see an attention to detail and a level of service that's missing in the larger hotels in the area.

OVER $250

A bit like staying on a French country wine estate, the **Vintners Inn** (4350 Barnes Rd., 707/566-2607 or 800/421-2584, www.vintnersinn.com, $275-425) sprawls amid 50 acres of manicured gardens and vineyards just a few miles north of Santa Rosa. It's ideally located for exploring the Russian River Valley, and quick access to the freeway (River Road exit) makes getting to points north a snap. All 44 rooms and suites are cozy and luxurious, some with fireplaces and all with either balconies or patios. Guests also have access to the inn's outdoor whirlpool tub, can reserve in-room spa services, and are treated to a half bottle of wine upon check-in. Breakfast is available at the **Vintners Inn Café** (7am-10am Mon.-Fri., and 7:30am-12:30pm Sat.-Sun.), which sits next to the celebrated **John Ash & Co.** (dinner daily 5pm-9pm).

Information and Services

In downtown Santa Rosa, the **Santa Rosa Visitors Center** (9 4th St., 707/577-8674 or 800/404-7673, www.visitsantarosa.com, 9am-5pm Mon.-Sat., 10am-5pm Sun.) shares space with the California Welcome Center and offers countless maps and brochures about accommodations, food, and wineries, plus activities in the city and surrounding region.

The serious local daily newspaper is the **Santa Rosa Press Democrat** (www.pressdemocrat.com). Check the Living and Entertainment sections for tourist information.

As a major city, Santa Rosa has plenty of medical services available. If you need help, try to get to **Santa Rosa Memorial Hospital** (1165 Montgomery Ave., 707/546-3210, www.stjosephhealth.org), which has an emergency room.

For banking needs, there is a **Bank of America** (10 Santa Rosa Avenue) and a **Wells Fargo** (200 B Street).

Getting There and Around

Santa Rosa is 50 miles north of San Francisco on U.S. 101. Be aware that traffic on this major corridor can get congested, particularly during the morning commute and 3pm-7pm Monday-Friday. It also slows on sunny summer afternoons when people go to cool themselves along the Russian River. Fortunately, the side roads that lead to various tasting rooms and recreation spots are seldom crowded. Taking exit 489 will get you to the heart of Santa Rosa. West of the freeway is the historic Railroad Square, while downtown is on the east side.

To avoid traffic headaches, **Golden Gate Transit** (415/455-2000, www.goldengatetransit.org, $13) runs buses between San Francisco and Santa Rosa.

SEBASTOPOL AND VICINITY

Low-key and a bit alternative, Sebastopol is undoubtedly the artistic heart of Sonoma County. The relatively low cost of living, liberal politics, natural beauty, and small-town vibe have attracted artists that include heavyweights like Tom Waits and Jerry Garcia as well as independent painters, sculptors, and ceramists. Downtown Sebastopol contains a number of shops where local artists sell their works, along with bookstores, record stores, and the odd place selling tie-dyed T-shirts. Recently, Sebastopol's hipness was confirmed with the opening of **The Barlow,** a large compound of shops, restaurants, and vendors reflecting Sebastopol's arty, earthy, and epicurean tendencies. The 12-acre development was the site of a former apple cannery that processed apples from the surrounding farmland. Grapes now dominate Gravensteins, but the few remaining orchards give fragrance and beauty to the already scenic country roads, especially during the spring bloom.

The nearby town of **Graton** remains true to its small-town agrarian roots, with a population hovering just over 1,200 people. Its charming two-block "downtown" is home to a couple beloved eateries, a tasting room, and a gallery. Farther west, where farmland yields to redwoods, **Occidental** (population 1,100) began as stop on the Northern Pacific Coast Railroad and has drawn writers and artists for over a hundred years (hence, the Bohemian Highway upon which it sits).

Wineries

Located at the edge of the lush Green Valley AVA, the wineries of Sebastopol produce some of the Russian River's best chardonnay and pinot noir, although you would never know it by the friendly and casual vibe of the tasting rooms here. This is especially true of the walk-in wineries, but those requiring reservations get fancier. Most sit on or near the Gravenstein Highway, but others require a detour (and a map) to smaller country roads.

HANNA WINERY

The specialty at **Hanna Winery** (5353 Occidental Rd., Santa Rosa, 707/575-3371, www.hannawinery.com, 10am-4pm daily, tasting $15) is a crisp, steel-fermented sauvignon blanc. Not only is it a hit with critics, it is exactly what you want to drink soaking in the Russian River sun on the winery's

wraparound front porch or beneath the great live oak out front.

Inside, the tasting room makes the most out of the views and sunlight with large picture windows. You'll taste estate wines that hail from the vineyards surrounding the winery, plus those at its other location in Healdsburg, and from its Bismark Ranch vineyards, high up in the Mayacamas Mountains, the highest-elevation vineyard in Sonoma. The Bismark red wines, including cabernet sauvignon, cabernet franc, and zinfandel, are powerful and often highly rated by critics. At the other end of the scale is the fruity rosé made from petite sirah and zinfandel, an ideal accompaniment to a picnic.

MERRY EDWARDS WINERY

Merry Edwards was one of California's first women winemakers, and during her illustrious 40-plus year career she has won a James Beard Award, been inducted into the Culinary Institute of America's Hall of Fame, and even developed her own pinot noir grape clone. Tasting at the **Merry Edwards Winery** (2959 Gravenstein Hwy., Sebastopol, 707/823-7466, www.merryedwards.com, 9:30am-4:30pm daily, free tasting) is not only refreshingly free of pretention, it is also just free, but you probably won't make it out the door without purchasing at least one bottle of Merry's stellar wine. Anxious to avoid the overcrowded, "pour and ignore" Napa tourist tasting model, each member of Merry Edwards's tasting staff will work with only one party of tasters at a time. Instead of forcing your way through a crowd to garner 12 inches of bar space, you'll be led to a table with comfortable chairs that's already set with four glasses ready to hold the sauvignon blanc, chardonnay, and pinot noirs you'll sip.

DUTTON-GOLDFIELD WINERY

At the corner of the Gravenstein Highway and Graton Road, **Dutton-Goldfield Winery** (3100 Gravenstein Hwy. N., Sebastopol, 707/823-3887, www.duttongoldfield.com, 10am-4pm daily, tasting $20) pours tastings

Apples in Grape Country

Although almost every imaginable fruit and vegetable seems to be grown in Sonoma, the most celebrated crop in the Russian River Valley (apart from grapes) is perhaps the apple, and in particular the small yellow and red Gravenstein with its strong aroma and taste.

Highway 116, which runs through Sebastopol and Graton, is also called the Gravenstein Highway for the large number of orchards it used to pass. The orchards are now disappearing, along with the Gravenstein apple itself, as they give way to new vineyards. At one point apple orchards covered 15,000 acres of Sonoma County, but by 2015 there were roughly 2,200 acres left, and Gravensteins accounted for only one-third of that total. Slow Food Russian River, the local chapter of the Slow Food movement, is now campaigning to raise the profile of this humble little apple among consumers, retailers, and restaurants to slow any further decline.

The Gravenstein is the earliest-ripening apple in the region, starting in late July. Farms offering apples are generally clustered around Sebastopol and Graton, and many are only open during the summer and fall.

- **Kozlowski Farms** (5566 Gravenstein Hwy. N., Forestville, 707/887-1587, www.kozlowski-farms.com, 9am-4:30pm Mon.-Fri., 10am-5pm Sat.-Sun. year-round)

- **Gabriel Farm** (3175 Sullivan Rd., just off Graton Rd., Sebastopol, 707/829-0617, www.gabrielfarm.com, 10am-3pm Sat.-Sun. Aug.-Oct.)

- **Walker Apples** (10955 Upp Rd., off Graton Rd., Sebastopol, 707/623-4310, 9am-5pm daily Aug.-mid-Nov.) sells a staggering 27 varieties of apples.

- **Ratzlaff Ranch** (13128 Occidental Rd., Sebastopol, 707/823-0538, 9am-5pm Mon.-Wed. and Fri. year-round) grows Gravensteins along with other apples and pears.

- **Hale's Apple Farm** (1526 Gravenstein Hwy. N., 707/823-4613, 9am-5pm daily July-Nov.)

- **Andy's Produce Market** (1691 Gravenstein Hwy. N., Sebastopol, 707/823-8661, www.andysproduce.com, 8am-7:30pm daily)

- **Mom's Apple Pie** (4550 Gravenstein Hwy. N., Sebastopol, 707/823-8330, www.

of limited-production wines. Started in 1998, the winery is a collaborative effort of Dan Goldfield, a well-known winemaker, and Steve Dutton, a member of the family that farms the renowned vineyards of Dutton Ranch in the Green Valley AVA. The cool tasting room matches the elegant and earthy cool climate of its pinot noir (both blends and several exquisite single-vineyards), chardonnay, syrah, and even zinfandel. Several unique food pairings are available to be enjoyed inside or on the patio, including pinots paired with charcuterie (by appointment, $40), whites and reds with cheese (by appointment $30), and a sushi flight that goes oddly well with the unoaked pinot noirs and chardonnays (noon-2pm Wed.-Sun., by appointment $40).

RED CAR WINERY

Vintage Hollywood meets the Sonoma Coast at **Red Car Winery** (8400 Graton Road, Sebastopol, 707/829-8500, 10am-5pm daily, tasting $20). The winery's name is an homage to the red electric trolley cars that crisscrossed Los Angeles during the early 20th century—the city remains a muse for owners Carroll Kemp and Mark Estrin, a former Tinseltown producer/screenwriter team. The hip tasting room has a rustic-chic appeal, with comfortable couches, antiques store memorabilia, and vinyl spinning on a turntable. For the price of tasting you'll get five generous pours of reserve whites to reds, including their well-balanced artisan blends as well as pinot noir and chardonnay that have received wide recognition.

the Gravenstein

momsapplepieusa.com, 10am-6pm daily year-round) sells homemade apple pies, made with delicious Gravensteins August-November.

If that isn't enough, plan a trip to Sebastopol during the **Gravenstein Apple Fair** (Ragle Ranch Regional Park, 500 Ragle Rd., Sebastopol, 707/837-8896, www.gravensteinapplefair.com, adults $15, children 6-12 $10, under 6 free). This two-day event in the middle of August celebrates the Gravenstein with live music, arts and crafts, livestock, and plenty of food, wine, beer, and cider.

More information about all the fruits and vegetables grown here and the farms that sell them is available from **Sonoma Country Farm Trails** (707/837-8896, www.farmtrails.org). You might also see the free *Farm Trails* map and guide at wineries and farms in the region.

DUTTON ESTATE WINERY

Up the road, another Dutton family endeavor makes wine from its renowned Dutton Ranch. The modest tasting room of the **Dutton Estate Winery** (8757 Green Valley Rd., Sebastopol, 707/829-9463, www.duttonestate.com, 10am-4:30pm daily, tasting $15-20) barely hints at its highly rated, limited-production wines. Sauvignon blanc, chardonnay, pinot noir, and syrah are the only wines made here, but there are lots of different versions of them from specific vineyards and sometimes specific blocks within a vineyard. Discovering some of the nuances of the tiny Green Valley sub-appellation with the more expensive vineyard-specific wines entails a higher tasting fee. Complimentary small bites are served

regardless of which tasting you pick. You are also invited to bring your own bag lunch and picnic surrounded by Dutton Estate's gorgeous vineyards. To learn more about the winemaking process here, book a private **VIP Tour and Tasting** ($45) that includes a walk through the vineyards, barrel tastings, and a flight of small bites to accompany a taste of the current release wines.

★ IRON HORSE VINEYARDS

Iron Horse Vineyards (9786 Ross Station Rd., Sebastopol, 707/887-1507, www.ironhorsevineyards.com, 10am-4pm Mon.-Thurs., Fri.-Sun. by appointment only, tasting $25), is well off the beaten track down a one-lane road that winds through orchards, over a creek, and (perhaps) past some wild turkeys before climbing up the palm-lined driveway to the winery. The rustic simplicity of the barn-like building and its indoor-outdoor tasting bar belies the pedigree of the sparkling wines made here—they have been served to presidents and won numerous accolades from wine critics over the past 30 years.

All the grapes for the sparkling wines are sourced from the winery's vineyards in the surrounding Green Valley AVA, the coolest part of an already cool Russian River Valley appellation. It's an ideal place to grow chardonnay and pinot noir, both of which Iron Horse also bottles as outstanding still wines that are worth tasting. Try the unoaked chardonnay—one of the best examples of this new breed of food-friendly chardonnays. Tours ($30) are offered by appointment weekdays only at 10am, and for another $20, on Monday mornings they are led by the winemaker David Muskgard. But with such panoramic views over the valley from right behind the tasting area, you might be content just to sit back and relax in the bucolic setting.

Downtown Sebastopol Tasting Rooms

You won't find any tasting rooms along Sebastopol's Main Street, but **The Barlow** (between McKinley St., Petaluma Ave., and Hwy. 12, 707/-824-5600, http://thebarlow. net) is home to six pouring flights of Russian River chardonnay and pinot noir. The best of these is **Marimar Estate** (6780 McKinley St., 707/823-9910, http://marimarestate.com, 11am-6pm daily, tasting $15), which makes only estate chardonnay and pinot noir from vineyards in the Russian River Valley and its sub-appellation, the cooler, Green Valley AVA. Owner and proprietor Marimar Torres originally hails from Spain and a family that has been making wine since the 17th century. This heritage comes through in her food-friendly wines, which pair particularly well with Spanish cuisine. If you don't have any paella recipes on hand at home, you can buy one of her cookbooks available in the tasting room.

Resembling your great aunt's parlor, this comfortable tasting room also offers flights of five whites and reds ($15) and wines by the glass ($10-12), and chocolate pairing with candlelight (4pm-6pm Fri.-Sat., $15).

A few doors down, you know you've entered the hipster center of Sebastopol's wine world when you enter **Wind Gap** (6789 McKinley St., 707/331-1393, Ste. 170, www.windgap-wines.com, Mon. and Wed. 2pm-6pm, Thurs. and Sun. noon-6pm, Fri.-Sat. noon-8pm, tasting $16-25), with its succulents, reclaimed wood, growlers, and turntable. Pick between several flights of Wind Gap's cool-climate varietals, such as chardonnay, pinot noir, and syrah, or a glass ($7-15) of its Fixie and Skinny Jeans blends, which employ the latest and coolest trends in winemaking from the concrete egg to carbonic maceration. What does that all mean? The tattooed and friendly tasting room staff is happy to explain while they pour a splash to see if you like it. Should you want to hang with the local industry types who swing by for a glass or two after work, order a glass of wine (the Trousseau Gris is a must) or a pint of the hard cider.

Wineries by Appointment
CLAYPOOL CELLARS FANCY BOOZE CABOOSE

Across from The Barlow in the Gravenstein Station, hipster turns rock-and-roll eccentric at the **Claypool Cellars Fancy Booze Caboose** (6761 Sebastopol Ave., #500, Sebastopol, 707/861-9358, http://claypoolcellars.com, daily by appointment, tasting $10). The repurposed train car is the official tasting zone for Pachyderm wines, the winery of Les Claypool, best known as the quirky bassist and frontman of the rock band Primus. Inside the Southern Pacific caboose you might rub elbows (literally, it's tiny) with artists and local bohemians. Sip Purple Pachyderm pinot noir and Pink Platypus rosé, nibble M&Ms, and immerse yourself in the artwork that lines the walls, some by Claypool himself. What started as a money-saving endeavor evolved into a viable undertaking for Claypool, who describes himself as "not much of a wine guy" until moving to the Russian River Valley. Fans of Primus needn't worry though, the band continues to record and tour.

PAUL HOBBS WINERY

From Healdsburg via Argentina to Graton might seem like a tortuous route for a winemaker, but the founder of **Paul Hobbs Winery** (3355 Gravenstein Hwy. N., Sebastopol, 707/824-9879, www.paulhobbswinery.com, 10am-2pm Mon.-Fri. by appointment, tour and tasting $65) picked up some valuable winemaking experience along the way. Now Hobbs makes highly rated, vineyard-designate chardonnay, syrah, and pinot noir from Russian River vineyards, and a cabernet sauvignon using Napa fruit. Prices of the wines, like their ratings, are high. Tasting here is more like Napa Valley than Sonoma and the Russian River. The price for a tour and tasting of five wines is a hefty $65, and for $135, your flight can be paired with small bites.

LYNMAR ESTATE

Despite Led Zeppelin and AC/DC piping in softly in the background, tasting at the beautiful **Lynmar Estate** (3909 Frei Rd., Sebastopol, 707/829-3374, http://lynmarestate.com, 10am-4:30pm daily, tasting $20-60, by appointment only) is a refined affair. Tastings are seated on the bistro-like patio surrounded by fragrant gardens of trailing veggies, fruit-heavy apple trees, blossoming flowers, and buzzing bumblebees, with the estate's lush Quail Hill vineyards beyond. Much of what is found in the garden will wind up on your plate should you opt for the Lynmar Lunch ($65), a three-course, 90-minute meal paired with Lynmar wine. Pizza and Pinot ($60) come together in the small redwood grove on select summer Sundays. While you may detect whiffs of Napa here, the wines are all Russian River. The winery produces nine chardonnays and 15 pinot noirs; most are estate, some are blends, and others are vineyard specific, showcasing the various microclimates of this corner of the Russian River Valley. Tastings

include two chardonnays and two pinots, plus a special welcome wine in the summer (likely the wonderful pinot noir rosé) and a pour of an extra pinot noir that your server is particularly excited about that day. Despite the cost and sleek professionalism of Lynmar, guests are encouraged to linger, enjoy the gardens, and the sunshine. If you do, be sure to ask for a bowl of popcorn sprinkled with something unusual from the garden.

INMAN FAMILY WINES

The focus of the **Inman Family Wines** (3900 Piner Rd., Santa Rosa, 707/293-9576, www.inmanfamilywines.com, 11am, 12:30pm, and 2pm Thurs.-Mon., tasting $20) is wine that is nurtured and cultivated in small lots in the Russian River Valley. Healthy soil, natural winemaking, and sustainable business practices are hallmarks here. Owner/general manager/winemaker Kathleen Inman's passion for the pinot noir grape is evident in the bright, balanced wines she produces. Inman prides herself on her hands-on approach to the business—you might even see this multitasking entrepreneur pouring her beloved pinots in the tasting room—and the winery's dedication to sustainability. This includes everything from sustainable farming to eco-friendly labels, recyclable packaging, and using suppliers that share the Inman family's vision and philosophy. In keeping with that, visitors who drive electric automobiles can charge up at Sonoma County's first privately owned public charging station while sipping Russian River Valley pinot noir or the snappy Sonoma chardonnay.

BATTAGLINI ESTATE WINERY

At the cluttered and homey tasting bar at **Battaglini Estate Winery** (2948 Piner Rd., Santa Rosa, 707/578-4091, www.battaglini-wines.com, daily by appointment, tasting $15) you'll find only zinfandels, chardonnays, and petite sirahs; however, the expression of each of these grapes approaches perfection. You'll also see a few unusual manifestations, such as a late-harvest dessert chardonnay. For the most fun you can have during the crowded harvest season, join Battaglini in the fall for the Stomp event ($130), during which you'll literally take off your shoes and start stomping in a bucket of grapes, followed by a fun buffet lunch.

Entertainment

Sebastopol is a bit on the sleepy side when it comes to nightlife, but live local bands, DJ dance nights, and the occasional open-mike night can be found at the **Hopmonk Tavern** (230 Petaluma Ave., Sebastopol, 707/829-7300, www.hopmonk.com, 11:30am-close daily). There's something going on nearly every night, particularly in summer, when the dance action can also sometimes spill out onto the patio. Check the website for upcoming events. Covers for live bands range $5-30, and most come on around 8pm. There's also a late-night menu for anyone looking for some food to wash down the microbrews made here.

Beer lovers may want to make a detour to **Woodfour Brewing Company** (6780 Depot St., Sebastopol, 707/823-3144, http://woodfourbrewing.com, noon-9pm Tues.-Sun., noon-7pm Mon.), which brews an astonishing array of complex German, French, Belgium, and American beer. Pick a traditional sour wheat ale, the flagship French farmhouse lager, or the black lager fortified with Taylor Maid cold-brew coffee. Pints are only $5, and a tasting flight is $10. With an atmosphere of a hip restaurant instead of a beer nerds tasting room, Woodfour serves farm-to-table pub food and house-made comfort snacks like potato chips and beer nuts.

Food

For years, the restaurants in laid-back Sebastopol catered to commuting locals and health-conscious back-to-the-land types. But as Sebastopol has become the hip center of North Sonoma, its cuisine has shifted to farm-to-fork fare, albeit on the quirky side. A few miles up the Gravenstein Highway, tiny **Graton** has always had a reputation for

excellent dining, which easily outsizes its under 1,200 population. In **Occidental** to the west, you'll find comfort food similar to that served during its heyday at the turn of the 20th century.

SEBASTOPOL

The Barlow is the center of Sebastopol's nascent dining scene, and at the center of The Barlow is the area's hippest farm-to-table restaurant, ★ **zazu** (6770 McKinley St., 707/523-4814, 5pm-10pm Mon. and Wed., 11:30am-10pm Thurs., 11:30am-midnight Fri.-Sat., 9am-10pm Sun., $18-33). The restaurant is best known for its house-cured bacon and salumi made from an heirloom variety Black Pig that the owners/chefs raise. The pork-heavy menu changes daily, but don't pass up the divine Black Pig bacon-wrapped dates or the grilled romaine salad topped with tender pork belly. Like the ingredients that fill its plates, the wine list is also locally sourced, and there is always a $5 glass of red and white available to help keep the check down. For something stiffer pick one of the house-made cocktails, best enjoyed on the outside patio.

Also at The Barlow is the ultracasual **Ultra Crepes** (6760 McKinley St., #120, 707/827-6187, http://ultracrepes.com, 8:30am-10pm daily, $6-9), which serves a selection of sweet and savory crepes. You'll find classics like the ham and cheese and the monte cristo, along with those to satisfy any sweet tooth, including one with bacon and maple syrup. The menu is on the slim side, but for the price, size, and variety, Ultra Crepes is the place to go for an affordable meal out, be it breakfast, lunch, or dinner.

Not far away, coffee plus pastries and small bites can be found at **Tailor Maid Farms** (6790 McKinley St., 707/634-7129, www.taylormaidfarms.com, 6:30am-6pm Mon.-Thurs., 6:30am-7pm Fri., 7am-7pm Sat., 7am-6pm Sun., $8), the reclaimed wood-filled café of this popular local roaster. Free wireless Internet and upstairs seating draw locals hammering away on their keyboards, catching up

GRATON

Halfway between Forestville and Sebastopol is the tiny rural town of Graton, home to some destination dining. The best known is the **Underwood Bar & Bistro** (9113 Graton Rd., 707/823-7023, www.underwoodgraton.com, 11am-10pm Tues.-Sun., dinner entrées $15-30), where lots of dark wood, plush red booths, and a nickel-plated bar add some class beyond the historic exterior. The Mediterranean-inspired bistro menu features tapas plates (you can't beat the oysters) and hearty main dishes like Catalan fish stew and duck confit with pancetta and an orange reduction. There's a late-night tapas menu served after 10pm on weekend nights.

Across the road (and sharing the same owners) is a rustic local gathering spot that doubles as a country store, the **Willow Wood Market Café** (9020 Graton Rd., 707/823-0233, www.willowwoodgraton.com, 8am-9pm Mon.-Sat., 9am-3pm Sun., $15-21). The well-priced breakfast, lunch, and light dinner menu is always popular with locals, and the polenta is legendary in these parts. It is becoming a victim of its own success, however, with lines that snake out the door on the busiest lunchtimes, although the back patio provides a bit more space. On a Sunday morning, this is where those in the know come for a brunch of Willow Wood Monte Cristo washed down with a mimosa.

OCCIDENTAL

You won't find many places to eat in wooded Occidental, but the **Union Hotel** (3731 Main St., 707/874-3555, http://unionhoteloccidental. com, 6am-9pm daily, $15-30), which has been serving hungry visitors since 1941, has it all. Inside the relatively small 1879 building you'll find hearty Italian comfort food and a more casual pizzeria, complete with red-checkered tablecloths. There is also a café, open at 6am, which makes a mean espresso and serves tasty homemade muffins and pastries, and a saloon where stiffer drinks start flowing at 11am. Curiously enough, the Union Hotel also offers free overnight RV parking with dinner.

zazu at The Barlow

with the paper, or out for a coffee date with friends.

On Main Street, **K&L Bistro** (119 S. Main St., 707/823-6614, http://klbistro. com, 11am-11pm daily, $15-32) has been a popular Sebastopol mainstay thanks to its combination French-style bistro food, cocktails, friendly service, and two (yes, two!) daily happy hours (3pm-6pm and 9:30pm-11pm) that offer $4 beer, $5 wine, and $1.50 oysters. Many locals insist that K&L has the best french fries in the Russian River Valley, and that its mac and cheese is better than mom's.

Also on Main Street, the **Gypsy Café** (162 N. Main St., 707/861-3825, http://gypsy-cafe. com, breakfast and lunch 8am-2:30pm Wed.-Mon., dinner 5:30pm-9pm Fri., $8-13) sticks to Sebastopol's roots with a casual menu of comfort food with plenty of healthy options. Brightly painted with an exposed brick wall, Gypsy Café is a friendly option for breakfast and lunch. Dinner is served every Friday night accompanied by live music.

PICNIC SUPPLIES

To take your lunch with you, make a stop at the **Community Market** (6762 Sebastopol Ave., #100, Sebastopol, 707/407-4020, www. srcommunitymarket.com, 8am-10pm daily), a worker-owned co-op in The Barlow. This large grocery has a full deli that makes hot and cold sandwiches to order, plus a variety of salads and prepared food to pack in your picnic. Farther up the Gravenstein Highway, **Andy's Produce Market** (1691 Gravenstein Hwy. N., Sebastopol, 707/823-8661, www.andysproduce.com, 8am-7:30pm daily) is part organic produce market and part grocery store. In addition to the piles of fresh produce, the market sells breads, cheeses, olives, and sandwiches. In late summer it's the place to find countless varieties of local apples, and throughout the summer you'll often find a barbecue fired up outside.

FARMERS MARKETS

For food straight from the fields, Sebastopol's **farmers market** is held on Sunday mornings (10am-1:30pm year-round) at the Sonoma Plaza on Weeks Way. Fruits, veggies, cheese, nuts, honey, bread, pastries, prepared goodies, hot food, and plenty of flowers are on hand, along with live music at this festive community gathering spot.

Accommodations

Despite its many charms and growing notoriety, Sebastopol offers few accommodations. The very best is the expensive but lovely **Avalon Bed and Breakfast** (11910 Graton Rd., Sebastopol, 707/824-0880, www. avalonluxuryinn.com, $299-499). With only three guest rooms, the inn seeks to channel the woodsy charms of its mystical island namesake, complete with high-end decorator flourishes. All guest rooms have king beds, fireplaces, and access to the garden hot tub. Because Avalon was purpose-built as a bed-and-breakfast, each guest room is actually a suite with plenty of space to spread out and enjoy a longer stay. At breakfast, you'll be served an organic feast made with local produce and loving attention to the details of preparation.

If you're in the market for something a little less splendid, try **The Sebastopol Inn** (6751 Sebastopol Ave., Sebastopol, 707/829-2500, www.sebastopolinn.com, $119-269). Rooms are a cut above your standard hotel accommodations with homey furnishings. Most rooms have a refrigerator and microwave, and all guests get to enjoy the heated pool and hot tub. The on-site coffeehouse hosts live music on weekend afternoons, and its location is an easy stroll to Sebastopol's shops and eateries.

A little off the beaten track in the redwood-enshrouded town of Occidental is the delightfully rambling Victorian ★ **Inn at Occidental** (3657 Church St., Occidental, 707/874-1047, www.innatoccidental.com, $299-399), a quirky yet luxurious bed-and-breakfast. None of the 16 whimsical rooms and suites are alike, although all have fireplaces and are stuffed with odd pieces of folk art, as are many of the inn's common areas. A hot breakfast is served every morning in the Wine Cellar Dining Room, complete with a large stone fireplace.

Information and Services

For maps of the area, souvenirs, newspapers, and wine-tasting coupons, swing by the **Sebastopol Chamber of Commerce Visitors Center** (265 S. Main St., 707/823-3032, www.sebastopol.org, 10am-5pm Mon.-Fri., 10am-3pm Sat.). If you arrive after hours, they have a 24-hour information kiosk outside.

Published in Sebastopol, the *Sonoma West Times and News* (www.sonomawest. com) covers local happenings and upcoming events and comes out every Thursday. You can find a **Bank of America** at 7185 Healdsburg Avenue and a **Wells Fargo** at 7151 Bodega Avenue.

Getting There and Around

Sebastopol is west of Santa Rosa, accessed by Highways 116 and 12. The heart of downtown

Sebastopol is the intersection of Sebastopol Avenue (Hwy. 12) and Main Street (Hwy. 116). Note that Sebastopol Avenue becomes the Bodega Highway once it hits downtown Sebastopol and extends all the way to, you guessed it, Bodega Bay.

To reach Sebastopol from U.S. 101, take either the exit for Highway 12 west in Santa Rosa or the exit for Highway 116 west at Cotati, eight miles south of Santa Rosa. Highway 116 is the most direct route to continue to the Russian River from Sebastopol.

GUERNEVILLE AND VICINITY

There are wineries in the Guerneville area, but most people come here to float, canoe, or kayak the gorgeous Russian River, winding from Healdsburg all the way to the Pacific Ocean at Jenner. In addition to its busy summertime tourist trade, **Guerneville** is also a very popular gay and lesbian resort area, particularly of San Franciscans looking for a weekend getaway. The rainbow flag flies proudly here, and the friendly community welcomes all.

To the east, **Forestville** is a loose conflagration of backcountry roads populated by rural homes and the occasional winery, with a small downtown commercial corridor just off Highway 116.

Wineries

Many of the Russian River wineries sit along the meandering Westside Road, which has been dubbed the "Rodeo Drive of Pinot Noir" due to the number of high-end pinot producers strung along it. Once Westside Road reaches River Road, a map is an essential tool to find the hidden gems around Forestville and beyond.

RUSSIAN RIVER VINEYARDS

While you haven't quite made it to the Russian River at **Russian River Vineyards** (5700 Gravenstein Hwy., Forestville, 707/887-3344, www.russianrivervineyards. com, noon-8pm Thurs.-Tues., tasting $15), the friendly staff help create a classy small-winery tasting experience in the weathered redwood tasting room. You'll enjoy full-bodied, fruity pinot noirs, pinot noir rosés, and a couple Sonoma Coast chardonnays. Private tours and tastings are available ($30) as is a food and wine pairing ($55). If the shadows begin lengthening and you want to stick around for dinner, take a table at the winery's **Cork Restaurant** (noon-8:30pm Thurs.-Tues., $20-45), which serves earthy plates of locally sourced gourmet food in a 1890s farmhouse. On sunny days be sure to take advantage of the back patio, where live music plays daily 5:30pm-8:30pm and brunch is served 12:30pm-3:30pm Saturday and Sunday.

MARTIN RAY WINERY

Although housed in the oldest continually operating winery in Sonoma and named after one of California's pioneering modern winemakers, the **Martin Ray Winery** (2191 Laguna Rd., Santa Rosa, 707/823-2404, www.martinraywinery.com, 10am-5pm daily, tasting $10-20) is actually a relatively modern operation with few links to the site's historic past or the man after whom it is named. The winery itself dates back to 1881, and a few of the massive redwood fermenting tanks from the early 1900s are still on display outside the modest tasting room at the end of the long driveway. Since then it has undergone countless transformations, including as a maker of sacramental wines during Prohibition.

Today the winery is a casual, affordable stop, perfect for spur of the moment wine-tasting. For $10 you'll taste five of its current release wines, ranging from the Russian River sauvignon blanc to a Sonoma cabernet. Up it $5 and have a seated tasting of six vineyard-designate wines in the garden, and for another $5 enjoy a six-pour library tasting. Tours are available for $35, while picnicking in the gardens comes at no extra charge. Boxed lunches and cheese and charcuterie platters ($12-18) are available with 48-hour advance notice.

JOSEPH SWAN VINEYARDS

If you're looking to taste some famous Russian River pinot noir, be sure to stop by **Joseph Swan Vineyards** (2916 Laguna Rd., Forestville, 707/573-3747, www.swanwinery.com, 11am-4:30pm Sat.-Sun., by appointment Mon. and Fri., tasting $10). Joseph Swan got into the winemaking game when he bought a run-down farm in Forestville in the late 1960s with a plan to grow grapes and make wine during his retirement. He went about it with such a perfectionist passion and with so many good winemaking connections, however, that he became one of a small group of pinot pioneers in the Russian River Valley—a group that helped put the region firmly on the world pinot noir stage. Today his son-in-law continues Swan's legacy, producing beautifully crafted single-vineyard pinots, chardonnays, syrahs, and zinfandels. The small, rustic winery tasting room is off the beaten path, down tiny Trenton Road at the northern end of Laguna Road.

RUSSIAN HILL ESTATE WINERY

A narrow drive wends its way up a hill covered in meticulously manicured vines. At the top, a stately, colonnaded building is home to **Russian Hill Estate Winery** (4525 Slusser Rd., Windsor, 707/575-9428, www.russianhillestate.com, 10am-4pm daily, tasting $10). This family-owned and operated winery is dedicated to the production of world-class pinot noir and syrah, but the crisp, fruit-forward chardonnay is also worth a taste. In contrast to the heavy oak found in other Sonoma regions, Russian River chards have higher acid levels, resulting in dry, refreshing wines. The tasting room patio offers spectacular views of rolling hills, historic hop kilns, California oaks, and the cool coastal fog that contributes to this region's climate and rich soil.

MARTINELLI WINERY

One of the most noteworthy zinfandels made in the Russian River Valley comes from the Jackass Vineyard of **Martinelli Winery** (3360 River Rd., Windsor, 707/525-0570 or 800/346-1627, www.martinelliwinery.com, 10am-5pm daily, tasting $12-25), planted in the 1800s. That notable vineyard's name has absolutely no historical significance, instead referring to the sort of farmer who would consider farming such a steep and rugged slope. Not much of the popular Jackass zin is made each year, but to try it, your best bet is to book either the Library Tasting (10am, 12:30pm, and 3pm daily, $50) or the Collectors Flight (daily $75). For considerably less ($12-25), you can sample other less exclusive wine in Martinelli's vast portfolio, including more than a half-dozen pinot noirs, plus chardonnays, syrahs, zinfandels, and an intensely aromatic muscat, an unusual wine for this area.

The rustic winery makes a charming stop along the Russian River Wine Road, not far from U.S. 101. The Martinellis have been a fixture here since the early 1900s as grape and apple growers. Should you want to linger, wine and cheese pairings (10am, 12:30pm, and 3pm by appointment, $40) as well as a prepared lunch to accompany a tasting of five wines (10am, 12:30pm, 3pm by appointment, $50) are available.

HARTFORD FAMILY WINERY

A little off the beaten track, but closer to the Russian River, is the big white barnlike winery and mansion of this pinot noir and chardonnay specialist. **Hartford Family Winery** (8075 Martinelli Rd., Forestville, 707/887-8030, www.hartfordwines.com, 10am-4:30pm daily, tasting $15) makes serious point-scoring regional and single-vineyard pinot noir, chardonnay, and zinfandel, all from cool-climate vineyards and well worth tasting. For $15 you get a flight of six wines—three are multi-vineyard, and three are single vineyard. On nice days, an outside seated tasting is available for the same price, but you may want to call ahead and reserve a table. Library tastings are also available ($35), as are wine and cheese pairings ($45).

Best Wineries for Lunch

Some wineries have full-service restaurants just a stagger away from the tasting room, while others have filling pairing options that offer more value than doing lunch and tastings separately. Be advised that reservations for food and wine pairings are standard.

- **Dutton-Goldfield Winery, Sebastopol:** Sushi pairs with unoaked pinots and chardonnays oddly well at this Russian River winery on the Gravenstein Highway. You can also opt for plates of cheese and charcuterie to go with your Green Valley flight, either in the stylish tasting room or out on the patio.

- **Lynmar Estate, Sebastopol:** The $65 for the Lynmar Lunch may seem steep, but when you consider that it includes a three-course meal paired with Lynmar's excellent chardonnays and pinot noirs in a setting surrounded by fragrant and elegant gardens, it's worth the price. Keep your eyes peeled for the Pizza and Pinot pairing, offered on select summer Sundays in the winery's small redwood grove.

- **Russian River Vineyards, Guerneville:** Out on the patio not quite overlooking the Russian River (although the vineyard views are lovely), you can taste full-bodied pinots paired with small bites. For something more substantial, the winery's restaurant, Cork, serves lunch and dinner in an 1890s farmhouse. Live music keeps it fun 5:30pm-8:30pm daily.

- **Kendall-Jackson Wine Estate and Gardens, Guerneville:** The seven-course wine and food pairing serves smoked duck, lamb with toasted farro, and pork belly sliders with reserve wines. It's a steal at $40 and impresses foodies and oenophiles alike. A little less extravagant is the cheese and wine pairing (six wines paired with six local cheeses with smoked almonds, fennel jam, and beet cracklings, $30), but it's a good option for a light lunch.

- **J Vineyards & Winery, Guerneville:** Take your bubbles in the Bubble Room, where five sparkly vintages are paired with five courses for a decadent one-hour lunch.

- **Michel-Schlumberger, Dry Creek Valley:** Dine alfresco surrounded by vineyards at this Spanish-inspired winery in the Dry Creek Valley. Book a formal food and wine pairing or take your flight of estate wine to the terra-cotta tile terrace with a cheese and charcuterie plate.

- **Francis Ford Coppola Winery, Geyserville:** Panini poolside, or lamb Marrakesh served on white linen? At Coppola's Wine Wonderland, the choice is yours. Two restaurants, a full bar, and a tasting room (and of course the pool) are part of this delightful spot in the Alexander Valley.

NORTHERN SONOMA
RUSSIAN RIVER VALLEY

★ KENDALL-JACKSON WINE
ESTATE AND GARDENS

Just off U.S. 101, **Kendall-Jackson Wine Estate and Gardens** (5007 Fulton Rd., Fulton, 707/571-7500, www.kj.com, 10am-5pm daily, tasting $10-20) surprises even serious oenophiles with the quiet elegance of its tasting room and the extensive sustainable gardens and demonstration vineyards surrounding the buildings. Inside, the moderately priced wine-tasting is a surprising delight considering the grandeur of the surroundings. If you are planning to be in the area for lunch, consider booking a seven-course wine and food pairing ($40), which includes reserve wines with bites of smoked duck, lamb with toasted farro, and pork belly slider. A little less extravagant is the cheese and wine pairing ($30): six wines paired with six local cheeses plus smoked almonds, fennel jam, and beet cracklings. Just be aware that in high season (May-Oct.) you might need to make a reservation well in advance—KJ doesn't have too many tables. Take a tour of the gardens offered daily at 11am, 1pm, and 3pm ($25) and you may even get the opportunity to taste fresh wine grapes close to harvest.

★ KORBEL CHAMPAGNE CELLARS

This collection of stone, brick, and wood buildings dating from the 19th century at the edge of redwood forests makes an astonishing 1.7 million cases of sparkling wine a year. While it may not have the cachet (or the wines) of other champagne houses, **Korbel Champagne Cellars** (13250 River Rd., Guerneville, 707/824-7000, www.korbel.com, 10am-5pm daily, free tasting) offers perhaps the best value for money among sparkling wine producers.

Three Korbel brothers, immigrants from the Bohemia region of what is now the Czech Republic, founded the winery in 1882 after making their money in the local redwood lumber business. Wine production gradually took over from their other businesses as the quality of their sparkling wines and brandies improved and word spread. Over its history, Korbel has been poured at five presidential inaugurations, and today its champagnes are eminently affordable, as are the cabernet, pinot noir, chardonnay, and zinfandel table wines, and even the brandy and barrel-aged port. In the complimentary tasting room, you may pick any four to taste, after which the prices look even better.

Korbel Champagne Cellars

How the bubbles get into the wine and how the Korbel brothers got into the wine business are both covered in an entertaining free tour offered daily. A tour of the rose garden is offered twice a day Tuesday-Sunday mid-April-mid-October. After all that touring you can lounge on the deck of the small delicatessen (707/824-7313, 9am-4:30pm daily), shaded by redwood trees with a gourmet sandwich and even a beer.

PORTER CREEK WINERY

Serious cork dorks recommend the tiny tasting room at **Porter Creek Winery** (8735 Westside Rd., Healdsburg, 707/433-6321, www.portercreekvineyards.com, 10:30am-4:30pm daily, tasting $15), which casual tasters might otherwise miss at a bend on a winding road. Turn onto the dirt driveway, pass the farm-style house (the owner's family home), and park in front of a small converted shed—the tasting room. This is old-school Sonoma wine-tasting. Porter Creek has been making its precious few cases of wine each year for the last 30 years or so. Porter Creek's wines are almost all reds (mainly pinot noir) and a couple chardonnays, made from grapes grown organically within sight of the tasting room. You might even see the owner-winemaker walking through his vineyards with his family on a sunny afternoon in the off-season.

THOMAS GEORGE ESTATES

Just up the road, **Thomas George Estates** (8075 Westside Rd., Healdsburg, 707/431-8031, www.thomasgeorgeestates.com, 11am-5pm daily, tasting $20) pours largely chardonnay and pinot noir, as well as a viognier, zinfandel, and a pinot noir rosé, made from grapes grown in its four vineyards scattered around the Russian River Valley. During the weekend, tasting takes place in the 8,000-square-foot cave, which also boasts a reserve tasting room and a library. To fully explore the cave and the rest of the winery, which started as a hop kiln in 1920, book a tour available Thursday-Sunday at 11am and 1:30pm. If you want a bit of sunshine, the winery has also made its outside picnic areas a priority. Tables with bright red umbrellas dot the stately open glen, and two picnic tables sit down the hill near the bocce ball courts. Outside food is welcome (although you can reserve a boxed lunch plus private seated tasting for $45), and all tables are first-come, first-served.

ARMIDA

Come to the **Armida** (2201 Westside Rd., Healdsburg, 707/433-2222, www.armida.com, 11am-5pm daily, tasting $20) tasting room for the gorgeous scenery and the funky facilities, but stay for the wonderful wines. The driveway meanders up a Russian River hillside to a cluster of geodesic domes set amid lovely and sustainable landscaping. Bring a picnic to enjoy on the big deck overlooking the duck pond, bocce ball courts, and the valley beyond. Before you get to eating, though, wander into the tasting room to check out some of the truly tasty Russian River red wines. You'll get your choice of structured pinot noirs and jammy zinfandels. The flagship wine, Poizin, is well represented in the wines and logowear in the small gift shop that shares space with the tasting bar. Armida sells Poizin in a coffin-shaped box—ask nicely and they might open a bottle for you to taste (even if they don't, it's still worth buying).

★ HOP KILN WINERY

Between Westside Road and the Russian River is one of Sonoma's best-preserved old hop kilns, a towering wooden building where hops were once dried before being used to make beer. The hop vines of Sonoma have long since been replaced by grapevines, but the **Hop Kiln Winery** (6050 Westside Rd., Healdsburg, 707/433-6491, www.hopkiln-winery.com, 10am-5pm daily, tasting $10-20) has kept much of the cavernous interior of the 1905-era building intact, including the old stone drying ovens.

In spite of its giant home, the winery itself is a fairly small operation, producing reasonably priced pinot grigio, chardonnay, pinot noir, pinot noir rosé, and a sparkling pinot noir rosé. There are plenty of picnic tables around the building, including some next to a rather murky pond. The winery stocks a host of vinegars, oils, and mustards, but not much in the way of more filling picnic fare, so you'll have to bring your own.

J VINEYARDS & WINERY

Unlike many wineries that cling to old-world traditions, **J Vineyards & Winery** (11447 Old Redwood Hwy., Healdsburg, 707/431-3646, www.jwine.com, 11am-5pm daily $20-75) loves the cutting edge of the California wine scene. J specializes in California-style sparkling wines, but the tasting room is a triumph of modern design. At the main tasting bar, $20 buys generous pours of five wines from the lengthy menu of red, white, sparkling, and dessert wines. If the spacious tasting room is overrun, a common occurrence on weekends, the more exclusive Bubble Room takes the tasting experience (and the price) up a notch. Thursday-Sunday, you'll get the chance to sample the sparkly vintages as they are meant to be enjoyed with a seated tasting of five reserve wines paired with four courses, plus dessert ($95). The food is filling and inventive, making it a worthwhile stop for both oenophiles and foodies alike. There are four seatings each day and reservations are mandatory. If it's already booked up or you're not inclined to shell out $95 for a high octane lunch, there's a similarly structured but slightly less indulgent tasting menu ($50/couple) available on the outdoor terrace Friday-Sunday during the summer by appointment. The Legacy Reserve Lounge pours flights of five reserve wines for $30, and for an additional $20, yours can be paired with cheese and charcuterie (daily by appointment). The sparkling winemaking process is the focus of the 1.5-hour appointment-only tours that finish with a wine-tasting (11:30am and 2:30pm daily).

RODNEY STRONG VINEYARDS

Founded in 1959, **Rodney Strong Vineyards** (11455 Old Redwood Hwy., Healdsburg, 707/431-1533, www.rodneystrong.com, 10am-5pm daily, tasting free-$15) comprise 12 estate vineyards in the Russian River Valley, Alexander Valley, Chalk Hill, and the Sonoma Coast. The name belongs to Rod Strong, a distinguished Broadway dancer and pioneering Sonoma County vintner, who was the first to plant pinot noir in the Russian River Valley. In 1989, Rodney Strong Vineyards was purchased by Tom Klein, a fourth-generation California farmer and Stanford graduate, who works hard to maintain old man Strong's level of excellence. Advocates of sustainable practices, their solar energy system is one of the largest of any winery worldwide, and they were the first carbon-neutral winery in Sonoma County. The winery offers a number of tasting options from the complimentary tasting of two Sonoma wines to the wine flights on the terrace paired with cheese and charcuterie (Fri.-Sun., $20-30). Tours are complimentary and held daily at 11am and 2pm by appointment, and you are welcome to spread your picnic blanket on the lawn or at one of the many nearby tables.

FOPPIANO VINEYARDS

One of the oldest wineries in the Russian River Valley, **Foppiano Vineyards** (12707 Old Redwood Hwy., Healdsburg, 707/433-7272, www.foppiano.com, 11am-5pm daily, tasting $10) dates from 1896 and is also one of the few historic wineries that continued to operate right through Prohibition. Today, Foppiano is still making a small list of premium red wines. Their signature wine is a powerful, inky petite sirah, unusual for the area. Other wines include the estate pinot noir, chardonnay, and sauvignon blanc. Tours are available by appointment of the vineyards, winery, and estate ($15-20) and conclude in the farmhouse-style tasting room for a flight of estate wines. To make an afternoon of it, order a boxed lunch (24-hour advance notice,

$20) or bring your own to their tables out front and enjoy the vineyards.

Wineries by Appointment

PORTER BASS

If it's a sunny day and you are passing through Guerneville, make an appointment to taste at **Porter Bass** (11750 Mays Canyon Rd., Guerneville, 707/869-1475, www.porterbass.com, tasting $10). Tucked up into the mountains, surrounded only by vineyards and redwood forest, this one-man operation makes less than 1,000 cases of estate chardonnay, zinfandel, and pinot noir a year. Luke Bass is the owner, farmer, winemaker, and tour guide and has lived on the property since his parents (who still live there) bought it and planted it in grapes in the early 1980s. Today the land is certified biodynamic, and when you visit, Bass is happy to explain the process of biodynamic farming, show off the small cave and bottling room, and talk about his family's history on the land. The tasting room is a plank of hardwood beneath a walnut tree surrounded by camping chairs, where Bass pours healthy tastes of anything he has available. Appointments are easy to come by and can be made a day in advance, and even hours before on Saturday. Bottle prices range $36-55.

GARY FARRELL WINES

On the other end of the spectrum (and on the other side of the river), **Gary Farrell Wines** (10701 Westside Rd., Healdsburg, 707/473-2909, www.garyfarrellwines.com, daily by appointment, tasting $30-55) offers elegant seated tastings on the outside terrace, where you can soak in the sun and the views, as well as the wine. Pinot noir and chardonnay dominate the portfolio, but limited-release sauvignon blanc and zinfandel are usually poured as well. For $10 more you can learn about the winemaking process on the 10:30am tour and tasting.

MACROSTIE WINERY

In 2015, **MacRostie Winery** (4605 Westside Rd., Healdsburg, 707/473-9303, www.

macrostiewinery.com, 11am-5pm Mon.-Thurs., 10am-5pm Fri.-Sun., tasting $20-25) traded in its laid-back tasting room in a Carneros loading dock for a Healdsburg address, sleek Napa stylings, and exquisite northern Sonoma views. Perched on a knoll above its rolling vineyards, the steel, glass, and concrete indoor/outdoor tasting room pours seated flights of its highly regarded and elegantly understated chardonnay and pinot noir, including one from MacRostie's own local Wildcat Mountain vineyard, a windswept hillside that the family first planted in 1998. You can opt for a vertical tasting of pinot noir or a flight of six wines. The winery only requires reservations on weekends, but to enjoy the relaxed luxury of tasting here it is strongly suggested to call ahead on weekdays as well.

DE LA MONTANYA WINERY

As Westside Road narrows, dotted with checkerboard vineyards and ancient oaks dripping with Spanish moss, be sure to keep your eyes peeled for **De La Montanya Winery** (999 Forman Ln., Healdsburg, 707/433-3711, 11am-4:30pm daily, tasting $10). Owner Dennis De La Montanya has a palate for lesser-known varietals and an irreverent sense of humor. Eighteen different wines, ranging in size from 1 to 12 barrels, are crafted from a broad spectrum of varietals. Signature wines include tempranillo, pinot noir, zinfandel, gewürztraminer, and a late-harvest sauvignon blanc dessert wine. The winery and tasting room, referred to as "The Barn," has a laid-back, welcoming vibe with cheeky, playful descriptions of the vintages. Outside is an outdoor kitchen, a garden picnic area with stunning views, and a bocce court, which are reserved for club members on the weekends. While the winery is appointment-only Saturday-Sunday, walk-ins are welcome during the week (although reservations are recommended).

ACORN WINERY

Acorn Winery (12040 Old Redwood Hwy., Healdsburg, 707/433-6440, www.acornwinery.com, 10am-4pm daily, tasting $15), with its modest tasting bar in the corner of Bill and Betsy Nachbauer's garage, couldn't be further from the winemaking behemoths of Rodney Strong and Foppiano it sits between. The Nachbauers are former corporate lawyers who bought their 26 acres of vineyards here in 1990 and started making their own wine six years later using equipment at other wineries but barrel aging (and tasting) in their garage. Production now is about 3,000 cases a year and a thoroughly Italian affair. Wines include zinfandel, sangiovese, dolcetto, and field blends including Medley, a blend of 15 varietals that redefines the term "complex." Being popular, however, most of the wines sell out fast each year.

LIMERICK LANE

Limerick Lane (1023 Limerick Ln., Healdsburg, 707/433-9211, www.limericklanewines.com, 10am-5pm daily) makes excellent syrah and zinfandel from vines planted in 1910. Both routinely score above 90 points with Robert Parker and *Wine Spectator,* and the 2012 Russian River zinfandel was named number 12 on the *Wine Spectator*'s Top 100 Wines of the World 2015 list. However, stepping into the pretty but laid-back tasting room you would never know the acclaim this winery receives. Without any pretention, you can enjoy a flight of four wines for $15. Be sure to ask if the Rocky Knoll zinfandel is available to taste. The tasting room staff is happy to chat about winemaking and farming the land, and even to show off the crush pad and vineyards outside on this 30-acre estate. Limerick Lane is family owned and operated, with the chief winemaker/farmer/founder living next door in a modest home with his family and black labs. While it is appointment-only, if there are enough people working in the tasting room, walk-ins are never turned away.

Entertainment

Guerneville and its environs have probably the most diverse entertainment scene in the Russian River Valley, befitting the eclectic population that swells in the summer with an influx of both gay and straight revelers. Much of Guerneville's nightlife caters to the gay scene with a curious mix of rustic bars enhanced with Day-Glo furnishings, all open late (and a few open unusually early, too) and all along a three-block stretch of Main Street downtown. The oldest of these is **The Rainbow Cattle Company** (16220 Main St., 707/869-0206, www.queersteer.com, noon-2am daily), which has been mixing the vibes of a down-home country saloon with a happening San Francisco nightspot since 1979. Think cocktails in mason jars, wood paneling, and leather nights. This is just the kind of queer bar where you can bring your mom or your straight-but-not-narrow friends, and they'll have just as much fun as you will.

It may not look like much from the road, but the **Stumptown Brewery** (15045 River Rd., 707/869-0705, www.stumptown.com, 11am-midnight Sun.-Thurs., 11am-2am Fri.-Sat.) is *the* place to hang out on the river. Inside this atypical dive bar is a pool table, Naugahyde bar stools, and a worn wooden bar crowded with locals. Out back is a second bar and an outdoor deck with tables overlooking the river. The brewery only makes a few of the beers sold on tap, but they are all great and perfect to enjoy by the pitcher. If you are feeling a little woozy from the beer and sunshine, Stumptown also serves a menu of burgers and grilled sandwiches—a perfect excuse to stay put.

Craft cocktails, tequila-style have come to Guerneville with **El Barrio** (16230 Main St., 707/604-7601, http://elbarriobar.com, 4pm-9pm Mon. and Wed.-Thurs., 4pm-11pm Fri, noon-11pm Sat., noon-9pm Sun.). Flights of mescal, tequila, and bourbon along with original cocktails are poured inside the black historic storefront on Main Street. You'll also find a slim menu of south-of-the-border bites to soak up the libations in this stylish bar.

A few miles east of Guerneville and almost an institution in the area is the **Rio Nido Roadhouse** (14540 Canyon 2 Rd., off River Rd., Rio Nido, 707/869-0821, www.

rionidoroadhouse.com, 11:30am-midnight Mon.-Fri., 9am-midnight Sat.-Sun.), which combines a rustic bar, restaurant, and poolside entertainment. Here you can lounge on a lawn next to bikers and aging hippies, surrounded by redwoods, soaking up the alcohol and the last rays of sun while tucking into some freshly barbecued ribs and listening to a local blues band. It can be quite a trip, even for Guerneville. Bands play most weekend evenings throughout the year, and the pool is open Memorial Day-Labor Day.

Recreation

Two big wilderness areas, miles of river, tracts of forest, and a limited population make almost any sort of outdoor pursuit possible in the Russian River Valley, whether on land or on water.

★ THE RUSSIAN RIVER

While the Russian River gently snakes through the vineyards and forests, expect to see it dotted with folks swimming, canoeing, or simply floating in inner tubes serenely downstream, often with a six pack or even a bag of white wine tethered to the back and chilling in the water (although drinking on the river is not recommended). The river flow is relatively smooth this far downstream, even in the winter when the water is higher and faster, so don't expect any adrenaline-pumping rapids. Do expect to have to slather on the sunscreen on a hot summer day, however, and not to care if you tip over and take an unexpected dip in the river. Thankfully, the water is not too cold.

Guerneville and its surrounding forest are the center for fun on the river. On the north bank, **Johnson's Beach & Resort** (16245 1st St., Guerneville, 707/869-2022, www.johnsonsbeach.com, 10am-6pm daily May-Oct.) rents canoes, kayaks, and pedal boats for $40 a day or $15 per hour. Inner tubes are also available, but can only be used at the beach. Johnson's Beach also has a safe, kid-friendly section of the riverbank that is roped off for small children. Parents and beachcombers

Russian River Beaches

It can get hot in the summer—too hot for even a chilled chardonnay to take the edge off. Luckily, the cool waters of the Russian River are always only a short drive away. As summer temperatures soar and the water level falls, the river is relatively calm and benign compared to the swift torrent it can become in the winter and spring. It's still fairly cold though, with plenty of hidden obstacles underwater. The dozens of small beaches exposed as the water level falls in the summer are technically public land, but getting to them usually involves crossing private or restricted areas. That puts many out of reach unless you're floating down the river in a canoe. It is still possible to get to some key beaches from the road, however.

- **Monte Rio Community Beach:** West of Guerneville in the tiny town of Monte Rio, the community beach (20488 Hwy. 116) welcomes all to its sandy shores beneath the Bohemian Highway Bridge. The beach has its own parking lot, is ADA accessible, and has a kayak, canoe, and SUP concession, plus a snack bar that sells ice cream and cold drinks. Volleyball courts and barbecues are free and first-come, first-served.

- **Johnson's Beach:** This family beach in the middle of Guerneville, just a few hundred yards off Main Street, is where a makeshift dam is set up each summer to create a lagoon for swimming or paddling around in a rented canoe. It's crowded in summer, but the atmosphere is fun. This is the spot to rent canoes, kayaks, inflatables, and beach umbrellas, as well as the site of the town's Fourth of July bash and the annual Jazz on the River festival. Parking costs $5.

- **Sunset Beach:** Just east of Guerneville, Sunset Beach has plenty of parking, plus pit toilets, picnic areas, as well as a day-use fee of $7. Despite its proximity to the road, the beach is secluded by a thicket of redwood trees and offers wonderful upriver views of the historic Hacienda Bridge. Dogs are welcome on leash.

- **Steelhead Beach:** To reach this beach, take River Road east toward Forestville. On the north side of the road near Burkes Canoe Trips is the entrance ($7 day-use fee). The large parking lot and boat ramp at the main beach hint at the spot's popularity for fishing and canoeing. A couple of trails heading east from the parking area lead to a more secluded stretch of beach that is better for swimming.

- **Mom's Beach:** Officially known as Forestville River Access, Mom's Beach is a favorite among locals for sunbathing, swimming, and fishing. This beach has its name for a reason: There is plenty of sand to stretch out in and the kids will enjoy the shallow water perfect for wading in. Parking is free.

- **Wohler Bridge:** The historic bridge on Wohler Road (just off the southern end of the Westside Rd.) has a small parking lot ($7), a boat ramp on the west side of the bridge, and some limited parking along the road. Walk back to the other side of the bridge, hop over the steel gate, and follow the gravel trail for about 0.5 mile, past the Water Agency yard. Bear right at a small fork until you reach the meadow and generally sandy beach just beyond. This is a popular beach with nude sunbathers and has gained a reputation as a gay cruising area.

can even rent beach chairs and umbrellas for use on the small beach, and the boathouse sells beer and snacks, rounding out what you might need for a day on the Russian River. Admission to the beach is free, but parking in the lot costs $5.

Farther east in Forestville, **Burkes Canoe Trips** (8600 River Rd., Forestville, 707/887-1222, www.burkescanoetrips.com, May-Sept.,

$65/day) also rents canoes and kayaks. Paddle or simply float 10 miles downriver, stopping at the many secluded beaches along the way, to Guerneville, where courtesy shuttles run back to base every half hour all day long.

Shuttled trips are also available at **Kings Sport & Tackle** (16258 Main St., Guerneville, 707/869-2156, www.kingsrussianriver.com, 8am-6pm daily May-Oct., kayak rentals

$45-65/day). For an extra $15, you can pre-arrange a pickup or drop-off from Monte Rio four miles downstream or Forestville upstream eight miles back to the launch location at Johnson's Beach. Stand-up paddleboards are also available ($60/3 hours, $85/full day), although shuttle service is not available. The store also sells a variety of beach and river gear, including inflatable boats and inner tubes.

Kings is also the place to go for anglers eager to fish for bass, bluegill, catfish, or steelhead salmon. Fishing equipment and licenses are available. Also ask about the myriad rules and regulations: Barbed hooks cannot be used, only artificial lures (no bait) are allowed during the summer, and chinook salmon must be released immediately if hooked. Fly fishers can cast their lines nearby off **Wohler Bridge** (9765 Wohler Rd., Forestville) and **Steelhead Beach** (9000 River Rd., Forestville).

★ ARMSTRONG REDWOODS STATE NATURAL RESERVE

The 805-acre **Armstrong Redwoods State Natural Reserve** (17000 Armstrong Woods Rd., Guerneville, 707/869-2015, www.parks.ca.gov, 8am-sunset daily, $8 per vehicle) just a few miles up Armstrong Woods Road from the center of Guerneville is, as its name suggests, home to some neck-twistingly tall redwoods. The shady and damp forest provides welcome relief from the summer heat and is now the largest remaining old-growth redwood forest in Sonoma County. Some of its trees survived the region's vast 19th-century logging operations and were ironically saved by a lumberman—Colonel James Armstrong—who bought the land in the 1870s to preserve the last tracts of the very same forest he profited from.

The easiest walk ever to a big tree is the 0.1-mile stagger from the **visitors center** (707/869-2958, 11am-3pm daily) to the tallest tree in the park, named the **Parson Jones Tree.** If you saunter another 0.5 mile, you'll reach the **Colonel Armstrong Tree,** which is believed to be about 1,400 years old and

the oldest in the park. It grows next to the Armstrong Pack Station—your first stop if you're doing heavy-duty hiking. From the Pack Station, another 0.25 mile of moderate hiking leads to the **Icicle Tree,** named for its unusual burl formations.

The more adventurous can choose a longer hike up out of the redwoods to the oak and madrone forests on the ridges higher up. One such hike is the relatively quick 2.3-mile **Pool Ridge Trail Loop,** which climbs 500 feet up a series of switchbacks before looping back down into the forest. Dogs and bikes are not allowed on any of the trails.

To just look up at the trees, unpack your picnic at any one of the tables less than a mile from the entrance. Grills and nearby restrooms make it easy to extend your stay.

AUSTIN CREEK STATE RECREATION AREA

Adventurous outdoorsy types might want to drive straight through Armstrong Redwoods to **Austin Creek State Recreation Area** (17000 Armstrong Woods Rd., Guerneville, 707/869-2015, www.parks.ca.gov, day use $8), a 5,700-acre wilderness with 20 miles of hiking trails, chaparral and oak woodlands, rolling hills, and meandering creeks. It's rough going on 2.5 miles of steep, narrow, treacherous dirt road to get to the main entrance and parking area; no vehicles over 20 feet long and no trailers of any kind are permitted. But once you're in, some great—and very difficult—hiking awaits you. The eponymous **Austin Creek Trail** (4.7 miles one-way) leads down from the hot meadows into the cool forest fed by Austin Creek. To avoid monotony on this challenging route, create a loop by taking the turn onto **Gilliam Creek Trail** (4 miles one-way), which dives down to Schoolhouse Creek. This way you get to see another of the park's cute little creeks as you walk back to the starting point.

RIVERFRONT REGIONAL PARK

About three miles south of J Vineyards on Eastside Road, **Riverfront Regional Park**

(7821 Eastside Rd., Healdsburg, 707/565-2041, www.sonoma-county.org/parks, sunrise-sunset daily, $8) is the perfect retreat to stretch your legs or sit in the shade of a redwood grove and enjoy a picnic. The former gravel-mining operation here left behind a series of small lakes that look very inviting on a hot summer day but are strictly off-limits to swimmers. You can, however, cruise around the lake on a stand-up paddleboard, which are available to rent from **Russian River Paddleboards** (707/479-6432, www.russianriverpaddleboards.com, $30/hour, $90/day), which has an outpost here. Several miles of trails around the 300-acre park give plenty of chances to see the wildlife on and around the lakes, however, and fishing in the lakes for bass is allowed with a current license. There are picnic areas with restroom facilities and barbecue pits, along with a volleyball court and a horseshoe pit. Just beyond that is the Russian River, where you can swim if you're brave enough. There's no official river access and no real beach, but it's easy enough to get down to the water if you're desperate to cool off.

GOLF

Stroll among the redwoods without donning hiking boots at the **Northwood Golf Club** (19400 Hwy. 116, Monte Rio, 707/865-1116, $15-45), just west of Guerneville. The historic par-36, nine-hole course was conceived by members of the exclusive gentlemen's retreat the Bohemian Grove, just across the road. It was designed by famous course architect Alistair McKenzie (who also designed the Augusta National course), and completed in 1928. Junior rates are available, as are club rentals and pull carts.

Food

Guerneville has always been known for having solid diner, burger, and beer fare. In other words, Guerneville was never a dining destination, until now. Recently, San Francisco money has begun to move into town, adding a bit of polish and urban sensibility to the rustic restaurant scene.

GUERNEVILLE

Representing the Guerneville old guard, **Main Street Bistro** (16280 Main St., 707/869-0501, www.mainststation.com, 4pm-11pm Mon.-Tues. and Thurs., noon-midnight Fri.-Sat., noon-11pm Sun., $9-30) offers a big menu filled with homey, casual grub. The mainstay is handmade pizza; you can grab a quick slice for lunch or bring friends and order a whole pie for dinner. In the evenings, locals and visitors come down to munch sandwiches and pizza, drink beer, and listen to live entertainment on the small stage.

Another is **Pat's Restaurant** (16236 Main St., 707/869-9904, www.pats-restaurant.com, 8am-2pm daily, $10), the kind of diner that travelers hope to find. It's homey, casual, and the place the locals come to sit at the counter and have breakfast all day long.

At night it is another restaurant entirely, and that's not speaking figuratively. The diner is home to ★ **Dick Blomster's Korean Diner** (www.dickblomsters.com, 5pm-9pm Sun.-Thurs., 5pm-10pm Fri.-Sat., $15-25), where comfort food is served up Korean style, with crazy twists such as deep-fried pickles, kimchi aioli, sake ice cream, and hash browns with a seafood medley. The dessert specialty? A peanut butter sandwich dipped in pancake batter and fried with pop-rocks. Not joking. And it's delicious. If you want a stiff one to go with your KFC (Korean Fried Crack, or Korean-style fried chicken served with a Captain Crunch waffle), you can order a large cocktail from the bar next door. Dick Blomster's is easily the hippest restaurant in Wine Country.

If a hot afternoon on the river makes you crave oysters, you're in luck: Guerneville's newest spot is **Seaside Metal Oyster Bar** (16222 Main St., 707/604-7250, http://seasidemetal.com, 5pm-9pm Sun. and Wed.-Thurs., 5pm-10pm Fri.-Sat., $10-24). From the creators of San Francisco's beloved Bar Crudo, Seaside Metal has a slim menu of oysters, shellfish, and crudo plates of raw fish, gently flavored veggies, and toppings such as wasabi tobiko, horseradish crème fraîche, and rosemary salt. To wash it all down, there is a large menu of beer and wine.

The elder statesman of the new guard is **Big Bottom Market** (16228 Main St., 707/604-7295, www.bigbottommarket.com, 8am-5pm Wed.-Mon., $8-12), a café that serves its coffee via French press and has a small but select local wine list. The food to go with your beverage of choice includes excellent cold and hot pressed sandwiches, savory bread pudding, and a wide assortment of biscuits, so dense and satisfying they can be a meal on their own. There are plenty of artisan jams, jellies, chocolates, and other treats for sale, including picnic supplies, but the atmosphere with touches of brushed metal of beautiful wood-topped tables will make you want to linger.

Guerneville may be on the culinary map of Wine Country now, but it was ★ **boon eat + drink** (16248 Main St., 707/869-0780, http://eatatboon.com, lunch 11am-3pm Mon.-Tues. and Thurs.-Sun., dinner 5pm-9pm Sun.-Thurs., 5pm-10pm Fri.-Sat., $16-28) that first got it there. Light and airy with splashes of

boon eat + drink

metal and bright colors, this bistro is related to the nearby (and equally hip) boon hotel + spa, where some of the vegetables are grown. Lunch usually consists of a simple menu of panini, small plates, and the grass-fed Boon burger ($15). For dinner, hearty mains combine lamb shank with mint pesto or flat iron steak with truffle fries. You really can't go wrong here—unless you can't get in!

You could say that the forces behind boon eat + drink and Big Bottom Market cornered the market on Guerneville's tourist economy when they bought the Guerneville Bank. Originally opened in 1921, it is now the **Guerneville Bank Club** (16290 Main St., 707/666-9411, www.guernevillebankclub.com, 11am-9pm Sun.-Thurs., 11am-10pm Fri.-Sat.), a collective that houses a gallery, a boutique home furnishing store, and the Russian River Historical Society. But most importantly for those with serious sweet tooths, it is the home of **Chile Pies Baking Company** and **Nimble & Finn's Handmade Ice Cream.** Inside the stylized space that pays appropriate homage to its 1920 banking past, you can order a slice of the house specialty, green chile pie à la mode, or a double scoop of organic maple bourbon bacon brittle topped with artisanal candies.

If all you're looking for is beer and barbecue, grab a patio table at **Stumptown Brewery and Smokehouse** (15045 River Rd., 707/869-0705, www.stumptown.com, 11am-midnight Sun.-Thurs., 11am-2am Fri.-Sat., $10-13), in the heart of Guerneville. Satisfying sandwiches filled with brisket and pulled pork, along with some veggie options, go great with its heady microbrews, like Red Rocket and Racer 5.

MONTE RIO

A scenic place to grab a bite is the **Village Inn Restaurant** (20822 River Blvd., 707/865-2304, http://villageinn-ca.com, dinner 5pm-close Wed.-Sun., $14-25) in Monte Rio. The beautifully restored building and its dining patio peek out from the redwoods onto the banks of the river. Most of the bistro-style main courses are hearty, rustic Italian-inspired dishes that can be washed down with wine from the award-winning list.

FORESTVILLE

You would not expect world-class food to find a home out in the woods east of Guerneville, but that's fast becoming the reputation of the restaurant at the Michelin-starred **Farmhouse Inn and Restaurant** (7871 River Rd., Forestville, 707/887-3300 or 800/464-6642, www.farmhouseinn.com, dinner 5:30pm-close Thurs.-Mon., prix fixe menu three-course $95, four-course $110). Chef Steve Litke lets the veritable treasure trove of local produce do the talking here, with dishes like oven-roasted bluenose sea bass and the squab and wild mushroom terrine. Following the trend of many high-end Wine Country restaurants, Litke has exchanged the traditional menu for a prix fixe menu. The menu changes nightly and diners get to choose three or four courses, including dessert. Wine pairing is an additional $69 or $79, depending on the number of courses.

PICNIC SUPPLIES

There is no shortage of stores and delis stocked with supplies tucked in the redwoods. In Forestville, the **Kozlowski Farms** store (5566 Gravenstein Hwy. N., Forestville, 707/887-1587, www.kozlowskifarms.com, 9am-4:30pm Mon.-Fri., 10am-5pm Sat.-Sun.), hidden down a driveway a few yards north of Ross Station Road, has a deli and offers a different kind of tasting—the countless jams, jellies, sauces, and chutneys it makes.

Along the Russian River Wine Road, the **Korbel Delicatessen** (13250 River Rd., Guerneville, 707/824-7313, 9am-4:30pm daily), right next door to the winery's tasting room, makes fat sandwiches and gourmet salads to go. Eat on the small deck outside or head off into the wilds.

And in downtown Guerneville, almost thumbing its nose at neighboring 24-hour Safeway, is the little organic grocery store **Food for Humans** (16385 1st St., Guerneville, 707/869-3612, 9am-8pm daily), an eminently better place to buy produce. Down the street, **Big Bottom Market** (16228 Main St., Guerneville, 707/604-7295, www.bigbottommarket.com, 8am-5pm Wed.-Mon.) has delicious boxed lunches ($17), take-out sandwiches, plus plenty of chips, dips, and drinks for any picnic basket.

FARMERS MARKETS

To take advantage of the Russian River Valley's agricultural bounty, make a stop at the **Guerneville's farmers market** every Thursday evening (3pm-7pm May-Oct.) at the Guerneville Plaza at River Road (Hwy. 116) and Armstrong Redwoods Road.

Accommodations

The bohemian resort town of Guerneville and the surrounding area offer the widest range of accommodations in northern Sonoma, from so-called river resorts that have seen better days to some classier and reasonably priced B&Bs or luxurious inns. As usual, camping is by far the cheapest option, and there's plenty of the great outdoors to choose from, including the wilds of the backcountry and the relative comforts of the grounds of some of those resorts along the river. Many of these spots are especially gay-friendly, some with clothing-optional hot tubs.

UNDER $150

Riverfront balconies, a private beach, and beautifully landscaped grounds combine to make **Rio Villa Beach Resort** (20292 Hwy. 116, Monte Rio, 877/746-8455, www.riovilla.com, $136-245) an ideal Russian River getaway. With only 12 guest rooms—including some with kitchens—you're guaranteed privacy. A generous continental breakfast is available in the morning, and the Russian River is mere steps away.

The **Creekside Inn & Lodge** (16180 Neeley Rd., Guerneville, 707/776-6586 or 800/776-6586, www.creeksideinn.com, $98-300) is indeed right beside the creek otherwise known as the Russian River. It is just a few minutes' stroll to Guerneville's main street. The rooms with the shared bath in the main house are the cheapest, while the suites, which boast a small sitting area, balcony, and private bathroom go to only $185. The several acres of grounds include a pool and eight cottages, from studios to two-bedrooms, all of which are equally affordable, never rising above $300. While this may seem spendy, the rooms at the high end are actually solar-powered suites that come with fully equipped kitchens and can sleep four.

Built in the 1920s, **Fern Grove Cottages** (16650 Hwy. 116, Guerneville, 707/869-8105, www.ferngrove.com, $119-289) offers equal measures of tranquility and activity among the redwoods at the far western end of town. The collection of well-spaced cottages includes studio, one-bedroom, and two-bedroom accommodations with some twists, including wet bars, hot tubs, and fireplaces. They are relative bargains, though the two-night minimum in the summer kicks the price tag up. On-site amenities include a pool, a bar, and a giant picnic area that's a hive of activity in the summer.

Cabins are also available at **Johnson's Beach & Resort** (16245 1st St., Guerneville, 707/869-2022, www.johnsonsbeach.com, $135-165). Also built in the 1920s, these board and batten cottages have minimal furnishings, a frugal charm, and a central location. Some include kitchenettes. You trade in quietude sleeping so close to the action, but for families and deep sleepers, the pros may outweigh the cons.

$150-250

The **West Sonoma Inn** (14100 Brookside Ln., Guerneville, 707/869-2474, www.westsonomainn.com, $149-179) is a refreshing change from the rustic nature of many of the lodging options in the area. The 36-room self-styled resort and spa is surprisingly cheap considering its relatively central location and the modern decor and amenities that include down comforters, fireplaces in most rooms, luxury bathrooms, and nice views.

The cheapest accommodations are the two Vineyard rooms and two Creekside rooms, while the best values are the Deluxe Vineyard or Courtyard rooms, which are more spacious and have either panoramic views or a cozy fireplace. More expensive suites are available, as are full cottages.

The experience of the ★ **Sonoma Orchid Inn** (12850 River Rd., Guerneville, 707/869-4466 or 888/877-4466, www.sonomaorchidinn.com, $149-249) is made by its amazing owners. The best (and spendiest) rooms have microwaves and small fridges, while on the economy end of the spectrum, the guest rooms are tiny but cute, with private baths and pretty decorations. Best of all, the owners of the Sonoma Orchid will offer to help you with absolutely anything you need. They not only recommend restaurants and spas, they'll make reservations for you. They've got knowledge about the local wineries, hikes, river spots, and just about everything else in the region. The inn is perfect for visitors who've never been to the area: It's dog/kid-friendly, clothing is mandatory in the communal hot tub, and it's welcoming to travelers of all stripes.

On the road to Armstrong Redwoods, ★ **boon hotel + spa** (14711 Armstrong Woods Rd., Guerneville, 707/869-2721, www.boonhotels.com, $170-290) is the antithesis of Guerneville's woodsy funkiness. In almost a rebuff to its environs, boon hotel + spa is minimal in the extreme, with a palette of white, slate, and chrome. Many of the 14 guest rooms have freestanding cast-iron fireplaces, private patios, and fridges, while all have beds vast enough to get lost in the fair-trade organic cotton sheets. True to its name, there is a pool and hot tub (both saltwater, for a little twist) and plenty of facial and massage options to work out the kinks. In the morning, wake up to a pressed pot of locally roasted coffee; in the evening, chill out with a cocktail by the pool.

A few miles west of Guerneville in Monte Rio is the **Village Inn** (20822 River Blvd., off Bohemian Hwy., Monte Rio, 707/865-2304, www.villageinn-ca.com, $155-250), a tastefully restored Victorian home set in the redwoods on the south bank of the river. All 10 rooms have private bathrooms and a view of something, whether trees or the river. The bargains here are the three queen studios in the main inn, which have comfy club chairs and views of the river from their private balconies. The cheapest rooms are in the separate lodge, while the most expensive deluxe king studio has a big private deck overlooking the river. Amenities include flat-screen TVs, wireless Internet access, and mini-fridges so you can chill a bottle of Russian River chardonnay to enjoy on the balcony.

Standing sentinel at a sharp bend in Wohler Road just half a mile south of Wohler Bridge is the historic ★ **Raford House** (10630 Wohler Rd., Healdsburg, 707/887-9573 or 800/887-9503, www.rafordinn.com, $180-275), once part of a huge hop-growing estate in its Victorian heyday but now a charming inn with verandas overlooking acres of vineyards. All five rooms have private bathrooms and are decorated in a tasteful and fairly restrained Victorian style. Rooms at the front of the house have the best views. Standard amenities include a CD player/radio, wireless Internet access, an evening wine reception, and a hot organic breakfast served every morning in the dining room.

OVER $250

A little piece of the Mediterranean landed in the redwoods just south of Guerneville in the form of the **Applewood Inn** (13555 Hwy. 116, Guerneville, 707/869-9093, www.applewoodinn.com, $225-375). Three salmon-pink villas are nestled around a manicured central courtyard, the oldest of which is the 1922 Belden House with the cheapest (and smallest) rooms, starting at $225. The more modern Piccola Casa and Gate House, both built since 1996, contain the bigger and more expensive rooms, costing over $300. At these prices, the tranquil surroundings, swimming pool, in-room luxuries, and available spa therapies are to be expected, as is a no child policy. The big building at one end of the courtyard houses

Revival (5:30pm-9pm Sun.-Mon. and Thurs., 5:30pm-10pm Fri.-Sat., $29-32), the hotel's sleek Mediterranean-influenced California restaurant.

Just a stone's throw from the Russian River, tucked away in the woods just off busy River Road, is the **Farmhouse Inn and Restaurant** (7871 River Rd., Forestville, 707/887-3300 or 800/464-6642, www.farmhouseinn.com, $595-995). Nestled among the trees, this compound of luxury cottages and suites is centered around a main house dating from 1872 and a heated pool and hot tub surrounded by the spa and gardens. Make an appointment with the in-house alchemist to find the best herbal concoction for your massage, wrap, or scrub ($195-310), or book the 90 Body Melt and massage ($260), or the couples only Roll in the Hay ($350 pp) scrub and massage combination. Once your appetite has been whetted, take a seat at the Michelin-starred restaurant. Cap your evening roasting complimentary gourmet s'mores on the communal fire pits. The price for all this luxury is high, but if you are looking for a polished Guerneville experience, this is it.

CAMPING

There are plenty of resort campgrounds along the Russian River, but many cater to summer crowds and RVs, usually charging a premium price for the extensive services and facilities they offer. In all cases, reservations are essential during the busy summer months.

To pitch your tent in the heart of Guerneville, book one of the 37 campsites at **Johnson's Beach & Resort** (16245 1st St., Guerneville, 707/869-2022, www.johnsonsbeach.com, $40). Overlooking the river beneath a sparse canopy of walnut and sycamore trees, the campground is a hive of summertime activity and boasts hot showers, laundry facilities, and a game room. Don't expect much privacy or wilderness solitude.

One of the more reasonable campgrounds is **Burkes Canoe Trips** (8600 River Rd., Forestville, 707/887-1222, www.burkescanoetrips.com, $12/pp/day), hidden in the redwoods right next to the river (and the road) just north of Forestville. The full-service campground, open May-October, has 60 sites for tents or RVs. This is also a popular place to rent canoes. The year-round **River Bend Resort** (11820 River Rd., Forestville, 707/887-7662, http://riverbendresort.net) is one of the smaller of the riverside resort campgrounds, with 49 open or secluded sites for tents ($35/night, $40 for the premium riverside sites) and small RVs ($60-70). There are also eight "camping cottages" that sleep just three people and have space for a tent outside, but cost a relatively steep $89-99 per night.

Stay inside a stylized Airstream trailer at the posh **Autocamp** (14120 Old Cazadero Rd., Guerneville, 888/405-7553, http://autocamp.com, $139-325). The 24 trailers nestled in the redwoods sleep four and are equipped with comfy mattresses and luxurious linens, bathrooms with "spa-inspired" walk-in showers complete with boutique toiletries, sleek interiors and outdoor furniture, and personal fire pits. For less money, you can opt for the fancy tent cabins, which likewise have top-notch beds, a cozy interior, a cooler, and an outdoor space to make the most of the environs. While these do not come with personal bathrooms, those found in the communal Club House are certainly a step up from most campgrounds and include expensive toiletries. The mid-century-inspired clubhouse has a store stocked with wine, beer, and gourmet goodies.

The more serene campgrounds are well off the beaten track at the primitive but scenic creek-side campgrounds high up in the **Austin Creek State Recreation Area** (17000 Armstrong Woods Rd., Guerneville, 707/869-2015, www.parks.ca.gov, $25). The road up into the park through Armstrong Redwoods State Natural Reserve ends at the **Bullfrog Pond Campground,** with 24 sites, toilets, and drinking water. No vehicles over 20 feet long are allowed into the park, so the camping experience is free of humming RVs. Out of the 24 sites, you can reserve 16 (www.hipcamp.com, $35). The

remaining seven walk-in sites are first-come, first-served and cost $25. For these you must stop by the Armstrong Redwoods park office (17000 Armstrong Woods Rd., Guerneville, 707/869-2958, 11am-3pm daily). You can also inquire about, or get permits for, the three backcountry sites ($25) that are roughly four miles from the parking lot. But if you arrive after hours, you can register (for the Bullfrog Pond sites, at least) at the self-pay kiosk at the campground.

Information and Services

The most important tool for visiting the Russian River Valley is the excellent free map published by the **Russian River Wine Road** (www.wineroad.com), an organization representing wineries and other businesses throughout northern Sonoma. The map is pretty easy to find at all major wineries and covers all the major roads in the Russian River Valley and up into the Dry Creek and Alexander Valleys. More area-specific maps are available to download on the website. Another resource is the **Russian River Valley Winegrowers Association** (www.rrvw.org), whose website produces a helpful interactive map.

Physical maps and other information about the region are available at the drop-in office of the **Russian River Chamber of Commerce and Visitor Center** (16209 1st St., Guerneville, 707/869-9000 or 877/644-9001, www.russianriver.com, 10am-5pm daily) in the center of Guerneville. There's also an outpost at **Korbel** (13250 River Rd., Guerneville, 707/869-4096, 10am-4pm daily summer, 10am-3pm Tues.-Sun. fall-spring), in the old station house that is now the ticket office.

There isn't much in the way of services in Guerneville, but you will find a **Bank of America** at 16390 Main Street and a **Wells Fargo** at 16405 River Road.

Getting There and Around

Guerneville sits squarely on the Russian River at the intersection of Highway 116 and River

Road. The most direct access is via U.S. 101 north of Santa Rosa, taking the River Road/Guerneville exit and following River Road west for 15 miles to downtown Guerneville. You can also opt for the more scenic and less crowded route by taking Highway 116 off U.S. 101 near Cotati, south of Santa Rosa. Named the Gravenstein Highway for its path through the apple orchards of Sebastopol, Highway 116 winds about 22 twisty miles through Sebastopol, Graton, and Forestville to emerge onto River Road in Guerneville.

Healdsburg

Farther up the Russian River and U.S. 101, Healdsburg sheds the woodsy rustic vibe of the Russian River Valley in exchange for Victorian charm. Established in 1867, Healdsburg is one of the more appealing Wine Country towns, with the right mix of history, modernity, shops, and wine, as well as a population of 11,000—large enough to prevent the town's economy from lurching too far in favor of wine tourism. There is still plenty of Wine Country paraphernalia here, however, and there are often-voiced concerns that the town is becoming a "bourgeois playland."

Healdsburg is also the nexus of three American Viticulture Areas (AVAs): the Russian River AVA, best known for producing pinot noir and chardonnay; Dry Creek AVA, famous for its zinfandel and sauvignon blanc; and the Alexander Valley AVA, which produces predominantly cabernet sauvignon and merlot. From the heart of town, Westside Road heads down into the Russian River Valley, Dry Creek Road to its namesake's valley, and Healdsburg Avenue heads north into the Alexander Valley. But it's just as easy to ditch the car and sample wines from those appellations and many more in the numerous downtown tasting rooms and wineries, all within walking distance from the plaza.

DOWNTOWN TASTING ROOMS

There are more wineries represented here than most people can comfortably visit in a day, and more than in any other Wine Country town. In fact, there are well over 30. So many, in fact, that wineries are upping their ante with some outlandish style, unbelievable deals, and classy food pairings.

SIDURI

Russian River pinot noir is the star at **Siduri** (241 Healdsburg Ave., 707/433-6000, www.siduri.com, 11am-7pm Sun.-Wed., 11am-8pm Thurs.-Sat., tasting $20), which has quietly carved out a huge reputation for its single-vineyard pinot noirs sourced from just about every great pinot-growing region on the West Coast. Since making its first case of wine 1994, the winery's pinots have received countless stellar ratings. In fact, the big news is when Siduri *doesn't* receive a 90-plus point rating for one of its wines, which generally cost $35-55 per bottle. For years, the only way to taste Siduri's wine was to make an appointment at its warehouse located in an industrial stretch of Santa Rosa. Recently, however, Siduri has opened this sleek tasting lounge in the heart of Healdsburg, providing a guest experience to match its high-caliber wines. You can opt for a flight of five wines ($20), add a food pairing for ($45), or simply order everything à la carte. The lounge serves wine by the glass ($13-18) and a wonderful small bites menu that includes crab rolls, pork belly, and fried chicken sliders ($5-25).

CELLARS OF SONOMA

Among the wines from the eight small vintners represented at **Cellars of Sonoma** (20 Matheson St., 707/578-1826, 11am-6pm daily, tasting $15), the standout is La Sirena from winemaker Heidi Peterson Barrett. Barrett is best known for making cult cabernets such

Healdsburg

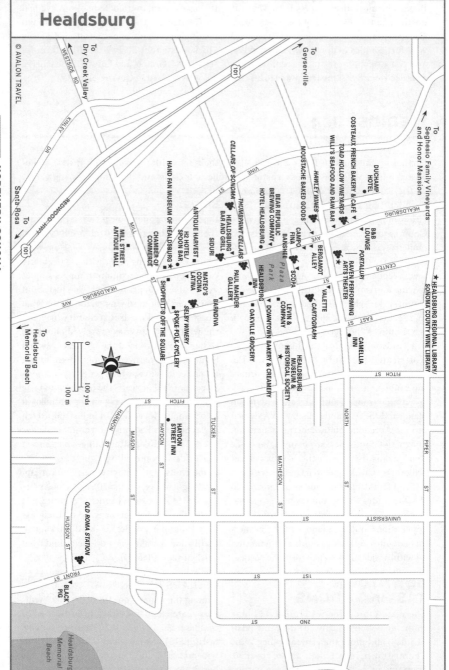

© AVALON TRAVEL

To Dry Creek Valley

WESTSIDE RD

KINLEY RD

To Santa Rosa

REDWOOD HWY

101

To Geyserville

To Seghesio Family Vineyards and Honor Mansion

101

HEALDSBURG

CENTER

HEALDSBURG REGIONAL LIBRARY/
SONOMA COUNTY WINE LIBRARY

COSTEAUX FRENCH BAKERY & CAFÉ

WILLI'S SEAFOOD AND RAW BAR

TOAD HOLLOW VINEYARDS

DUCHAMP HOTEL

B&B LOUNGE

PORTALUPI

HAWLEY WINES

MOUSTACHE BAKED GOODS

VINE ST

CELLARS OF SONOMA

BEAR REPUBLIC BREWING COMPANY

HOTEL HEALDSBURG

BANSHEE

CAMPO FINA

AVE

BERGAMOT ALLEY

RAVEN PERFORMING ARTS THEATER

HAND FAN MUSEUM OF HEALDSBURG

ANTIQUE HARVEST

THUMBPRINT CELLARS

HEALDSBURG BAR AND GRILL

H2 HOTEL/ SPOON BAR

SIDURI

SCOPA

VALETTE

EAST ST

CARTOGRAPH

CAMELLIA INN

MILL ST

MILL STREET ANTIQUE MALL

CHAMBER OF COMMERCE

MATEO'S COCINA LATINA

PAUL MAHDER GALLERY

HEALDSBURG
Plaza
Park

HEALDSBURG INN

LEVIN & COMPANY

HEALDSBURG MUSEUM & HISTORICAL SOCIETY

HEALDSBURG AVE

SHOFFEIT'S OFF THE SQUARE

SELBY WINERY

SPOKE FOLK CYCLERY

BARNDIVA

OAKVILLE GROCERY

DOWNTOWN BAKERY & CREAMERY

FITCH ST

NORTH ST

PIPER ST

0   100 yds
0   100 m

To Healdsburg Memorial Beach

HARMON ST

MASON ST

HUDSON ST

FITCH ST

HAYDON ST

HAYDON STREET INN

TUCKER ST

MATHESON ST

FITCH ST

UNIVERSITY ST

PIPER ST

OLD ROMA STATION

FRONT ST

FRONT ST

BLACK PIG

1ST ST

1ST ST

2ND ST

Healdsburg
Memorial
Beach

Healdsburg to Geyserville Tasting Tour

For an ideal Healdsburg breakfast, take a table on the outside patio at **Costeaux French Bakery & Café** and indulge in fresh French pastries or a hearty breakfast. Afterwards, wander over to **Antique Harvest** and nearby **Mill Street Antiques** to hunt for antiques and locally made arts and crafts. If you're ready for some Russian River chardonnay, make your way to **Selby Winery** and **Banshee** for some flights before heading over to **The Shed** to supply your picnic basket. Make the short drive to **Seghesio Family Vineyards** for a glass of sangiovese, a round of bocce ball, and a dose of history. Follow Alexander Valley Road to the old community of **Jimtown,** where **Medlock Ames** will greet you with a flight of estate Alexander Valley wines beneath its grape arbor. Alternatively, if a taste of Alexander Valley cabernet has piqued your interest, head to nearby **Hawkes.** To try the king of cabernet, trek to the north end of the valley to **Silver Oak Cellars,** where you can compare and contrast Alexander Valley and Napa cabernets. Backtrack to Geyserville to continue your cabernet journey at **Meeker,** known for its big wines as well as staying open until 6pm. For something lighter, **Pech Merle** pours a cool and refreshing Rose de Syrah in its cool and refreshing tasting room. Stay in Geyersville for comforting yet sophisticated Italian food at **Catelli's.**

as Screaming Eagle, a six-liter 1992 vintage that sold at the Napa Valley Wine Auction in 2000 for $500,000. However, you can taste her syrah for the price of the $15 tasting, along with three other boutique wines. Cellars of Sonoma offers casual tasting outside on the sunny patio or inside its industrial chic tasting room.

THUMBPRINT CELLARS

Touting itself as a "micro-winery," **Thumbprint Cellars** (102 Matheson St., 707/433-2393, www.thumbprintcellars.com, 11am-6pm daily, tasting $10-20) was started as a hobby for winemaker Scott Lindstrom-Dake in the late 1990s and has rapidly grown to become a member of the boutique brigade. In the small and relaxed tasting room, you'll get to enjoy local art and a flight of three ($10) or five ($20) fruit-forward wines from the Alexander and Dry Creek Valleys that include syrah, zinfandel, and cabernet sauvignon, plus chardonnay and viognier. The Russian River pinot noir is one of the few cooler-climate wines but is just as approachable as the others. Food pairing is also available and features locally made cheese and charcuterie.

HAWLEY WINES

John Hawley, winemaker and proprietor of **Hawley Wines** (36 North St., 707/473-9500, www.hawleywine.com, 11am-6pm daily, tasting $10-20), certainly knows how to make Sonoma wine, and lots of it. He started his winemaking career in the 1970s as a winemaker at the giant Clos du Bois and Kendall-Jackson wineries. In the mid-1990s he started making small quantities of wine under his own label: nine or so different varietals sourced from a wide variety of northern Sonoma vineyards, including the family's own estate on Bradford Mountain in the Dry Creek Valley.

The tasting room, a block away from the square, is relaxed and warm with carved wood, a bar made from old wine barrels, and the impressionist paintings of vineyards and other Northern California landscapes by its resident artist, Dana Hawley. There are two tasting options: four pours for $10 and nine pours for $20. On the current release menu look out for the acclaimed barrel-fermented viognier, a late-harvest zinfandel, and a merlot from the Bradford Mountain estate that usually sells out fast.

NORTHERN SONOMA
HEALDSBURG

TOAD HOLLOW VINEYARDS

The toad in this hollow is actually owner Todd Williams, the half-brother of late actor Robin, who has sported the amphibious nickname since his youth. His winery, **Toad Hollow Vineyards** (409A Healdsburg Ave., 707/431-8667, www.toadhollow.com, 11am-5:30pm daily, tasting $8) is best known for its oak-free chardonnay, sourced from the 103 acres of estate vineyards, but it also makes estate pinot noir and merlot, a pinot noir rosé, and one or two unique (and uniquely named) wines, including the red blend called Erik's the Red, which is produced from a staggering 15 different types of grape. The two sparkling wines are not local, however, but imported from France. For $8, you can enjoy nine pours at the gnarled redwood bar. And if the wines don't entertain, their colorful labels, painted by San Francisco artist Maureen Erickson, might. Serious wines sport a very conservative-looking toad, while the fun wines see the toad in party mood.

PORTALUPI

If you only go to one tasting room in Healdsburg, make it **Portalupi** (107 North St., 707/395-0960, www.portalupiwine.com, 11am-7pm daily, tasting $10-20). You'll find Russian River pinot noirs and zinfandel, and Italian additions like a barbera, a port classically made from carignane, and the Vaso di Marina, a blend of pinot noir, zinfandel, and cabernet sauvignon. As a nod to Jane Portalupi's grandmother, who used to make wine herself in her native village in Italy, the wine comes in a liter ($26). The sole white on the menu is the Carneros vermentino, an Italian varietal known for its notes of jasmine and subtle acids and minerality.

The lush, inky quality of Portalupi's wines is perfectly matched by its sophisticated slate and purple tasting room filled with two large couches. You can taste a flight or order by the glass. Cheese and salami plates are also available ($20) and a seated food and wine pairing costs $25. Despite the tasting room's small size, this is a great place to hang out (or wait for a table at a nearby restaurant), particularly when the large glass doors are open.

BANSHEE

The cool interior of **Banshee** (325 Center St., 707/395-0915, www.bansheewines.com, 11am-7pm daily, tasting $15-30) makes you want to linger. This boutique winery specializes in distinctive chardonnay and pinot noir from the Sonoma Coast inland, and offers a flight of five wines for $15 and a flight of five reserve wines for $30. While the $15 price tag is tempting, splurge on the reserve flight, which includes the incomparable Heintz vineyard chardonnay. With notes of pear, lemon, and vanilla bean, along with a bright mineral structure, it is a standout Russian River chardonnay. You can get the Heintz by the glass ($15) along with over a dozen Banshee wines ($10-15). Snacks from the beloved Jimtown Store are also available ($8-12), and if you are in hangout mode, you are welcome to select a record to play on the tasting room's turntable.

CARTOGRAPH

Cartograph (340 Center St., 707/433-8270, www.cartographwines.com, noon-6:30pm daily, $15), another favorite among tasting room locals, is one of the youngest and smallest wineries in downtown Healdsburg, having started in 2008 making just 1,300 cases of mainly vineyard-specific pinot noir. The winery also specializes in white Alsatian varietals including a totally dry gewürztraminer. You'll be able to taste the full range of current release wines in the flight of five wines offered in the stylish but spare (particularly compared to the younger wineries around here) tasting room.

SELBY WINERY

Selby Winery (215 Center St., 707/431-1288, www.selbywinery.com, 11am-5:30pm daily, tasting $5-10) makes wine using fruit from vineyards all over Sonoma, with an emphasis on the nearby Russian River Valley, Alexander Valley, and Dry Creek Valley. The Russian

River Valley chardonnay is perhaps the best wine here and regularly wins praise from the critics. The reserve chardonnay has even been served at the White House. Other wines include a Russian River pinot noir, a couple of nicely structured syrahs, including a dry syrah rosé, and some nice zinfandels, including a juicy port. Most of the red Bordeaux varietals are also in the winery's large portfolio, including a nice malbec from the nearby Chalk Hill appellation. All can be tasted for $5 in the tiny, relaxed tasting room, where you're as likely to see a few locals hanging out as you are visitors. There's a $10 tasting fee for a flight of reds.

OLD ROMA STATION

A pleasant 10-minute walk from the plaza right across from the Russian River sits **Old Roma Station** (51-57 Front St. and 412-428 Hudson St., www.oldromastation.com), an old complex of warehouses. It was once home to the Roma Winery, a Victorian-era winery that shipped fortified wines by rail from its own station before the trains were halted by Prohibition. Often referred to by locals as the Front Street Wineries, most of the dozen wineries here offer tastings every day, but some are appointment only, and a few are closed for a few days midweek.

Standouts include **Pezzi King Vineyards** (707/431-9388, www.pezziking.com, 11am-5pm daily, tasting $5), which specializes in Dry Creek zinfandels and cabernets, along with a nice Russian River Valley chardonnay; **Sapphire Hill Vineyards** (707/431-1888, www.sapphirehill.com, 11am-4:30pm daily, tasting $10), where you can sidle up to the bar and taste a variety of small-lot Russian River chardonnay, pinot noir, and zinfandel while munching on plenty of bar snacks like caramel popcorn and raspberry jalapeño brownies; and the collective inside the collective, **Hudson Street Wineries** (707/433-2364, www.hudsonstreetwineries.com, 11am-4:30pm Thurs.-Mon., tasting $10). Here, five wineries share the quaint tasting room. **Bluenose Wines** specializes

in Dry Creek zinfandel, Sonoma County chardonnay, and petite sirah; from **Kelly & Young** come a Sonoma County sauvignon blanc and a Bordeaux-style rosé; **Owl Ridge** makes Dry Creek sauvignon blanc and zinfandel, plus Alexander Valley cabernet sauvignon; **Shippey Vineyards** also produces Dry Creek petite sirah, petite sirah rosé, and heritage clone zinfandel; and from **Willowbrook** come three pinot noirs and one vineyard-designate zinfandel. All five wineries produce less than 300 cases of each vintage, making them the boutiques of the boutiques.

SEGHESIO FAMILY VINEYARDS

One of the old Italian family wineries that helped define the northern Sonoma wine industry over the past hundred years is about a 20-minute walk (or 5-minute drive) from Healdsburg Plaza in a building dating from the 1890s. Although it is not surrounded by bucolic vineyards and fields, the ample gardens at **Seghesio Family Vineyards** (700 Grove St., 707/433-3579, www.seghesio.com, 10am-5pm Sun.-Thurs., 10am-6pm Fri.-Sat., tasting $15) make it the best place to picnic and play a game of bocce within easy reach of the plaza.

The winery was founded in 1902 by Edoardo Seghesio and remains a family affair to this day. The wines are sourced from 400 acres of vineyards throughout the Russian River, Alexander, and Dry Creek Valleys. You'll find excellent and bargain-priced Sonoma County zinfandel as well as age-worthy zin from the tiny Rockpile appellation, plus Italian varietals including the limited-production Venom, sourced from the oldest sangiovese vines in the United States and named for the rattlesnakes that thrive in the hilltop vineyard.

The Italian wines pair well with the artisan cheese and house-made charcuterie plate offered Friday-Sunday by appointment in the Founder's Flight tasting option ($30) or alfresco dining out in the oak shaded picnic grounds. Just buy a bottle after your tasting.

SIGHTS

Healdsburg's biggest draw is its central plaza, which was donated to the city by the founder of Healdsburg, Harmon Heald, in the 1850s. On any day of the week you can still see Healdsburg's residents enjoying this spot of green beneath a canopy of mature trees. Many of these were planted over a century ago and include Canary date palms, orange and lemon trees, and a rare dawn deciduous redwood from China. The benches scattered around the plaza are perfect for a quiet conversation over a cup of coffee, indulging in a good book, or getting away from the office (the plaza is blanketed in Wi-Fi). The plaza plays host events throughout the year, such as the **Healdsburg Antique Fair** (707/431-3325, www.healdsburg.com) held for one day every June.

You can learn more about the town's history at the **Healdsburg Museum & Historical Society** (221 Matheson St. 707/431-3325, www.healdsburgmuseum.org, 11am-4pm Wed.-Sun., free), housed in an old neoclassical library a few blocks from the plaza. The museum is a treasure trove of information and photos illustrating the town's Victorian heyday and its Native American roots. Serious history buffs can pore through oral histories, official records, and newspapers going back to the 1860s.

The modern Healdsburg library is home to the **Sonoma County Wine Library** (139 Piper St., Healdsburg Regional Library, 707/433-3772, www.sonomalibrary.org/wine, 10am-6pm Tues.-Fri., 10am-4pm Sat.), where a collection of over 5,000 books on wine, subscriptions to more than 80 wine periodicals, photos, prints, and wine labels await both the amateur wine lover and serious oenophile. Among the 1,000 or so rare wine books, you'll find treatises on the history, business, and art of wine from as far back as 1512. The library is a perfect place for wine drinkers who want to take their habit or hobby to the next level.

More esoteric history awaits you just off the square between the visitors center and the H2Hotel. The tiny **Hand Fan Museum of Healdsburg** (219 Healdsburg Ave., 707/431-2500, www.handfanmuseum.com, 11am-4pm Wed.-Sun.) seeks to tell the cultural histories of Europe, America, and Asia through the creation, decoration, and use of fans. It doesn't take long to view and enjoy both the permanent collection and seasonal exhibits at this fun little museum. You might be surprised to discover the level of artistry put into some of the fans here, be they paper or lace, antique or modern. And you'll learn a little bit about how fans were and are used in various societies (the 17th-through 19th-century courting practices and sexual invitations in some European countries included intricate movements of a lady's fan, directed at the gentleman of the hour).

ENTERTAINMENT

Raven Performing Arts Theater

Hats off to Healdsburg's fiercely independent **Raven Performing Arts Theater** (115 North St., 707/433-6335, www.raventheater.org) for keeping it real in the middle of Wine Country. The theater is owned by a performing arts cooperative that stages five plays per year—primarily award-winning and established works. Recent offerings have included Arthur Miller's *After the Fall* and Christopher Durang's *Beyond Therapy*. For the last show each season, the Ravens produce a big dramatic musical; productions have included *Evita* and *Hello Dolly!*

Around the corner is Healdsburg's own arty "multiplex." The **Raven Film Center** (415 Center St., 707/522-0330, www.srentertainmentgrp.com) has four movie theaters squeezed into this historic building (though one is about the size of an average living room), so there's usually a combination of mainstream, independent, and documentary films showing 3-5 times every day (entrance on Center St., admission $10, matinees $7.50). For a more unique Wine Country movie experience, order a glass of Sonoma wine ($8-11) or a pint of craft beer ($6-7) and a gourmet panini ($7.50) to go with your flick.

Nightlife

A couple of local hangouts keep the bar scene in Healdsburg real too, staying open all day, every day until 2am. Both **John & Zeke's Bar & Grill** (420 Healdsburg Ave., 707/433-3735, 10am-2am daily) and the **B&B Lounge** (1239 Healdsburg Ave., 707/433-5960, 10am-2am Mon.-Fri, 8am-2am Sat.-Sun.) have grumpy bartenders and shun Wine Country frills for good old-fashioned barroom entertainment like jukeboxes, pool, and darts. The B&B is more popular with locals and slightly less of a dive.

For a beer and maybe some food, head over to the **Bear Republic Brewing Company** (345 Healdsburg Ave., 707/433-2337, http://bearrepublic.com, 11:30am-9pm Sun.-Thurs., 11am-11pm Fri.-Sat.), where locals are known to grab a Racer 5 IPA and chill out after work. Beer, wine, and cocktails can be found down the street at the other pub in town, the **Healdsburg Bar & Grill** (245 Healdsburg Ave., 707/433-3333, www.healdsburgbarandgrill.com, 11am-9pm Mon.-Fri., 9am-9pm Sat.-Sun.). Here you'll find specialty drinks like the Hummingbird, which features St. Germaine; the Cucumber Collins made with Effen Cucumber Vodka and jalapeño and lime juice; and an assortment of "adult milkshakes" spiked with rum, Bailey's, or Jack Daniels served on the large outside patio busy until the place closes at 9pm.

The slim **Bergamot Alley** (328A Healdsburg Ave., 707/433-8720, www.bergamotalley.com, noon-1am Tues.-Sat., noon-midnight Sun.) is all exposed brick, cool lighting, microbrews, European wines sold by the glass, and a turntable that plays full albums from start to finish (i.e., no playlists here). There are small offerings to nibble on, like spiced popcorn and candied jalapeños. You are even invited to bring your own snacks, so long as they are not alcoholic beverages. Basically, Bergamot Alley has the vibe of the coolest basement hangout spot you can think of.

SHOPPING

Wine-tasting, dining, and shopping form the trifecta of the Healdsburg experience. For many years, Healdsburg was known for its slightly funky antiques scene, some of which remains, but the true bargain hunting has been replaced by higher-end boutiques. In fact, the town has gone so upscale that many residents jokingly call it "HealdsBeverly Hills." Still, there are some old treasures and lots of cool shops for browsing.

If antiques are what you're after, several stores line Healdsburg Avenue and nearby side streets. **Antique Harvest** (225 Healdsburg Ave., 707/433-0223, www.antiqueharvest-healdsburg.com, 10:30am-5:30pm Mon.-Sat., 11am-5:30pm Sun.), sharing a block with the sleek H2Hotel, is a cavernous and crowded space filled with furniture, kitchenware, knickknacks, and collectibles. While it may be disorganized and those with claustrophobia may want to stick to the sidewalk displays, true antiques hunters may get lost here. Across the street, **Shoffeitt's Off the Square** (208 Healdsburg Ave., 707/433-5556, 10am-5pm daily) is another treasure trove of antique housewares, which spills out onto the back patio and features furniture locally made out of wine barrels. A short distance away, **Mill Street Antiques** (44 Mill St., 707/433-8409, 10:30am-5pm Thurs.-Mon., 11am-5pm Tues.-Wed.) boasts more than 20,000 square feet of floor space that is home to numerous local dealers and craftspeople.

Vintage bric-a-brac takes a stylish turn at **Studio Barndiva** (237 Center St., 707/431-7404, www.studiobarndiva.com, 10am-6pm daily), a spin-off of the **Barndiva** restaurant (231 Center St., 707/431-0100, www.barndiva.com, lunch noon-2:30pm Wed.-Sat., dinner 5:30pm-9pm Wed.-Thurs. and Sun., 5:30pm-10pm Fri.-Sat., brunch 11am-2pm Sun., $27-35). Wine Country clichés are nowhere to be seen among this showcase of weird and wonderful artistic creations from local and global

Northern Sonoma Festivals and Events

Whatever the time of year, there's always some sort of festival or wine-related event going on in this part of the world.

JANUARY

Wineries have to think of something to bring in customers in the depths of winter, hence the **Winter Wineland** event (707/433-4335, www.wineroad.com) held around the middle of the month. More than 100 of the region's wineries take part. For the ticket price of $45, visitors get the VIP treatment and samples of limited-release wines. There's even a special designated-driver ticket price of $5.

MARCH

The region's annual **Barrel Tasting** (707/433-4335, www.wineroad.com), held on the first two weekends of the month, is a great excuse to visit as many wineries as possible in a day and sample wines straight from the barrel, whether you're interested in buying wine futures or not. Tickets are $50 or $10 for designated drivers.

APRIL

The **Passport to Dry Creek Valley** ($80-135), held on the last weekend of the month, gets visitors into almost every winery in the valley, even those usually open by appointment only. Every one of them has some sort of theme for the weekend and puts on quite a party, with plenty of food and, of course, wine. The mock passports are stamped at every winery; passports are limited so book early. Contact the **Winegrowers of Dry Creek Valley** (707/433-3031, www.wdcv. com) for more information.

JUNE

Before wine there was the Wild West, which is celebrated every year at the **Russian River Rodeo** (707/865-9854, www.russianriverrodeo.org, tickets $10-12), held the third weekend of the month at Duncans Mills, a 15-minute drive west of Guerneville. Over in Healdsburg, the beginning of June marks the beginning of the annual **Healdsburg Jazz Festival** (707/433-4633, www.healdsburgjazzfestival.com), a weeklong series of concerts at venues around the city. This is followed by the one-day **Healdsburg Antique Fair** (707/431-3325, www.healdsburg.com), where the town's antiques sellers lay out their wares in the plaza. It is a free event. June also kicks

artisans, and prices of many of the unique creations are not as expensive as the hipper-than-thou atmosphere suggests. At 2:30pm Wednesday-Sunday, food starts flowing from the restaurant to the gallery, with light entrées served with beer, wine, and cocktails ($16-27).

Modern art has found a home at the **Paul Mahder Gallery** (222 Healdsburg Ave., 707/473-9150, www.paulmahdergallery. com, 10am-6pm Wed.-Mon.). Large installations, multimedia work, paintings costing $10,000, and galleries within the gallery let visitors know this is not your ordinary Wine Country art gallery. Instead, the space, an 8,500-square-foot Quonset hut that was

formerly an antiques collective, is more akin to a San Francisco art museum. You are invited to browse the heady space and be inspired.

Book lovers, music aficionados, epicureans, and home cooks alike will undoubtedly fall in love with **Levin & Company** (306 Center St., 707/433-1118, www.levinbooks.com, 9am-9pm Mon.-Sat., 10am-6pm Sun.), an independent bookstore that has been around 25 years. Inside, current fiction and nonfiction titles share shelf space with one of the best selections of culinary and wine books around. CDs of jazz, classical, and pop music can also be found here.

off **Rodney Strong's Summer Concert Series** (11455 Old Redwood Hwy., Healdsburg, 707/431-1533, www.rodneystrong.com, June-Sept.), in which major musical acts from the B-52s to Smokey Robinson perform in front of picnickers on the winery's vast lawn.

AUGUST

They named a highway after this apple, so why not have a festival in its honor as well? The **Gravenstein Apple Fair** (800/207-9464, www.gravensteinapplefair.com, adults $15, children 6-12 $10, under six free) in Sebastopol is held around the middle of the month at the town's Ragle Ranch Park. The event includes music, crafts, and plenty of apple-flavored fun. More raucous fun can be had farther down the road at the **Russian River Beer Revival and BBQ Cook Off** (707/869-0705, www.stumptown.com, $100) at the Stumptown Brewery. The annual event features live music, beer tasting from 30 different breweries, and lots and lots of barbecue.

SEPTEMBER

The big blowout wine event of the year is the **Sonoma Wine Country Weekend** (855/939-7666, www.sonomawinecountryweekend.com), a three-day wine, food, and arts extravaganza held during the beginning of the month at the region's wineries. The main event is the **Taste of Sonoma County,** which is usually held at a winery near Healdsburg. You must reserve a spot for each event, which cost $85-165.

Celebrate the end of summer on the beach in Guerneville at the **Russian River Jazz and Blues Festival** (707/869-1595, www.omegaevents.com, $50-80), usually held the third weekend of the month. Top jazz musicians, fine wine, late summer sun, and the option of simply floating on the river all combine to make a unique experience. Tickets for the weekend event are available starting in April from the festival organizers.

NOVEMBER

With all the creative names for food and wine events apparently exhausted for the year, this month's reason to eat and drink to excess is called simply **A Food & Wine Affair.** Many of the region's wineries match their wines with all sorts of food on the first weekend of the month. All you have to do is get from one winery to another. Tickets ($60-80, $30 designated drivers) and information are available from the **Russian River Wine Road** (707/433-4335 or 800/723-6336, www.wineroad.com).

Moustache Baked Goods (381 Healdsburg Ave., 707/395-4111, www.moustachebakedgoods.com, 11am-7pm daily) pulls mean shots of Four Barrel espresso. Along with coffee, you'll be tempted to pick up one of their handmade Oreo cookies, colorful macarons, or devilishly delicious cupcakes displayed in the antique-looking display case.

RECREATION
Healdsburg's Russian River

Snaking through the south side of town, the Russian River is a great place to cool off and relax on a hot Healdsburg day. Across the Veterans Memorial Bridge lies **Healdsburg**

Veterans Memorial Beach (13839 Old Redwood Hwy., 707/433-1625, http://parks.sonomacounty.ca.gov, sunrise-sunset daily, parking $7), a stretch of sandy and rocky shoreline along the river with a grassy picnic area, swimming shallows, and a few concessions. Known just as Memorial Beach, this is a popular spot with locals with kids in tow, so you may find the parking lot full on summer weekends. If so, hunt for parking across the bridge in the residential area. On foot, the beach is only a 15-minute walk from downtown Healdsburg. Dogs are allowed on leash on the lawn only, and alcohol is strictly prohibited.

During the summer (generally May-Oct.), **River's Edge Kayak & Canoe Trips** (13840 Healdsburg Ave., 707/433-7247, www.riversedgekayakandcanoe.com, trips $50-120) can help you get out on the water. Located across the street from Memorial Beach, the company offers two self-guided tours in either canoes ($100-120) or kayaks ($50-120). After checking in between 8:30am-11:30am, you'll be shuttled 5 or 16 miles up the river and left to paddle downstream with lots of tips for the best beaches, swimming holes, and picnic spots along the way. The public is allowed on all the beaches along the Russian River that fall below the winter high-water mark—basically every beach you see during the summer.

If you are more interested in joining a guided tour, another local outfit, **Russian River Adventures** (20 Healdsburg Ave., 707/433-5599, http://russianriveradventures.com, adults $45-60, children $25-30, dogs $10), offers guided paddles down a secluded section of the river in stable, sturdy inflatable canoes. Dogs, children, and even infants are welcome. Trips usually last 2-6 hours, with little white water and lots of serene shaded pools.

Ballooning

Not to be left out, Healdsburg has its own balloon outfit ready to show you the serenity of floating over the vineyards. **Up and Away** (707/836-0171, www.up-away.com, $235) meets at **The Shed** (25 North St., 707/431-7433, http://healdsburgshed.com, 8am-9pm Wed.-Mon.) in downtown Healdsburg. From there, you'll be ferried to the launch site and then lofted into the air above the Russian River and Alexander Valleys. Following your flight, you'll be brought back to The Shed for a gourmet champagne breakfast. Tack on a bike tour of local breweries for an additional $113.

Golf

Touting itself as a Wine Country golf course, the **Tayman Park Golf Course** (927 S. Fitch Mountain Rd., 707/433-4275, www. taymanparkgolfcourse.com) is actually in a Healdsburg residential area, a five-minute drive from downtown, but it does have some nice views west toward Dry Creek and the Russian River Valley. It's a 9-hole course that can also be played as an 18-hole par-68 course. Greens fees are $19-22 for 9 holes, depending on the time of the week, and $25-29 for 18 holes. Golf-cart rental starts at $8.

Cooking Classes

Spend some time in the kitchen at **Relish Culinary Adventures** (14 Matheson St., 707/431-9999 or 877/759-1004, http://relishculinary.com). A block off the plaza, this mom-and-pop culinary school offers hands-on classes in its sleek new demonstration kitchen that are both intimate and entertaining. Learn how to make handmade pasta, market-fresh pizzas, mushroom tarts, and fresh ricotta. Classes cost $98-110 and come with a glass of wine.

FOOD

Healdsburg is blessed with a number of great restaurants, from edgy fine dining California cuisine to farm-to-food truck fare along the Russian River. Its real strength lies in the number and diversity of mid-range restaurants that are casual, affordable, and excellent. Despite the breezy atmosphere of Healdsburg's culinary scene, dinner reservations are a good idea, especially in summer.

California Cuisine

The high-ceilinged, concrete, wood, and glass dining room of the H2Hotel's **Spoonbar** (219 Healdsburg Ave., 707/433-7222, http://spoonbar.com, 5pm-9pm Mon.-Thurs., 3pm-9:30pm Fri.-Sat., 3pm-9pm Sun., $23-32), which opens out to bustling Healdsburg Avenue, feels slightly cafeteria-like, but what comes out of the kitchen is a far cry from a high school lunch tray. Instead, servers carry out plates of beef tartare, crab and scallop pasta, and beet risotto. Matching the sophisticated entrées are snacks such as chicken cracklings and ahi poke; a wine list that

Barndiva

After six years of being at the helm of Dry Creek Kitchen, Dustin Valette has opened his own restaurant in the space of the beloved Zin Restaurant. **Valette** (344 Center St., 707/473-0946, www.valettehealdsburg. com, 5:30pm-9pm daily, $25-37) serves farm-to-table food that is crisp and original (think cocoa nib-crusted duck served with pickled green peaches) in a space that is both rustic and elegant, cozy and modern. But the stars here are the house-made charcuterie and the wine list, which has earned a *Wine Spectator* award for excellence.

Down Center Street, the big wood barn housing **Barndiva** (231 Center St., 707/431-0100, www.barndiva.com, lunch noon-2:30pm Wed.-Sat., dinner 5:30pm-9pm Wed.-Thurs. and Sun., 5:30pm-10pm Fri.-Sat., brunch 11am-2pm Sun., $27-35) looks very Wine Country from the outside, but inside the vibe is more Manhattan. As at the best Wine Country restaurants, the food is French inspired but aims to reflect the *terroir* of the place. Ingredients are for the most part locally sourced and made into such specialties as caramelized day boat scallops, bacon-wrapped pork tenderloin, and braised and roasted rabbit. The wine list is likewise largely local, with the occasional French and Italian vintages thrown in. Keeping up with the times (and its Manhattan vibe), Barndiva also has an impressive cocktail menu that in the parlance of the day is "retro-fresh."

If you want a Victorian setting for dinner, there is probably no better option than the restaurant at **Madrona Manor** (1001 Westside Rd., 707/433-4321, www.madronamanor.com, 6pm-9pm Wed.-Sun.) just outside Healdsburg. Eating here is as much about the sumptuous five-room Victorian setting and candlelit table decorations as the food, though the very expensive and stylish modern cuisine gets rave reviews and has earned a Michelin star every year since 2008. You can pick between two nine-course prix fixe menus: the Grande Dame ($165) or the vegetarian A Walk Thru the Garden ($155). Wine pairing is an extra $120, and service is included in the price. For

ranges from local to European; and a artisanal cocktail menu that includes fun-loving concoctions such as Remember the Maine (rye whiskey and absinthe), Shark Week (cocoa-infused bourbon and walnut liquor), and the Burning Shrub (tequila, jalapeño, and grapefruit).

Dry Creek Kitchen (317 Healdsburg Ave., 707/431-0330, http://drycreekkitchen. com, 5:30pm-9:30pm Sun.-Thurs., 5:30pm-10pm Fri.-Sat., $29-39) is located in the H2Hotel's sister property, Hotel Healdsburg. Just as the hotel is elevated in charm and luxury, the Dry Creek Kitchen has been a California cuisine mainstay since 2001. Today, unpretentious and seasonal fare is served on white linen both inside the smart dining room and on the alfresco sidewalk patio overlooking the square. The focaccia served in its cast-iron pan that arrives before the appetizers and the modestly priced tasting (five courses, $79) and prix fixe (Mon.-Thurs., three courses, $36) menus endear this California eatery to diners.

something less ornate, the restaurant has a shorter tasting menu (three courses, $65) and an à la carte menu that ranges from $5 snacks to $52 wagyu steak available in the lounge.

The epicurean catchall in Healdsburg is ★ **The Shed** (25 North St., 707/431-7433, http://healdsburgshed.com, 8am-9pm Wed.-Mon., $5-28), perhaps the most glamorous shed you've ever seen. Inside this bright and airy understatement, you'll find a sit-down restaurant, a take-out counter, deli cases, a coffee bar, a fermentation bar serving a variety of kombucha, plus crockery, cookbooks, and wine. The chic country vibe encapsulates Healdsburg's aspirations of the modern landed gentry. Whether you take a seat at the restaurant or the communal tables outside, you can practically see the fields from which the beautiful food is sourced. For a filling and economic option, check out the daily bruschetta special: a slice of artisanal sourdough topped with fresh veggies, cheese, and local olive oil.

American

If you are craving a burger, then the place to go is the spacious **Healdsburg Bar & Grill** (245 Healdsburg Ave., 707/433-3333, www.healdsburgbarandgrill.com, 11am-9pm Mon.-Fri., 9am-9pm Sat.-Sun, $10-23), with plenty of seating in its saloon-style interior and outside on its shady patio. As its name and the giant outdoor barbecues suggest, plenty of big hunks of char-grilled meat form the basis of the classic pub menu. There's a half-decent wine list and a wide variety of carefully crafted cocktails.

There's more pub-style dining and food at the **Bear Republic Brewing Company** (345 Healdsburg Ave., 707/433-2337, www.bearrepublic.com, 11:30am-9pm Sun.-Thurs., 11am-11pm Fri.-Sat. $9-18), right behind the Hotel Healdsburg. The microbrews are the main attraction, however, and can be enjoyed right in the shadow of stainless steel brewing tanks on the patio outside. A plentiful kids menu makes this a great option for families who might need it most.

Italian

While its antipasti dishes like grilled calamari and Venetian-style sardines won't necessarily win awards for inventiveness, the unpretentious ★ **Scopa** (109A Plaza St., 707/433-5282, www.scopahealdsburg.com, 5:30pm-10pm Mon.-Sat., $16-22) has won over locals for its perfect execution, intimate yet energetic vibe, and very reasonable prices. Being so popular makes securing one of the tables wedged into the long, narrow, space a challenge, so consider eating at the small bar instead. If you're in town midweek, make sure to book a reservation for Wine Maker Wednesdays, when a local winemaker works the floor pouring glasses and selling bottles of his or her favorite vintages. On these days in particular, the restaurant fills up with local industry types, making for a fun, wine-filled night out.

If you can't get a table at Scopa, head around the corner to its sister restaurant, the even more casual **Campo Fina** (330 Healdsburg Ave., 707395-4640, www.campofina.com, 11:30am-10pm daily, $15-23). You'll find everything from oysters on the half shell to antipasti plates to panini to main courses like breaded pork loin. Outside, the semi-covered patio has plenty of tables, plus bocce ball courts and the wood oven, from which come some of the best thin crust pizzas in the Bay Area. Thankfully, the full bar keeps patrons' thirst quenched, and the plentiful snack menu holds the munchies at bay.

Mexican

At ★ **Mateo's Cocina Latina** (214 Healdsburg Ave., 707/433-1520, www.mateoscocinalatina.com, 11:30am-9pm Wed.-Mon., $15-33) the flavors of the Yucatán are served surrounded by white plaster walls, colorful textiles, and wood furniture, all of which echoes California's own Latin history. It is a pleasant reprieve from Wine Country haute style, but the menu will no doubt impress. Order several of the finger food tacones or save yourself for the *Cochinita Pibil,* a slow-roasted suckling pig that is the restaurant's signature dish. To wash down the spice there is a well-balanced drink menu of a dozen microbrews, local wines, and a whole host of tequila-inspired cocktails. True aficionados will swoon over the range of tequilas, reserve anejo tequilas, and mescals available.

Seafood

The biggest problem with **Willi's Seafood and Raw Bar** (403 Healdsburg Ave., 707/433-9191, www.starkrestaurants.com, 11:30am-9pm Sun.-Thurs., 11:30am-10pm Fri.-Sat., small plates $9-15) is that there are just too many tasty dishes to choose from. Thankfully, all are small plates and hover around the $10 mark. Pick from oysters on the half shell, ceviches and crudos, steamers and skewers, and intricately executed small plates that incorporate local produce, fresh seafood, and bright international flavors. Like its beloved sister restaurant, Willi's Wine Bar in Santa Rosa, it is extremely popular and often necessitates reservations, particularly for large groups (which may be the best way to dine here).

Bakeries and Cafes

For an independent cup of coffee in Healdsburg, **Flying Goat Coffee** (324 Center St., 707/433-3599, www.flyinggoatcoffee.com, 7am-7pm daily) sits conveniently opposite the square and pours strong cups of small-batch roasted coffee. Add some pastries and European flair by making a stop at the **Costeaux French Bakery & Café** (417 Healdsburg Ave., 707/433-1913, www.costeaux.com, 7am-4pm Mon.-Thurs., 7am-5pm Fri.-Sat., 7am-1pm Sun., $12-16). It sells the usual crusty bread and other bakery fare together with some tasty breakfasts and deli lunches that can be enjoyed on the big patio next to the sidewalk. Likewise, filling breakfasts and decadent pastries are the specialty of the **Downtown Bakery & Creamery** (308A Center St., 707/431-2719, www.downtownbakery.net, 6am-5:30pm Mon.-Fri., 7:30am-5pm Sat., 7am-4pm Sun., $7-10), on the south side of the plaza.

Casual Dining

During the summer, stake out a riverfront table at ★ **Black Piglet** (52 Front St., www.zazurestaurant.com, 11:30am-3:30pm daily May-Oct., $12), the Healdsburg outpost of the popular farm-to-table restaurant zazu in Sebastopol. Here, the food truck specializes in pork sandwiches, including an over-the-top BLT, and pulled pork and Black Pig (the heritage pig started by zazu owners) salami sandwiches. Vegetarians can also find something they might like with the grilled fontina sandwich that comes with apple cider slaw. Fragrant gardens, bocce ball courts, and wines by the glass by the Davis Family Vineyards, which also shares the waterfront, make eating here a full afternoon activity.

Another option is ★ **The Wurst** (22 Matheson St., 707/395-0214, www.wurstrestaurant.com, 11am-9pm Mon.-Thurs., 11am-9:30pm Fri.-Sat., 11am-8:30pm Sun., $7-9), which serves greasy baskets of sausage sandwiches, burgers, fries, onion rings, plus milk shakes and root beer floats. The variety of house-made sausages is amazing, and the sides and specialty toppings are truly special. While this is pure American fast-food fare, the modern industrial interior and patio remind you that you are in Healdsburg, as does the quality of the food itself. If you're looking for something easy, with kids, on a summer evening, this is your place.

Picnic Supplies

The southwest corner of Healdsburg's plaza is dominated by the bustling **Oakville Grocery** (124 Matheson St., 707/433-3200, 9am-5pm daily). Picnic central, it has just about everything, including wine, needed for either a gourmet alfresco feast or just some simple bread and cheese. If your provisions look too tasty to take on the road, grab a shaded table out front on the large patio, although on busy weekend days they can be hard to come by. **The Shed** (25 North St., 707/431-7433, http://healdsburgshed.com, 8am-9pm Wed.-Mon., $5-28), on the other side of the plaza, has coffee, kombucha, and boutique sodas, plus cheese, deli sandwiches, and full box lunches.

When getting your morning pastries, don't forget the sandwiches and bread available at the **Costeaux French Bakery & Café** (417 Healdsburg Ave., 707/433-1913, www.costeaux.com, 7am-4pm Mon.-Thurs., 7am-5pm Fri.-Sat., 7am-1pm Sun.) and at the **Downtown Bakery & Creamery** (308A Center St., 707/431-2719, www.downtownbakery.net, 6am-5:30pm Mon.-Fri., 7:30am-5pm Sat., 7am-4pm Sun.).

Farmers Markets

If you're after something really fresh, the **Healdsburg Farmers Market** (www.healdsburgfarmersmarket.org) is held 9am-noon Saturday mornings May-November in the parking lot of the **Plaza Park** (North St. and Vine St.), one block west of the plaza itself. Those in the know say it's one of the best farmers markets in this part of Sonoma. On Wednesday afternoons, 3pm-6pm June-October, the market sets up on North Street between Grove and Foss.

ACCOMMODATIONS

Despite its size and the abundance of shopping, tasting rooms, and restaurants, Healdsburg has relatively few reasonable lodging options. Most tend to be pricey B&Bs, and the two larger hotels come with a hefty price tag. Cheaper and a greater diversity of lodging options are available to the north in the Alexander Valley and south in the Russian River Valley, but the town of Healdsburg itself seems to work hard to retain its sense of exclusivity.

Under $150

Few options exist for those on a budget other than chain hotels and motels. One of the better discount options is the **Dry Creek Inn** (198 Dry Creek Rd., 707/433-0300, www.drycreekinn.com, $109-150), a Best Western property less than one mile from the plaza but perilously close to the freeway at the Dry Creek Road exit. Amenities that include free wireless Internet access, a large pool area, and a complimentary hot breakfast make the stay a little more bearable.

$150-250

This could be classified as the Victorian frills price category, into which fall the many small family-owned inns and B&Bs in often historic houses. There might be some inflexibilities inherent to such small establishments (check whether smoking, pets, or children are allowed, and ask about the sometimes-strict cancellation policies), but the advantage is that the owners usually know the area like the backs of their hands and can offer great local insights and, of course, a great breakfast.

One of the relative bargains in a crowded field of frilly B&Bs is the **Camellia Inn** (211 North St., 707/433-8182 or 800/727-8182, www.camelliainn.com, $139-269). Flowers abound on the walls and fabrics inside the elegant 1869 house and in the gardens, which contain more than 50 varieties of camellia, some planted by renowned horticulturist Luther Burbank, who was a friend of the original owners. Unusual for a B&B, there is a small swimming pool, as well as massages in the Sun Room ($95-185) by the resident masseuse. Four of the nine guest rooms have gas fireplaces, and all but one have in-room bathrooms. The aptly named budget room ($139-159) has a private bathroom, but it is across the hall.

The ★ **Haydon Street Inn** (321 Haydon St., 707/433-5228, www.haydon.com, $205-450) sits on a quiet residential street about a 10-minute walk from the plaza. Built in 1912, the Queen Anne-style house is perfectly maintained with original detailing, quaint antiques, and period flourishes. Each of the nine rooms is individually decorated, and all have private baths, with the exception of the Plum Room, whose bathroom is across the hall. One of the owners, John Harasty, was an executive chef by trade, so expect a sumptuous three-course breakfast and wonderful hors d'oeuvres (maybe even a pizza or two made from the wood-fired oven out back) at the inn's nightly wine hour.

The town of Healdsburg might have a surplus of historic Victorian houses, but the ★ **Madrona Manor** (1001 Westside Rd., 707/433-4231, www.madronamanor.com, $235-495), just outside the town at the southern end of the Dry Creek Valley appellation, puts them all in the shade. This enormous pile of Victorian opulence is the centerpiece of an eight-acre hilltop estate dating from the 1880s and is on the National Register of Historic Places.

Spread among five buildings, the elegant 21 rooms and suites contain plenty of genuine and reproduction antiques as well as most amenities, except for televisions. Here, entertainment comes in the form of watching the fire burn in your own private fireplace or seeing the sun set from your private deck. Room rates are not as high as the opulence suggests, with the cheapest rooms located in the Carriage House and Manor House. If the romantic setting, landscaped grounds, and swimming pool aren't enough to keep you from ever leaving during your stay, then the manor's renowned restaurant might be. It serves the sumptuous breakfast included in the rate and a stylish, though pricey, dinner (on the big porch in the summer) with an outstanding wine list that leans heavily on the local appellations.

Over $250

Jumping to the next price bracket is the nine-room **Calderwood Inn** (25 W. Grant St., 707/395-0929 or 800/600-5444, www.calderwoodinn.com, $264-399), another standout in the crowded Victorian B&B scene. The Queen Anne Victorian boasts gardens that were laid out by famed horticulturalist Luther Burbank and has a beautifully (and tastefully) restored interior, right down to the reproduction Victorian wallpaper. The spacious rooms all have garden views and private bathrooms. Be advised, no children under 18 are allowed.

At this price range, Victorian frills start to yield to more contemporary style, nowhere more so than at the **Hotel Healdsburg** (25 Matheson St., 800/431-2800, www.hotelhealdsburg.com, $300-599) on the plaza. Neutral tones, clean lines, and white but plush linens dominate the aesthetic of each room, whether you get the "economy" Sonoma King or the luxurious 800-square-foot Plaza Suite. All guests have access to the tranquil outdoor pool and small fitness room, while the minimally named **The Spa** offers a wide range of spa treatments and massages for $125 and up. Downstairs is the pricey and equally contemporary restaurant, the **Dry Creek Kitchen** (317 Healdsburg Ave., 707/431-0330, http://drycreekkitchen.com, 5:30pm-9:30pm Sun.-Thurs., 5:30pm-10pm Fri.-Sat., $29-39).

A similar modern aesthetic at a slightly lower price is offered by the hotel's sister property just down the road, the **H2Hotel** (219 Healdsburg Ave., 707/431-2202, www.h2hotel.com, $215-299). As seems to be the norm for trendy new hotels, the green credentials of the sleek building are impeccable, from the undulating grass-covered "living" roof to the solar heating and water collection system and right down to the furniture in each room, made from reclaimed wood or sustainable bamboo. Still, it is hard to know what to make of the hotel's style with its rather institutional exterior dressed up with arty balconies for all 36 rooms. There is an impressive list of luxury features, from high-definition TVs to custom organic bathroom amenities. Complimentary bike rentals, a fireside lounge and bar, and the downstairs restaurant, **Spoonbar** (219 Healdsburg Ave., 707/433-7222, http://spoonbar.com, 5pm-9pm Mon.-Thurs., 3pm-9:30pm Fri.-Sat., 3pm-9pm Sun., $23-32)—a destination in itself—all add to the package.

Slightly more reasonable though slightly less contemporary is the **Healdsburg Inn** (112 Matheson St., 800/431-8663, www.healdsburginn.com, $295-450). The inn is part of the Four Sisters hotel chain, so comfort and an elevated level of amenities are guaranteed. All rooms have bay windows or balconies, claw-foot or jetted spa bathtubs, and simple modern decor that blends with the original features of the Victorian building to create a sort of contemporary-lite character. Afternoon cookies and wine are usually on offer, and the inn will also lend you bikes, although being right on the plaza you might not need them.

Even more luxury, tranquility, and contemporary style can be found at the even more expensive and effortlessly hip ★ DuChamp Hotel (421 Foss St., 707/431-1300 or 800/431-9341, www.duchamphotel.com, $375-425). A short walk from the plaza, this exclusive compound offers only six pool- and creek-side villas. There's every luxury amenity you can imagine and a few you can't, such as a 50-foot lap pool, private terraces, and its private-label champagne (made by Iron Horse Vineyards). Private tastings can also be arranged at the nearby DuChamp Estate Winery (280 Chiquita Rd., 707/570-7774, www.duchamp-winery.com, by appointment, tasting $10), which makes only syrah.

At Honor Mansion (891 Grove St., 707/433-4277 or 800/554-4667, www.honor-mansion.com, $450-605) you'll probably feel that you are getting your money's worth. Each of the 13 guest rooms and suites has been furnished and decorated with exquisite attention to even the smallest details, including private baths stocked with high-end toiletries. Many also have fireplaces and private patios, and naturally, all guest rooms come with a full gourmet breakfast each morning. The Honor Mansion also has a lap pool, a tennis court, a croquet lawn, a bocce pit, a putting area, and outdoor professional massage service.

INFORMATION AND SERVICES

As befitting such a desirable destination, the Healdsburg Chamber of Commerce and Visitors Bureau (217 Healdsburg Ave., 707/433-6935, www.healdsburg.com, 10am-4pm Mon.-Fri., 10am-3pm Sat.-Sun.) is centrally located, just off U.S. 101 when you come into town on Healdsburg Avenue. The friendly staff will be happy to load you up with maps, brochures, and helpful tips.

For a bit of local flavor, the *Healdsburg Tribune* (www.sonomawest.com) is published every Thursday. And for any aches and pains, the Healdsburg District Hospital (1375 University Ave., 707/431-6300) has a 24-hour emergency room. But if all you want to do is grab some cash, there is a Bank of America (502 Healdsburg Avenue) and a Wells Fargo (999 Vine Street).

GETTING THERE AND AROUND

Healdsburg is an easy destination as it sits on U.S. 101, 14 miles north of Santa Rosa. To reach downtown Healdsburg, take exit 503 (Central Healdsburg exit). From Guerneville just continue east on River Road. You'll pass through Forestville and Fulton before hitting 101, where you will turn north. If you're coming from Calistoga, continue north on Highway 128 for 17.4 miles. At Jimtown it will intersect with Alexander Valley Road, upon which you head straight. After 3.3 miles, you'll turn left onto Healdsburg Avenue, which will take you into the heart of Healdsburg. Once you are in town, Healdsburg is fairly easy to navigate, although finding parking is not always. Parking around the plaza is limited to three hours, but due to the increased congestion in town, Healdsburg has been considering installing parking downtown.

To avoid parking headaches, Healdsburg is great to navigate by bike. Many hotels now offer loaner bikes, but they can also be rented at Wine Country Bikes (61 Front St., 707/473-0610, www.winecountrybikes.com, 9am-5pm daily). Road bikes, tandem bikes, and hybrids are available for $39-145 per day. Rentals can also be found at the Quonset hut in downtown Healdsburg that houses Spoke Folk Cyclery (201 Center St., 707/433-7171, www.spokefolk.com, 10am-6pm Mon.-Fri., 10am-5pm Sat.-Sun.), where you can rent a bike for $60 per day.

Dry Creek Valley

This compact valley is perhaps one of the easiest parts of northern Sonoma to visit in a day and certainly one of the easiest to get around by car or bike.

The Dry Creek Valley begins right after Healdsburg and runs north to the huge Lake Sonoma Recreation Area, which offers some of the best outdoor recreation opportunities in Sonoma County. Between Healdsburg and the lake, there are vineyards, barns, and small wineries full of charm, many run by eccentric characters.

Although the wine industry got an early start here when French and later Italian immigrants planted grapes in the late 1800s, Prohibition killed everything off, and for much of the 20th century the valley was full of plum and pear orchards. It was not until the early 1970s that grape growing started to pick up again, and the 7,000 acres of prune orchards that once filled the valley with their bounty shriveling in the hot sun are now long gone.

During that agricultural transition, little else apparently changed in the valley, and the only development seems to have been winery related. Just two main roads run up the valley, on either side of Dry Creek itself: West Dry Creek Road and the original Dry Creek Road, which eventually becomes Skaggs Springs Road and heads off over the coastal hills to the ocean. Apart from a couple of roads traversing the valley and cutting through the eastern hills to the freeway and Alexander Valley beyond, that's about it.

Development did significantly change one thing: the valley's eponymous creek. Dry Creek used to dry up to nothing more than a few puddles by the end of the summer, like the many smaller creeks running down the valley sides still do today. Since the dam that created Lake Sonoma was completed in the 1980s, however, Dry Creek has become wet year-round.

The Wines

Dry Creek is perhaps best known for its zinfandels, which can sometimes take on an overbearing, jammy style in the hotter parts of the valley. But zinfandel vines do not dominate the valley as much as the wine's prevalence might suggest, accounting for only about a quarter of the almost 10,000 acres of vineyards in the **Dry Creek AVA.** That's a big total acreage for such a small and narrow valley, especially when you consider the sprawling Russian River Valley AVA to the south only contains a few thousand more acres.

About 4,000 acres in the Dry Creek Valley are planted with cabernet sauvignon and merlot, particularly on the cooler western hillsides around places like the renowned Bradford Mountain. The hotter valley floor with its richer, alluvial soils grows excellent sauvignon blanc and, increasingly, semillon. Other varietals hint at the valley's French and Italian heritage, with syrah and petite sirah coexisting with small amounts of sangiovese and carignane.

The ideal mix of growing conditions for so many grape varietals results from the two ranges of low mountains that flank the valley—the 1,500-foot coastal hills on the valley's western side and the lower hills on the eastern side that separate it from the Alexander Valley. These hillsides have thousands of acres of benchland and canyons where growers can usually find just the right degree of heat needed for ideal ripening of most grape varietals. The hills also shield the valley from direct influence of the cold coastal air, yet just enough cool air and fog are funneled up from the Russian River Valley to prevent things from getting too hot and sticky, particularly at night.

At the far northern end of the valley, on the hot rocky ridges overlooking Lake Sonoma, is the aptly named **Rockpile AVA,** established in 2002. Don't expect to be visiting wineries

Dry Creek Valley and Alexander Valley

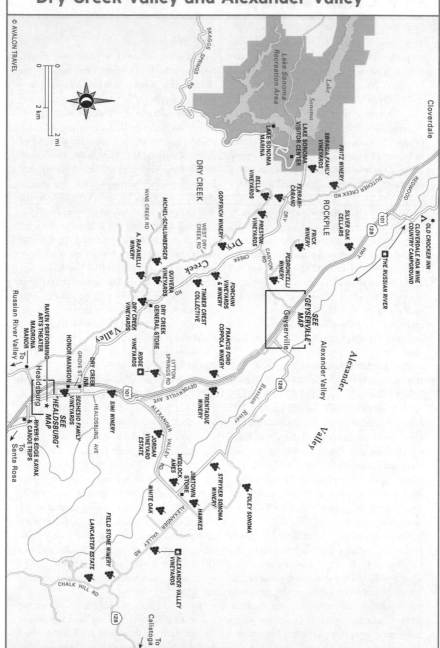

© AVALON TRAVEL

here, though, because there are none. In fact, there are few paved roads. The 200 acres of vineyards are planted predominantly with zinfandel and cabernet, producing intensely flavored wines for the few wineries lucky enough to own land here.

WINERIES

This part of the world offers perhaps the most eclectic mix of wineries, from rustic homespun operations of families that have been making wine for generations to the splashier newcomers reflecting the increasing popularity of the Dry Creek Valley as a major wine destination. Most wineries (even some newcomers) are fairly small, and many still offer some sort of free tasting, although more are now charging a modest fee for a basic tasting, usually $10. Nearly all the wineries also have some sort of outdoor space for picnics.

★ RIDGE VINEYARDS

To experience the world of Dry Creek zins, make a stop at **Ridge Vineyards** (650 Lytton Springs Rd., Healdsburg, 707/433-7721, www.ridgewine.com, 11am-4pm Mon.-Thurs., 11am-5pm Fri.-Sun., tasting $5-20), which makes over a dozen different versions sourced

from vineyards as far south as Paso Robles and as far north as Geyserville. Ridge is also best known for its cabernet sauvignons, particularly those sourced from its Monte Bello vineyards in Santa Cruz. In 1976, Ridge's Monte Bello cabernet placed fifth out of 10 in the notorious Judgment of Paris. Forty years later in the anniversary competition it placed first.

Ridge's mid-century origins (the winery was founded in 1962) come through in its style and commitment to sustainability, which includes 400 rooftop solar panels that supply most of the winery's power. The green ethos extends to the guest experience with the tasting room, contemporary in style and constructed out of recycled materials, and the full use of expansive canopied decks. Here you taste wines while overlooking the vineyards, smelling the earth, and feeling the breeze. Tasting is surprisingly affordable. For $5 you'll get a flight of five single-vineyard wines (three zinfandel and one cabernet). The estate vineyard flight costs $10, and for an additional $10, your pourer will add a taste of Monte Bello cabernet, which runs $185 a bottle. If you can't get enough of the Monte Bello, opt for the vertical tasting of three vintages for $60. To learn more about Ridge, book a

the view at Ridge Vineyards

tour and tasting (11am and 2pm daily by appointment, $30).

DRY CREEK VINEYARD

Built in 1973 not far from Dry Creek itself, this ivy-clad winery was the first to be built in the valley since the repeal of Prohibition. Although it is by no means the oldest in the valley and far more commercial than most of its neighbors, **Dry Creek Vineyard** (3770 Lambert Bridge Rd., Healdsburg, 707/433-1000 or 800/864-9463, www.drycreekvineyard.com, 10:30am-5pm daily, tasting $15) has, without a doubt, played an important role in transforming the valley from prune orchards to vineyards. What it lacks in homey charm it makes up for by producing some of the best white wines in the valley, including its flagship, the fumé blanc and the estate chenin blanc. Not be left out, the heritage clone and old vine zinfandels are well worth the visit. Tours are available (11am and 2pm Mon.-Fri., $30 by appointment) as is a Flight Through Dry Creek Valley (11am, 1pm, and 3pm Sat.-Sun., $30 by appointment), which pours and discusses the unique qualities of wine from the Dry Creek Valley. The picnic tables surrounded by lawn, flower gardens, and shading trees beg for a picnic, so grab a bottle of the bargain-priced Regatta white blend or chenin blanc and relax while planning the rest of your day.

TIMBER CREST COLLECTIVE

The distinctive red barn up the hill next to Dry Creek Road marks the location of a collective winemaking facility shared by some of the valley's best small wineries, **Timber Crest Farms** (4791 Dry Creek Rd., Healdsburg, www.timbercrest.com). The driveway is marked by a well-populated signpost next to the road. Four wineries make wines and have modest tasting rooms here—in some cases just a counter propped on barrels. Tasting is more about the wine and the unpretentious vibe than the surroundings. Indeed, the wineries are small enough that it's likely to be the winemakers themselves doing the pouring.

The heart of the collective is **Family Wineries** (707/433-0100 or 888/433-6555, http://familywines.com, 10:30am-4:30pm daily Mar.-Dec., 10:30am-4:30pm Thurs.-Mon., Jan.-Feb., tasting $10), itself a collective of six small family-owned and operated wineries. Inside the stand-alone tasting room at the top of the drive, the collective is a cross section of northern Sonoma wineries that range from a five-generation family affair centered in Geyserville to a relatively recent upstart that makes wine in an Oakland warehouse from Dry Creek grapes. This variety is reflected in the more than 30 varietals and blends available to taste. The tasting room also has an eclectic general store where you can buy specialty condiments, fine linens, and Wine Country knickknacks.

Nearby, **Amphora Winery** (707/431-7767, www.amphorawines.com, 11am-4:30pm, tasting $10) makes nearly 20 different varietals, including many unusual Italian varietals such as teroldego, aglianico, and Alicante bouschet as well the usual zinfandel, cabernet, malbec, and pinot noir. Pottery is the owner's other passion, in particular the creation of the amphorae that inspired the winery's name and appear on the wine labels.

Another longtime Dry Creek producer, **Peterson Winery** (707/431-7568, www.petersonwinery.com, tasting 11am-4:30pm daily, tasting $10) makes small lots of about a dozen different wines. There are several very good and well-priced zinfandels, but it is some of the more unusual (and unusually named) blends that stand out here, including a cheap and cheerful Rhône blend called Zero Manipulation. You also can't go wrong with any of the single-vineyard wines (cabernet, syrah, and zinfandel) sourced from Fred Peterson's Bradford Mountain vineyard in the southwest corner of the valley.

Perched above the valley, **Papapietro Perry Winery** (707/433-0422, www.papapietro-perry.com, 11am-4:30pm daily, tasting $15) pours only pinot noirs and zinfandels. Sourced from Dry Creek, Russian River, and Anderson Valley vineyards, the wines here have earned quite a reputation. Although not all the vineyard- and clone-specific pinots are likely to be available to taste, there will still be a dizzying array of wines for any pinot or zin lover to try.

At the tasting bar of **Kokomo Winery** (707/433-0200, www.kokomowines.com, 11am-4:30pm daily, tasting $10), you can choose five pours from the current release wines, which are likely to include Dry Creek and Russian River sauvignon blanc, chardonnay, pinot noir, zinfandel, and a cabernet. Kokomo also offers wine and cheese pairing in the barrel room for $25.

FORCHINI VINEYARDS & WINERY

The Forchini family has been growing grapes in the Dry Creek and Russian River Valleys since the 1970s but only started making wines in the mid-1990s, and today makes only 3,000 cases of wine each year. As a result, the **Forchini Vineyards & Winery** (5141 Dry Creek Rd., Healdsburg, 707/431-8886, www. forchini.com, 11am-4:30pm Fri.-Mon., by appointment Tues.-Thurs., tasting $10) has a charming homey character that makes you feel like a privileged guest.

The small tasting room is in the main house and features a sunny deck next to the cabernet vines lining the driveway. The portfolio includes a well-balanced Dry Creek cabernet sauvignon; the zinfandel, which is a typically intense Dry Creek style; and, representing the Russian River vineyards, a big, rich chardonnay and a more reserved pinot noir. The cheap and cheerful Papa Nonno blend, made in the style of an easy-drinking Tuscan table wine, is primarily zinfandel and makes a great picnic wine.

PEDRONCELLI WINERY

It no longer sells jug wines like it did up to the 1950s, but **Pedroncelli Winery** (1220 Canyon Rd., Geyserville, 707/857-3531 or 800/836-3894, www.pedroncelli.com, 10am-4:30pm daily, tasting $5) still produces some very approachable wines at the cluster of buildings on Canyon Road. None of the wines

sell for more than $25 and most are under $15, making this a good place to buy a picnic wine or stock up with some everyday drinkers.

The winery has been a family affair since John Pedroncelli bought the run-down former Canota winery and 90 acres of vineyards in 1927. Today the winery makes sauvignon blanc, chardonnay, zinfandel, sangiovese, petite sirah, and cabernet sauvignon, all in the style of robust, easy-drinking table wines. Zinfandel is something of a specialty here, and the portfolio includes the Mother Clone zin, sourced from clones of Victorian-era vines. Nearly all the wines are sourced from Dry Creek Valley vineyards with one notable exception—a Russian River Valley pinot noir that's pretty good for its modest price.

FRICK WINERY

Proceeds from the sale of a '57 Chevy helped get Bill Frick started in the wine business in 1976 near Santa Cruz. He moved to this small hillside winery at the end of sleepy Walling Road at the far northern end of Dry Creek Valley in the late 1980s.

The six acres of estate vineyards at **Frick Winery** (23072 Walling Rd., off Canyon Rd. or Dutcher Creek Rd., Geyserville, 707/857-1980, www.frickwinery.com, noon-4:30pm Fri.-Sun., weekends only in winter, free tasting) are mainly planted to Rhône varietals, and Bill is perhaps Dry Creek's most ardent Rhône Ranger. The small production includes syrah, viognier, cinsault, and C-Squared, which is a blend of cinsault and carignane. More unusual still is the grenache blanc, a white version of this varietal that is rarely seen in California. Fittingly, the cottage tasting room is small, cozy, and doesn't accommodate large groups, meaning you will get a fun low-key tasting of some great French-style wines.

FERRARI-CARANO VINEYARDS AND WINERY

No other Dry Creek winery could be further from the down-home and generations-old Frick and Pedroncelli than the

Ferrari-Carano Vineyards and Winery (8761 Dry Creek Rd., Healdsburg, 707/433-6700 or 800/831-0381, www.ferraricarano. com, 10am-5pm daily, tasting $10-15) owned by the Carano family, whose sister businesses include the Eldorado Hotel and Casino in Reno and the luxury **Vintners Inn** in Santa Rosa. The pink Italianate mansion known as Villa Fiore (which translates to House of Flowers, a fitting name when the spring bulbs are in full bloom) and the acres of gardens are an island of manicured extravagance in the rustic charm of Dry Creek Valley.

Equally grandiose is the huge vaulted cellar that can house up to 1,500 barrels of aging wine down the grand stairs from the main tasting room. Here you can select from a whole raft of highly rated single-vineyard chardonnays and a wide range of reds, from single varietals to blends including Bordeaux-style blends for a tasting fee of $25. A sumptuous den that has been routinely voted best tasting room by local publications, the Enoteca Lounge is a respite from the bustling, Mediterranean-style main tasting room and gift shop and the somewhat unexceptional wines poured there.

SBRAGIA FAMILY VINEYARDS

Sbragia Family Vineyards (9990 Dry Creek Rd., Geyserville, 707/473-2992, www.sbragia. com, 10:30am-5pm daily, tasting $20) makes the most of its southern exposure, offering sweeping views of the Alexander Valley below. Thankfully, the wines are as beautiful as the scenery.

While very much a family operation, the winery has a serious pedigree. Ed Sbragia spent 32 years at Beringer Vineyards in the Napa Valley, where he earned a reputation for producing some of Napa's greatest cabernets. His skill at creating highly extracted yet elegant wines, together with his connections to some of the best growers in Sonoma and Napa, makes Sbragia one of the best wineries in the valley. All the wines here are single-vineyard

versions from both the family's own vineyards and other growers.

For $20, you can taste both the winery's Dry Creek and Napa Valley wines, including a Dry Creek merlot, a highly rated chardonnay, and a spicy and jammy zinfandel, plus chardonnay from Oakville and cabernet from Mount Veeder in the Napa Valley. The sunlit tasting room opens out onto a large concrete deck overlooking the valley. Take your tasting here with table service ($20) or order a charcuterie plate ($30) to create an impromptu picnic. Plenty of shaded tables dot the property, and while the winery sells some light picnic fare in its tasting room, it does welcome outside food.

FRITZ UNDERGROUND WINERY

Fritz Underground Winery (24691 Dutcher Creek Rd., Cloverdale, 707/894-3389 or 800/418-9463, www.fritzwinery.com, 10:30am-5pm daily, tasting $15-20) bills itself as an "underground winery," but that doesn't stand for some radical politics to match its earthship aesthetic. In fact, the winery owes its name and styling in part to the energy crisis of the late 1970s, when it was built by Jay and Barbara Fritz. The patio and domed tasting room are above two levels of winery workings deep underground, so no pumps, coolers, or air-conditioning are needed, saving power and adding to its modern-day green credentials. If seeing the extent of this subterranean marvel sounds intriguing, make sure you visit Fritz on a weekend and book a tour, which takes you "top to bottom" and often includes a barrel tasting (11am Sat.-Sun., $30).

While the inner workings of the winery occur deep underground, the tasting room has lovely views of the vineyards, with a stone patio for picnicking and tasting just outside. The estate and other Dry Creek Valley vineyards provide grapes for zinfandel, sauvignon blanc, and cabernet. The Russian River wines include chardonnay and pinot noir, both of which have become as highly regarded as some of the Dry Creek wines.

QUIVIRA VINEYARDS

Although the winery is named after a mythical place where Spanish explorers expected to find untold riches in the 1500s, there's nothing fictitious about the qualities of the vineyard-designate zinfandels, the flavorful sauvignon blanc, and the aromatic grenache made by **Quivira Vineyards** (4900 W. Dry Creek Rd., Healdsburg, 707/431-8333, www.quivirawine.com, 10am-4:30pm daily, tasting $10). Quivira was one of the first wineries in Sonoma to have its vineyards certified biodynamic and its power sourced from its vast array of solar panels. You can learn more about the winery's commitment to sustainability on its appointment-only tours offered at 10am and 2pm daily ($25), but the fruit of the grounds can best be enjoyed at the tasting room, which also sells an assortment of estate honeys and preserves, or by grabbing a bottle of sauvignon blanc or rosé and planting yourself at one of its many picnic tables.

MICHEL-SCHLUMBERGER

In a beautiful mission-revival building surrounding a tranquil courtyard, **Michel-Schlumberger** (4155 Wine Creek Rd., Healdsburg, 707/433-7427 or 800/447-3060, www.michelschlumberger.com, 11am-5pm daily, tasting $10-20) is tucked away up Wine Creek Canyon and surrounded by 100 acres of undulating benchland vineyards that create a multitude of different growing conditions, from the cool heights of nearby Bradford Mountain down to the hotter canyon floor.

Unusual for the Dry Creek Valley, there is only one zinfandel in the wine portfolio here, as the cooler hillsides favor cabernet sauvignon, merlot, pinot blanc, and chardonnay. The cabernets, particularly the reserve, are outstanding illustrations that the Dry Creek Valley is good for growing more than just zinfandel. The estate tasting is a flight of five wines in the tasting room, the terra-cotta tile terrace, or in the courtyard alongside the burbling pool. For $25, you can make it a seated tasting paired with a cheese and charcuterie plate, or a more formal food and wine pairing can take the place of lunch (noon and 2pm, Fri.-Sun., $55). Tours of the estate are offered daily at 11am, 1pm, and 3pm, cost $40, and conclude with a seated tasting of the estate-grown wines.

★ PRESTON FARM & WINERY

Located at the tip of the narrow flower-filled West Dry Creek Road, **Preston Farm & Winery** (9282 W. Dry Creek Rd., Healdsburg, 707/433-3372, www.prestonfarmandwinery.com, 11am-4:30pm daily, tasting $5) is the quintessential back-to-the-land fantasy come to life. At this idiosyncratic establishment established in the 1970s, you'll find a farmhouse tasting room pouring organic wines and selling homemade sourdough bread, organic vegetables, farm-fresh eggs, and olive oil that come one way or another from the 125 acres just outside the door.

Not to let down the fantasy, the wines are excellent. The farm grows 13 different varietals including a 100-year-old block of zinfandel plus Rhône and Italian varietals. Don't miss the highly regarded petite sirah, the spicy barbera, and the lovely sauvignon blanc rosé. On Sunday, be sure to step down into the barrel room for a taste of the jug wine, a zinfandel-based blend whose affordability ($36) and drinkability make it ideal for a picnic or casual dinner party.

Along with the wine you can buy some organic vegetables grown on the farm, as well as olive oil and artisan bread from a commercial bakery on-site. The selection of locally produced foods rivals that in some delis and makes this an ideal place to buy everything you need for an impromptu picnic next to the bocce courts outside in the company of the winery cats.

BELLA VINEYARDS

As its name suggests, **Bella Vineyards** (9711 W. Dry Creek Rd., Healdsburg, 866/572-3552, www.bellawinery.com, 11am-4:30pm daily, tasting $10) is one of the prettiest wineries in the area, with a farm-like setting overlooking

Unpack Your Picnic Basket

There is no shortage of tranquil places to have a picnic, from the beaches of the Russian River to the shade of the redwoods at the Armstrong Redwoods State Natural Reserve just north of Guerneville. Or head to one of the many picnic-friendly wineries and pick up a bottle of wine to go with lunch.

- **Thomas George Estates, Guerneville:** This Russian River winery has made its picnic grounds almost as much of a priority as its wines. Grab a bottle of its pinot noir rosé and find a table under a bright red umbrella on the stately open glen or at one of the picnic tables near the bocce ball courts.

- **Rodney Strong Vineyards, Guerneville:** Spread your picnic blanket on the expansive lawn or find a table nearby to go with your Russian River chardonnay.

- **Foppiano Vineyards, Guerneville:** Foppiano has a shaded picnic area overlooking the vineyards and $20 estate wines to go with your provisions. The winery also makes boxed lunches ($20) with 24-hour advance notice.

- **Korbel Champagne Cellars, Guerneville:** Shaded by redwood trees, this free winery has a full delicatessen and affordable booze to fuel any picnic outside on its spacious deck.

- **Armstrong Redwoods State Natural Reserve, Guerneville:** Unpack your picnic at a table beneath a canopy of sky-high redwood trees. Grills and nearby restrooms make it easy to extend your stay.

- **Dry Creek Vineyard, Dry Creek:** This ivy-clad winery has stunning gardens, green lawns, and plenty of shaded tables that beg for a picnic—particularly one paired with the bargain-priced Regatta white blend.

- **Preston Farm & Winery, Dry Creek:** You'll find everything you need for the perfect country picnic at this farm/winery. Homemade sourdough bread, fresh fruit, cheese, and olive oil are all available for purchase, along with the excellent sauvignon blanc rosé and a very drinkable jug wine.

- **Fritz Underground Winery, Dry Creek:** While the winery may be underground, the shaded picnic tables are out on the stone patio overlooking the vineyards in the wilds outside of Dry Creek.

- **Medlock Ames, Healdsburg:** Grab a bottle of sauvignon blanc and head out to the garden for a picnic beneath olive trees near the bocce ball courts. This winery is also dog- and kid-friendly.

the valley. But the pristine caves with vines growing literally right above the entrance add a touch of class to the tasting experience. Tasting wines underneath a vineyard certainly is a cool summer diversion at this hot northern end of the valley.

Adding to the experience, of course, is the wine itself. Bella has been a rising star in the valley and is particularly known as a producer of outstanding single-vineyard zinfandels, the best of which are sourced from old vines in each of Bella's three vineyards, including the robust and complex Lily Hill zinfandel from the vineyard around the winery. The winery also makes a rosé, a grenache, a couple of petite sirahs, and a syrah, all from Sonoma County.

Wineries by Appointment

A. RAFANELLI WINERY

Up a long driveway off West Dry Creek Road, just south of Wine Creek Road, is where the fourth generation of Rafanellis now makes its limited-production wines at the **A.**

Rafanelli Winery (4685 W. Dry Creek Rd., Healdsburg, 707/433-1385, http://arafanelliwinery.com, daily, complimentary tasting). Intense zinfandel accounts for more than half of the wines made here, and the rest is cabernet and merlot sourced from the hillside vineyards. All the wines have attained an almost cultlike status, so the winery tends to attract those serious about their zins. The views from the vegetable garden next to the old redwood barn are also pretty spectacular, which along with the difficulty getting an appointment only adds to the slightly exclusive atmosphere.

GÖPFRICH ESTATE VINEYARD AND WINERY

There is more than the family's German heritage to the **Göpfrich Estate Vineyard and Winery** (7462 W. Dry Creek Rd., Healdsburg, 707/433-1645, www.gopfrichwinery.com, Fri.-Sat., complimentary tasting). In addition to limited-production cabernet, zinfandel, and syrah wines from the Dry Creek estate, Göpfrich also sells limited quantities of fragrant, late-harvest German white wines including riesling, huxelrebe, and silvaner from its sister winery in the Rheinhessen region of Germany.

Lake Sonoma Recreation Area

There is no mistaking the tip of the Dry Creek Valley when you spy the massive earthen dam on the north end. The Warm Springs Dam completed by the Army Corps of Engineers in 1983 not only made Dry Creek's name obsolete by providing a year-round source of water but also resulted in Lake Sonoma, which became **Lake Sonoma Recreation Area** (3333 Skaggs Springs Rd., 707/431-4533, www.parks.sonoma.net), one of the best regional recreation areas around. The large lake (2,700 surface acres, to be precise) has the region's best bass fishing, in addition to plenty of swimming and boating opportunities, while the 17,000 acres of hot oak-studded hills surrounding it have more than 40 miles of trails for hikers, bikers, and horseback riders. Make the **Milt Brandt Visitor Center** (3333 Skaggs Springs Rd., Geyserville, 707/431-4533, 8:30am-3:30pm Wed.-Sun., hours vary) your first stop upon visiting, where you'll get plenty of information, some basic necessities (water, sunscreen), and learn about the area's ecosystems, as well as about the Pomo Native American Tribe, which lost some of its sacred sites when Lake Sonoma was created.

Preston Farm & Winery has a homey charm.

The main access points to the lake and trails are Stewarts Point Road, just south of the Warm Springs Bridge; Rockpile Road, north of the bridge; and the grassy **Yorty Creek Recreation Area,** at the end of Shady Lane/Hot Springs Road, from Cloverdale. A public boat launch at Warm Springs Bridge lets you launch your own ski or fishing boat for a $3 fee, and the **Lake Sonoma Marina** (707/433-2200, www. lakesonoma.com) off Stewarts Point Road farther west offers boat ($35-100/hour or $210-570/day), kayak ($20-25/hour or $75-85/day), and canoe rentals ($20/hour or $70/day), as well as slip rentals.

A couple of the easier and more accessible hiking trails start at the **South Lake Trailhead** (on Stewarts Point Rd. about 0.5 mile south from its junction with Skaggs Springs Rd., just before the marina turn-off). From there it's a quick jaunt up the hill to the **Overlook,** with great views of the lake. Or take the **South Lake Trail** for a longer hike, ducking in and out of groves of madrone and pine along the way. At about two miles, head right; it's then about 0.75 mile down to the Quicksilver Campground, where you can duck into the lake for a swim, if you came prepared. Alternatively, go left and stay on the South Lake Trail for as long as you want. More trails start at another trailhead across the bridge off Rockpile Road. A trail map is available at the visitors center.

Mountain bikers will have to be content with just one loop on the **Half-a-Canoe Trail,** which starts at the No Name Flat Trailhead, about 1.5 miles north of the bridge on the left. The loop is about 4.5 miles of mostly fire road with a short section of single-track.

Temperatures around the lake regularly top 100°F in the summer, so take plenty of water, whatever you do (the lake water is not drinkable). Other natural hazards include the occasional rattlesnake, disease-carrying ticks, and poison oak. You might be lucky enough to see the odd jackrabbit, a wild pig, or a rare peregrine falcon.

FISHING AND BOATING

The **Congressman Don Clausen Fish Hatchery** (behind the recreation area visitors center) was built to beef up the steelhead, chinook, and coho salmon populations in the Russian River and its tributaries and to mitigate some of the detrimental effects caused by construction of the Warm Springs and nearby Coyote Valley Dams. The main fishing draw on the lake is the healthy stock of largemouth bass, which love the submerged trees that were left in the Dry Creek arm of the lake when it was flooded. The bass record stands at just over 15 pounds, though most reportedly weigh less than 10 pounds. There are also smallmouth bass, catfish, crappies, sunfish, trout, and numerous other species, including some landlocked steelhead.

When the water is clearest, during the summer, sight fishing is possible in the shallower waters close to the shore, as is bank fishing, particularly at the Yorty Creek Recreation Area. The lake is primarily a boat-fishing lake, however, and boats can be rented at the **Lake Sonoma Marina** (707/433-2200, www. lakesonoma.com, $35-100/hour or $210-570/day), just off Stewarts Point Road about 0.5 mile south of Skaggs Springs Road.

There are three places to launch boats on Lake Sonoma—a trailer ramp at the Lake Sonoma Marina ($10 to launch), a big public ramp just across the bridge ($3), and a cartop launch area at Yorty Creek ($3). Check with a ranger for the boating rules. If fishing or high-octane boating doesn't appeal, canoes and kayaks can be rented at the marina ($10-15/hour).

Unless you're fortunate to be camping at one of the hike-in or boat-in campsites, there are not many places with decent shoreline access for swimming on the lake. The only official swimming beach is at the Yorty Creek Recreation Area.

CAMPING

To stay in the Dry Creek Valley you have to camp, so thankfully Lake Sonoma is a tent-camping mecca, especially if you have a boat.

There are nearly 200 sites scattered along its 50 miles of shoreline. For car campers, there's just one developed drive-in campground: **Liberty Glen** (877/444-6777, www.recreation.gov, $25). About a mile across the bridge from the visitors center, it has 95 sites for tents and RVs (no electrical hookups), a dump station, flush toilets, and hot showers.

Around the lake there are more than 100 hike-in or boat-in primitive campsites, most of them on the Warm Springs arm of the lake. The most easily accessible on foot are the **Island View** or **Quicksilver Campgrounds,** though the heat and terrain make the 2.5-mile hikes to them fairly strenuous during the summer months.

Most of the campgrounds are small, with an average of about 10 tent sites. None have drinking water, but all have fire rings and chemical toilets. Apart from the usual wildlife warnings (look out for rattlesnakes, and ticks that carry Lyme disease), visitors should also keep an eye out for feral pigs, descendants of domestic pigs brought by early settlers.

Also worth noting: Some campsites are located on lake areas designated for waterskiing, and the constant drone of powerboats and Jet Skis can spoil an otherwise idyllic scene. More peace and quiet can be found near parts of the lake designated as wake-free zones (marked on the free map available at the visitors center). Quicksilver is the quieter of the two most accessible hike-in campgrounds. Reservations cost $20 during the summer months (877/444-6777, www.recreation.gov). A minimum two-night stay is required on weekends during the summer season, and on holiday weekends the minimum is three nights.

FOOD

Befitting Dry Creek's rustic beauty, the valley's only commercial establishment is the ★ **Dry Creek General Store** (3495 Dry Creek Rd., Healdsburg, 707/433-4171, http://drycreekgeneralstore1881.com, 6:30am-5pm Mon.-Thurs., 6:30am-5:30pm Fri.-Sat., 7am-5pm Sun., $6-13), which has existed in some form or another since the 1880s. Inside the historic general store browse the collection of cookware, tableware, and local gourmet goodies while you wait for your sandwich to be prepared. The deli makes an impressive selection of hot, cold, and grilled sandwiches, along with a full case of salads and hot dishes that straddle comfort Americana and epicurean Wine Country. When your food is finished grab a bottle of vino and find a seat either out front or in the garden. Should you find

The Dry Creek General Store and Dry Creek Bar have been around since the 1880s.

yourself needing a real drink, the **Dry Creek Bar** next door is open daily from 3pm. Grab a beer, sit outside, and watch the wine tasters drive by. Closing time varies and usually depends on how many people are left propping up the bar.

INFORMATION AND SERVICES

You won't find a visitors center in the Dry Creek Valley; instead, swing by the **Healdsburg Chamber of Commerce and Visitors Bureau** (217 Healdsburg Ave., Healdsburg, 707/433-6935, www.healds-burg.com, 10am-4pm Mon.-Fri., 10am-3pm Sat.-Sun.) for tips, maps, and the occasional wine-tasting coupon. More comprehensive information about the wines and the wine-makers of the Dry Creek Valley is available from the **Winegrowers of Dry Creek Valley** (707/433-3031, www.wdcv.com). The association does a sterling job ensuring the area's wineries get national attention and organizes the sell-out Passport to Dry Creek Valley weekend event, a two-day party involving nearly all valley wineries on the last weekend in April.

Any fuel or banking needs should be taken care of in Healdsburg (as there are no banks or gas stations here), and cell phone reception can be unreliable, particularly in the northern part of the valley.

GETTING THERE AND AROUND

The base of Dry Creek is just five miles northwest of downtown Healdsburg across U.S. 101, conveniently connected by Dry Creek Road. Navigating up the valley couldn't be easier. The majority of wineries are on either Dry Creek Road (a fairly fast two-lane road) or West Dry Creek Road (more of a slow-going country lane); they run parallel to each other, straddling the creek.

The relatively quiet roads in the Dry Creek Valley make it a great place to tour by bike. In Healdsburg, **Wine Country Bikes** (61 Front St., Healdsburg, 707/473-0610, www.winecountrybikes.com, 9am-5pm daily) rents bikes ($39-85/day) and offers a casual six-hour tour ($139) of Dry Creek that includes stops at a couple wineries and a gourmet picnic catered by the Oakville Grocery. Rentals also can be found at **Spoke Folk Cyclery** (201 Center St., Healdsburg, 707/433-7171, www.spokefolk.com, 10am-6pm Mon.-Fri., 10am-5pm Sat.-Sun.), where you can rent a bike for $60 per day.

Geyserville and the Alexander Valley

The 20-mile-long Alexander Valley starts southeast of Healdsburg and stretches north to the small town of Cloverdale. In between there is only one town of note: the hamlet of **Geyserville**, which for years has been destined to become the next big Wine Country resort town, only to stubbornly remain its old sleepy self, despite the recent additions of several tasting rooms and two excellent restaurants.

Geyserville wasn't always so quiet. Back in the late 1800s the nearby geysers drew visitors from far and wide, and the resulting influx of money helped build the town's grand Victorian homes. Now the only signs of the area's underground hot water supply are the clouds of steam sometimes visible from the 19 geothermal plants in the hills east of Geyserville (an area known simply as The Geysers). The area is one of the world's largest geothermal energy sources.

The Wines

The **Alexander Valley** is the northernmost appellation in Sonoma and also one of the hottest, despite the fact that the Russian River floodplain is wide enough to allow some of the more persistent fog to creep this far north on summer nights. Summer temperatures in Geyserville can often be 10 degrees higher than in Healdsburg just a few miles south.

With the ripening power of the sun and heat, together with the rich alluvial soils deposited by the Russian River over millions of years, it's relatively easy to guess what style of wine can be made here—big and opulent. Indeed, Alexander Valley cabernets have a softness and suppleness that they attain in few other places. There was good reason why the cabernet specialist Silver Oak Cellars chose this valley in 1993 for its first vineyard and winery outside the Napa Valley. Alexander Valley cabernets are characterized by soft tannins and lush fruit with hints of dark chocolate, making them perhaps the easiest drinking in California, if not necessarily the most complex or long-lived. Other varietals grown here include chardonnay, which ripens easily to make rich and flavorful wines, along with merlot, zinfandel, and increasing quantities of syrah and sangiovese. The appellation expanded in 1990 to include the vineyards creeping up the hillsides, particularly on the eastern side of the valley where the mountains climb to more than 2,500 feet. As growers experiment with the cooler hillside vineyards, subtler styles of wine are being created, different than the blockbusters from the fertile, sun-drenched valley floor.

At the southern end of Alexander Valley, east of Santa Rosa, is the **Chalk Hill** appellation, which derives its name from soils that contain chalk-like volcanic ash, similar to those at the northern end of the Napa Valley. It's directly in the path of the cooler Russian River Valley air and mostly contained within the easternmost part of the Russian River appellation. The few wineries here are perhaps best known for some tangy chardonnays and sauvignon blanc.

Between the Alexander Valley and Calistoga in the Napa Valley sits the **Knights Valley** appellation, a primarily grape-growing region with just a couple of small wineries. The soils are both gravelly and volcanic, and the AVA is completely shielded from the cool ocean air, making it the hottest of Sonoma's appellations and perfect for growing sauvignon blanc and cabernet sauvignon.

WINERIES

With the exception of a couple big Napa-esque wineries, tasting here is a fairly low-key affair. Most of the big wineries are located on Geyserville Avenue, which runs parallel to the freeway between Healdsburg and Geyserville, and on Highway 128, which runs from the Chalk Hill appellation, separating the Napa and Alexander Valleys, up to Geyserville.

SIMI WINERY

Brothers Pietro and Giuseppe Simi came from Tuscany in the 1860s and set themselves up as winemakers and traders in San Francisco before moving to the current site of **Simi Winery** (16275 Healdsburg Ave., Healdsburg, 800/746-4880, www.simiwinery.com, 10am-5pm daily, tasting $10), just north of Healdsburg, in 1881. In its heyday, the winery boasted Sonoma's first public tasting room—a 25,000-gallon redwood tank set up at the side of the road. It was evidently a roaring success, but the current tasting room is a more modern affair inside the historic stone cellar building, which dates from the late 1800s.

The winery is best known for its chardonnay, sourced from the Russian River Valley, and its cabernets, from the Alexander Valley, both of which garner consistently good reviews. Other wines include sauvignon blanc, pinot noir, and merlot sourced from a variety of vineyards in Sonoma County. A flight of five wines is $10, or you can taste à la carte for $3 a glass. Tours followed by a tasting are offered twice daily at 11am and 2pm ($20, reservations recommended).

TRENTADUE

As you walk up to the magnificent Italianate tasting room at **Trentadue** (19170 Geyserville Ave., Geyserville, 707/433-3104, www.trentadue.com, 10am-5pm daily, $5-10)

Geyserville

© AVALON TRAVEL

just off U.S. 101, the first thing you'll notice is the gardens sweeping out toward the vineyards. Many of Trentadue's vintages are made from estate-grown grapes, including Italian varietals in keeping with the Tuscan heritage of the winery's founding family. Inside the high narrow tasting room, a tasting bar pours largely red (sangiovese, pinot noir, merlot, zinfandel, and carignane), plus a cuvee and sauvignon blanc. These wines top out at $30 but generally hover around $20. The stars of the show are unquestionably the ports; Trentadue makes an array of different styles and flavors of the famed fortified dessert wines. The limited-production blended La Storia wines regularly score over 90 points in the press yet start at well under $30. These can be tasted by appointment for $25 in the reserve La Storia Room, accompanied by small bites. To get outside, book a seated tasting of current release wines either under the arbor or out in the courtyard ($20 by appointment), or join the gondola tour offered every

day by appointment and costing $25. This is a particular treat during harvest time.

FRANCIS FORD COPPOLA WINERY

You have to give "Francis," as he is known by all the staff here, credit; he isn't trying to bill the **Francis Ford Coppola Winery** (300 Via Archimedes, Geyserville, 707/857-1471, www. franciscoppolawinery.com, 11am-6pm daily, tasting $18) as something it is not. Called a "Wine Wonderland," the winery has a concierge desk, restaurant, full bar, a gift store selling a surprisingly wide variety of tableware, bocce ball, and a pool, complete with *cabines* to rent for the day and a poolside café. In fact, only the acres of grapevines surrounding the buildings indicate that this is a winery. Even the tasting bar is housed inside a museum of memorabilia of Coppola's different films. Still, the pours are plentiful, and even complimentary for a taste of two less expensive table wines.

It may be easy to deride the winery's theme

park-like atmosphere, but if you have squirrelly kids in tow or simply want to soak in the Alexander Valley rays, it becomes easier to get on board with Francis's vision. The **pool** is open 11am-6pm daily in the summer and Friday-Sunday in the fall and spring. Passes cost $35 for adults and $15 for children 3-14. *Cabines* (pronounced kab-eens) with private showers and a place to keep your clothes are available for rent. The hefty price ($170-215/day) does include four pool passes, use of four towels and chaise lounges, and a deck of playing cards.

The **Poolside Café** serves panini, salads, and gelato, delivered right to your lounge chair. So, no outside food, please. For a more elegant meal, the restaurant, **Rustic** (11am-9pm, $16-45), serves a mash-up of high-quality food from ribs to Neapolitan-style pizzas to specialties like lamb Marrakesh. Seating is either on the back veranda, which overlooks the quiet of the valley, or inside the high-beamed dining room. Nearby, the tasting room/Coppola museum pours flights and glasses of Coppola's midrange wines. You won't find his more elegant, handcrafted Inglenook wines here, but something perfect for a picnic or a casual dinner back home. And for those who want something stiffer for their Wine Country getaway, a backlit bar shakes, stirs, and serves well-made cocktails.

FIELD STONE WINERY

On the opposite end of the valley and spectrum from Coppola's largesse is the small **Field Stone Winery** (10075 Hwy. 128, Healdsburg, 707/433-7266 or 800/544-7273, www.fieldstonewinery.com, 10am-5pm daily, tasting $10), the southernmost winery on the beautiful Highway 128. Built from stones unearthed during construction in 1977, Field Stone was one of the first of a wave of modern underground wineries built in the Wine Country. Grapes from the 50 acres of estate vineyards, together with some from the Russian River Valley and Mendocino, go into

highly regarded cabernet, merlot, sangiovese, and the winery's signature, petite sirah. Whites include a limited-production viognier, sauvignon blanc, chardonnay, and a sangiovese rosé.

Oak trees shade two small picnic areas outside the small tasting room, sometimes shared with the local wild turkeys, and staff might be willing to take you on an impromptu tour if it's not too busy.

★ ALEXANDER VALLEY VINEYARDS

Alexander Valley Vineyards (8644 Hwy. 128, Healdsburg, 707/433-7209 or 800/888-7209, www.avvwine.com, 10am-5pm daily, free tasting) shares the name of the historic valley for good reason. In the 1960s the founders of the winery bought a large chunk of the original homestead once owned by Cyrus Alexander, the mountain man who became a ranch manager and finally a landowner credited with planting the valley's first vineyards in 1846.

Whether Alexander ever made wine from those grapes is not known, but today's vineyards provide the grapes for two decadent blends, Temptation Zin and Redemption Zin, and the Bordeaux-style Cyrus flagship wine. The wine routinely gets rave reviews, and in 2013 a 2008 vintage magnum sold for a record-breaking $215,000 at a Texas wine auction.

Historical sites pepper the current estate, including a wooden schoolhouse built by Alexander in 1853 and the Alexander family grave site up the hill behind the winery. Complimentary tasting is in the homey tasting room elevated for great views. Also complimentary are the tours of the expansive wine caves available daily at 11am and 2pm. If you are just dying to pay something, sign up for the Wine and Cheese pairing (10:30am, 1pm, 3pm daily, 48-hour advance reservation required, $25) or the Vineyard Hike tour and tasting (10:30am, 48-hour advance reservation required, $50).

WHITE OAK

At the Spanish-inspired **White Oak** (7505 Hwy. 128, Healdsburg, 707/433-8429, www.whiteoakwinery.com, 10am-5pm daily, tasting $20), you'll find a wide variety of wines from the Alexander, Russian River, and the Napa Valleys. While white-wine drinkers enjoy the sauvignon blanc and chardonnay, big reds are the specialty of the house. Cabernet sauvignon and zinfandel lovers flock to White Oak for the fabulous regular releases and occasional special library selections. At the walk-in tasting bar, you can select four pours, which are paired with cheese from a Healdsburg cheese maker. If you have lunch in mind, bring your picnic to the picnic tables dotting the green gardens overlooking the vineyards of old vine zinfandels. Tours (10am-4pm daily, reservations required, $25-30) at White Oak give participants a special look at wine-tasting, describing and illustrating the various components that make up a wine's fragrance.

HAWKES

Sitting at what could be called the hub of the Alexander Valley, **Hawkes** (6734 Hwy. 128, Healdsburg, 707/433-4295, http://hw.winemindeddesign.com, 10am-5pm daily, tasting $15) specializes in estate cabernet sourced from its vineyards in Alexander Valley and Chalk Hill. The Hawkes family has been in the wine business since 1972 when Stephen Hawkes first planted chardonnay in Chalk Hill. Since then, the family farm expanded with the planting of more vineyards throughout the southern Alexander Valley and began turning those grapes into wine under the direction of Stephen's son Jake. The Chalk Hill chardonnay is the first you'll taste in the current release flight, followed by an estate merlot and two cabernets, one blended and the other single vineyard. For $10 more you can take your tasting out on the deck surrounded by vineyards for the more private Vineyard Tasting. Those who share Jake's powerful love of cabernet sauvignon may want to sign up for the Rare Single Vineyards tasting ($75), which tastes cabernets from Hawkes's three vineyards while delving into a discussion of the meaning of *terroir,* climate, and winemaking in the production of this varietal.

MEDLOCK AMES

Medlock Ames (3487 Alexander Valley Rd., Healdsburg, 707/431-8845, www.

Hawkes is the cabernet specialist of the Alexander Valley.

medlockames.com, 10am-4:30pm daily, tasting $15) is a must-stop in the heart of the Alexander Valley. For years, to visit this small eco-conscious winery you had to make a trek to its 380-acre certified organic **Bell Weather Ranch on Chalk Hill** (13414 Chalk Hill Rd., Healdsburg, 707/431-1418), where vineyards of chardonnay, sauvignon blanc, cabernet sauvignon, and merlot share space with organic gardens, wildlife corridors, and its 100 percent solar-powered, gravity-flow winery. You can still book a tour ($35) of Medlock Ames's beautiful ranch, which lasts 90 minutes (wear comfortable shoes) and finishes with a seated tasting paired with local cheese and carefully crafted small bites.

Medlock Ames's new tasting room is more convenient but no less charming. The building, which previously housed the Alexander Valley Store & Bar, was given a sustainable makeover, and the grounds outside are dotted with picnic tables, organic garden boxes, and a bocce ball court. The patio is covered by a lovely grapevine trellis and is the best place to enjoy the current release flight of five wines ($15). You'll get a mix of new releases plus the Small Lot Collection, including the Snakepit Red, a delicious blend of merlot and cabernet, so named for its memorable sharpness and the viper-filled vineyard from which the grapes hail. Other standouts include a sauvignon blanc aged in 4 percent neutral oak that rounds out the varietals' telltale edge, and the cabernet-based Estate Red with soft tannins and an equally soft price point of $38. Wines are also available by the glass ($9-15), and there are bar bites ($5-10) and a wine and cheese pairing ($20). Medlock Ames is dog- and kid-friendly, accommodates outside food in the picnic areas, and stays open until 5:30pm on Sundays June-August, hosting live music and food trucks.

As if this winery couldn't get cooler, the winery rehabbed the **bar** half of the Alexander Valley Store & Bar and now pours retro-fresh cocktails with ingredients from the gardens outside starting at 5pm Thursday-Tuesday.

FOLEY SONOMA WINERY

While Stryker Sonoma Winery is now **Foley Sonoma Winery** (5110 Hwy. 128, Geyserville, 707/433-1944 or 800/433-1944, www.strykersonoma.com, 10am-5pm daily, tasting $10), the winery is no less striking, housed in a contemporary glass, wood, and concrete structure that won an architectural award. The huge glass-walled tasting room overlooks 26 acres of estate vineyards from which are made plush cabernet, merlot, old vine zinfandel, and chardonnay, plus small amounts of cabernet franc, malbec, and petit verdot used in interesting blends or as standalone vintages. A flight is only $10, but you may want to drink in the scenery, as it were, with a seated tasting with views of the vineyards ($30) that includes an antipasti cheese and charcuterie platter. To traipse around the vineyards, book a 90-minute Grape to Glass tour (by reservation, $40).

ROBERT YOUNG ESTATE WINERY

Chardonnay dominates the 14 varietals grown on the 320 acres of Alexander Valley vineyards owned by the **Robert Young Estate Winery** (4960 Red Winery Rd., Geyserville, 707/431-4811, www.ryew.com, 10am-4:30pm daily, tasting $10), and a rich, full-bodied version of this varietal is what the winery is best known for. In fact, there is a Robert Young clone of the chardonnay grape. Much of the rest of the estate is planted with merlot and cabernet, both of which go into the flagship Scion blend.

The Young family first settled this part of the world in 1858, but it was Robert Young who planted grapes here in the 1960s, slowly transforming what had been prune orchards and grazing land into hundreds of acres of vineyards, planting the very first cabernet sauvignon vines in the valley in 1963, and chardonnay in 1967. Robert died in 2009 at the ripe old age of 91, but there are still plenty of other Youngs who call the beautiful estate home. Tours of this six-generation family farm are available Saturday and Sunday at 10:30am by reservation.

SILVER OAK CELLARS

In the north end of the Alexander Valley, the temple for red-wine lovers is the Sonoma outpost of **Silver Oak Cellars** (24625 Chianti Rd., Geyserville, 707/942-7082, www.silveroak.com, 10am-5pm Mon.-Sat., 11am-5pm Sun., tasting $20-60), which makes just one wine—cabernet sauvignon. If you like cabernet, you'll undoubtedly like Silver Oak's powerful, velvety version that some say has an unusual aroma from being aged for years in only American oak barrels. You might not like the price, however. The Alexander Valley cabernet is $75 per bottle, and the Napa version made at the Oakville winery is over $100. Despite this, the tasting is low-key and includes four wines from both Napa and Alexander Valleys. To stretch your palate, book an appointment-only ($30) Silver Oak-Twomey Reds tasting, which includes its carefully crafted merlot from sister winery **Twomey** (1183 Dunaweal Ln., Calistoga, 707/942-2489, www.twomey.com, 10am-5pm Mon.-Sat., 11am-5pm Sun., tasting $15-20). You might also be able to taste the more moderately priced port that's only available at the winery.

Geyserville Tasting Rooms

There isn't much of a downtown Geyserville; in fact, "downtown" means one historic block at the intersection of Geyserville Avenue and Highway 128. Nevertheless, the cozy spot is worth the short detour off the highway, as seven wineries now fill the 19th-century buildings. An added bonus: The tasting rooms stay open later than almost anywhere else in Wine Country, making them a great end-of-the-day destination.

MEEKER

The first to arrive, **Meeker** (21035 Geyserville Ave., 707/431-2148, www.meekerwine.com, 10:30am-6pm daily, tasting $10) is known for its big reds, often code here for strong tannins with heavy fruit on the nose, thrown together with unusual bits of white pepper, cola, coffee, and vanilla. For the modest fee, you'll taste what they have on hand, which is generally five wines that include zinfandel, cabernet, a Bordeaux blend, petite sirah, and merlot. While it is evident that proprietor Charley Meeker has his hand in everything related to winemaking, including selecting the grapes and creating (or resurrecting in the case of his Fossil blend) new Bordeaux-style blends, this is most (at least visibly) evident in the Winemaker's Handprint merlot, in which every bottle is covered in painted handprints of, you guessed it, Charley Meeker.

MERCURY WINES/ RAMAZZOTTI WINES

For wines that don't take themselves quite so seriously, swing by the joint tasting room of **Mercury and Ramazzotti Wines** (21015 Geyserville Ave., 11am-6pm daily Mar.-Nov., 11am-5pm daily Dec.-Feb.). Both wineries were started during the 2000s and have a wide selection of Alexander Valley whites and reds. **Mercury Wines** (707/857-9870, www.mercurywine.com, tasting $5) was started by winemaker Brad Beard, an Arizona native, and is named for the quicksilver mining history of the area. Its label and vibe, however, are pure pop culture. The standouts are the reds made in the European tradition, co-fermented, with big heavy fruit exemplifying the best of the Alexander Valley. But Mercury is also a great place to taste. Beard's brother, Grady, is usually behind the counter and always up for some fun, and you'll be met at the door with lots of big dog kisses from the resident black lab, unsurprisingly named Freddie Mercury.

While Beard may be a transplant from Phoenix, the **Ramazzotti** (707/814-0016, www.ramazzottiwines.com, tasting $10) clan grew up in the Alexander Valley and are second-generation Italian Americans, representing the Italian heritage of the area. You can see it reflected in the wines they make. While there is the standard chardonnay, cabernet franc, and grenache, there are also Italian varietals such as barbera and sangiovese, as well as unique Tuscan blends. All of their wines are co-fermented, giving them a particular depth and complexity of flavor. Both wineries make less than 1,000 cases a year. Neither sells bottles for more than $55 and most prices hover around $30.

ROUTE 128 WINERY

At **Route 128 Winery** (21079 Geyserville Ave., 707/696-0004, www.route128winery. com, noon-6pm Fri.-Sat., 11am-5pm Thurs. and Sun., tasting $10) you'll also be greeted by a big black lab (this one's name is Ralph), and you'll taste wines that are unfiltered and co-fermented. The winery is a "hobby gone awry," as owner and winemaker Pete Opatz likes to say. Opatz and his wife, Lorna, have been in the wine business for 30 years, and you'll likely find Lorna pouring your wine during the four days the tasting room is open. From the estate vineyard in the tiny appellation of Yorkville Highland (1,000-2,200 feet above sea level straddling the Anderson and Alexander Valleys in southern Mendocino) come the winery's viognier, zinfandel, syrah, and a couple of blends. The High-Five is a particular standout, but it sells out quickly as only one barrel is made. The unassuming tasting room is tucked to the side of the antique barn, Gin'Gilli's Vintage Home. Recently redone, the bar is made from reclaimed barrel staves, and a shuffleboard table entices tasters to linger.

PECH MERLE

You'll want to linger at the stylish digs of **Pech Merle** (21001 Geyserville Ave., 707/891-3015, www.pechmerlewinery.com, 11am-6pm daily, tasting $10-15). Surfboards, electric blue electric guitars, boats converted to bookshelves, radiators made into a coffee table, and even a ski life chair adorn the polished concrete-floored, exposed brick tasting room. There are numerous places to sit, including at the bar, where a friendly staff pours flights of the winery's small portfolio. You'll find Dry Creek sauvignon blanc and zinfandel, Russian River pinot noir, and Alexander Valley cabernet. If

you're lucky the Alexander cabernet franc will be on the reserve tasting menu ($15), but thanks to its accolades, this unusual stand-alone varietal is usually sold out. If there is something that particularly tickles your taste buds, like the excellent (and affordable) Ivy Rose de Syrah, Pech Merle also serves wine by the glass (whites $7, reds $10).

LOCALS TASTING ROOM

Meeker may be the first winery to set up shop on Geyserville Avenue, but **Locals Tasting Room** (Geyserville Ave. at Hwy. 128, 707/857-4900, www.tastelocalwine.com, 11am-6pm daily, free tasting) is the first wine cooperative in the state and one of the few tasting rooms to offer complimentary tasting. This is because, with 70 wines open at any time, owner Carolyn Lewis says, people usually will find something they want to take home—and with good reason. Most of the wines sit at $20-40, and there is a broad mix of wineries, representing wines from as far south as the Central Coast up to Mendocino and most points between. Locals also has its own wine club incorporating most of the wineries represented here, making it one of the more varied and worthwhile clubs to join.

Wineries by Appointment
LANCASTER ESTATE

You might miss the turnoff from Highway 128 to Chalk Hill Road, but you won't miss the striking modern gates of the **Lancaster Estate** (15001 Chalk Hill Rd., Healdsburg, 707/433-8178, www.lancaster-estate.com, 10am-5pm daily, tour and tasting $35). This small but exclusive maker of cabernet sauvignon offers a tour of the vineyards, state-of-the-art winemaking facility, and caves before retiring to what seems like a private salon for tastings of the Bordeaux-style red wines, which range from the limited-production Nicole's Red blend to the flagship Lancaster Estate cabernet. To stay longer, tack on another $10 and book a wine and cheese pairing following the tour.

JORDAN VINEYARD ESTATE

While Judy Jordan focuses on bubbly and pinot noir at the J Vineyards & Winery in the Russian River appellation, father Tom crafts rich fruit-forward cabernet sauvignon and crisp chardonnay at the château-style **Jordan Vineyard Estate** (1474 Alexander Valley Rd., Healdsburg, 707/431-5250 or 800/654-1213, www.jordanwinery.com, daily by appointment, tasting $30, tour and tasting $40).

The beautifully manicured estate is perhaps the most picturesque winery setting in the valley and best appreciated on the hour-long tour (11am daily) that culminates in a tasting of wines and the estate olive oil together with some tasty morsels of food. Cabernet lovers might want to opt for the library tasting, which includes current releases of red and white wines along with several older vintages of the estate cabernet sauvignon, accompanied by a cheese plate (10am and 2pm daily).

FOOD

While most people head to Healdsburg after a day of tasting in the Alexander Valley, tiny Geyserville is increasingly becoming a secret dining destination. That may seem odd, especially as there are only three restaurants in town, but they are all excellent.

Italian

For a long time the renowned Taverna Santi was the heart of Geyserville's restaurant scene. **Catelli's** (21047 Geyserville Ave., Geyserville, 707/857-3471, www.mycatellis.com, 11:30am-8:30pm Tues.-Thurs., 11:30am-9:30pm Fri., noon-9:30pm Sat., noon-8:30pm Sun., $17-24) originally opened in 1936 and now has been reclaimed by the next generation of Catellis and rechristened under their name. It only so happens that one member of this next generation happens to be a celebrity chef who has appeared on *Iron Chef* and *Oprah*. Steering the restaurant back to her family's roots, but with an added dedication to healthy local food, Domenica Catelli and her brother, Nick, have created an earthy, high-quality Italian eatery. Homey sides like fries get a touch of truffle

oil, and meatball sliders are made with local organic beef. There are plenty of pasta dishes, and entrées are happily geared toward sophisticated comfort food.

A few doors down from Catelli's, ★ **Diavola** (21021 Geyserville Ave., Geyserville, 707/814-0111, www.diavolapizzeria.com, 11:30am-9pm daily, $14-25) lures locals from as far away as Healdsburg. Inside the rustic brick-walled interior, the restaurant dishes up seasonal Italian-inspired food, including amazing thin-crust pizzas from the central wood-burning oven. However, the chef's true passion is butchering and curing meat, skills he developed during his seven-year-long apprenticeship in Italy. That is why you'll find traditional dishes accented with items such as crispy pork belly or pork cheek.

Breakfast

For breakfast, the place to go (in fact the only place) is the **Geyserville Grille** (21712 Geyserville Ave., Geyserville, 707/857-3264, 7:30am-3pm Tues.-Wed., 7:30am-8pm Thurs. and Sun.-Mon., 7:30am-9pm Fri.-Sat., $10-15) at the Geyserville Inn. While it may be the only place to get a plate of eggs, fortunately everything on the menu is good. Hearty plates of crab cake omelets, vanilla French toast, and breakfast burritos pair perfectly with the sunny wraparound porch of the Craftsman-style building. If you are too late for breakfast, simply go for the burger or the fish-and-chips. Either way, you can't go wrong. Besides, there is plenty of espresso, mimosas, or Bloody Marys to wash anything down.

Picnic Supplies

It may not look like much, but the **Geyserville Market & Deli** (21010 Geyserville Ave., Geyserville, 707/431-7090, 9am-5pm daily) has just about everything you need for snacks or a picnic lunch in Alexander Valley. The deli has a great assortment of local cheeses, plus freshly made sandwiches and tacos, and it sells local wines, many of which you can't find outside the area.

Across the street, you can also pick up

supplies at **Diavola** (21021 Geyserville Ave., Geyserville, 707/814-0111, www.diavolapizzeria.com, 11:30am-9pm daily). Just inside the door is a deli case full of the house-made sausages and pork belly along with a half a dozen different sauces. While many of these may not be best for a picnic without a barbecue present, the containers of pickled white anchovies, marinated olives, roasted peppers, and even the guinea ham terrine certainly would be.

The premier spot to go, in fact *the* place to make a detour for, is the bright yellow and green ★ **Jimtown Store** (6706 Hwy. 128 at Alexander Valley Rd., Healdsburg, 707/433-1212, 7am-3pm Mon., Wed.-Fri., 7:30am-5pm Sat., 7:30am-3pm Sun., $7-14), with its bright red vintage pickup truck parked outside. This general store, in operation since 1895, is a quirky combination of old-fashioned American country store and gourmet sensibility. You'll find house-made gourmet jams, jellies, and condiments; penny toys; housewares; and, best of all, hot lunches. The chalkboard menu presents a tasty assortment of smoked-brisket sandwiches, chili, buttermilk coleslaw, and chorizo and provolone grilled-cheese sandwiches. You can enjoy table service in the back, unwrap your sandwich on benches outside, or pick up one of their prepared box lunches to go (48-hour notice required, $17).

ACCOMMODATIONS

There are only a few options of where to stay in the Alexander Valley. Thankfully, prices are reasonable, and there is great food along with plenty of tasting rooms nearby.

At the lowest end of the price range is the conveniently located **Geyserville Inn** (21714 Geyserville Ave., Geyserville, 707/857-4343 or 877/857-4343, www.geyservilleinn.com, $140-200), a modern two-floor building resembling an upscale motel at the northern edge of town. Request an east-facing room to get a view of the vineyards and mountains rather than the freeway, which is a little too close for comfort. The larger (and more expensive) of the 41 rooms have a fireplace, and many have a balcony or patio. Next door is the homey **Geyserville Grille** (21712 Geyserville Ave., Geyserville, 707/857-3264, 7:30am-3pm Tues.-Wed., 7:30am-8pm Thurs. and Sun.-Mon., 7:30am-9pm Fri.-Sat., $10-15), which serves breakfast and lunch daily.

Nestled among the homes of central Geyserville along the main road is the Victorian-style ★ **Hope-Merrill House** (21253 Geyserville Ave., Geyserville, 707/857-3356 or 800/825-4233, www.hope-inns.com, $179-319). The richly decorated interiors were restored in painstaking detail by the Hope family in the 1980s, and they put many of the historic Healdsburg B&Bs to shame. There are eight guest rooms in the 1870 Victorian, which features silk-screened wallpapers, coffered ceilings, and original woodwork. Only one room, the sumptuous Sterling Suite, has a television, though others have some features that more than compensate, from fireplaces and chaise lounges to whirlpool and claw-foot tubs to free wireless Internet access. Downstairs you'll find the dining room, where a hearty breakfast is served, while outside a saltwater pool is the perfect place to cool down after a hot day wine-tasting.

INFORMATION AND SERVICES

Tiny Geyserville has very little in the way of services. Even the small **Geyserville Chamber of Commerce** (21060 Geyserville Ave., 707/276-6076, www.geyservillecc.com, 12:30pm-4:30pm Fri.-Sun.) only opens its doors a few days a week. Still, the website has lots of helpful information, or you can stop by the visitors center in Healdsburg for more information before heading north. Another resource for the area's wines together with a comprehensive winery map can be found on the **Alexander Valley Winegrowers Association** website (www.alexandervalley.org).

As you might expect, the Alexander Valley has limited to no services, including, at times, reliable cell phone service. So get any banking, gas, or medical needs taken care of in Healdsburg before heading north.

GETTING THERE AND AROUND

The Alexander Valley runs on a diagonal from southeast of Healdsburg aiming northwest to the town of Cloverdale. U.S. 101 flanks the west side while Highway 128 runs from Calistoga, through Chalk Hill, connecting to 101 at Geyserville, eight miles north of Healdsburg. Alexander Valley Road connects to Highway 128 at the tiny hub of Jimtown. Geyserville is 25 miles north of Calistoga and 21 miles north of Santa Rosa. Like the Dry Creek Valley, the Alexander Valley is fairly easy to navigate. Most of the wineries are located just off Highway 128, which travels all the way to Calistoga, or off Geyserville Avenue, which hugs U.S. 101 to Alexander Valley Road (which eventually becomes Healdsburg Avenue).

San Francisco

Look for ★ to find recommended
sights, activities, dining, and lodging.

Highlights

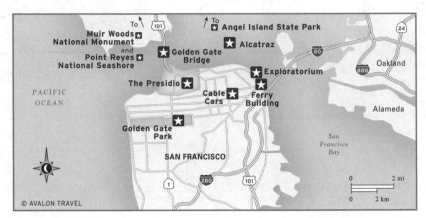

★ **Cable Cars:** Nothing is more iconic than climbing San Francisco's steep hills on a historic cable car (page 274).

★ **Ferry Building:** The 1898 Ferry Building has been renovated and reimagined as the foodie mecca of San Francisco (page 275).

★ **Exploratorium:** Kids and adults love to explore San Francisco's innovative and interactive science museum (page 278).

★ **Alcatraz:** Spend the day in prison at the famous former maximum-security penitentiary in the middle of the bay (page 279).

★ **The Presidio:** The original 1776 El Presidio de San Francisco is now a national park (page 283).

★ **Golden Gate Bridge:** Nothing beats the view from one of the most famous and fascinating bridges in the country (page 284).

★ **Golden Gate Park:** Home to stunning museums, botanical gardens, and outdoor festivals, the park is the place to be any day of the week (page 284).

★ **Angel Island State Park:** A visit to the largest island in the bay packs a lot into a short amount of time (page 293).

★ **Muir Woods National Monument:** Stand among trees nearly 1,000 years old and 200 feet tall in one of the nation's earliest national monuments (page 294).

★ **Point Reyes National Seashore:** Point Reyes is home to tule elk, desolate beaches, dairy farms, lighthouses, and remote wilderness trails (page 295).

The regular grid pattern found on maps of San Francisco leaves visitors unprepared for the precipitous inclines and stunning water views in this town built on 43 hills.

Geographically and culturally, San Francisco is anything but flat, and what level ground exists might at any moment give way. While earthquakes remake the land, social upheavals play a similar role, reminding locals that the only constant here is change. In the 1950s, the Beats challenged postwar conformity and left a legacy of incantatory poems and independent bookstores. The late 1960s saw a years-long Summer of Love, which shifted consciousness as surely as quakes shift tectonic plates. Gay and lesbian liberation movements sprang forth in the 1970s, as did a renewed push for women's rights. Since then, tech culture has taken root and continues to rapidly evolve as groundbreaking companies and visionaries choose to make the city their home.

Although San Francisco is one of the most visited cities in the United States, it often seems like a provincial village or a series of villages that share a downtown and a roster of world-class icons. Drive over the Golden Gate or the Bay Bridge as the fog is lifting and your heart will catch at the ever-changing beauty of the scene. Stand at the base of the Transamerica Pyramid, hang off the side of a cable car, or just walk through the neighborhoods that make the city more than the sum of its parts. Despite the hills, San Francisco is a city that cries out to be explored on foot.

PLANNING YOUR TIME

Try to spend at least **one weekend** in San Francisco, and focus your time downtown. Union Square makes a great home base, thanks to its plethora of hotels, shops, and easy access to public transportation, but it can be fairly dead at night. You can easily spend another full day exploring the Presidio, visiting Golden Gate Park's excellent museums, and taking a scenic, foggy stroll across the Golden Gate Bridge.

San Francisco's weather tends toward blanket fog and chilly wind, with bright spots of sun being the exception. Come prepared with a warm coat and a sweater, and leave the shorts at home.

Previous: Alcatraz; the Golden Gate Bridge. **Above:** the Transamerica Pyramid.

One Day in San Francisco

San Francisco may only be roughly seven miles long and seven miles wide, but it packs in many historic neighborhoods, some of the West Coast's most iconic landmarks, and dozens of stomach-dropping inclines along the way. Exploring all its hills and valleys takes some planning.
Start your day at the **Ferry Building.** Graze from the many vendors, including **Blue Bottle Café, Cowgirl Creamery,** and **Acme Bread Company.**
After touring the gourmet shops, catch the Muni F line (Steuart St. and Market St., $2.25) to Jefferson Street and take a stroll along **Fisherman's Wharf.** Stop into the **Musée Mécanique** to play a few coin-operated antique arcade games. Near Pier 39, catch the ferry to **Alcatraz**—be sure to buy your tickets well in advance. Alcatraz will fill your mind with amazing stories from the legendary island prison.
After you escape from Alcatraz, walk west along Bay Street to catch the Powell/Mason **cable car.** From the Powell Street Muni, take the N Judah line ($2.25) to 9th Avenue and Irving Street, then follow 9th Avenue north into **Golden Gate Park,** where you can delve into art at the fabulous **de Young Museum** or science at the **California Academy of Sciences.** Stroll the scenic **Japanese Tea Garden** and get a snack at their Tea House.
For dinner, head to the bustling Mission District, where new eateries are always popping up. Opt for Mexican cuisine at **La Taqueria** or raw fish at **Anchor Oyster Bar.** Alternatively, make a reservation in advance to eat at **State Bird Provisions.**
The next day, head north across the **Golden Gate Bridge** for your Wine Country adventure!

Sights

UNION SQUARE AND DOWNTOWN
★ Cable Cars

Perhaps the most recognizable symbol of San Francisco is the **cable car** (www.sfmta.com), originally conceived by Andrew Smith Hallidie as a safer alternative for traveling the steep, often slick hills of San Francisco. The cable cars ran as regular mass transit from 1873 into the 1940s, when buses and electric streetcars began to dominate the landscape. Dedicated citizens, especially "Cable Car Lady" Friedel Klussmann, saved the cable car system from extinction, and the cable cars have become a rolling national landmark.

Today you can ride the cable cars from one tourist destination to another for $7 per ride. A full day "passport" ticket ($20, also grants access to streetcars and buses) is totally worth it if you want to run around the city all day. Cable car routes can take you up Nob Hill from the Financial District or from Union Square along Powell Street, through Chinatown, and out to Fisherman's Wharf. Take a seat, or grab one of the exterior poles and hang on! Cable cars have open-air seating only, making for a chilly ride on foggy days.

The cars get stuffed to capacity with tourists on weekends and with local commuters at rush hours. Expect to wait an hour or more for a ride from any of the turnaround points on a weekend or holiday. But a ride on a cable car from Union Square down to the Wharf is more than worth the wait. The views from the hills down to the bay inspire wonder even in lifetime residents. To learn a bit more, make a stop at the **Cable Car Museum** (1201 Mason St., 415/474-1887, www.cablecarmuseum.org, 10am-6pm daily Apr.-Oct., 10am-5pm daily Nov.-Mar., free), the home and nerve center of the entire fleet. This sweet little museum depicts the life and times of the cable cars,

an iconic cable car

while an elevated platform overlooks the engines, winding wheels, and thick steel cable that keep the cars humming. You can even glimpse into the 1873 tunnels that snake beneath the city.

Grace Cathedral

Local icon **Grace Cathedral** (1100 California St., 415/749-6300, www.gracecathedral.org, 8am-6pm daily) is many things to many people. The French Gothic-style edifice, completed in 1964, attracts architecture and Beaux Arts lovers by the thousands with its facade, stained glass, and furnishings. The labyrinths—replicas of the Chartres Cathedral labyrinth in France—appeal to meditative walkers seeking spiritual solace. Concerts featuring world music, sacred music, and modern classical ensembles draw audiences from around the bay and farther afield.

To view some of the church's lesser-seen areas, sign up for the 1.5-hour **Grace Cathedral Grand Tour** (10am select days, $25). Docent-led tours are also available

(1pm-3pm Mon.-Fri., 11:30am-1:30pm Sat., 12:30pm Sun.), although time and availability varies. Check the website for more information or to send a request for a specific date.

★ Ferry Building

Restored to its former glory, the 1898 **Ferry Building** (1 Ferry Bldg., 415/983-8030, www.ferrybuildingmarketplace.com, 10am-7pm Mon.-Fri., 8am-6pm Sat., 11am-5pm Sun., check with businesses for individual hours) stands at the end of the Financial District at the edge of the water. Learn about the history of the edifice just inside the main lobby, where photos and interpretive plaques describe the life of the Ferry Building.

Today, the building is home to the famous **Farmers Market** (415/291-3276, 10am-2pm Tues. and Thurs., 8am-2pm Sat.). Permanent shops provide top-tier artisanal food and drink, from wine and cheese to high-end kitchenware, while fresh produce and organic meats are on display outside. Local favorites Cowgirl Creamery and Acme Bread Company maintain storefronts here. For immediate gratification, a few incongruous quick-and-easy restaurants offer reasonable eats.

On the water side of the Ferry Building, you can actually catch a ferry with the **Blue and Gold Fleet** (www.blueandgoldfleet.com), **Golden Gate Ferry** (www.goldengateferry.org), or **Bay Link Ferries** (https://sanfranciscobayferry.com).

San Francisco Museum of Modern Art

The **SFMOMA** (151 3rd St., 415/357-4000, www.sfmoma.org, 10am-5pm Fri.-Tues., 10am-9pm Thurs., adult $25, senior $22, ages 19-24 $19, 18 and under free), as it's fondly called, is a local favorite. It's an architectural wonder with ample gallery space for rotating special exhibitions and for its growing permanent collection, which includes notable work from Henri Matisse, Shiro Kuramata, Wayne Thiebaud, Richard Diebenkorn, and Chuck Close.

Downtown San Francisco

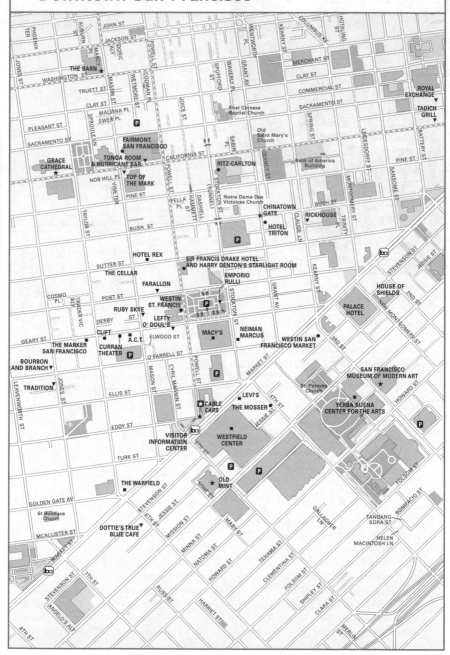

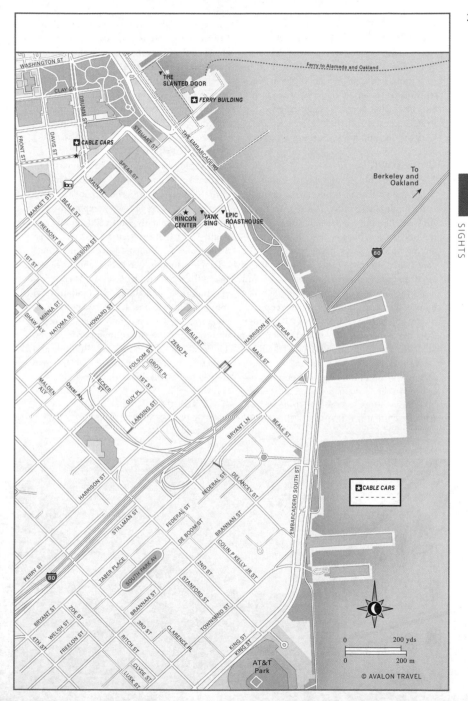

NORTH BEACH AND FISHERMAN'S WHARF

North Beach has long served as the Little Italy of San Francisco, a fact still reflected in the restaurants in the neighborhood. North Beach truly made its mark in the 1950s when it was, for a brief time, home to many writers in the Beat Generation, including Jack Kerouac, Gary Snyder, and Allen Ginsburg.

Chinatown

The massive Chinese migration to California began almost as soon as the news of easy gold in the mountain streams made it to East Asia. And despite rampant prejudice, the Chinese not only stayed, but persevered and eventually prospered. Many never made it to the gold fields, preferring instead to remain in bustling San Francisco to open shops and begin the business of commerce in their new home. They carved out a thriving community at the border of **Portsmouth Square** (Kearney St. between Clay St. and Washington St.), then center of the young city, which became known as Chinatown. Along with much of San Francisco, the neighborhood was destroyed in the 1906 earthquake and fire.

Today visitors see the post-1906 visitor-friendly Chinatown that was built after the quake, particularly if they enter through the **Chinatown Gate** (Grant Ave. and Bush St.) at the edge of Union Square. In this historic neighborhood, beautiful Asian architecture mixes with more mundane blocky city buildings to create a unique skyline. Small alleyways wend between the touristy commercial corridors, creating an intimate atmosphere.

★ Exploratorium

Lauded both as "one of the world's most important science museums" and "a mad scientist's penny arcade," the **Exploratorium** (Pier 15, 415/528-4444, www.exploratorium. edu, 10am-5pm daily, adults $30, seniors and youth 13-17 $25, children 4-12 $20, children 3 and under free) houses 150 playful exhibits on physics, motion, perception, and the senses that utilize its stunning location. Make a reservation ($15) to walk blindly (and bravely) into the Tactile Dome, a lightless space where you can "see" your way only by reaching out and touching the environment around you. The location between the Ferry Building and Fisherman's Wharf makes a crowd-free trip impossible, especially on the weekends.

Coit Tower

Built in 1933 as a monument to benefactor

the Ferry Building

Lillie Hitchcock Coit's beloved firefighters, Coit Tower (1 Telegraph Hill Blvd., 415/249-0995, http://sfrecpark.org, 10am-6pm daily May-Oct., 10am-5pm daily Nov.-Apr., entrance free, tour $7, call for tour times) has beautified the city just as Coit intended. Inside the art deco tower, the walls are covered in the recently restored frescoes painted in 1934 depicting city and California life during the Great Depression. For a fee (adults $8, seniors and youth $5, children 5-11 $2, children 4 and under free), you can ride the elevator to the top, where on a clear day, you can see the whole city and bay. Part of what makes Coit Tower special is the walk up to it. Rather than contributing to the acute congestion in the area, consider taking public transit to the area and walking up Telegraph Hill Boulevard through Pioneer Park to the tower, then descending either the Filbert or Greenwich steps toward the Embarcadero. It's long and steep, but there's no other way to see the lovely little cottages and gardens of the beautiful and quaint Telegraph Hill.

Lombard Street

You've no doubt seen it in movies: Lombard Street (Lombard St., one way from Hyde St. to Leavenworth St.), otherwise known as "the crookedest street in the world." The section of the street that visitors flock to spans only one block, from Hyde Street at the top to Leavenworth Street at the bottom. However, the line of cars waiting their turn to drive bumper-to-bumper can be just as legendary as its 27 percent grade. Bypass the car and take the hill by foot. The unobstructed vistas of San Francisco Bay, Alcatraz Island, Fisherman's Wharf, Coit Tower, and the city are reason enough to add this walk to your itinerary, as are the brick steps, manicured hydrangeas, and tony residences that line the roadway.

Fisherman's Wharf

Welcome to the tourist mecca of San Francisco! While warehouses, stacks of crab pots, and a fleet of fishing vessels let you know this is still a working wharf, it is also *the* spot where visitors to San Francisco come and snap photos. Fisherman's Wharf (Beach St. from Powell St. to Van Ness Ave., backs onto Bay St., www.fishermanswharf.org), reachable by Muni F line and the Hyde-Powell cable car, sprawls along the waterfront and inland several blocks, creating a large tourist district.

The Wharf, as it's called by locals, features all crowds, all the time. Be prepared to push through a sea of humanity to see sights, buy souvenirs, and eat seafood. Still, many of the sights of Fisherman's Wharf are important (and fun) pieces of San Francisco's heritage, like the Fisherman's and Seaman's Memorial Chapel (Pier 45) and the Musée Mécanique (Pier 45, 415/346-2000, www.museemechanique.org, 10am-7pm Mon.-Fri., 10am-8pm Sat.-Sun., free), an arcade dating back more than a century.

★ Alcatraz

Going to Alcatraz (415/561-4900, www.nps.gov/alcatraz), one of the most famous landmarks in the city, feels a bit like going to purgatory; this military fortress-turned-maximum-security prison, nicknamed "The Rock," has little warmth or welcome on its craggy, forbidding shores. While it still belonged to the military, the fortress became a prison in the 19th century to house Civil War prisoners. The isolation of the island in the bay, the frigid waters, and the nasty currents surrounding Alcatraz made it a perfect spot to keep prisoners contained, with little hope of escape and near-certain death if the attempt were ever made. In 1934, after the military closed down its prison and handed the island over to the Department of Justice, construction began to turn Alcatraz into a new style of prison ready to house a new style of prisoner: Depression-era gangsters. A few of the honored guests of this maximum-security penitentiary were Al Capone, George "Machine Gun" Kelly, and Robert Stroud, "the Birdman of Alcatraz." The prison closed in 1963, and in 1964 and 1969 occupations were staged by Indians of All Tribes, an exercise

North Beach and Fisherman's Wharf

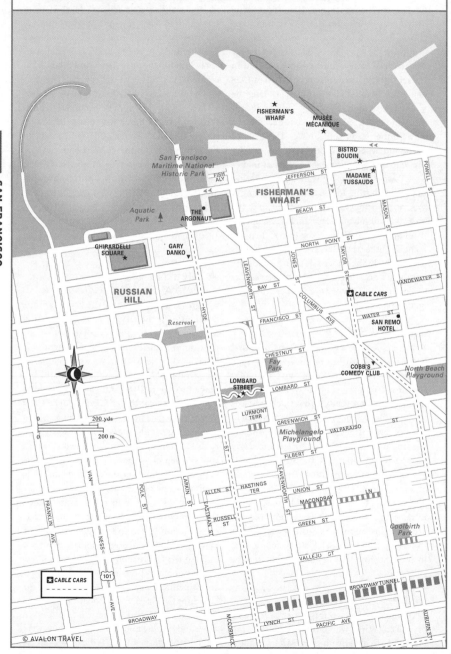

FISHERMAN'S WHARF ★
MUSÉE MÉCANIQUE ★

BISTRO BOUDIN ★

San Francisco Maritime National Historic Park

FISH ALY

JEFFERSON ST

MADAME TUSSAUDS ★

POWELL ST

Aquatic Park

THE ARGONAUT ●

FISHERMAN'S WHARF

BEACH ST

MASON ST

GHIRARDELLI SQUARE ★

GARY DANKO ▼

NORTH POINT ST

TAYLOR ST

JONES ST

VANDEWATER ST

RUSSIAN HILL

LEAVENWORTH ST

BAY ST

COLUMBUS AVE

★ CABLE CARS

HYDE ST

Reservoir

FRANCISCO ST

WATER ST

SAN REMO HOTEL ●

CHESTNUT ST

Fay Park

COBB'S COMEDY CLUB ●

North Beach Playground

LOMBARD STREET ★

LOMBARD ST

LURMONT TERR

GREENWICH ST

VALPARAISO ST

Michelangelo Playground

0   200 yds
0   200 m

FILBERT ST

VAN NESS AVE

POLK ST

LARKIN ST

EASTMAN ST

ALLEN ST

HASTINGS TER

RUSSELL ST

LEAVENWORTH ST

UNION ST

MACONDRAY LN

GREEN ST

Coolbirth Park

FRANKLIN AVE

NESS AVE

VALLEJO CT

★ CABLE CARS

101

BROADWAY TUNNEL

BROADWAY

MCCORMICK ST

LYNCH ST

PACIFIC AVE

AUBURN ST

© AVALON TRAVEL

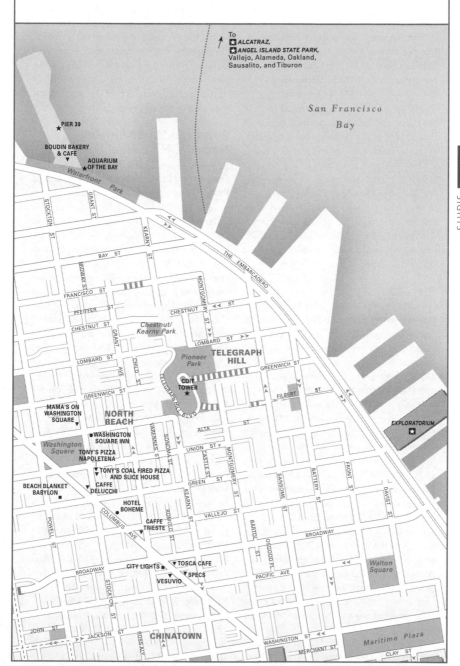

To
✚ *ALCATRAZ,*
✚ *ANGEL ISLAND STATE PARK,*
Vallejo, Alameda, Oakland,
Sausalito, and Tiburon

San Francisco
Bay

★ PIER 39

BOUDIN BAKERY
& CAFE
▼
AQUARIUM
★ OF THE BAY
Waterfront   Park

STOCKTON

GRANT ST

KEARNY

ST

BAY ST

MIDWAY ST

FRANCISCO ST

THE EMBARCADERO

MONTGOMERY

PFEIFFER

CHESTNUT ST

CHESTNUT   ST

GRANT

Chestnut/
Kearny Park

ST

LOMBARD ST ▶▶

LOMBARD ST

Pioneer
Park

TELEGRAPH
HILL

GREENWICH ST

AVE

CHILD ST

TELEGRAPH HILL BLVD

COIT
TOWER
★

FILBERT ST

LOMBARD ST

GREENWICH ST

MAMA'S ON
WASHINGTON
SQUARE
▼

NORTH
BEACH

VARENNES ST

SONOMA ST

ALTA ST

EXPLORATORIUM
✪

Washington
Square

● WASHINGTON
   SQUARE INN

TONY'S PIZZA
NAPOLETENA

▼ TONY'S COAL FIRED PIZZA
   AND SLICE HOUSE

CAFFE
DELUCCHI
▼

UNION ST ▼

MONTGOMERY

CASTLE ST

SANSOME

BATTERY

FRONT ST

DAVIS ST

BEACH BLANKET
BABYLON ■

HOTEL
BOHEME
●

KEARNY

GREEN ST

VALLEJO ST

POWELL

COLUMBUS

AVE

CAFFE
TRIESTE

ROMOLO ST

BARTOL

OSGOOD PL

BROADWAY

Walton
Square

ST

CITY LIGHTS ■

BROADWAY

▼ TOSCA CAFE

▼ SPECS

STOCKTON

VESUVIO ▼

PACIFIC AVE

JOHN ST

JACKSON ST

ROSS ALY

CHINATOWN

WASHINGTON ST ◀◀

Maritime Plaza

MERCHANT ST

CLAY ST

that eventually led to the privilege of self-determination for North America's original inhabitants.

Today Alcatraz acts primarily as an attraction for visitors to San Francisco. **Alcatraz Cruises** (Pier 33, 415/981-7625, www.alcatrazcruises.com, 8:45am-1:35pm daily, adults $36, children 5-11 $22, 4 and under free) offers ferry rides out to Alcatraz and tours of the island and the prison. Tours depart from Pier 33, and prices are steep, but family tickets are available for $108 and include passage for two adults and two kids of any age. Buy tickets at least a week in advance, especially if you'll be in town in the summer and want to visit Alcatraz on a weekend. Tours often sell out, especially the evening tour (3:50pm daily, adults $43, children 5-11 $26, 4 and under free), which has been voted one of the best tours in the Bay Area.

Pier 39

One of the most visited spots in San Francisco, **Pier 39** (www.pier39.com) hosts a wealth of restaurants and shops. If you've come down to the pier to see the sealife, start with the unusual **Aquarium of the Bay** (415/623-5300, www.aquariumofthebay.com, 10am-8pm daily, closing times vary throughout the year, adults $25, seniors and children 4-12 $15, family rate of two adults and two kids, $68). This 300-foot, clear-walled tunnel lets visitors see thousands of species native to the San Francisco Bay, including sharks, rays, and plenty of fish. For a special treat, take the Behind the Scenes or Feed the Sharks tour. Farther down the pier, get close (but not *too* close) to the local colony of **sea lions.** These big, loud mammals tend to congregate at K-Dock in the West Marina. The best time to see the sea lions is winter, when the population grows into the hundreds. To learn more about the sea lions, head for the interpretive center on Level 2 of the **Sea Lion Center** (415/262-4735, www.sealioncenter.org, 10am-5pm daily, free).

A perennial family favorite, the **San Francisco Carousel** (10am-7pm Sun.-Thurs.,

10am-8pm Fri.-Sat., $3 per ride) is painted with beautiful scenes of San Francisco. Riders on the moving horses, carriages, and seats can look at the paintings or out onto the pier. Kids also love the daily shows by local street performers. Depending on when you're on the pier, you might see jugglers, magicians, or stand-up comedians on the **Carousel Stage** (noon-8:50pm daily, free).

San Francisco Maritime National Historical Park

The real gem of the Wharf is the **San Francisco Maritime National Historical Park,** which spreads from the base of Van Ness to Pier 45. At the **visitors center** (499 Jefferson St., 415/561-7000, www.nps.gov/safr, 10am-4pm daily), not only will rangers help you make the most of your visit, but you can also get lost in the labyrinthine museum that houses an immense Fresnel lighthouse lens and engaging displays that recount San Francisco's history. For $10 you can climb aboard the historical ships at permanent dock across the street at the **Hyde Street Pier** (9:30am-5pm daily). The shiniest jewel of the collection is the 1886 square-rigged *Balclutha,* a three-masted schooner that recalls times gone by, complete with excellent historical exhibits belowdecks. There are also several steamboats, including the workhorse ferry paddle-wheel *Eureka* and a cool old steam tugboat called the *Eppleton Hall.* Farther down at Pier 45, World War II buffs can feel the claustrophobia of the submarine **USS *Pampanito*** (415/775-1943, www.maritime.org, 9am-close daily, adults $20, senior $12, children 6-12 $10, under 6 free) or the expansiveness of the Liberty ship **SS *Jeremiah O'Brien*** (415/544-0100, www.ssjeremiahobrien.org, 9am-4pm daily, adults $20, seniors and children 5-12 $10, children under 5 free).

The art deco **Aquatic Bathhouse Building** (900 Beach St., 415/447-5000, www.nps.gov/safr, 10am-4pm daily, free), built in 1939, houses the Maritime Museum, where you can see a number of rotating exhibits alongside its brilliant WPA murals.

MARINA AND PACIFIC HEIGHTS

The Marina and Pacific Heights shelter some of the amazing amount of money that flows in the City by the Bay. Starting at the Marina Green along the bay, you'll find a couple of yacht harbors, plenty of open space, great dining, and shopping that only gets better as you go up the hill.

Palace of Fine Arts

The **Palace of Fine Arts** (3301 Lyon St.) was originally meant to be nothing but a temporary structure—part of the Panama-Pacific International Exposition in 1915. But the lovely building designed by Bernard Maybeck won the hearts of San Franciscans, and a fund was started to preserve the palace beyond the exposition. Through the first half of the 20th century, efforts could not keep it from crumbling, but in the 1960s and 1970s, serious rebuilding work took place, and today the Palace of Fine Arts stands proud, strong, and beautiful. It houses the **Palace of Fine Arts Theatre** (415/563-6504, www.palaceoffinearts.org), which hosts events nearly every day, from beauty pageants to conferences to children's musical theater.

★ The Presidio

A visit to the **Presidio** (Bldg. 36, Graham St. and Lincoln Blvd., 415/561-4323, www.nps.gov/prsf, visitors center 10am-4pm Thurs.-Sun., free) will remind visitors that this used to be an army town. Capping the northwestern part of the city, the Presidio has been a military installation since 1776. When defense budgets shrank at the end of the Cold War, the military turned it over to the National Park Service, making it a historical park in 1994.

To orient yourself among the more than 800 buildings that make up the Presidio, start at the visitors center in the beautiful Main Post. You'll also find the **Walt Disney Family Museum** (104 Montgomery St., 415/345-6800, www.waltdisney.org, 10am-6pm Wed.-Mon., adults $20, seniors $15, children 6-17 $12, children 5 and under free); George Lucas's **Letterman Digital Arts Center** (Chestnut St. and Lyon St., www.lucasfilm.com), where you can snap a photo with a life-size Yoda statue; **Crissy Field,** which runs along the bay and includes the World War II grass airfield; and the breathtaking **Fort Point** (end of Marine Dr., 415/556-1693, www.nps.gov/fopo, 10am-5pm Fri.-Sun.) with its Civil War-era fortifications.

the Palace of Fine Arts

★ Golden Gate Bridge

People come from the world over to see and walk the **Golden Gate Bridge** (U.S. 101/ Hwy. 1 at Lincoln Blvd., 415/921-5858, http:// goldengatebridge.org, southbound cars $7.50, pedestrians free). A marvel of human engineering constructed in 1936 and 1937, the suspension bridge spans the narrow "gate" from which the Pacific Ocean enters the San Francisco Bay. Pedestrians are allowed on the **east sidewalk** (5am-6:30pm daily Nov.-Apr., 5am-9pm daily Apr.-Oct.). On a clear day, the whole bay, Marin Headlands, and city skyline are visible. Cyclists are allowed on both sidewalks (check the website for times), but be aware of pedestrians not keeping their eyes on where they are going.

GOLDEN GATE PARK AND THE HAIGHT

The neighborhood surrounding the intersection of Haight and Ashbury Streets (known locally as "the Haight") is best known for the wave of countercultural energy that broke out in the 1960s. Haight Street terminates at the entrance to Golden Gate Park.

★ Golden Gate Park

Dominating the western half of San Francisco,

Golden Gate Park (main entrance at Stanyan St. at Fell St., McLaren Lodge Visitors Center at John F. Kennedy Dr., 415/831-2700, www.golden-gate-park.com) is one of the city's most enduring treasures. Its 1,000-plus acres include lakes, forests, formal gardens, windmills, museums, a buffalo pasture, and plenty of activities. Spend a day hiking the beautiful trails, enjoying a free summer concert, or exploring the scores of sights.

The **de Young Museum** (50 Hagiwara Tea Garden Dr., 415/750-3600, http://deyoung.famsf.org, 9:30am-5:15pm Tues.-Thurs. and Sat.-Sun., 9:30am-8:45pm Fri. Apr.-Nov., 9:30am-5:15pm Tues.-Sun. Dec.-Mar., adults $15, seniors $10, children 17 and under free) is staggering in its size and breadth: You'll see everything from pre-Colombian art to 17th-century ladies' gowns. View paintings, sculpture, textiles, ceramics, "contemporary crafts" from all over the world, and rotating exhibits that range from King Tut to the exquisite Jean Paul Gaultier collection.

A triumph of the sustainable scientific principles it exhibits, the **California Academy of Sciences** (55 Music Concourse Dr., 415/379-8000, www.calacademy.org, 9:30am-5pm Mon.-Sat., 11am-5pm Sun., adults $35, students, seniors, and children

a historic home in the Presidio

12-17 $30, children 4-11 $25, children 3 and under free) drips with ecological perfection. Wander through a steamy endangered rainforest contained inside a giant glass bubble or travel through an all-digital outer space in the high-tech planetarium. The Academy of Sciences takes pains to make itself kid-friendly, with interactive exhibits, thousands of live animals, and endless opportunities for learning.

The **Japanese Tea Garden** (75 Hagiwara Tea Garden Dr., 415/752-4227, http://japaneseteagardensf.com, 9am-6pm daily Mar.-Oct., 9am-4:45pm daily Nov.-Feb., adults $8, seniors $6, children 5-11 $2, children 4 and under free) is a haven of peace and tranquility. The planting and design of the garden began in 1894 for the California Exposition. Today the flourishing garden displays a wealth of beautiful flora, including stunning examples of rare Chinese and Japanese plants.

The 55-acre **San Francisco Botanical Garden** (9th Ave. at Lincoln Way, 415/661-1316, www.sfbotanicalgarden.org, 7:30am-6pm daily early Mar.-Sept., 10am-5pm daily Oct.-early Mar., adults $8, students and seniors $6, children 5-11 $2, families $17, under age 5 and city residents with ID free) is home to more than 8,000 species of plants from around the world, including a California Natives garden and a shady redwood forest.

For a trip to San Francisco's Victorian past, step inside the steamy **Conservatory of Flowers** (100 John F. Kennedy Dr., 415/831-2090, www.conservatoryofflowers.org, 10am-6pm Tues.-Sun., adults $8, students and seniors $6, children 5-11 $2, children under 4 free). Built in 1878, the striking wood and glass greenhouse is home to more than 1,700 plant species that spill out of containers, twine around rainforest trees, climb trellises reaching the roof, and rim deep ponds where eight-foot lily pads float serenely on still waters.

The Legion of Honor

A beautiful museum in a town filled with beauty, **The Legion of Honor** (100 34th Ave. at Clement St., 415/750-3600, http://legionofhonor.famsf.org, 9:30am-5:15pm Tues.-Sun., adults $15, seniors $10, children 17 and under free) sits on its lonely promontory in Lincoln Park, overlooking the Golden Gate. A gift to the city from philanthropist Alma Spreckels in 1924, this French Beaux Arts-style building was built to honor the memory of California soldiers who died in World War I. From its beginning, the Legion of Honor was a museum dedicated to bringing European art to the

the de Young Museum

population of San Francisco. Today visitors can view gorgeous collections of European paintings, sculpture, decorative arts, ancient artifacts from around the Mediterranean, thousands of paper drawings by great artists, and much more. Special exhibitions come from the Legion's own collections and museums of the world.

Food

UNION SQUARE AND DOWNTOWN

Blue Bottle Café (66 Mint Plaza, 510/653-394, www.bluebottlecoffee.net, 7am-7pm daily, $5-15) is a popular local chain with multiple locations around the city. The Mint Plaza location is Blue Bottle's only café with a full food menu. Other locations include the Ferry Building (1 Ferry Bldg., Ste. 7, 7am-7pm daily) and a Hayes Valley kiosk (315 Linden St., 7am-6pm Mon.-Sat., 8am-6pm Sun.). Expect a line.

Even on a weekday morning, there will be a line out the door of ★ Brenda's French Soul Food (652 Polk St., 415/345-8100, http://frenchsoulfood.com, 8am-3pm Mon.-Tues., 8am-10pm Wed.-Sat., 8am-8pm Sun., $12-17). People come in droves to this Tenderloin eatery for its delectable and filling New Orleans-style breakfasts. Unique offerings include crawfish beignets, an Andouille sausage omelet, and beef cutlet and grits.

Hidden in a tiny alley that looks like it might have been transported from Saint-Michel in Paris, ★ Café Claude (7 Claude Ln., 415/392-3505, www.cafeclaude.com, 11:30am-10:30pm Mon.-Sat., 5:30pm-10:30pm Sun., $21-28) serves classic brasserie cuisine to French expatriates and Americans alike. Café Claude is open for lunch through dinner and features live music 7pm-10pm Thursday-Saturday.

Make reservations in advance at San Francisco legend Farallon (450 Post St., 415/956-6969, www.farallonrestaurant.com, 5:30pm-9:30pm Mon.-Thurs., 5:30pm-10pm Fri.-Sat., 5:30pm-9pm Sun., $37-49). The theme here is underwater: dark, cave-like rooms, a unique Jellyfish Bar, and lots of seafood on the pricey-but-worth-it menu.

At Dottie's True Blue Café (28 6th St., 415/885-2767, 7:30am-3pm Mon. and Thurs.-Fri., 7:30am-4pm Sat.-Sun., $9-14), the menu is simple: classic egg dishes, light fruit plates, and an honest-to-goodness blue-plate special for breakfast as well as salads, burgers, and sandwiches for lunch. The service is friendly and the portions are huge. Expect lines up to an hour long for a table at this locals' mecca, especially on weekend mornings.

At The Slanted Door (1 Ferry Plaza, Ste. 3, 415/861-8032, http://slanteddoor.com, 11am-2:30pm and 5:30pm-10pm Mon.-Sat., 11:30am-3pm and 5:30pm-10pm Sun., $22-48), owner Charles Phan utilizes organic local ingredients in both traditional and innovative Vietnamese cuisine, creating a unique dining experience. The light afternoon tea menu (2:30pm-4:30pm daily) can be the perfect pick-me-up for weary travelers.

Established in 1849, the ★ Tadich Grill (240 California St., 415/391-1849, www.tadichgrill.com, 11am-9:30pm Mon.-Fri., 11:30am-9:30pm Sat., $22-45) still serves fresh caught fish and classic miner fare. The menu combines perfectly sautéed sand dabs, octopus salad, and the Hangtown Fry, an oyster and bacon frittata. Mix that with the business lunch crowd in suits, out-of-towners, and original dark wooden booths from the 1850s and you've got a fabulous San Francisco stew of a restaurant.

How could you not love a steak house with a name like Epic Roasthouse (369 Embarcadero, 415/369-9955, www.epicroasthouse.com, lunch 11:30am-2:30pm Mon.-Fri., dinner 5:30pm-9:30pm Sun.-Thurs., 5:30pm-10pm Fri.-Sat., brunch 11am-2:30pm Sat.-Sun., $34-90)? Come for the wood-fired grass-fed beef; stay for the prime views over San Francisco Bay. The Epic Roasthouse sits almost underneath the Bay Bridge, which dazzles with its light display after the sun goes down.

NORTH BEACH AND FISHERMAN'S WHARF

Tourists at Boudin's **Bakers Hall** (160 Jefferson St., 415/928-1849, www.boudinbakery.com, 8am-9:30pm Sun.-Thurs., 8am-10pm Fri.-Sat., $8-15) can order a steaming bowl of clam chowder in a fresh bread bowl and watch how the bread is made in its demonstration bakery. Upstairs, have a more formal dinner at **Bistro Boudin** (415/351-5561, 11:30am-10pm Sun.-Thurs., 11:30am-10:30pm Fri.-Sat., $15-40), which serves elegant American food and a whole host of oysters in its dark wood dining room overlooking the wharf. Boudin has another café location at **Pier 39** (Space 5 Q, 415/421-0185, 7:30am-10pm daily, $8-15).

In North Beach, the family-owned **Caffe Trieste** (601 Vallejo St., 415/392-6739, www.caffetrieste.com, 6:30am-10pm Sun.-Thurs., 6:30am-11pm Fri.-Sat., cash only) first opened its doors in 1956 and is rumored to be where Francis Ford Coppola penned the original *Godfather* screenplay.

★ **Mama's on Washington Square** (1701 Stockton St., 415/362-6421, www.mamas-sf.com, 8am-3pm Tues.-Sun., $10-14) is legendary for breakfast—and so is the line. Starting from down the block, the line flows through the heart of the restaurant to the counter where you place your order, then wait for a table to open up. To minimize your wait, arrive at Mama's when it opens or go after noon.

Park Tavern (1652 Stockton St., 415/989-7300, http://parktavernsf.com, 5:30pm-10pm Mon.-Thurs., 11:30am-2:30pm and 5:30pm-11pm Fri., 10am-2:30pm and 5:30pm-11pm Sat., 10am-2:30pm and 5:30pm-10pm-Sun., $24-42) serves meat and fish dishes as well as exquisite appetizers in its elegant dining room.

Nine-time World Pizza Champion Tony Gemignani runs ★ **Tony's Pizza Napoletana** (1570 Stockton St., 415/835-9888, www.tonyspizzanapoletana.com, noon-10pm Mon., noon-11pm Wed.-Sun., $15-30), where four different pizza ovens cook eight distinct styles of pizza. The chef's special Neapolitan-style pizza margherita is simple pizza made to perfection.

MARINA AND PACIFIC HEIGHTS

Famed chef Traci Des Jardins took over the 1895 mess hall in the Main Post and turned it into the **Commissary** (Presidio, 101 Montgomery St., 415/561-3600, www.thecommissarysf.com, 5:30pm-9:30pm Mon.-Sat., $24-36). The cuisine is a blend of San Franciscan and Spanish influences and utilizes such ingredients as cod, anchovies, chorizo, and peppers.

To get the very best food truck experience, plan a Sunday afternoon at the **Off the Grid Presidio Picnic** (Presidio, Main Post Lawn, 415/339-5888, http://offthegridsf.com, 11am-4pm Sun. Apr.-Oct., $7-20), where eight trucks, 17 tents, and two carts roving through the crowds sell everything from Bloody Marys to Vietnamese soup. The Presidio Picnic is a party with live DJs and plenty of dogs, kids, hipsters, Frisbees, and picnic blankets.

There is no escaping the hipster cred of ★ **State Bird Provisions** (1529 Fillmore St., 415/795-1272, http://statebirdsf.com, 5:30pm-10pm Sun.-Thurs., 5:30pm-11pm Fri.-Sat., $30), but this restaurant is unpretentiously serving carefully crafted California fusion dishes dim sum-style. While the pace is brisk, the servers are friendly and attentive, even stopping to help select a beer or wine for your eclectic meal.

CIVIC CENTER AND HAYES VALLEY

Housed in a former bank, ★ **Nopa** (560 Divisadero St., 415/864-8643, http://nopasf.com, 6pm-midnight Sun.-Thurs., 6pm-1am Fri.-Sat., $17-30) serves hip farm-to-table food on long communal tables. Upscale comfort food is made with the best ingredients, a global sensibility, and excellent execution. But it's impossible to get a table without a reservation.

Suppenküche (525 Laguna St., 415/252-9289, www.suppenkuche.com, 5pm-10pm Mon.-Sat., 10am-2:30pm and 5pm-10pm Sun., $15-21) brings Bavaria to the Bay Area. For dinner, expect German classics with a focus on Bavarian cuisine. The spaetzle, pork, and sausage will harden your arteries right up. Suppenküche also has a **Biergarten** (424 Octavia St., 415/252-9289, http://biergartensf.com, 3pm-9pm Wed.-Sat., 1pm-7pm Sun.) two blocks away.

MISSION AND CASTRO

Locals love ★ **Tartine Bakery** (600 Guerrero St., 415/487-2600, www.tartinebakery.com, 8am-7pm Mon., 7:30am-7pm Tues.-Wed., 7:30am-8pm Thurs.-Fri., 8am-8pm Sat.-Sun., $5-15). Tartine's bakers use organic flour, sea salt, and locally sourced produce and cheeses to craft its culinary creations, and the French-Italian-California fusion pastries and panini have brought this bakery its word-of-mouth success.

Range (842 Valencia St., 415/282-8283, www.rangesf.com, 6pm-close Tues.-Thurs., 5:30pm-close Fri.-Sun., $27-32) is consistently rated one of the top Bay Area restaurants, serving up expertly crafted California cuisine. An inventive cocktail list doesn't hurt.

Frances (3870 17th St., 415/621-3870, www.frances-sf.com, 5pm-10pm Sun. and Tues.-Thurs., 5pm-10:30pm Fri.-Sat., $26-34) has been winning rave reviews ever since it opened its doors. The California-inspired French cuisine is locavore-friendly, with an emphasis on sustainable ingredients and local farms. The short-but-sweet menu changes daily and includes such temptations as caramelized Atlantic scallops and bacon beignets. Reservations are strongly advised.

★ **Delfina** (3621 18th St., 415/552-4055, www.delfinasf.com, 5:30pm-10pm Mon.-Thurs., 5:30pm-11pm Fri.-Sat., 5pm-10pm Sun., $11-30) gives Italian cuisine a hearty California twist. From the antipasti to the entrées, the dishes speak of local farms and ranches, fresh seasonal produce, and the best Italian-American taste that money can buy.

Much of the rich heritage of the Mission district is Hispanic, which makes it *the* place to find a good taco or burrito. It is generally agreed upon that **La Taqueria** (2889 Mission St., 415/285-7117, 11am-9pm Mon.-Sat., 11am-8pm Sun., $6-12) makes the best burrito in the city. Critics rave, as do locals grabbing dinner on their way home.

For great seafood in a lower-key atmosphere, head for the ★ **Anchor Oyster Bar** (579 Castro St., 415/431-3990, www.anchoroysterbar.com, 11:30am-10pm Mon.-Sat., 4pm-9:30pm Sun., $20-34), an institution in the Castro since 1977. The raw bar features different varieties of oysters, while the dining room serves seafood, including local favorite Dungeness crab.

GOLDEN GATE PARK AND THE HAIGHT

The **Beach Chalet Brewery** (1000 Great Hwy., 415/386-8439, www.beachchalet.com, 9am-10pm Mon.-Thurs., 9am-11pm Fri., 8am-11pm Sat., 8am-10pm Sun., $14-30) is an attractive brewpub and restaurant directly across the street from Ocean Beach. Out back, sister restaurant **Park Chalet** (http://parkchalet.com, noon-9pm Mon.-Thurs., noon-10pm Fri., 11am-10pm Sat., 10am-9pm Sun., $15-24) offers a similar menu with outdoor seating and jumping live music on the weekends.

One of the most famous locations in San Francisco is the ★ **Cliff House.** The high-end eatery inhabiting the famed facade is **Sutro's** (1090 Point Lobos Ave., 415/386-3330, www.cliffhouse.com, 11:30am-3:30pm and 5pm-9:30pm Mon.-Sat., 11am-3:30pm and 5pm-9:30pm Sun., $28-46), where expensive plates of steak, lamb, and salmon are best with a glass of California wine. The more casual (and affordable) **Bistro** (9am-3:30pm and 4:15pm-9:30pm Mon.-Sat., 8:30am-3:30pm and 4:15pm-9:30pm Sun., $16-33) serves big bowls of cioppino at an ornately carved zinc bar. The **Lounge** (9am-11pm Sun.-Thurs., 9am-midnight Fri.-Sat.) is the best deal in the house, where you can order off a limited menu or just sip coffee and drinks without all the fuss.

Accommodations

Both the cheapest and most expensive places tend to be in Union Square, SoMa, and the Financial District. Consistently cheaper digs can be had in the neighborhoods surrounding Fisherman's Wharf. Valet parking and overnight garage parking can be excruciatingly expensive. Check with your hotel to see if they have a "parking package" that includes this expense.

UNION SQUARE AND DOWNTOWN
Under $150

The ★ **Golden Gate Hotel** (775 Bush St., 415/392-3702 or 800/835-1118, www.goldengatehotel.com, $135-190) offers small, charming rooms with friendly, unpretentious hospitality. You'll find a continental breakfast every morning in the hotel lobby. There are only two rates: the higher rate ($215) gets you a room with a private bathroom, while the lower rate ($145) gets you a room with a bath down the hall. Pets are welcome.

The Mosser's (54 4th St., 415/986-4400, www.themosser.com, $109-289) inexpensive rooms have European-style shared baths in the hallway and bright modern decor that nicely complements the century-old building. Pricier options include bigger rooms with private baths. With a rep for cleanliness and pleasant amenities, including morning coffee and comfy bathrobes, this hotel provides visitors with a cheap crash space in a great location convenient to sights, shops, and public transportation.

$150-250

The **Hotel Bijou** (111 Mason St., 415/771-1200, www.hotelbijou.com, $140-220) is a fun spot. Whimsical decor mimics an old-fashioned movie theater, and a tiny "movie house" downstairs runs double features, free to guests, every night—with only movies shot in San Francisco. The rooms are small, clean, and nicely appointed.

Only half a block down from the square, the **Sir Francis Drake** (450 Powell St., 415/392-7755 or 800/795-7129, www.sirfrancisdrake.com, $149-415) has its own history beginning in the late 1920s. Here at the Drake you'll find a bit less opulence in the lobby but a bit more in the guest rooms. The Beefeater doorman (almost always available for a photo), the unique door overhang, and the red-and-gold interior all add to the character of this favorite.

The ★ **Hotel Triton** (342 Grant Ave., 415/394-0500, www.hoteltriton.com, $135-389) adds a bit of whimsy and eco-chic to the stately aesthetic of Union Square. Jerry Garcia decorated a room here, and Häagen-Dazs tailored its own suite, complete with an ice cream-stocked freezer case. The rooms are tiny but comfortable and well stocked with ecofriendly amenities and bath products. The flat-panel TVs offer a 24-hour yoga channel, and complimentary yoga props can be delivered to your room on request.

Hotel Rex (562 Sutter St., 415/433-4434 or 800/433-4434, www.jdvhotels.com, $179-400) channels San Francisco's literary side, evoking a hotel in the early 1900s when bohemians such as Jack London, Ambrose Bierce, and even Mark Twain roamed and ruminated about the city. Rooms are comfortable and spacious, decorated with the work of local artists and artisans. The dimly lit lobby bar is famous in the city for its literary bent—you may have a fascinating conversation as you enjoy your evening glass of wine.

Over $250

A San Francisco legend, the **Clift** (495 Geary St., 415/775-4700, www.clifthotel.com, $299-400) has a lobby worth walking into. The high-ceilinged industrial space is devoted to modern art. Yes, you really are supposed to sit on the antler sofa and the metal chairs. By contrast, the rooms are almost spartan in their simplicity, with colors meant to mimic the city skyline. Stop in for a drink at the Redwood Room, done in brown leather and popular with a younger crowd.

At the 1904-built **Westin St. Francis** (335 Powell St., 415/397-7000 or 888/627-8546, www.westinstfrancis.com, $259-500), the hotel's robber-baron and Jazz-Age past is evident as soon as you walk into the immense lobby. The hotel's two wings are the original section, called the Landmark Building, and the 1972 renovation is The Tower. There are 1,200 rooms, making it the largest hotel in the city. Rooms in the historical section are loaded with lavish charms like ornate woodwork and chandeliers, while the modern rooms are large and sport fantastic views of the city and the bay.

The **Fairmont San Francisco** (950 Mason St., 415/772-5000, www.fairmont.com, $350-595) opened shortly after the 1906 earthquake, designed in the Beaux Arts style of the time. It has a tower addition; rooms are large with marble baths and even more spectacular views than the historical rooms.

Hotel Vitale (8 Mission St., 415/278-3700 or 888/890-8688, www.hotelvitale.com, $365-650) professes to restore guests' vitality with its lovely rooms and exclusive spa, complete with rooftop hot soaking tubs and a yoga studio. Many of the good-size rooms also have private deep soaking tubs, and many have views of the Embarcadero and the bay.

The **Palace Hotel** (2 New Montgomery St., 415/512-1111, www.sfpalace.com, $400-700) has enjoyed its reputation as the grande dame of all San Francisco hotels since 1875. In 1919 President Woodrow Wilson even negotiated the terms of the Treaty of Versailles over lunch at the Garden Court here. Today guests take pleasure in beautiful bedrooms, exercise and relax in the full-service spa and fitness center, and dine in the Palace's three restaurants. A meal in the exquisite Garden Court dining room is a must, though you may forget to eat as you gaze upward at the stained-glass domed ceiling.

NORTH BEACH AND FISHERMAN'S WHARF

Under $150

The **San Remo Hotel** (2237 Mason St., 415/776-8688 or 800/352-7366, www.sanremohotel.com, $89-249) is one of the best bargains in the city. The rooms boast the simplest of decorations and none have telephones or TVs, and the bathrooms are located down the hall. Downstairs, Fior d'Italia is the oldest Italian restaurant in the country and has a generous happy hour seven days a week.

$150-250

The **Washington Square Inn** (1660 Stockton St., 415/981-4220, www.wsisf.com, $209-359) doesn't look like a typical California B&B, but more like a small, elegant hotel. The inn offers 16 rooms with queen or king beds, private baths, elegant appointments, and fine linens. Standard rooms are "cozy" in the European urban style, while some have spa bathtubs and others have views of Coit Tower and Saints Peter and Paul Church. A few of the amenities include a generous continental breakfast brought to your room daily, afternoon tea, a flat-screen TV in every room, and free wireless Internet.

Over $250

In a district not known for its luxury, **The Argonaut** (495 Jefferson St., 415/563-0800 or 800/790-1415, www.argonauthotel.com, $209-579) in Fisherman's Wharf stands out. Housed in an exposed-brick 1907 warehouse, the hotel embraces its nautical connections to the nines. Many rooms have great views of the bay, and its location is ideal, only steps away from Aquatic Park, Pier 45, Ghirardelli Square, and the excellent Maritime Museum.

MARINA AND PACIFIC HEIGHTS

$150-250

The rooms at the ★ **Marina Motel** (2576 Lombard St., 415/921-9406, www.marinamotel.com, $119-349) may be small, but the place is big on charm and character. This friendly little motel, decorated in French-country style, welcomes families with kids and dogs. Just ask for the room type that best suits your needs when you make your reservations. Rooms are pleasantly priced for budget travelers.

The **Hotel del Sol** (3100 Webster St., 415/921-5520 or 877/433-5765, www.jdvhotels.com, $169-229) embraces its origins as a 1950s motor lodge, with the rooms decorated in bright, bold colors with whimsical accents, a heated courtyard pool, and the ever-popular free parking. Family suites and larger rooms have kitchenettes. The Marina locale offers trendy cafés, restaurants, bars, and shopping within walking distance as well as access to major attractions.

The stately **Queen Anne Hotel** (1590 Sutter St., 415/441-2828, www.queenanne.com, $149-250) is thoroughly Victorian. Sumptuous fabrics, ornate antiques, and rich colors in the rooms and common areas add to the feeling of decadence in this boutique bed-and-breakfast. Small, moderate rooms offer attractive accommodations on a budget, while superior rooms and suites are more upscale. Continental breakfast is included, as are a number of high-end services.

A Pacific Heights jewel, the **Jackson Court** (2198 Jackson St., 415/929-7670, www.jacksoncourt.com, $239) presents a lovely brick facade in the exclusive neighborhood. The 10-room inn offers comfortable, uniquely decorated queen rooms and a luscious continental breakfast each morning.

Over $250

The **Inn at the Presidio** (42 Moraga Ave., 415/800-7356, www.innatthepresidio.com, $310-385) is inside historical Pershing Hall right in the center of the Presidio. Built in 1903, the large brick building was formerly home to single military officers. In the classic rooms and suites (some with fireplaces), subtle contemporary furnishings complement the framed photos and other Presidio memorabilia sprinkled throughout. On-site amenities include a breakfast buffet, wine and cheese reception, free wireless access, a covered front porch with rocking chairs overlooking the Main Post, and an outdoor deck with fire pit. There is an $8 fee for self-parking, or take advantage of the PresidiGo shuttle.

Tucked in with the money-laden mansions of Pacific Heights, ★ **Hotel Drisco** (2901 Pacific Ave., 415/346-2880 or 800/634-7277, www.hoteldrisco.com, $297-369) offers elegance to discerning visitors. You get quiet, comfy rooms that include a "pillow menu"; continental breakfast with a latte, smoked salmon, and brie; hors d'oeuvres and a glass of wine in the evening; and bicycles on loan.

Transportation

AIR

San Francisco International Airport (SFO, 800/435-9736, www.flysfo.com) isn't within the city of San Francisco; it is actually about 13 miles south in the town of Millbrae, right on the bay. You can easily get a taxi ($43-63) or other ground transportation ($16-20) into the heart of the city from the airport. BART (www.bart.gov) is available from SFO's international terminal and will deliver you to downtown San Francisco for $8. Some San Francisco hotels offer complimentary shuttles from the airport as well. You can also rent a car here.

As one of the 30 busiest airports in the world, SFO has long check-in and security lines much of the time and dreadful overcrowding on major travel holidays. On an average day, plan to arrive at the airport two hours before your domestic flight and three hours before an international flight.

TRAIN

Amtrak (800/872-7245, www.amtrak.com) does not run directly into San Francisco. You can ride into San Jose, Oakland, or Emeryville station, and then take a connecting bus into San Francisco.

BUS

Greyhound (200 Folsom St., 800/231-2222, www.greyhound.com) offers bus service to San Francisco from all over the country.

MUNI

The **Muni** (www.sfmta.com, adults $2.25, youth and seniors $1.25, children 4 and under

free) transit system can get you where you want to go in San Francisco as long as time isn't a concern. Tickets can be purchased from any Muni driver; underground trains have ticket machines at the entrance. Exact change is required, except on the cable cars, where drivers can make change for up to $20. See the website for a route map, ticket information, and schedules.

CAR

The **Bay Bridge** (toll $4-6) links I-80 to San Francisco from the east, and the **Golden Gate Bridge** (toll $7.50) connects Highway 1 from the north. From the south, U.S. 101 and I-280 snake up the peninsula and into the city. Be sure to get a detailed map and good directions to drive into San Francisco—the freeway interchanges, especially surrounding the east side of the Bay Bridge, can be confusing, and the traffic congestion is legendary. For traffic updates and route planning, visit **511.org.**

If you absolutely must have your car with you, try to get a room at a hotel with a parking lot and either free parking or a parking package for the length of your stay.

Car Rental

All the major car rental agencies have a presence at the **San Francisco International Airport** (SFO, 800/435-9736, www.flysfo.com). In addition, most reputable hotels can offer or recommend a car rental. Rates tend to run $20-100 per day and $165-450 per week (including taxes and fees), with discounts for weekly and longer rentals.

North Bay

Marin County, in the North Bay, is San Francisco's backyard. Beginning with the Marin Headlands at the terminus of the Golden Gate Bridge, there is a nearly unbroken expanse of wildlands from San Francisco Bay to Tomales Bay. Here you'll find rugged cliffs plunging into the Pacific, towering redwoods, and verdant pastures.

★ ANGEL ISLAND STATE PARK

Angel Island (415/435-5390, www.parks. ca.gov, 8am-sunset daily, rates vary by ferry company) has a long history, beginning with regular visits (though no permanent settlements) by the Coastal Miwok people. During the Civil War the U.S. Army created a fort on the island in anticipation of Confederate attacks from the Pacific. The attacks never came, but the Army maintained a base here. Today many of the 19th-century military buildings remain and can be seen on the hour-long **tram tour** (415/435-3392, http://angelislandsf.com, 11:45am and 2pm daily Mar.-Sept., 11.45pm Mon.-Tues., 11:45am and

2pm Wed.-Sun. Oct., 11:45 and 2pm Sat.-Sun. Nov.-Feb., $10-15), on foot, or on a docent-led two-hour **Segway tour** (10:30am and 1pm daily, $68). Later, the Army built a Nike missile base on the island to protect San Francisco from possible Soviet attacks. The missile base is not open to the public but can be seen from roads and trails.

Angel Island's history also has a sobering side. Between 1910 and 1940, it served as an immigration station for inbound ships and as a concentration camp for Chinese emigrants attempting to escape turmoil in their homeland. Europeans were waved through, but Chinese were herded into barracks as government officials scrutinized their papers. After months and sometimes years of waiting, many were sent back to China. Poetry lines the walls of the barracks, expressing the despair of the immigrants who had hoped for a better life. The **Immigration Station** (11am-3pm Wed.-Sun., adults $5, children 6-17 $3, under 6 free) is open to visitors and docent-led tours are also available (11am and 12:30pm Wed.-Fri., 11am, 12:30pm, and 1:45pm Sat. Sun., $7).

the view of Marin from Angel Island

Angel Island is a destination for both casual and serious hikers. Multiuse trails of varying difficulty crisscross the island. Adventurous trekkers can scale Mount Livermore via either the **North Ridge Trail** or the **Sunset Trail**. Each runs about 4.5 miles round-trip for a moderate, reasonably steep hike. At the top, enjoy gorgeous bay views. For the best experience, make a loop, taking one trail up the mountain and the other back down. If you're up for a long paved-road hike, take the **Perimeter Road** (five miles, moderate) all the way around the island.

Pick up a boxed lunch or take a table at the **Angel Island Café** (415/435-3392, www.angelisland.com, 10am-3pm daily May-Oct., $9-14), which serves hot sandwiches, wraps, salad, soup, and ice cream. Open summer only, the nearby **Angel Island Cantina** (11:30am-4:30pm Fri.-Sun., $7-14) serves burgers, tacos, oysters, beer, wine, and pitchers of mimosas and sangria.

Getting There

The harbor at Tiburon is the easiest place to access Angel Island, located in the middle of San Francisco Bay. The private **Angel Island-Tiburon Ferry** (21 Main St., Tiburon, 415/435-2131, www.angelislandferry.com, adults $15, seniors $14, children 6-12 $13, children 3-5 $5, bicycles $1) can get you out to the island in about 10 minutes and runs several times a day. You can also take the **Blue and Gold Fleet** (415/705-8200, www.blueandgoldfleet.com, one-way adult $8, senior and children 5-11 $4.50) to Angel Island from San Francisco's Pier 41. Ferries depart San Francisco 9:45am-3pm, and the last ferry back departs Angel Island at 3:50pm. Although the ferry out of Tiburon has more sailings during the day, the last ferry is still early (3pm-5pm daily), with very few sailings on weekdays during the winter.

Ferries have plenty of room for you to bring your own bicycle, or you can rent one at the **main visitors area** (415/435-3392, http://angelislandsf.com, Sat.-Sun. Mar.-Nov., daily Apr.-Oct., $13.50 per hour, $50 per day) near the ferry dock. Rentals must always be returned at 3pm.

Tiburon is located on a peninsula about eight miles north of the Golden Gate Bridge. From San Francisco, take U.S. 101 north to the Tiburon Boulevard (CA 131) exit. Stay to the right and follow the road along the water for nearly six miles until you reach the small downtown area.

★ MUIR WOODS NATIONAL MONUMENT

Established in 1908 and named for naturalist and author John Muir, **Muir Woods National Monument** (1 Muir Woods Rd., 415/388-2596, www.nps.gov/muwo, 8am-sunset daily, adults $10, under 16 free) comprises acres of staggeringly beautiful redwood forest. More than six miles of trails wind through the redwoods and accompanying Mount Tamalpais area. These are some of the most stunning—and accessible—redwoods in the Bay Area.

The visitors center is a great place to begin your exploration. The **Muir Woods Visitors Center** (9am-sunset daily) abuts the main parking area and marks the entrance to Muir Woods. In addition to maps, information, and advice about hiking, you'll also find a few amenities. Inside the park, slightly past the visitors center, is a **café** (415/388-7059, www.muirwoodstradingcompany.com, 9am-5:30pm daily, closing hours vary) where you can purchase souvenirs and food.

Many lovely trails crisscross the gorgeous redwood forest. First-time visitors should follow the wheelchair- and stroller-accessible **Redwood Creek Trail** (one mile, easy). Leading from the visitors center on an easy and flat walk through the beautiful redwoods, this trail has an interpretive brochure (pick one up at the visitors center) with numbers along the way that describe the flora and fauna. Hikers can continue the loop on the **Hillside Trail** for an elevated view of the valley.

Getting There

Muir Woods is accessed via the long and winding Muir Woods Road. From U.S. 101, take the Stinson Beach/Highway 1 exit. On Highway 1, also named the Shoreline Highway, follow the road under the freeway and proceed until the road splits in a T junction at the light. Turn left, continuing on Shoreline Highway for 2.5 miles. At the intersection with Panoramic Highway, make a sharp right turn and continue climbing uphill. At the junction of Panoramic Highway and Muir Woods Road, turn left and follow the road 1.5 twisty miles down to the Muir Woods parking lots on the right.

If you're visiting on a holiday or a summer weekend, get to the Muir Woods parking areas early—they fill fast, and afternoon hopefuls will not find a spot. Lighted signs on U.S. 101 will alert you to parking conditions at the main parking lot. To avoid the traffic hassle, the **Muir Woods Shuttle** (415/226-0855, http://www.marintransit.org/routes/66.html, Sat.-Sun. Apr.-May and Sept.-Oct., daily June-Aug., $5 round-trip, under 16 free) leaves from various points in southern Marin County, including the Sausalito ferry terminal.

★ POINT REYES NATIONAL SEASHORE

The Point Reyes area boasts acres of unspoiled grassland, forest, and beach. Cool weather presides even in the summer, but the result is lustrous green foliage and spectacular scenery. **Point Reyes National Seashore** (1 Bear Valley Rd., 415/464-5100, www.nps.gov/pore, dawn-midnight daily) stretches between Tomales Bay and the Pacific, north from Stinson Beach to the tip of the land at the end of the bay. Dedicated hikers can trek from the bay to the ocean or from the beach to land's end. The protected lands shelter a range of wildlife. In the marshes and lagoons, a wide variety of birds—including three different species of pelicans—make their nests. The pine forests shade shy deer and larger elk. A few ranches and dairy farms operate inside the park. Grandfathered in at the time the park was created, these sustainable, generations-old family farms give added character and historical depth to Point Reyes.

The Point Reyes area includes the tiny towns of Olema, Point Reyes Station, and Inverness.

SAN FRANCISCO
NORTH BAY

the entrance to Muir Woods National Monument

Point Reyes Historic Lighthouse

The rocky shores of Point Reyes make for great sightseeing but incredibly dangerous maritime navigation. In 1870 the first lighthouse was constructed on the headlands. Its first-order Fresnel lens threw light far enough for ships to avoid the treacherous granite cliffs. Yet the danger remained, and soon after, a lifesaving station was constructed alongside the light station. It wasn't until the 20th century, when a ship-to-shore radio station and newer lifesaving station were put in place, that the Point Reyes shore truly became safer for ships.

The **Point Reyes Historic Lighthouse** (415/669-1534, www.nps.gov/pore, 10am-4:30pm Fri.-Mon.) still stands today on a point past the visitors center, accessed by descending a sometimes treacherous, cold, and windblown flight of 300 stairs, which often closes to visitors during bad weather. Still, it's worth a visit. The Fresnel lens and original machinery all remain in place, and the adjacent equipment building contains foghorns, air compressors, and other safety implements from decades past.

Visitors Centers

The **Bear Valley Visitors Center** (1 Bear Valley Rd., 415/464-5100, 10am-5pm Mon.-Fri., 9am-5pm Sat.-Sun. May-Nov., 10am-4:30pm Mon.-Fri., 9am-4:30pm Sat.-Sun. Nov.-May) acts as the central visitors center for Point Reyes National Seashore. In addition to maps, fliers, and interpretive exhibits, the center houses a short video introducing the region. You can also talk to park rangers, either to ask advice or to obtain beach fire permits and backcountry camping permits.

The **Ken Patrick Visitors Center** (Drakes Beach, 415/669-1250, 9am-5pm daily summer, 9:30am-4:30pm Sat.-Sun. fall-spring) sits right on the beach in a building made of weathered redwood. Its small museum focuses on the maritime history of the region.

Getting There

Point Reyes is only about an hour north of San Francisco by car, but getting here can be quite a drive. From the Golden Gate Bridge, take U.S. 101 north to just south of San Rafael. Take the Sir Francis Drake Boulevard exit toward San Anselmo. Follow Sir Francis Drake Boulevard west for 20 miles to the small town of Olema and Highway 1. At the intersection with Highway 1, turn right (north) to Point Reyes Station and the Bear Valley Visitors Center.

A slower but more scenic route follows

Point Reyes Historic Lighthouse

Highway 1 into Point Reyes National Seashore and provides access to the trails near Bolinas in the southern portion of the park. From the Golden Gate Bridge, take U.S. 101 north to the Mill Valley/Stinson Beach exit. Follow Shoreline Highway for almost 30 miles through Stinson Beach and past Bolinas Lagoon to the coast. From the lagoon, it's 11 miles north to Point Reyes Station. Expect twists, turns, and slow going as you approach Point Reyes.

You can get gas only in Point Reyes Station. There are full-service grocery stores in Point Reyes Station at **Palace Market** (11300 Highway 1, 415/663-1016, www.palacemarket.com, 8am-9pm daily) and in Inverness at **Inverness Store** (12784 Sir Francis Drake Blvd., 415/669-1041, 9am-7pm daily).

Background

The Landscape

GEOLOGY

Some 150 million years ago, probably long before vines had evolved from the primordial jungles, what we today know as Napa and Sonoma Counties was at the bottom of a giant ocean lapping up against massive volcanoes that eventually formed California's Sierra Nevada mountain range, about 100 miles east of today's Napa Valley.

Much of modern-day California did not come into existence until the tectonic plates that make up the earth's crust had played their game of geological push and shove, generating massive creases in the earth's surface that pushed up the seafloor, creating mountains and shifting and splitting ancient continents to create the map of the world we recognize today.

From a winemaker's point of view, the geological history of California is ultimately what makes this area such a great wine-growing region. The ancient soils, valleys, and mountains combine into some of the most perfect places on earth to grow grapes.

Franciscan Formation

The section of the earth's crust that ended up creating California is the Farallon plate, immortalized in the tiny Farallon Islands that lie about 20 miles off the coast of San Francisco. Where the plate pressed against its neighbor, the massive North American continental plate just west of the Sierra Nevada, it lost the shoving battle and ended up being forced under the larger continental plate in what is known in geological terms as a subduction zone.

As the Farallon plate was squeezed closer to the hot core of the earth under immense pressure, it generated huge quantities of molten rock, fueling prehistoric volcanoes which over millions of years built the mountains we know today. The process is continuing today all around the Pacific Ocean, particularly farther north where there's a reminder of the recurring tectonic activity every time Mount St. Helens or one of Alaska's many volcanoes sparks into life.

Geologists believe that as those prehistoric mountains got bigger and heavier from spewing out lava over the course of millions of years, they literally squashed the earth's crust and created a surrounding bulge hundreds of miles wide, much like pressing the edge of your finger into soft mud will cause the goop around it to bulge up.

That big undersea bulge then acted like a giant spatula, scraping off big chunks of the Farallon plate as it dived under its neighbor in the subduction zone and depositing them over millions of years to create what we now know as modern coastal California, including Napa and Sonoma. These geological scrapings are known as the Franciscan formation and form the bedrock of Northern and Southern California.

Volcanoes

The mountains and valleys of coastal California are altogether more recent additions to the Franciscan formation—recent at least in terms of geological timelines. About five million years ago, fissures in the bedrock opened up all over the land and spawned violent volcanoes that spewed out lava, ash, and giant boulders, rearranging the surface of the land and blanketing it with deep layers of volcanic rock and ash.

In the Napa Valley, evidence of these ancient volcanoes is easy to see. Mount St. Helena is an ancient volcano that once blew

---

Previous: vineyards in the Spring Mountain appellation; morning fog over Robert Mondavi Winery.

its top, flattening nearby trees, which were buried, fossilized, and eventually uncovered in the area where Calistoga's Petrified Forest is today. Nearby, Calistoga's hot springs, geyser, and the volcanic mud that visitors submerge themselves in are reminders of the cauldron that still bubbles deep underground, and just southeast of Calistoga is an area called Glass Mountain, so called because of the lumps of black glass-like volcanic obsidian found in the soil.

While the volcanoes were adding their own ingredients to what would become the complex mix of soils in the Wine Country, enter the giant geological blender known as the San Andreas Fault, a huge gash in the earth's crust.

The mountains and valleys of Napa and Sonoma were formed in the last three million years as the Pacific plate, another giant chunk of the earth's crust under the Pacific Ocean, slid northward along the San Andreas Fault, eventually breaking up the Farallon plate in front of it. As it progressed, unleashing an earthquake with every sudden move, it slowly compressed the edge of the neighboring North American continental plate and, over millions of years, buckled the land on the other side of the fault line, pushing up ridges of the Franciscan bedrock through the deep volcanic deposits covering it and creating the series of coastal mountain ranges and valleys that today define this part of Northern California.

The Mayacamas Mountains between the Napa and Sonoma Valleys, for example, were formed by this buckling. The plates are still moving today, ever so slowly, though the only reminders we have of this ongoing evolution of the planet's geology are the occasional earthquakes that rattle California.

The Franciscan and volcanic soils were further mixed up over the millennia by rivers and streams that carved their way down through the rocks, picking up sediment and dumping it miles away. The resulting patchwork of Franciscan, volcanic, and sedimentary soils is a winemaker's dream and helps explain why Northern California's Wine Country can turn out so many diverse styles of wine. Napa Valley alone is said to have up to 33 distinct types of soil.

CLIMATE

The soils aren't everything, of course. The mountains, hills, and valleys that make the geographical patchwork of the region also create a patchwork of climates, sheltering some areas from cool ocean winds, channeling the cool air to others, and exposing different slopes to different amounts of sunshine throughout the day. Throughout Napa and Sonoma, and indeed much of the greater San Francisco Bay Area, microclimates are the norm. It might be a cool, murky August morning in San Francisco, but just 10 miles away the sun will be out and the weather balmy. Even within one sunny valley the temperature can vary widely in just a few miles.

The average maximum temperature in the city of Napa in July and August (the hottest months of the year) is about 82°F, according to historical climate data. In St. Helena, halfway up the Napa Valley, it averages about 89°F, and in Calistoga, far away from the cooling influence of the San Francisco Bay air, it averages 92°F. Carneros, meanwhile, is right next to the bay and usually only reaches the mid-70s at best.

Elsewhere in the area the extremes are just as great. In northern Sonoma, the top of the Alexander Valley bakes in average temperatures of nearly 92°F in July, while down in the fogbound Russian River Valley, Occidental chills out at about 75°F.

For a winemaker, different climates are measured using a method called heat summation (also known as the Winkler Scale), which categorizes climates into regions on a scale from 1 to 5 depending on how hot the average daily temperature is during a vine's main growing season, April-October. Different grapes grow and ripen best in each climate region.

If California were a country, it would be one of the few on Earth that have areas corresponding to all five growing regions.

Northern California's Wine Country alone contains four of the five regions (though some say it has only three), which means there's an ideal climate for almost any type of grape.

Winemakers also have an easier job here than their colleagues in many other parts of the world, particularly in Europe, because rainfall is almost nonexistent for much of the summer, so grapes can ripen in the plentiful sun and avoid damp-related fungal disease like mildew. Similarly, hail and damaging winds are almost unheard of here during the summer. Most rain falls between November and April, and apart from the rare summer thunderstorm or late spring shower, it is generally dry from late May through October.

Fog

One of the defining aspects of the weather along the Northern California coast is the fog—damp, chilly marine fog that creeps, and sometimes charges, inland from the cold Pacific Ocean during the summer through every gap it can find in the mountains. Perhaps no aspect of the weather here is more important. Fog takes the edge off the sometimes vicious summer heat and sun, keeps the nights cool, and slows the ripening of grapes in many places to a perfect tempo. It also generates the damp conditions in which California's famous coastal redwoods thrive, from Santa Cruz to Crescent City and nowhere more so than in the Russian River Valley, which is essentially a fog freeway, providing a direct channel from the ocean through the coastal hills and inland.

The factors that generate the fog, however, actually start hundreds of miles away in the sun-baked Central Valley of California. As the temperature there rises on summer days, so does the hot air, lowering the atmospheric pressure near the ground. Something has to replace all that rising air and even out the pressure. Imagine, then, a giant sucking noise as cool air is pulled in from the ocean to do just that.

Because the ocean is so cold, thanks to some chilly Alaskan currents, it actually condenses water from the air (much like cold air does to your breath), forming a deep bank of fog that sits, menacingly, just off the coast. The onshore winds generated by the inland sun drag that fog onto the coast.

How far inland it gets depends on all sorts of factors, from the time of year to the prevailing atmospheric pressure. During summer days it usually hugs the coast. At night it can advance inland as far as the southern part of Napa Valley, Dry Creek Valley, burning off rapidly as the sun heats things up.

Many additional factors have recently been found to influence fog formation, from weather over the Rocky Mountains to the currents in the South Pacific. But all winemakers care about is that the fog helps make a great bottle of wine.

UNIQUE VINEYARD CONDITIONS

The combination of diverse soils and diverse microclimates offers just about everything a winemaker could want. There are very few grapes that have not been able to grow somewhere in California, and the current diversity of grape varietals (or lack thereof) has more to do with marketing than weather.

The French have a term for the unique conditions of a place that a grape is grown: *terroir*. It describes the combination of geological, geographical, and climate-related aspects of the land, including soil, slope, elevation, sun exposure, wind levels, and temperature patterns. California has a vast number of distinct *terroirs*.

Terroir explains why grapes grown in one vineyard will make a wine that tastes different from that made from grapes in a neighboring vineyard. So-called vineyard-designate wines sourced from one specific vineyard rather than multiple vineyards take advantage of that difference. There can even be a difference in the wine made from different sections, or blocks, of an individual vineyard.

It explains why the Napa Valley's Stag's Leap Wine Cellars can make very different wines from different blocks of one of its vineyards, for example, and why Stags Leap District cabernets as a whole taste different from those produced in the Rutherford District just a few miles up the road.

Best Soils and Climate

Almost without exception, the best soils for growing wine grapes are well drained and relatively infertile. Drainage is important to prevent the vines and grapes from getting too damp and potentially rotting, and also to encourage the vines to grow deep roots in search of a stable source of water. Some of the oldest vines are known to have sent roots down as deep as 100 feet.

Drip irrigation systems are common sights in California vineyards, but they often have more to do with producing a financially viable quantity of grapes per acre than keeping the vines alive. Without some artificial water the vines might well survive but would not look nearly so lush with leaves and plump grapes by the end of the summer.

Fertility (or the lack of it) is a less important factor, although it's not by chance that some of the world's most distinctive and flavorful wines come from vineyards that thrive on fairly barren, rocky land, including steep mountainsides where even native plants struggle to grow.

Ultimately, grape growers are trying to produce a stressed vine—one that has to relentlessly search for water and survive on meager nutrients. This is not exactly the aim of most gardeners, who water and feed their plants to make them as big and lush as possible. The theory goes that a stressed vine will produce fewer and smaller grapes, but they will have a far more concentrated flavor. The same principle (taken to an extreme) explains why a shriveled raisin has a far more concentrated and powerful flavor than a plump Thompson seedless grape grown with the aid of plenty of water and fertilizer.

Climate plays an equally important role in how a wine turns out, determining how quickly a grape ripens and the level of ripeness it is ultimately able to reach as measured by its sugar content. Temperatures during the day and night are affected by sun exposure, wind patterns, and countless other factors. Climate helps explain why a cabernet produced from vineyards on the west-facing slopes of a valley, which get sun during much of the warmest part of the day, will taste slightly different from that made from a vineyard on an east-facing slope that might get less sun due to morning fog.

Appellation or AVA?

The diversity of grape-growing conditions is recognized around the world in various national systems of defining geographical regions based on their specific soils and climate. Such systems have given rise to the names of famous types of wine all over the world, from Bordeaux to Burgundy, Chianti to Barolo. In the United States, such regions are called American Viticultural Areas, or AVAs, though many people simply call them appellations, after the French word meaning almost, but not quite, the same thing.

An appellation describes a geographical area, like an entire state or even a country. An AVA is based on a unique growing region only, one that can be shown to have conditions (soils, climate, etc.) that make it stand apart from other areas around it. An appellation can be an AVA, but not all are. If wine were an appellation, then specific types of wine would be the viticultural areas. In the same vein, California is an appellation, and the Napa Valley is an AVA.

The federal Bureau of Alcohol, Tobacco, and Firearms (ATF) is the arbiter of AVAs and dishes them out only when wineries in a specific area have been able to prove that theirs is a unique place to grow grapes. Such proof usually comes in the form of an analysis of soils, climate, and physical features of the land. The petitioning and granting of an AVA takes many years, as is typical of most federal government processes, and is usually led by one or a group of wineries. Winemaking politics often complicate matters, especially when some wineries don't want to be included in an AVA for some marketing reason or another, leading to some very drawn-out application processes and sometimes arbitrary AVA boundaries.

The first AVA was established in 1980 in, of all places, Augusta, Missouri, and they are still being established today. The biggest in the country in terms of area is the Upper Mississippi River Valley, covering nearly 30,000 square miles in parts of four different states. The smallest is Cole Ranch in Mendocino County, California, covering about a quarter square mile.

In Northern California there was a rush to get AVA status following the 1976 Judgment of Paris. Not surprisingly, the Napa Valley was the first California AVA, and second in the nation, being granted its status only eight months after that in Augusta, Missouri. As of 2016 there are now 138 AVAs in California, a figure that is constantly growing. There can also be AVAs within AVAs, often called sub-appellations (again a technically incorrect term in some cases, but often used anyway) or nesting AVAs. The Napa Valley AVA, for example, contains a patchwork of 16 smaller AVAs, each producing its own distinctive style of wine. The appellation of Sonoma County contains 15 AVAs, some of which overlap. If defining the land is so complicated, it's no wonder that the wines are so varied.

One interesting pattern exists in the Napa Valley. Since 1989, thanks to an arcane labeling law designed to protect the exclusivity of the Napa Valley name, no Napa County viticultural areas can fall outside the Napa Valley AVA. That's why many of the smaller AVAs in the Napa Valley, such as Mount Veeder and Spring Mountain, end abruptly at the county border. The one exception is Los Carneros AVA, which sprawls across the southern portion of the Napa Valley and west into Sonoma County. It defies Napa Valley borders only because it was created before the 1989 law was enacted.

History

Northern California is widely regarded as the historic center of the state's wine industry, with its roots tied to the Spanish missions and the era of Mexican land grants.

CALIFORNIA'S EARLY WINE INDUSTRY
Spanish Missions

California's missions played a crucial, though controversial, role in California's history, including its winemaking history. Their inexorable march northward from Mexico to Northern California introduced important winemaking skills thanks to the demand for sacramental wines. The missions also marked the beginning of the end for the lifestyles and cultures of the region's Native Americans, who had lived off the land for thousands of years.

In present-day Sonoma, Mission San Francisco de Solano was the 21st California mission and the last one built. It was established by Father Jose Altimira, who arrived in the Sonoma Valley in 1819. Once the mission had been dedicated in 1824, the missionaries quickly set about their religious purpose. With the aid of the Mexican army, Native Americans were converted to Christianity whether they wanted to be or not. Within six years the mission had also established a big farming operation, with thousands of head of sheep and cattle, and had planted some of the region's first vines.

The new mission was founded not only to continue the spread of Christianity but also to provide food for the ailing missions in present-day San Francisco and San Rafael, which were struggling to sustain themselves. It was also the first and only mission in California created under Mexican rule, and it's likely that part of its purpose was to help prevent any expansion of a trading outpost established by Russian hunters nearby on the Sonoma coast at Fort Ross.

Just three years later, trouble rode into town in the form of a 25-year-old Mexican army lieutenant, Mariano Guadalupe Vallejo, who was sent north from the Presidio in San Francisco to rattle some sabers at the Russians and establish a military post at Sonoma. Vallejo would remain in Sonoma for the next half century and play a pivotal role in the creation of modern California.

By the time the missions were secularized by the Mexican government in 1835, Vallejo's garrison at Sonoma was well established and had created a Mexican-style plaza (present-day Sonoma Plaza) as a parade ground. Vallejo was ordered to take over the mission, and he promptly started to divide the buildings and land between friends and relatives. Meanwhile, the garrison and the town started to grow in importance, and Vallejo was promoted to colonel, the highest rank he ever achieved (despite this, he somehow became commonly known as "General Vallejo," a title that sticks to this day). As the military importance of his garrison in peaceful California slowly dwindled, he started living the good life, amassing land and planting vineyards.

The Land Grants

As the military commander and later Director of Colonization in Mexico's Northern Frontier, Vallejo controlled much of the land in today's Napa and Sonoma Counties and was under orders to dole it out to Mexican citizens for development. In reality he doled it out to friends, relatives, and business associates.

The land was snatched up by names that would eventually become a big part of modern wine history, including Agoston Haraszthy, a Hungarian immigrant who planted some of the earliest European vineyard cuttings and is credited with dragging the California wine industry from its missionary roots into the modern era through his Buena Vista Winery in the Sonoma Valley.

Over in the Napa Valley, George Yount was granted the 18-square-mile Rancho Caymus in 1836, an area that today includes Yountville. He built up a huge agricultural business and is credited with planting the first grapes in the Napa Valley. He made small quantities of wine but never became one of the valley's big early producers. Another Napa Valley pioneer, Edward Bale, was granted a huge swath of land in 1844 near present-day St. Helena by way of marriage to Vallejo's niece. He planted some vines, and his friend Charles Krug, a Napa wine pioneer, made wine for him.

Up at the northern end of the Sonoma Valley, in 1859, Scotsman Charles Stuart bought some of Vallejo's land and named his home and ranch Glen Ellen, after Ellen, his wife. The name was eventually adopted by the town that developed in the area, and Stuart's ranch was renamed Glen Oaks. It still exists today. Captain Henry Boyes was another beneficiary of Vallejo's land and would go on to establish his mineral baths, Boyes Hot Springs, another name that eventually became a town.

Also in northern Sonoma, Captain Henry Fitch was granted 48,000 acres of land around present-day Healdsburg, about a quarter of which he later gave to Cyrus Alexander (after whom Alexander Valley is named) in recognition of the help that the former mountain man had been in managing Fitch's huge acreage.

As the early agricultural pioneers got started on these vast new swaths of land, California's potential wealth grew more and more apparent. More American settlers began crossing over the Sierra Nevada, and many were soon itching for independence.

The Bear Flag Revolt

As Americans began pouring into California, the Mexican government became apoplectic. It tried to round up these American illegals and dissuade others from coming to California, an ironic reversal of roles compared to today's flow of Mexican migrant workers into California. Near Sacramento, Captain John Sutter was welcoming the new immigrants at his fort, riling the Mexican government even more. Not helping matters was the arrival of U.S. Army captain John C. Frémont in California on a mapping expedition.

As tensions rose, Vallejo tried to stay neutral, walking a fine line between supporting various parties in the increasingly fragmented Mexican government and remaining friendly with the new American immigrants.

Soon tensions boiled over. In 1846, word came that Mexican general Castro was planning to drive out the Americans at Sutter's Fort. Some of the settlers believed that Vallejo, who had met with Castro several times, was part of the plan to reexert Mexican authority, and they launched a preemptive attack on Vallejo's small garrison at Sonoma.

A ragtag group of about 30 men rode the 120 miles from Sacramento to Sonoma on the night of June 13, 1846, and barged into Vallejo's unprotected residence, La Casa Grande, to arrest him. He was taken the next day to Sacramento, where he remained under arrest until August. That day the members of the raiding party made a flag for their newly declared California Republic, and that Bear Flag replaced the Mexican emblem over Sonoma Plaza.

The U.S. Navy, which had a ship off the coast, soon stepped into the power vacuum created by the Bear Flaggers and raised the Stars and Stripes over Sonoma Plaza on July 9, 1846, claiming California for the United States with little in the way of a fight. Coincidentally, a few months earlier, U.S. president James Polk had declared war on Mexico after his request to buy Texas and California had been rejected. News of the war didn't reach California until mid-July. Two years later when the war was over, California and other Southwest states were officially ceded by Mexico.

The Early Wine Boom

As if by design, gold was discovered in the Sierra foothills not long after California became a U.S. territory. Beginning in 1848, the gold rush brought a tidal wave of European immigrants to California, many of whom made their fortunes not from gold but by supplying the massive new economy with agricultural products.

The sheer scope of the immigrant influx is staggering and considered by historians to be the largest mass migration in human history. The nonnative population of California was believed to have been around 15,000 people in 1847. Six years later it was an estimated 300,000, and most of those people were under age 40. Some of Napa and Sonoma's early pioneers were among them.

By now, the missionaries, General Vallejo, and the early wine pioneers had shown that the region was well suited to growing just about everything, including grapes. The twin catalysts of the Mexican land grants and the gold rush had given a huge boost to California's agricultural industry. The next few decades would see wine production surge as all the newly arrived Europeans put their winemaking and wine drinking experience to use.

By 1876 the Sonoma Valley alone was producing 2.3 million gallons of wine a year. Around this time many of the immigrants that would shape the Napa and Sonoma wine industry had started to arrive from Europe, lured by the early successes of pioneering winemakers in the Napa and Sonoma Valleys like Charles Krug, Jacob Gundlach, and the Beringer brothers.

Outlying areas like the Alexander Valley and Dry Creek Valley were being planted with vines, and the Italian-Swiss Colony, a winemaking cooperative, was established near Cloverdale. Then the scourge of phylloxera struck. It is a devastating disease caused by a small aphid-like insect that attacks the roots of vines and slowly kills them by preventing the plant from absorbing water and nutrients. Phylloxera wiped out many vineyards in Europe in the late 1800s but is actually native to the United States. In fact, California's wine industry was doing so well in the late 1800s in part because the devastation in Europe wiped out exports and left

Haraszthy's Legacy

Although German and Italian families founded some of the oldest wineries still operating in this part of Sonoma, it was a Hungarian immigrant named **Agoston Haraszthy** who became the area's first big commercial winemaker, and in doing so helped change the face of the California wine industry.

Within a decade of arriving in the state, he had established the pioneering Buena Vista Winery in the Sonoma Valley and was producing some of the best wines in the United States. A decade later he was gone. While his contribution to California's wine industry was important, it was not quite as important as might be suggested by some of the accolades heaped upon him over the centuries.

Haraszthy is often called the Father of California Viticulture, for example, despite the fact that by the time he started bottling wine at Buena Vista the state was already producing about 240,000 gallons of the stuff. He is also sometimes credited with introducing the ubiquitous zinfandel grape to California, but there is some evidence that it arrived in the state even before he did.

One thing that is safe to say is that Haraszthy helped introduce European grapes and European-style commercial wine production to an industry still dependent on its missionary roots. He also had an entrepreneur's sense of self-promotion, which might explain his larger-than-life image.

His wine odyssey started in Wisconsin, of all places. He arrived there from Hungary and helped create what is now Sauk City, but the harsh Wisconsin winter quickly killed the vines he tried to cultivate. In 1849, like modern-day snowbirds, he headed west to the kinder, gentler climate of Southern California.

In San Diego, Haraszthy entered politics as a state legislator, and a combination of political and agricultural aspirations gradually drew him north. The 560-acre plot of land he bought in the Sonoma Valley in 1856 was quickly planted with many European grape varietals, and soon the Buena Vista Winery, with its hand-dug caves, boasted the largest vineyard in the United States and was producing award-winning wines.

He also reportedly helped plant vineyards for other Sonoma families that became (and still are) big names in the wine industry themselves, including Krug, Gundlach, and Bundschu.

By the 1860s, Haraszthy was combining his political and viticultural interests, promoting California wine across the country and getting state funding to travel around Europe to study winemaking techniques.

He returned in 1862 with thousands of vine cuttings collected in almost every European country, from Spain to Turkey. Among them are believed to be the cabernet sauvignon, pinot noir, sauvignon blanc, riesling, and semillon varieties that have become mainstays of the California wine industry.

Exactly what he brought back is open to debate, however, since cataloging and naming conventions in those days were unreliable. Some of those well-known grapes might also have stealthily arrived in California long before, and many others that he brought back never took hold.

Haraszthy's downfall was as sudden as his success. In 1863, facing financial problems, he sold his wine business to the Buena Vista Viticultural Society, a conglomerate in which he held almost half the shares, and took a management position. But within three years he was accused of mismanagement and Enron-style fraud in an attempt to create the biggest winemaker in California; in 1866 he quit.

What happened after this is still a bit of a mystery. Haraszthy left California in 1868 to run a sugar plantation in Nicaragua, but he disappeared in the rain forest and is believed to have been killed by a crocodile.

It's hard not to raise a glass to an immigrant who, in the space of 25 years, had been the co-founder of a Wisconsin town, a businessman, a politician, and a crocodile's meal. But as you raise that glass of mass-produced Sonoma Valley red wine, also consider that it might not taste quite the same (or be as cheap) if not for Agoston Haraszthy.

Americans on the East Coast gasping for wine from other sources.

It would only be years later, after most California vineyards had themselves been decimated, that vines with resistant rootstock were replanted in Northern California by Jacob Gundlach, one of the Sonoma Valley's early wine pioneers.

Not long after Northern California's wine industry had started to recover from phylloxera and was once again booming, it took another economic hit, one from which it barely recovered.

Prohibition

The 18th Amendment of the U.S. Constitution, which ushered in the era of Prohibition in 1919, was born not out of government meddling but of an increasingly powerful temperance movement that had its roots in the puritanical beliefs that go back to Plymouth Rock. Not helping matters was the increasing drunkenness of American society during the 1800s, which resulted in widespread public disgust and calls for change.

By some estimates, average Americans were drinking almost three times the amount of whiskey and other spirits in the mid-1800s as they do today. The more people drank, the more temperance movements tended to spring up all over the country in response. Eventually, the so-called "Drys" gained the political clout to pass laws in many states that banned public drinking, finally getting the Volstead Act, and with it Prohibition, passed in Congress. Winemakers had hoped that, being an upper-class drink, wine would be exempt from the legislation. In the end, though, the commercial production, sale, and transportation of any form of alcoholic drink were banned.

As with any piece of legislation, it didn't take long for people to find the loopholes and take advantage of weak enforcement. Bootleggers and gangsters set up a huge underground liquor network, and the wine industry got in on the act. Despite all commercial wine being banned, there were more acres of vineyards in existence during Prohibition than before it, and the price of grapes actually increased even as the quality of the grapes generally declined. Grape juice concentrate or bricks of compressed grapes were shipped all over the country, sometimes even accompanied by yeast tablets, for individuals to make their own wine behind closed doors, which was perfectly legal.

Although many grape growers flourished, wineries did not, and many closed. The few that remained open did so by making sacramental wine, which was still legal (as wine historians like to say, a lot of people found religion during Prohibition) or wine for government functions, also legal. After all, leaders still had to be able to entertain foreign dignitaries with fine wine even when the rest of the country had to do without.

In many ways, Prohibition marked the end of one chapter of California's winemaking history. In some areas, virtually all the wineries closed, never to reopen. Fruit trees replaced vines in many of today's winemaking valleys and held sway until relatively recently.

In Napa and Sonoma, a handful of wineries continued to operate during Prohibition, making sacramental wines, including Beringer Vineyards (the oldest continuously operating winery in the Napa Valley), Beaulieu Vineyard, Buena Vista Winery (its Carneros facility is the oldest continuously operating winery in California), and Sebastiani Vineyards. Still others turned to farming or supplying grapes until Prohibition was repealed, then resumed winemaking, while a few wineries continued to make wine and store it in the hope that Prohibition would soon end.

It took 14 years for Prohibition to come to an end; it was finally repealed in 1933, when the 21st Amendment was passed by Congress. In those 14 years, California's wine industry had been gutted. Most wineries had closed, important winemaking skills had been lost, and the public had lost the taste for fine wines, instead preferring homemade hooch. Making matters worse, the few remaining wine producers emerged from the shadow of Prohibition only to sink into the gloom of the deepest economic crisis in American history, the Great Depression.

Picking Up the Pieces

Following the repeal of Prohibition, winemakers were left with broken wineries, vineyards that had been planted with grapes that shipped well rather than grapes that made good wine, and a nonexistent domestic market for wine. For an industry in such a dire state, recovery was surprisingly fast.

In some ways the wine industry took several steps back after repeal, turning out bulk and fortified wines of far lower quality than the world-class wines made by the new European immigrants some 30 years earlier. The few big wineries that did survive, especially those in the Napa and Sonoma Valleys, continued to make some high-quality wines, but they too jumped on the bulk bandwagon.

They were joined by former grape growers who had made a tidy profit during Prohibition, including the Gallo brothers who, in 1933, established a winery that would morph into the world's largest wine producer half a century later. Other new wineries prospered from the sale of massive quantities of cheap wines. Fine-wine production remained a rarity and the preserve of the modest number of old-school wineries that had largely been left behind in the new winemaking environment, where size mattered.

After all booms come busts, and it was no different for the booming California wine industry. By the end of the 1930s, the industry was suffering a monumental post-repeal party hangover as the market imploded under the weight of too much bad wine. Prices crashed and the number of wineries dramatically declined, but there was a silver lining. The formation of two important marketing organizations in the 1930s, the Wine Institute and the Wine Advisory Board (the board has long since been disbanded), would give California's wine industry some much-needed strategic direction as it once again picked itself up after World War II.

The Modern Era

The California wine industry emerged from the frugal war years as production of cheap wines sourced from cheap grapes once again soared as it had after Prohibition. The difference this time was that improved marketing had created more buyers of cheap wine than in the 1930s, but important figures in the industry still recognized the need to improve quality and wean the public onto finer wines. This was the period when the pioneers of California's modern wine industry would start to appear—figures like André Tchelistcheff at Beaulieu Vineyard in the Napa Valley and, perhaps most importantly, the Mondavi family.

One of the key figures in the start of the modern age of fine winemaking was Robert Mondavi in the Napa Valley. His father, Cesare Mondavi, was one of the many producers of bulk wine in the Napa Valley after Prohibition, and his two sons, Robert and Peter, were already getting some experience helping run the bulk business. When Cesare bought the old Charles Krug winery in 1943, the family's attention increasingly turned to fine wines, but following a family feud after Cesare's death, Robert was forced out of the family business.

With wine already in his blood, he started his own Robert Mondavi Winery in 1966, the first new winery to be built in Napa since the repeal of Prohibition. It proved to be one of the most important symbols for growth in the fine-wine industry in the region, and Mondavi is often cited as one of the figures who proved that a dream of starting a great winery from scratch could become reality. Whether by luck or by design, Mondavi's venture coincided with a surge in the popularity of fine wines, and in the following decade hundreds more wineries were established by dreamers hoping to catch the same wave, including many of today's biggest winemaking names.

From the 1940s to the 1970s, the number

of wineries in California steadily declined as production of fine wine slowly replaced massive output of cheap wine. In 1945 there were just over 400 wineries in the state. By 1970 that number had dwindled to about 240 wineries. The industry had reached another nadir by 1970, but it would rise yet again, this time with a strategy that would last. By the end of the 1970s, the number of wineries had more than doubled, to over 500.

There was no single person or event that helped usher in this modern wine era in California. Instead, it has been linked to the more general growth in modern technology. The world became smaller as air travel and television introduced millions to previously unknown cultures and ideas. There was a population boom in the United States and an economic boom that introduced the modern consumer age. And, it seems, the wine industry's marketing efforts finally started to click.

The Judgments of Paris

The reputation of California's modern wines was cemented at an international wine-tasting event in Paris in 1976. British wine writer and critic Stephen Spurrier, already familiar with the rising quality of California's wines, suggested a taste-off between what he regarded as the best Californian and best French wines in an event to celebrate the American bicentennial.

Five California chardonnays and five cabernet sauvignons were pitted against the same number of French white Burgundies and red Bordeaux wines. The all-French panel of esteemed judges had to taste blind in case the French national disdain for New World wines at the time influenced their conclusions. Having set all this up, Spurrier must have been pretty confident the California wines would do well, but he reportedly did not expect them to win.

The tasting panel placed a 1973 cabernet sauvignon from Stag's Leap Wine Cellars in the Napa Valley at the top of the reds, followed by three Bordeaux wines and a cabernet from Ridge Vineyards. The California whites did even better. A 1973 Chateau Montelena chardonnay was judged to be the best white wine, and two other California chardonnays were placed in the top five (from Chalone Vineyard and Spring Mountain Vineyards).

The shock wave of the French being beaten at their own game reverberated around the wine world. The French were gutted. California winemakers never looked back.

The French tried to salvage some pride, suggesting that California wines might well taste better upon release but would not age as well as their French counterparts. That theory was disproven when the tasting was re-created 30 years later. The so-called Judgment of Paris was retried in 2006, when the same 1970s-vintage wines were pulled from cellars and tasted again. Once again the California wines trounced the French, perhaps more decisively than in the original tasting. The top five reds were all from California, led by the 1971 Ridge Monte Bello cabernet sauvignon and the 1973 Stag's Leap cabernet.

Marketing types proclaimed that this proves California wines can age as well as the best Bordeaux. Critics suggested it was simply a gimmick, and the wines of 30 years ago bear no resemblance to wines made today. It was a fun exercise nonetheless, even if it only proves that California can indeed make good wines (as judged by the French).

The events leading up to the 1976 tasting were recounted in the 2008 movie *Bottle Shock*. The producers of the film were accused by Stephen Spurrier of taking too much artistic license in the name of entertainment, and he was particularly annoyed at his depiction in the film, but it nonetheless provided an entertaining portrayal of an important turning point in California's winemaking history.

CALIFORNIA'S MODERN WINE INDUSTRY

Economy

The wine industry is to the Napa and Sonoma Valleys and large parts of northern Sonoma what the movie business is to Los Angeles—an integral part of the cultural and social fabric. Everyone seems to have some link to the wine business, whether directly or indirectly, and given the industry's sheer size it's hardly surprising.

If California were a country, it would be the fourth-largest producer of wine in the world after France, Italy, and Spain. The state's wine industry made nearly 640 million gallons of wine in 2015, according to the Wine Institute, or more than 90 percent of all the wine produced in the United States. That makes California's wine industry an over $30 billion industry in terms of U.S. retail sales, but it brings a lot more money to the state in other ways.

An estimated 24 million tourists visit many of the state's 4,600 bonded wineries each year, and the wine industry accounts for more than 325,000 jobs in California directly and indirectly. All told, the value of the wine industry to California's overall economy was estimated at nearly $60 billion in 2016, and the economic impact on the U.S. economy was more than $114 billion, according to one research report.

Napa and Sonoma dominate California's wine industry, though not by sheer size; Santa Cruz and other parts of Northern California's Wine Country are bit players by comparison. Together the two counties contain almost half of all the wineries in the state, even though they account for less than one-fifth of the state's total acreage of wine-grape vineyards. The important factor is quality. Huge quantities of cheap wines are churned out in the Central Valley of California, but Napa, Sonoma, and other important Northern California wine regions produce a big proportion of the state's premium wines, the fastest-growing category of wines that sell for premium prices.

Consumption Trends

Luckily, the rest of the world likes to drink wine, because Americans apparently don't. Although an impressive 918 million gallons of all types of wine were consumed in the United States in 2015, much of it made in California, consumption per person is only about 2.8 gallons, or about 11 bottles, per year.

Per capita consumption in the United States is actually about not much more than it was in the mid-1980s, but it has been increasing at quite a pace. Still, by 2015 people in the United Kingdom were drinking over twice as much wine on average as their U.S. counterparts, the Austrians almost three times more, and the French over four times more. Even Slovaks, Finns, and Swedes drink more wine than the average American. And the top per-capita wine consumer in 2015? Vatican City.

It's not that Americans in general don't drink much wine, just that most Americans don't drink any at all. Nearly all the wine consumed is drunk by less than one-fifth of the population (and Californians drink about a fifth of all the wine consumed in the United States). A wide range of factors might explain the country's low rate of wine consumption, including its puritanical roots, the legacy of Prohibition, and even the climate.

One important factor is simply that the U.S. population does not have a great wine-making legacy. Wines have only been made in California in commercial quantities for 150 years, which might seem like a long time but is the blink of an eye when you consider that the Romans fueled their orgies with the stuff some 2,000 years ago. Moreover, the waves of recent American immigrants from Central America and Asia also tend to have little previous exposure to wines.

Europeans have been making wine for thousands of years, and it is as much a part of the culinary culture in many European countries as, say, apple pie is in the United States. American consumers tend to view wine as a special-occasion drink, something to be enjoyed once in a while rather than every day.

While it's true that high-quality wine might be a little too expensive for most people to open a bottle every day, consider that wine in an open bottle can remain fresh for 4-5 days if stored correctly. If you prefer to save an expensive wine for a special occasion, consider stocking up with "house wine," which still

Unsung Heroes

They pick the grapes, prune the vines, and help manage the vineyards, but the workers toiling away during the long hot summers in Northern California are largely the unsung heroes of the wine industry, ensuring winemakers have the best vines and grapes to work with but rarely remembered when the cork is pulled.

As is the case in much of the rest of the state's agricultural sector, most of these workers are migrants from Latin America. They do the work that locals usually won't touch for the money offered, which in many cases is barely above the state's minimum hourly wage. Without question, the migrant labor pool is a valuable competitive asset for California's winemakers and the state's agriculture industry as a whole.

Despite the low wages paid to workers, it still costs almost double the amount per ton to harvest grapes and maintain vines by hand than by machines. Increasing mechanization has drastically reduced the number of vineyard workers in the past few decades, but they remain a critical part of the wine industry, particularly in the premium growing areas like Napa and Sonoma, where hand-picking the valuable grapes is much preferred over letting a machine bludgeon its way through the vines. Steep mountain vineyards in Northern California also pose problems for machines and require the human touch to manage and harvest them.

By some estimates, 82 percent of the vineyard workers in California are from Mexico and Central America, so it's no surprise that after decades of toiling in the vineyards, an increasing number of Mexican American families are cashing in on the skills, knowledge, and contacts they have developed.

Since the early 1990s, more than a dozen Mexican families have started their own wineries in Sonoma and Napa. Former migrant worker Reynaldo Robledo, for example, started working in California's vineyards in the 1960s, later established his own vineyard management company, and finally realized his dream to make his own wine. He founded the Robledo Family Winery in Carneros, which in 2003 became the first Mexican American winery to open a public tasting room.

His story and those of the numerous other newly minted Mexican American winemaking families are just part of the latest chapter for California's wine industry, which owes a historical debt to immigrants from all over the world, from the Victorian pioneers like Charles Krug and Samuele Sebastiani to the Gallo and Mondavi families, who helped put California's wine industry on the international map after Prohibition.

tastes good but at a price far more inviting for an everyday drink.

Chardonnay remains the most popular wine, even though that popularity has waned slightly in recent years. Cabernet sauvignon, merlot, pinot grigio/gris and pinot noir are not far behind in popularity. Those four varietals together accounted for just over half the wines sold in U.S. food stores in 2014, and overall sales of red wines were slightly higher than sales of white.

The Power of Marketing

Take a trip to wineries in Napa and Sonoma and you'd be lucky to find any wine for sale under $30, which might give the impression that wine is generally an expensive drink. But

those pricey wines account for only a fraction of the wine made in California. A trip to the local supermarket or liquor store will confirm that most wine sold in the United States is of the cheap and cheerful kind, usually packaged in big 1.5-liter bottles or magnums. In fact, the majority of wine sold in the United States in 2014 cost less than $9 per bottle, according to the Wine Institute. That represents about the same alcoholic bang for the buck as beer.

So-called premium wine, costing over $10 per bottle, is where the big money is for the wineries, however, so that's where the marketing dollars tend to get spent. It's also the fastest-growing segment of the wine industry in the United States, although there are signs that the continuing recession has slowed the growth in sales of the most expensive wines.

Wineries in the best winemaking regions of Northern California have high costs to recoup. Land for vineyards in the Napa Valley costs on average $310,000 per acre. It then costs $25,000-50,000 per acre to prepare and plant it with vines. Add the costs of managing that vineyard and actually making, bottling, and distributing the wine, and some wine prices start to seem justified.

But it's also in a winery's best interests to try to wean consumers onto the expensive stuff because then they'll probably be consumers for life. Research shows that once your palate is used to a $50 cabernet, you're highly unlikely ever again to choose a jumbo bottle of $5 generic red wine to go with dinner. You'll buy as much of the $50 wine as you can afford.

Gaining and retaining consumers is a tough balancing act for the wineries from a marketing point of view. On the one hand they want to lure new premium-wine consumers into the fold by promoting their wines as an easy entry into some sort of elite Wine Country lifestyle. But as wineries push pricey wines and all the pretensions that go along with them onto non-wine drinkers, they risk scaring the uninitiated away altogether. Just visiting the Napa Valley, with its $25 tasting fees, can be enough to scare some people off. The industry sometimes doesn't seem to help itself either. One new winemaker in Sonoma recounted asking some industry colleagues how he should price his new wine. He was told not to price it too low or no one would take it seriously. It goes to show that price is not necessarily a firm measure of quality, but just one of many indicators.

Fortunately, the wine industry sometimes gets some marketing help from unlikely places. Touting the health benefits of moderate amounts of wine has always been a surefire, if temporary, way to get more Americans to drink the stuff. The increasing marketing of food and wine together is also helping to increase consumption—cooking shows now routinely feature advice from wine experts.

Perhaps the best example of popular culture's influence on the wine industry is the Oscar-winning 2004 movie *Sideways,* a comedy-drama that follows two aging bachelors on a voyage of self-discovery through the Santa Barbara Wine Country, which did wonders for sales of pinot noir. As the movie's characters waxed lyrical about the joys of a good pinot, American consumers apparently decided to discover the joys themselves, and sales of pinot noir in California jumped by a third in the year leading up to the 2005 Academy Awards compared to the previous year, according to statistics from A. C. Nielson, which monitors sales at retail outlets. Although Santa Barbara pinots were the stars of the movie, Northern California's pinots benefited just the same.

The 2008 movie *Bottle Shock,* about the famous 1976 Judgment of Paris, had less of an effect on overall wine sales, but did reportedly bring more tourists to the already-popular Napa Valley and reminded the world how good California wine can be.

Wine and Health

In 1991, CBS aired a *60 Minutes* program titled "The French Paradox," which reported that the French population has a far lower incidence of heart attacks than the American population despite getting less exercise, eating more fatty foods, and smoking more. According to some medical experts, this apparent health paradox could be explained by the fact that the average French person drinks a lot of wine.

The American wine industry could not have asked for better publicity. In the month following the broadcast, wine sales reportedly jumped by 44 percent compared to the same period a year earlier. Although the sales spurt didn't last, and research has since suggested that the French paradox is far more complex than can be explained simply by higher wine consumption, the wine industry gained a new marketing angle for its wines.

Wine and some other alcoholic beverages have been shown to indeed have health benefits. In the case of the French paradox, however, it is thought that the health benefits have as much to do with overall lifestyle and food consumption patterns as they do with drinking wine.

Low stress (the French take far more vacations than most Americans) and a Mediterranean diet rich in fish, fresh vegetables, and oils, for example, could be factors. Regular wine drinkers also tend not to be binge drinkers, avoiding all the potential health hazards associated with overconsumption of alcohol.

The jury is still out on whether alcoholic beverages, and wine in particular, have direct effects on long-term health. Statistical studies performed all over the world suggest that moderate wine drinkers (those that drink 1-2 glasses a day) seem to suffer from lower rates of heart diseases and certain cancers, but no one yet knows exactly why or what other factors might be involved.

Some research has focused on a family of chemicals found in the skins of red grapes (and therefore found only in red wines) called polyphenols, which are believed to be natural antioxidants. Some polyphenols have specifically been shown in laboratory tests to reduce the likelihood of arteries getting clogged.

As is the case with many health-related issues, there seems to be a new study done every year that in some way contradicts results from the last. It's enough to give anyone a headache even before drinking too much wine.

In one study published in the science journal *Nature* in 2005, for example, researchers in Denmark reported that levels of "good" cholesterol increased in test subjects who drank red wine and not in those who drank grapeskin extract rich in polyphenols or water. That seemed to suggest lifestyle and simply alcohol content are more important factors than chemicals in the wine. Then, in 2006, a Harvard Medical School study found that another naturally occurring substance in red wine called resveratrol could offset the bad effects of high-calorie diets in mice.

Later that year, another family of chemicals found in wine, procyanidins, was determined to help lower the risk of heart attacks by blocking a chemical signal in the body that normally constricts blood vessels. Moreover, wines from southwest France and southern Italy were found to contain higher levels of procyanidins, perhaps lending credence to the supposed benefits of the Mediterranean diet.

And the studies keep coming. In 2008, researchers at the University of Nebraska found that resveratrol lowered the risk of breast cancer, while in 2009 three independent studies linked lower rates of esophageal cancer with moderate wine drinking, and another linked resveratrol with a reduced risk of developing Alzheimer's. That same year, women diagnosed with non-Hodgkins lymphoma were found less likely to die if they drank some wine or beer. One of the most recent studies includes the discovery of an enzyme found in red wine that decreases the body's ability to excrete testosterone, thus increasing the levels of the hormone. The marketing strategy has yet to come out on that. However, much of the good news (at least for oenophiles) came to an end with a 2015 study by Harvard researchers that linked moderate daily consumption of red wide with a 13 percent higher risk of certain types of cancer, particularly breast cancer, for women, and a 26 percent chance of liver, colon, and esophagus cancers for men.

Whether research will ever be able to discover the secrets behind the French paradox, or how wine can improve your love life, is anyone's guess. While much of the media focus has been on the supposed beneficial effects of drinking wine, there are some less-well-publicized downsides to drinking wine, even in moderate amounts, aside from the headaches, impaired driving ability, and worse things that everyone knows about.

As anyone who has drunk several glasses of a Napa cabernet with dinner probably has discovered, red wine stains the teeth. But it does more than just this temporary cosmetic damage; the acids in both red and white wines wear away the protective enamel on teeth (white wines are the worst offenders), making them more susceptible to decay. For wine tasters who often swill hundreds of wines around in their mouths each week, it is a very significant problem, and regular fluoride treatment is often recommended to replace minerals lost from the teeth.

But even for the occasional wine drinker there can be an effect, not least because wine is consumed over several hours, giving those acids plenty of time to start working on the teeth. Recommendations to prevent damage range from drinking plenty of water to help dilute the acidity and get your saliva flowing, to eating cheese at the end of the meal. Cheese neutralizes acids, and it has been suggested the calcium in cheese might even harden the enamel weakened by the wine's acid.

Wine 101

CALIFORNIA GRAPE VARIETALS

The diversity of California's wine industry and the multitude of growing conditions are illustrated by the vast number of grape varietals grown in the state. There are more than 40 types of red wine grapes grown in over 300,000 acres of vineyards, and over 34 types of white wine grapes grown in almost 200,000 acres of vineyards. It's a dizzying array of varietals but dominated by just a handful.

Certain grapes will only grow in certain conditions, while others will grow anywhere. Chardonnay, for example, is the everyman's grape, able to grow happily almost anywhere in the Wine Country. Pinot noir is fussy and will only grow in a narrow range of cooler climates—and makes good wine in an even narrower range.

Red Wine Grapes

Cabernet sauvignon is by far the most important red wine grape in California, accounting for about a quarter of all red grapes grown in the state. It is easy to ripen in the California sun and capable of making both powerful, tannic wines in hotter climates and lighter, more austere wines in cooler mountain regions, all of them usually capable of long-term aging if they are well-made and all having the telltale aromas of cassis (black currant), blackberry, green bell pepper, cedarwood, and leather.

Merlot is the second most widely planted red wine grape in California, though its popularity peaked in the 1990s and is now waning. It is usually blended with cabernet sauvignon in Bordeaux wines, but in California is often made into an easy-drinking wine that is less tannic and plumper than most cabernet sauvignons. Sometimes its subtler flavors can be lost, resulting in a bland wine, but a well-made merlot has just as much structure as other reds.

Pinot noir has for a long time been well behind other top varietals due to its finicky nature, which limits the areas where it can be successfully grown. However, with the movie *Sideways,* the acreage planted in pinot noir has steadily increased. Pinot noir is said to have the most complex flavors and be able to communicate the unique properties of the *terroir* like no other grape, but only if grown in the right conditions—not too hot, yet just warm enough to ripen the grapes sufficiently. Classic pinot flavors and aromas include cherry, raspberry, strawberry, violet, and any number of earthy overtones. Cooler parts of California are some of the few areas of the world where great pinot noirs are made, the most famous being the Burgundy region of France. It is also one of the most important grapes for making champagne.

Zinfandel is not far behind pinot noir in terms of total acreage planted and is often considered a California native, though recent genetic studies have shown it probably originally came from southern Europe.

Zinfandel can come in many styles, from intense, jammy, and tannic wine to a subtler spicy wine with cherry and berry flavors and nice structure—typical of cooler-climate styles. A characteristic of zinfandel vines is that individual grapes can vary dramatically in size within bunches, so they ripen at different speeds. This can result in some being overripe when picked, leading to high sugar levels and even higher alcohol levels in the wines, together with an almost raisiny flavor. Old vines tend to have a smaller crop with more uniform grape size and are favored by winemakers—some zinfandel vines are over a century old.

Syrah is the rising star of California's red wines and the fifth most planted red grape in the state. Its traditional home is the Rhône region of France, and it is often made into Rhône-style wines in cooler parts of California, exhibiting telltale black pepper and chocolate flavors and an almost purple color. It makes a much denser, more powerful wine when grown in hotter climates, including parts of California and in Australia, where it is commonly known as **shiraz.**

Petite sirah is normally used as a blending grape, particularly in zinfandels, but it is also increasingly bottled on its own. The resulting wine is one of the darkest colored you'll see and has a trademark intensity with plenty of dark fruit and peppery flavors that can (and often do) support some fairly robust tannins. It can age well but is at its best when blended with Rhône varietals to give it a little more complexity. Despite the different spelling, petite sirah is genetically related to syrah, although most of the petite sirah grown in California has actually been found to be a varietal called durif, which is itself a cross between petite sirah and another varietal called peloursin. The confusion is yet another example of how California's pioneer winemakers were often a little too casual or simply inaccurate when documenting newly planted grapes.

White Wine Grapes
Chardonnay is the king of white grapes in California. It accounts for almost 100,000 acres, or more than half the total acreage planted with white varietals, and about a quarter of all wine made in California in 2014. It grows almost anywhere and can be made into wines of a multitude of styles to suit almost every palate, depending on the winemaking process. Overoaking is a common fault of California chardonnays, as is an overreliance on high levels of malolactic fermentation, which gives the wines a sweet, buttery, and slightly generic flavor. Chardonnay is also one of the most important champagne grapes.

Pinot gris/pinot grigio is quickly rising to the top of California's varietals. In 2001, less than 3,000 acres were devoted to the grapes. Since then, the number has quadrupled with over 15,000 acres planted in 2014. A cool-climate grape, pinot grigio is related to pinot noir and produces a lovely table wine that is aromatic, low in acidity, with soft tannins. While it has traditionally shared the vineyard with its more famous cousin, pinot grigio is spreading to warmer growing regions around the state, proving its versatility.

Sauvignon blanc is one of the most important white grape varietals in Bordeaux, where it is usually blended with semillon, and it is growing in popularity in California. In cool climates like its home in France and parts of California, it makes a refreshingly crisp, aromatic wine, often with unusual aromas of grass and herbs. In warmer climates it makes a more intense style of wine from which winemakers sometimes coax richer, more tropical fruit flavors. These richer styles are often called **fumé blanc** but are still made from the same sauvignon blanc grape.

Viognier is an increasingly fashionable white varietal originally from the Rhône region of France that exploded onto the California wine scene in the 1990s. In 1992 there were just 100 acres planted of this varietal; by 2014 there were over 3,000 acres. It does well in California's warm climate, where it ripens enough to create full-bodied, elegant wines with a distinctive exotic, floral aroma and rich texture. It is sometimes used in small quantities as a blending grape in red wines.

Watch out for sometimes excessive levels of alcohol (often over 15 percent) that can give the wine a "hot," or overly alcoholic, taste.

Riesling is regarded as the king of white wines on its home turf in Germany and is increasingly popular in California thanks to its ability to make different styles of wine depending on the climate and winemaking process. Some rieslings are too sweet and lack structure, but the best wines from places like the Anderson Valley in Mendocino have a unique balance of acidity, tropical fruit flavors, powerful aromas, and a lightness that makes them some of the most complex in the white wine world. Also look for a delicious dessert wine made from so-called botrytized grapes, which have been infected by the botrytis mold either naturally on the vine or artificially after harvest. The mold has the effect of dehydrating the grape, concentrating the sugars and flavors into an uncommon intensity.

Gewürztraminer is another Alsatian grape that has found a home in the cooler parts of California, most notably the Anderson Valley in Mendocino, and produces wonderfully complex wine with telltale floral aromas and a refreshing acidity that makes them great with food. Most gewürztraminer is made in a dry style, but grapes are also often harvested later than usual to make a rich and equally complex dessert wine.

HOW WINE IS MADE

For thousands of years civilizations have made wine, and the chemical process of fermentation that turns the sugar in grape juice into alcohol in wine is the same as it's always been. The actual process of making wine has changed drastically, however, particularly since the science behind fermentation was first discovered in the mid-1800s. Since then, winemaking has become ever more refined to get the best out of particular grapes and to make different styles of wine, some for aging and others for mass consumption.

The year that appears on a wine bottle, known as the wine's vintage, is the year that the grapes are harvested and winemaking begins. The processes used to make red and white wines are similar but with a few important differences. One of the most important is that red wines are made by fermenting the juice in contact with the skins of the grapes. The skins contain the pigments that make red wine red; juice from virtually all grapes, whether red or white, is relatively colorless. Cut a red grape in half, scoop out the flesh, and it will be almost identical in color to flesh from a white grape.

Grapes are brought from the vineyards to the crush pad at the winery, where they are unloaded onto a conveyor and fed into a **crusher-destemmer,** a machine that chops off the stems but lets the grapes through, gently crushing them in the process so the juice can seep out. In the case of the best grapes destined for more expensive wines, human sorters often pull out withered, unripe, or otherwise unworthy grapes and stems from the conveyor so only the best get through. Once grapes are crushed and destemmed, the winemaking process begins.

Although red and white winemaking techniques differ in many ways, they both involve a fermentation stage during which naturally occurring yeasts on the skins of the grapes, often supplemented by the addition of other yeast strains for certain flavor characteristics, get to work on the grape juice and turn the naturally occurring sugar into alcohol. Fermentation can be carried out in giant wooden tanks (the old-fashioned way), temperature-controlled stainless steel tanks (the modern way), or even open-top concrete tanks (old-fashioned but still widely used in California for some wines, like pinot noir).

Almost as important as the type of fermentation vessel used is how the wine gets in and out of it. A lot of modern wineries use standard food-grade pumps and pipes to move the wine between each stage of winemaking. The more traditional method of moving the liquid around is gravity flow—literally letting gravity do the work. This is how it used to be done before the age of modern pumps and

How Many Grapes in a Glass?

Understanding the winemaking process is a bit easier if it's brought down to a personal scale—how many grapes go into the bottle of wine you're drinking. The Sonoma County Grape Growers Association has helpfully worked it out for us.

An average vineyard yields about 5 tons, or 10,000 pounds, of grapes per acre (it's actually far less for the best vineyards and most expensive wines). All those grapes make about 13.5 barrels of wine, which is 797 gallons, or 3,985 bottles.

Do the math and it turns out that one bottle of wine is made using about 2.4 pounds of grapes, so one glass comes from just under 10 ounces of grapes.

This is little more than a back-of-an-envelope calculation, however, and will depend on all sorts of factors, from the type of grape to the style of wine being made.

The Napa Valley Vintners Association has slightly different figures. It says a ton of grapes makes on average 720 bottles of wine, so each bottle contains about 2.8 pounds of grapes. It also helpfully calculates that one average vine plant produces enough grapes to make 4-6 bottles of wine each year.

BACKGROUND
WINE 101

electricity. Many old (and an increasing number of modern) wineries are designed around the gravity flow principle, whereby each stage of the winemaking process is at a progressively lower level of the winery. Purists argue that gravity-flow winemaking minimizes the amount of contact the wine has with processing equipment and the heat it generates. It also saves a considerable amount of power.

California winemaking differs from that in some other parts of the world in that winemakers cannot add any sugar to the wine (known as chaptalization). Luckily, the weather is hot enough and the sun strong enough that ripening grapes to their necessary sweetness is generally not a problem in California. Very little else can be added to wines during fermentation either, except for yeast and clarifying agents, but winemakers have plenty of ways to manipulate wines after fermentation. More sugar can be added in the form of additional grape juice, acid levels can be increased with the addition of tartaric or citric acid, and alcohol levels can be lowered if necessary using a process called reverse osmosis. Such manipulation of the finished product is more common than wineries and winemakers want you to believe.

Alcohol and many naturally occurring chemicals act as preservatives in bottled wine, but a chemical that is usually added for its additional preservative action is sulfur dioxide, and this is responsible for the statement on wine labels that a wine "contains sulfites." Sulfur dioxide is added to wines before bottling to prevent the growth of bacteria that could spoil the wine, and it is also sometimes added at the beginning of the winemaking process to kill naturally occurring yeasts, some of which might impart slightly funky flavors to a wine. In most cases, however, natural yeasts are an important part of the winemaking process, though often supplemented by other strains of yeast, all of which create wines with slightly different characteristics.

The headaches that some people claim are caused by sulfites in wine, particularly cheap wine, could also be due to naturally occurring histamines. Some people experiment with taking an antihistamine before drinking wine.

Making Red Wine

After destemming and crushing, the grapes are either pumped or flow by gravity into the fermentation vessel, where fermentation begins and usually continues for a couple of weeks.

During fermentation, the grape skins, seeds, and remaining small pieces of stem float to the top and form a thick crust that has to be constantly broken and remixed with the fermenting wine to ensure all the pigments in the grape skins and the other desirable chemicals like tannins are leached out of this "cap" of crud. These days the wine from the bottom of the fermentation tank is usually pumped over the cap and filters back down through it, or a giant mixer-like system keeps all the skins and stems constantly circulating through the fermenting wine.

Traditionally, the cap was broken up and pushed back down into the wine by hand using a big wooden paddle, and this punching-down technique is still used in some smaller wineries today, especially to produce pinot noir—a wine that requires more work to extract the color from the grape skins.

Once the winemaker determines that enough pigment and tannins have been extracted from the skins and fermentation has gone on long enough, the liquid is transferred into barrels or stainless steel storage tanks. This liquid is known as the free-run juice and goes into the best wine. Sometimes the free run is blended with some of the more concentrated and tannic press wine, generated when the leftover skins and other mulch in the cap are pressed to extract all the remaining juice, which is then stored separately. In some cases fermentation is stopped by chilling the wine and filtering out the yeast, but fermentation will also stop naturally when alcohol levels rise high enough to kill the yeast—usually about 15 percent by volume.

The blending of the free-run wine and the press wine is just part of the important **blending** process. Wines from different vineyards, sometimes from different parts, or blocks, of the same vineyard, are usually made and stored separately and will have slightly different characteristics. They are blended together at a later stage by the winemaker, often together with small quantities of wines made from different grapes, to make the final product. Labeling laws determine how the final wine is described on the bottle.

Most of the premium wines made in Napa and Sonoma are aged in oak barrels once they have been blended—the barrels you often see stacked on giant racks in caves or cool storage rooms of wineries. This barrel aging not only lets the wine continue to develop its taste and aroma through ongoing chemical reactions but also imparts new flavors and aromas that come from the barrels themselves. It is also when most red wines undergo **malolactic fermentation,** which is not fermentation at all but a bacterial reaction that converts the tart malic acid in a wine to the softer lactic acid.

Buying the barrels and storing them is expensive and reserved for the best wines that can command premium prices. Cheaper wines made to be drunk right away are bottled straight from the stainless steel tanks in which they were blended. Sometimes oak chips are added to those tanks to impart some of the important oaky flavors, a method still frowned upon by European winemakers.

Before wines are bottled or left to age in barrels, they are purified using a process called **fining,** which uses a coagulant to remove all the particles of dead yeast, excess tannins, and other crud suspended in the liquid. The coagulant can be anything from types of clay to egg whites or gelatin and is simply dropped into the wine, where it attaches itself to particles and pulls them down to the bottom of the barrel or tank. In fine wines that need to age further, the freshly cleaned wine is siphoned off into clean barrels to ensure this gunk does not interfere with the aging process, a process known as **racking.** After usually six months or a year (longer for the very best age-worthy wines) the wine from barrels will be bottled, often after being filtered to remove the last of the sediment. Cheaper wines stored in stainless steel tanks are usually bottled soon after fining.

Some more expensive red wines are made without the crusher-destemmer step; instead, whole bunches of grapes with the biggest stems removed are left to ferment using the yeasts naturally occurring on the skins. The grapes eventually burst and the fermented juice escapes.

Making White Wine

White wine production leaves out many of the steps involved in making red wines and is an altogether quicker process. The speed of the winemaking and the fact that most California white wines are not aged for long (if at all) before bottling explain why a bottle of white wine often has a much more recent vintage date on the label than a red.

Winemakers don't want white grape juice to sit in contact with grape skins and stems for long because that would introduce all sorts of bitter flavors, so the grapes often go through not only the crusher-destemmer but also a press, which gently squeezes the juice out. The first juice out of the grapes is the best and is often reserved for the best wines, much like the best olive oils are the "first cold-pressed." The last juice to be squeezed out picks up some of the bitterness from the skins, seeds, and stems and is destined for cheaper wines.

Most California white wines are fermented in giant stainless steel vessels, and fermentation is carefully controlled using giant refrigeration jackets incorporated into the outside of the tanks to ensure a wine retains some sweetness—white wines, even dry whites, generally contain more residual sugar and have less alcohol than most reds. Because of this extra refrigeration the fermentation time for white wines is usually longer than that of reds.

During fermentation, dead yeasts and other particles, known as the **lees,** will slowly drop to the bottom and are sometimes left in contact with the fermented wine to add distinct yeasty, toasty aromas. This is often the case with more expensive white wines that are fermented and aged in barrels.

Once fermentation is complete, the wine is fined and filtered and either bottled or transferred to barrels for aging, which adds the oakiness that California chardonnays are so famous for. White wines often undergo some degree of malolactic fermentation, which turns a crisp white wine into a rich,

buttery-tasting one. If a winemaker does not want malolactic fermentation to occur, the wine undergoes some additional filtering and might also be treated with sulfur dioxide to kill the bacteria responsible for the reaction.

Making Champagne

The cool climate of Carneros and the Russian River Valley is ideally suited for growing the two most important champagne grape varietals, chardonnay and pinot noir. A few other grapes are also often used, including small amounts of pinot blanc and pinot meunier. (Producers of the Spanish sparkling wine, cava, use totally different grapes more suited to the local Spanish climate.)

Most California champagne-style wines are blends of both pinot noir and chardonnay, with some exceptions. A blanc de blancs champagne is made only from chardonnay grapes and has the lightest, most delicate style. A blanc de noirs is still a white wine but made exclusively from dark-skinned grapes like pinot noir, giving it a fuller body. Somewhere in between the two is rosé, or pink, champagne, which is made by adding a small amount of red wine to the white blend.

The key to making champagne is to bottle the wine while it is still fermenting so the yeast will continue to do its work and generate both alcohol and the all-important gas that creates the fizz, carbon dioxide. The fizziness was likely discovered by accident when the cold winters of the Champagne region stopped barrel fermentation in its tracks before the wine was bottled. Once the wine was bottled and the weather warmed up, fermentation started again, only this time inside the sealed bottle, where the carbon dioxide (dissolved in the liquid as carbonic acid) had nowhere to go. As pressure built up, the corks popped off (and the fizzy wine was immediately drunk by people assuming it had gone bad) or the bottles simply exploded from the immense pressure.

English merchants taking delivery of barrels of French wine were probably the first to experience this peculiar phenomenon of

Five Fizzy Facts

- **Champagne making is a high-pressure business.** The pressure inside a champagne bottle, created by the dissolved carbon dioxide gas (carbonic acid), is about 90 pounds per square inch, or about three times the pressure in a car tire. That's why the glass of champagne bottles is so thick and the cork can shoot so far.

- **Champagne isn't just for celebration.** More than 80 percent of sparkling wine sales occur between November and January, but it is a style of wine that can be enjoyed at any time of year and with a wide range of foods. Try it as an aperitif or instead of chardonnay at the beginning of a meal.

- **Not all bubbles are created equal.** The more expensive the champagne, the smaller the bubbles and the smoother and creamier it feels in your mouth. The priciest French champagnes barely taste fizzy at all. The cheapest supermarket sparklers feel like fizzy water or soda in your mouth.

- **Champagne gets you tipsy more quickly.** The carbonation in sparkling wine is thought to relax the valve between your stomach and small intestine, where alcohol is absorbed by the blood more quickly. So while still wines stay in the stomach longer, champagne enters the small intestine more quickly and really does go to your head faster.

- **Better champagne glasses make for better bubbles.** The tall, slender champagne glasses, known as flutes, help keep the wine sparkling for longer and show off the bubbles better. Most good-quality flutes have a small etching at the bottom that encourages the bubbles to form. That's why you'll usually see a long, straight line of bubbles rising from the very bottom of the glass.

exploding wine. At the time, back in the late 1700s, England was also home to a state-of-the-art glassblowing industry, so once the wine sellers understood what was going on with the wine, they were able to develop bottles thick enough to contain it.

The full potential of this new style of fizzy wine was quickly realized, and modern champagne production began. The biggest challenge for the early champagne houses was to remove the sediment of dead yeast and other by-products of fermentation from the bottle without losing the fizz; otherwise the champagne would end up murky.

The process, developed in 1805 and known as *méthode champenoise,* is still largely unchanged today. Bottles of half-fermented champagne are stored neck-down in large racks; traditionally they were turned on an exact schedule over many months to get the sediment to work its way down to the cork, a process known as riddling. Today, of course, the riddling is all done by computer-controlled

machines (despite what many champagne houses would have you believe).

Then comes the process of disgorging, during which the sediment is carefully removed. In today's automated version, the neck of the bottle is frozen, the cork is removed, and the compressed gas in the wine shoots the frozen plug of muck out. Finally comes dosing, when the bottle is topped off with wine and some sugar (more sugar for the sweeter wines, less for the dry styles) before being recorked and allowed to continue fermenting in peace.

It's a precise and expensive process, which is why it's reserved for the high-end champagnes. Cheaper sparkling wines are today more likely to be made in large stainless steel tanks that are pressurized to keep the carbon dioxide dissolved in the wine before it is filtered and bottled.

Making Port

Dark, juicy ports have become increasingly popular in recent years, and some sort of port

Trends and Buzz Words

With nearly 24 million tourists visiting annually and 4,600 bonded wineries in California to choose from, marketing is a powerful tool. Wineries struggle to differentiate themselves, employing everything from fine art and medieval castles to how they approach wine making itself. While winemaking is itself centuries old, the large margins of Napa Valley provide plenty of room for the curious winemaker to experiment. These trends that range from vineyard management to vessels for winemaking often give marketers the perfect nuggets with which to pitch their wines to consumers. Buzz words float over Wine Country like hot-air balloons, shifting direction with any change in the weather. Don't be surprised if on your tour of Wine Country some new trend is on the tip of everyone's tongue.

· **Organic:** Organic agriculture is not new to Wine Country; in fact, many Napa Valley wineries that started in the 1970s and early 1980s were the first large-scale champions of organic farming, eschewing synthetic fertilizers, herbicides, and pesticides in favor of natural methods to combat weeds, pests, and disease. In order for a wine to be labeled organic, not only must the vineyards be certified organic, but also the wine itself cannot contain added sulfites, a preservative common in wine.

· **Biodynamic:** Pioneered by Rudolph Steiner, the godfather of Waldorf Education, biodynamics attempts to re-create the natural interactions of the environment. This includes promoting biodiversity on the farm, utilizing animal husbandry, planting and harvesting in concert with the moon's cycles, and using elements in the soil to boost health.

· **Boutique Winery:** This is perhaps the slipperiest term in Wine Country. At the most basic level it means small (i.e., producing less than 10,000 cases a year), but other descriptors also attach themselves, like "artisanal" and "crafted," which capture the imagination and make the assumption that boutique wineries are superior to large wineries. Ah, marketing! Of course, some of the world's best wine comes from large established wineries, while boutique wineries are just as capable as making bad wine.

· **Concrete Egg:** Fermenting wine in concrete goes back centuries, but the new oval shape has made the concrete egg the biggest (or at least heaviest) winemaking trend in recent years. Proponents claim that the oval shape allows for a gentle circulation of the wine, adding complexity; the interior's tiny pockets of oxygen help preserve the wine's aromatics; concrete's breathable quality is like oak without imparting any flavor; and the thick walls help guard against fluctuating temperatures. Some seasoned winemakers and aficionados disagree on some of these points, but one thing is for certain: The eggs made in France cost nearly as much to ship as to make, and this cost is often passed on to the consumer.

can now be found at most wineries. Not all of it is good, however. Some is nothing more than an overly sweet red dessert wine that has about as much complexity as concentrated, alcoholic grape juice. Others approach (though don't yet reach) the sophistication of the best ports made in the country where they were invented—Portugal. The name is derived from the Portuguese coastal city of Oporto, from where the wines were shipped to their main market, England.

Traditional ports are made using the Portuguese grape varieties tinta barroca, tinta roriz, tinto cao, and touriga, though a lot of California ports use more common regional varietals, particularly zinfandel and syrah.

The process starts out similar to the red winemaking process, but the fermentation is stopped in its tracks when the wine is poured into a fortified spirit like brandy, which has enough alcohol to kill the yeast that was turning the wine's sugar into alcohol. The result is a half-fermented wine still containing plenty of unfermented sugar but with a high alcohol level (usually around 20 percent) thanks to the addition of the brandy.

Because fermentation of red wine is stopped halfway, the winemaker has to work hard to ensure that enough color has been extracted from the grape skins before the wine is poured off into the brandy. In Portugal that is still often achieved by the age-old custom of crushing the grapes with bare feet to thoroughly grind up the skins. Not many California wineries will admit to that.

The best ports in the world are aged for many years in barrels, sometimes many decades, and eventually attain a pale, tawny color. These are the most expensive tawny ports. Most California ports are made to be drunk relatively young, although they can also be aged in the bottle just like regular wines.

Wine Barrels

Oak was traditionally used for making barrels because it was strong, had a fine grain and so was watertight, and was plentiful in the forests of Europe. Early winemakers also discovered that wines picked up some pleasant flavors and smells when stored in oak barrels, which is why oak has remained the most desirable wood to use when aging wines.

Most barrels used in winemaking today are made of oak, but not all oak is the same when it comes to making wine. Just as different varietals of grape have different flavors and smells, different types of oak also have different characteristics that a winemaker can incorporate into the winemaking process. Even the same type of oak from different forests can have distinct properties.

French oak is the most highly prized because of the soft, subtle flavors it gives a wine. It is also the most expensive. A typical French oak barrel costs a winery $800-3,500, compared to about $360-500 for a barrel made from American oak, which tends to add more pronounced flavors to a wine. As French oak is priced out of the market, the oak from Eastern Europe, particularly Hungary and Slovakia, is becoming more popular and has some of the same characteristics as its French cousin but at far less cost to the winery.

Some of the most distinctive flavors and smells added to a wine by aging it in oak barrels include vanilla, leather, tobacco, cloves, and cedar. Those flavors will be stronger the newer the barrel is. Wineries often age wine in a mixture of new and old barrels, both to save money and to get the right mixture of strong and mellow flavors from the oak. They will also often use a mixture of American and European oak to get the right balance of flavors and aromas.

When barrels are made by a cooper (an art in itself), they are usually **toasted** by lighting a fire inside the half-finished barrel to create a thin layer of burnt wood. This toasted wood imparts its own set of flavors and smells to the wine, including the rich chocolate, caramel, and nutty characteristics typical in barrel-aged wines, particularly reds.

The Wine-Making Year

A winegrower's year is a busy one, and January is about the only time they can take significant time off for a well-earned vacation. Most of us have more flexible vacation time and can choose when to visit Wine Country based on all sorts of factors, including the weather, the scenery, events, and where the winegrowers are in their yearlong process of creating great wines.

January: The vineyards are bare, the weather is cool and wet, and the Wine Country is at its quietest. This is also the time of year that the vines are pruned. Straggly bare stems are cut back to the thick branches and trunks of the vine. In the cellar, racking of the red wines is under way.

February: More vineyard maintenance and pruning are carried out, but the wet weather has by now started all the wildflowers blooming, including cover crops like the bright yellow wild mustard that fills the rows between vines in many parts of the Wine Country between now and April. Racking and blending the wines for barrel aging continues.

March: New vines are planted, and bottling lines at wineries spring into action, bottling wines designed to be drunk young (like many whites) that were made the previous year.

April: Buds are open on the vines, and the new growing season begins in the vineyard as the weather finally starts to dry out and warm up. The danger of late frosts often gets the giant wind machines going to keep the air moving and prevent ice from forming on the delicate shoots.

May: Vines are now growing vigorously, and wineries are gearing up for the summer rush of tourists.

June: The vines are tied to the wires and posts of the trellises to make sure the grapes get as much sun as possible later in the year. The vines also start flowering, so rain is an unwelcome, though rare, disruption. Bottling of older wines begins before the heat of summer sets in.

July: Flowering is over, and grapes are starting to form. Spraying with organic or other chemicals starts, to safeguard the developing grapes from pests and diseases.

August: This is the first month that red grapes will really start to look red as they continue to grow. Pruning of excess leaves sometimes takes place to ensure grapes are not shaded and can fully ripen. Smaller, less-developed clusters of grapes might also be cut off so the vine can concentrate all its energy and nutrients into the remaining grapes. Wineries start to clear space for the imminent harvest.

September: The first harvesting begins, with the earliest-ripening grapes in the hottest areas picked first (in particularly hot years or those with an early summer, harvesting sometimes starts in August). Most grapes in Northern California's premium growing regions are picked by hand, usually by migrant workers. This is the best time to surreptitiously taste just how sweet wine grapes are if you see any dangling over the shoulder of country roads. Wineries themselves are hives of activity as tons of grapes start to be brought in by truck.

October: Harvesting finishes, and the vineyards start to look a little more bare, though the vines will keep their leaves for another month or so. The crush is well under way at wineries, and steel tanks rapidly fill up with wine.

November: The vineyards start to turn shades of red and yellow as the weather starts to cool, and the leaves finally drop when the nights get cold enough. In wineries, the wine is starting to be transferred from the fermentation vats into barrels to begin aging.

December: Many wineries offer barrel tasting of new wines, and the winemaker will start to plan the blends that will ultimately be bottled.

Reading Wine Labels

Thanks to strict labeling regulations overseen by the federal Bureau of Alcohol, Tobacco, and Firearms, it is tough for wineries to mislead consumers about what goes into a bottle of wine, but there is a little more to a wine's content than might meet the eye.

The year on the bottle is the **vintage date** and indicates the year in which at least 95 percent of the grapes that went into the wine were harvested.

Usually underneath the vintage is the **appellation of origin,** which is where the dominant grapes in the wine were grown. It is usually a geographical area (appellation) like California or Sonoma County or a specific American Viticultural Area (AVA), such as Rutherford, Napa Valley, or Dry Creek Valley. In the case of an appellation, at least 75 percent of the grapes in the wine must have come from that area. In the case of an AVA, at least 85 percent of the grapes must be from the area identified on the bottle.

The type of grape the wine is made from, or **varietal designation,** is usually displayed above or below the appellation of origin. If a specific grape varietal is identified (cabernet sauvignon or sauvignon blanc, for example), then at least 75 percent of the grapes the wine is made of must be that named varietal. That leaves a lot of leeway for winemakers to blend small quantities of other grapes into a wine to add to its character; sometimes these blending grapes will be identified elsewhere on the label, other times not.

If less than 75 percent of the grapes in a wine are one varietal, then a winery will either simply call it red or white wine or will come up with a snappy and unique name to describe the blend. Such a wine is known as a **proprietary wine** or blend. Meritage (rhymes with heritage) is a name unique to the United States that is sometimes used to describe a blend of Bordeaux varietals, either red or white.

The final words to look for on labels are **estate bottled,** which means that all of the grapes in a wine came from land owned or controlled by the winery, and the wine was made and bottled on the winery premises. So-called estate wines tend to be among a winery's best and most expensive. Sometimes a wine is made using grapes from only one vineyard, in which case the vineyard is identified on the label (although it doesn't have to be) and the wine is known as a single-vineyard or vineyard-designate wine.

HOW TO TASTE WINE

The involved process of thoroughly smelling and tasting a wine is one reason why aficionados love the stuff and a big reason that novices tend to be intimidated. Some people seem to regard wine almost as an intellectual pursuit. Others just like the taste or want to get drunk.

On one level, it seems ludicrous to spend so long detecting every nuance of flavor in a wine. After all, when a plate of food arrives in a restaurant, we don't sit for five minutes smelling it to try to detect every ingredient and how it was cooked. Then again, there is probably no other drinkable liquid on earth that can pack as many complex aromas and flavors into a glass as wine can, and certainly no other food product that can reflect so completely the place that it came from.

With the magic worked by winemakers, simple grape juice can be transformed into wines that mimic the smells and tastes of a remarkable range of fruits, vegetables, and countless other substances. From a scientific point of view, however, there's no magic involved—grapes actually contain many of the same chemicals that give other fruits and vegetables their distinctive smells. Wine reviews often read like a shopping list for the produce department at a local supermarket.

Wine appreciation cannot be taught. It has to be learned by experience. One reason that many people are confused by those slightly pretentious-sounding reviews is that they cannot actually recognize many of the smells or tastes being referred to. Someone who has never smoked a cigar, for example, is not going to understand what a reviewer is referring to when he describes a cabernet sauvignon as having an aroma of "cigar box." Everyone knows what chocolate tastes and smells like, though, so a "chocolaty" cabernet will instantly ring a bell in most people's minds.

The sort of diverse smell and flavor database that critics use takes time (and an extremely varied diet) to develop. Patience is the best way to learn—it takes a while to develop a palate that can detect the subtle nuances of wine and years to build up a useful tasting memory that you can draw on to recognize and describe wines or their aromas.

When in doubt, simply listen to how everyone else describes the wine, or just ask whoever is pouring the wine at a winery what exactly you are supposed to be smelling or tasting. On a few occasions you might not get much help from a harried staffer, but usually they are happy to give a quick description.

Alternatively, an intensive wine-tasting course can shorten the process of learning all the smells and tastes by setting out every imaginable fruit, vegetable, and other organic substance in dishes, allowing students to directly match aromas from the foods to the aromas in wines (something you can also do at home with whatever you have in your kitchen).

Of course, the world of smells and tastes is unique to each individual. There are some fairly standard categories of the basic flavors and aromas of wines. Beyond them, it's fine to make up your own comparisons, and the more recognizable they are the better. For fun, make up your own personal wine descriptions every day—pinot noir can sometimes smell a little like a traffic jam on the St. Helena Highway on a hot summer afternoon, for example. Alternatively, just ignore all the fancy words and simply say "it smells and tastes good." Just never use the word "Yummy."

The fact that critics don't always agree with each other illustrates just how subjective the art of describing wines really is. Take these three excerpts from reviews in three major wine magazines of a 2001 merlot from Pride Mountain Vineyards. All three have a few common threads, but they could equally be describing totally different wines:

- Possesses gorgeous aromas of creosote, damp earth, sweet black cherry as well as currant fruit, and a chocolaty aftertaste.

- Rich in spicy currant, exotic spice, and ripe blackberry fruit, turning spicy and exhibiting pretty mocha-scented oak.

- Smoky aromas of black raspberry, coffee, and nutty oak. Lush, fat, and sweet, with layered flavors of black raspberry and sweet oak.

Looking at Wine

There's no denying it: Wine looks inviting. Whether it's the pale yellow of a sauvignon blanc, the golden hue of chardonnay, or the deep purple of a syrah, the purity of color in wines is striking. How a wine looks in the glass can also give some clues about what you're about to drink. Try to look at it against a white background (the tasting room menu, for example). Overall the wine should be crystal clear and a bright, vivid color. Any hint of cloudiness is generally not a good sign.

White wines range from a pale yellow in young and light wines like sauvignon blanc to a darker gold in some heavier whites such as some styles of chardonnay that have been aged in oak. White wines darken as they age; a hint of brown might be a sign of a well-aged wine, but for most California whites it's usually the sign of a wine that's past its prime.

Red wines have a much wider range of colors, from deep red in the case of cabernet sauvignon to deep purple in a young syrah and a paler brick red in pinot noir. The color of red wines fades as they age and the pigment molecules react with other chemical components of the wine, so the deeper the color, the younger the wine.

Smelling the Wine

There's no other drink that can match the array of aromas in a wine, and experiencing all those smells is one of the great pleasures of tasting wine. Trying to identify and describe them is one of the great challenges. Wineglasses are designed to concentrate the aroma of a wine and channel it straight to your nose. Most of what we taste is actually what we smell, so smelling a wine is the key to enjoying it and discovering its complexities.

Professionals smell the wine to learn more about it, such as the main grape varietals it contains and the region it came from, especially in blind tastings that are designed to be as objective as possible. Most people smell wine just to enjoy and appreciate the glorious aromas before drinking it. Identifying those aromas is really nothing more than a bit of fun that might one day be useful if someone asks you to identify a wine with no label.

Swirl the glass two or three times to help release the aromas, and then take a deep sniff and try to identify all the aromas. Take as many sniffs as you want. Some wines have an intense smell, others subtler ones.

Most of the up-front smells are the aromas that come directly from the fruit in the wine, and such fruity smells are the biggest category of aromas in the world of wine-tasting. Another big category of aromas is vegetative, or anything that smells like it came from a plant, whether grass, bell pepper, or tobacco. Some of the most enticing aromas are those of exotic flowers.

Classic aromas for white wines include apple and pear, citrus fruits, tropical and stone fruits, grass, bell pepper, honey, and melon.

Opportunities for Study

Where better to get some professional wine training than in the heart of Wine Country? It's easy to learn a lot just by visiting wineries and talking to the staff, but to really come to grips with wine, it might be worth taking a crash course in the art of making and enjoying wine.

- **Culinary Institute of America** in the Napa Valley offers a variety of wine appreciation classes including the Wine 101 classes, Tasting Wine Like a Pro series, and the intensive Wine Lover's Boot Camps. With the exception of the boot camps, which are a hefty two- to five-day commitment at $895-2,195, most classes last 2.5 hours and cost $95. For a full catalog of these and other courses, together with schedules and sign-up information, visit the website for the institute's Food Enthusiast Courses (https://enthusiasts.ciachef.edu/).

- **Napa Valley Wine Academy** is dedicated to educating the next generation of somme- liers, but thankfully this downtown Napa school offers a few courses for the lay wine apprecia- tor. Wine 101 courses are offered daily 10am-noon for $100 with a 24-hour advance reservation. For $1,995, step into the shoes of a winemaker at harvest for three days in which you'll tour vineyards, meet winemakers, and have a hand in the process.

- **Bell Wine Cellars** in Yountville specializes in wine education with its variety of tours and tastings. The Grape to Glass tour (10:30am, 1pm, and 3pm daily by appointment, $50) will get you out into the vineyards, while the Sensory Tasting (by appointment, $75) will teach you how to parse out different flavors and aromas through a series of blind tastings. At the Blending Seminar (by appointment, $150) you'll learn to create your own blend, guided by an expert.

- **W.H.Smith** is a Calistoga winery known for its cabernets and pinot noirs, as well as the Wine Sensory Experience it offers at its tasting room. The two-hour class is held every day at 10am with a maximum of only eight students at a time. For $65, students learn how to identify different aromas and flavors in wine, as well as how each are cultivated by the winemaker in the first place.

For red wines there might be aromas of any number of berries, cherries, raisins, plums, licorice, and black pepper. The lists are almost endless. Some of the subtler underlying smells come from the barrel, yeasts, and other wine- making factors. They include vanilla, oak, nuts, butterscotch, and chocolate.

Wine aromas are supposed to be pleasant, but sometimes bad smells creep in and are an indicator of a wine gone bad. Most are pretty obviously bad, like the rotten egg smell of hy- drogen sulfide, the vinegary smell of oxidized wine, or the sherry-like smell of cooked, or maderized, wine.

A corked wine—one that has been contam- inated by mold on the cork—can sometimes be harder to detect. Often the characteristic musty or mildewy smell is so fleeting that it might be missed and quickly overpowered by other aromas. Another indicator of mold con- tamination is a strong smell of wet cardboard.

Tasting the Wine

Taking a sip of wine will be the ultimate test of whether to buy it or not. Most wine smells pleasant enough (unless you have an aversion to fruit or the wine is bad), but not all wines will taste good to everyone. This is where sub- jectivity becomes most evident.

More aromas than you initially smelled might be detectable once a wine is in your mouth, as the body's heat vaporizes chemi- cals that you could not previously smell. The "flavors" of fruit are actually aromas hitting the back of your nose—most of what we think we taste is actually an aroma.

Our taste buds can only detect four fun- damental tastes—sweet, sour, bitter, and salty—but those four are enough to determine whether a wine is in balance and ultimately good to drink. There's also a fifth element that taste buds can detect, known as umami, which can best be described as a savory character.

What complicates matters is that everyone has a different threshold for those five tastes. Sweet to one person might be sour to another—it all depends on the structure of our mouths and the wiring of our brains.

The amounts of alcohol, tannin, residual sugar, and acid in a wine can all be detected by swirling it around in your mouth for about 10 seconds, making sure it coats every part of your mouth to hit all the different taste buds.

The sum of these tastes is more important than each one individually. How they all interact together is a reflection of a wine's balance, yet another highly subjective measurement of overall quality. Some people prefer sweeter wines; others prefer a little more acidity to make their mouths water. Some don't like the astringency of tannins, while others like the solid taste they can give to a powerful wine. Generally, however, people describe a wine as balanced when all these tastes are about equal to each other.

Aftertaste (the pleasant kind) is almost as important as the main taste. Poor wines have no aftertaste, and once the wine is swallowed, that's it. Good wines leave your taste buds tingling for anywhere from a few seconds to almost a minute, and aromas will waft around in your mouth almost as long.

Another aspect of a wine that is worth noting is its body. Much like water will feel lighter in your mouth than milk, a light-bodied white wine will have a different presence in your mouth than a full-bodied red like a zinfandel.

The Aroma Wheel

Recognizing smells is always easier than naming them, which is why tasting wine is more fun when you know what you're supposed to be smelling. The wine's label or a winery's description will often include a list of aromas the winemaker has identified in the wine, which can be useful, but the ultimate tool to train yourself to recognize aromas is the Aroma Wheel.

An educator at the University of California at Davis created the Aroma Wheel, and even professionals use it when describing wines.

It broadly categorizes aromas and bouquets, then subcategorizes them and gives specific examples. If you smell something fruity, for example, the wheel will break down fruity smells into categories such as citrus, berry, and tropical fruit, then break each of those subcategories down further into examples of specific fruits.

Aroma Wheels ($6) are often sold among the wine paraphernalia in the tasting rooms of large wineries or can be bought online (along with Aroma Wheel T-shirts for those who live for wine) at www.winearomawheel.com. The website also includes information on how to use the wheel.

WINE AND FOOD

Probably as intimidating to many people as smelling and tasting wine is the question of how to match a wine with food, or vice versa. Like everything else to do with wine, it ultimately boils down to personal taste and personal experience, but there are some underlying principles worth knowing about.

Learning from scratch how your favorite wine interacts on your palate with your favorite foods will increase your appreciation for both the wine and the food. Along the way you'll probably discover the few combinations that really are best avoided and a few others that make your taste buds sing.

There really are no rules to pairing food and wine, despite what some connoisseurs might say. Instead, think of any advice you are given as merely guidelines that will help make the voyage of discovering your favorite food and wine combinations quicker and easier.

These guidelines are constantly in flux. Cuisine trends change and so do winemaking trends. The old adage of white wine with fish and red wine with red meat is somewhat irrelevant. It all depends on the style of a particular wine, how the meat or fish is prepared, and what goes into the accompanying sauces and dishes. One guideline to pairing food and wine is based on sensory adaptation. An acidic wine will taste less acidic if paired with a fairly acidic food. Vinaigrette dressing on a salad, for example, will mellow out a wine that would otherwise taste too tart. Similarly, a sweet wine will taste less sweet if drunk with a dessert, which is why dessert wines taste far too sweet if drunk on their own.

Some food and wine interactions are more confusing. Saltiness of food has a profound effect on how a wine tastes, for example. A salty dish will give the impression of neutralizing some of the acidity of a particularly tart wine, making it taste smoother and fruitier. Foods with some inherent bitterness, such as green vegetables, can actually enhance the bitterness of some wines.

Perhaps one of the classic pairings is a bold red wine with steak, and for good reason. The concentrated protein in red meat serves to soften the taste of tannins in wine, taming what would normally be an astringent, tannic monster into a softer and fruitier beast altogether. A barrel-aged Napa cabernet, for example, would be perfectly balanced with a steak but would taste like a hunk of wood if you still have some left over when the crème brûlée arrives, as the sugar in the dessert overpowers the fruit in the wine, leaving just those woody tannins to dominate.

For a thoroughly educational experience, try drinking just one wine, white or red, with a multiple-course meal to see how its taste dramatically changes with each course. It might not be fun for some courses, but the basics of food and wine interaction very quickly become evident. Some of the simplest foods can prove to be the hardest to find a good wine match. Cheese, for example, does not (as many people believe) go terribly well with many red wines. Try port for rich cheeses like stilton or a dry white wine like sauvignon blanc for sharper cheeses like goat cheese.

Wine in Restaurants

If you've ever wondered how restaurants can justify charging more than $50 for a wine that you just bought in a tasting room for $30, the answer is fairly simple. The markup helps restaurants cover their overhead costs, especially those related to the wine. It pays for the salary

of a sommelier (so make sure you use his services), some of the salaries of the waitstaff, spoilage of wine (by some estimates, about 5 percent of all restaurant wines go bad before being opened), the cost of storing wine (wine cellars cost a lot of money), and all sorts of other costs of doing business, from the electricity bill to broken wineglasses that can cost a restaurant thousands of dollars a year to replace.

In general, cheap wines have higher markups, percentage-wise, than expensive wines. Those from well-known regions or made from popular grape varietals also tend to have higher markups because they're guaranteed sellers. The pricing ploys can be cynical, but there is a way to beat them. One way to save money on wine in restaurants is to bring your own. Corkage fees (the fee charged by the restaurant for you to bring and open your own wine) vary but are generally about $20 in Napa and Sonoma restaurants. It sounds pricey, but it's worth considering if you plan to drink an expensive wine. Some places offer free corkage on certain days of the week, however, and many others offer free corkage on one bottle of your own wine for every bottle you buy from their wine list. Ask about the corkage policy of the restaurant when making a reservation.

Having ordered a bottle in a restaurant, there is yet another wine ritual to go through. This restaurant ritual is all about finding those wines that you don't want to drink. When a server brings a bottle of wine to the table and shows it to you like some trophy, double-check that it is in fact the wine you ordered. Take note of the vintage because it's not uncommon for a restaurant to receive new vintages and forget to update its wine list.

When the wine is opened, the cork will often be handed to you or placed gingerly on the table. It might make a nice souvenir but is actually given to you to check whether it's in good condition. A good cork should feel springy and soft. A dried-out and hard cork suggests that the wine was not stored well and should be a warning to pay close attention when you taste the wine. Don't bother smelling the cork—it will just smell of cork. And don't bother doing anything at all with synthetic corks.

Finally, the server will pour a tasting room quantity of wine into your glass. The idea is to check that the wine is the right temperature and that it is not oxidized or corked. If you simply don't like it, you're stuck with it, though many wines will sometimes taste a bit rough when first opened. Always give the wine a few minutes in the glass before drinking to let it open up and show off its full range of aromas and tastes.

Restaurants are usually pretty good about chilling white wines before serving, but red wines can sometimes feel like they have been stored above a hot oven in the kitchen. In those cases it's fine to ask for an ice bucket to cool the bottle down. Red wine is generally best drunk at 60-70°F.

AGING WINE

The whole point of aging wine for some people is to make it more valuable. For most of us, however, aging wine is all about making it taste better after a few years of development. Youthful wine is like a youthful person— brash, unsure of itself, and a bit awkward. Like people, a wine mellows, gets more complex, and becomes a more well-rounded individual the older it gets. At least that's the theory.

As wine ages it undergoes a complex chemical process that only scientists fully understand. For the rest of us, the aging of wine is a process full of mystery and myths. One common myth is that all wine gets better as it ages. Sadly, that's not true, so don't start stocking a cellar with $10 bottles of cabernet. A poorly made wine that is not in balance when young will not turn into a finely balanced masterpiece after a few years.

A wine almost has to be designed to be aged by the winemaker. Moreover, a wine capable of aging for a decade or more might taste a little unappealing when young. A wine made to be drunk young will probably taste flat and generally awful after 10 years.

Another myth is that age-worthy wine gets better and better as it gets older. While that's almost true for some of the most famous Bordeaux wines, most modern wines are created to be drunk relatively young and will reach a peak after a certain number of years, then go downhill fast. Wineries don't help matters by making sweeping statements that a wine will "continue to improve for 10-15 years." It all depends on how it's stored. In many cases that wine will be barely drinkable after 10 years unless stored under almost perfect aging conditions.

Unfortunately, winemakers and wineries are the only sources of information on how a wine might age, because there are no hard-and-fast rules. One way to get a fairly good idea of how a particular wine will age is to taste some so-called library wines, those from previous vintages that are kept by wineries in part so they themselves know how their wines change with age. Most good wineries either offer library tasting to the public for a fee or will happily oblige if it will likely result in the sale of a case of expensive wine.

In California, virtually no white wines are made to be aged, and they should be consumed within a couple of years. Some that are more age-worthy tend to be chardonnays from mountain vineyards like those on Mount Veeder in the Napa Valley.

It's harder to determine which California red wines will age well. In very general terms, good-quality red port will happily age the longest, followed by a decent cabernet sauvignon, syrah, zinfandel, merlot, and finally pinot noir, which is often at its peak after a couple of years.

Price can also offer a hint at a wine's aging potential, though this test sometimes falls foul of marketing and overpricing. A $100 bottle of Napa Valley cabernet will probably only be bought by serious collectors, for example, who are unlikely to crack it open that night but will instead cellar it for years to either enjoy themselves or sell for a profit to another collector. Winemakers and wineries often have that sort of buyer in mind when they craft the style of wine.

STORING WINE

Research has shown that most American consumers drink wine very soon after buying it, so storage is not a big issue. Aging wine, even for a few years, however, requires a little care to ensure it does not spoil. A pretty iron wine rack on top of a fridge opposite a sunny kitchen window will be useless for anything but short-term storage.

Wine likes to be dark, still, and kept at a fairly constant temperature somewhere from 50-70°F, conditions found in most basements or even a dark interior closet in many homes. The most ideal storage conditions will also be cool (below 60°F) and damp (over 60 percent relative humidity), though these last two requirements can be tough to achieve without digging your own cave or buying some sort of specially designed storage cellar.

Although excessive heat makes wines age a little too fast to achieve their full potential, a constantly fluctuating temperature is the biggest enemy. As the temperature goes up and down during the day, the wine will expand and contract in the bottle, causing the cork to move slightly in the bottle neck and potentially suck in air. That air will gradually oxidize the wine and spoil it.

If a wine is stored in very low humidity, the cork might also dry out and expose the wine to air. Keeping the cork moist so it retains a good seal with the neck of the bottle is the main reason for storing wine sideways.

SHIPPING WINE

The 21st Amendment to the U.S. Constitution ended Prohibition in 1933 but still plagues the wine industry today because it allows states to continue to regulate the sale and distribution of all types of alcoholic beverages.

Since repeal, a patchwork of rules and regulations unique to almost every state has evolved. If you plan to buy wine at a California winery or on the Internet and have it shipped to your home state, you might be out of luck, although an important U.S. Supreme Court decision in May 2005 on interstate shipping laws is slowly reshaping the archaic laws all across the country.

Before May 2005, there were 23 states that banned any direct shipping of wine and other alcoholic drinks from out of state to consumers. Even buying the wine yourself and sending it home in a FedEx box to avoid having to carry it was illegal. Many of those states allowed shipments from producers within the state, however, and some allowed wine shipments from out of state as long as it came through designated in-state distributors.

That discrimination between in-state and out-of-state wineries was the basis of the May 2005 Supreme Court decision that struck down such shipping laws in both New York and Michigan. The court ruled that such discrimination against out-of-state businesses was in violation of the Commerce Clause of the U.S. Constitution, which ensures free trade between states. Although the ruling only affected two states, by definition it called into question the laws in the other states that similarly ban out-of-state wine shipments.

Importantly, however, the Supreme Court left the 21st Amendment untouched in its ruling, so many of those states are still free to enact legislation to either ban or put restrictions on all distribution of alcoholic beverages, whether from within or outside the state.

They could go the route of the 17 states that, along with the District of Columbia, allow direct shipping but with restrictions. Though all stop short of an outright ban, the restrictions vary state by state and can be complex. Some allow shipment of only limited quantities of wine, others leave the rules up to each individual county within the state, and still others limit shipments from individual wineries. These rules also change regularly. Luckily, California wineries are on top of the ever-changing situation, and as of 2016 they will generally be able to ship wine for personal consumption to all states except Alabama, Delaware, Mississippi, Oklahoma, Pennsylvania, South Dakota, and Utah. Be sure to ask your favorite winery about the latest laws, because everything might well have changed again by the time this book is published.

International shipping tends to be prohibitively expensive and involves considerable taxes, though some wineries will oblige. If you plan to take wine overseas yourself, be sure to check the liquor import laws of the countries in question. Unfortunately, taking wine on a plane yourself became much harder when airlines banned carriage of liquids in cabin baggage. Packing a few bottles of wine in checked luggage is an option, but make sure the bottles are well protected from the sometimes rough baggage handlers. Most wineries sell shipping boxes with plenty of padding.

WINE CLUBS

Chances are that you will be told about a winery's wine club while at the tasting room bar. Every winery has a wine club of some sort, and many dream up fancy names to make them sound more exclusive (some actually are exclusive and have long waiting lists to join).

Wine clubs are an important marketing tool for wineries and can be one of the only distribution channels for small boutique wineries. They can also be a great way for visitors to Wine Country to get discounts on their favorite wines even if they live hundreds of miles away or when the wines are not widely distributed. Make sure you read the rules carefully, however. The small print sometimes commits new members to buying far more than they anticipate.

When new members sign up for a wine club and hand over a credit card number, they often get an on-the-spot discount on wines (the club discount varies, but it's generally 10-20 percent). More importantly for the winery, the new club members have also agreed to buy at least one (sometimes more) wine club shipment in the future before they are able to cancel their membership. Those shipments contain wines that the winery chooses, not the customer, and are subject to often sizable shipping fees that can more than offset the club discount (if you live near the winery, you can usually avoid shipping fees by collecting the wine yourself).

Wine club shipments are usually made once every three or four months, and there's often a choice of different tiers of membership, offering different styles (red or white) or quantities of wine in each shipment. There are also plenty of other "exclusive" membership privileges, from discounts on gifts to free reserve wine-tastings, some more worthwhile than others, depending on how far you live from the winery.

Essentials

Getting There

AIR

There are four major international airports within a few hours' drive of most parts of Napa and Sonoma Counties. San Francisco International Airport, Oakland International Airport, and San Jose's Norman Y. Mineta International Airport all serve the cities of the San Francisco Bay Area, and Sacramento International Airport serves its namesake city and parts of California's Central Valley.

The biggest airport by far is **San Francisco International Airport** (SFO, 800/435-9736, www.flysfo.org), known locally as SFO. It is served by nearly 50 airlines at last count, about two-thirds of which are international carriers. All major domestic U.S. airlines serve SFO (United Airlines has by far the largest number of flights), as do a number of low-cost carriers, including Southwest Airlines, JetBlue, and Virgin America.

Driving from SFO to Napa or Sonoma takes about 1.5 hours if traffic is good but involves hitting San Francisco city streets for a few miles to reach the Golden Gate Bridge. In rush hour, add at least a half hour to that. Alternatively, you can stick to the freeway and take the Bay Bridge to I-80 East. While you may bypass the inevitable slow ride through city streets, I-80 between Oakland and Vallejo, where you turn west on Highway 37, can get sticky even during non-commute times.

The Oakland and San Jose airports get their "international" tag from just a handful of international flights, and most of the airlines serving them are domestic. Flying into either can often be cheaper than going to SFO, but the drawback is that direct flights from major U.S. cities tend to be less common and connections might be necessary.

Oakland International Airport (OAK, 510/563-3300, www.flyoakland.com) is just across the bay from San Francisco and is served by 13 airlines, including two of the big domestic airlines (American Airlines and Delta) as well as two major low-cost carriers (JetBlue and Southwest) and a handful of charter airlines. Driving time from Oakland's airport to Napa is about an hour. Driving to Healdsburg in northern Sonoma can take more than two hours.

San Jose's **Norman Y. Mineta International Airport** (SJC, 408/392-3600, www.sjc.org) is served by American, Delta, and United, and low-cost carriers including Southwest, Virgin America, and JetBlue. The airport is about a 45-minute drive south of SFO, putting it farther from Napa and Sonoma.

Sacramento International Airport (SMF, 916/929-5411, www.sacramento.aero) is smaller than the three Bay Area airports and considerably farther away, about a 1.5-hour drive to Napa and longer to destinations to the west.

The only commercial airlines to service the tiny **Charles M. Schulz Sonoma County Airport** (STS, 707/565-7240, www.sonomacountyairport.org) in Santa Rosa are Alaska Airlines, Allegiant Air, and American Airlines. These offer direct flights to and from Seattle, Portland, Los Angeles, Orange County, Las Vegas, Phoenix, and San Diego.

RAIL

The days of easily being able to visit much of Napa and Sonoma by train are long gone—about 100 years gone, to be exact. Railroads that brought Victorian visitors to Sonoma's lush forests and Calistoga's spa resorts were driven out of business by the car, which has since come to dominate transportation in California.

Emeryville, next to Oakland, is the main Amtrak hub of the Bay Area these days. Four train routes stop here: The California Zephyr travels from Chicago via Denver; the Capitol Corridor services Auburn, Sacramento, Emeryville, Oakland, and San Jose and is a popular route with local commuters; the Coast Starlight travels down the West Coast from Seattle to Portland and ends in Los Angeles; and the San Joaquin services the Central Valley. Despite fun perks like the dining and lounge cars, train travel is not for those with limited vacation time, since it takes considerably longer than traveling by car, and to get from Emeryville to parts of the Wine Country requires transferring onto Amtrak bus services.

From the **Emeryville station** (5885 Horton St.) there are connecting bus services to San Francisco and some of the bigger Napa and Sonoma towns, including Napa, Santa Rosa, and Healdsburg. Times and frequencies of all these services vary depending on the day and season, so contact **Amtrak** (800/872-7245, www.amtrak.com) for more information.

BUS

Most major cities in Wine Country can be reached by a combination of long-distance and local bus services (and Amtrak bus service). Many of the smaller towns and most of the wineries, however, are off the beaten path and can be reached only with your own wheels, though it's certainly an option to go to Napa, Healdsburg, or Sonoma by bus and rent a bicycle for a couple of days of touring.

Getting to those cities by bus might take a while. The long-distance **Greyhound Lines** buses (800/231-2222, www.greyhound.com) serve only the major Bay Area cities of San Francisco, Oakland, and San Jose, plus Santa Rosa in Sonoma.

Local bus service from Santa Rosa on the **Sonoma County Transit** bus network (707/576-7433 or 800/345-7433, www.sctransit.com) connects to Guerneville, Healdsburg, Glen Ellen, and Sonoma. San Francisco is the best place to head to for using Greyhound Lines for connections to Santa Rosa. While there are no direct connections to Napa by bus, it is reachable aboard the **San Francisco Bay Ferry** (415/291-3377, https://sanfranciscobayferry.com, adults $14, seniors and children 5-18 $7, 4 and under free), which also departs from San Francisco. It offers daily service, multiple times per day, to Vallejo. From the ferry terminal, **VINE**'s (707/251-6443 or 800/696-6443, www.ridethevine.com) Route 11 runs directly to downtown Napa and on to Yountville, St. Helena, and Calistoga.

Getting Around

CAR

Almost everyone gets around by car in California, and it's no different in Napa and Sonoma, where public transportation links are even thinner on the ground than in urban areas. With so many people in cars, congestion is a constant problem.

Thanks to a booming tech economy and tight housing market, the San Francisco Bay Area is now behind only Los Angeles as the most congested part of the nation. Rush hour on the area's freeways now stretches three hours at each end of the day, even on weekends: 7am-10am and 4pm-7pm, expect slow freeway traffic at almost any major junction, bottleneck, or bridge.

Up in the Wine Country the roads are smaller but are also often congested during rush hour, and especially on summer weekends when visitors from local cities flock to their favorite wineries.

The worst roads are in the busiest parts of Wine Country—**Highway 12** between Sonoma and Kenwood in the Sonoma Valley, and **Highway 29** between Napa and St. Helena in the Napa Valley. The jams on **Highway 37,** which connects U.S. 101 to I-80 and leads to Napa and Sonoma via Highway 121, can also be legendary, particularly when there is a race at Sonoma Raceway. In northern Sonoma, the **U.S. Highway 101** freeway through Santa Rosa tends to get clogged during the rush hours almost every day, though mercifully the roads from the freeway into the Russian River Valley are far quieter, except sometimes the River Road (Hwy. 116) through Guerneville, which can be a traffic jam on hot summer weekends or when there's an event in town.

You can help the traffic flow by making sure you know where you're going and driving at the same clip as other drivers. If you're being tailgated by more than one car on a narrow, winding road, pull over at the nearest turnout or turnoff to let the faster traffic pass. And on two-lane roads with a center turn lane, use that lane both for turning left to avoid holding up traffic behind you and also to merge into traffic when turning left onto that main road.

Gas in the San Francisco Bay Area is some of the most expensive in the nation due to a combination of higher state and local taxes, higher costs for gas stations, and tight supply of the special, cleaner-burning formulation that is required in the state. The most expensive gas by far is in San Francisco. Some of the cheapest is in the most unlikely places off the beaten track, like Forestville in the Russian River Valley and Kenwood in the Sonoma Valley. Although there's sometimes no rhyme or reason to explain the difference in prices between one gas station and the next, Arco usually offers the cheapest gas and will sometimes be matched by other local gas stations. The prevalence of gas stations generally means you'd be hard-pressed to run out of gas anywhere in Napa and Sonoma, but don't set off on a drive over a winding mountain road if the gas warning light is already on.

Much of Napa and Sonoma is within easy reach of a freeway. From San Francisco, take U.S. 101 north out of the city and over the Golden Gate Bridge ($7.50 toll, payable southbound only). About a 20-minute drive north of the bridge is Highway 37 East, which connects with Highway 121, which leads to Carneros, the Sonoma Valley, and the Napa Valley. Continue on U.S. 101 to Santa Rosa (about 45 minutes from the bridge) for jumping-off points to the Russian River Valley, and drive a further 15 minutes for Healdsburg, the Dry Creek Valley, and Alexander Valley.

Driving from downtown San Francisco to Napa can sometimes be quicker via I-80 East, which crosses the **Bay Bridge** ($4-6 toll, payable westbound only) then turns north and crosses the Carquinez Bridge about 25 minutes later ($5 toll, payable northbound only). Shortly after is the Sonoma Boulevard/Highway 29 exit, which leads to the southern end of the Napa Valley.

Jumping from Napa to Sonoma is relatively easy but requires navigating many two-lane roads, which are often twisty mountain rides. From Napa, the main highway to Sonoma is Highway 121, which connects Napa to Carneros and intersects with Highway 12. The Oakville Grade takes a more adventurous route from Oakville over the Mayacamas Mountains to Glen Ellen, while farther up the valley Petrified Forest Road in Calistoga reaches U.S. 101 just north of Santa Rosa at Mark West Springs Road. Highway 128 runs the length of the Napa Valley from Rutherford, past Calistoga, and eventually meets U.S. 101 at Geyserville, connecting Napa with the Alexander Valley and the rest of northern Sonoma.

Rental Cars

All the major car-rental companies are represented at the three main Bay Area airports, and most also have locations in downtown San Francisco, Oakland, San Jose, Santa Rosa, and Napa. Prices vary wildly, although they tend to be more expensive in California than in other parts of the nation, particularly at the airports. Deals are always available, and it's worth noting that four-day rentals usually cost the same as weekly ones.

Always check what your own car-insurance

policy, credit cards, or travel insurance will cover before renting a car so you don't buy unnecessary (and often pricey) car, medical, or personal possession insurance at the rental counter. Liability insurance is required by law for all drivers in California, so if you have no car insurance of your own, you'll have to buy it from the rental company. Credit cards will not always cover it.

For current prices and availability, contact:

- **Alamo** (855/354-6962, www.alamo.com)
- **Avis** (800/633-3469, www.avis.com)
- **Budget** (800/218-7992, www.budget.com)
- **Dollar** (800/800-5252, www.dollar.com)
- **Enterprise** (800/261-7331, www.enterprise.com)
- **Hertz** (800/654-3131, www.hertz.com)
- **Thrifty** (800/334-1705, www.thrifty.com)

You can also get some good deals and make reservations through major online travel agencies, including **Orbitz** (www.orbitz.com), **Travelocity** (www.travelocity.com), and **Expedia** (www.expedia.com). Check whether there are any discounts from your airline, too.

BIKE

Biking is a potentially fun way of seeing parts of Napa and Sonoma but one that few people seem to try, if the lack of bicycles on the roads is anything to go by. Choose your route well, however, and the rewards of experiencing the warm air and all the unique smells of Wine Country are many. Plan badly and you'll be cursing all day long.

The roads in much of Wine Country can make biking more exciting than you'd like. Small roads tend to be winding and narrow, with the ever-present danger of inattentive (or drunk) drivers failing to see cyclists or give them enough clearance. While accidents seem to be few, close shaves are more common, so be well aware of approaching cars and always cycle in single file as close to the edge of the road as possible. Make sure you wear a helmet, and don't plan on drinking much. Biking drunk is illegal, and it increases your risk of having an accident, whether from being hit by a car or running off the road down a ravine.

Drinking and strenuous exercise are also a recipe for dehydration and heatstroke. Hot summer days might not be the best time to go biking in much of Napa and Sonoma, except in the cooler parts of the Russian River Valley and down in Carneros. If you do go in the summer, plan on taking a picnic and whiling away the hottest mid- and late-afternoon hours somewhere off the bike. Spring and fall are the best times to venture out on two wheels. Winter is out, unless you like wet-weather riding or happen upon one of the occasional warm, dry spells.

Bike Tours

Some of the best places to see wineries by bike include the Dry Creek Valley, a relatively flat and compact area crammed with small wineries, many just a few minutes' ride from Healdsburg's bike shops. Healdsburg is also the jumping-off point for rides down the Westside Road into the Russian River Valley and into the Alexander Valley, though distances are longer and wineries farther apart.

The handful of wineries and historic sites around the city of Sonoma are also perfect for a bike tour. They are close together and only a short ride from Sonoma's main bike-rental shops near the downtown plaza. From Sonoma it is a slightly longer ride down into Carneros, but once you're there, the flatlands and wetlands are fun to explore on a bike. Wineries here tend to be farther apart, however, and the weather can be on the cool and murky side, even in summer.

The Napa Valley has some good areas for biking, but the size of the valley and the crowds mean you'll have to plan a route carefully to avoid traffic and long distances. Try sticking to Coombsville, the Calistoga area, or the wineries along the Silverado Trail in the Rutherford appellation, just a few minutes' ride from St. Helena. The Napa Valley Vine Trail, linking communities (and wineries) along Highway 29, is in the works with a few sections completed as of this printing.

Travel Tips

CONDUCT

Despite seemingly endless official rules and regulations, there's a refreshing anything-goes attitude to life in Northern California. The multicultural population is so used to bizarre behavior by its fellow citizens that people barely bat an eye at characters who might leave outsiders staring in disbelief.

The Wine Country is generally a wealthy enclave in a wealthy part of California, a place where money talks and lifestyle is everything. Like the rest of California, it's also a place of sharp economic contrasts. Migrant workers in the vineyards harvesting grapes are at one end of the economic scale, while corporate winery executives are at the other. As is the norm in California, each group seems to happily tolerate the other.

Dress

California virtually invented business casual attire, and it's rare to see a shirt and tie, especially in Napa and Sonoma. About the only places that require you to pay attention to what you wear are golf courses (collared shirt and appropriate shoes) and a handful of top restaurants (smart casual for women, jacket and tie for men).

Drinking and Smoking

The legal drinking age in California is 21. While tasting rooms rarely check ID, expect to have it handy if you look under age 30. This is especially true in bars and clubs, and even restaurants.

The legal smoking age in California is also 21, as of 2016. Smoking has been banned in many places throughout the state; don't expect to find a smoking section in any restaurant or an ashtray in any bar. Smoking is illegal in all bars and clubs, but some have outdoor patios. Taking the ban one step further, many hotels, motels, and inns throughout Northern California are strictly nonsmoking, and you'll be subject to fees of hundreds of dollars if your room smells of smoke when you leave.

Furthermore, there's no smoking in any public building, and even some of the state parks don't allow cigarettes. There's often good reason for this; the fire danger in California is extreme in the summer, and one carelessly thrown butt can cause a genuine catastrophe.

Tipping

As is the case in the rest of the nation, tipping is a voluntary but necessary practice in restaurants, bars, taxis, and for services given by valets or hotel concierges. A 15 percent tip is average, though more (20 percent) is normal in this land where money talks. Most restaurants will automatically add a standard 18 percent gratuity to the bill for parties of more than six or eight people. If that's the case, you have no obligation to add any further tip when signing the credit card slip, even though there will still be a spot for one.

Tipping is definitely not necessary in winery tasting rooms. In fact, you risk offending the generally well-paid staff if you do try to slip them a fiver, however helpful they have been. If you feel a strong urge to return a favor, simply buy a bottle or two of wine.

When ordering in bars, tip the bartender or waitstaff $1 per drink. For taxis, plan to tip 15-20 percent of the fare, or simply round the cost up to the nearest dollar. Cafés and coffee shops often have tip jars out. There is no consensus on what is appropriate when purchasing a $3 beverage. Often $0.50 is enough, depending on the quality and service.

Tipping is also expected in hotels and B&Bs. You'll often find an envelope on the desk for the housekeeping staff. Depending on the type of accommodations, $1-5 per night is the standard rate.

Wine Country on a Budget

Go where inexpensive or complimentary tasting is the norm. The Alexander, Dry Creek, and Russian River Valleys offer the best deals overall. Here is a list of the best complimentary tasting rooms in Napa and Sonoma.

- **Heitz** (page 88): Free flight of superb cabernets

- **Jacuzzi Family Vineyards** (page 176): Free flight of Italian varietals (and estate olive oil)

- **Cline Cellars** (page 176): Free tasting of Rhône varietals and access to historic sites and beautiful picnic grounds

- **Korbel Champagne Cellars** (page 220): Free tasting of bubbly, tour, and access to shaded picnic spots

- **Merry Edwards Winery** (page 209): Free seated tasting of award-winning pinot noir

- **Alexander Valley Vineyards** (page 263): Free tasting and cave tour

Clip coupons. Vouchers for free or two-for-one tastings are available at most visitors centers or chambers of commerce, and in free local magazines like *Wine Country This Week.* Many winery websites offer printable vouchers for discounted tastings, as do NapaValley.com and WineCountry.com.

Talk to your concierge. Many hotels and inns arrange free or discounted tastings for their guests at local wineries.

Buy a bottle. The cost of a tasting can often be deducted from a wine purchase.

Go in the off-season. In the winter and spring, hotel rates drop by as much as 50 percent. More wineries offer deals to lure in customers, as do restaurants and other attractions.

Go with a local. Many wineries offer free tastings to Napa Valley residents.

Avoid wine altogether. Many museums and recreation options are free. Visit **The Hess Collection** (page 46) or spend the day at a beach in the Russian River Valley (page 225).

TRAVELERS WITH DISABILITIES

California is one of the most progressive states in the country when it comes to access for people with disabilities, and its state laws often go beyond the requirements of the federal Americans with Disabilities Act, which requires that all new public buildings must be disabled-accessible and older ones must be retrofitted if readily achievable.

Major wineries that are open to the public without an appointment, together with museums and other sights, all generally have wheelchair access ramps and restrooms for disabled people. Appointment-only wineries often stay appointment-only partly because of the prohibitive cost of meeting the various building and safety codes required for commercial public buildings, including accessibility for people with disabilities. Small B&Bs and inns often do not have to comply with the strict laws because their historic buildings cannot easily be made accessible.

Napa and Sonoma Counties are ostensibly rural areas, so access for people with disabilities is always going to be far from universal. One organization that can help people with disabilities plan visits within Northern

California is **Access Northern California** (http://accessnca.org). It has specific information on accommodations and sights with access. Also contact local chambers of commerce or visitors centers for more specific information.

TRAVELING WITH CHILDREN

Most, but not all, winery activities are geared toward adults. Wineries generally allow children onto the premises, but anyone under 21, California's legal minimum drinking age, cannot taste any wines. And wineries without wine-tasting tend to be pretty boring places, especially for kids.

If there are children in tow, careful planning can avoid tears of boredom and frustration. Some wineries offer educational tours that can be fun for kids and adults alike. Others have other attractions, ranging from art to historic cars. In all cases double-check that children are welcome, because some wineries, such as the Castello di Amorosa castle, that might seem to offer plenty of entertainment for kids have an age limit.

Plenty of sights and museums have something to offer inquisitive young brains. The Petrified Forest or Old Faithful Geyser near Calistoga will delight and amaze children (though not necessarily adults), as will an adult-supervised ride in a canoe on the Russian River or a turn on a carnival ride or the narrow-gauge railroads at Train Town in Sonoma.

Also worth noting is that a lot of higher-priced B&Bs and resorts do not allow children under a certain age, and some do not allow children at all. The reasons vary—in some cases the policy is to protect precious antiques, in other cases simply to ensure that the peace and tranquility that guests are paying top dollar for is not shattered by screaming kids. Always check the policy on young guests when booking a room.

TRAVELING WITH PETS

Wine Country might not be terribly kid-friendly, but it is most definitely not dog-friendly. Dogs are actively discouraged or banned in many wineries, even those that have their own resident winery pooch. They are also not allowed in rooms of many lodgings, though an increasing number of hotels and motels accept pets for an additional nightly fee, usually $25. On many hiking trails, dogs are either not allowed at all or must be on a leash at all times.

Worse still (from the dog's point of view), the hot summer weather makes cars thoroughly uncomfortable places to be even for short periods of time. Dogs should never be left for long periods in a car in the California sun, even with the windows slightly cracked.

MAPS

Beware the cartoonish maps in many of the free magazines that blanket the Wine Country. Many of them are highly inaccurate for anything other than determining the approximate location of wineries and other major sights. Even for that purpose they can sometimes be unreliable, putting wineries on the wrong side of the road, for example, or giving little idea of distances involved. As road maps they should certainly not be relied on. Many small roads are missing from them, and other roads turn out to be dead ends or are misnamed.

The chamber of commerce at the bigger wine country towns, particularly in the Napa and Sonoma Valleys, produce excellent maps that are available at their visitors centers. However, the most reliable road maps for planning a trip covering Napa and Sonoma are published by the veteran map companies, though many have narrowed their focus to cities or to larger regions such as Northern California. Either way, most of these maps don't have wineries or other sights marked on them but are good for general navigation, especially when used in conjunction with this book or the winery maps published by local wine associations in each region.

The **American Automobile Association** (AAA) no longer publishes a specific Wine Country map, but does have reliable regional maps as well as more detailed road maps for Napa, northern Sonoma, and the greater San Francisco Bay Area. They are available from your local AAA office and are free for members. Check www.aaa.com for your local office; to order maps online, visit www.calstate.aaa.com.

Rand McNally publishes several excellent Northern California maps that include some but not all of the major wine regions. Rand McNally maps are usually available at bookstores and can also be ordered online at www.randmcnally.com. Other options include *Napa-Sonoma Wine Country Pocket Guide* and *Napa/Sonoma Wine Country Road & Recreation Map* by **Great Pacific Map** (206/236-3060, www.greatpacificmaps.com), available online or in bookstores.

Health and Safety

DRINKING AND DRIVING

Driving (and even cycling) under the influence of alcohol is a serious offense in California. Both state and local police are well aware that visitors to Wine Country might have overindulged, and they will often be on the lookout for erratic driving in popular wine-tasting areas on busy weekends.

The blood alcohol limit for driving in the state is 0.08 percent, a level you can reach very quickly in a tasting room. Most wineries will pour about one ounce of wine per taste (some might be stingier, but use one ounce as a guideline), which means that by visiting one winery and tasting (and swallowing) four wines, you will already be well on the way to that limit.

People weighing less than 150 pounds who taste another flight of four wines at another winery in a two-hour period will likely be at their legal limit already. Those over 150 pounds will have a little more leeway, but not much.

The penalties for a DUI conviction are severe, including a fine ranging $200-7,000 and time in jail, not to mention the potential loss of your driver's license and a big jump in insurance premiums if you are able to get it back. If you are a driver involved in an accident that causes bodily harm while your blood alcohol is over the legal limit, the penalties are even stiffer.

Trying to calculate how much can be drunk before reaching the limit is a notoriously inexact science. It depends not only on how much alcohol is consumed but also the person's weight, gender, metabolism, and how much food he or she has eaten over the previous few hours. Drinking a lot of water while tasting might ward off headaches but will do little to lower the blood alcohol level.

The only way to guarantee you are safe to drive is not to drink at all. Instead, use a designated driver, or if that's not an option, learn to spit wine out after smelling the aromas and swirling it around your mouth. If you really want to experience the lingering aftertaste of a $100 cabernet, then swallow just one wine out of all those you taste. There are usually plenty of spitting containers on tasting room counters. Just double-check that it's not the water jug you're about to empty your wine into.

OUTDOORS

The Wine Country might be all about luxury pampering, but the wilds here are also a major draw for visitors and can be just as wild as anywhere else in California. Experiencing Napa and Sonoma is as much about experiencing the great outdoors as the wine, but there are some basic outdoor rules to be aware of, particularly if you've had some wine. Even a few tastes of wine can be enough to potentially impair your judgment.

On the hiking or mountain-biking trail, make sure you know where you're going, and never go alone in case you get into trouble. Also be aware that many of the trails in Napa

Best Towns to Park and Taste

To replace driving with walking, considering spending a day in one of Wine Country's historical towns that are filled with excellent tasting rooms, restaurants, and shops.

· **Napa:** This working-class town has worked hard to revitalize its historical riverfront downtown. Amid Victorian buildings, you'll find plenty of boutique tasting rooms and collectives, plus scores of restaurants and the famed Oxbow Public Market, the biggest foodie emporium in Napa and Sonoma.

· **Sonoma:** Sitting compactly around the historical plaza, downtown Sonoma is home to nearly two dozen tasting rooms, which range in specialty from bubbly to big and bold cabernets. Along the way, historical sites, hiking trails, specialty shops, and plenty of places to eat vie for attention.

· **Healdsburg:** The Victorian grande dame of Wine Country has over 30 tasting rooms filling its historic storefronts, plus great restaurants, boutique shops, and a leafy town square where you can relax under trees planted over a century ago.

· **Geyserville:** This small city has a grand total of five tasting rooms, three restaurants, and one bar. However, these pretty much take up all of the tiny and quaint Main Street, and are all worth a stop. The restaurants are so popular they draw devotees from as far away as Santa Rosa.

and Sonoma might start off in cool, damp woods but will often climb up to scrubland with little shade and often searing heat in the summer. Sunscreen, sunglasses, and a hat are mandatory in California during the summer, far less important during the winter. Luckily, most large wineries sell baseball caps should your bare head be overheating.

On the water, whether the Russian River or the many lakes, take the usual water-safety precautions. Don't jump in unless you know what's under the water, especially in the Russian River, where all sorts of treelike debris (washed downstream during the winter and spring) might lurk just below the surface of the often-murky water. Always wear a life jacket when in a boat, and avoid doing anything on or in the water when you've had too much to drink.

Lyme Disease

Potentially the most dangerous animal for outdoor hikers in many parts of California, particularly parts of Napa and Sonoma, is also one of the smallest. The western black-legged tick, which thrives in most lowland hills and meadows, can transmit Lyme disease, one of the most common vector-transmitted diseases in the United States.

The good news is that Lyme disease is easily treated with antibiotics if caught early. The bad news is that it can be difficult to detect early, with many of the initial symptoms (including fever, aches and pains, headaches, and fatigue) often mistaken for other ailments. If left untreated, Lyme disease can develop into a serious degenerative illness, and the longer it goes untreated the harder it is to cure with antibiotics.

The best protection is to wear long pants and sleeves to avoid picking the ticks up in the first place. Plenty of insect repellent also helps. If you are bitten by a tick and it is still attached, do not try to pull it off with your fingers because the head will likely stay embedded. Remove ticks with tweezers by grasping the tick's head parts as close to your skin as possible and applying slow steady traction. Do not attempt to get ticks out of your skin by burning them or coating them with nail polish remover or petroleum jelly.

Always check for ticks after being outdoors in woodland or grassy meadows, and watch for the telltale circular rash that usually appears around tick bites from three days to a month after being bitten. Also be aware that any flu-like symptoms might be a sign of Lyme disease. If in any doubt, see a doctor.

Wildlife

Much of California's other wildlife is not a great danger for visitors. Mountain lions, also known as pumas or cougars, do live in many of the hills and forests around urban areas, especially those where deer (their favorite prey) are common, but they are rarely seen and usually stay well away from humans, especially big groups of noisy humans (one reason never to hike alone).

Attacks by mountain lions are extremely rare. In fact, you're more likely to get struck by lightning. Sightings are more common, though still relatively rare. If you do happen across a lion on a hiking trail and it doesn't instinctively run the other way, try to make yourself look as large as possible to scare it, then slowly back away. Mountain lions are big cats—males can weigh up to 150 pounds and grow up to eight feet long from head to tip of the tail—but they'd rather not pick a fight with something their own size. In the rare instance a lion does attack, fight it with whatever comes to hand, like rocks and sticks. It's a strategy that has saved plenty of victims, as cats, no matter what size, don't like to get hurt or overly inconvenienced.

One thing you should not do is turn and run—mountain lions can run faster. Dogs should be kept on a leash (it's the law in most wilderness areas) to avoid agitating mountain lions, and also for the well-being of the dog, which would be easy prey. If you see a big cat in the brush next to the trail, do not try to approach it. Remember that you are trespassing on their territory, so if you let them get on with their lives, you'll likely be left alone.

Another animal that can do some damage to humans but is rarely seen is the western diamondback rattlesnake, the most common of the eight varieties of rattler found in California. The snakes are brown with a triangular head and a dark diamond pattern running down their backs. They also have that distinctive rattle that should be a warning to walk the other way if you hear it.

Rattlesnakes live throughout Napa and Sonoma, preferring hot rocky or grassy areas. When tromping through such areas, always be aware of where you're stepping, and if climbing on rocky ledges, make sure you can see where you're putting your hands. If you are bitten, reduce any movement. Next, get immediate medical help. Thankfully, the venom is rarely fatal with the proper medical attention.

Snakes will usually head the other way when they hear anyone approaching, but if you do see one and it refuses to budge, back off and give it a wide berth. Also be especially alert for rattlers in the spring when the snakes are just emerging from hibernation and tend to be groggy, hungry, and mean.

Poison Oak

Poison oak is a deciduous shrub, usually 2-4 feet tall, with glossy leaves resembling those of a real oak tree. The leaves have scalloped edges and are arranged in clusters of three. In the late summer and fall, they take on a pretty rusty red color. Those leaves and stems contain an oil, similar to that in poison ivy, called urushiol, that causes an allergic skin reaction in an estimated three-quarters of the population, even after only brief exposure.

Even in the winter the bare stems remain just as dangerous to passing skin and can be hard to spot. Even burning a small amount of poison oak on a campfire generates dangerous smoke that, if inhaled, can lead to a potentially fatal inflammation of the lungs.

The plant is common all over California, particularly in shady lowland woods and meadows. You will almost certainly encounter it alongside hiking trails, and it's particularly abundant after wet winters. Learn to identify it, and avoid it if at all possible.

Wear long pants and sleeves and wash both clothes and skin as soon as possible if you even *think* you have been in contact with poison oak. Rashes can take a few days to appear, but once they do, there's little you can do to get rid of them, and they'll likely spread as your body's immune system battles to neutralize the poisons and becomes even more sensitized in the process. The oil stays active for months, sometimes years, on surfaces like hiking boots and clothes (and dogs), and can rub off on skin at any time and cause a rash, so wash these too if you think they have been contaminated. Any regular laundry detergent will remove the oil.

If you do get a rash, do not scratch it, and make sure it is covered to prevent infection. Contrary to popular belief, the ooze from the rashes cannot spread the toxins, but it can attract bacteria that will further irritate the skin. Mild rashes will usually go away in a few days. The more seriously afflicted could be driven mad for many weeks by a growing rash, and some might require treatment with anti-inflammatory steroids, though the application of readily available hydrocortisone cream is the usual treatment.

Some specialized cleansing products that will neutralize the toxic oils are worth using if you're highly allergic. They are sold under the Tecnu brand name and are available at most pharmacies.

Dehydration and Heatstroke

Dehydration is a perennial enemy for about half the year in Napa and Sonoma, whether from tasting too much wine or from any sort of exertion in the heat. Most of Northern California is warm May-November and can get downright hot July-September, especially in the inland valleys.

Parts of the Russian River Valley, Carneros, and coastal regions will often be cooler because of fog and cool ocean breezes, but even these areas can heat up quickly in the summer when the sun comes out or the breezes die. The other half of the year, November-May, is the rainy season, though even in November, April, and May there can be some very warm spells of weather.

Drink plenty of water, especially if hiking, but even when frolicking on or in the water on a hot day. For serious hiking in hot weather, at least a half quart of water per hour is recommended (in small doses, not all at once). Wear a hat to help prevent both sunburn and heatstroke, a potentially fatal condition created when the body is no longer able to cool itself sufficiently, causing symptoms including headache, confusion, and muscle cramps.

The water you do drink should always come from a bottle or a tap. Most of California's rivers and lakes contain parasites and bacteria that, although not fatal, can play havoc with digestive systems for several days and might require treatment. If camping at a primitive site near a stream or lake, consider taking a water filter so you don't have to carry all your water in with you.

Resources

Glossary

acetic acid: All wines contain a minuscule amount of acetic acid (vinegar), but bad wine will have enough (over about 0.1 percent) to actually start smelling of vinegar—not a good thing.

acid/acidity: The natural acids (citric, malic, tartaric, and lactic) in a wine create a tartness that is supposed to act as a counterpoint to sugary sweetness, balancing the wine.

aftertaste: The flavors that linger on your palate after swallowing the wine. The longer the aftertaste, the better—sometimes you can still taste wines almost a minute after swallowing.

aging: The process of storing a wine in barrels or bottles for a few months to many decades so it develops character and more desirable flavors. White wines tend to turn from a greenish hue in young wines to a yellowish cast/tone to a gold/amber color as they age. Reds usually have a purple tone when young, turning to a deep red (Bordeaux wines and cabernet, for example) or a brick-red color (burgundy wines and pinot noir, for example), detectable at the surface edge in a wineglass, as they age.

alcohol: The colorless and flavorless chemical created as a byproduct of fermentation that gets you drunk but also acts as a preservative for the wine. The higher the sugar content of the grape when picked, the higher the alcohol content of the wine. Californian red wines tend to have alcohol content of over 13 percent, sometimes as high as 16 percent in the case of some zinfandels.

angular: Describes a tart wine with a sharp edge to its taste. The opposite of a round, soft, or supple wine.

appellation or AVA: The specific area a wine comes from. Technically, appellation is a term used simply to describe a geographic area. To be classified as an American Viticultural Area, or AVA, by the federal Bureau of Alcohol, Tobacco, and Firearms (ATF), an area must be shown to have unique soil, climate, or other growing conditions that will distinguish its wines from those grown in other areas. When an AVA, such as Napa Valley or Carneros, is named on the label, at least 85 percent of the grapes must have come from there (100 percent in Washington and Oregon). There can also be AVAs within AVAs. The Napa Valley, for example, is a single AVA that contains 16 other AVAs, commonly referred to as sub-appellations.

approachable: An approachable wine is easy to enjoy and generally made to be drunk without aging.

aroma: The smell of a wine that comes from the fruit or smells like fruit. As wine ages, some of the fruit-related smells dwindle and are replaced by more complex smells from chemicals created during the aging process, referred to as the bouquet.

aromatic: Describes wines that have a strong flowery or spicy character.

astringent: The rough, puckery taste that most people describe as sour and that often comes from a high tannin content. Astringent wines normally mellow with age.

austere: Slightly hard and acidic wines that seem to lack depth of flavor. Such wines may soften a bit with age and develop more subtle complexity than fuller wines. Austere wines are often from cool growing regions, especially mountain areas.

Bacchus: The Roman god of wine and a name sometimes seen in jokey marketing material.

balance: A balanced wine is what winemakers strive to make, one in which no flavor or aroma overpowers another. Acid balances the sweetness, fruit against oak and tannin. You'll know a balanced wine when you taste one.

barrel: A wooden vessel used to store wine before it is bottled, made of oak and charred (toasted) on the inside to impart specific flavors and color to the wine. On any winery tour you'll likely pass racks of oak barrels (sometimes called *barriques*) that are usually the standard size of 59 gallons, or about 225 liters. American oak barrels cost between $360-500 new. Highly prized French oak barrels cost more than $800 each. Barrels are usually used and reused for several vintages, then end up as planters or are discarded.

barrel fermenting: The fermentation of wine in barrels to impart specific flavors and texture. It often gives a richer flavor to white wines, though is sometimes overused and will make a wine "over-oaked." In red wines, barrel fermenting will impart more tannins to the wine so it can age for longer. The increasingly common alternative is to age wines in stainless steel or concrete eggs.

big: Wine with a big, robust, and full-bodied character, usually because of high alcohol content. Dry Creek Valley zinfandel is an example of a "big" wine.

bitter: One of the four basic tastes that your taste buds can detect. Some wines are supposed to have slight bitterness, but too much is a bad thing. It comes from unripe grapes or from too many stems being crushed with the grapes (that's why many wineries destem grapes first).

blanc de blancs: Sparkling wine or champagne made purely from white grapes like chardonnay. Other white sparklers might contain the juice from the dark-skinned pinot noir grape and are called blanc de noirs.

blending: The mixing of different types of wine (cabernet, merlot, or syrah, for example) or of wines made from the same grape but from different vineyards. Blending different wines is part of the winemaker's art and is done to create a wine of particular character, much like different shades of paint are blended to create the desired tone.

body: How heavy the wine feels in your mouth, a perception created by the alcohol, glycerin, and sugar content of a wine. An Alexander Valley cabernet sauvignon is a full-bodied wine, while a Carneros chardonnay is lighter bodied.

Bordeaux blend: A wine (usually red) made from a blend of some or all of the main grape varietals used to make wine in the French region of Bordeaux—cabernet sauvignon, merlot, cabernet franc, malbec, petit verdot, and carmenère in the case of red wine; sauvignon blanc, semillon, and muscadelle in the case of white. See also *meritage.*

botrytis: A gray fungus (also known as noble rot) that attacks grapes in humid conditions, shriveling them up like raisins and concentrating the sugar and acid content. Wines made from affected grapes are sweet and complex, and are often sold as dessert wines.

bouquet: Often confused with the aroma, the bouquet refers specifically to the scent in a wine that comes from the aging process in either the barrel or bottle, rather than from the fruit.

brawny: Term used mainly to describe young red wines (especially in California) with high alcohol and tannin levels.

briary: An aggressive, prickly taste in young wines, sometimes described as peppery.

brix: A measure of the sugar content in a grape, used to determine when grapes should be harvested. The final alcohol content of a wine is often related to the brix reading of the grapes when harvested.

brut: Refers to a dry (but not the driest) champagne or sparkling wine with less than 1.5 percent residual sugar.

burgundy: A catchall term to describe red and white wine from the Burgundy region in

France. Real red burgundies are usually pinot noir. Cheap Californian burgundies are usually misusing the term for totally unrelated wine.

buttery: An obvious taste often found in white wines, particularly Californian chardonnay.

carbonic maceration: A method of fermenting the juice while still inside the grape, by placing whole grapes within a vessel and allowing gravity to crush the grapes at the bottom. The result is light, fruity wines low in alcohol and tannins.

cava: A sparkling wine from Spain made in a similar style to champagne but using different grapes.

Champagne: A region in northern France best known for production of sparkling wine by a very specific method, known as the *méthode champenoise,* using chardonnay, pinot noir, and pinot meunier. Since 2006, American wineries are no longer allowed to call sparkling wines made this way "champagne."

chaptalization: The addition of sugar to wine before or during fermentation to increase the final alcohol content. It is legal in France, where cooler weather often means grapes do not have enough sugar when harvested, but not legal (and not necessary) in California.

charmat method: The process of making cheaper sparkling wines by carrying out the secondary fermentation (the one that creates the bubbles) in large steel vats under pressure rather than in the bottle like the more expensive *méthode champenoise* used to make fine champagnes.

chewy: Usually used to describe powerful tannins in red wines like cabernet that give it an almost viscous mouthfeel, making you almost want to chew it before swallowing.

citrus: An aroma and flavor reminiscent of citrus fruits, especially grapefruit, in many white wines, particularly those from cooler growing regions like Carneros and the Russian River Valley.

claret: An old English term used to describe red wines from Bordeaux. In France, "clairet" is a particular Bordeaux that is produced like red wine, but the wine must stay in contact with the skins for the first 24 hours during its making.

clone: A genetic variation of a grapevine. In a wine and vineyard context, usually the specific genetic type of vine picked to match the local growing conditions or the desired style of wine.

cloudy: Used to describe a wine that is a little hazy when viewed through the glass rather than crystal clear. Except in some rare occasions, a cloudy wine is not a good thing and might also have an unpleasant smell.

complex: The ultimate flattery for winemakers is to call their wines complex. Everything from the aroma to the long aftertaste is in balance and harmony.

cooked: Leave wine in a hot car for a day, open it, and it will probably taste odd. It has been cooked (see *maderized*).

cooperage: All the containers a winery uses to store and age wine, including barrels, vats, and tanks. They are made by coopers.

corked: The brief taste or smell of wet cardboard in a wine that is caused by bacteria in a contaminated cork interacting with chemicals in the wine. It can often be very subtle, so many people might not realize a wine is corked, and it is harmless to drink.

creamy: The silky taste and texture of a white wine that has undergone malolactic fermentation. Often accompanied by the faintest smell of creamy foods like crème brûlée.

crisp: A definite but not undesirable tartness and acidity usually used to describe white wines and often accompanied by the aroma of citrus fruits. White wines from cool climates like Carneros are often crisp.

crush: Literally the crushing of the grape skins to release the juice and start the fermentation process. Crush is the term also used to describe the process of harvesting and transporting the grapes of a particular year prior to making the wine.

cuvée: A French term to describe the blend of wines from different grapes and different years. The term is most often used for champagne and sparkling wines, but can be applied to any wine blend.

decanting: The slow and careful pouring of aged red wine into a broad, shallow glass container to ensure the sediment from aging stays in the bottle and to then allow the wine to breathe, or start to release its aromas, before drinking.

demi-sec: A slightly sweet sparkling wine or champagne containing 3.5-5 percent residual sugar.

dessert wine: A sweet red or white wine usually drunk in small amounts with dessert. The sweetness of desserts would mask the much smaller amount of sugar in a normal wine and make it taste bitter or acidic. Sweet dessert wines are often made from late-harvest grapes, picked when they are riper and their sugar content is higher. The botrytis fungus can also be used to make these sweeter wines.

dry: Describes a red or white wine that has been fermented until less than 0.2 percent of the natural sugars remain. Although a dry wine will not taste sweet, it might still taste fruity.

dumb: My favorite wine term—it means, literally, a wine with nothing to say. Flavors and aroma might have been muted by over-chilling a white wine or simply because a red wine is at a certain stage of aging when it is in between youthfulness and adulthood (often when about 5-6 years old).

earthy: Fine pinot noir is always earthy, possessing an aroma and/or flavor that could have come straight from the ground. Think of what a handful of damp soil smells like, and that's the earthiness. Different soil smells a different way, and the pros can often detect the type of soil or region a wine comes from simply by recognizing the smell of that earth. Or so they say. A lot of wines have the potential to be earthy, but other aromas and flavors often mask the distinctive smell.

elegant: How to praise a well-balanced and graceful wine. The opposite would be "rustic."

enology: The science and study of wine-making, often spelled *oenology* outside the United States. An *oenophile* is someone who loves wine.

estate bottled: Refers to wine made from vineyards that are both owned by the winery and in the same appellation or AVA as the winery. In addition, the entire winemaking process from fermentation to bottling has to occur at that winery. Non-estate wines are made from grapes bought from other growers or grown in another appellation.

fat: Describes the texture of a full-bodied wine with lots of fruit. A full-bodied wine without enough acidity to balance the fruit is often called flabby.

fermentation: The process that turns grape juice into wine. A biochemical process in yeast cells converts the sugar in grape juice into alcohol and carbon dioxide. Usually that gas is simply allowed to escape, but in the secondary fermentation process used to make sparkling wines it is retained in the wine under pressure and released as the bubbles when a bottle is opened.

filtering: The easy way to remove particles from a wine to ensure it is clear before being bottled. Pumping wine through filters can, however, damage the flavor of a wine. Fining is a more laborious but better way to clarify wine.

fining: The process of adding a natural, non-reactive substance like gelatin or crushed eggshell to a tank of wine to slowly remove suspended particles as it falls to the bottom. It takes longer than simple filtering.

finish: Also sometimes called the aftertaste, this is the lingering impression of the wine on your palate after swallowing. It might be long or short (or absent), acidic or sweet. Generally, a longer finish denotes a better wine.

firm: A wine that has some acidic astringency, much like firm unripe fruit. Like unripe fruit, a firm wine is usually young and will ripen with age, mellowing its acidity. But sometimes it won't.

flat: Wines with too little acidity are said to be flat and uninteresting.

flowery: A white wine that has an aroma reminiscent of flowers.

forward: A forward wine is one that has all its best aromas and flavors right up front and screams "drink me now." You'll usually hear the term *fruit forward* used to describe cheap red wines in which the fruity flavors overpower all others (if there are even others present).

fruity: A generic term used to describe whatever aroma and flavor comes from the grape itself. Strangely enough, wine does not usually smell of the one fruit used to make it but of everything from grapefruit to honeydew melon, depending on the type of grape and how the wine was made. Fruity wines are not necessarily sweet wines.

funky: Believe it or not, this is a real wine-tasting term used to describe a certain unidentifiable yeasty aroma that some wines have. You'll have to be a professional wine critic to recognize the smell. Most people simply call any unidentifiable smell or taste "funky." Just don't say it in front of a winemaker.

grassy: Sauvignon blanc is often described as grassy. Imagine the smell of freshly cut grass. Too much grassiness is not a good trait.

green: A term often applied to sauvignon blanc. It describes the slightly leafy taste of a wine made with underripe fruit.

hollow: When there's really nothing between the first initial taste of a wine and the aftertaste. Something's missing in the middle for any number of reasons.

horizontal tasting: No, not drinking wine while lying down, but tasting the same type of wine from the same year but from different wineries. It's fun to line up a horizontal tasting of, say, cabernets from different Napa Valley appellations to learn how different growing conditions affect wine.

hot: You'll know a hot wine when the back of your throat burns after swallowing, as though you just downed a shot of vodka. It's caused by too much alcohol in the wine and not enough of everything else. This is a normal character of fortified wines like port and sherry but a no-no in regular wines like cabernet sauvignon. Cheap, high-alcohol zinfandels are often hot.

jammy: Word most often used to describe Californian zinfandel. Imagine the taste of a spoonful of blackberry jam.

late harvest: Picking grapes as late as possible so their sugar content is as high as possible to make a sweeter wine, usually a dessert wine.

lean: More body would be good, sort of thin in the mouth, often too much astringency; sometimes used as a compliment for certain styles.

lees: The leftover yeast and other crud that falls to the bottom of barrels or fermentation tanks or is removed by fining. It is also sometimes called mud. Makers of white and sparkling wines sometimes leave it in the bottle so it can impart a yeasty, toasty flavor and smell to aged wines. That technique is called fermenting wine *sur lies*.

legs: Spot the novice wine taster cracking jokes about "great legs." Swirl wine around the glass, then stop and watch clear rivulets cling to the side of the glass. They are the legs, and how fat or long they are actually has nothing to do with the quality of the wine. Instead they have everything to do with how much alcohol and glycerin there is in the wine, what the temperature is, and even how clean the glass is.

length: Pretty much the same as finish, namely how long the flavors and aromas of a wine last on the back of your throat after swallowing; the longer, the better.

maderized: What might happen to your wine if you leave it in a hot car for too long. It is a distinctive brown color and smell caused by exposure of wine to excessive heat and oxygen. Also sometimes called "oxidized." Even if you haven't smelled the Portuguese fortified wine madeira, you'll know when a wine has maderized. It doesn't smell like wine anymore.

malolactic fermentation: A secondary chemical process (not technical fermentation at all) that nearly all red wines undergo and white wines are sometimes put through to give them a smoother, less acidic flavor (often described as creamy or buttery). It converts the harsh-tasting malic acid that naturally occurs in wine into the softer lactic acid plus carbon dioxide. Wineries often use the process to make a more popular style of easy-drinking chardonnay, though sometimes they overdo it and create a wine that lacks any sort of acidity at all and is just flat.

meritage: Californian wines have to contain at least 75 percent of one grape varietal to be labeled as such, but some of the best red wines are blends of some of the five varietals used in Bordeaux wine, with no grape in the majority. Californian winemakers, not wanting to use the term *Bordeaux blend,* instead came up with a new term to describe blended red wines: meritage. It remains an uncommon term, however, and most wineries instead come up with their own proprietary names for their blends.

mouthfeel: How a wine feels rather than tastes in your mouth. Use any description you want. Ones I use too much include "velvety" and "soft."

musty: A flaw that makes a wine smell like your grandmother's dank old attic. It is caused by mold getting into the wine sometime during the winemaking or bottling process.

nonvintage: Most wines are made with grapes harvested in a single year (vintage). Nonvintage wines are made by blending wines made in different years, and they have no year on their label. Some cheap red wines are nonvintage and made by using up surplus wine from different years. The best champagnes are also nonvintage so the winemakers can make sure the wine is of consistent high quality every year.

nose: The most important tool for wine tasting, but in most cases used to describe the overall smell of a wine, a combination of the aroma and bouquet.

oaky: The taste or smell of freshly sawn oak, toast, or vanilla that comes from aging wine in oak barrels that have usually been charred, or toasted, on the inside. A hint of oakiness in red wines is considered a good thing and is a matter of taste in white wines. Oak aromas and flavors should never overpower the fruit in a wine, as they do in some "over-oaked" chardonnays. There's an entire vocabulary used to describe oak smells and tastes, all of which depend on factors ranging from where the oak tree was grown to the size of the wood's grain to its toast level.

open up/opening up: Some bottled cellar-aged red wines possess the peculiarity that, when the cork is first pulled and the wine poured, the full flavors do not immediately make an appearance. However, after the passage of several minutes in an open glass goblet, the wine develops unsuspected flavor characteristics that can verge on the sublime. This phenomenon is referred to as "opening up." These flavors can disappear just as fast in just 30 minutes, leaving a subsequent impression of a flat, stale, over-the-hill, or mediocre wine.

overripe: A grape precondition necessary for making certain styles of Californian zinfandel wines. Left on the vine to dry in the sun, certain grape varietals will develop the desirable raisiny character and concentrated sugar necessary for making specialty wines such as the Hungarian tokay.

oxidized: As soon as a bottle of wine is opened, it is exposed to the oxygen in the air and starts to oxidize, usually a good thing for an hour or two. If it has been exposed to air for too long, however, either due to a leaky cork during storage or from being left open on a kitchen counter for a week, it will start to smell like cheap sherry and turn brown. At that point it is oxidized. With excessive heat as well, it will become maderized.

peppery: A term that usually goes hand-in-hand with *spicy* to describe the slightly pungent quality of wines like gewürztraminer and some styles of syrah and zinfandel.

phylloxera: A small aphid-like insect that attacks the roots of vines and slowly kills them by preventing the plant from absorbing water and nutrients. It wiped out many vineyards in Europe in the late 1800s but is actually native to the United States, where it has periodically ravaged California vines, particularly in the early 1900s. Most vines are now grafted onto resistant rootstock, though some are not, and limited outbreaks still periodically occur.

Pierce's disease: A virus that infects grapevines and kills them in 1-5 years. It is spread by a leafhopper-type insect called the glassy-winged sharpshooter. Though the disease is not yet endemic in Northern California's vineyards, authorities are worried it could soon be and have imposed strict plant quarantine laws to prevent its spread.

plump: Almost a fat wine but not quite.

pomace: The mashed-up residue of skin, seeds, stems, and pulp left after grapes are pressed to release the juice. In California it's often used as fertilizer. In Italy they distill it to make grappa.

racking: A traditional method of wine clarification that involves transferring wine from one barrel to another to leave sediment and other deposits behind.

reserve wine: This term actually means nothing in California thanks to the total lack of official definition. In general, a reserve wine is made from the best grapes (they are reserved specially) and often aged for longer to create a higher-quality wine than a winery's normal offerings. In practice the term is often as much about marketing as good wine. Some wineries give their best-of-the-best wines other labels like "special selection."

residual sugar: The percentage, by weight or volume, of the unfermented grape sugar that remains in wine when it is bottled. The driest wines have less than 0.5 percent residual sugar, though many have slightly more to give them a fuller flavor.

rootstock: The roots of a grapevine, which often come from a different species than the leaves. Many vines are a combination of two different plants. The stems and leaves might come from one, and they are grafted, or grown onto, roots from another chosen either for its suitability for certain growing conditions or resistance to disease.

rough: If a wine feels like it's taking the lining off your throat with its tannins, it's described as rough. Some rough wines smooth and mellow with age.

Rutherford dust: A slightly mineral flavor said to be present in some of the classic cabernets grown in the Rutherford appellation of Napa Valley.

sediment: The small quantity of particulate matter often found at the bottom of well-aged red wines, generated during the aging process. Sediment includes a lot of the phenols that give wine its color, so as a wine gets really old the color literally starts dropping out of it. Sediment is harmless but best left in the bottle for presentation's sake.

soft: A wine with low acid or tannin content that has little impact on your taste buds.

sommelier: The person responsible for the wine cellar, wine service, and wine list in a restaurant. If you have no clue which wine to order, ask to speak to the sommelier, and he or she can usually help.

sour: Almost a synonym for acidic. It implies the presence of acetic acid plus excess acid components. (It is also one of the four basic taste sensations detected by the human tongue.)

spicy: Almost a synonym for peppery, but it implies a more nuanced flavor suggesting delicate Indian spices rather than those that get up your nose.

supple: A red wine with a mouthfeel that lies somewhere between lean and fat; usually an easy drinker.

tannin: The reason many people don't like red wines. Tannin is a naturally occurring chemical (a phenol) in grape skins, seeds, and stems as well as the wood of barrels. It gives red wines their backbone, helps preserve them, and has an astringent taste. Young wines, particularly those meant for aging, can be highly tannic but will mellow and soften with age. Other overly tannic wines taste rough or harsh and might never mellow. White wines generally contain very little tannin.

tartaric acid: If you ever see what looks like small shards of glass in a bottle of white wine, they are probably crystals of tartaric acid, a harmless acid that is in all white wines and can crystallize under certain conditions.

terroir: A French term for all the environmental characteristics of a vineyard, including every conceivable nuance of the soils, climate, and geography. The *terroir* is said to give the grapes grown there a unique flavor profile, and the best wine experts in the world can identify (allegedly) the exact vineyard that the grapes in a wine came from.

tobacco: A common description of a flavor often found in cabernet sauvignon that refers to the smell of fresh tobacco leaves. *Cigar box* is a common term often used in its place. Like all those flavor descriptions, it's easier to identify if you have actually experienced the smell firsthand by smelling and smoking a cigar.

ullage: The small gap between the wine in the bottle and the cork. It should be almost nonexistent and is formed by the evaporation of wine through the cork or cork leakage. If the ullage gets too big, it will contain enough oxygen to start oxidizing the wine.

vanilla: A desirable aroma and taste component of many red wines that comes from the compound vanillin in oak barrels. Newer barrels have more vanillin than older barrels. Smell a bottle of vanilla essence used in cooking to help identify the subtle equivalent in a wine.

varietal: A wine made from a particular type of grape, such as pinot noir, chardonnay, cabernet sauvignon, and so on, that shows the distinct characteristics of that type of grape. A varietal wine must contain more than 75 percent of the grape variety Identified on the label. Blended wines made from more than one type of grape, such as many European wines identified more by their region than the grape (Bordeaux and Chianti, for example), are not varietal wines.

vertical tasting: Tasting a number of different vintages of one varietal of wine from the same winery, starting from the youngest and working to the oldest. Vertical tasting can help identify the best years for a particular wine and show how it changes as it ages.

vineyard-designate: Describes a wine that is made using grapes from a single, named vineyard only. These wines are usually more expensive and higher quality than those made with grapes from multiple vineyards.

vintage: The year grapes are harvested, which is the year on the bottle label. Making the wine and bottling it often takes several more years, so a 2013 wine might not be released until 2015 or beyond.

Vitis vinifera: The main grapevine species behind all the great wines of the world, and one that is often grafted onto rootstock from other *Vitis* species. All the major varietal grapes are members of the *Vitis vinifera* species, including chardonnay, cabernet sauvignon, pinot noir, sauvignon blanc, and so on.

yeast: Single-celled fungi that use enzymes to turn the natural sugars in grape juice into alcohol and carbon dioxide gas (and energy for themselves) through a biochemical process called fermentation. Different wild and genetically modified yeasts are used by winemakers, each performing differently and imparting a slightly different flavor to the wine. Wild yeasts often live naturally on grape skins, and winemakers will simply rely on them. A few wild yeasts can, however, give an undesirable yeasty odor to wines.

Suggested Reading

CUISINE

Wine Country cuisine is all about using the freshest local produce, and recipes in many of the Wine Country cookbooks tend to rely heavily on the kind of ingredients you might not necessarily find in your local supermarket. Still, they make a nice reminder of what to strive for in re-creating an idyllic Wine Country lifestyle and will probably be a fun reminder of memorable meals in the Napa and Sonoma restaurants that inspire many of them.

Bernstein, Sondra. *Plats du Jour: The Girl & the Fig's Journey Through the Seasons.* New York: Simon & Schuster, 2011. Here are 28 three-course meals, all arranged by season, that reflect the culinary fun to be had in the popular Sonoma restaurant.

Brown, Carrie, and John Werner. *The Jimtown Store Cookbook.* New York: HarperCollins, 2002. The Jimtown Store is the little store that could, hidden away in the heart of the Alexander Valley but still managing to compile a no-nonsense collection of classically stylish yet simple Wine Country recipes that cross all culinary borders.

Chiarello, Michael. *Bottega: Bold Italian Flavors from the Heart.* San Francisco: Chronicle Books, 2010. From the celebrity chef and his celebrated Yountville restaurant comes this classic of home Italian cooking. While you may not invest in duck prosciutto or lavender limoncello, the recipes are a mouthwatering reminder of Napa's rustic Italian food.

Higgins, Michelle. *Decanting Napa Valley: The Cookbook.* Yountville: Decanting Wine Country. Decanting Wine Country, 2010. Reading like a who's who of the Napa Valley, this cookbook/wine pairing guide/homage to Wine Country life is the valley condensed into 388 pages. You'll find beautiful photos, expertly chosen pairing menus, and small essays that outline the history of the valley and the culinary life that put it on the map.

Keller, Thomas. *Ad Hoc at Home* New York: Artisan Press, 2009. If you can't afford to eat at French Laundry or would rather spend $200 on a case of wine, then buy this giant cookbook from the little bistro of Keller's and learn how to make some simple yet sophisticated family-style food to go with your new wine purchase.

Keller, Thomas. *Bouchon Bakery.* New York: Artisan Press, 2012. For some bread, pastries, or even Ho-Ho's to go with your Ad Hoc meal, pick up this bakery bible. The table of contents ranges from high French classics to low (but oh so good) American pop culture favorites.

Orsini, Dominic. *Silver Oak Cookbook: Life in a Cabernet Kitchen—Seasonal Recipes from California's Celebrated Winery.* New York: Rizzoli, 2016. For a meal to match that special Napa or Alexander Valley cabernet, pick up this book. Recipes range from mascarpone bruschetta to Gouda crème brûlée, with simple yet elegant dishes such as beef short ribs and roasted lamb with fennel slaw in between. Each is paired with the best varietal (so your sauvignon blanc, merlot, and pinot noir won't go to waste) to bring out the best on the plate and in the glass.

Pawlcyn, Cindy. *Mustards Grill Napa Valley Cookbook.* Berkeley, CA: Ten Speed Press, 2001. This is one of the more digestible Wine Country cookbooks from this famous Yountville restaurant, with plenty of relatively simple recipes based on hearty American fare with twists of sophistication.

This is the restaurant credited with starting the Wine Country food scene.

Sone, Hiro, and Lissa Doumani. *Terra: Cooking from the Heart of Napa Valley.* Berkeley, CA: Ten Speed Press, 2001. This cookbook, from one of St. Helena's best restaurants, contains often sophisticated and tricky recipes drawing on French, Italian, and Japanese cuisine, but it helps makes their preparation as simple as possible with plenty of handy kitchen tips.

HISTORICAL LITERATURE

Fisher, M. F. K. *The Art of Eating: 50th Anniversary Edition.* New York: Houghton Mifflin Harcourt, 2004. One of the Sonoma and Napa Valleys' most famous writers, who ended up living in Glen Ellen, Fisher was also one of the best-known food writers in the United States in her later years. This compilation of five of her books is a collection of autobiographical information and musings on food preparation, consumption, and nutrition. She was described by John Updike as "the poet of appetites."

London, Jack. *The Valley of the Moon.* Berkeley, CA: University of California Press, 1999. Although not one of this prolific Victorian author's better-known books, this is a clear homage to the beauty of the Sonoma Valley, a mythical nirvana to the story's two protagonists, who try to escape their harsh working-class roots in Oakland for a simple country life. The story mirrors the life of London himself, who eventually moved from Oakland to live in the Sonoma Valley, a place he adored. First published in 1913.

Stevenson, Robert Louis. *The Silverado Squatters.* Rockville, MD: Wildside Press, 2004. The Victorian author is better known for his classic book *Treasure Island,* but he spent a few days of his honeymoon in a cottage at the abandoned Silverado Mine just outside Calistoga. He wrote an entertaining account of the colorful characters he met and places he visited in the surrounding area, including early wineries and some sights still there today. First published in 1884.

NAPA VALLEY

Conaway, James. *Napa: The Story of an American Eden.* Boston: Mariner Books, 2002. With a compelling narrative style, Conaway tells the story of the key people, families, and politics that helped make the Napa Valley what it is today—a land of dreams, obsessions, money, and wine.

Conaway, James. *The Far Side of Eden.* Boston: Mariner Books, 2003. Conaway picks up where his previous book, *Napa: The Story of an American Eden,* left off to chart the rise and impact of new money in the Napa Valley's recent social and winemaking history through the boom years of the 1990s.

Flynn Siler, Julia. *House of Mondavi: The Rise and Fall of an American Wine Dynasty.* New York: Gotham, 2008. This is a well-researched and riveting tale of the Napa Valley's greatest families, beginning when Cesare Mondavi passes through Ellis Island and continuing through the scandals that almost cost Robert Mondavi his empire.

Mondavi, Robert. *Harvests of Joy: How the Good Life Became Great Business.* San Diego: Harcourt, 1998. No family has had more of an impact on the modern wine industry of the Napa Valley, and indeed California, than the Mondavis, and Robert Mondavi in particular. Here the man himself gives the inside information on what makes it all tick.

Peterson, Richard G. *The Winemaker.* Journey from the end of Prohibition to today's wine world with Peterson, a winemaker who has seen it all. His lively and at time humorous story brings many of California's legendary figures to life, from the Gallos to Andre Tchelistcheff at Beaulieu Vineyards.

Swinchatt, Jonathan. *The Winemaker's Dance: Exploring Terroir in the Napa Valley.* Berkeley, CA: University of California Press, 2004. A dense book—for wine or science enthusiasts only—that explains how the Napa Valley came to be the way it is and how its geology and geography make it such a fine place to grow grapes.

Taber, George. *Judgment of Paris: California vs. France and the Historic 1976 Paris Tasting That Revolutionized Wine.* New York: Scribner, 2006. Learn about the players, the wine, and what happened that changed California and the wine world forever. Included in the story is a very readable history of winemaking in the United States, particularly in the West.

SONOMA VALLEY

Deutschman, Alan. *A Tale of Two Valleys: Wine, Wealth and the Battle for the Good Life in Napa and Sonoma.* New York: Broadway, 2003. Deutschman continues where James Conaway left off with his book *The Far Side of Eden,* chronicling the flood of dot-com wealth into both the Napa and Sonoma Valleys and the changes it wrought in Wine Country society. His style is brasher than Conaway's and might not be to everyone's liking.

Sullivan, Charles. *Sonoma Wine and the Story of the Buena Vista Winery.* San Francisco, CA: Board and Bench Publishing, 2015. Sonoma wine gets the spotlight in this easy to read history of the Valley of the Moon. Central to the story is California's first commercial winery, Buena Vista Winery, and its founder, the eccentric Agoston Haraszthy, while the scope stretches from the 17th century onward.

WINE REFERENCE

Acitelli, Tom. *American Wine: A Coming of Age Story.* Chicago: Chicago Review Press, 2015. Through the voices of America's biggest food and wine players, from Robert Parker and Julia Child to Cesar Chavez, Acitelli chronicles the rise of American wine. Beginning in the 1960s, the book moves with ease (and without jargon) through the Judgment of Paris to today, when the United States can claim to be the top maker of fine wine in the world.

Bonne, Jon. *The New California Wine: A Guide to the Producers and Wines Behind a Revolution in Taste.* Berkeley, CA: Ten Speed Press, 2013. From the wine editor of the *San Francisco Chronicle* comes a definitive and fresh take on today's wine. Bonne employs his experience, contacts, and writing skill to craft a guide to California's unique winemaking landscape that includes the state of industry, regional profiles, and a comprehensive list of the best producers.

Kolpan, Steven, Brian Smith, and Michael Weiss. *Exploring Wine: The Culinary Institute of America's Guide to Wines of the World.* 3rd edition. New York: Wiley, 2010. This giant tome is a crash course in winemaking, wine appreciation, and the wines of the world, with the added authority of being from the Culinary Institute of America (CIA), which offers some of the most highly regarded wine and food education courses in the country. That probably explains the unbelievably comprehensive chapter on pairing food and wine that, like many chapters, tends to read more like a textbook.

MacNeil, Karen. *The Wine Bible.* New York: Workman Publishing, 2015. A book to be found on many winery office desks, not least because MacNeil and her husband are Napa Valley winemakers themselves. It has an altogether more chatty, approachable style than the CIA guide and contains information on just about every wine and wine-related term you will come across, although it sometimes lacks depth.

Pinney, Thomas. *A History of Wine in America from Prohibition to the Present.* Berkeley, CA: University of California Press, 2007. This exhaustive tome details the characters, trends, and policies that shaped both the West and East Coast wine industries from the 1930s to the turn of the century.

Robinson, Jancis. *The Oxford Companion to Wine.* 4th edition. *Oxford University Press, 2015.* A massive tome that is widely regarded as the most exhaustive and accurate encyclopedia of everything you ever wanted to know about wine, from a well-known British wine writer and master of wine.

Internet Resources

These Internet resources are either free or have some useful information that is free. They supplement the more specific regional Internet resources listed in each chapter. Most major magazines are not included because they operate subscription-based websites.

The Wine Institute
www.wineinstitute.org
The main lobbying organization for the national wine industry, with all the background you could want on wine-related laws, regulations, and statistics.

WINE
Vinography
www.vinography.com
An entertaining and sometimes brutally honest blog from a well-informed San Francisco wine enthusiast.

Winery Sage
www.winery-sage.com
A direct, easy-to-use online encyclopedia for California's wineries, appellations, or varietals. The blog often highlights out-of-the-way places and small wine-related events.

Wine Business Online
www.winebusiness.com
All the latest industry news, events, jobs, and other business-related wine information for industry insiders.

RECREATION
Bay Area Hiker
www.bahiker.com
Maps, photos, and information about some of the best hikes in the Bay Area and Wine Country from the author of a popular regional hiking book.

International Wine Research Database
http://iwrdb.org
An authoritative, searchable database of wine, winemaking, wine history, and grape growing from the Sonoma County Wine Library.

Index

List of Maps

Also Available

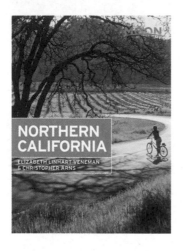

NORTHERN CALIFORNIA
ELIZABETH LINHART VENEMAN & CHRISTOPHER ARNS

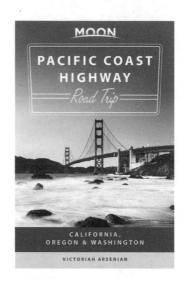

MOON
PACIFIC COAST HIGHWAY
Road Trip

CALIFORNIA, OREGON & WASHINGTON

VICTORIAH ARSENIAN

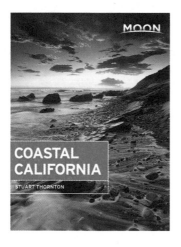

MOON
COASTAL CALIFORNIA
STUART THORNTON

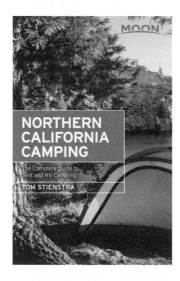

MOON
NORTHERN CALIFORNIA CAMPING
The Complete Guide to Tent and RV Camping
TOM STIENSTRA